WITHDRAWN

Small Business and Entrepreneurship

Visit the *Small Business and Entrepreneurship* Companion
Website at **www.pearsoned.co.uk/storeygreene** to find
valuable **student** learning material including:

- Exclusive *Financial Times* video interviews with entrepreneurs
  and small business owners.

- Annotated weblinks to real life companies and organisations
  cited in the book.

- Flashcard glossary to help with revision.

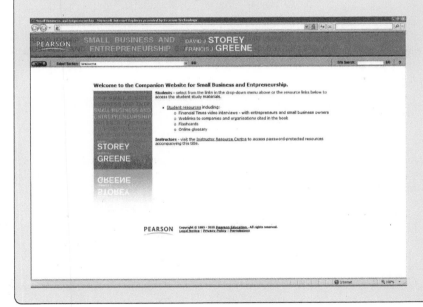

Small Business and Entrepreneurship

David J. Storey and
Francis J. Greene

Financial Times
Prentice Hall
is an imprint of

Harlow, England • London • New York • Boston • San Francisco • Toronto • Sydney • Singapore • Hong Kong
Tokyo • Seoul • Taipei • New Delhi • Cape Town • Madrid • Mexico City • Amsterdam • Munich • Paris • Milan

Pearson Education Limited
Edinburgh Gate
Harlow
Essex CM20 2JE
England

and Associated Companies throughout the world

Visit us on the World Wide Web at:
www.pearsoned.co.uk

First published 2010

© Pearson Eduction Limited 2010

ISBN: 978-0-273-69347-5

British Library Cataloguing-in-Publication Data
A catalogue record for this book is available from the British Library

Library of Congress Cataloging-in-Publication Data
Storey, D. J.
   Small business and entrepreneurship / David J. Storey and Francis J. Greene. — 1st ed.
      p. cm.
   Includes bibliographical references and index.
   ISBN 978-0-273-69347-5
   1. Small business.   2. Entrepreneurship.   I. Greene, Francis J.   II. Title.
   HD2341.S74 2010
   658.02'2—dc22

                                                                        2009050275

10 9 8 7 6 5 4 3 2
13

Typeset in 10/12 pt Minion by 35
Printed and bound by Rotolito Lombarda, Italy

The publisher's policy is to use paper manufactured from sustainable forests.

Brief contents

Contents

Part 1   Understanding small businesses and entrepreneurship   1

Part 3 · Business closure

Part 4 · Business growth

Part 7

Case studies   463

Supporting resources

Visit www.pearsoned.co.uk/storeygreene to find valuable online resources:

Companion Website for students

- Exclusive *Financial Times* video interviews with entrepreneurs and small business owners.
- Annotated weblinks to real life companies and organisations cited in the book.
- Flashcard glossary to help with revision.

For instructors

- Instructor's Manual, including:
  - Entrepreneurial attitudes: Self-assessment exercises for use with students.
  - Exercises to use in classes and seminars.
  - Discussion points and learning objectives for all chapters and topics.
  - Solutions to end-of-chapter questions.
- PowerPoints for all chapters.
- Case study teaching notes.

Also: The Companion Website provides the following features:

- Search tool to help locate specific items of content.
- E-mail results and profile tools to send results of quizzes to instructors.
- Online help and support to assist with website usage and troubleshooting.

For more information please contact your local Pearson Education sales representative or visit www.pearsoned.co.uk/storeygreene.

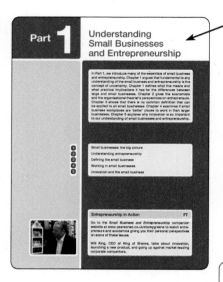

Part openers introduce the chapters in each section, and briefly list chapter contents.

Key learning objectives help you focus on the main aims as you begin to read the chapter.

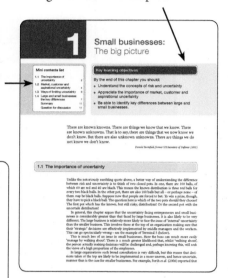

Mini contents lists at the head of each chapter display the topics discussed.

Illustrations are short case studies of entrepreneurial businesses, many including full-colour photographs.

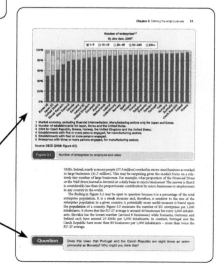

Classic research summaries present essential insights from academic studies of entrepreneurship and small business.

Figures illustrate colourfully the evidence behind each subject.

Questions in the chapters ask you to reflect as you read.

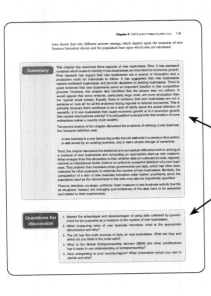

A full list of **References** for each chapter assists your further reading.

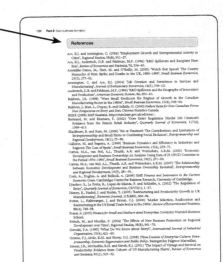

A **Summary** of the chapter clinches the important points that have been presented.

Questions for discussion at the end of each chapter encourage broader thinking about what you've just read.

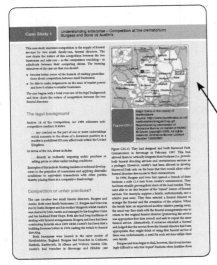

Glossary definitions, found in bold type throughout the text, are comprehensively listed at the end of the book.

Case studies unique to this book are presented in Part 7, offering in-depth perspectives, and including **Questions** and **Exercises**.

On the Companion Website
Exclusive *Financial Times* video interviews, annotated weblinks, and flashcard glossary definitions are available at www.pearsoned.co.uk/storeygreene.

Preface

Our, admittedly casual, review of books on small businesses and entrepreneurship suggests that there are two main types.

The first is 'how to do it books' which come in several guises. Some are 'war stories'. These are written by entrepreneurs – or their ghost writers – about how they made their fortune and provide advice to others on how their example might be followed. Another variant is 'practical' books on how to start or run a business. Typically, they include chapters on what factors to take into account in writing a business plan, or what sources of finance are available to a fledgling business. A third variant is books that imply that there are a finite number of actions that a business owner has to take to make his or her firm (very) successful.

These 'practical' books are unified in several important respects. First, the word 'theory' never appears – other than perhaps to point out that the word will not appear. After all, these books are 'practical'. Second, many of these books seek to avoid the use of any 'evidence' beyond that of the views of the writer about his or her own experience, or newspaper articles reporting the views of others. Even where there is some reference to evidence, it tends to point in a single direction. There is no room for diversity or contradiction. Business is simple and the task of practical books is to point out simple 'home' truths. The world described in practical books is one of certainties. Words such as 'luck' or 'chance' or 'probability' do not appear.

The second type of book is 'academic' textbooks. These are 'serious' books, which too often take the simplest of ideas and convert them into unnecessarily complex and 'academic' theories. Words – jargon – are used as a barrier to entry rather than a means of understanding matters.

Our view, and the philosophy underpinning this book, is that both types of book have potential merits. 'Practical' books offer intuitive and appealing examples of business activities. 'Academic' textbooks, meanwhile, have the advantage of moving beyond simple (and potentially misleading) certainties.

Our aim in this book is to combine the good characteristics of both types of book. Where the evidence is clear, then we say it is clear. But, much more often than not, the 'evidence' is far from clear. There are not five, six, or even twenty-six things that an individual can do to guarantee the creation of a successful business. We make it clear that the evidence supporting many of the common assertions is either contradictory or even non-existent. Examples include the assertions that entrepreneurs easily 'learn' or that training improves business performance.

However, wherever possible, we seek to favour simplicity over complexity. Inevitably, there will be the use of what some may view as jargon, but we hope it is used sparingly and never for its own sake. One novelty of the book is that in very many chapters we make use of a 'classic' article. We make use of these because we believe that there is great merit in understanding 'academic' theory but in a way that is approachable and accessible.

We also provide a range of 'in chapter' examples and longer case studies that will 'practically' illuminate the 'academic' material. To achieve an easy reading style, we have foregone the use of footnotes and do not require you to have more than very basic mathematical skills.

We hope you like our efforts. Please provide us with feedback so that we can improve for the future.

Acknowledgements

Although there are only two authors of this book, it would not exist without the help and support of many others.

A textbook is primarily the distillation of other people's ideas. Sometimes we know who those people are because they are our friends and colleagues. In other cases we document and reference the work of individuals that we have never met. A third group are people who influence how and what we think, but where even we do not realise the role they have played. We apologise to this third group, but the contribution of the first two groups is reflected in the index.

There are, however, people that we know did contribute to the book. We would therefore like to begin by offering thanks to colleagues at the Centre for Small and Medium-Sized Enterprises (CSME) at Warwick Business School. Nigel Sykes, Roger Mumby-Croft, Stuart Fraser, Margi Levy, Kevin Mole and Stephen Roper have either read chapters or provided material to support the development of the book. The CSME support staff, Elaine Pollard and Sharon West, have been invaluable to us in writing this book. They have edited it, read it, or had it read to them, and it has been their 'baby' as much as ours. We thank them for their 'over and above the call of duty' contribution.

Outside of CSME, there are several individuals who have helped us considerably. First, thanks go to Roger Wigglesworth, who read and commented on virtually the whole text. Known to many as New Zealand's SME policy authority, Roger's contribution provided the expected insights into the politics of SME policy but also a gift for exposing our stylistic limitations!

A second group of thanks go to those who have contributed to the cases used in the book. Two cases were specially written for us by Claire Crawford of the Institute of Fiscal Studies and by Lorraine Morley of Morley Associates whilst Rhoder Brown helped co-write the finance case. Stuart Roberts of Two Seasons, Justin Burgess of Burgess & Sons and Graham Whitworth of Sprue Aegis plc helped us with the case studies written on their businesses. All of these contributions have undoubtedly strengthened the book.

We would also like to thank Matthew Walker of Pearson Education for patiently supporting the development of the book. We originally agreed to write the book back in 2004. We made a start in 2005, had another go in 2007, and then got into the seemingly endless final strait in 2008/9.

Throughout this marathon, Pearson Education has sought the views of six referees, most of whom were given the text in four separate blocks. We do not know who these referees are, but we would like to acknowledge their contribution. Receiving referees' comments is salutory. Sometimes you agree with them but very often you don't. However, our most frequent reaction has been to go away and grudgingly recognise that they have a point since what appears on the page is not quite what we meant to say. We thank all six referees for their insights and support.

Our final thanks, though, must go to Andrew Harrison at Pearson Education. He has read and provided invaluable commentary on each and every one of the 250,000 words in this book. Since the book has basically been written three times, this means he has provided commentary to over 750,000 words. We thank him a great deal for his help and support.

Although all these people have helped us with this book, any errors or omissions are down to us. Finally, we dedicate this book to 'Abbster', 'Annabanana', 'Booboo', 'Fatz', 'Doozie', 'Miley' and 'Trick'.

Publisher's acknowledgements

We are grateful to the following for permission to reproduce copyright material:

Figures

Figures 3.1 and 3.2 from OECD (2008) *Measuring Entrepreneurship: A digest of indicators*, OECD: Paris, Figures A1 and A2, http://www.oecd.org/dataoecd/53/23/41664409.pdf; Figure 3.3 from Eurostat (2008) *Enterprises by Size Class: Overview of SMEs in the EU*, Eurostat: Brussels, adapted from the original Figure 2, p. 4 and Table 3, p. 3, published on http://epp.eurostat.ec.europa.eu/cache/ITY_OFFPUB/ KS-SF-08-031/EN/KS-SF-08-031-EN.PDF, responsibility for the adaptation lies entirely with Pearson Education; Figure 3.5 from 'UK self-employment jobs', http://www.statistics.gov.uk/StatBase TSDSeries1. asp, Crown Copyright material is reproduced with the permission of the Controller, Office of Public Sector Information (OPSI); Figure 3.11 from A. Stel (2005) 'COMPENDIA: Harmonising business ownership data across countries and over time', *International Enterpreneurship and Management Journal* 1(1), 105–23, with kind permission from Springer Science and Business Media; Figure 4.2 from Rand Corporation (2006) *Are Small Businesses Riskier than Larger Ones?*, Figure 1, Rand Corporation: Santa Monica, CA; Figure 4.3 from A. Parent-Thirion, E. Fernández Macías, J. Hurley and G. Vermeylen (2007) *Fourth European Working Conditions Survey Report: Lack of information on workplace risks, by company size (%)*, Figure 3.10, p. 33, source: Fourth European Working Conditions Survey 2005 © Foundation for the Improvement of Living and Working Conditions, www.eurofound.europa.eu, European Foundation for the Improvement of Living and Working Conditions, Dublin; Figure 4.4 from A. Parent-Thirion, E. Fernández Macías, J. Hurley and G. Vermeylen (2005) *Fourth European Working Conditions Survey: Violence and harassment, by company size*, Figure 4.4, p. 37, source: Fourth European Working Conditions Survey 2005 © Foundation for the Improvement of Living and Working Conditions, www.eurofound.europa.eu, European Foundation for the Improvement of Living and Working Conditions, Dublin; Figure 4.5 from A. Parent-Thirion, E. Fernández Macías, J. Hurley and G. Vermeylen (2007) *Fourth European Working Conditions Survey: Number of days of health-related leave*, Table 7.3, p. 66, source: Fourth European Working Conditions Survey 2005, © Foundation for the Improvement of Living and Working Conditions, www.eurofound.europa.eu, EFILWC: Dublin; Figure 5.3 adapted with permission from R. Agarwal and B.L. Bayus (2002) 'The market evolution and sales take off of product innovations', *Management Science*, 48(8), 1024–41, © The Institute for Operations Research and the Management Sciences, 7240 Parkway Drive, Suite 300, Hanover, Maryland 21076; Figure 6.2 from P. Mueller, A. van Stel and D.J. Storey (2008) 'Small Business Economics: The effects of new firm foundation on regional development over time – the case of Great Britain', *Small Business Economics* 30(1), 59 –71, with kind permission from Springer Science and Business Media; Figure 6.7 from S. Vale (2006) from *The International Comparability of Business Start-up Rates*, Figure 3.2, OECD: Paris; Figure 7.2 from E. Oldsman and K. Hallerg (2004) from *Evaluating Business Assistance Programmes: Evaluating local economic and employment development – How to assess what works among programmes and policies*, Figure 10.4, OECD: Paris; Figure 8.1 from OECD (2008) *Women and Men in OECD Countries (00 2006 3B 1 P) – No. 83841 2006*, p. 18, OECD: Paris, http://www.oecd.org/dataoecd/23/36/ 37954993.pdf; Figure 8.2 from CBS, http://www.cbs.nl/en-GB/menu/themas/bedrijven/publicaties/ artikelen/archief/2005/2005-1805-wm.htm, © CBS-NL Statistics, www.cbs.nl; Figure 8.3 from ONS (2006), http://www/statistics.gov.uk/cci/nugget.asp?id=463, Crown Copyright material is reproduced with the permission of the Controller, Office of Public Sector Information (OPSI); Figure 8.4 from K. Clark and S. Drinkwater (2006) 'Pushed out or pulled in? Self-employment among ethnic minorities in England

and Wales', *Labour Economics*, 7(5), 603–28, copyright (2006) with permission from Elsevier; Figure 9.1 from New Zealand Ministry of Economic Development (2008) *SMEs in New Zealand: Structure and dynamics 2008*, p. 22, Table 9, New Zealand Ministry of Economic Development: Wellington; Figures 10.4 and 10.5 from J. Baldwin, T. Gray, J. Johnson, J. Proctor, M. Rafiquzzaman and D. Sabourin (1997) *Statistics Canada, Failing Concerns: Business bankruptcy in Canada*, Catalogue 61-525, released 1 April 1998, http://www.statcan.gc.ca/pub/61-525-x/61-525-x1997001-eng.pdf; Figure 11.1 from P. Schreyer (2000) *High-growth Businesses and Employment: OECD Science, Technology and Industry Working Papers, 2000/3*, Figure 1, OECD: Paris; Figure 11.2 from L. Hull and R. Arnold (2008) *New Zealand Firm Growth as Change in Turnover*, Ministry of Economic Development: Wellington; Figure 12.1 from L.E. Greiner (1972) 'Evolution and revolution as organizations grow', *Harvard Business Review*, 50(4), 37–46, reprinted by permission of *Harvard Business Review*, copyright © 1972 by the Harvard Business School Publishing Corporation, all rights reserved; Figure 12.2 from Cluster Mapping Project, Institute for Strategy and Competitiveness, Harvard Business School, all rights reserved; Figure 14.1 from D. Pilat, A. Cimper, K. Olsen and C. Webb (2006) *The Changing Nature of Manufacturing in OECD Economies: STI Working Paper 2006/9*, Figure 1, OECD: Paris; Figure 14.2 from M.E. Porter (1980) *Competitive Strategy: Techniques for analysing industries and competitors*, Macmillan: London, reprinted with the permission of The Free Press, a Division of Simon & Schuster, Inc., from *COMPETITIVE STRATEGY: Techniques for Analyzing Industries and Competitors* by Michael E. Porter, copyright 1980, by The Free Press, all rights reserved; Figure 14.3 from K. Dunnell (2009) 'National statistician's article: measuring regional economic performance', *Economic and Labour Market Review*, 3(1), 18–30, Crown Copyright material is reproduced with the permission of the Controller, Office of Public Sector Information (OPSI); Figures 16.1, 16.2 and 16.4 from S. Fraser (2009) 'How have SME finances been affected by the credit crisis?' BERR/ESRC Seminar, London, Crown Copyright material is reproduced with the permission of the Controller, Office of Public Sector Information (OPSI); Figure 16.3 from A.N. Berger and G.F. Udell (1998) 'The economics of small business finance: the roles of private equity and debt markets in the financial growth cycle', *Journal of Banking and Finance*, 22(6–8), 613–73, copyright (1998) with permission from Elsevier; Figure 19.4 from C. Wren (1996), 'Grant equivalent expenditure on industrial subsidies in the post-war United Kingdom', *Oxford Bulletin of Economics and Statistics*, 58(2), 317–53, Wiley-Blackwell; Figure 20.1 from *White Paper on Small and Medium Enterprises in Japan, 2006: Small and medium enterprises at a turning point – Strengthening ties with overseas economies and population decline in Japan*, JSBRI, 2006 White Paper on Small and Medium Enterprises in Japan, Ministry of Economic Trade and Industry (METI, 1-3-1 Kasumigaseki Chiyoda city 100-8912 Tokyo) and Japan Small Business and research Institiute (JSBRI, Sanbancho-KS Bldg, Sanbancho 2, Chiyoda city 102-0075 Tokyo); Figure 20.2 from B. Powell (2002) 'Explaining Japan's recession', *The Quarterly Journal of Austrian Economics*, 5(2), 35–50, with kind permission from Springer Science and Business Media; Figure 20.4 from F. Bourguignon (2005) *World Development Report 2005: A better investment climate for everyone*, Box 2, World Bank: Washington, copyright 2005 by World Bank, reproduced with permission of World Bank in the format Textbook via the Copyright Clearance Center; Figure 20.5 from International Finance Corporation (2009) *Enterprise Surveys: Corruption*, http://www.enterprisesurveys.org/exploretopics/ ?topicid=3, (2009) Enterprise Surveys Online by the World Bank, World Bank: Washington, copyright 2009 by World Bank, reproduced with permission of World Bank in the format Textbook via the Copyright Clearance Center; Figure 20.6 from International Finance Corporation (2009) *Enterprise Surveys: Corruption,* http://www.enterprisesurveys.org/exploretopics/?topicid=8, (2009) Enterprise Surveys Online by the World Bank, World Bank: Washington, copyright 2009 by World Bank, reproduced with permission of World Bank in the format Textbook via the Copyright Clearance Center; Figure 20.7 from International Finance Corporation (2009) *Enterprise Surveys: Corruption*, http://www. enterprisesurveys.org/exploretopics/?topicid=1, (2009) Enterprise Surveys Online by the World Bank, World Bank: Washington, copyright 2009 by World Bank, reproduced with permission of World Bank in the format Textbook via the Copyright Clearance Center; Figure 20.8 from F. Bourguignon (2005) *World Development Report 2005: A better investment climate for everyone*, Figure 5.8, World Bank: Washington, copyright 2005 by World Bank, reproduced with permission of World Bank in the format Textbook via the Copyright Clearance Center; Figure 7.2 from E. Oldsman and K. Hallerg (2004) *Evaluating Business Assistance Programmes: Evaluating local economic and employment development – How to assess what works among programmes and policies*, OECD: Paris.

Maps

Map 1.1 from http://www/touristnetuk.co.uk/hertfordshire/images/map.gif, reproduced by permission of Ordnance Survey on behalf of HMSO © Crown copyright 2009, all rights reserved, Ordnance Survey Licence Number 100030901.

Tables

Table 2.2 from G.D. Meyer, H.M. Neck and M.D. Meeks (2002) 'The entrepreneurship–strategic management interface', in Hitt, M.A., Ireland, R.D. Camp S.M. and Sexton, D.L. (eds), *Strategic Entrepreneurship: Creating a new mindset*, Wiley-Blackwell; Table 3.1 from Eurostat (2008) *Enterprises by Size Class: Overview of SMEs in the EU*, Eurostat: Brussels, http://ec.europa.eu/enterprise/enterprise_policy/sme_definition/index_en.htm, © European Communities, 1995–2009; Appendix 3.1 from Eurostat (2008) *Enterprises by Size Class: Overview of SMEs in the EU*, 31, Eurostat: Brussels, adapted from the original Figure 2, p. 4 and Table 3, p. 3, published on http://epp.eurostat.ec.europa.eu/cache/ITY_OFFPUB/KS-SF-08-031/EN/KS-SF-08-031-EN.PDF, responsibility for the adaptation lies entirely with Pearson Education; Table 3.3 from F.J. Greene, K.F. Mole and D.J. Storey (2008) *Three Decades of Enterprise Culture: Entrepreneurship, economic regeneration and public policy*, Palgrave MacMillan; Table 4.2 from B.A. Kirchhoff and P. Greene (1998) 'Understanding the theoretical and empirical content of critiques of US job creation research', *Small Business Economics*, 10(2), 153–69, with kind permission from Springer Science and Business Media; Table 4.3 from J. Forth, H. Bewley and A. Bryson (2006) *Small and Medium-sized Enterprises: Findings from the 2004 workplace employment relations survey*, Table 7.4, Department of Trade and Industry: London, Crown Copyright material is reproduced with the permission of the Controller, Office of Public Sector Information (OPSI); Tables 5.2, 5.6 and 5.8 from S. Robson and G. Haigh (2008) 'First findings from the UK Innovation Survey 2007', *Economic and Labour Market Review*, 2(4), 47–53, Palgrave, Crown Copyright material is reproduced with the permission of the Controller, Office of Public Sector Information (OPSI); Table 5.7 from Innovation in Australian Business, 2005 (accessed 19 March 2009), http://www.abs.gov.au/AUSSTATS/abs@nsf/Lookup/8158.0Main+Features12005?OpenDocument, source: Australian Bureau of Statistics; Table 6.2 from BERR (Department for Business, Enterprise and Regulatory Reform) (2008), Crown Copyright material is reproduced with the permission of the Controller, Office of Public Sector Information (OPSI); Table 7.1 from C.G. Brush, T.S. Manolova and L.F. Edleman (2008) 'Properties of emerging organizations: an empirical test', *Journal of Business Venturing*, 23(5), 547–66, copyright (2008) with permission from Elsevier; Table 7.2 from S.C. Parker and Y. Belghitar (2006) 'What happens to nascent entrepreneurs? An econometric analysis of the PSED', *Small Business Economics*, 27(1), 81–101, with kind permission from Springer Science and Business Media; Table 9.3 from M.P. Taylor (1999), 'Survival of the fittest? An analysis of self-employment duration in Britain', *Economic Journal*, 109(454), C140–55, Wiley-Blackwell; Table 9.4 from N. Harada (2007) 'Which firms exist and why? An analysis of small firm exits in Japan', *Small Business Economics*, 29, 401–14, with kind permission from Springer Science and Business Media; Table 11.2 from F. Delmar, P. Davidsson and W.B. Gartner (2003) 'Arriving at the high-growth firm', *Journal of Business Venturing*, 18, 189–216, copyright (2003), with permission from Elsevier; Table 12.1 from M. Scott and R. Bruce (1987) 'Five stages of growth in small business', *Long Range Planning*, 20(3), 40–52, copyright (1987), with permission from Elsevier; Table 16.1 from S. Fraser (2005) *Finance for Small and Medium-sized Enterprises: A report on the 2004 UK Survey of SME Finances. ESRC UK Data Archive: SN 5326*, Bank of England: London; Table 16.2 from F.J. Greene, K.M. Mole and D.J. Storey (2008) *Three Decades of Enterprise Culture*, Palgrave, p. 156; Table 16.3 from A.D. Cosh and A. Hughes (eds) (2007), *British Enterprise: Thriving or surviving?*, Centre for Business Research, University of Cambridge, Cambridge; Table 16.4 from S. Fraser (2009) 'How have SME finances been affected by the credit crisis?, BERR/ESRC seminar, London, Crown Copyright material is reproduced with the permission of the Controller, Office of Public Sector Information (OPSI); Table 17.1 from FAME database (2009), http://www.bvdep.com/en/FAME.html?gclid=COLk7Y6Ro5wCFaAA4wodcDXpjw, FAME (2009) published by Bureau Van Dijk; Table 19.3 from R. Spires and M. Rooke (2005) *Small Business Service Mapping of Government Services for Small Business Final Report*, PACEC: Cambridge; Table 20.1 from World Bank (2009) *Doing Business 2010* (2009) Doing Business online by World Bank, http://www.doingbusiness.org/economyrankings/, World Bank: Washington, copyright 2009 by World Bank, reproduced with permission of World Bank in the format Textbook via the Copyright Clearance Center; Table 20.2 from M.W. Crain (2005) *The Impact of Regulatory Costs on Small Firms*, SBA: Washington; Table 20.3 from World Bank (2009) *Doing Business 2010*, (2009) Doing Business online by World Bank, http://www.doingbusiness.org/economyrankings/ World Bank: Washington, copyright 2009 by World Bank, reproduced with permission of World Bank in the format Textbook via the Copyright Clearance Center; Table 21.1 from T. Graham (2004) *Review of the Small Firms Loan Guarantee*, HM Treasury: London, Crown Copyright material is reproduced with the permission of the Controller, Office of Public Sector Information (OPSI); Table 21.2 from Eurostat (2008) *Entrepreneurial Diversity in a Unified Europe*, European Commission: Brussels, adapted from the original Tables 5 and 6 published on http://ec.europa.eu/enterprise/policies/sme/files/support_measures/migrant/eme_study_en.pdf, p. 26, responsibility for the adaptation lies entirely with Pearson Education.

Text

Epigraph on page 14 from W. Baumol (1990) 'Entrepreneurship: productive, unproductive and destructive', *Journal of Political Economy*, 98(5), 893–921, © 1990 by the University of Chicago Press; Box on page 16 from *New York Times*, 31 October 2008, © 31 October 2008 The New York Times, all rights reserved, used by permission and protected by the Copyright Laws of the US, the printing, copying, redistribution, or retransmission of the Material without express permission is prohibited; Box on page 58 from 'Stay out of my way, baby', *The Sunday Times*, 4 November 2007, © The Sunday Times, 4 November 2007/nisyndication.com; Box on page 164 from R. Bridge 'How to cope when your business goes bust', *The Times*, 10 February 2008, © The Times, 10 February 2008/nisyndication.com; Box on page 164 from 'Hong Kong sisters commit suicide after business failure', *The China Daily*, 31 March 2007; Box on page 234 from the *Guardian*, 28 November 2008, copyright Guardian News & Media Ltd 2008; Box on page 240 from 'No-frills boss who keeps one foot on the ground', *Guardian*, 10 October 2008, copyright Guardian News & Media Ltd 2008; Extract on page 261 from *The Times*, 26 March 2008, © The Times 26 March 2008/nisyndication.com; Box on page 286 from *Sunday Times*, 27 April 2008, © Sunday Times 27 April 2008/nisyndication.com; Box on page 301 from growthbusiness.co.uk, http://www.growthbusiness.co.uk/channels/raising-finance/venture-capital/2080/why-i-turned-down-2-million.thtml, GrowthBusiness.co.uk; Box on page 306 from 'One in the eye for the big boys', *Daily Telegraph*, 2004, © Telegraph Media Group Limited 2004; Box on page 337 from British Bankers' Association, 14 December 2005, http://www.bba.org.uk/bba/jsp/polopoly.jsp?d=103&a=143, British Bankers' Association; Box on page 363 from S.N. Kaplan, B.A. Sensoy and P. Stromberg (2009) ' Should investors bet on the jockey or the horse? Evidence from the evolution of firms from early business plans to public companies', *Journal of Finance*, 64(1), 75–115, Wiley-Blackwell; Box on page 424 from T. Jersild and Z. Skopljak (2008) 'How to double business entry in two years', in *Celebrating Reform*, World Bank, Washington: p. 15 Celebrating Reform 2008: Doing Business Reform Case Studies by Jersild T. and Skopljak Z. Copyright 2009 by World Bank. Reproduced with permission of World Bank in the format Textbook via Copyright Clearance Center; Box on page 428 from Here's one place where rip-off showbiz agencies are banned, thanks to Plaid Cymru, *The Mirror*, 23 April 2009.

In some instances we have been unable to trace the owners of copyright material, and we would appreciate any information that would enable us to do so.

Introduction

> The differences in the administrative structure of the very small and the very large firms are so great that in many ways it is hard to see that the two species are of the same genus . . . We cannot define a caterpillar and then use the same definition for a butterfly.
>
> *Edith Penrose,* The Theory of the Growth of the Firm *(1959: 19)*

Up until the 1980s, most students studying business and management completed their degree without ever learning anything about entrepreneurship and small businesses. Only large businesses seemed to exist. They were the norm and, if they appeared at all in textbooks, then entrepreneurs and small businesses were a 'special' case. Even now, a casual read of the business pages of newspapers highlights an almost exclusive focus on large, normally multinational, businesses whose shareholders are dominated by impersonal financial institutions with large boards of directors. The media interest in large businesses either focuses upon the factors that influence their share price or on their social responsibility – or lack of it.

In contrast, small businesses have been almost anonymous and certainly less glamorous. The private life of the managing director of a 'household name' retailer is of much more interest to newspaper readers even outside the business pages. What the owner of the local shop does is of concern probably only to his or her immediate family.

The aim of this is book is to provide the 'big picture' on entrepreneurship and small businesses. We apply broad brush strokes, looking for what occurs in most situations, but knowing that it will not always be relevant to *all* entrepreneurs and businesses in *all* situations. Entrepreneurs and small businesses – partly because there are so many of them – are just too diverse. Also, we do not favour the approach of examining individual businesses or entrepreneurs in such detail that no general pattern ever seems to emerge. Our approach is to identify when the evidence is clear but acknowledge that – more often than we would like – either the knowledge base remains limited or nothing applies to *all* entrepreneurs and small businesses.

Still, two things remain obvious. First, that the large business is not the norm. Instead, the 'small business' – which can be anything from your local family butcher to a high-tech spin-off from a university – is always the most common type of business wherever you come from in the world.

Second, as the above quotation from the economist Edith Penrose makes clear, small businesses are not scaled-down versions of larger businesses. They behave differently; they are organised differently; and they respond to very different incentives compared with large businesses.

Key features of the book

There are four key features of this book.

1. In each of the chapters (coloured white), a thorough and comprehensive *international* survey of the theory and empirical evidence base on entrepreneurship and small businesses,

with a glossary of key terms (see end of the book), is provided. Here we use the term 'international' to refer primarily, but not exclusively, to developed economies.

2. Short case studies, questions for discussion and examples of 'classic' research are provided in the chapters.

3. 'Stand alone' longer case studies (coloured blue) are at the end of the book. These explore – for classroom discussion purposes – particular theoretical and managerial issues developed in the chapters.

4. Two larger case studies (coloured blue). The first is a five-part case study that longitudinally follows the start up and development of a business. The second is a four-part case study/exercise on developing public policy.

How the book should be read

Table I.1 highlights that there are seven parts to the book. For each part, a detailed theoretical and empirical understanding of entrepreneurship and small businesses is developed. Our consistent view is that there is nothing like a good theory for informing good practice. To support this, each chapter ends with a series of questions that can be used either for classroom discussion or for assessment purposes. The longer case studies – which are at the end of the book – are also designed to help you critically reflect on small business activities.

The first part of this book serves to introduce key themes. Chapter 1 argues that fundamental to any understanding of the small business and entrepreneurship is the concept of uncertainty. Chapter 1 defines what this means and what practical implications it has for the differences between large and small businesses. The key point here is that small businesses lack 'market power' (see also Case study 1 at the end of the book which examines the issue of market power between two family-owned funeral businesses). This means that they cannot influence the price in their marketplace and so – to be successful in the medium term – generally cannot compete on price alone. They have to find other ways to attract customers such that its products or services have 'quality' advantages (e.g. have a better customer focus).

In Part 1, another core theme is the question of what we mean by entrepreneurship and small businesses. Chapter 2 gives the economist's and the organisational theorist's perspectives on entrepreneurs. What we learn here is that there are differing motivations behind why people seek to establish and develop a business, depending on what perspective we look at for inspiration.

Closely linked to this theme is Chapter 3 in which we show that there is no common definition that can be applied to all small businesses. Typically, **small and medium-sized enterprises** (SMEs) are seen as having 250 or fewer employees in Europe. In North America, the employment-based measure used to define small businesses is 500 or fewer employees. In truth, an almost endless set of categories can be offered, from formal numeric definitions to qualitative definitions that emphasise the outcomes of a business, such as supporting a particular 'lifestyle'. However, for comparison purposes, the 250 employment threshold is used the most often.

These issues of defining what is involved in understanding the small business and what is the status of an 'entrepreneur' are explored in Case study 2 (at the end of the book) which examines the practical consequences that result when it is difficult to decide if someone is an 'entrepreneur'. Case study 7, Part 1, also examines how difficult it is for policymakers to arrive at a definition of 'entrepreneurship' and how 'entrepreneurship' should be measured over time.

Chapter 4 examines if small business workplaces are 'better' places to work in than larger businesses. In examining 'better', we consider different dimensions of a 'better' workplace such as job tenure, pay, training, health and safety and job satisfaction. Our review of this

Table I.1	Routes through the book

Chapter no.	**Part 1: Understanding small businesses and entrepreneurship**
1	Small businesses: the big picture
2	Understanding entrepreneurship
3	Defining the small business
4	Working in small businesses
5	Innovation
	Part 2: New business formation
6	Defining and measuring start ups
7	Nascent entrepreneurship and social networks
8	The economics of start ups
	Part 3: Business closure
9	Defining and measuring business closure
10	Analysing business closure
	Part 4: Business growth
11	Defining business growth
12	Analysing and measuring business growth
13	Business growth – pre start-up factors
14	Business growth – at start-up factors
15	Business growth – post start-up factors
	Part 5: Finance in the small business
16	Theories of entrepreneurial finance
17	Debt finance
18	Equity finance
	Part 6: Public policy and the small business
19	Public policy, small businesses and entrepreneurs
20	Macro policies towards small businesses and entrepreneurs
21	Policy in practice
	Part 7: Case studies
Case study 1	Understanding Enterprise – Competition at the crematorium: Burgess and Sons vs Austin's
Case study 2	Understanding Enterprise – Dragonfly Consulting: self-employed or employee?
Case study 3	Formation and Growth – The changing fortunes of Runner & Sprue
	Part 1 Runner & Sprue's business plan
	Part 2 Developing and commercialising Runner & Sprue
	Part 3 The IPO
	Part 4 Reaching for the 'Stars and Stripes'
	Part 5 Growing pains?
Case study 4	Finance – Four options facing Two Seasons
Case study 5	Business Closure – Tahir Moshan: running out of time?
Case study 6	Business Closure – The English Grocer: right idea, wrong time?
Case study 7	Public policy in your hands
	Part 1 Defining 'entrepreneurship'
	Part 2 Measuring 'entrepreneurship'
	Part 3 Policy choices
	Part 4 Assessing the policy choice
	Appendix A monitoring and evaluation primer
Case study 8	Tax and the small business – Tax breaks, high stakes
	Glossary, references and index

evidence highlights that there is a high level of heterogeneity in the small business workplace which is increasingly reflected in theoretical understandings of small business employment relationships. Overall, however, the evidence is clear: workers are less well paid but 'happier' in small businesses.

Chapter 5 explores why innovation is so important to our understanding of small businesses and entrepreneurship. It examines how innovation is measured, how innovation occurs at the 'macro' level and whether it is small or large businesses that are more likely to be innovative. This is important because the most famous innovation scholar – Joseph Schumpeter – memorably changed his mind on the matter. He began believing that it was new and small businesses that caused 'gales of creative destruction' (this is often called 'Schumpeter I'). However, he ended up believing that it was only large businesses that had sufficient access to resources, both to undertake Research and Development on a sufficient scale to achieve major scientific breakthroughs, and to effectively commercialise those developments ('Schumpeter II').

Chapter 5 examines both Schumpeter Mark I and II and also how innovation is typically measured and generally understood. The longitudinal business study at the end of the book examines – over its five parts – the particular challenges that an innovative business experiences as it develops from a new start up through to a growth business.

Part 2 examines new businesses. Chapters 6, 7 and 8 examine three main features of new businesses. In Chapter 6, the importance of new businesses is identified. The chapter then proceeds to show that the concept of new business formation is rather imprecise. This is not helped because economists and other social scientists have differing reasons for focusing on new businesses. For the economist, new businesses are of interest primarily because of what they promise in terms of outcomes such as economic development. Other social scientists place greater emphasis on the journey or process which the individual goes through in creating a new business. Chapter 7 considers the types of factors that influence nascent entrepreneurship (people in the process of setting up a business) and the role played by social networks. In Chapter 8, we consider the economic treatment of new businesses. It identifies those individuals, or groups of individuals, that *actually* start a new business and highlights their key characteristics.

The first part of the longitudinal business case on Runner & Sprue presents their actual business plan (Case study 3). Parts 2 and 3 of this case examine the early development of this business.

You will see that Part 3 in Table I.1 – business 'closure' (Chapters 9 and 10) – is placed before business growth (Chapters 11 to 15). This may seem odd. After all, the anticipation might be that businesses come into existence in order to develop. In practice, the prime purpose of a new business is to survive. Chapter 9 argues that business closure is a vital area of importance to anyone interested in small businesses – indeed that it is the ever-present threat of closure that is at the heart of 'smallness'. It then goes on to examine the issues involved in defining business closure and the key issues involved in measuring the number and rates of business closure. In Chapter 9, the focus is on presenting five approaches to business closure. These five approaches are: 'gambler's ruin', population ecology, resource-based closure approaches, 'utility' and entrepreneurial learning. We introduce each approach and, for each, we provide empirical evidence for and against each of the approaches. What emerges is that a 'stylised' feature of small businesses is that they are much more likely to fail than large businesses. This is recognised as an important influence on the behaviour of business owners themselves, on their suppliers and customers and on those that provide finance and credit to the business owner.

To complement this part, there are two longer case studies on business failure at the end of the book. One deals with an entrepreneur, Tashir Mohan, who was formerly highly successful. This case study investigates the reasons for his 'failure'. The second is a case study of a 'failed' small grocery shop, The English Grocer.

Chapters 11 to 15 turn to the important issue of business growth. This is Part 4. Chapter 11 examines why fast-growth businesses are important, how they have been defined and measured, and what 'stylised facts' have been developed out of our understanding of business growth. Chapter 12 introduces six approaches to business growth. These are: evolutionary approaches, social networking approaches, managerial approaches, resource-based views, economic approaches and the role of luck or chance. Finally, Chapters 13 to 15 examine the empirical evidence for the factors that have been used to explain fast growth. This is done by examining entrepreneurial characteristics ('pre' start-up factors), business characteristics ('at' start-up) and business strategy factors ('post' start-up). In these chapters we identify factors that have been shown to be associated with business growth. In Chapter 15, we summarise the theoretical and empirical evidence on business growth. The conclusion is stark: there are very few 'magic bullets' that explain why some businesses grow rapidly and others do not. Researchers, unsurprisingly, are much better at providing explanations of why a business has grown – backcasting – than forecasting which businesses will grow. We also attribute a much greater role to chance or 'luck' than is the case in most entrepreneurial textbooks.

This part of the book is also reflected in the longer case studies at the end of the book. In particular, the longitudinal business case study charts the development of the business as it tries to break into the US market and faces – in the fifth and final part of the case – harsh strategic choices in its attempts to cement its competitive position.

The fifth part of the book examines small business finance. There are three finance chapters. In Chapter 16, we describe the basic forms of finance available to the new and established business. In Chapter 17, we present theories of entrepreneurial finance. We, therefore, examine the range of 'signals' available to both the lender (the bank) and the borrower (small business) and the evidence on finance gaps, discrimination and any financial constraints in debt finance. Chapter 18 considers equity finance. That chapter examines the role and activities of two types of equity financiers: 'business angels' and 'venture capitalists'. We subsequently examine how these equity financiers 'signal' to entrepreneurs, how they monitor the activities of entrepreneurs and how they use particular techniques to value the business.

Besides the in-chapter examples and the longer longitudinal case study, there is also a dedicated finance case study on a company called Two Seasons (Case study 4). This examines the finance options (debt, equity, trade sale) available to an entrepreneur seeking to grow a business.

The final part considers the role of public policy. There are three chapters in this section. Chapter 19 provides an overview of the main issues involved in public policy. This chapter, therefore, covers why policy makers are typically attracted to supporting entrepreneurs and small businesses and what justifications are used to legitimate such support. Chapter 20 considers the impact that 'macro' influences (e.g. economic conditions, taxation, regulation) have on the development of entrepreneurship and small businesses. Finally, Chapter 21 examines the impact of policies targeted at entrepreneurs and small businesses. The chapter reviews five main areas of public support – enterprise culture, finance, advice and assistance, supporting technology and innovation and the development of particular groups (e.g. women, ethnic minorities).

What emerges from these three chapters on public policy is that very often the government departments responsible for leading public policy in this area lack the necessary financial 'muscle' to effectively support smaller businesses. Equally, there is very little evidence from our review that public support is a significant positive benefit to entrepreneurs and small businesses.

Supporting these public policy chapters is a five-part case study/exercise on public policy. The first part returns to Chapter 1 and asks: what is an appropriate definition of entrepreneurship for a policy maker? The second asks for an assessment to be made on how a policy maker should measure entrepreneurship. The third part asks for a particular policy choice to be identified and worked through. The fourth part asks: how do we know if a particular policy works? To support this, a 'primer' on monitoring and evaluation is provided to help guide on how policy should be assessed.

Part 1 Understanding Small Businesses and Entrepreneurship

In Part 1, we introduce many of the essentials of small business and entrepreneurship. Chapter 1 argues that fundamental to any understanding of the small business and entrepreneurship is the concept of uncertainty. Chapter 1 defines what this means and what practical implications it has for the differences between large and small businesses. Chapter 2 gives the economists and the organisational theorist's perspectives on entrepreneurs. Chapter 3 shows that there is no common definition that can be applied to all small businesses. Chapter 4 examines if small business workplaces are 'better' places to work in than larger businesses. Chapter 5 explores why innovation is so important to our understanding of small businesses and entrepreneurship.

Entrepreneurship in Action   FT

Go to the *Small Business and Entrepreneurship* companion website at www.pearsoned.co.uk/storeygreene to watch entrepreneurs and academics giving you their personal perspectives on some of these issues.

Will King, CEO of King of Shaves, talks about innovation, launching a new product, and going up against market-leading corporate competitors.

1

Small businesses:
The big picture

Key learning objectives

By the end of this chapter you should:

- Understand the concepts of risk and uncertainty
- Appreciate the importance of market, customer and aspirational uncertainty
- Be able to identify key differences between large and small businesses.

There are known knowns. There are things we know that we know. There are known unknowns. That is to say, there are things that we now know we don't know. But there are also unknown unknowns. There are things we do not know we don't know.

Donald Rumsfeld, former US Secretary of Defense (2002)

1.1 The importance of uncertainty

Unlike the notoriously rambling quote above, a better way of understanding the difference between risk and uncertainty is to think of two closed pots. In one, there are 100 balls, of which 60 are red and 40 are black. This means the known distribution is three red balls for every two black balls. In the other pot, there are also 100 balls but all – or perhaps none – of them *may* be black balls. Suppose now that people are forced to bet. To win a prize, though, they have to pick a black ball. The question here is which of the two pots should they choose? The first pot which has the known, but still risky, distribution? Or the second pot with the uncertain distribution?

In general, this chapter argues that the uncertainty facing entrepreneurs and small businesses is considerably greater than that faced by large businesses. It is also likely to be very different. The large business is relatively more likely to face the issue of 'internal' uncertainty than the smaller business. This involves those at the top of an organisation making sure that their 'strategic' decisions are effectively implemented by middle managers and the workers. This can go spectacularly wrong – see the example of Terminal 5 (below).

This is much less of an issue in small businesses. Here the boss can much more easily 'manage by walking about'. There is a much greater likelihood that, whilst 'walking about', the person actually making decisions will be challenged and, perhaps knowing this, will seek the views of a high proportion of the employees.

In large organisations such broad consultation is very difficult, but this means that decisions taken at the top are likely to be implemented in a more uneven, and hence uncertain, manner than is the case for smaller businesses. For example, Forth *et al.* (2006) reported that

Illustration	The opening of Terminal 5

Despite its impressive appearance, Heathrow's Terminal 5 was plagued with problems when it first opened.

Terminal 5, the £4.3 billion passenger terminal at London Heathrow, was opened in 2008. Prior to its opening, Willie Walsh, the British Airways Chief Executive said: 'Terminal Five is a fantastic facility and our customers will really enjoy the space, comfort and convenience it offers'. On its first days of opening, hundreds of flights were cancelled and some 15,000 bags were lost as the baggage system collapsed. Willie Walsh was forced into a very public apology: 'I'd again like to apologise to those customers who have suffered disrupted journeys or baggage delays'. A variety of reasons were blamed for the fiasco: poor staff training; the size of the terminal; the 'newness' of the baggage system; and poor management. Although Willie Walsh did not resign, the directors of operations and customer services left the company. Ultimately, none of these events could have been easily predicted. Senior managers at BA had real difficulties in 'translating' their strategy down to their workforce. The consequence is that some of them lost their jobs.

69 per cent of workers in small businesses agreed that 'those at the top are best placed to make decisions about this workplace' whilst this view was shared by only 46 per cent of large business employees. In part this may also be because the person at the top of a large organisation does not know what is really going on. Harris and Ogbonna (2009) illustrate how customer-contact employees in a large business hide customer complaints, but those that do emerge from such staff are then subsequently likely to be concealed by their supervisory and managerial staff. Such concealment is more difficult in a small business.

However, these behavioural advantages do not protect small businesses from 'external' uncertainties. In this chapter, we examine three kinds of external uncertainty: market, customer and aspirational. We then consider what small businesses and entrepreneurs can generally do to limit such uncertainty, and the key differences between large and small businesses.

1.2 Market, customer and aspirational uncertainty

There are three dimensions to external uncertainty. These are market, customer and aspirational uncertainty. We examine each of these in turn.

Market uncertainty

One key difference between small and large businesses is their access to market power. Large businesses, acting either independently or with others, may be able to influence prices in a market by withholding supplies. This power of influence may make the large business a **price maker**. In contrast, the small business lacks this market power and has to accept that the price received for its product/service is beyond its control. This makes the small business a **price taker**.

One illustration of this lack of competitive strength is that very many small businesses are heavily dependent on a single customer or a small group of customers. This has changed little over time. As long ago as 1971, the Bolton Report found that more than one-third of all small manufacturers made a quarter or more of their sales to a single customer. More recently, Kitson and Wilkinson (2000) reported that 37 per cent of small and medium-sized enterprises (SMEs) relied on one customer for more than one quarter of their sales. Perhaps even more strikingly, 20 per cent of businesses that employed 1–9 employees (micro businesses) obtained *at least* half their sales from a single customer. This compares with only 4 per cent of medium-sized businesses (20–249 employees). This suggests that the smaller the business, the more likely it is to be heavily reliant on a single customer.

Small businesses also tend to be concentrated in sectors in which there are few obstacles to entry such as needing large amounts of capital to start the business (i.e. **entry barriers** are low). Similarly, they are also likely to choose sectors where there are few cost advantages from having a bigger operation (i.e. the **scale economies** are limited). Examples include hairdressers, window cleaners and taxi drivers, but also an increasing number of small businesses are found in the IT and business service sectors. So, where entry is easy, competition is likely to be fierce and uncertainty for the individual business is likely to be high.

Small businesses may respond to this market uncertainty by seeking to compete on the basis of price, by lowering their own costs at every opportunity. However, since large businesses are much more likely to have lower costs owing to scale economies, this approach is potentially problematic. Indeed, Saridakis *et al.* (2008) showed that new businesses that report their key competitive advantage over rivals to be price are less likely to exhibit short-term survival than new businesses that emphasise other factors, such as customer service or innovation.

A second approach is to seek to identify some form of **niche**. A niche is a small, restricted marketplace, in which higher than average profits can be made by offering some form of specialist service or product. This niche could be geographical (e.g. the only shop in the locality); the provision of a specialist service (e.g. a 24-hour call-out service); or it may also be an ability on the part of the owner to identify customer requirements more accurately than rival businesses. Unfortunately, small business niches tend to be temporary, meaning that if above average profits are being earned, and entry barriers are low, then competitors are likely to enter the niche, and erode profit margins.

The consequences or 'downside losses' of making an incorrect decision may also be considerable. As Chapters 9 and 10 show, approximately 30–40 per cent of businesses starting today will not be in existence in three years' time.

Many of these businesses will cease without incurring any losses either to the owners or to the creditors, but the fact that they do cease implies that many owners made an incorrect decision in starting them in the first place. Nevertheless, there are serious debts for some and the fear of incurring such debts is an understandably powerful influence on the psychology and behaviour of entrepreneurs.

Customer uncertainty

A second source of uncertainty for the small business is its customer(s). One of the assumptions of Knight (1921) was that employees could be (fairly) certain of receiving a wage. By contrast, he assumed that entrepreneurs buy inputs for their business at a *certain* price but only sell their output for an *uncertain* price. In other words, they know what their costs are but are unsure how many of their products they can sell, or for what price. Hence, the income of the entrepreneur is the *uncertain* revenue minus the *certain* costs whilst the income for the employee is the *certain* wage that they know they are going to get at the end of the week or month.

The impact of this uncertainty is seen in different ways. For example, if the customer is a larger business, a small business may seek to reduce customer uncertainty by becoming a sub-contractor to the customer. In this relationship the customer agrees, normally for a period of time, to purchase all or a high proportion of the output of the (small) business. This constitutes a guarantee to the small business and, in this sense, reduces its uncertainty.

However, whilst the uncertainty associated with sales falls, in a subcontracting relationship, the (large) customer is likely to impose additional requirements upon the (small) business. The customer may require the product to be produced in a very specific way, using predetermined materials. In negotiating the elements of the contract, the (small) business may be required to divulge costings and so have a reduced opportunity for profit making. In short, whilst subcontracting is one response to uncertainty, it is likely to lead to lower profit margins. There may be a trade-off between uncertainty and profitability.

However, Johnson *et al.* (1999) found that short-term growth in small businesses appears unrelated to customer dependence. They attribute this to two conflicting influences. If the (large) customer is expanding then the (small) supplier is likely also to grow, but if the (large) customer is declining then the (small) supplier will contract. Since either is possible then it is difficult to forecast whether those businesses that are more heavily dependent upon a small number of customers will grow more or less slowly than those with a more diverse customer base. What is clear is that, all else being equal, the dependent business is more risky.

Aspirational uncertainty

We have already noted that small businesses are characterised by diversity. Whilst it may be broadly valid to assume that the bulk of large businesses seek to enhance shareholder value or profit maximise in the medium term, the same appears much less the case for smaller businesses. Some businesses may only seek to generate 'pin money' for their owners. More typically, small businesses provide interesting employment for their owners, even though these individuals could obtain a much higher income as an employee (Hamilton 2000).

Another reason may be that owners wish to build a business or keep it running – even if profits are low – in order to pass it on to their family. Alternatively, it may be a hobby that happens to generate some income. A final group may believe that there is a chance they may strike it rich. They recognise the chance is low but they also recognise that for this to happen they have to be in business. In short, small business owners are likely to have a wide range of motivations and aspirations and it is unwise to assume that these are exclusively, or even primarily, monetary (Gimeno *et al.* 1997). Also, individual business owners are likely to respond very differently to market conditions and external circumstances.

Whilst there exists this diversity of aspirations, a desire to grow the business is the exception rather than the rule, particularly for the smallest businesses. Whilst growth is discussed more fully in Chapters 11 to 15, it is important to note the evidence of Hakim (1989). She found that, in a survey of approximately 750,000 UK businesses, 55 per cent had no plans for growth, at a time when the UK economy was growing. This finding was clearly influenced by business size, with 60 per cent of businesses with fewer than 3 workers having no growth aspirations, compared with only 2 per cent of those with 25–49 employees. Hence, the smaller the operational size of the business the less likely it is to seek to increase its scale.

Also impacting on aspirations is the number of owners. If we relax the implicit assumption that a single business is owned by one person, then we can see that owning more than one business (**portfolio entrepreneurship**) or having a team running a business means an even greater diversity of aspirations amongst those owning and managing small businesses.

There is also likely to be a link between the aspirations of the (small) business owner and their personal characteristics. So, whilst the population of small businesses may exhibit considerable diversity, research has addressed the link between business aspirations and owner characteristics. For example, Arabsheibani *et al.* (2000) have clearly shown that entrepreneurs are more optimistic about their own prospects and abilities than the population as a whole. This is set out in the Classic research (below).

The owners of small businesses are likely to have a combination of objectives for operating their business. These include ensuring the business survives, that it provides for their family needs, provides enough disposable income, and for a minority, meets their growth ambitions. Hence, whilst the assumption of a profit-maximising business seeking to generate shareholder value may be valid for larger enterprises, it is wholly inappropriate when considering smaller businesses.

In summary, this section has identified three types of external uncertainty: market, customer and aspirational. Small businesses tend to be price takers, reliant on few customers and have a wide range of aspirations for their business.

Classic research	Arabsheibani, G., de Meza, D., Maloney, J. and Pearson, B. (2000) 'And a Vision Appeared unto Them of Great Profit: Evidence of Self-deception Among the Self-employed', *Economics Letters*, 67, 35–41.

Using 20,000 observations from the British Household Panel Survey 1990–6, Arabsheibani *et al.* show that:

- Amongst the self-employed, 4.6 times as many forecast an improvement in their finances whilst subsequently experiencing a deterioration as forecast a deterioration but subsequently experienced an improvement.
- For employees the ratio was only 2.9.

This correlates with Cooper *et al.* (1988) who found that 68 per cent of entrepreneurs believed that the odds of their business succeeding were better than for others in the same sector whilst only 5 per cent thought it was worse.

The conclusion drawn from this research is that if people are generally optimistic about events outside their control, then entrepreneurs are drawn disproportionately from the 'super' optimist category. In other words, entrepreneurs are significantly more optimistic than the average person.

1.3 Ways of limiting uncertainty

An implicit assumption so far has been that most people prefer certainty to uncertainty. However, one situation where this may not apply is where the potential pay-offs are significantly higher under uncertainty. For example, reconsider the two pots example used at the start of the chapter. If the pay-off was greater (or the losses were lower) for the uncertain pot, then the uncertain pot becomes more likely to be chosen.

Small businesses may also seek to increase the positive pay-off, reduce the negative pay-off, or try to improve the odds facing them. We now set out four ways in which small businesses seek to achieve this.

First, the small business owner can register his or her business as a limited liability company. This means that the owners/directors are not personally liable for the debts of the company if it is liquidated, unless it has been trading fraudulently. This may help minimise any downside losses for which the owners/directors *may* be held personally responsible. The choice of legal form may also be influenced by issues of credibility and taxation. A new business may be viewed as more credible by customers and by financial institutions if it becomes incorporated, since it then has to register formally and produce reports on an annual basis which enter the public domain. In this sense, the choice of legal form is one that not only reduces downside losses but also enhances upside gains. Perhaps reflecting this, both Harhoff *et al.* (1998) and Schutjens and Wever (2002) for Germany and the Netherlands, respectively, show that incorporation is associated with faster growth. Taxation issues may also influence this choice (see Crawford and Freedman 2008). We discuss this evidence in greater detail in Chapters 14 and 20.

A second way in which smaller businesses address uncertainty is to focus upon short-term survival rather than upon longer-term profitability. Given that the owners of small businesses face the real prospect of business closure leading possibly to financial ruin for themselves and their family, it is to be expected that they will have, on average, shorter time horizons than those making similar decisions in larger businesses. Evidence of this is reflected in the nature of the investments they make. For example, it is quite rational for a small business owner to invest less heavily in workforce training, than a large business. This is because any pay-off from this training will only materialise in the medium to long term when, of course, the small business may not exist.

A third response to uncertainty is that small businesses invest less heavily in fixed plant and equipment (e.g. machinery) which may have a more restricted range of uses, than is the case for larger businesses. This is because in the event of an unexpected change in demand for the product or service, such equipment could become obsolete. Since small businesses are more likely to face such changes it is quite rational for them to invest less in such equipment even if this leads to a higher cost base.

A fourth response to uncertainty amongst small business owners is to establish a portfolio of businesses rather than a single enterprise. In this case if there is a risky, but potentially profitable opportunity, the small business owner may choose to establish a new independent company. The basic logic for this is that it spreads the risks faced by the entrepreneur, because the poor performing business can be closed without endangering the business interests of the entrepreneur as a whole. Evidence of the scale of portfolio entrepreneurship suggests this is common. Westhead and Wright (1998) found that 12 per cent of new businesses were founded by an individual who currently owned another business (**portfolio entrepreneur**) whilst 25 per cent of businesses were owned by individuals that had been in business previously but were not owners when starting their existing businesses (**serial entrepreneurship**). Greene *et al.* (2008) also obtained broadly similar findings: they found 17 per cent were portfolio entrepreneurs and 31 per cent were serial entrepreneurs.

Overall, this section has presented four ways the small business can limit uncertainty. These are incorporation, having short survival-based time horizons, limiting investment and portfolio entrepreneurship. These issues are explored more fully in Case study 1 (Understanding enterprise – Competition at the crematorium).

1.4 Large and small businesses: the key differences

Drawing upon the above case and the earlier discussion of uncertainty, Table 1.1 summarises 17 key dimensions – other than size *per se* – by which small and large businesses differ from each other. For each of these dimensions, Table 1.1 provides empirical evidence.

Table 1.1	The key differences between small and large businesses	
Aspect (evidence)	**Small business**	**Large business**	**What difference does it make?**
1. Risk of failure (Honjo 2000; Harhoff *et al.* 1998; Hart and Oulton 1996)	Much more likely to cease trading than large businesses. It is the risk of failure that most fundamentally distinguishes small from large businesses.	Whilst large businesses do fail, often spectacularly and with considerable media coverage, the risk of failure is not as ever-present as it is with small businesses.	Makes small businesses more focused on short-term survival. They have to focus on cash rather than profit. Makes some small businesses want to grow fast to become larger and so reduce failure risk. Makes external funding organisations more selective about funding small businesses.
2. Market power (see Case study 1: Understanding enterprise – Competition at the crematorium)	No market power to set prices – except sometimes in very local markets. They have to seek to compete in other ways such as service, quality, and timeliness.	Much more likely to have power to set prices, although this has to be used carefully to avoid attracting the attention of competition authorities.	Market prices are strongly influenced by large businesses that, through scale economies, should be able to set low prices. The competitive focus of small and large businesses is likely to differ sharply. Small businesses are seen to incur 'external uncertainty' because of their lack of market power.
3. Management (Cosh *et al.* 2005)	The small business is generally owned and managed by the same individual(s).	Owners are normally private shareholders or financial institutions, with management being undertaken by professionals who generally are only modest owners of shares.	In small businesses the interests of the owners and the managers correspond; this is much less likely to be the case in large businesses. For example, since remuneration 'packages' for managers are clearly linked to business size, managers may favour takeovers that increase scale, without necessarily leading to a higher share valuation in the longer run. Such pressures are less likely within smaller businesses.
4. Motivation of owner (Gray 2002; Hart and Oulton 1996)	Some are 'lifestyle' owners of small businesses whose object is primarily to obtain a comfortable living for themselves or to pass on their business to family members. In contrast, others may wish to grow their business rapidly.	Traditionally, the owners or shareholders of large businesses seek to maximise the value of the company. The task of management is to achieve this maximisation of shareholder value.	There is much greater diversity of small business performance. The smaller the business the more diverse the performance, at least in part because of the greater diversity of motivation of the owners.
5. Brand (Shocker *et al.* 1994; Hatten and Schendel 1977)	No brand value – apart from some local loyalty.	Brand can be a major positive factor influencing sales. It provides the customer with awareness leading to confidence and ultimately loyalty.	Protecting a positive brand image is vital for large businesses.
6. Strategy (Man *et al.* 2002; Rangone 1999)	Has to be flexible, since it lacks the opportunity to reap scale economies. So more likely to be shifting to new products/services and new customers.	The large business will seek to exploit its price advantages, and advantage obtained by heavy investment in people, plant or research and development.	The development of new markets and particularly new industries has often been pioneered by smaller businesses. Once those industries have become established, average business size increases, in part because scale economies become more important.

Table 1.1 continued

7. Internal organisation (Curran and Blackburn 2001)	Informal. Because their business is small, the owner can make decisions and ensure they are implemented. There is little incentive to document decisions. However, in some cases the informality can be a cloak for exploitation.	Procedural. In a large organisation there are many middle managers who can 'water-down' decisions made by the top managers. One way to ensure that everyone is aware of decisions, and why they were taken, is for this to be communicated in writing.	The central managerial concern in large businesses is to ensure that decisions made at the top of the organisation are implemented in full throughout the whole of the organisation. Large businesses are, therefore, much more likely to suffer from 'internal uncertainty', defined as an inability to deliver a product or service consistently throughout the organisation. Much managerial time in large businesses is devoted to addressing this issue, with formality and 'procedures' being implemented. In contrast, the owner of a small business is often constantly in direct contact with customers.
8. Wages and benefits for workers (Brown et al. 1990; Troske 1999)	Small businesses generally pay lower wages and provide fewer fringe benefits.	Larger businesses pay higher wages and provide more fringe benefits.	Large and small businesses hire different types of worker. The small business worker is more likely to be either old or young, attracted by a team ethic and less likely to have formal qualifications.
9. Human resources (Vickers et al. 2005; Forth et al. 2006)	At their best, small businesses provide a happy environment in which to work. At their worst, they can be unsafe, exploitative, working environments.	Large businesses are more likely to attract prime age workers, with formal qualifications, and those seeking a career.	Overall, job satisfaction appears to be higher in small than in large businesses. Large business workers are likely to receive a higher remuneration package but small business workers may derive greater satisfaction from flexibility and sense of teamwork.
10. Training and Recruitment (Carroll et al. 1999; Storey 2005)	Small businesses provide less formal training and recruit new staff through informal channels.	Large businesses are much more likely to provide formal training and use formal channels to recruit new staff.	Small businesses, because they emphasise the use of informal procedures, are viewed by some as 'backward'. But this is to misunderstand the motivations and constraints of small business owners. What is less clear is whether small businesses provide more informal training than large ones.
11. Investment policies (Cosh and Hughes 1994)	Small businesses spend relatively less on fixed equipment, especially that which cannot easily be converted to alternative uses in the event of changes in demand.	Heavy investment is central to achieving scale economies that underpin the cost advantage of large businesses.	Investment, and capital stock per employee, is much higher in small than large businesses.
12. Sources of finance (Ang 1991)	Small business owners have a pecking order which favours internal to external sources of finance. External providers of finance have imperfect information on small businesses.	Large businesses have a wide choice of sources of finance. Information imperfections are much less than with small businesses.	Small businesses are funded primarily from the owner's savings and retained profits. Commercial banks providing short-term loans are also important in most countries. Use of external equity is rare. Small businesses pay higher interest rates on borrowed funds than large businesses.

Table 1.1 continued

Aspect (evidence)	Small business	Large business	What difference does it make?
13. Innovation (van Praag and Versloot 2007)	Small businesses are more likely to commercialise innovations but less likely to adopt innovations.	Large businesses' innovation capitalises on heavy expenditure on formal Research and Development.	Whilst most small businesses do not innovate, and many fewer undertake formal Research and Development, those that do are able to bring novel ideas to the marketplace quickly if they are able to access suitable funding.
14. Competitive advantages (Jennings and Beaver 1997)	Flexible, responsive to the customer, and innovative.	Able to undertake investment and provide a more comprehensive service.	Large businesses can reap scale economies, so they are more likely to be able to compete on price. They are also able to supply a wider range of linked services, avoiding the need for customers to have to shop around.
15. Political influence (Dannreuther 1999)	The individual small business, acting alone, will have minimal impact on government. Only by joining a lobby organisation can this be overcome. Unfortunately, most small business owners are not, by nature, 'joiners' which means that the members of small business lobby organisations are not 'typical' small businesses – except in countries where membership is compulsory.	Large businesses are widely consulted by governments, even at the early stage when legislation is considered. Since there are only small numbers of large businesses, this consultation is easy and convenient for government.	Large businesses have considerable power and can influence the formulation of government policy. If legislation is introduced, the cost of complying with it is relatively much higher for small than for large businesses. However, large businesses argue that, whilst they comply fully with legislation, smaller businesses can avoid enforcement by avoiding the scrutiny of government.
16. How it sees itself	The small business sees itself as customer focused, placing emphasis on service.	The large business sees itself as reliable, with a reputation to uphold.	
17. How it sees the other	The small business is seen by the large business as lacking credibility, as potentially unreliable, and as a transient 'fly by night'.	The small business sees the large as bureaucratic, distanced from the customer, yet seeking to exploit its muscle in the marketplace.	
Key words	Uncertainty. Diversity. Flexibility. Failure.	Reliability. Brand. Market power. Influence.	

Summary

This chapter has made the case that small businesses differ radically from large businesses in a number of dimensions other than size. Many of these stem from the small business being more likely to cease trading than larger enterprises, reflecting in part its lack of market power and credibility. The external environment for small businesses is also more uncertain than for large businesses.

We argue that these external uncertainties directly influence the way that small businesses organise themselves – the 'internal' differences. If it is to survive and prosper, the small business needs to be flexible. This implies placing much less emphasis when making business decisions upon the longer term, and more upon being agile in the short to medium term.

The key advantage of the small business is that, whilst the external uncertainty they experience is greater than for large businesses, they experience less internal uncertainty. In a small business, the owner observes more closely what is going on, so there is much less emphasis on formality or written procedures. Small businesses even choose their workers in a different way to large businesses, focusing much less on formal qualifications. Instead, they place more emphasis upon 'attitude' and what others whose judgement they trust say about the worker. The person making the choice is much more likely to be the owner in a small business, whereas in a large business it is more likely to be a human resource 'professional'.

However, all of the above points are generalisations. Small businesses, partly because there are so many of them, exhibit huge diversity and probably every one of the above generalisations is untrue for some small businesses. This is more clearly illustrated in Case study 1 – Competition at the crematorium – where a small business was able to exert real market power over a competitor, even if a lack of market power is generally viewed as a central characteristic of a small business.

Question for discussion

One implication from this chapter is that small businesses – and their owners – have more diversity in their private and business objectives than owners of large businesses. This does not seem to sit comfortably alongside the idea that small businesses operate in more intensely competitive markets in which failure to profit maximise would be expected to endanger the survival of the business.

Do you think it is true that small business owners have more diverse sets of objectives than those who own larger businesses?

References

Ang, J.S. (1991) 'Small Business Uniqueness and the Theory of Financial Management', *Journal of Small Business Finance*, 1(1), 1–13.

Arabsheibani, G., de Meza, D., Maloney, J. and Pearson, B. (2000) 'And a Vision Appeared unto Them of Great Profit: Evidence of Self-deception among the Self-employed', *Economics Letters*, 67, 35–41.

Bolton, J.E. (1971) *Report of the Committee of Inquiry on Small Firms*. Cmnd. 4811. London: HMSO.

Brown, C., Hamilton, J. and Medoff, J.L. (1990) *Employers Large and Small*. Cambridge, MA: Harvard University Press.

Carroll, M., Marchington, M., Earnshaw, J. and Taylor, S. (1999) 'Recruitment in Small Firms: Processes, Methods and Problems', *Employee Relations*, 21(3), 236–50.

Cooper, A.C., Woo, C.Y. and Dunkelberg, W.C. (1988) 'Entrepreneurs' Perceived Chances for Success', *Journal of Business Venturing*, 3(2), 97–108.

Cosh, A. and Hughes, A. (1994) 'Size, Financial Structure and Profitability: UK Companies in the 1980's', in Storey, D.J. and Hughes, A. (eds), *Finance and the Small Firm*. London: Routledge, 18–63.

Cosh, A., Guest, P. and Hughes, A. (2005) *Board Share Ownership and Takeover Performance*. Cambridge: Centre for Business Research, University of Cambridge.

Crawford, C. and Freedman, J. (2008) *Small Business Taxation*. London: Institute for Fiscal Studies.

Curran, J. and Blackburn, R.A. (2001) *Researching the Small Enterprise*. London: Sage.

Dannreuther, C. (1999) 'Discrete Dialogues and the Legitimation of EU SME Policy', *Journal of European Public Policy*, 6(3), 436–55.

Forth, J., Bewley, H. and Bryson, A. (2006) *Small and Medium-sized Enterprises: Findings from the 2004 Workplace Employment Relations Survey*. London: Department of Trade and Industry.

Gimeno, J., Folta, T.B., Cooper, A.C. and Woo, C.C. (1997) 'Survival of the Fittest? Entrepreneurial Human Capital and the Persistence of Under-performing Firms', *Administrative Science Quarterly*, 42, 750–83.

Gray, C. (2002) 'Entrepreneurship, Resistance to Change and Growth in Small Firms', *Journal of Small Business and Enterprise Development*, 9(1), 61–72.

Greene, F.J., Mole, K.F. and Storey, D.J. (2008) *Three Decades of Enterprise Culture*. London: Palgrave.

Hakim, C. (1989) 'Self-employment in Britain: Recent Trends and Current Issues', *Work, Employment and Society*, 2(4), 421–50.

Hamilton, B.H. (2000) 'Does Entrepreneurship Pay? An Empirical Analysis of the Returns to Self-employment', *Journal of Political Economy*, 108(3), 604–31.

Harhoff, D., Stahl, K. and Woywode, M. (1998) 'Legal Form, Growth and Exit of West German Firms: Empirical Results from Manufacturing, Construction, Trade and Service Industries', *Journal of Industrial Economics*, 66(4), 453–88.

Harris, L.C. and Ogbonna, E. (2009) 'Hiding Customer Complaints: Studying the Motivations and Forms of Service Employees' Complaint Concealment Behaviours', *British Journal of Management*, Published Online, 16 February.

Hart, P.E. and Oulton, N. (1996) 'Growth and Size of Firms', *Economic Journal*, 106(438), 1242–52.

Hatten, K.J. and Schendel, D.E. (1977) 'Heterogeneity within an Industry: Firm Conduct in the US Brewing Industry 1952–71', *Journal of Industrial Economics*, 26(2), 97–113.

Honjo, Y. (2000) 'Business Failure of New Firms: An Empirical Analysis Using a Multiplicative Hazards Model', *International Journal of Industrial Organisation*, 18(4), 557–74.

Jennings, P. and Beaver, G. (1997) 'The Performance and Competitive Advantage of Small Firms: A Management Perspective', *International Small Business Journal*, 15(2), 63–75.

Johnson, P., Conway, C. and Kattuman, P. (1999) 'Small Business Growth in the Short Run', *Small Business Economics*, 12(2), 103–12.

Kitson, M. and Wilkinson, F. (2000) 'Markets, Competition and Collaboration', in Cosh, A. and Hughes, A. (eds), *British Enterprise in Transition*. Cambridge: Centre for Business Research, University of Cambridge.

Knight, F. (1921) *Risk, Uncertainty and Profit*. Boston, MA: Houghton Mifflin.

Man, T.W., Lau, T. and Chan, K.F. (2002) 'The Competitiveness of Small and Medium Enterprises: A Conceptualisation with Focus on Entrepreneurial Competencies', *Journal of Business Venturing*, 17(2), 123–42.

Rangone, A. (1999) 'A Resource-based Approach to Strategy-based Analysis in Small–Medium-sized Enterprises', *Small Business Economics*, 12(3), 233–48.

Saridakis, G., Mole, K. and Storey, D.J. (2008) 'New small firm survival in England', *Empirica*, 35(1), 25–39.

Schutjens, V.A.J.M. and Wever, E. (2002) 'Determinants of New Firm Success', *Papers in Regional Science*, 79, 135–59.

Shocker, A.D., Shrivastava, R.K. and Ruekert, R.W. (1994) 'Challenges and Opportunities Facing Brand Management', *Journal of Marketing Research*, 31(2), 149–58.

Storey, D.J. (2005) *The Competitive Experience of UK SMEs: Fair and Unfair.* Report to the Competition Commission, London.

Troske, K.R. (1999) 'Evidence on the Employer Size-wage Premium from Worker-establishment Matched Data', *Review of Economics and Statistics*, 81(1), 15–26.

van Praag, C.M. and Versloot, P.H. (2007) 'What Is the Value of Entrepreneurship? A Review of Recent Research', *Small Business Economics*, 29(4), 351–82.

Vickers, I., James, P., Smallbone, D. and Baldock, R. (2005) 'Understanding Small Firm Responses to Regulation: The Case of Workplace Health and Safety', *Policy Studies*, 26(2), 149–69.

Vossen, R.W. (1998) 'Relative Strengths and Weaknesses of Small Firms in Innovation', *International Small Business Journal*, 16(3), 88–94.

Westhead, P. and Wright, M. (1998) 'Novice, Serial and Portfolio Founders: Are They Different?', *Journal of Business Venturing*, 13(3), 173–204.

2 Understanding entrepreneurship

Key learning objectives

By the end of this chapter you should:

- Be able to identify key differences between productive, unproductive and destructive entrepreneurship
- Understand the key features of economic and organisational theory interpretations of entrepreneurship
- Evaluate the major areas of debate between these two approaches.

When conjectures are offered to explain historic slowdowns or great leaps in economic growth, there is the group of usual suspects that is rounded up – prominent among them is the entrepreneur. When growth has slowed, it is implied that a decline in entrepreneurship was partly to blame (perhaps partly because the culture's 'need for achievement' has atrophied). At another time and place, it is said, the flowering of entrepreneurship accounts for unprecedented expansion.

William Baumol (1990)

2.1 Introduction

Here is a heretical question. Are we sure that entrepreneurs play a valuable role in society? One aim of this chapter is to assess their worth. We show that the answer depends on what the rules and incentives are. We then consider two main approaches to understanding entrepreneurs which Casson (1982) defines as 'someone who specialises in making judgemental decisions about the co-ordination of scarce resources' (p. 23). The first approach is that of the economists. We then examine the organisational theorist approach.

Both the economist and the organisational theorist emphasise that entrepreneurship occurs when information about opportunities is imperfectly known. At the very least, this gives rise to opportunities because entrepreneurs are able to exploit price differences between two areas (or differences between current and future prices). The chapter explores the major features of both the economist and organisational theorist approaches and also highlights their differences. It suggests the economist's approach is more focused on choices and outcomes of entrepreneurial activity. The organisational approach also places emphasis on these features but gives greater importance to entrepreneurial processes and to cognition.

2.2 Entrepreneurs: good or bad? Not enough or just not the right sort?

If a person is called 'enterprising' or 'entrepreneurial', this is normally – but not always – seen as a compliment. In a dynamic and constantly changing world, it is thought to be desirable to be entrepreneurial because it conjures up a picture of an individual who sees opportunities and is willing to exploit them. Classic examples of this may include people like the founder of Microsoft, Bill Gates. Others might include the eighteenth-century banker, Mayer Rothschild; the nineteenth-century oil magnate, John Rockefeller; or Estée Lauder in the twentieth century.

But, like many frequently used words, 'enterprising' or 'entrepreneur' often have different meanings for different people. Baumol (1990), in a 'Classic research' article (below), analysed the mixed historical perception of entrepreneurs. This is a classic article because he distinguishes between three types of entrepreneurs: productive, unproductive and destructive. An example of a productive entrepreneur is perhaps someone like Ingvar Kamprad. He began his entrepreneurial activities at an early age before setting up IKEA, the Swedish furniture chain, which now has branches throughout the world.

Unproductive entrepreneurs tend to be involved in some form of bureaucracy. A fictional example of this may be Lionel Hutz, the lawyer from 'The Simpsons' cartoon programme. Hutz may be described as an 'ambulance chaser' because he preys on the misfortunes of others by looking to represent them in court, usually on some spurious health and safety issue.

An example of a destructive entrepreneur may be someone like 'The Godfather' played by Marlon Brando in the film of the same name. From humble Sicilian roots, 'The Godfather' achieves a position of authority through corruption, illegal gambling and prostitution. But this is not just Hollywood fantasy. Antonopoulos and Mitra (2009) document that the scale and enterprise in bootlegging cigarettes out of Greece cost the Greek taxpayer tens of millions of euros annually. A second example is that of the 'pirates of Somalia'. What is destructive about these types of behaviour is that they have negative impacts on wider society.

Illustration	Somalia's pirates flourish in a lawless nation

Destructive entrepreneurs make profits while others suffer: the pirate economy of Somalia is just one example.

Boosaaso, Somalia – this may be one of the most dangerous towns in Somalia, a place where you can get kidnapped faster than you can wipe the sweat off your brow. But it is also one of the most prosperous. Money changers walk around with thick wads of hundred-dollar bills. Palatial new houses are rising up next to tin-roofed shanties. Men in jail reminisce, with a twinkle in their eyes, about their days living like kings. This is the story of Somalia's booming, not-so-underground pirate economy. The country is in chaos, countless children are starving and people are killing one another in the streets of Mogadishu, the capital, for a handful of grain. But one particular line of work – piracy – seems to be benefiting quite openly from all this lawlessness and desperation. This year, Somali officials say, pirate profits are on track to reach a record $50 million, all of it tax free. 'These guys are making a killing', said Mohamud Muse Hirsi, the top Somali official in Boosaaso.

Source: *New York Times*, 31 October 2008.

In essence, Baumol argues that an individual with exactly the same entrepreneurial abilities could become a productive, unproductive or destructive entrepreneur. Baumol argues what determines that choice are the 'rules of the game'. So, an entrepreneurial individual will choose to be productive, unproductive or destructive depending on these rules and how they are enforced. Classic justifications are that in the former Soviet Union the 'rules of the game' encouraged entrepreneurial individuals to become state governors rather than business owners. When the rules changed, these same individuals shifted to becoming oil oligarchs.

To some, Baumol's paper is highly contentious (see Classic research, below). He suggests that if society thinks it has too few entrepreneurs, it might be tempted to try to develop a more entrepreneurial attitude amongst its citizens. However, Baumol argues this would be ineffective on two grounds. First, it is far from clear whether it is possible to promote an 'entrepreneurial mindset' in any society. Second, even if this were possible, such efforts would be pointless because most societies have no shortage of people with this mindset. If a society appears to lack entrepreneurs, it is because those people are using their skills in an unproductive/destructive way, rather than in a productive way.

| Classic research | Baumol, W.J. (1990) 'Entrepreneurship: Productive, Unproductive and Destructive', *Journal of Political Economy*, 98(5), 893–921. |

Baumol's view is that each society – both in the past and in the present – displays three types of entrepreneurship:

- Productive entrepreneurship is innovation leading to wealth creation and economic development which advances not only the individual but wider society. Baumol cites the historical example of the Cistercian monks of the Middle Ages. These monks were able to acquire land, invest in animal flocks and create and maintain water mills.

- Unproductive entrepreneurship is some form of bureaucracy that typically benefits an individual but not necessarily society. Baumol uses the example of lawyers in the US and Japan. He notes that, relative to the US, Japan has fewer lawyers and fewer lawsuits devoted to economic issues. He argues that in Japan there are subsequently fewer opportunities for 'rent-seeking' by lawyers. Another example (although not used by Baumol) is that of Stella Liebeck who successfully sued McDonald's in the US. Whilst a passenger in a car, Liebeck spilled coffee over her legs. Because she was burned, she was subsequently awarded $2.7 million in damages. Her lawyer presumably was vastly better paid as an 'unproductive' lawyer than as a 'productive' coffee maker.

- Destructive entrepreneurship also benefits the individual more than society. Baumol suggests that in both ancient Rome and medieval China one of the 'acceptable' ways of gaining wealth was through 'political payments'. Bribery and corruption are still a central problem in many societies. The World Bank (2004) has estimated that $1 trillion is paid in bribes every year, representing 3 per cent of the world's gross domestic product.

Baumol's point is that entrepreneurs are always with us in every society. The task of society is to ensure that the 'rules of the game' are such that the benefits to the individual are greater by being a productive, rather than an unproductive or destructive entrepreneur. So, it might well be that in some countries 'natural' entrepreneurs join the secret police, the bureaucracy or establish crime syndicates, whereas in other countries they begin legitimate businesses that become world brands.

Implications

We don't need to focus on trying to change the supply of entrepreneurs, because these people are always with us. We only need to change the incentive structures they face. These are the 'rules of the game'. These incentives might be changing taxation rates, making it easier to start and operate a business, or making unproductive or destructive entrepreneurship less attractive.

An implication of Baumol's approach is that society should *not* focus upon changing the attitudes of its people. Instead, it should seek to channel such individuals into productive, rather than destructive/unproductive activities. In short, there is never a shortage of entrepreneurs, merely an imperfection in their distribution between productive and unproductive or destructive activities. A classic example of this is the analysis of De Soto (1989). He showed that in Peru very many farmers did not legally own their land. Without legal title to their land, they found it difficult to raise external finance. Getting insurance was also impossible, except from those offering 'protection'. By policy makers giving legal title to farmers, Peru was able to begin the process of switching people from unproductive or destructive entrepreneurship and towards productive entrepreneurship.

This emphasises that entrepreneurship is about making imperfectly informed *choices*. If entrepreneurs are those who set up a business, then individuals make a choice between setting up a business and other forms of activity – the most likely of which is being an employee, but it may take the form of illegal or criminal activity, unemployment or retirement. Of course, although the word choice is used in this context, it does not necessarily imply that this is a fully informed choice – the individual's knowledge of their entrepreneurship ability may be very imperfect. Second, entrepreneurship can be either 'good' or 'bad'. This means that we must be very clear about precisely what we mean by entrepreneurship in order to be able to measure or quantify it. Only by so doing can we then, for example, understand whether there is any link between entrepreneurship and economic and social welfare and, if so, how this might be measured.

Before we turn to defining entrepreneurship, we would like you to undertake the following exercise. It asks you to do four things. First, it asks you to decide what sorts of activities 'entrepreneurs' get involved with. It then asks you to think of some negative/positive words that you can associate with 'entrepreneurs'. Finally, it asks you to evaluate if entrepreneurs are a force for 'good' or 'bad'. The aim is to try to decide which of these meanings you are most comfortable with and, crucially, why you hold these opinions.

Questions

1   What is an entrepreneur?
   ● Someone who starts a new business?
   ● Someone who runs their own business?
   ● Someone who runs a successful business?
   ● Someone who takes over a (failing) business and turns it around?
   ● Someone who runs an 'informal'/criminal business?

   Why do you think that one (or more) of these activities constitute being an entrepreneur? What does this say about how you think about entrepreneurs?

2   What negative words do you associate with entrepreneurs?

3   What positive words do you associate with entrepreneurs?

4   On balance, do you think that entrepreneurs are a force for 'good' or 'bad'?

2.3 Defining entrepreneurs and entrepreneurship

As the economist Edith Penrose (1959) once said, '*Entrepreneurship is a slippery concept… not easy to work into formal analysis because it is so closely associated with the temperament or personal qualities of individuals*'.

Despite these difficulties, various researchers have sought to grasp this slippery concept by formulating their own definitions and approaches. Davidsson (2004), for example, provides a very readable synthesis of these matters, linking it neatly to the conduct of research on the topic. Our approach is to distinguish between:

1 the economist approach; and

2 the organisational theorist approach.

Common to both is that entrepreneurs do not exist where there is perfect certainty about the future – that is, where everyone has the same view (see Chapter 1).

Instead, when there is less than perfect certainty, there is the potential for entrepreneurs to exist. In its purest form, entrepreneurship potentially exists when an individual judges that there is a price difference between a product/service in one market and its price in another, and it is possible to exploit that price difference to make a profit.

Here are two examples. First, suppose that the price of a product in one town is higher than in another town. If the goods can be purchased in the low price town and sold at a higher price in another town then this, in principle, constitutes an entrepreneurial opportunity. Ingvar Kamprad, the IKEA entrepreneur, began his entrepreneurial career by exploiting this very difference. The young Kamprad found he could buy matches in bulk from the Swedish capital, Stockholm, and then sell them on in smaller batches, for a profit, to people in his local village.

Second, suppose the current price of a product is judged to be less than its expected future price, then there is the opportunity for making a profit by purchasing the product today and selling it later when the price has risen. For example, the billionaire financier, George Soros, was said to have gained financially by buying shares in the French bank Société Générale prior to its takeover and then benefiting from the subsequent doubling of the share price. Although he denied the charge, Soros was fined by a French court for profiting from inside knowledge of a takeover bid for the bank.

These two activities are referred to as **arbitrage**. In the first case it is **spatial arbitrage** and in the second it is **temporal arbitrage**. Common to both examples is the concept of imperfect information. Taking the temporal arbitrage case, the individual cannot know the future for certain and has to make a judgement that prices will have risen sufficiently to provide them with a reward. Entrepreneurship is about both 'imperfect information' and about 'making a judgement'.

A second common element of the examples above is that they describe **pure arbitrage** (difference in two prices). This is a necessary but not a sufficient condition for entrepreneurship to take place for four reasons. First, the entrepreneur may incur costs which eliminate any profit. In the case of the spatial arbitrage example, there may be transport costs in moving the goods from one town to another. In the temporal arbitrage example, these costs may include storing the goods until the price rises. Second, some entrepreneurial opportunities require finance or capital, for example to buy or store products. The availability of reasonably priced capital may be crucial in exploiting any opportunities.

A third reason is that, although the price difference exists, not all individuals are aware of it. Information may be restricted to only a small number of individuals and only they can exploit the opportunity. Fourth, even amongst those that are aware of the entrepreneurial opportunity, not all will choose to exploit it. This might be because they have different attitudes to risk. Some will be risk-lovers; others may be risk-averse whilst others may be risk-neutral. In principle, we would expect business opportunities to be more likely to be developed by risk-lovers than by those who are risk-averse. But it may also be that the profit-making opportunity is not as good as other ways for that individual to obtain income, or that they are too lazy to exploit it, or that they think they have better things to do with their time.

These choices are now explored by looking in detail at the economist's and organisational theorist's approach to entrepreneurship. Both approaches suggest that individuals make choices under uncertainty. Where they differ is that the economists emphasise choices and information processing. Organisational theorists tend to emphasise cognitive processes.

2.4 The economist approach

Economists still debate what entrepreneurship constitutes. Key areas of debate are around risk, innovation and entrepreneurial characteristics. But, beginning with the eighteenth-century economist, Cantillion, an important distinction has been made between entrepreneurs, on the one hand, and employees on the other. This clear distinction continues to be at the heart of economic approaches to entrepreneurship. The basic premise is that employees are assumed to be certain to get their wages, whereas entrepreneurs only obtain their income – also called profit – if their judgement proves correct. In short, the entrepreneur's income is uncertain, whereas that of the employee is not.

Integral to this is that entrepreneurs, in making choices, do so because they are seeking to maximise their utility. This is often in terms of the expectation that entrepreneurs seek to increase their income (profit). Not all economists, though, see utility exclusively in terms of income. Morton and Podolny (2002) show that wine producers in California are frequently individuals who have sought explicitly to escape the high-tech 'rat race'. Hamilton (2000) also shows that those who work for themselves (self-employed) could earn on average 35 per cent more as employees, implying that the non-pecuniary benefits of entrepreneurship are considerable, and that an exclusive focus upon monetary earnings can easily lead to misunderstanding.

One continuing area of debate amongst economists is around risk and uncertainty. In Chapter 1, we argued that risk is measurable in the sense that, whilst an individual outcome is not certain, if it is (continuously) repeated, then it becomes possible to assign probabilities to outcomes. This is not the case with uncertainty '. . . because the situation dealt with is in a high degree unique' (Knight 1921).

For example, take traffic accidents. Here there is a chance that all of us may incur a cost by damaging our own, or someone else's, car. Whilst we are individually 'uncertain' about whether this will occur in the future, insurance companies do estimate the likelihood of it happening. Indeed, their ability to make money depends on being able to estimate the risk (i.e. the likelihood and cost) of road accidents. They need to know the liabilities of specific groups of individuals of having an accident and what is the appropriate premium to charge such groups.

Attitudes to risk are an aspect of entrepreneurship that economists have developed. Table 2.1 seeks to identify this and other key themes that economists have developed in examining entrepreneurship. Whilst the concepts of arbitrage appear common to almost all economic writing, Table 2.1 illustrates that the focus of attention differs sharply between different writers in four main ways.

One area is in terms of risk. Kihlstrom and Laffont (1979) assume that a key function of the entrepreneur is to bear the risk and then retain any profits that are subsequently derived. This role is primarily performed by institutions that are providers of capital, but who do not

Table 2.1	Economic theories of entrepreneurship

Functions	Authors	Discussion
Arbitrageur	All	Arbitrage underlies all discussions about the entrepreneur.
Assumer of risk	YES: Kihlstrom and Laffont (1979)	The profits from entrepreneurship are the rewards for accepting risk.
	NO: Schumpeter (1934, 1942)	Profiting from risk bearing reflects ownership of capital, not entrepreneurship.
Decision making under uncertainty	YES: Knight (1921)	Entrepreneurship income is uncertain, and some people may have more talent than others. Even so, people move to entrepreneurship from being employees when the risk-adjusted rewards are greater. In principle, everyone can be an entrepreneur if the price is right.
Special personal insights or qualities	YES: Blanchflower and Oswald (1998)	Only a fixed proportion of the population has 'entrepreneurial vision'. So only that fraction of the population will ever be entrepreneurs.
	YES: Schumpeter (1934, 1942)	The entrepreneur is a special person who sees opportunities that others do not.
	NO: Kihlstrom and Laffont (1979)	Everyone sees and has access to the same opportunities, but only those with low risk-aversion seek to exploit them.
Risk-lover	YES: Kihlstrom and Laffont (1979)	Entrepreneurs have low risk-aversion. If they had high risk-aversion, they would be employees. Hence, it is attitudes to risk that distinguish entrepreneurs from employees.
	NO: Knight (1921)	Attitude to risk is not a factor that distinguishes entrepreneurs from employees.
Innovator	Schumpeter (1934, 1942)	The key role of the entrepreneur is to innovate, not to bear risk.
Disequilibrium creator	Schumpeter (1934, 1942)	The act of innovating creates new market conditions, so creating disequilibrium in the market.
Equilibrium creator	Kirzner (1973)	It is the disequilibrium in the market that creates the entrepreneurial opportunity – so the entrepreneur is moving the market back towards equilibrium.
Manager, co-ordinator, employer and organiser	Casson (1982)	The crucial role of the entrepreneur is to make judgemental decisions about the co-ordination of scarce resources.

Source: derived from Ripsas (1998) and Hebert and Link (1989).

themselves undertake the entrepreneurial act. This is in contrast with Schumpeter (1934) who argued that these profits from risk reflected ownership rather than entrepreneurship.

A second area of debate is whether entrepreneurs are 'special people'. Economists, again, have differing views. Blanchflower and Oswald (1998) assume that only a fixed proportion of the population has what it takes to be an entrepreneur – which might be qualities such as foresight, information or determination. Alternatively, Knight's (1921) view is that whilst individuals may differ in terms of entrepreneurial talent, there is an income level at which everyone would be an entrepreneur. In short, if the benefits of being an entrepreneur so exceeded those of being an employee then everyone would shift to being an entrepreneur.

A third area of debate is whether entrepreneurs are simply those individuals who are more comfortable with risk – in the jargon they have 'low risk-aversion'. Again, Knight would argue that whilst there may be differences in attitudes to risk, this is not a key element in the entrepreneurial decision. To Knight, it was a simple choice between uncertain income from entrepreneurship and a certain or guaranteed income as an employee. But, to Kihlstrom and Laffont, the key element was that the expected value of an opportunity would encourage some individuals to shift from being an employee to becoming an entrepreneur, whereas others would not make the shift. This assumption of heterogeneity in risk-aversion is based upon the idea that some people are less influenced in their risk taking as their incomes rise than others.

Table 2.1 also reflects the debate about the role of innovation and its link with entrepreneurship. This is a subject considered more fully in Chapter 5. In basic terms, some economists believe that innovation has at least some linkages with entrepreneurship. Schumpeter (1934, 1942) – the architect of much of the original thinking on innovation – believed that an entrepreneur was someone who innovated (rather than assumed the risk of the innovation) and brought about, through creating new market conditions, disequilibria in the market. An entrepreneur (innovator) is someone who creates and develops new ways of doing things. For example, young entrepreneurs like Jerry Yang and David Filo (Yahoo!) and Mark Zuckerberg (Facebook) have been responsible for creating new ways of exploiting the potential of the internet.

Other economists see entrepreneurship in more mundane terms. Kirzner (1973) argues that the principal role of entrepreneurs is to bring markets *back* into equilibrium. To return to the example of the two towns, we saw that that there was a difference in price for a product (market disequilibrium) between the two towns. Suppose the entrepreneur moves the product from low price town A to the high price town B. This will lead to pressure for lower prices in B and for the prices in the two markets to become more aligned, so reducing or eliminating the disequilibrium.

However, this 'market-adjustment' view has also been criticised. To some it is unsatisfactory because it offers no explanation of why or how this *process* takes place. It does not explain why some individuals undertake these entrepreneurial acts when others do not. But, perhaps more importantly, it assumes that the presence of the opportunity induces the individual to act. In other words, the opportunity exists before, and causes, the entrepreneurial action. This sits uncomfortably with the concept of entrepreneurs as individuals who enact entrepreneurial opportunities. It seems perhaps more plausible that it is the action of entrepreneurs that creates market opportunities rather than vice versa.

Finally, Table 2.1 sets out Casson's (1982) view of the entrepreneur. He defined the entrepreneur as: '*Someone who specialises in making judgemental decisions about the co-ordination of scarce resources*'.

In his later writing, Casson (1999) sees the key role of the entrepreneur as being to process information when that information is both costly and volatile. Casson argues that the economic environment is continuously disturbed by outside events, which may be either temporary or permanent. The entrepreneur who runs a business has to respond to these events or shocks by making decisions – for example, whether to invest in new plant and machinery, to develop new products or services or whether to shed labour. To make such decisions, the entrepreneur is assumed to require information which is costly.

Casson also argues that not all entrepreneurs choose to collect the same amount of information. Nor is their decision making likely to be uniform. Casson suggests that those who are better able to collect and process information are likely to be better entrepreneurs.

In summary, there are major differences in the way that economists view entrepreneurship. Still, four themes are now widely accepted:

1 The individual exercises a *choice* between becoming an entrepreneur or an employee and is able to switch between them.

2 The choice to switch between the two depends on the utility of each 'state'.

3 The recognition that the income from being an entrepreneur is more risky than that from being an employee.

4 The choice is also influenced by differences between individuals in terms of their entrepreneurial talent and attitudes to risk.

2.5 The organisational theorist approach

Organisational theorists have, like economists, exhibited considerable diversity in their approach to studying entrepreneurs. We will now explore this diversity and go on to suggest that where it differs from the approach of the economist is that it emphasises more strongly the importance of cognition and behaviours.

Table 2.2 identifies eleven different organisational theory definitions of entrepreneurship, of which only two (Schumpeter and Kirzner) have been included in the earlier Table 2.1. Like the economist approaches, there exist areas of different interpretations. For example, Timmons (1997) focuses on the individual, seeing entrepreneurship as a way of thinking and acting about opportunities. Meanwhile, Morris (1998) talks about individuals and teams, in differing contexts, coming together to create 'value'. Stevenson *et al.* (1989) see entrepreneurship as a process by which individuals pursue opportunities without regard to capabilities or resources. Drucker (1985) also emphasises that it has to do with 'the act of innovation'.

Low and MacMillan (1988), Gartner (1988), Rumelt (1987) and Sharma and Chrisman (1999) all emphasise that this innovation is largely in terms of creating a new business.

This emphasis on the unit of analysis being the new business brings its own problems. First, it is individuals or teams who *do* business, not businesses. Within this, it is clear that there are differences in the profile of people who choose to set up a new business. For example, some people approach it for the first time (**nascent entrepreneurs**) some have prior experience (**serial entrepreneurs**) whilst some are currently running a business (**portfolio entrepreneurs**).

Table 2.2	Selected definitions of entrepreneurship
Author	**Definition**
Drucker (1985)	Entrepreneurship is an act of innovation that involves endowing existing resources with new wealth-producing capacity.
Stevenson *et al.* (1989)	Entrepreneurship is the pursuit of an opportunity without concern for current resources or capabilities.
Rumelt (1987)	Entrepreneurship is the creation of new business, *new* business meaning that they do not exactly duplicate existing businesses but have some element of novelty.
Low and MacMillan (1988)	Entrepreneurship is the creation of new enterprise.
Gartner (1988)	Entrepreneurship is the creation of organisations, the process by which new organisations come into existence.
Timmons (1997)	Entrepreneurship is a way of thinking, reasoning, and acting that is opportunity obsessed, holistic in approach, and leadership balanced.
Venkataraman (1997)	Entrepreneurship research seeks to understand how opportunities to bring into existence future goods and services are discovered, created and exploited, by whom, and with what consequences.
Morris (1998)	Entrepreneurship is the process through which individuals and teams create value by bringing together unique packages of resource inputs to exploit opportunities in the environment. It can occur in any organisational context and results in a variety of possible outcomes including new ventures, products, services, processes, markets and technologies.
Sharma and Chrisman (1999)	Entrepreneurship encompasses acts of organisational creation, renewal or innovation that occur within or outside an existing organisation.

Source: Meyer *et al.* (2002).

Second, not all new businesses are the same. Some are new **corporate ventures**; others are bought out by the existing managers (**managerial buy outs**). Another model is **social enterprises** (businesses run for social purposes) or those 'cloned' or **franchised** from an existing business (e.g. McDonald's is largely run on a franchise basis). These forms are all different but potentially could be seen as new enterprises.

Given such issues, researchers have wondered if there can be any clearly defined organisational approach to the study or understanding of entrepreneurship. Shane and Venkataraman (2000: 217) argue that:

> Entrepreneurship has become a broad label under which a hodgepodge of research is housed. What appears to constitute entrepreneurship research today is some aspect of the setting (e.g. small businesses or new businesses), rather than a unique conceptual domain.

Shane and Venkataraman argue for an alternative view of entrepreneurship. The 'classic' research below can be seen as an archetypal – and widely cited – expression of organisational theorists' views on entrepreneurship.

Classic research	Shane, S. and Venkataraman, S. (2000), 'The Promise of Entrepreneurship as a Field of Research', *Academy of Management Review*, 25(1), 217–26.

Shane and Venkataraman suggest three distinctive advantages of entrepreneurship. First, it is the mechanism by which society learns about new products and services. Second, it helps rectify temporal and spatial inefficiencies. Finally, it is a major driver underlying wider social and economic change. Despite the importance of entrepreneurship, they note no unifying conceptual definition for entrepreneurship. As organisation theorists, they argue that the concern should be with three sets of research questions about entrepreneurship;

(i) Why, when and how opportunities for the creation of goods and service come into existence.

(ii) Why, when and how some people and not others discover and exploit these opportunities.

(iii) Why, when and how different modes of action are used to exploit entrepreneurial opportunities.

They examine these questions by adopting a disequilibrium approach to entrepreneurship and argue that entrepreneurship is broader than creating a new business.

Shane and Venkataraman's focus is upon the dual phenomena of both the presence of lucrative opportunities and the presence of enterprising individuals. They subsequently define the field of entrepreneurship as:

> 'The scholarly examination of how, by whom and with what effects opportunities to create future goods and services are discovered, evaluated and exploited' (p. 218).

Fundamental to this approach are four key assumptions:

1 Entrepreneurial opportunities exist – but are not known to everyone.

2 People have different perceptions on the value (financial or non-financial) of an opportunity.

3 Some people will choose to pursue these opportunities.

4 Acting on these opportunities will result in differing outcomes, both profitable and unprofitable.

At face value, the assumptions of Shane and Venkataraman are also the focus of the economic approaches. Where, however, the economic and the organisational perspectives diverge is that the economists' approach tends to emphasise choices and information processing. In the organisational explanation, the focus was initially on the traits or characteristics of the entrepreneur. In essence, there was an interest in 'who' the entrepreneur was and 'why' they became an entrepreneur. Organisational theorists have gone on to examine how individuals cognitively gather, process and evaluate information in entrepreneurial contexts. In contrast, economists tend not to be interested in the 'why' question. They think that they know the answer, which is that entrepreneurship provides greater 'utility' than other labour-market 'states'.

Entrepreneurial traits

As with some economic approaches, there is an urge in many organisational approaches to ascertain if entrepreneurs are 'special' people. Fundamentally, is there a single trait or set of traits that allow for the identification of an entrepreneurial personality? Chell (2008) argues that there are three traits – either on their own or in combination – that are important.

The first of these is the **need for achievement (NAch).** McClelland (1961) argued that people with high levels of NAch are achievement motivated, undertake tasks of moderate difficulty, actively seek out taking responsibility and welcome feedback on their actions. This seems to resonate with features of entrepreneurship. Entrepreneurship is – relative to employment – risky. It also involves a high degree of individual responsibility but, in return, offers higher levels of 'job' satisfaction (see Chapter 4).

A second characteristic commonly associated with entrepreneurship is **locus of control**. This is derived from Rotter's (1966) social learning theory. Rotter suggested that some individuals have an *internal* locus of control. Such individuals believe that the achievement of a goal is due to their own actions. In contrast, those with an *external* locus of control believe that outside events or 'fate' determines the likelihood of achieving a goal. The suggestion is that those with an internal locus of control are more likely to become entrepreneurs because they believe they have control over their own destiny.

Finally, there is **risk-taking propensity**. The argument here is that because risk taking is so fundamental to entrepreneurship it must follow that entrepreneurs are individuals with greater propensities to take risks. A more sophisticated approach is to suggest that entrepreneurs are better able to evaluate risks. Moreover, as McClelland (1961) suggested with NAch, they are likely to take calculated risks, particularly in situations when they perceive the situation will lead to positive outcomes (Kahneman *et al.* 1982).

There is a range of other potential traits that the entrepreneur may possess. Entrepreneurs may have a higher **desire for autonomy** (meaning they value freedom and independence). Related to any locus of control, entrepreneurs may also be **over-optimistic** about their likely chances of being successful (see Chapter 1). Similarly, alongside any risk taking propensity, entrepreneurs may be better able to cope with situations where information is limited and events uncertain (**tolerance for ambiguity**).

However, despite a huge range of studies, the evidence on whether, and if so why, entrepreneurs are 'special people' remains weak. Chell (2008) suggests that researchers have struggled to identify if one single trait or a combination of traits explains the entrepreneurial 'personality'. Gartner's (1988) review also severely questions the value of entrepreneurial trait research. He argues that trait approaches assume that the entrepreneur has a fixed and identifiable personality type. This ignores the fact that the enterprise population is very fluid. For example, Henley (2004), using British Household Panel Study data for 1991–1999, found that that only 78 per cent to 85 per cent of the self-employed in any one year were in self-employment in the previous year.

To reach his conclusion, Gartner reviewed a wide range of studies, using a diverse set of definitions for the 'entrepreneur'. Despite this diversity he concluded that 'a startling number of traits and characteristics have been attributed to the entrepreneur and a "psychological profile" of the entrepreneur assembled from these studies would portray someone larger than life, full of contradictions and conversely so full of traits that (s)he would have to be a sort of generic "Everyman"' (p. 57).

That, though, is unlikely to be the last word on entrepreneurial traits. Nicolaou *et al.* (2008) investigated entrepreneurial activities and attitudes amongst 870 pairs of identical twins and 857 pairs of same gender twins. Since the 870 pairs of identical twins share the same genetic material whilst the 857 pairs of same gender twins share, on average, half of their genetic material, the logic is that any differences in entrepreneurial activity may be attributable to genetic factors. Nicolaou *et al.* (2008) found this to be case. For example, 48 per cent of the variance in the likelihood of becoming self-employed was explained by genetic factors. The issue, however, for Nicolaou *et al.* (2008) is that they are unable to tell which genetic factors are responsible for their results.

In summary, a common problem faced by trait-based views of the entrepreneur is the inability to readily and accurately identify what are the elements of the 'entrepreneurial personality'. Moreover, even if this could be resolved, which elements of this 'entrepreneurial personality' *cause* entrepreneurial behaviour? The response from an organisational theorist like Aldrich (1999) is that there is little value in pursuing such questions. He concludes: '*Research on personal traits seems to have reached an empirical dead end*' (p. 76).

Cognitive approaches

Some organisational theorists have, instead, turned towards understanding how people think and react in different situations rather than focussing on entrepreneurial traits. This stems from a realisation that people do not follow apparently rational choices or the 'laws of probability' when decisions are made under uncertainty. Take the following as an example. You are offered a choice of accepting a sure win of £500 or taking a 50 per cent chance of winning £1,000. Which one will you choose? Although probability states that both options have the same expected value, most people will choose a sure win of £500.

In contrast, you are offered a 50 per cent chance on losing £1,000 or a sure loss of £500. Again, which one will you choose? Although both options have the same expected value – most people take the gamble.

One explanation for these choices is that human rationality is bounded: all of us have limits to how much attention, memory or 'brain power' we can give any task (Simon 1957). Kahneman *et al.* (1982) also argued that people who make decisions in uncertain situations – like entrepreneurial ones – use cognitive heuristics (mental shortcuts or 'rules of thumb'). There are three main types: representative heuristics, availability heuristics, and anchoring and adjustment heuristics.

A **representative heuristic** assumes that an action or event can be categorised and understood based on similarities with other situations – it is 'like for like'. Chapters 8 and 9 show that one of the stylised 'facts' about small businesses is that the fate they are most likely to face is closure. Despite this, entrepreneurs may choose to ignore the likelihood of such events occurring to them. Similarly, individuals may start a business based on a very limited knowledge or evidence and yet assume that it is representative. They may also assume that a 'normal' event is, in fact, 'rare' or unlikely to happen to them. For example, suppose amongst the potential entrepreneur's group of friends there is an individual whose business closes. This is a likely event but the potential entrepreneur may decide that, in fact, it is a rare occurrence.

A second prominent mental shortcut is to rely on information that is available (**availability heuristic**), because it is easily retrieved or recalled. For example, the decision to set up a business may be based on a short-term or partial analysis of market trends because the entrepreneur has insufficient time, interest or capability to fully investigate the market.

Finally, people tend to make use of an **anchoring and adjustment heuristic**. Suppose that there are two individuals each wanting to buy a franchise in the next 12 months. The first individual is told that the current price of the franchise is £600,000 whilst the second individual is told that the current price is £1.2 million. How do differences in these reference points or 'anchors' influence the likely price paid for the franchise? On average, the first individual with an 'anchor' of £600,000 will tend to pay less than the individual with the £1.2 million anchor. Both individuals will still tend to make insufficient adjustments: so the first individual may pay £850,000 whilst the second individual may pay £1 million.

The use of these cognitive heuristics may be particularly apparent in entrepreneurial contexts. Besides the potential types of biases mentioned above, entrepreneurs may be prone to other biases like having an **illusion of control** (overestimate personal control over outcomes); be more susceptible to the **planning fallacy** (believe that their plan can be put in place quicker than is actually possible) or try to **impression manage** (like politicians who 'spin' events, the entrepreneur may believe that their business failed because of others and/or external events).

Hence, although entrepreneurial contexts are still important (e.g. availability of finance, quality of support networks, prior experience), organisational theorists like Shane and Venkataraman (2000) argue that cognitive perceptions of how risks and opportunities are constructed are still pivotal.

Three cognitive concepts are often used to explain how individuals evaluate opportunities and risks (Delmar 2000). One is **self-efficacy**. This is defined as '. . . the belief in one's capabilities to organise and execute the courses of action required to manage prospective situations' (Bandura 1997: 2). This may seem like the earlier locus of control, in that a person's self-efficacy may be linked to beliefs about their ability to control their own destiny. Where self-efficacy differs, however, is that it is situational: you may believe you have ability in one area of your life but not necessarily in other parts. The implication here then is that people with high levels of self-efficacy are more likely to welcome entrepreneurial contexts. Those who are successful in such entrepreneurial contexts are also likely to believe that they will continue to be successful. Success breeds success whilst failure leads to failure. Cognitive concepts such as self-efficacy do not hold that these results are fixed or immutable. People can be trained to change their beliefs about a particular behaviour leading to alternative outcomes.

A second favoured concept is **intrinsic motivation**. This suggests that individuals who perform tasks for their own sake are likely to be better motivated than individuals who are motivated by some external feature. For example, it might be anticipated that the entrepreneur may gain greater levels of intrinsic motivation from their business than an employee who may only gain satisfaction from the wage they receive. The implication, like with self-efficacy, is that when intrinsic motivation coincides with goals directed to business success, then business success is more likely to occur.

Finally, there is the concept of **intentionality**. Here individuals are, for example, more likely to set up a business if this is their intention. This, in turn, relies on subjective perceptions, social norms (e.g. do the entrepreneurs' friends and family see it as a 'good' thing) and if the perception is desirable and feasible (self-efficacy) (Krueger 2000).

The central problem with these cognitive conceptualisations when applied to entrepreneurship is that there is still some distance between the presence of self-efficacy, intrinsic motivation or intentions and how these translate into entrepreneurial actions. Equally, cognitive approaches remain relatively under-researched (Delmar and Davidsson 2006).

Summary of the two approaches

At one level, both the economist and the organisational theorist are concerned with similar questions about how individuals come to evaluate and exploit entrepreneurial opportunities. At heart, the main differences between the two approaches is that economists tend to be more concerned with the role of price information and the 'outcomes' of economic activity (e.g. starting or growing a business). The organisational theorist has also an interest in price information and outcomes because they help shape the nature of entrepreneurial opportunities. However, the organisational theorist is more likely to place emphasis on *how* outcomes are achieved and the cognitive or psychological attributes of the entrepreneur. At the risk of over-simplification, the economist views the 'process' question as easy to answer and uninteresting. Individuals switch from one 'state' to another depending on the expected utility. The economist is interested in who moves and when. The answer to the 'why' question is because they think it is better for them.

Summary

This chapter began by introducing the heretical question of the value of entrepreneurship. Baumol (1990) suggests that entrepreneurship can be productive, unproductive or destructive. He also implies that there is little point in seeking to change the 'mindset' of individuals because entrepreneurs are always with us. What matters, instead, are the 'rules' under which entrepreneurship operates. The implication is that societies that align incentives to productive entrepreneurship are more likely to produce entrepreneurs that benefit the rest of society.

The chapter also identified two approaches to understanding entrepreneurship. Both approaches agree that entrepreneurship occurs in situations where knowledge is imperfect and that there are arbitrage opportunities for individuals who can spot, evaluate and exploit either temporal or spatial opportunities. Casson (1982) defined an entrepreneur as 'someone who specialises in making judgemental decisions about the co-ordination of scarce resources'. Where they differ is that economic approaches fundamentally see entrepreneurship as one amongst a number of labour-market choices. Organisational theories are much more interested in the factors influencing entrepreneurial decision making and seek to identify cognitive factors influencing such choices.

Questions for discussion

1 Is more entrepreneurship always desirable?

2 Under what circumstances can there be 'insufficient entrepreneurs'?

3 If entrepreneurship is to be stimulated, should this be by changing attitudes or by changing the 'rules of the game'?

4 Provide examples of productive, unproductive and destructive entrepreneurship. How might policy makers tilt the balance in favour of productive entrepreneurship?

5 In what key respects do the organisational and economic approaches to entrepreneurship differ?

6 Do entrepreneurs have traits or cognitive biases that make them different from other individuals?

7 Can you train individuals to be entrepreneurs?

8 Which is a better explanation of entrepreneurship – the economic or organisational approach?

References

Aldrich, H. (1999) *Organizations Evolving*. London: Sage.

Antonoupolos, G.A. and Mitra, J. (2009) 'The Hidden Enterprise of Bootlegging Cigarettes out of Greece', *Journal of Small Business and Entrepreneurship*, 22(1), 1–8.

Bandura, A. (1997) *Self-Efficacy: The Exercise of Control*. New York: W. H. Freeman.

Baumol, W.J. (1990) 'Entrepreneurship: Productive, Unproductive, and Destructive', *Journal of Political Economy*, 98(5), 893–921.

Blanchflower, D.G. and Oswald, A.J. (1998) 'What Makes an Entrepreneur?', *Journal of Labor Economics*, 16(1), 26–60.

Carlsson, B. and Karlsson, C. (eds) *Entrepreneurship, Small and Medium-sized Enterprises and the Macroeconomy*. Cambridge: Cambridge University Press, 45–78.

Casson, M.C. (1982) *The Entrepreneur: An Economic Theory*. Oxford: Martin Robinson.

Casson, M.C. (1999) 'Entrepreneurship and the Theory of the Firm', in Acs, Z., Carlsson, B. and Karlsson, C. (eds) *Entrepreneurship, Small and Medium-sized Enterprises and the Macroeconomy*. Cambridge: Cambridge University Press, 45–78.

Chell, E. (2008) *The Entrepreneurial Personality: A Social Construction*. London: Routledge.

Davidsson, P. (2004) *Researching Entrepreneurship*. Boston, MA: Springer.

De Soto, H. (1989) *The Other Path*. New York: Basic Books.

Delmar, F. (2000) 'The Psychology of the Entrepreneur', in Carter, S. and Jones-Evans, D. (eds), *Enterprise and Small Business; Principles, Practice and Policy*. London: Prentice Hall, 132–54.

Delmar, F. and Davidsson, P. (2006) 'Firm Size Expectations of Nascent Entrepreneurs', in Davidsson, P., Delmar, F. and Wiklund, J. (eds), *Entrepreneurship and the Growth of Firms*. Cheltenham: Edward Elgar, 87–108.

Drucker, P.F. (1985) *Innovation and Entrepreneurship: Practice and Principles*. New York: HarperCollins.

Gartner, W.B. (1988) ' "Who is an Entrepreneur?" Is the Wrong Question', *American Journal of Small Busines*s, 12(1), 11–32.

Hamilton, B.H. (2000) 'Does Entrepreneurship Pay? An Empirical Analysis of the Returns to Self-employment', *Journal of Political Economy,* 108(3), 604–31.

Henley, A. (2004) 'Self-Employment Status: The Role of State Dependence and Initial Circumstances', *Small Business Economics*, 22(1), 67–82.

Herbert, R.F. and Link, A.N. (1982) *The Entrepreneur: Mainstream Views and Radical Critiques*. New York: Praeger.

Herbert, R.F. and Link, A.N. (1989) 'In Search of the Meaning of Entrepreneurship', *Small Business Economics*, 1(1), 39–50.

Kahneman, D., Slovic, P. and Tversky, A. (eds) (1982) *Judgement under Uncertainty: Heuristics and Biases*. Cambridge: Cambridge University Press.

Kihlstrom, R.E. and Laffont, J.-J. (1979) 'A General Equilibrium Entrepreneurial Theory of Firm Formation Based on Risk Aversion', *Journal of Political Economy*, 87(4), 719–48.

Kirzner, I.M. (1973) *Competition and Entrepreneurship*. Chicago, IL: University of Chicago Press.

Knight, F. (1921) *Risk, Uncertainty and Profit*. Boston, MA: Houghton Mifflin.

Krueger, N.F. (2000) 'The Cognitive Infrastructure of Opportunity Emergence', *Entrepreneurship Theory and Practice*, 24(3), 5–23.

Low, M. and MacMillan, I.C. (1988) 'Entrepreneurship: Past Research and Future Challenges', *Journal of Management*, 14, 139–61.

McClelland, D.C. (1961) *The Achieving Society*. Princeton, NJ: Van Nostrand.

Meyer, G.D., Neck, H.M. and Meeks, M.D. (2002) 'The Entrepreneurship: Strategic Management Interface', in Hitt, M.A., Ireland, R.D., Camp, S.M. and Sexton, D.L. (eds), *Strategic Entrepreneurship: Creating a New Mindset*. Oxford: Blackwell, 19–44.

Morris, M. (1998) *Entrepreneurial Intensity: Sustainable Advantages for Individuals, Organizations and Societies*. Westport, VA: Quorum Books.

Morton, F.M.S. and Podolny, J.M. (2002) 'Love or Money? The Effects of Owner Motivation in the California Wine Industry', *Journal of Industrial Economics*, 50(4), 431–56.

Nicolaou, N., Shane, S., Cherkas, L., Hunkin, J. and Spector, T.D. (2008) 'Is the Tendency to Engage in Entrepreneurship Genetic?', *Management Science*, 54(1), 167–79.

Penrose, E. (1959) *The Theory of the Growth of the* Firm. Oxford: Oxford University Press.

Ripsas, S. (1998) 'Towards an Interdisciplinary Theory of Entrepreneurship', *Small Business Economics*, 10(2), 103–15.

Rotter, J.B. (1966) 'Generalized Expectancies for Internal Versus External Control of Reinforcement', *Psychological Monographs*, LXXX, 1–28.

Rumelt, R.P. (1987) 'Theory, Strategy and Entrepreneurship', in Teece, D.J. (ed.), *The Competitive Challenge*. New York: Harper & Row, 137–58.

Schumpeter, J. (1934) *The Theory of Economic Development*. Cambridge, MA: Harvard University Press.

Schumpeter, J.A. (1942) *Capitalism, Socialism, and Democracy*. New York: Harper and Brothers.

Shane, S. and Venkataraman, S. (2000) 'The Promise of Entrepreneurship as a Field of Research', *Academy of Management Review*, 25(1), 217–26.

Sharma, P. and Chrisman, J.J. (1999) 'Reconciling the Definitional Issues in the Field of Corporate Entrepreneurship', *Entrepreneurship Theory and Practice*, 23, 11–26.

Simon, H. (1955) 'A Behavioural Model of Rational Choice', *Quarterly Journal of Economics*, 69(1), 99–118.

Simon, H. (1957) 'A Behavioral Model of Rational Choice', in *Models of Man, Social and Rational: Mathematical Essays on Rational Human Behavior in a Social Setting*. New York: Wiley.

Stevenson, M.J., Roberts, H. and Grousbeck, I. (1989) *New Business Ventures and the Entrepreneur*. Homewood, IL: Irwin.

Timmons, J.A. (1997) *New Venture Creation: Entrepreneurship for the 21st Century*. Boston, MA: Irwin McGraw-Hill.

Venkataraman, S. (1997) 'The Distinctive Domain of Entrepreneurship Research: An Editor's Perspective', in Katz, J. and Brockhaus, R. (eds), *Entrepreneurship, Firm Emergence and Growth*. Greenwich, CT: JAI Press, 119–38.

World Bank (2004) *Doing Business in 2004: Understanding Regulation*. Washington, DC: World Bank.

3

Defining the small business

Key learning objectives

By the end of this chapter you should:

- Understand the issues involved in defining smaller-sized businesses
- Grasp the importance of small businesses to developed and developing economies
- Account for the changes in business populations over time.

3.1 Introduction

The previous chapter considered the entrepreneur. This chapter shifts the 'unit of analysis' to the small business. Both the entrepreneur and the small business share similarities. Our view is that the unifying characteristic of both is that they operate in uncertain environments. The skill of the entrepreneur, as Casson (1982) argues, is to make good decisions about the co-ordination of scarce resources when faced by these uncertainties. Chapter 1 also showed that the nature and character of the *external* uncertainty facing small businesses is considerably greater than that facing larger businesses.

Yet, there can also be marked differences. The entrepreneur is a person, whilst the business is a business. The individual can act in an entrepreneurial manner – for example, by undertaking arbitrage (potentially gaining profits from price differences) – without ever becoming a business. Conversely, a small business may exist for many years without ever being innovative in the sense of doing something different from the competition. Furthermore, the small business may effectively be the trading activities of a single person.

These similarities and differences show that there is some overlap between the 'entrepreneur' and the 'small business'. This is evident in the statistical treatment of individuals and businesses. Indeed, in most countries the most consistent and comprehensive data – broadly covering entrepreneurs – is on individual self-employment. Countries, however, also provide data on enterprises and distinguish between small, medium and large sized businesses.

In this chapter, we begin by seeking to define key terms such as self-employment and small businesses. We then use our definitions, particularly of small businesses, to present data on the size structure of enterprises in a range of developed countries. This proves to be more difficult than might have been imagined because the definitions are the subject of some dispute, and the data available is not consistent either over time or between countries.

Nevertheless, what emerges is that the small business is by far the most common size of enterprise in the world. In Europe, for example, large businesses comprise only 0.2 per cent of all enterprises and provide far fewer jobs than smaller businesses.

Small businesses have also been seen as being instrumental in leading an 'entrepreneurial revolution' over the last 30 years (Audretsch and Thurik 2000). This chapter concludes by reflecting on whether there is sufficient evidence from changes in the enterprise population to warrant such claims. It acknowledges that today we may talk more about entrepreneurship than 20 years ago, and the type of entrepreneurship may also differ, but whether we actually practise it more remains in our view unproven. Instead, the Baumol (1991) notion, introduced in Chapter 2, that entrepreneurship varies little over time seems more compatible with the evidence.

3.2 Defining the self-employed

No agreed definition of self-employment exists. Internationally, one of the clearest definitions is 'Self-employment jobs ... are those jobs where the remuneration is directly dependent upon the profits derived from the goods and services produced. The incumbents make the operational decisions affecting the enterprise, or delegate such decisions while retaining responsibility for the welfare of the enterprise' (OECD 2000: 191).

However, two main problems remain in defining the self-employed. Statistically, those who own and run their own business are often regarded as self-employed in labour-market statistics, even if they employ others in their business. For tax purposes, though, these same individuals can be classed as employees since they work for *their* business. The implication is that different countries have different ways of counting the self-employed. This makes cross-country statistical comparisons difficult.

A second practical problem is the grey area between when someone is an employee and when they are self-employed. This matters because in many countries, the self-employed enjoy tax advantages unavailable to employees (see Chapter 20). Individuals have an incentive to convince tax authorities that they are self-employed. Establishing if someone has self-employment status is usually straightforward because the individual contracts to provide goods and services (see Case study 2 – Dragonfly Consulting: employer or employee?). However, in the UK at least, four tests are applied in difficult cases:

1 **Control** (e.g. does the individual have to obey orders and do they have discretion on hours of work?)

2 **Integration** (e.g. are they part of disciplinary/grievance procedures; are they included in occupational benefit schemes?)

3 **Economic reality** (e.g. how do they get paid; are they free to hire others; do they provide their own equipment; how do they pay tax; who covers sick/holiday pay?)

4 **Mutuality of obligation** (e.g. how long does the contract last; how regular is the work; does the individual have the right to refuse work?)

3.3 Defining the small business

We require three characteristics from a satisfactory definition of a small business. First, it must genuinely reflect the characteristics of 'smallness' identified in Chapter 1. These include the absence of market power, the high element of risk and uncertainty, and the autonomy of running your own business. Second, we require a definition that enables valid comparisons to be made within the same country between different sectors and regions. Third, we require a definition to be consistent when comparisons are made over time so that accurate assessments can be made, for example, of whether a country becomes more or less 'enterprising' over a ten-year period.

Definitions of the small business

Probably the most influential conceptual definition of a small business was provided by the Bolton Report in 1971. This was a seminal report because it was one of the first times that a national government had sought to investigate the experiences of small businesses. Bolton said that the small business had to:

● be owned and managed by the same individual(s);
● be legally independent; and
● have a small share of the marketplace.

The emphasis placed by Bolton on combining ownership and management is to distinguish the small business from large businesses, which tend to be managed by professional managers on behalf of shareholders. In a large business, owners and managers tend to be different

| Illustration | Enterprise or establishment? |

Carrefour's local branches are small establishments, but are all part of one large enterprise.

An example of a small enterprise might be a shop which is owned by a single individual or a family. If they only own this one shop, the business is referred to as a single-establishment enterprise. In contrast, take the same size shop with the same number of workers in the store but, crucially, owned by one of Europe's largest retailers, Carrefour. Some of Carrefour's shops are small establishments but they are part of a large enterprise. On the other hand, the independent shop is a small enterprise and a small establishment. Crucially, the small independent shop cannot rely on provision of funding or common services from its parent organisation. It stands or falls on its own. In this it differs from the Carrefour establishment.

groups of individuals. The emphasis upon legal independence is to reflect the distinction between a small **enterprise** and a small **establishment**.

Finally, the emphasis placed by Bolton on having a small share of the market – or exceptionally a larger share of a very tiny marketplace – is to reflect the absence of market power amongst small businesses. This makes the Bolton definition similar to the US definition. The Small Business Act (1953) defined a small business as 'one that is independently owned and operated and which is not dominant in its field of operation'.

The Bolton qualitative definitions for the small business have been extensively analysed. Curran and Blackburn (2001) emphasise three points of issue with Bolton's (1971) definition. First, that small businesses are both numerous and varied in the ways they do business. Second, a small business in one sector might not be viewed as a small business in another. Third, they ask what is the appropriate measure for defining 'smallness': should it be the number of employees, the sales of the business, its profits, or its assets?

To address these issues, we return to what is required for an adequate definition of a small business. If international comparisons are to be made, particularly over time, then any definition based upon monetary values is likely to be problematic. This is because exchange rate differences influence monetary values. So, too, do differences in inflation rates. Monetary approaches may, therefore, provide an unreliable picture of small business numbers.

Curran and Blackburn favour a 'grounded approach'. Here business owners themselves define whether they consider their business to be 'small'. The main advantage of this approach is that it may better capture the multi-dimensional character of small businesses. This may be important in understanding the behaviour of the small business. Its main disadvantage is the impossibility of producing easily harmonised statistics on small businesses. This is important for two reasons. First, all governments see they have a role in supporting small businesses (see Chapters 19–21). To judge their impact, they need statistics to see if their efforts have been worthwhile for the taxpayer. Second, small business owners often apply to government for advice, support and finance. They too need simple eligibility criteria that define 'smallness' to see if they qualify for such support. Therefore, the grounded approach may not be the most helpful or practical way for governments to define eligibility.

The statistics produced by governments about small businesses, despite the best efforts of government statisticians, are imperfectly harmonised. In the European Union, there is a standardised definition used for defining **small and medium-sized enterprises** (SMEs). These definitions are shown in Table 3.1.

There are three points to note from the definitions.

1 The use of the term SME. This is the most common European term to describe small businesses. It includes all enterprises with up to 250 employees.

2 The sub-categories of SMEs are: micro businesses with an upper employment threshold of fewer than 10 employees; small businesses with an employment threshold of between 10 and 49 employees; and medium-sized businesses with between 50 and 249 employees.

3 It is not only the number of employees that influences the definition. Other elements include turnover (sales) and assets (balance sheet).

Table 3.1	EU SME definitions			
Enterprise category	**Headcount**	**Turnover**	**or**	**Balance sheet total**
Medium-sized	< 250	≤ €50 million		≤ €43 million
Small	< 50	≤ €10 million		≤ €10 million
Micro	< 10	≤ €2 million		≤ €2 million

Source: EU (2008).

Unfortunately, the EU definition of 'smallness' does not correspond with other developed countries. In both Canada and the US, the upper size limit for small businesses is 500 employees. However, in many countries, including the US, size thresholds can also vary depending on the sector. For example, a 'smallness' threshold for US wholesalers is 100 employees whilst in the non-goods producing sectors it is typically set at annual receipts of US$6 million (SBA 2008).

Japan also has its own definition of small businesses:

- in the retail and service sectors, small businesses are those whose capital/investment does not exceed ¥50,000,000 or 50 regular employees;

- the thresholds for wholesalers are ¥100,000,000 or 100 employees; and

- other sectors (e.g. manufacturing) have thresholds of ¥300,000,000 or 300 employees (OECD 2004: 11).

The economies of less developed and intermediate developed countries are even more dominated by small businesses than is the case for developed nations. For this reason, it is appropriate for the large business threshold in these countries to be low by the standards of developed countries. For example, India defines large businesses as those with more than 20 employees (Indian Ministry of Statistics 2006).

3.4 International business size distributions

Despite the absence of shared small business definitions, the OECD (2008) has provided estimates of the number of enterprises by employment size class. These are shown in Figure 3.1. This shows that nearly all of the businesses in each of the countries are SMEs (fewer than 250 employees). The only exceptions to this appear to be Japan, Korea and the US. Part of this may be explained by the fact that the data for these countries is for establishments rather than enterprises. This may lead to 'double counting' because enterprises may have more than one establishment. However, the US, in particular, still appears to have greater numbers of large businesses than any other country judging by Figure 3.1.

Question   How can the US be seen as the most entrepreneurial country in the world if it has more businesses that are large than any other country?

In general, however, the picture is clear. In most countries, at least 80 per cent of businesses are micro sized (1–9 employees). Figure 3.1 also shows that the number of larger sized businesses (250+ employees) typically represents less than 1 per cent of all businesses. For example, in the 27 countries of the European Union, there were 19.65 million enterprises. Of these, 91.8 per cent (18.04 million) were micro businesses, 6.9 per cent (1.35 million) were small and 1.1 per cent (0.21 million) were medium-sized businesses. **In other words, only around 40,000 businesses or 0.2 of businesses in the 27 EU economies employed more than 250 employees** (Eurostat 2008).

Figure 3.2 shows the number of people engaged by employment size class. The key result from Figure 3.2 is that around 60 per cent of total employment is in SMEs with the other 40 per cent being in large businesses. Indeed, in the 27 countries of the EU, there were 127 million people employed in 2005 (Eurostat 2008). Of these, two-thirds (85 million) worked in

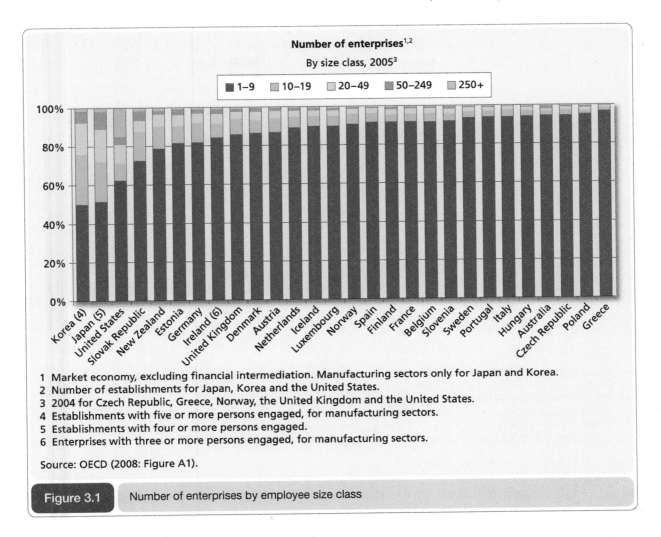

Number of enterprises[1,2]

By size class, 2005[3]

Legend: 1–9 | 10–19 | 20–49 | 50–249 | 250+

1 Market economy, excluding financial intermediation. Manufacturing sectors only for Japan and Korea.
2 Number of establishments for Japan, Korea and the United States.
3 2004 for Czech Republic, Greece, Norway, the United Kingdom and the United States.
4 Establishments with five or more persons engaged, for manufacturing sectors.
5 Establishments with four or more persons engaged.
6 Enterprises with three or more persons engaged, for manufacturing sectors.

Source: OECD (2008: Figure A1).

| Figure 3.1 | Number of enterprises by employee size class |

SMEs. Indeed, nearly as many people (37.5 million) worked in micro-sized business as worked in large businesses (41.7 million). This may be surprising given the media's focus on a relatively tiny number of large businesses. For example, what proportion of the *Financial Times* or the *Wall Street Journal* is devoted on a daily basis to micro businesses? The answer is that it is considerably less than the proportionate contribution by micro businesses to employment in any country in the world.

The finding in Figure 3.2 may be open to question because it is a percentage of the total enterprise population. It is a **stock** measure and, therefore, is sensitive to the size of the enterprise population in a given country. A potentially more useful measure is based upon the **population** of a country. Figure 3.3 measures the number of EU enterprises per 1,000 inhabitants. It shows that the EU-27 average is around 40 businesses for every 1,000 inhabitants. Slovakia has the lowest number (around 8 businesses) while Romania, Germany and Ireland each have around 20 SMEs per 1,000 inhabitants. In contrast, Portugal and the Czech Republic have more than 80 businesses per 1,000 inhabitants – more than twice the EU-27 average.

| Question | Does this mean that Portugal and the Czech Republic are eight times as entrepreneurial as Slovakia? Why might you think this? |

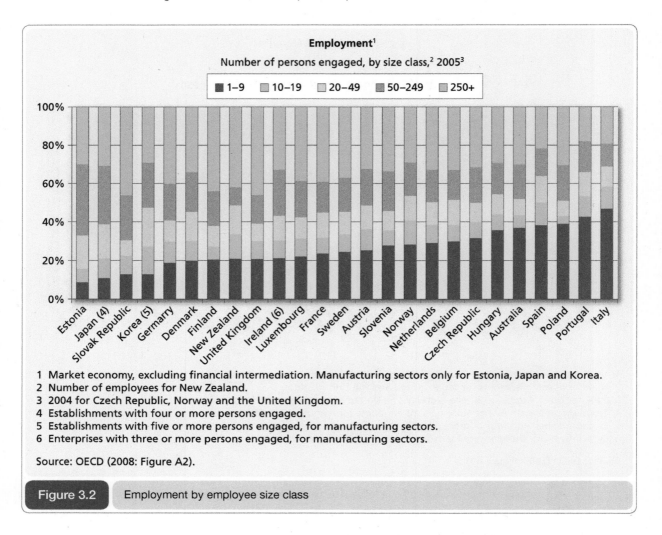

Employment[1]

Number of persons engaged, by size class,[2] 2005[3]

Legend: 1–9 | 10–19 | 20–49 | 50–249 | 250+

1 Market economy, excluding financial intermediation. Manufacturing sectors only for Estonia, Japan and Korea.
2 Number of employees for New Zealand.
3 2004 for Czech Republic, Norway and the United Kingdom.
4 Establishments with four or more persons engaged.
5 Establishments with five or more persons engaged, for manufacturing sectors.
6 Enterprises with three or more persons engaged, for manufacturing sectors.

Source: OECD (2008: Figure A2).

Figure 3.2 Employment by employee size class

Worldwide

Table 3.2 presents further data on 'formal' businesses in 48 selected countries. This data is split into each of the other main continents of the world (eastern Europe, North America, Caribbean and Latin America, South America, Africa and Asia and Australasia). It is based upon IFC (2006) data, supplemented by World Bank Development Indicators data from 2008. The data has four significant features:

1 The table shows the most recent data available in 2008. However, the actual age of the data varies widely between countries. Bolivian data are for 1995 – so a decade out of date – whereas the most recent data from countries such as Armenia are from 2005.

2 There is a wide variation in how individual economies define their SME population. For example, medium-sized companies range from more than 10 employees (Albania), 21–50 (Malawi), 50–199 (Chile) to 100–499 (Canada). This makes collecting internationally comparable data very difficult.

3 The data include no information on the number of large businesses in a given economy. The structure of the 'SME sector' figures refers only to the percentages of all SMEs. Nevertheless, it is clear that micro businesses (however defined) make up the vast majority of SMEs. Typically, medium-sized businesses tend to represent fewer than 5 per cent of SMEs.

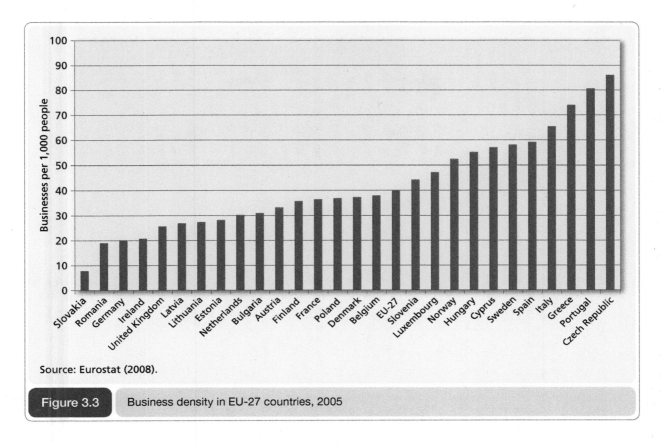

Source: Eurostat (2008).

Figure 3.3   Business density in EU-27 countries, 2005

4 The numbers of SMEs and the business density (SMEs per 1,000 people) results appear to under-estimate the likely SME populations. For example, it is difficult to believe that China had only 8 million businesses in 2000 (Table 3.2). Indeed, more recent Chinese data (NBSC 2005) indicates that the number of self-employed alone was 39 million in 2006. These official figures on numbers of enterprises are likely to under-estimate – sometimes quite seriously – the number of micro businesses. There are three main reasons for this:

(a) Smaller businesses are less likely than large businesses to be required to register with the government.

(b) Entrepreneurs may feel able to operate in the informal economy without risk of prosecution.

(c) Finally, the 'harmonised' data are likely to select a high, rather than a low size threshold for registration.

The overall effect of these influences is that the actual number of micro enterprises is likely to be considerably higher than the official figures – implying that the 'share' of micro enterprises in the economy is even higher than that in official data. This may be a particular problem in some economies. For example, the more recent Chinese data on self-employment (NBSC 2005) ignores the numbers of self-employed Chinese farmers. As such, China is likely to have far more self-employed individuals than the 39 million reported in official figures.

Recent evidence from the Indian Ministry of Statistics (2006) indicates that it has a business population of 42 million and a business density of 39. However, it should not be assumed that under-numeration of businesses is only a characteristic of lower-income countries. The

Table 3.2 International SME definitions, distributions and participation

Economy	Year of SME data	SME definitions (number of employees, unless otherwise noted)[a]			Country SME characteristics — Structure of the SME sector (% of all SMEs)			SME participation in the economy	
		Micro	Small	Medium	Micro	Small	Medium	SMEs	SMEs per 1,000 people
Eastern Europe									
Albania	2004[g]	1	2–10	>10	94.3	3.8	1.9	38,331	12.23
Armenia	2005[g]			<100				99,805	33.07
Azerbaijan	2003[g]		<50	50–249	80.1		19.9	49,527	6.01
Belarus	2002[g]	0–9	10–49	50–249	68.6	29.0	2.3	25,108	2.53
Bosnia and Herzegovina	2003[g]	0–9	10–49	50–249	85.3	11.3	3.4	14,986	3.85
Estonia	2001	0–9	10–49	50–249	77.8	18.7	3.5	32,801	24.0
Georgia	2005[g]	0–9	10–49	50–249	48.7	38.2	13.1	33,860	7.57
Latvia	2001	0–9	10–49	50–249	73.0	22.3	4.7	32,571	13.8
Moldova	2001	0–19	20–75		80.3	19.7		20,518	4.8
Russian Federation	2005[g]	FE & IE[d]	<100	<250	60.0	10.6	29.5	6,891,300	48.14
Serbia and Montenegro	2003[g]	0–9	10–49	50–249	87.0	9.4	3.6	68,220	9.12
Ukraine	2005[g]		<50					343,786	7.3
Uzbekistan[f]	2003	0–10	11–40	41–100				229,600	9.0
Africa									
Algeria	2001			<250				580,000	18.8
Botswana	2005[g]	0–4[b]	5–49	50–99	57.4	40.1	2.5	13,137	7.16
Egypt, Arab Rep.	2002			<99				2,500,000	42.2
Malawi	2000	0–4	5–20	21–50	91.3	8.5	0.2	747,396	72.5
South Africa	1997	0–9[e]	10–49	50–100[e]	92.0	7.0	1.0	900,683	22.0
Tanzania	2002[g]	1–5	6–20					2,700,000	75.81
North America									
Canada	2005[g]	0–9	10–99	100–499	75.2	23.1	1.7	2,245,245	69.49
US	2004[g]	0–9	10–99	100–499	79.3	19.9	0.8	5,868,737	19.99

Table 3.2 continued

Caribbean and Latin America

Country	Year								SMEs/1,000 pop.
Costa Rica	2004[g]	0–10	11–30	31–100	79.7	20.3		40,921	9.62
El Salvador	2001[g]	0–4	5–49	50–99	97.3	2.6	0.1	461,642	73.32
Guatemala	1999	0–10	11–25	26–60	77.7	16.7	5.6	173,699	15.7
Jamaica	1996	1–2	3–4	5–9				93,110	37.2
Mexico	2004[g]	0–30	31–100	101–500	96.0	3.1	0.9	2,891,300	28.33
Nicaragua	1999[g]		≤100					158,859	31.59
Panama	1999[g]	i ≤ 150,000	i ≤ 1,000,000	i ≤ 2,500,000	83.5	13.7	2.8	39,636	13.7

South America

Country	Year								SMEs/1,000 pop.
Argentina	1999[g]	a ≤ 170,000	a ≤ 1,000,000	a ≤ 8,300,000	91.4	7.8	0.8	894,169	24.49
Bolivia	1995	0–10	11–19	20–49	99.7	0.2	0.1	501,333	67.0
Brazil	2001	0–9	10–49	50–249	92.9	6.2	0.9	4,903,268	27.35
Chile	2004[g]	0–4	5–49	50–199	82.8	15.1	2.1	700,000	43.41
Colombia	2003[g]	0–9	10–49	50–199	96.1	3.9		664,000	15.2
Paraguay	2002[g]	1–5	6–20	21–100	77.5	16.6	5.9	548,000	98.44
Peru	2004[g]	0–10	11–49	50–199	95.8	3.3	0.9	658,837	24.44
Venezuela, RB	2000	0–10	11–50	51–100	76.9	23.1		11,314	0.5

Asia and Australasia

Country	Year								SMEs/1,000 pop.
Australia	2000	0–9	10–99	100–499	73.0	24.8	2.2	1,075,000	54.0
China	2000							8,000,000	6.3
Hong Kong, China	2004[g]	0–4	5–19	20–99	87.4	7.7	4.9	263,959	38.88
Indonesia	2002[g]	1–5	5–19	20–99				41,362,315	195.27
Japan	2004[g]	0–4	5–19	20–99	57.2	35.2	7.5	5,712,191	44.71
Korea, Rep.	2004[g]	0–4	5–19	20–99	73.4	18.0	8.6	2,998,223	62.36
Malaysia	2005[g]	Manuf. <100, non-manuf. <50						518,996	20.23
New Zealand	2004[g]	0–9	10–99	100–499	92.6	7.0	0.4	334,031	81.72
Philippines	2003[g]	0–4	5–19	20–99	91.4	8.2	0.4	808,634	9.96
Singapore	2004[g]	0–4	5–19	20–99	68.9	24.9	6.2	136,363	32.17
Thailand	2002[g]	0–4	5–19	20–99	79.4	18.5	2.0	842,360	13.66
Vietnam	2004[g]	<30	<200					90,935	1.11

(a) Annual sales (in US dollars).
(b) Includes working proprietors and unknown.
(c) Data are APEC's best guess for 2000 or the latest available data (1998–2000).
(d) FE = farm enterprises; IE = individual enterprises.
(e) Except in the mining, electricity, manufacturing, and construction sectors.
(f) The SME definitions apply only to manufacturing.
(g) Data from World Bank Development Indicators (April 2008): Data only applies to the number of SMEs and SMEs/1,000 population.

Sources: Marta Kozak International Finance Corporation, 2006; World Bank Indicators, April 2008.

UK has, according to EU estimates, 1,535,000 businesses (Eurostat 2008), but other statistics from the UK suggest that the overall enterprise population is more than 4 million (see section below). Even this only counts businesses 'known' to the government.

Questions

- If smaller businesses dominate the economies of poorer countries, why should prosperous economies want more small businesses?
- If you were to plot the data on the numbers of businesses and the importance of SMEs, and then link it to data on gross domestic product (or another measure of national income), what patterns do you think would emerge?

Overall, in this section the picture that emerges is that the standardised data on which SMEs statistics are compiled tend to be based upon registered businesses. This is likely to considerably under-estimate the numbers of SMEs in both developed and developing economies. Nonetheless, it remains clear that the vast majority of businesses in the world are SMEs and that micro businesses are the most common enterprise type in the world. However, business density varies markedly from country to country. Even in the same continent, Canada has a business density of 70 whilst the US has a business density of 20 businesses per 1,000 people.

3.5 A general picture of the changing importance of small businesses: the UK case

Figures 3.1 and 3.2 showed the best available data on the *current* size distribution of businesses. We now examine *changes* in this size structure over time. This is important because of the need to understand the role of SMEs in economic development. We begin by looking first at the UK and then we assess whether the changes in the UK enterprise population are typical of any changes that occurred in other developed economies.

We present two conflicting arguments. The first is that there have been wholesale changes in the UK enterprise population since the 1980s. The alternative is that little has actually changed over the same period.

In presenting 'for' and 'against' arguments, we have to rely upon piecemeal data because there is no continuous, comprehensive and reliable data on small businesses. We must rely, therefore, on data from self-employment statistics and the variety of methods by which the enterprise population has been calculated.

Data on changes in the enterprise population

The oldest reliable data on SMEs in the UK come from the now defunct Census of Production. Beginning in 1924, data were published on a periodic basis, and from this data it was possible to calculate the proportion of total manufacturing employment in small establishments in the UK. The data are an imperfect measure of small businesses for the following reasons. First, they refer only to the manufacturing sector and not to all sectors. Second, they refer to small establishments which are not identical to small enterprises because small establishments may be workplaces which are owned by larger businesses. Third, the definition of 'small' is the establishment having fewer than 200 workers whereas the current definition of an SME is 250 employees. Despite these imperfections, the data have the great merit of being available between 1924 and 1988 and are shown in Figure 3.4.

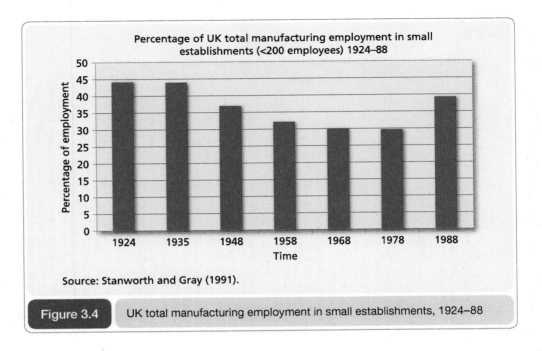

Percentage of UK total manufacturing employment in small establishments (<200 employees) 1924–88

Source: Stanworth and Gray (1991).

| Figure 3.4 | UK total manufacturing employment in small establishments, 1924–88 |

It shows that in 1924 almost 45 per cent of manufacturing employment was in small establishments but that, by the time of the 1968 and 1978 surveys, this had fallen to 30 per cent. However, a striking increase then occurs by the time of the 1988 survey, raising the proportion of employment in small establishments to close to 40 per cent.

Two key factors may explain this U-shaped pattern:

● Between the 1920s and the 1960s, the competitive advantage of UK manufacturers seemed to be more likely to be based on cost advantages. Under these circumstances large businesses are able to reap scale economies and so outperform smaller businesses.

● The UK manufacturing sector was broadly uncompetitive – particularly in the 1950s to 1970s – and suffered severely during the 'oil shocks' of the 1970s and the recession of the early 1980s. Many large businesses went bankrupt and so part of the explanation for the increased share of small businesses is attributable to the disappearance of many large enterprises during these severe recessionary periods. In other words, the increasing share of employment in small businesses was only partly due to their 'good' performance, and is more likely to reflect the 'bad' performance of large businesses.

The second oldest set of data available is on self-employment (individuals who may or may not have their own employees but who classify themselves as being self-employed – the majority of whom are business owners). Figure 3.5 displays data for the period of 1959–2007. It shows that between 1959 and 1979, self-employment rates were stable at around 8 per cent of the working population. Throughout the 1980s, the rate of self-employment increased, reaching 13.75 per cent in 1990. By the mid-1990s, the rate had surpassed 14 per cent, but fell to around 12 per cent at the start of this century. Since then, the rate has risen to around 13 per cent.

There are three main explanations for these dramatic changes:

● The Thatcher governments (1979–91) were the first to actively promote self-employment.

● Unemployment was high in the 1980s and individuals saw self-employment as a viable alternative to a long period without work.

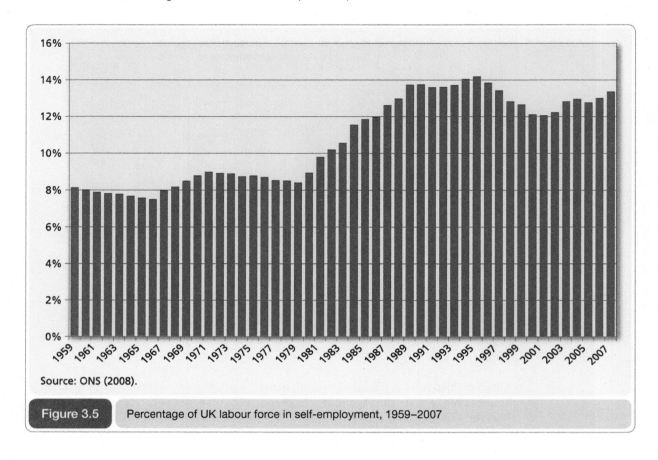

Source: ONS (2008).

Figure 3.5   Percentage of UK labour force in self-employment, 1959–2007

● The service economy has expanded rapidly since the early 1980s. This is perhaps more resistant to traditional economies of scale because '. . . the most important competitive advantages are "personal attention to client needs", "specialised expertise or products" and "established reputation"' (Bryson *et al.* 1997: 352).

The final piece of evidence relates to changes in the enterprise population. This is presented in Figure 3.6. These data begin in 1980 and relate to the stock of Value Added Taxation (VAT) registered businesses and the total number of UK businesses. As a measure of the business population, VAT is sensitive to increases in VAT thresholds. Nonetheless, Figure 3.6 shows a steady increase from 1.3 million businesses in 1980 to nearly 2 million in 2006. The increase of the business population data is more dramatic. Although incomplete (missing data in the 1980s), it shows that the enterprise population was nearly 2.5 million in 1980. By the end of the 1980s, it had increased to 3.7 million. It remained at this level for most of the 1990s before increasing to 4.5 million in 2006. Overall, this represents a near doubling of the enterprise population over a 25-year period.

Again, in tandem with the explanations for the increase in self-employment, other supplementary explanations may be offered:

● There was a continuation of governmental support for the development of an 'enterprise culture'.

● The labour market has continued to restructure. Individuals no longer envisaged stable employment or working for one business all of their working life. Instead, they increasingly saw self-employment as a viable labour-market choice even if only for a limited period.

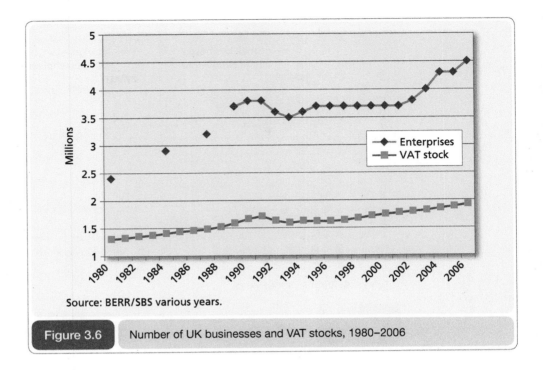

Source: BERR/SBS various years.

| Figure 3.6 | Number of UK businesses and VAT stocks, 1980–2006 |

- Macro-economic stability impacted on enterprise levels: the enterprise population contracted after the sharp recession of the early 1990s but increased as the macro-economy stabilised.

- The nature of competitive advantage has continued to shift towards 'quality' rather than 'cost' advantages. Smaller businesses with behavioural advantages (e.g. flexibility, service, speed) were potentially more competitive than larger and more bureaucratic businesses.

The stability of the enterprise population

The data in the previous section constitutes the 'good news' that Britain has become more enterprising. We now set out the contrary case which suggests that 'entrepreneurship' has not been reborn since the early 1980s. We examine the actual employment contribution of SMEs; any changes in the age composition of the self-employed; and the regional balance of SMEs.

Figure 3.7 shows the shares of total employment in small businesses (fewer than 50 employees) and medium-sized businesses (50–249 employees). It shows that in 1980 small businesses' share of employment was below 40 per cent. This increased over the next 20 years. However, since 2000, the small business share of employment has returned to about its 1980 level. In 1980, medium-sized enterprises provided 17 per cent of all jobs. Since then, as Figure 3.7 shows, there has been a fairly uniform decline in employment in medium-sized businesses to around one in ten workers. Why this matters is because small businesses, and more particularly medium-sized businesses, are seen as the 'backbone' of developed economies. Cooke and Morgan (1998) argue that Germany's *Mittlestand* (its medium-sized businesses) are central to the economic success of its regional economies.

The second piece of data is on the age of the self-employed. If there has been a change in attitudes over the last 25 years, then the expectation is that younger people will be more likely to become self-employed. Alternatively, if Baumol (1990) – see Chapter 2 – is correct, then changing 'attitudes' will make little or no difference to who *actually* become self-employed. Figures 3.8 and 3.9 present data on female and male self-employment over nearly 25 years. Both Figures 3.8 and 3.9 show a similar pattern. Although the male self-employment rate is

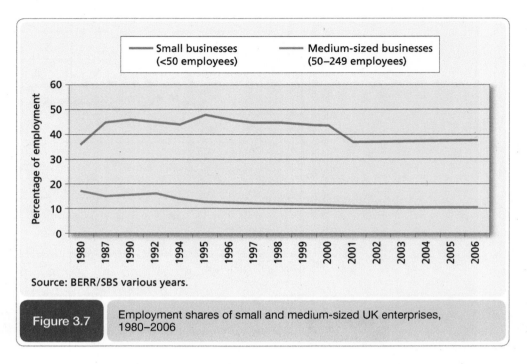

Source: BERR/SBS various years.

| Figure 3.7 | Employment shares of small and medium-sized UK enterprises, 1980–2006 |

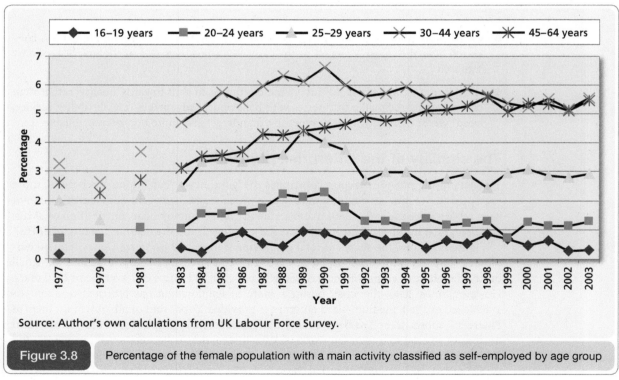

Source: Author's own calculations from UK Labour Force Survey.

| Figure 3.8 | Percentage of the female population with a main activity classified as self-employed by age group |

always much higher, the temporal pattern is quite clear. Self-employment rates rise continuously from 1977 until 1989/90 and then, for young and middle-aged workers, fall. By 2000, the proportions of these age groups that were self-employed had returned to the same levels as in 1979.

The only notable exception to this pattern is older people. The proportion of 45–64-year-old self-employed females increased continuously from 1979 onwards. A similar pattern is

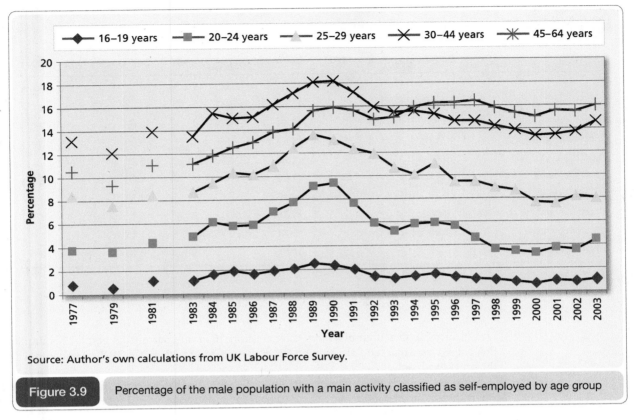

Source: Author's own calculations from UK Labour Force Survey.

| Figure 3.9 | Percentage of the male population with a main activity classified as self-employed by age group |

evident for older males, although at a less dramatic rate. This is an interesting finding since these individuals were *not* the focus of policy attention to change 'attitudes' during this period. In contrast, the key target group of interest to policy makers was that of young people, whose 'attitudes' were regarded as being most amenable to change. However, the case can be made that the 'rules of the game' changed for older individuals. Many such individuals were made redundant when they were willing and able to work. Others may, though, have taken early retirement or simply left the employee 'rat race' to generate incomes for themselves in self-employment occupations often associated with their hobbies or interests. So, despite the focus of policy makers to change the attitudes of the young, the upsurge of self-employment came from those at the opposite end of the age spectrum for whom the 'rules of the game' had changed.

Our final piece of evidence regarding the UK enterprise population relates to the regional picture. Here we examine whether there have been changes in self-employment in different parts of England over time. We feel more comfortable in presenting this data since it is derived from the census for 1981, 1991 and 2001, rather than being derived from samples of individuals or businesses used for official data. The disadvantage of census data is that it is not able to detect changes between the census dates, but, since our purpose is to provide a 'long view', this limitation is of only modest importance.

Table 3.3 shows self-employment rates for 1981, 1991 and 2001 for the English regions. Before examining the differences between the regions it is reassuring to note that the temporal patterns in self-employment reported in Figure 3.5 are confirmed in this census-based table. Self-employment rose by at least two percentage points in all of the English regions between 1981 and 1991.

The aggregate changes between 1991 and 2001 were, as might have been expected, much less. Whilst all regions with the exception of the South West of England reported a growth, the increase for seven of the other regions was less than a single percentage point. Only London

Table 3.3	Self-employment rates in the English regions: 1981, 1991 and 2001					
	Self-employment	**1981**	**Self-employment**	**1991**	**Self-employment**	**2001**
	%	Rank	%	Rank	%	Rank
South West	12.93	1	15.20	1	14.94	1
South East	10.45	2	13.10	2	13.68	2
East of England	10.12	3	12.68	3	13.35	3
London	9.61	4	11.83	4	13.28	4
East Midlands	8.77	5	11.26	5	11.50	5
North West	8.23	6	10.48	6	11.22	6
Yorkshire and Humberside	8.00	7	10.48	6	11.12	7
West Midlands	7.91	8	10.44	8	11.11	8
North East	5.45	9	7.61	9	8.59	9

Source: Greene *et al.* (2008).

saw an increase in self-employment rates of more than one percentage point. This implies that there was a marked flattening of self-employment growth in the 1990s compared with the previous decade.

However, what is most remarkable about Table 3.3 is that it seems like a 'league table' where there is no promotion or relegation between the divisions. The West Midlands, Yorkshire and Humberside, North East and North West are always in the lower league. Within that league they do change positions, but only slightly. In contrast, the South East, South West, London and the East are always in the higher league but never change their place in the 'league'. The dividing line is the stereotypical English region – the East Midlands which, over three censuses, never moves from fifth place.

The reasonable inference from Table 3.3 is that whilst there has been an overall increase in self-employment in all English regions over the period, the growth was much faster in the 1980s than in the 1990s. Second, that the group of English regions with high rates of self-employment in 1981 are the same as those with high rates in 2001. Conversely, those with low rates in 1981 continued to have low rates 20 years later.

Pulling together all the data sets on the UK or its constituent parts, and recognising there is a risk of drawing overly strong conclusions, our interpretation is the following:

- For probably the first 70 years of the twentieth century, SMEs were of declining importance in terms of provision of employment.

- A change occurred during the 1970s with manufacturing SMEs providing an increased share of manufacturing jobs.

- This step increase lasted for 20 years and probably applied to sectors other than manufacturing, fuelled by changes in the labour market, in business practices, sources of competitive advantage and political support for SMEs.

- But, in the 2000s, the increase has either stopped or slowed considerably.

- Despite these changes, the share of employment in SMEs has tended to fall; there is little statistical evidence of increased self-employment rates amongst younger people; and, within the UK, if a regional league table of entrepreneurship existed, it would probably point to almost no changes in the relative positions of regions over 30 years.

3.6 Is the British pattern typical of other developed countries?

We have noted the need for careful interpretation of data sources and the difficulties of making valid comparisons over time, even within a single country. Drawing cross-national comparisons over time is even more problematic than making comparisons for a single country.

The need is to look beyond 'easy' or 'headline' statements about enterprise and instead look at long-term changes. So, again, our task is to present the most appropriate data, together with the key issues, and derive some broad conclusions on whether the long-term patterns observed in Britain apply in other, primarily European, countries.

The only relevant data that has been collected, in a broadly similar manner and over a long period of time, is that on self-employment. Two analyses are now presented using:

● official self-employment data; and

● a data set that combines enterprise data and self-employment data – COMPENDIA.

Self-employment data for six developed countries over virtually half a century until 2004 are shown in Figure 3.10. They show an interesting range of temporal patterns, but the overall pattern is one of little change. Taking 1956 as the base year, the self-employment rates range from 27 per cent in Italy to about 7 per cent in the UK. In 2004, Italy continues to have the highest rate at about 27 per cent whilst the US has the lowest at about 8 per cent. However, because in 2004 every country, with the exception of Italy, has rates of between 8 per cent and 14 per cent, the arithmetic mean rate is marginally *lower* in 2004 than half a century previously.

In the intervening period, however, there have been a range of interesting changes pointing to a broadly U-shaped pattern with self-employment falling and then subsequently rising

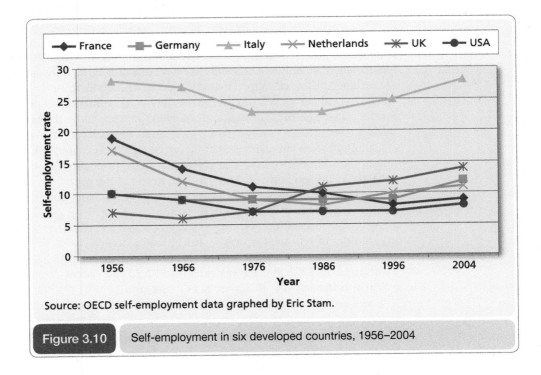

Source: OECD self-employment data graphed by Eric Stam.

| Figure 3.10 | Self-employment in six developed countries, 1956–2004 |

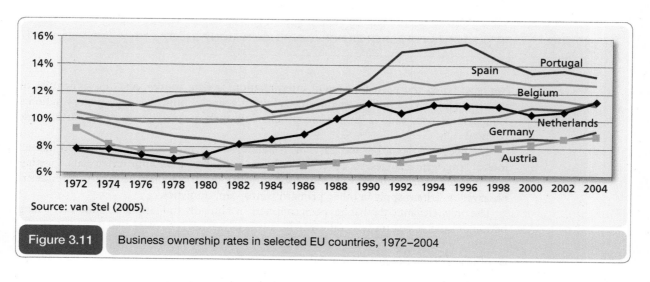

Source: van Stel (2005).

| Figure 3.11 | Business ownership rates in selected EU countries, 1972–2004 |

back to the level of half a century earlier. Clear examples of this U-shaped pattern are Italy and the Netherlands. Less clear examples are the US, Germany and the UK. In the US, the fall is clear but the rise is less clear. The UK and Germany are the reverse: here the fall is less clear but the rise is very clear. France, meanwhile, does not conform to any of these patterns. It shows an almost continuous decline in the proportions of self-employed.

A second source of data that has been assembled to enable international comparisons in enterprise to take place is COMPENDIA. It identifies the proportion of the population that can be classified as business owners – and may be considered as providing a guide to the question: what proportion of individuals, in an individual country, are owner-managers?

The data has been compiled by van Stel (2005) who seeks both to overcome the limitations of the self-employment data and supplement it with data on small enterprises. He uses OECD, EU and US data with the aim of controlling for differences in definition between countries (see section 3.2 on defining the self-employed). For example, German self-employment data includes individuals who are owners of incorporated businesses, whereas this group is excluded in the US. Other 'grey areas' include whether the self-employed include unpaid family workers and the extent to which agricultural and other related workers are included. Also, self-employment data derives generally from the Labour Force Survey in which individuals classify themselves – albeit with guidance – into one of several labour market states. This runs the risk of ill-informed judgements on the part of respondents – with this again being likely to vary between individuals, between countries and, probably, over time.

Taking all seven countries together, it can be seen from Figure 3.11 that in 1972 the proportion of the labour force in self-employment ranged from about 8 per cent to 12 per cent. By 2004, the range was between 9 per cent and nearly 13 per cent. Over 30 years, therefore, there is little evidence of any seismic change affecting the countries as a group. A single percentage point change for each country is fairly typical.

A second observation pointing to stability is that the countries with the highest, and the lowest, rates of self-employment in 1972 broadly occupy the same positions in 2004: Spain and Portugal have the highest rates in 1972 and the highest rates in 2004. In contrast, Germany, Austria and the UK had the lowest rates in 1972: 32 years later Germany and Austria continue to be the countries with the lowest rates in the group.

Some changes have occurred. As with Figure 3.10, the general pattern is for rates to rise at some point and then to either flatten out or to fall back. However, the timing of the change varies between countries. For example, as we have already seen, the UK rates rise in the 1980s, but then remain broadly constant until 2004. In contrast, the Netherlands, Austria, Germany and Belgium have a U-shaped pattern with all four countries showing declines in the 1970s.

Belgium then increases in the 1980s, but the increase does not occur in the Netherlands, Austria and Germany until the 1990s. By the end of the 1990s, however, the Belgian rate was in decline, along with both Spain and Portugal.

The overall pattern that emerges from the data is one of perhaps surprising stability over a long period of time, particularly given that during this time we have seen the following developments:

- three major world recessions;

- a massive shift of employment away from the primary and secondary sectors and into the service sector;

- a revolution in communications technology;

- a considerable increase in tertiary education; and

- the vast expenditure of taxpayers' money by governments seeking to create a more entrepreneurial economy.

Despite these profound macro changes, the changes in business ownership patterns are modest. Whilst there have been fluctuations, the reality is that self-employment rates increased by about 1 per cent over 32 years, and only the UK changes its relative position in the league table of countries identified.

Overall, it seems reasonable to conclude that amongst developed countries:

- Over a 30-year period, the proportion of the population that can be regarded as business owners/entrepreneurs has increased, but that over 50 years it has changed little.

- Even over the 30 years, the increase has been very small – perhaps around a single percentage point.

- The increase has not occurred in all countries – France shows a semi-continuous decline over the whole period.

- Not all countries changed at the same time. The US and the UK change in the 1980s, whereas Germany and the Netherlands change in the 1990s.

- Broadly, the same countries that were 'entrepreneurial' in 1972 continued to have a high proportion of business owners in 2004. The exception is the UK which moved into the more entrepreneurial category primarily because of changes in the 1980s.

- Several countries show declines in more recent years. Examples include the US, Portugal and Belgium.

So, to address the question of whether the UK patterns are broadly reflected in other countries, the answer is both yes and no. The similarities are that business ownership – as a measure of entrepreneurship – has increased over the last 30 years. This is the pattern for most developed countries with the notable exceptions of Japan and France.

Where the UK differs is that it seems to have had a step increase in business ownership in the 1980s and then little change afterwards. Most other European countries experienced a rise in the 1990s, rather than the 1980s, and any rise was much more gradual. The overall effect is that the UK is one of the few EU countries where business ownership rates are much higher in 2004 than 30 years previously.

Summary

This chapter has sought to define self-employment and small businesses. Both are difficult to define and quantify. There is also considerable doubt about measuring entrepreneurship either at an individual or societal level. These issues are discussed more fully in Case study 2: Dragonfly Consulting, and in Part 1 of Case study 7: Public policy in your hands. This chapter, like the case studies, shows that any definition of the small business typically tries to capture 'smallness' characteristics, such as a lack of market power, being owned and managed by the same individual and its legal independence. Converting these concepts into a statistical definition that enables valid comparisons to be drawn between countries, and over time, is a challenge.

No single definition of a small business applies in all countries, but the European Union definition of a small and medium-sized enterprise (SME) – based on having fewer than 250 employees, together with upper limits on sales and balance sheet valuations – is illustrative. Within the SME group are small businesses which are defined as having fewer than 50 employees.

Using such definitions we show that the vast majority of all enterprises in the world are SMEs. Indeed, based upon the EU definition of SMEs, we cannot identify any country in the world in which large businesses constitute more than 2 per cent of all enterprises. In contrast, what does vary markedly is business density (businesses per 1,000 population). Finally, despite their seeming invisibility to the media, it is clearly the case that SMEs are the dominant provider of employment.

The evidence on the UK in this chapter points to a dramatic enterprise population increase in the 1980s: the number of enterprises effectively doubled over this period. Despite this once-off change, there is also surprisingly stability. Within England, the regions with high rates of self-employment in 1981 continue to have high self-employment 20 years later. Second, over a 50-year period, self-employment rates have risen in many developed countries by only around 1 percentage point. Over a 30-year period, data that combines both self-employment and small business ownership suggests a considerable diversity of patterns between countries but a similar scale of increase to the 50-year change. Given that, during this time, there have been three world recessions, a huge shift of employment into the services sector and considerable technological change, the case is far from clear that there has been a long-run shift to greater entrepreneurialism in developed countries.

The evidence presented in this chapter points to small businesses clearly being a major source of employment and being the 'typical' business. The extent to which this has changed over a long period of time is less clear. So, whilst there is much more 'talk' about enterprise and entrepreneurship than was the case 30 or 50 years ago, it is harder to provide clear evidence of more 'action'.

Questions for discussion

1 Margaret Thatcher came to power in the UK in 1979, committed to moving Britain away from 'dependency' and towards 'enterprise'. What data might be used to assess if she was successful?

2 What measures could be used to decide if a country has become more enterprising? Taking a single country, describe the advantages and limitations of the data sources available in your chosen country to address that question.

3 If country A has a higher rate of new business formation than country B, does that make it more entrepreneurial? Give reasons for your answer.

4 Have developed countries become more entrepreneurial in the last 30 years? Provide evidence for your view.

5 Review the difficulties of defining a small business. How have these difficulties been resolved in practice?

6 How should the 'small business' be defined?

7 Is the UK economy now more entrepreneurial than it was 30 years ago?

References

Audretsch, D.B. and Thurik, A.R. (2000) 'Capitalism and Democracy in the 21st Century: From the Managed to the Entrepreneurial Economy', *Journal of Evolutionary Economics*, 10(1–2), 17–34.

Baumol, W.J. (1990) 'Entrepreneurship: Productive, Unproductive and Destructive', *Journal of Political Economy*, 98(5), 893–921.

Bolton, J. (1971) *Report of the Committee of Inquiry on Small Firms*, Cmnd. 4811. London: HMSO.

Bryson, J., Keeble, D.E. and Wood, P. (1997) 'The Creation and Growth of Small Business Service Firms in Post-industrial Britain', *Small Business Economics*, 9(4), 345–60.

Casson, M.C. (1982) *The Entrepreneur*. Oxford: Martin Robertson.

Curran, J. and Blackburn, R.A. (2001) *Researching the Small Enterprise*. London: Sage.

Eurostat (2008) *Enterprises by Size Class: Overview of SMEs in the EU*, adapted from Figure 2 and Table 3. Brussels: Eurostat, 31 April. http://epp.eurostat.ec.europa.eu/cache/ITY_OFFPUB/KS-SF-08-031/EN/KS-SF-08-031-EN.pdf.

Greene, F.J., Mole, K.F. and Storey, D.J. (2008) *Three Decades of Enterprise Culture: Entrepreneurship, Economic Regeneration and Public Policy*. London: Macmillan/Palgrave.

Indian Ministry of Statistics (2006) *Provisional Results of the Fifth Economic Census*. http://www.mospi.gov.in/economics_census_press_note.pdf.

NSBC (National Bureau of Statistics of China) (2005) *Communiqué on Major Data of the First National Economic Census of China (No. 1)*. http://www.stats.gov.cn/english/newsandcomingevents/t20060301402307658.htm (accessed 2 September 2009).

OECD (2000) *Employment Outlook*. Paris: OECD, June.

OECD (2004) *SME Statistics: Towards a More Systematic Statistical Measurement of SME Behaviour*. http://www.oecd.org/dataoecd/6/6/31919286.pdf.

OECD (2008) *Measuring Entrepreneurship: A digest of indicators*, Figures A1 and A2. Paris: OECD. http://www.oecd.org/dataoecd/53/23/41664409.pdf.

ONS (2008) *UK Self-Employment Jobs*. http://www.statistics.gov.uk/StatBase/TSDSeries1.asp.

SBA (2008) *US Small Business Administration Table of Small Business Size Standards Matched to North American Industry Classification System Codes*. http://www.sba.gov/idc/groups/public/documents/sba_homepage/serv_sstd_tablepdf.pdf.

Stanworth, M.J.K. and Gray, C. (eds) (1991) *Bolton 20 Years On: The Small Firm in the 1990s*. London: PCP/Small Business Research Trust.

Van Stel, A.J. (2005) 'COMPENDIA: Harmonising Business Ownership Data Across Countries and Over Time', *International Entrepreneurship and Management Journal*, 1(1), 105–23.

Appendix 3.1

Key indicators for enterprises in the non-financial business economy, by EU-27 countries, 2005

	Number of enterprises (000s)	Number of persons employed (000s)	Percentage of enterprises that are SMEs	Percentage of employed in SMEs
EU-27	19,602	85,000	99.8	67.1
Austria	272	1,589	99.7	67.4
Belgium	395	1,602	99.8	66.6
Bulgaria	240	1,318	99.7	72.6
Cyprus	43	174	99.9	84.3
Czech Republic	878	2,461	99.8	68.9
Germany	1,654	12,357	99.5	60.6
Denmark	202	1,129	99.7	66.0
Estonia	38	305	99.6	78.1
Greece	820	2,031	99.9	81.9
Spain	2,542	10,538	99.9	78.7
Finland	187	717	99.7	58.5
France	2,274	8,834	99.8	61.4
Hungary	556	1,783	99.8	70.9
Ireland	85	654	99.5	67.5
Italy	3,819	12,182	99.9	81.3
Lithuania	93	619	99.7	72.9
Luxembourg	21	120	99.6	70.8
Latvia	62	469	99.7	75.6
Netherlands	492	3,146	99.7	67.6
Norway	241	895	99.8	69.6
Poland	1,405	5,289	99.8	69.8
Portugal	848	2,676	99.9	82.0
Romania	410	2,463	99.5	60.8
Sweden	523	1,667	99.8	63.2
Slovenia	88	371	99.7	66.4
Slovakia	42	501	98.8	54.0
United Kingdom	1,535	9,636	99.6	54.0

Source: Eurostat (2008).
Notes: Includes no data from Malta but data from Norway (European Economic Area country).

4 Working in small businesses

Key learning objectives

By the end of this chapter you should:

- Understand the issues associated with estimating the extent to which job creation takes place in businesses of different size

- Be able to compare and contrast small and large business workplaces

- Critically evaluate if small businesses are 'better' places to work.

Sophos [a large Canadian IT company] was recognized [as Canada's top employer] for an excellent benefits package that, among other things, offers enrolement in the company's bonus program, a matching Registered Retirement Savings Plan (RRSP), and participation in Sophos's share option plan. Sophos was also acknowledged for a superior training and development program. Expanding and honing the current knowledge and skills of its employees is a main focus for the organization; the company offers comprehensive orientation programs, in-depth product training and external training opportunities.

Sophos (2009)

Stress is a fact of life, but in the City [of London] it is contagious and can encourage some pretty unhealthy habits. It is no coincidence that the City is Britain's busiest centre for Alcoholics Anonymous, Narcotics Anonymous and Gamblers Anonymous. One 43-year-old consultant who has chronic fatigue syndrome and has just quit the City says: 'Many employers provide comprehensive private medical insurance, which includes a free trip to The Priory [a health clinic] if things get out of hand. The trouble is, as soon as you've been given a clean bill of health you're back at your desk facing the same situation that led to depression and compulsive behaviour problems in the first place'.

The Times (2007)

I would say larger firms tend to be dictatorial. We have a very open approach, very transparent, and it tends to remove stress. As a company we try to ensure everybody knows what's happening and what the plans are. Big companies are more guilty of just telling staff what's going on. I was part of a multi-million-pound organisation for 17 years and that was considerably more stressful. Staff issues were a big problem. Smaller companies like ours are much more approachable. If you have a problem you can go straight to the owner and talk to them.

Richard Shacklock of Stewart and Shacklock (2007)

Kathryn worked as a retail assistant for her local newsagency. She had worked on a permanent part-time basis for over 12 months. One day she went to work and mentioned to her boss that she had not been offered any annual leave even though she was entitled to it after 12 months of service. The following day Kathryn was sacked.

Job Watch Australia (2002)

4.1 Introduction

The four examples above each illustrate different features of working for a large and a small employer. Sophos, the Canadian IT business, appears a 'model' employer, whilst the second quote points to the downsides of working (for a large business) in the stressful City of London. The third example suggests that in a small business employees can gain real benefits from working closely and collaboratively with others. On the other hand, the example from Australia points to the potential downsides of working for a small employer.

In this chapter, we ask in what ways is it better, worse, or simply different to be an employee in a small business. These are important questions. In Chapter 3, we saw that in the European Union 60 per cent of employed people – around 85 million in 2005 – worked in a small business. We also showed that about one in eight adults in the UK were self-employed, whilst in Italy, it is closer to one in five. In short, employment in small businesses matters to many people.

To examine these questions, we examine a range of key dimensions of a 'better' workplace: pay, training, health and safety and job satisfaction. This, again, is important because there is no single measure of what makes a workplace a 'better' place to work.

As our focus is the small business we use, for illustrative purposes only, the two polar opposites identified initially by Rainnie (1989). At one extreme is the 'small is beautiful' perspective where the owner and employees work harmoniously, shoulder to shoulder, for their common good. The polar opposite was described by Rainnie as the 'Bleak House'. He argues that internal social relations in small businesses are a reflection of '. . . fierce competition in product markets (which) leads to the need for close supervision and control and a dictatorial style of management' (Atkinson 2008: 449).

In practice, as we show, neither can be considered to be 'typical' of a small business, but nevertheless they are valuable benchmarks in reviewing the evidence on small business employment. The reality, as Ram *et al.* (2007) suggest, is that employment and social relations in small businesses reflect the huge diversity of contexts and choices made by employers and employees between these polar extremes.

To place our examination of the dimensions of the small workplace in context we begin by briefly reviewing the literature which has sought to answer the question: is it small or large businesses that are the main sources of job creation in an economy?

4.2 The direct employment effects of small businesses

New and small businesses have both a direct and an indirect impact on employment. This section reviews the evidence on the direct employment generation effects which have been available for at least 30 years. The evidence on the indirect effect of new businesses on subsequent employment is more recent and was pioneered by Fritsch and Mueller (2004). This is discussed more fully in Chapter 6.

There are two approaches to assessing whether it is large or small businesses that are the prime direct source of job creation: the first is the static approach and the second is the dynamic approach. Both approaches are now illustrated with reference to Table 4.1.

The static approach is so called because it takes two 'snapshots' (the base year 'snapshot' and the final year 'snapshot') of employment in large and small businesses, and compares the two.

To illustrate the static calculation, we assume the economy is comprised of only three businesses. Business 1 starts off in the base year as an EU-defined large business (more than 250 employees) employing 260 workers. In the final year, its employment has grown to 315 employees. Business 2 is a small business (fewer than 250 employees) with 200 employees that, in the final year, ends up with 260 employees. It, therefore, becomes a large business. Between the base and final years a new business (Business 3) is started. By definition, since it did not exist in the base year, it has zero employees. But in the final year it has 50 employees.

Overall, there are 460 employees in the base year and 625 employees in the final year. In total, employment has grown by 165 jobs.

In the base year 'snapshot', therefore, the two small businesses (200 and 0 employees) represent 43 per cent of total employment (200/460 employees). In the *final* year 'snapshot', only one business is small (50 employees). So, small businesses provide only 8 per cent (50/625) of total employment. Employment in small businesses has dropped by 35 per cent.

If data are only available on the size distribution of businesses in the base and final year then only the static calculation is possible. However, Table 4.1 also presents a different way of calculating employment change which generates very different conclusions. These calculations were first performed by Birch (1979) who had access to data on employment in 5.6 million business establishments in the US.

Birch's dynamic calculation is also illustrated in Table 4.1. It shows that there is one large business **in the base year** and its employment grows from 260 to 315 employees, adding

Table 4.1	The static and dynamic approaches to job generation		
	Base year	**Final year**	**Change between base and final year**
Business 1	260	315	+55
Business 2	200	260	+60
Business 3	0	50	+50
TOTAL EMPLOYMENT	460	625	+165
'Static' calculation of small business share	43%	8%	−35%
'Dynamic' calculation of small business share			
Small business change			+110 (66%)
Large business change			+55 (33%)

55 jobs. However, in the base year, there were two small businesses: one with zero employees and the other with 200 employees. In the **final** year their total employment was 310 employees or a growth of 110 employees. So, classifying businesses by their size in the base year, the small businesses had generated 110 jobs whereas the large businesses had generated 55 jobs. **Small businesses in this example had generated two thirds of the increase in jobs** – which was precisely the figure that Birch calculated for the US between 1969 and 1976, and was clearly a very different conclusion from that derived from the static calculation.

Kirchhoff and Greene (1998) also showed that how employment change is calculated can make a big difference to the interpretation of the importance of small businesses. Table 4.2 shows US job creation (1976–86) using both the 'static' and the 'dynamic' approaches. It clearly shows that the job contribution of small businesses was higher using the 'dynamic' approach but lower when the 'static' approach was used.

Birch's (1979) work, when it was first produced, was controversial. It was critiqued on the basis of deficiencies in the data (e.g. his data was not 'representative') and that his approach did not deal with random changes in employment change. This meant that his results were hard to replicate (Armington and Odle 1982) and that his results were potentially biased towards smaller businesses because, using Birch's methodology, employment changes are thought to be 'caused' by smaller businesses when, in fact, they are normal and natural fluctuations in employment (regression to the mean fallacy) (Davis *et al.* 1996).

Nonetheless, despite these criticisms, a range of international evidence has shown that smaller businesses are important contributors to job creation (Davidsson *et al.* 1998 (Sweden); Picot and Dupuy 1998 (Canada); Kirchhoff and Greene 1998 (US); and Broersma and Gautier 1997 (the Netherlands)). If smaller businesses are more likely to create jobs, the evidence also suggests that they are more likely to lose jobs. Voulgaris *et al.* (2005) showed, for example, that in Greek manufacturing – even after controlling for the regression to the mean fallacy – that smaller businesses experience more job growth and job losses than larger businesses. Similarly, Neumark *et al.* (2008) showed, for the US, that small businesses were more likely to experience job gains and losses. Overall, this emphasises that smaller businesses are much more likely to experience volatility or 'churn' in employment than larger businesses.

However, it is not simply the *quantity* of small business jobs that is of interest. We also are interested in whether they are 'good' jobs. So if, for example, the jobs created by small businesses were, in some sense, 'worse' than those provided in large businesses, then the role of small businesses in employment change might be regarded as less valuable to society. The next section – and subsequent sections – considers different measures of job 'quality' in smaller businesses.

Table 4.2	Job generation in the US: 1976–86, by percentage	
Size	**Static**	**Dynamic**
1–19	13.4	26.2
20–99	17.6	17.4
100–499	16.6	13.6
500+	52.5	42.8
TOTAL	100.0	100.0

Source: Kirchhoff and Greene (1998).

4.3 Pay

This section considers two questions relating to pay:

1   Do smaller businesses pay less than larger businesses?

2   Do they provide fewer fringe benefits (e.g. health insurance, holidays, pension arrangements) than larger businesses?

We clearly show that employees in small businesses obtain lower pay and fewer fringe benefits than employees in large businesses. We look at each of these issues in turn.

1 Do smaller businesses pay less than larger businesses?

Oi and Idson (1999) showed that not only do smaller businesses pay their workers less than larger businesses, but that they have done so for more than a century. They report that Moore (1911) found that Italian women workers in large textile businesses earned nearly 40 per cent more than women workers in small textile businesses. The UK's Bolton Report (1971) also showed that the difference in earnings between large and small business workers was about 20 per cent.

More recent evidence suggests that little had changed. Forth *et al.* (2006) showed that 11 per cent of employees in small workplaces were low paid (£4.50 per hour or less), compared with only 5 per cent of employees in large workplaces. They also showed that 14 per cent of large workplace employees were highly paid (£15 per hour or more) whilst only 7 per cent of workers earned high wages in small businesses.

Such results, however, may reflect differences in the characteristics of workers/businesses. For example, larger businesses may be able to pay higher wages because they:

● have more market power and hence higher profits;

● tend to employ a more qualified workforce and, subsequently, have to pay more for these workers;

● have more exacting performance standards and need to pay more to attract and retain staff; and

● find it difficult to distinguish between good and bad workers in a team so end up paying the same (high) wages to all in a particular team (Lallemand *et al.* 2005).

In contrast, small businesses may pay less because they are more likely to employ groups that are more prone to lower pay (e.g. women, younger people, the 'low' skilled). It may also be that the characteristics of the business may explain wage rates. Brown and Medoff (2003) found evidence that older businesses pay higher wages and – since younger businesses are likely to be smaller – this may explain why small businesses pay less than larger businesses. However, Brown and Medoff found this relationship to be much weaker when worker characteristics (e.g. skills of worker) were also included in the analysis. They also imply that the relationship between wages and business age is U-shaped, with very young and very old businesses paying the highest wages. More generally, Oi and Idson (1999) controlled for a range of worker characteristics. They found that worker characteristics reduced the scale of the so-called 'size-wage premium', but their US evidence implied that smaller businesses pay between 10 and 20 per cent less than larger businesses. Troske (1999) using US data, and EFILWC's (2007a) European data, also showed that, once worker characteristics are controlled for, it still appears that smaller businesses pay less than larger businesses.

McNabb and Whitfield (2000) showed that smaller establishments (10–24 employees) were most likely to have a high proportion of workers that were low paid. This proportion fell as establishment size rose. However, when low pay was related to business size, there is some evidence that very large businesses also had high proportions of low-paid workers. Nonetheless, McNabb and Whitfield confirmed that smaller businesses paid less and that they had a higher proportion of young people, women and the unskilled. Forth *et al.* (2006) also found that small business employees were more likely to experience pay being unilaterally set for them – without negotiation – by their manager. Finally, Agell's (2004) study of Swedish businesses showed a wider earnings spread amongst larger businesses. This effect is considerably reduced when worker composition characteristics are taken into account. However, Agell also showed that managers in large establishments consciously used income differentials to positively motivate the workforce. In contrast, small business managers believed that such a policy would have a counter-productive effect on employee motivation.

Van Praag and Versloot (2007) provide a helpful summary of the recent literature on the matter, with their findings closely corresponding with ours – pointing to a consistent 'size-wage premium' with large business employees being considerably better paid than those in small businesses.

2 Do they provide fewer fringe benefits (e.g. health insurance, holidays, pension arrangements) than larger businesses?

Brown *et al.* (1990) showed that smaller businesses provided fewer fringe benefits to their employees than large businesses. Belfield (1999) found, in his study of UK graduates, that not only were the salaries paid to graduates employed in large businesses higher, but that large

---

Illustration	Should small business employees be allowed maternity leave?

Question

Below are the views of Sylvia Tidy-Harris, the founder of Womenspeakers.co.uk. Do you believe that she has a point? Whose interest should be first – the employer or the employee?

Small firms shouldn't be forced to employ women of child-bearing age. Small businesses should be exempt from employing women of child-bearing age because the cost of dealing with maternity leave could cripple them. If one of the six staff in my public-speaking agency found she was pregnant and needed to have a year off, I would have to keep her job open – and to cover the job while she was on maternity leave, it would be very hard to find somebody else as committed, as that person would know that at the end of the maternity-leave period they were going to be booted out. It would be incredibly debilitating for my business – and any small enterprise hoping to grow.

Big companies may be able to cope with people going on maternity leave because they have a human resources department that can find somebody to move across from another division. But small businesses with only a few employees haven't got these resources – so they are likely to have to employ an expensive agency to help them . . .

I am not the only female boss who feels this way; others tell me the only person they want on maternity leave is themselves, it's just that I'm the only one with the guts to speak out. Nobody should be treated badly in a business. If you go and work for somebody, you shouldn't be discriminated against. But, equally, you shouldn't take advantage of the situation. I cannot understand how somebody can go for interview, knowing they are pregnant, and not have to tell the prospective employer. Employers should be allowed to ask more questions.

Source: 'Stay Out of My Way, baby', *The Sunday Times*, 4 November 2007.

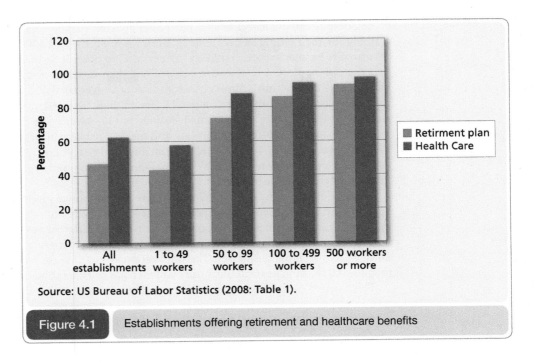

Source: US Bureau of Labor Statistics (2008: Table 1).

| Figure 4.1 | Establishments offering retirement and healthcare benefits |

businesses were much more likely to provide an employer pension fund: 29 per cent of new graduates working for a business with fewer than 25 workers received pension rights, compared with 83 per cent of those employed by a business with more than 500 workers. Belfield also showed similar, if less stark, differences for other fringe benefits such as health insurance, profit-sharing or merit/bonus pay.

Wagner's (1997) evidence was even clearer. He found that in Germany not only was there a substantial size-wage premium but that holiday entitlement and bonuses were lower in smaller businesses. The Kaiser Family Foundation (2008) also found that there were marked differences in the provision of fringe health benefits in the US. For example, 88 per cent of larger businesses (200 or more workers) – compared to 53 per cent of small businesses (3–199 workers) – were prepared to offer 'wellness' programmes (e.g. weight loss programmes, gym membership discounts or on-site exercise facilities). The US Bureau of Labor Statistics (2008) data in Figure 4.1 show that retirement and healthcare benefits are much more prevalent in larger businesses whilst the SBA (2005) also shows that workers in larger businesses are more likely to have a pension, more likely to have sick leave, and more likely to have paid holidays (vacations).

In short, the evidence consistently shows that smaller businesses provide fewer fringe benefits to employees than larger businesses.

4.4 Training

The provision of workforce training has the potential to provide wide-ranging benefits to both employers and employees. Bartel (2000) reviewed a large number of US studies and found that the annual returns to companies varied from 7 to 50 per cent. Blundell *et al.* (1999) reported that employees who make use of employer-provided and vocational training can expect their earnings to increase by at least 5 per cent.

Yet, despite this evidence, smaller businesses are considerably less likely to provide **formal** training for their employees than larger businesses. Forth *et al.* (2006) found, for example, that smaller businesses were less likely (59 per cent) to provide formal off-the-job training for experienced employees in the core occupations than medium-sized (85 per cent) or large workplaces (89 per cent). Similarly, Spanish data suggested that '. . . only 11.9 per cent of the employees in the smallest companies (fewer than 10 employees) receive any training, well below the 31.1 per cent in small businesses (10–49 employees), the 46.6 per cent in medium businesses (50–249 employees), and the 69.4 per cent in large businesses (more than 250 employees)' (EFILWC 2007*b*: 6). As Kitching and Blackburn (2004) and Patton (2005) confirm, there is plenty of evidence that small-business employees receive less formal training than employees in large businesses.

The question is why is this? Why – despite the supposed productivity benefits for the business and earning benefits for the employee – is relatively little formal workforce training provided in small businesses? We now provide two very different answers to this question.

One answer is that there are distinctive 'barriers' to formal training in small businesses that do not occur in large businesses. The implication is that if these barriers can be overcome, then formal training in small businesses will increase considerably.

This 'barrier' perspective suggests that small businesses would train more if:

- entrepreneurs were more aware of the benefits of training;
- the 'right' training (cost and appropriateness) was offered;
- the 'negative' attitudes held by the entrepreneurs towards training could be overcome.

At face value, a lack of awareness of the benefits of training seems to be a legitimate barrier but upon reflection it seems curious that entrepreneurs – who are often presumed to be able to identify and exploit opportunities – do not recognise and nurture the key skills of their workforce. This raises questions about the worth of increasing 'awareness' amongst entrepreneurs about the 'value' of training.

A second barrier is that training is viewed as more expensive for small than for large businesses (Beaver and Hutchings 2004). Patton (2005) also suggests that one other commonly held reason for the poor take up of training is that the available training is often inappropriate. For example, trainers may not offer a tailored programme that meets the needs of the small business. He also suggests there may be too many training programmes available, making it difficult for the small business to identify the 'right' training for their employees.

However, these arguments fail to take account of the fact that the entrepreneur has to continually make judgements about the cost, availability and appropriateness of a wide range of 'inputs' of capital and labour. It is assumed that they are able to make appropriate decisions on these matters – and yet somehow be unable to make good decisions on formal training.

The final barrier identified is that entrepreneurs hold negative attitudes towards training. Matlay (1999) argued that the provision of small business training is strongly influenced by the characteristics of the entrepreneur. Matlay found that training in small businesses is most likely to take place where the entrepreneur has educational qualifications and, since entrepreneurs were (generally) less likely to be educationally well qualified than those managing larger businesses, it is this which explains why small businesses are less likely to train. Again, there will be entrepreneurs who are 'prejudiced' against training but, if they were, this would be expected to be reflected in their poorer performance, and might be expected to lead to a change in behaviour. However, as Chapter 16 will show, there is little evidence of a direct link between formal training and business performance. This, again, raises questions about the 'barriers' argument.

Fundamentally, the 'barrier' perspective rests upon an implicit assumption that practices in small businesses ought to resemble the business practices of larger businesses. It assumes that, because large businesses provide formal training for their employees – and implicitly that they are 'better managed' than small businesses – small businesses should do likewise. Instead, what seems a more cogent explanation is that small business owners/managers make 'informed' rather than 'ignorant' decisions about training.

We assume that small businesses provide less formal training because it correctly reflects their market situation. So, rather than being 'ignorant' about the benefits of training, entrepreneurs make 'market'-based judgements about training. Overall, for the following reasons (Storey and Westhead 1999):

- Small businesses have fewer 'slack' resources than large businesses. So, if someone is being trained, there are fewer 'slack' resources (other staff) to cover their absence. This serves as a disincentive to train people. Also, arguably, 'good' training involves continuous investments (e.g. participation in refresher courses) by the worker and the business if long-term benefits are to be realised. This means – if nothing else – that the training costs per worker are likely to be higher in a small business because they have fewer workers over whom the costs can be spread.

- Training deepens and broadens the skill base of the individual worker making them more productive. The large business benefits from this because it offers a career path to its workers – what is called an internal labour market – so that the more productive workers are promoted to better paid jobs. In contrast, the entrepreneur, even if they recognise that training increases the productivity of a worker, also knows that there are likely to be fewer routes for promotion in the business. They fear that trained staff will be poached – probably by a larger business able to pay higher wages. The entrepreneur that provides formal training, therefore, incurs the cost of the training and then risks losing the worker.

- Most formal training – especially that provided from public funds – sees the successful trainee obtain a formal qualification. This has the advantage of confirming for another employer that the individual has a specified range of skills. However, it may also dissuade entrepreneurs from offering training because they fear that their newly qualified staff have a greater likelihood of being poached.

- Chapter 1 showed that small businesses tend to favour investments that have short period returns and are highly flexible to changing circumstances. Formal training fails on both counts: the return is at best in the medium term and formality – in terms of qualifications – is the focus rather than flexibility. So, even if the entrepreneur recognises that staff need training on current products, services and markets, they recognise – given the volatility of the marketplace – that these products, services and markets may well be radically different in the future.

- Training senior and middle managers from a single large organisation benefits from having people generally at the same stage of their managerial development and sharing a common corporate 'outlook'. It means there are 'scale economies' available to training providers that enable them to tailor the training to the specific requirements of the business. This makes it worthwhile for the training provider to develop a deep understanding of the company's markets, history, traditions and aspirations. This is not the case for those providing training for small business workers. Each small business will send only one or two employees, and there are likely to be huge sectoral and aspirational differences between small businesses, so tailoring training to specific business needs may not be feasible. There will also be diversity amongst those small business personnel attending courses – all of which eliminates any possible scale economies.

- Finally, we move away from small business employee training to that of training the entrepreneur. There are perhaps three main reasons why entrepreneurs are less likely to undertake formal training, in comparison with large business managers: 1) entrepreneurs believe that they are successful because of their 'personality'. Therefore, since personality is 'given', there is little point in training something that is not 'there'; 2) the best form of training is 'doing the job'; and 3) entrepreneurs might consider that the 'trainers' are likely to be less entrepreneurial: so there is little point in seeking 'training' from people with 'inferior' entrepreneurial skills.

Overall, the 'market-based' perspective on small business training provides a more cogent explanation of why it is that employees in small businesses are less likely to receive formal training than those in large businesses.

What is less clear, however, is the scale and nature of *informal* training. Patton (2005) describes informal training and learning as: 'a far more diffuse process and occurs throughout the organisation as individuals observe, imitate and learn from others on a fragmented and flexible basis'.

Kitching and Blackburn (2004) reported that most small businesses provide some informal training for their employees. So, measuring only the provision of formal training under-estimates the total amount of training provided in small businesses. Coetzer and Perry (2008) implied that such training is likely to be more effective in facilitating employee learning in small businesses than formal training.

What, however, remains unclear is whether the scale of informal training varies between large and small businesses. It seems quite possible that informal learning may be equally or perhaps even more prevalent in large than in small businesses. So, whilst this is an area for future research, the case is clear that workers in small businesses are less likely to receive formal training. This is not because of prejudice or ignorance on the part of entrepreneurs, but stems from an informed assessment of the costs and benefits of formal training provision. The evidence on informal training provision is much less clear.

4.5 Health and safety

One important measure of the quality of working life is health and safety. The widely held view is that small firms provide a less safe working environment than that provided by large employers. A comprehensive review of health and safety issues in small businesses was conducted by Hasle and Limborg (2006). They reached the following conclusions:

- There was strong evidence of higher accident risks in smaller businesses, with this being particularly clear for fatal or very serious accidents. Hasle and Limborg (2006), for the EU, found that the fatal injury rate per 100,000 employees was 6.8 in enterprises with fewer than 10 employees, 6.3 in enterprises with 10–49 employees and 2.7 in enterprises with more than 250 employees. Similar differences are evident in Figure 4.2 which shows US data on the rate of fatalities per 100,000 workers in US manufacturing. This clearly points to fatalities being higher in small businesses.

- Hasle and Limborg's review also points to a higher likelihood of exposure to physical or chemical hazards in small businesses.

- They also showed a correlation between sectors dominated by small businesses and poor safety records. Their evidence suggested that the high risk sectors were agriculture, construction, wood industry and printing.

Hasle and Limborg reviewed explanations for these patterns. They concluded that these patterns reflect:

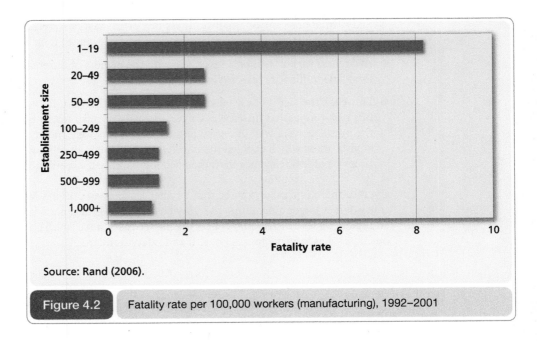

Source: Rand (2006).

| Figure 4.2 | Fatality rate per 100,000 workers (manufacturing), 1992–2001 |

- the narrower profit margins of small businesses, where entrepreneurs respond by seeking to cut costs wherever possible;

- the imperfect knowledge of entrepreneurs of the legal environment, perhaps reflecting their lack of specialist knowledge.

This lack of knowledge of workplace risks is identified in Figure 4.3. It clearly shows that amongst EU businesses the smaller the size of the business, the greater the likelihood of not being informed about workplace risks. Vickers *et al.* (2005) confirmed this amongst a sample of UK businesses. They found as follows:

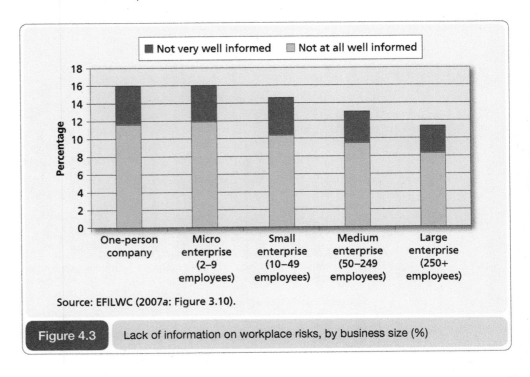

Source: EFILWC (2007a: Figure 3.10).

| Figure 4.3 | Lack of information on workplace risks, by business size (%) |

- Sixty-three per cent of small business owner/managers were unable to identify a single piece of health and safety legislation which was relevant to their business.

- Awareness varied with business size – with the owners of the smallest businesses being the least able to identify relevant legislation.

- However, the fact that owners were unaware of legislation did not necessarily imply these businesses operated unsafe or dangerous businesses. In many, but certainly not all, cases the premises were well managed because employers were motivated to provide a working environment which enabled them to retain employees. In other words the threat of legislation was of less relevance than the need for 'good housekeeping'.

Overall, there is clear evidence that smaller businesses provide less safe workplaces when compared to larger businesses. This may be explained by a general lack of awareness of health and safety issues but also may reflect the higher costs that a small business – relative to a large business – has to incur to meet health and safety standards.

4.6 Job satisfaction

Given that employees in larger businesses earn more, work in safer environments and have greater fringe benefits, it might be expected that such individuals would report higher job satisfaction than small business employees. However, the evidence, on balance, suggests that it is workers in smaller businesses that are more satisfied. One indicator of this is that violence and harassment are higher in larger businesses. Figure 4.4 shows that in the EU workers in a large businesses (250+ employees) are more likely to experience physical

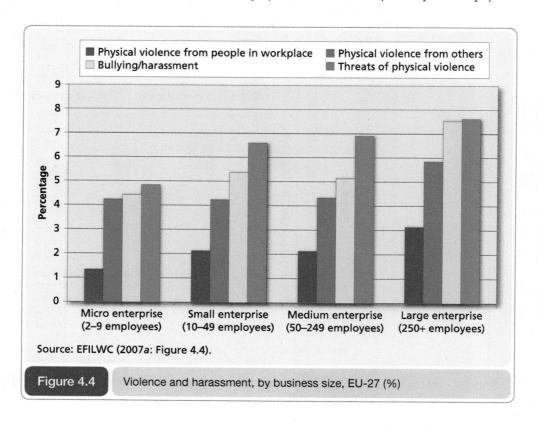

Source: EFILWC (2007a: Figure 4.4).

Figure 4.4   Violence and harassment, by business size, EU-27 (%)

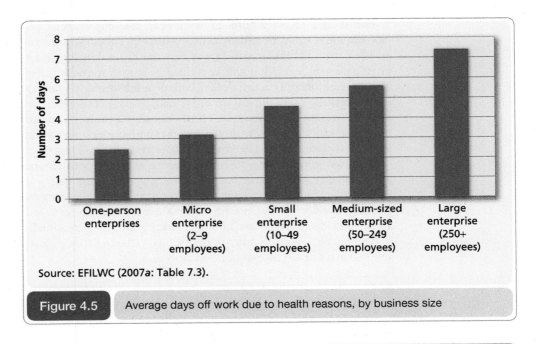

Source: EFILWC (2007a: Table 7.3).

| Figure 4.5 | Average days off work due to health reasons, by business size |

| Table 4.3 | Employees' trust in workplace managers (percentage agreeing or strongly agreeing with the statements), by business size |

Managers here . . .	Small	Medium sized	Large
. . . can be relied upon to keep their promises	65	49	46
. . . are sincere in attempting to understand employees' views	69	55	52
. . . deal with employees honestly	73	56	53
. . . treat employees fairly	72	59	53

Source: Forth et al. (2006), Table 7.4

violence, bullying/harassment and the threat of physical violence than those in micro-sized businesses (2–9 employees).

Figure 4.5 shows EU data on the average number of days taken off due to health related issues. It clearly shows that absenteeism is much higher in larger businesses.

Forth et al. (2006) also found that smaller businesses experienced lower levels of absenteeism and lower levels of voluntary resignations. They showed that employee trust varied markedly depending on the size of the business. Table 4.3 shows the percentage of employees 'agreeing or strongly agreeing' with four statements. Small business employees believed their managers were more likely to keep their promises, were more sincere in understanding employee views, were more likely to deal honestly with employees and treated them fairly.

The only contrary result is reported by van Praag and Versloot (2007). They reported results from Winter-Ebmer and Zweimuller (1999) which found small business employees were more likely to search for, and find, alternative employment than those in large businesses. From this, it was inferred that job satisfaction was lower amongst small business employees.

So, with that single exception, the evidence clearly points to higher satisfaction amongst small business employees. The central explanation provided for these findings is that they reflect the greater managerial informality that characterises smaller businesses (Ram et al. 2001).

Formality is reflected in the presence of written procedures, rules and policies to design, measure and regulate the employment relationship. The advantage of such processes is that they are likely to be administered by human resource professionals who are more likely to be aware of employment legislation and be trained in human resource issues. However, the key disadvantage of formality is that dealing with people becomes 'procedural' rather than 'personal'.

On virtually every dimension of formality smaller businesses are more informal workplaces. For example, Storey *et al.* (2010) identify 12 measures of formality. They then show that for all 12 measures formality increases as both business and workplace size increase. Only when workplaces exceed 250 employees does formality no longer increase.

However, from a management perspective, there are both advantages and disadvantages of **informality** which we define as a reliance upon custom and practice and an absence of written procedures. The advantage is that informal workplaces are more likely to have closer working relationships because employees are more likely to get to know other people than in a large and 'distant' business. Equally, entrepreneurs have potentially greater access to their staff and are able – again other things being equal – to develop closer bonds with their staff. The two main disadvantages of informality are:

● That the entrepreneur is unlikely to be a dedicated employment specialist. This means that more informal small businesses are less likely to be successful in employment tribunals because they are – regardless of the rights or wrongs of the case – less likely to follow the 'procedures' (Saridakis *et al.* 2008).

● That recruitment is likely to be done informally (Forth *et al.* 2006). A reliance on friends and family as employees may mean that that the chosen employees are not the 'best' available. Also, there is a chance that employees will be treated inconsistently. For example, the employee might get different responses depending on when they raised an issue with the employer; or when two employees get different responses from their employer to the same request.

Storey *et al.* (2010) showed, however, that job satisfaction is higher in more informal workplaces. To show this they compared formality with job satisfaction across different business sizes and their results are shown in Figure 4.6. They found that, as expected, job satisfaction was higher in smaller sized businesses. However, their interest was more in the type of workplace. Some workplaces are – as we saw in Chapter 3 – small but actually owned by a larger business whilst others are single enterprises. They, therefore, tested to see if there were any differences in job satisfaction between small enterprises, and 'small' establishments that were part of a larger

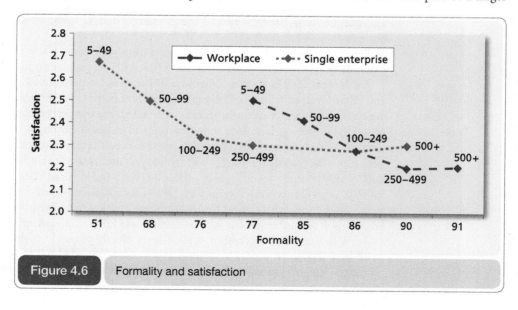

Figure 4.6   Formality and satisfaction

enterprise. The expectation is that the small single enterprise (e.g. the small independent grocery store) would be less formal than the small establishment (e.g. the grocery store that was part of a national chain). Their findings, shown as Figure 4.6, make it clear that job satisfaction is not only higher in small than in large establishments but also much higher in the single enterprise than in the equivalent sized small establishment. Only when single establishments reach 100 employees and workplaces reach 250 employees is size no longer an influence.

These results suggest that workplaces owned by larger enterprises have both more formality and a less contented workforce than workplaces of the same size owned by a small business.

Illustration	'Unfair' dismissal claims at Old Station Nursery

Sarah Steel, the Managing Director of Old Station Nursery, a provider of children's day nurseries and out-of-school clubs, believes that employment regulation in the UK has made it too easy for employees to claim unfair dismissal.

She says: 'Central to our business is the staff we employ. We are providing high quality care for children and so we have to ensure that we, in turn, take the training and development of our own staff very seriously'.

Putting staff and the children they look after at the forefront of the business has certainly proved successful. Since starting in 2002, the business has grown to 12 nurseries and a turnover of £3 million.

To support staff, it has sought and been successfully awarded Investors in People status (a UK training scheme award). It has also made use of an external human resource (HR) company to guide them through employment law.

Yet, despite this, Old Station Nursery still found itself on the 'wrong' end of unfair dismissal claims. Ms Steel explains: 'Like other businesses in 2008, we were faced by a downturn in the UK economy. We needed to make two people redundant. The redundancy process was carried out in conjunction with our external HR adviser to ensure that we met our obligations to the staff. This allowed any member of staff who had been selected for redundancy to appeal or to file a grievance during the course of the process and whilst they were still employed. Following the consultation process, two employees were selected for redundancy and the employees left us with the appropriate severance pay.'

That, though, was not the end of the matter. Although none of those made redundant filed a grievance complaint whilst they were still employed, they subsequently decided to issue legal proceedings against Old Station Nursery to take them to an employment tribunal.

'I was indignant', says Ms Steel, 'we had followed what we believed were all the right formalities and, yet, the employees still sought more money off us.' Ms Steel, however, felt that she had to pay up. 'It would have cost us between £5,000 to £8,000 to contest these claims. It was simpler to pay out £1,500 because we could not be absolutely sure that we had crossed all the 't's and dotted all the 'i's.'

Questions

1 How likely do you think it is that Old Station Nursery will experience further employment claims?

2 Do you think that employment regulations 'encouraging' unfair dismissal claims should be reformed?

3 Is Old Station Nursery an atypical employer? If so, is it right that employment regulations should be reformed?

4.7 A review of the small workplace

So far, we have seen that there are radical differences between employment relationships in small and large businesses. These are summarised in Table 4.4 which shows that:

- Large workplaces pay better, provide better fringe benefits, provide more formal training and are safer places in which to work.

- Small workplaces have a workforce that is more likely to trust its managers. Despite being paid less, they also appear 'happier'.

Does this then suggest that smaller workplaces are 'better' places to work? In response to this, two polar viewpoints have been suggested. One viewpoint is called the 'small is beautiful' approach and the other sees a small workplace as 'Bleak House' (Wilkinson 1999).

Central to the 'small is beautiful' approach is a sense that relationships between employees and managers are harmonious, there is little unnecessary formality and the working relationships are close to being that of 'one happy family'. This viewpoint is best summed up by the Bolton Report (1971) which stated that:

> Although sometimes physical conditions can sometimes be inferior in small businesses, most people prefer to work in a small group where communication presents fewer problems: the employee in a small business can more easily see the relation between what he is doing and the objectives and performance of the business as a whole. Where management is more direct and flexible, working rules can be varied to suit the individual. Each employee is also likely to have a more varied role, with a chance to participate in several kinds of work and better opportunities to learn and widen his experience. No doubt, mainly as a result of this, the turnover of staff in small businesses is very low and strikes and other kinds of industrial disputes are relatively infrequent. The fact that small businesses offer lower earnings than larger businesses suggests that convenience of location, and generally the non-material satisfactions of working in them, more than outweigh any financial sacrifice involved.
>
> *Cited in Storey (1994: 186)*

The polar contrast to 'small is beautiful' is that small workplaces are 'bleak houses'. For example, Rainnie (1989) argued that far from being harmonious workplaces, small workplaces are marked by exploitation, conflict, authoritarianism, poor safety records and unsatisfactory pay. Indeed, they are far from 'happy' families. Instead, Rainnie argues, very many small workplaces are indirectly dominated by large businesses that either compete with smaller businesses or 'control' them through sub-contractor relationships. In short, the most typical form of small business workplace is likely to be a 'sweatshop'.

Table 4.4	Small and large workplaces: a review	
	Small workplaces	**Large workplaces**
Average pay	Lower	Higher
Fringe benefits	Lower	Higher
Formal training	Lower	Higher
Informal training	A much greater focus on informal training	Not clear if large businesses also focus heavily on informal training
Recruitment	More informal	More formal
Safety	Less safe	Safer
Absenteeism	Lower	Higher
Reported job satisfaction	Higher	Lower

Illustration	Morecambe Bay cockle pickers

The deaths of 23 illegal immigrant workers at Morecambe Bay prompted a change in UK employment law.

On the evening of 5 February 2006, 23 Chinese cockle pickers were drowned on the notoriously dangerous quicksands of Morecambe Bay in north-west England by rapidly incoming tides. The workers, mainly impoverished former farmers from the Fujian province of China, were all illegal immigrants working for a gangmaster named Lin Liang Ran. On 24 March 2006, Lin Liang Ran was convicted on 21 counts of manslaughter (two bodies were never found but presumed drowned) and sentenced to 14 years in prison. He attributed the disaster to 'the top bosses, the English suppliers and their international clients, who put enormous pressure on us to produce'.

The workers resorted to cockling for three reasons: 1) when they couldn't send money home due to the low pay of their regular job such as working in a takeaway; 2) when seasonal casual work in food-processing factories dried up; and 3) when their vulnerable migration status led to fear of dealing with employers who might check up on their employment status. Gangmasters found Chinese workers to be cheaper and harder working than the locals. But it was prosperous local middlemen who – supplying seafood processing conglomerates such as Penclawdd Seafoods (owned by Dani Foods) – controlled the workload required and set the production targets for the 30–40 Chinese cocklers in each team and who were referred to as 'the bosses'. Frequent price-cutting also pushed gangmasters, such as Lin Liang Ran, to impose a harsher work regime to enhance productivity.

Health and safety was not part of the agenda for those involved in cockling. Workers were never told of the dangers of Morecambe Bay, never given tide timetables, and were not provided with safety equipment. Penclawdd Seafoods is said to work with 1,500 fisherman who use gang labour all over Britain and makes an annual profit of £4 million, but does not concern itself with the working conditions of cocklers.

In response to the tragedy at Morecambe Bay, the UK government enacted the Gangmasters (Licensing) Act (2004), which requires gangmasters to obtain a licence. Failure to do so results in a jail sentence of up to 10 years.

Source: Adapted from Legge (2009).

Wilkinson (1999) argued that the 'small is beautiful' and 'bleak house' approaches are stereotypes. Barrett and Rainnie (2002) also argue that there is a need for a more nuanced theoretical understanding of small business workplaces. In response, Ram and Edwards (2003) have argued that '. . . research has made substantial empirical and analytical progress' (p. 720). They suggest that this is in two main areas:

1 a better understanding of the ways social and economic structures impact on employment relationships in small businesses;

2 a better understanding of how human actors (owner-managers and employees) respond and make choices in particular social and economic contexts.

In terms of the first point, ever since the early work of Curran and Stanworth (1981), it has been understood that there are widespread sectoral differences in employment relations. The influence of economic and social pressures, however, is not confined just to more traditional sectors such as fishing, construction or manufacturing. For example, Ram (1999) examined a single professional consultancy business and found – as with 'low value added' sectors (Edwards and Ram, 2006) – that such businesses were shaped by the pressures of large business customers and competitors.

Whilst economic and social pressures may, overall, influence employment relations in small businesses, Ram and Edwards (2003) argue that this is too narrow a focus: what, typically, emerges with such a viewpoint is that small businesses are seen as exploitative and dominated either directly or indirectly by large businesses (Rainnie 1989).

Instead, Ram and Edwards (2003) believe it to be more insightful to better understand how human actors (owner-managers *and* employees) respond and make choices in particular social and economic contexts. How these choices are developed is demonstrated in the 'Classic research' article by Jones *et al.* (2006) (p. 71).

There are two reasons for choosing this article. The first is its methodological contribution. The article examines the employment of illegal immigrants by clothing and restaurant businesses. It does this by employing a qualitative research framework that uses two 'intermediaries' charged with identifying and interviewing employers and employees using the researchers' pre-developed qualitative interview schedule. Such 'sociological sampling' is an innovative and sensitive response to the difficulties of researching such 'hard to reach' groups.

The second reason is that it considers three different perspectives: 1) the national and social 'interest'; 2) the employers; and 3) the employees. Using these three viewpoints, it identifies the social and economic pressures that lead to the employment of illegal immigrants. The article argues against simplistic depictions of the 'exploitation' of illegal immigration. For example, the paper suggests that an understanding of the employment of illegal immigrants has to be understood within a context of family structures (the main source of employment in such businesses), cut-throat competition, and a sector whose 'culture' promotes long hours and low pay. Employers, therefore, often feel that they would prefer not to employ 'illegals' but have no choice.

Edwards *et al.* (2006) develop the influence of choices and contexts into a framework for understanding employment relationships in small businesses. This framework is shown in Table 4.5. It identifies seven examples of organisations potentially prevalent amongst small businesses. These range from the atomistic business or the 'sweatshop' through to the 'modern firm' which is able to set its own strategy. It suggests that six structural influences impact on each of these 'examples' of small business. For each of these six structural influences, Edwards *et al.* (2006) suggest a particular dichotomy between ideal types:

● Product market (competitive – control). Business as price takers (competitive) rather than price makers (control) (e.g. business operates in a distinctive niche allowing them more control over their marketplace).

● Labour market (open – restricted). Open or restricted recruitment of labour.

| Classic research | Jones, T., Ram, M. and Edwards, P. (2006) 'Ethnic-minority Business and the Employment of Illegal Immigrants', *Entrepreneurship and Regional Development*, 18(2), 133–50. |

They are employed because you can't get anyone else. It is very difficult to find workers these days, it could be the long hours, low pay and when you work in a restaurant you just work and sleep. Other places have closed through lack of staff. I'm scared of getting caught employing illegals but there is no choice.

(A restaurant owner, p. 139)

Just to survive in the clothing trade it has become a necessity to employ illegal workers. This is a risk I have to take just to keep my business running.

(p. 139)

The absence of a simple stereotypical 'exploitative' entrepreneur also extends to the perspective of the employee. Whilst employees recognise that their low pay and long hours exploit their labour, balanced against this is a recognition of their limited skills, a lack of alternative options and a sense that relative to their home country they are doing well: 'In almost every case, respondents measure their present lot against Third World rather than British standards, a point driven home by the case of Worker X, who declares himself well satisfied with his wage – "it's fine" – and yet he is earning only £100 a week for six days working until 1 a.m. and beyond' (p. 146).

The paper, therefore, is able to use these three viewpoints (national interest, employers and employees) to arrive at the following conclusion: 'the almost humdrum lives of our respondents [employers and employees] nevertheless embody the extremes of powerlessness and social exclusion, the ultimate victims of the current mismatch between economic and political forces in a globalized world' (p. 147).

| Table 4.5 | Edwards *et al.* (2006) framework |

	Example	Product market	Labour market	Resources	Choice	Rules	Style
1	The classic atomistic business. Very weak embeddedness.	Competitive	Open	+	Reactive	Universal	(No view)
2	The classic sweatshop. Strong but highly localised embeddedness.	Competitive	Restricted	–	Reactive	Particularist	Authoritative
3	The fraternal business. Strong embeddedness in local and occupational networks.	Control	Restricted	–	Reactive	Particularist	Authoritative participation
4	The traditional family business. Moderate degree of embeddedness in family and kin networks.	Control	Restricted	+	Reactive	Particularist	Participation
5	The modern business. Embeddedness is within the logics of the market economy.	Competitive	Open	–	Reactive	Particularist	Authoritative participation
6	Paternalism. Embeddedness similar to sweatshops, but ties with workers based on mutual obligations, and hence there is a complementary element of network support.	Competitive	Restricted	+	Reactive	Particularist	Participation
7	The modern business, embedded within the logics of the market economy.	Control	Open	+	Strategic	Universal	Participation

- Resources (positive – negative). Human and social capital is either able to positively or negatively respond to changing circumstances.
- Strategic choice (strategic – reactive). Business has a clear strategic direction or merely responds and reacts.
- Rules and routines (universalistic – particularistic). Business either has formalised or unwritten and informal rules and routines.
- Management style (authoritarian – participative). Power in the business held by owner-manager who has the potential to adopt an authoritarian or participative management style.

The essential point of this framework is to emphasise the need to recognise the context and choices available to small business employers and employees. It is also to realise that small businesses are extremely diverse; it is too simplistic to adopt a 'small is beautiful' or a 'bleak house' perspective on small business employment relations – although both do exist.

In part, this is because employees may self-select into particular types of business. This was recognised as long ago as 1970 by Ingham, who argued that workers self-selected into employment dependent on whether they valued financial or non-financial rewards. If they placed greater emphasis on teamwork, flexibility, role variety and personal relationships, Ingham argued that they were more likely to choose to work in a small business. Winter-Ebmer (1995) has also shown that very many employees choose small businesses – despite the higher likelihood that they will lose their jobs – because it fits in with their skills and abilities. In other words, although some employees may believe that working for a small business reflects their limited choice, for others it is a positive choice. Overall, therefore, although Edwards *et al.*'s (2006) model pays due consideration to the wide heterogeneity of employment relationships, there still persists a complex range of interactions in the small business workplace that requires further research.

Summary

The aim of this chapter has been to examine if small business workplaces are 'better' places to work in, than the workplaces of larger businesses. To examine this question, the chapter has considered a range of dimensions of 'better'.

The first was the scale and measurement of job losses and gains. We showed that an accurate quantification required adopting a 'dynamic' job accounting framework (Birch 1979). Using this framework, a range of international evidence suggests that smaller businesses are more likely to create jobs but that they are also more likely to lose jobs.

We then reviewed the evidence on whether job quality varied by business size. We found that larger businesses were likely to pay more, provide better fringe benefits, safer workplaces and were more likely to provide formal training for their workers.

This might imply that small business workplaces are 'bleak houses'. However, the reverse is the case when job satisfaction is used as a measure. The results clearly demonstrate that on a wide range of measures of job satisfaction, workers in small businesses rate their job more highly than workers in large businesses. This is attributed to large businesses imposing upon their employees considerably greater formality than is the case in small businesses. Indeed, a key lesson for large businesses that operate small workplaces is that, if they wish to raise employee job satisfaction, they should seek to emulate the informality characteristic of the small workplace.

Despite the power of this general finding, the chapter showed that it was important to remember the heterogeneity of small businesses. Edwards *et al.*'s (2006) framework explores some of this heterogeneity by identifying different examples of the small business workplace (e.g. sweatshop, 'modern' business). What also emerges from such research on small business employment relations is the need to consider the context (e.g. sector, 'culture' of sector, work patterns) and the choices of both employers and employees.

Questions for discussion

1 Assess the contribution made by Birch to understanding the role of small businesses in employment creation/destruction.

2 Review the arguments and evidence that small businesses would benefit by providing more formal training for their employees.

3 Are employees happier working in small businesses?

4 What are the costs and benefits of more informal employment structures in small businesses? If there are benefits, what are the reasons for this?

5 Why are large business employees paid more?

6 What characteristics of the small business workplace distinguish it from large businesses?

7 Are the Morecambe Bay cockle pickers just an isolated example of small business labour exploitation or indicative of a much wider problem?

References

Agell, J. (2004) 'Why are Small Firms Different? Managers' views', *Scandinavian Journal of Economics*, 106(3), 437–52.

Armington, C. and Odle, M. (1982) 'Small Business – How Many Jobs?', *Brookings Review*, Winter, 14–17.

Atkinson, C. (2008) 'An Exploration of Small Firm Psychological Contracts', *Work Employment and Society*, 22, 447–65.

Barrett, R. and Rainnie, A. (2002) 'What's So Special About Small Firms? Developing an Integrated Approach to Analysing Small Firm Industrial Relations', *Work, Employment and Society* 16(3), 415–32.

Bartel, A.P. (2000) 'Measuring the Employer's Return on Investments in Training: Evidence from the Literature', *Industrial Relations*, 39(3), 502–24.

Beaver, G. and Hutchings, K. (2004) 'The Big Business of Strategic HRM in SMEs', in Stewart, J. and Beaver, G. (eds), *HRD in Small Organisations: Research and Practice*. London: Routledge, 74–101.

Belfield, C.R. (1999) 'The Behaviour of Graduates in the SME Labour Market: Evidence and Perceptions'. *Small Business Economics*, 12(3), 249–59.

Birch, D. (1979) *The Job Generation Process*. Cambridge, MA: MIT Program on Neighborhood and Regional Change.

Blundell, R., Dearden, L., Meghir, C. and Sianesi, B. (1999) 'Human Capital Investment: The Returns from Education and Training to the Individual, the Firm and the Economy', *Fiscal Studies*, 20, 1–23.

Bolton, J. (1971) *Report of the Committee of Inquiry on Small Firms*, Cmnd. 4811. London: HMSO.

Broersma, L. and Gautier, P. (1997) 'Job Creation and Job Destruction by Small Firms: An Empirical Investigation for the Dutch Manufacturing Sector', *Small Business Economics*, 9(3), 211–24.

Brown, C. and Medoff, J.L. (2003) 'Firm Age and Wages', *Journal of Labor Economics*, 21, 677–97.

Brown, C., Hamilton, J. and Medoff, J.L. (1990) *Employers Large and Small*. Cambridge, MA: Harvard University Press.

Bureau of Labor Statistics (BLS) (2008) *Establishments offering retirement and healthcare benefits.* http://www.bls.gov/ncs/ebs/benefits/2008/ownership/private/table01a.htm (accessed 28 March 2009).

Coetzer, A. and Perry, M. (2008) 'Factors Influencing Employee Learning in Small Businesses', *Education + Training*, 50(8), 648–60.

Curran, J. and Stanworth, J. (1981) 'A New Look at Job Satisfaction in the Small Firm', *Human Relations*, 34(5), 343–65.

Davidsson, P., Lindmark, L. and Olofsson, C. (1998) 'The Extent of Overestimation of Small Firm Job Creation – An Empirical Examination of the Regression Bias', *Small Business Economics*, 11(1), 87–100.

Davis, J.J., Hatiwanger, J. and Schuh, S. (1996) 'Small Business and Job Creation: Dissecting the Myth and Reassessing the Facts', *Small Business Economics*, 8(4), 297–315.

Edwards, P. and Ram, M. (2006) 'Surviving on the Margins of the Economy: Working Relationships in Small, Low-wage Firms', *Journal of Management Studies*, 43(4), 895–916.

Edwards, P., Ram, M., Sen Gupta, S. and Tsai, C.J. (2006) 'The Structuring of Working Relationships in Small Firms: Towards a Formal Framework', *Organization*, 13(5), 701–24.

European Foundation for the Improvement of Living and Working Conditions (EFILWC) (2007*a*) *Fourth European Working Conditions Survey*. Dublin: EFILWC.

European Foundation for the Improvement of Living and Working Conditions (EFILWC) (2007*b*) *Quality of life in the Spanish workplace, 2003.* http://www.eurofound.europa.eu/ewco/surveys/ES0405SR01/ES0405SR01.pdf, (accessed 28 March, 2009).

Forth, J., Bewley, H. and Bryson, A. (2006) *Small and Medium-sized Enterprises: Findings from the 2004 Workplace Employment Relations Survey*. London: Department of Trade and Industry.

Fritsch, M. and Mueller, P. (2004) 'Effects of New Business Formation on Regional Development over Time', *Regional Studies*, 38(8), 949–60.

Grunewald, R. (2005) 'A Dynamic Economy Means Churning Employment', *Federal Reserve Bank of Minneapolis Gazette*, March.

Hart, P.E. and Oulton, N. (1999) 'Gibrat, Galton and Job Generation', *International Journal of the Economics of Business*, 6(2), 149–64.

Hasle, P. and Limborg, H.J. (2006) 'A Review of the Literature on Preventive Occupational Health and Safety Activities in Small Enterprises', *Industrial Health*, 44(1), 6–12.

Ingham, G.K. (1970) *Size of Industrial Organisation and Worker Behaviour*. Cambridge: Cambridge University Press.

Job Watch Australia (2002) *Unfair Dismissal Protection for Workers in Small Business*. Melbourne: Job Watch Inc.

Jones, T., Ram, M. and Edwards, P. (2006) 'Ethnic Minority Business and the Employment of Illegal Immigrants', *Entrepreneurship and Regional Development*, 18(2), 133–50.

The Kaiser Family Foundation (2008) *Employer Health Benefits: 2008 Summary of Findings*. Menlo Park, CA: Kaiser Family Foundation.

Kirchhoff, B.A. and Greene, P.G. (1998) 'Understanding the Theoretical and Empirical Content of Critiques of US Job Creation Research', *Small Business Economics*, 10(2), 153–69.

Kitching, J. and Blackburn, R. (2004) 'The Nature of Training and the Motivation to Train in Small Firms', *Small Business Research Centre Research Report*, RR 30, University of Kingston.

Lallemand, T., Plasman, R. and Rycx, F. (2005) 'Why Do Large Firms Pay Higher Wages? Evidence from Matched Worker – Firm Data', *International Journal of Manpower*, 26(7/8), 705–23.

Legge, K. (2009) 'Networked Organizations and the negation of HRM' in Storey, J. (ed.), *Human Resource Management: A Critical Text*. London: Routledge, 39–56.

Matlay, H. (1999) 'Employee Relations in Small Firms; A Micro-business Perspective', *Employee Relations*, 21(3), 285–95.

McNabb, R. and Whitfield, K. (2000) 'Worth So Appallingly Little': A Workplace-level Analysis of Low Pay', *British Journal of Industrial Relations*, 38(4), 585–609.

Moore, H.L. (1911) *Laws of Wages: An Essay in Statistical Economics.* New York: Augustus M. Kelley.

Neumark, D., Wall, B. and Zhang, J. (2008) 'Do Small Businesses Create More Jobs? New Evidence for the US from the National Establishment Time Series', *IZA DP 3888.* Bonn: Forschungsinstitut zur Zukunft der Arbeit.

Oi, W.Y. and Idson, T.L. (1999) 'Firm Size and Wages', in Aschenfelter, O. and Card, D. (eds), *Handbook of Labor Economics*, 33. London: Elsevier, 2165–214.

Patton, D. (2005) 'Training in Small Firms', in Marlow, S., Patton, D. and Ram, M. (eds), *Managing Labour in Small Firms.* London: Routledge, 83–108.

Picot, G. and Dupuy, R. (1998) 'Job Creation by Company Size Class: The Magnitude, Concentration and Persistence of Job Gains and Losses in Canada', *Small Business Economics*, 10(2), 117–39.

Rainnie, A. (1989) *Industrial Relations in Small Firms: Small isn't beautiful.* London: Routledge.

Ram, M. (1999) 'Managing Consultants in a Small Firm: A Case Study', *Journal of Management Studies*, 36(6), 875–97.

Ram, M. and Edwards, P. (2003) 'Praising Caesar Not Burying Him: What We Know about Employment Relations in Small Firms', *Work Employment and Society*, 17(4), 719–30.

Ram, M., Edwards, P., Gilman, M. and Arrowsmith, J. (2001) 'The Dynamics of Informality: Employment Relations in Small Firms and the Effects of Regulatory Change', *Work Employment and Society*, 15(4), 845–61.

Ram, M., Edwards, P. and Jones, T. (2007) 'Staying Underground – Informal Work, Small Firms, and Employment Regulation in the United Kingdom', *Work and Occupations*, 34(3), 318–44.

Rand Corporation (2006) *Are Small Businesses Riskier Than Larger Ones?* Santa Monica, CA: Rand.

SBA (2005) *Cost of Employee Benefits in Small and Large Businesses*, 262. Washington, DC: SBA.

Saridakis, G., Sen-Gupta, S., Edwards, P.K. and Storey, D.J. (2008) 'Employment Tribunal Cases: The Impact of Enterprise Size on Incidence and Outcomes', *British Journal of Industrial Relations*, 46(3), 469–99.

Shacklock, R. (2007) 'Is It More Stressful Working in a Small Business than a Big One?', *Cabinet Maker*, 27 July.

Sophos (2009) *Sophos Named in Canada's Top 100 Employers 2009.* http://www.sophos.com/pressoffice/news/articles/2008/10/canadas-top-employer-2009.html (accessed 28 March 2009).

Storey, D.J., Saridakis, G., Sen-Gupta, S., Edwards, P.K. and Blackburn, R.A. (2010) 'Linking HR Formality with Employee Job Quality: The Role of Firm and Workforce Size', *Human Resource Management*, (49)2.

Storey, D.J. and Westhead, P. (1999) 'Management Training in Small Firms: A Case of Market Failure?', *Human Resource Management Journal*, 7(2), 61–71.

The Times (2007) *Stress and the City*, 11 January http://business.timesonline.co.uk/tol/business/career_and_jobs/graduate_management/article1291101.ece (accessed 28 March 2009).

Troske, K.R. (1999) 'Evidence on the Employer Size-wage Premium from Worker-establishment Matched Data', *Review of Economics and Statistics*, 81(1), 15–26.

US Bureau of Labor Statistics (2008) *Establishments Offering Retirement and Healthcare Benefits.* http://www.bls.gov/ncsebs/benefits/2008/ownership/private/table01a.htm.

van Praag, M. and Versloot, P.H. (2007) 'What Is the Value of Entrepreneurship? A Review of Recent Research', *Small Business Economics*, 29(4), 351–82.

Vickers, I., James, P., Smallbone, D. and Baldock, R. (2005) 'Understanding Small Firm Responses to Regulation: The Case of Workplace Health and Safety', *Policy Studies*, 26(2), 149–69.

Voulgaris, F., Papadogonas, T. and Agiomirgianakis, G. (2005) 'Job Creation and Job Destruction in Greek Manufacturing', *Review of Development Economics*, 9(2), 289–301.

Wagner, J. (1995) 'Firm Size and Job Creation in Germany', *Small Business Economics*, 7(6), 469–74.

Wagner, J. (1997) 'Firm size and Job Quality: A Survey of the Evidence from Germany', *Small Business Economics*, 9(5), 411–25.

Wilkinson, A. (1999) 'Employment Relations in SMEs', *Employee Relations*, 21(3), 206–17.

Winter-Ebmer, R. (1995) 'Does Layoff Risk Explain the Firm-Size Wage Differential?', *Applied Economics Letters*, 2, 211–14.

Winter-Ebmer, R. and Zweimuller, J. (1999) 'Firm-Size Wage Differentials in Switzerland: Evidence from Job-Changers', *American Economic Review*, 89(2), 89–93.

5 Innovation

Key learning objectives

By the end of this chapter you should:

- Understand the key terms and measures in innovation.
- Be able to evaluate key explanations for how innovation occurs.
- Be able to discuss how business size impacts on innovation.

'A man need only build a better mousetrap and the world will beat a path to your door.'

Ralph Waldo Emerson

'The manufacturer who waits for the world to beat a path to his door is a great optimist. But the manufacturer who shows his "mousetrap" to the world keeps the smoke coming out his chimney.'

O.B. Winters

5.1 Introduction

We begin this chapter with a short quiz. There are three questions related to Table 5.1. First, in group 1, how many of the four names do you recognise? Second, in group 2, there are four more names. Again, how many of these are recognisable? Finally, what is the common theme that links the names in group 1 and group 2?

Our guess is that the names from group 1 are much less well known than those from group 2. Group 1 consists of four 'inventors' whilst group 2 consists of four 'innovators'. Elias Howe was the first American to hold a patent on the sewing machine. Yet, it is Issac Singer that

Table 5.1	Innovation quiz	
Group 1		**Group 2**
Elias Howe		Isaac Singer
Murray Spangler		W.H. Hoover
Douglas Engelbart		Apple Mackintosh
RC Cola		Coca Cola

we more commonly associate with the sewing machine because Singer manufactured and popularised the sewing machine, and literally stamped his name on it. A similar story occurred with the vacuum cleaner. One of the earliest inventors of the vacuum cleaner was Murray Spangler. He, however, sold his patent to W.H. Hoover and we are much more likely to call a vacuum cleaner a Hoover rather than a Spangler. Douglas Engelbert is credited with developing the computer mouse yet it was Apple Macintosh who 'commercialised' it in 1984. Finally, every one has heard of Coca Cola but RC Cola is a much less well known – and successful – cola. Yet, RC Cola was the first to introduce a diet cola in 1958, one of the first to introduce a caffeine-free cola and, again, one of the first colas to use pure cane sugar rather than fructose corn syrup to sweeten a cola.

What these examples suggest is that there is a difference between invention and innovation. We define invention as 'the first occurrence of an idea for a new product or process' whilst we define innovation as '. . . the first commercialisation of the idea' (Fagerberg 2003: 3). As Fagerberg (2003) also suggests, these definitions do not tell the whole story. Invention seems – as the quote attributed to the American poet and writer Ralph Waldo Emerson at the start of the chapter suggests – a solitary activity which is largely independent of the actual commercialisation and adoption of the particular 'mousetrap'. The quote from the American advertising executive O.B. Winters, however, suggests that this is only the start of the process. Turning an 'invention' into an 'innovation' requires, amongst other things, an understanding of the market, resources to produce the product/process and managerial capability. Indeed, Hope (1996) identifies that there have been 4,400 different patented 'mousetraps' in the US. Nearly all of these patents were given to 'amateur' inventors. Only a very few of these have ever been commercially successful.

Astebro (2003) also investigated the returns for Canadian inventors. He found that only 7 per cent of the inventions in his sample actually 'reached' the market. Of this 7 per cent that did make it to market, only 40 per cent of these actually made any money. This was also heavily skewed: six inventions (0.55 per cent) made 1,400 per cent returns, and one invention (0.09 per cent) made a return of 2,960 per cent. In general, however, the median return for those inventions that made it to market was −7 per cent. In other words, of the minority of inventions that did make it to market, the most common outcome was that the invention lost money.

Nonetheless, the introduction of new innovations is fundamentally important to economic growth: without technological change, economies would stagnate. For example, in the 1950s, the economist Robert Solow (1957) showed that 87.5 per cent of economic growth was due to technological changes. Cameron (1998) also summarises more recent data and concludes '. . . typically, a 1 per cent increase in the R&D capital stock is found to lead to a rise in output of between 0.05 per cent and 0.1 per cent' (p. 7). Ulku (2004) also shows that there is a positive relationship between per capita GDP and innovation in both developed and developing countries. In other words, new innovations are pivotal to increased productivity and wealth.

In this chapter, our first aim is to identify key terms in innovation. We begin by examining the contribution of the German economist Joseph Schumpeter (1883–1950) to our understanding of innovation. One of Schumpeter's main contributions was to introduce the notion that innovation was a disruptive and radical change to the way societies are ordered. In contrast, Freeman and Soete (1997) have argued that very many of what we call innovations are, in fact, incremental changes to how things are done. For example, a radical innovation may be the introduction of the mobile phone whilst an incremental innovation may be described as making it smaller or giving it extra functionalities (e.g. putting an MP3 player on it). This section also examines differences between product and process innovation. Finally, it examines three different measures of innovation: research and development (R&D), patents and innovation outcomes.

This chapter also focuses on the context for innovatory activity by large and small businesses. It shows that, in general, technology has a life cycle (the technology 'S' curve) and that technology typically follows a path that starts off with lots of product innovation which is then followed by relatively greater process innovation (technology paradigm approach).

These contexts are important because, in the final section of the chapter, we examine the innovating activities of small and large businesses. Yet again, we show that Schumpeter is important. We discuss his two approaches to understanding innovation by small and large businesses. What we find is that the vast quantity of innovation is done by larger businesses. However, other evidence suggests that small businesses play an important dynamic role in innovation (Audretsch 2002*b*).

5.2 Key terms in innovation

Schumpeter (1950) argued that innovation should be seen as a radical and disruptive departure from existing practice. He suggested that innovation was what typified capitalism. Capitalism, he suggested, was subject to what he termed '... the perennial gale of creative destruction ...' (Schumpeter 1950: 84) '... that incessantly revolutionizes the economic structure from within, incessantly destroying the old one, incessantly creating a new one' (Schumpeter 1950: 83).

Schumpeter defined five types of innovation:

1 Introduction of a new method of production.

2 Opening up of new market.

3 The conquest of a new source of supply of raw materials or half manufactured goods.

4 The creation of a new type of industrial organization.

5 Introduction of a new good or significant improvement.

These five types of innovation may be described as types of **radical** or disruptive innovation. For example:

- The assembly line used by Henry Ford represented a radical departure in terms of how cars were produced.

- The East India Company was one of the first of the European companies that specifically set out to exploit the Indian and Chinese markets.

- Bessemer's process of making steel allowed the mass production of steel.

- The introduction of limited liability partnerships represented a new type of industrial organisation.

- The introduction of personal computers in the 1980s represented a radical and disruptive shift in how computers were used.

Such innovation is often also called 'competence destroying' (Tushman and Anderson 1986) because, as Schumpeter suggests, they 'creatively destroy' existing forms of practice.

In contrast, 'competence enhancing' innovation seeks to extend the value of an existing innovation. Such innovations – often also called **incremental** innovations – are 'order-of-magnitude improvements in price/performance that build on existing know-how within a product class' (Tushman and Anderson 1986: 442). For example, Kellogg's is a well-known breakfast cereal food manufacturer that launched 'Live Bright Brain Health' snack bars. This was designed to take advantage of sales opportunities in the 'new' market segment of 'healthy' cereal snack bars. Vaona and Pianta (2008) describe such product enhancements as attempts by businesses to increase their 'technological competitiveness'. Whilst **product** innovations offer the potential for new or improved goods or services, incremental **process** innovations often principally offer the opportunity to cut costs. Vaona and Pianta (2008) describe this as 'active price competitiveness'. For example, the former UK prime minister, Margaret Thatcher, started off her working career as a chemist. She was involved in a research team that increased the amount of 'air' in ice cream. This meant that ice cream manufacturers could cut their raw material costs, whilst apparently continuing to churn out the same volume of ice cream.

The final issue in this section is to define how innovation is measured. There are essentially three measures:

1   'Input' measures such as research and development (R&D) expenditure or the number of R&D 'workers' employed.

2   'Intermediate output measures' such as number of patents.

3   Direct measures of innovation output such as surveying businesses about their innovative activity.

We now briefly examine each of these three measures in turn. We focus on their advantages and limitations in comparing large with small businesses.

'Input' measures such as research and development (R&D) expenditure or the number of R&D 'workers' employed

One measure of innovation is to count the number of 'knowledge' workers (e.g. scientists or engineers) or the amount a business spends on R&D. Both these approaches are 'input' measures. As Audretsch (2002*b*) suggested, there is not necessarily a correlation between these inputs and outputs (an innovation): 'R&D reflects only the resources devoted to producing innovative output, but not the amount of innovative activity actually realized' (p. 18). In short, it is the output of innovation that needs to be measured rather than the input of workers or expenditure.

Another limitation of both these measures is that they are likely to under-estimate the innovatory 'contribution' of smaller businesses (Roper 1999). This is because, where R&D activity does occur in a smaller business, it is more likely to be spread across the whole business rather than in a dedicated R&D 'department' (Santarelli and Sterlacchini 1990). In essence, R&D expenditure is a measure of money/labour resources expended rather than a measure of innovations gained. It is, therefore, of limited value as a measure of innovation, particularly in relation to smaller businesses.

'Intermediate output measures' such as number of patents

A potentially more favourable measure of innovation is intermediate measures such as the number of patents granted or applied for. A patent ensures the exclusive use of an invention to an individual or business, for a restricted period of time. Essentially, it is a negative right as those that hold patents can *prevent* other individuals or businesses using the invention without permission. If the patent is infringed, the patent holder can take legal action to stop the use of the invention by another party (an injunction) and seek damages. For example, the UK manufacturer Dyson successfully sued Hoover because it infringed its patent on its dual cyclone vacuum cleaner. The judgment prevented Hoover from making use of Dyson's invention (the injunction) and awarded damages to Dyson.

Governments award these legal rights to patent holders because they believe they provide a legal 'shelter' for innovatory activity. Without the protection of patents, the argument is that individuals and businesses would be less likely to innovate. This is because the development of an invention is likely to be time-consuming and may require considerable financial resources. Committing resources is less worthwhile when the period for recouping revenues is short, so patents provide the guarantee that time is made available for sales to be made without the threat of direct competition. Also, even when the invention is complete, it may take considerable additional resources to obtain a profitable revenue stream for the inventor. There is also the chance that a competitor – with access to the invention – may be in a better position to successfully exploit the invention because they have not had to incur the expenses in its development. Finally, whilst there can be personal financial benefits to the inventor, there are also benefits that accrue to the rest of society from an invention, for which the members of society do not pay. These (un-priced) benefits are called positive externalities or 'spillovers'.

Patents are typically limited to 20 years. This reflects an important judgement that legislators have to make: if they make the life of the patent too short, the risk is that too few resources are devoted to exploiting the innovation. On the other hand, if too long a life is granted for the patent, this risks the inventor being able to exclude other competitors and so being able to charge customers a higher price. In that case, the 'spillover' benefits of the invention to consumers are fewer, partly because diffusion of the innovation is slower and partly because the benefits are acquired by the inventor rather than the consumer.

There are two main advantages in using the number of patents granted as a measure of the scale of innovation in an economy. First, since obtaining a patent involves a fixed cost to the inventor, this is likely to limit the number of 'trivial' patents. Second, patents are a measure of innovative output and are, therefore, superior to input measures such as R&D expenditure.

A disadvantage with using patents to measure innovative activity is that they only cover one type of intellectual property protection that a business can seek whereas there are three other forms of intellectual property:

1　*Design rights*. These cover the internal or external shape or configuration of an original design. There is no requirement to formally register designs but, if they are registered, design rights typically last for up to 15 years in the UK. For example, Jimmy Choo, the maker of shoes and fashion accessories, threatened the UK retailer Marks & Spencers with legal action because it believed that Marks & Spencers' £9.50 handbag too closely resembled Jimmy Choo's £450 'Cosmo' handbag. Marks & Spencers agreed to withdraw from sale its bag and pay damages to Jimmy Choo.

2　*Copyright rights*. As with design rights, there is no need to formally register the copyright of:

- literature (e.g. novels, instruction manuals, computer programs, song lyrics, newspaper articles, website content and databases);

- drama (including dance or mime);

- music;

- art (e.g. paintings, engravings, photographs, sculptures, collages, architecture, technical drawings, diagrams, maps);

- recordings/broadcasts of sound and film.

Copyright rights come into existence automatically when the work is created. For artistic, literary, musical and dramatic works it lasts until the death of the author *plus* 70 years. For music, film and other TV or radio broadcasting recordings, copyright lasts 50 years from the *date of its first production* (at least in the EU). Creators of copyright material typically gain income from their material by receiving royalties.

3　*Trademark rights*. These typically are 'badges' of identity that help distinguish one good or service from another. These may cover names (e.g. McDonald's), straplines (e.g. L'Oreal's 'because you are worth it'), logos (e.g. Nike's 'swoosh' logo), colours (e.g. Heinz baked beans' turquoise colour) and shapes (Coca Cola's bottle) and sounds (e.g. Intel jingle). Again, there is no need to register but if businesses do, the ® shaped sign means that it has been formally registered. Trademarks can last indefinitely. Businesses tend to apply for trademarks because it prevents other businesses 'passing off' their goods or services. For example, the football club Arsenal took a street trader, Matthew Reed, to the European Court of Justice to stop him using their logos on his unofficial merchandise.

A second disadvantage of using patents or other forms of intellectual property rights to measure innovation is that the measure is biased towards larger businesses. The first reason for this is that patents are expensive and time consuming. Typically, patents have to be applied for each and every geographical territory. Hence, an Italian business may choose to patent their invention first in Italy then in Europe and then in other individual countries throughout the world. The European Patent Office (2005) estimated, for instance, that in 2005 the average cost of a Europe-wide patent that was enforced for 10 years was around €32,000. Such sums are likely to discourage patent activity amongst smaller businesses, which lack the resources of larger businesses. Arundel and Kabla (1998) also show that patent activity in Europe is more likely amongst certain sectors (e.g. pharmaceuticals, chemicals, machinery, and precision instruments) and that larger businesses are much more likely to patent than smaller businesses.

Illustration	Intellectual property rights: The Verve's bitter experience

Small businesses may not patent their idea because it can be very difficult to enforce their intellectual property rights. They may simply lack the resources or the will to pursue through the courts their legal rights given that they may eventually lose. For example, The Verve, a music group, had a 'hit' single with the song 'Bittersweet Symphony' in 1997. The song used four bars from a Rolling Stones song 'The Last Time'. The copyright for this Rolling Stones song is owned by Allen Klein who controls the back catalogue of the Rolling Stones. Klein successfully ensured that 100 per cent of the royalties for the song were given to his business ABKCO Records. Keith Richards and Mick Jagger from the Rolling Stones were also given song writing credits. Klein was also able – without the permission of The Verve – to license the song for a Nike and Vauxhall car advertisement.

Small businesses may make use of a range of alternative strategies to protect their innovation. For instance, they may decide to protect their idea through confidentiality agreements or, alternatively, believe that being 'first to market' is important or that their technology is difficult to replicate ('reverse engineer'). Finally, they may not seek formal intellectual property protection. For some, this is because any form of legal intellectual property protection eventually means that the 'new' knowledge has to come into the public domain. Some businesses may choose to keep their knowledge a 'trade secret' whilst other businesses recognise that the costs of enforcing and upholding their intellectual property can be prohibitive. However, as Table 5.2 shows, larger businesses are much more likely to rate both formal and informal ('strategic') methods of innovation protection as being of high importance. For example, larger businesses are more than twice as likely to rate patents as an important means of protecting their innovation. Indeed, except for two methods – 'lead time advantage on competitors' and 'copyright' – larger businesses are at least twice as likely as small businesses to use a method of protecting their innovation.

A third disadvantage of patent data or other such data that relies on registered intellectual property rights (e.g. trademarks) is that it is a measure of technological activity – the rate of invention – rather than innovation. As we saw with the 'mousetrap', there have been very many mousetraps invented but very few that actually made any money. A potentially better measure is to examine patent citations (how many times a particular patent is cited by others

Table 5.2	Enterprises rating different methods for protecting innovation as of 'high' importance		
	Percentage of all respondents		
	Size of enterprise (employees)		
	10–250	**250+**	**All**
Formal			
Confidentiality agreements	12	26	13
Trademarks	8	19	8
Copyright	8	14	8
Patents	6	15	6
Registration of design	5	14	6
Strategic			
Lead-time advantage on competitors	10	17	10
Secrecy	8	17	9
Complexity of design	4	9	5

Source: Robson and Haigh (2008).

seeking a patent) rather than the rate of patent activity (patent counts) as this may give some indication of its value to wider users.

Another similar measure is to use information on new product announcements derived from trade or specialist journals. The problem with new product announcements is that it is likely to be intrinsically biased: larger businesses have larger marketing budgets, making them more likely to make product announcements. Another problem is that announcing a new product is not necessarily an indicator of product 'innovation'. Yahaya and Abu-Bakar (2007) and Srinivasan et al. (2009) both report estimates suggesting that the failure rate of new product development is between 33 and 60 per cent. In essence, a simple measure of counting patents is a useful, but far from perfect, indicator either of the scale or economic significance of innovation in an economy. It is also a measure that is likely to favour large over small businesses. Indeed, Temperly et al. (2004) summarise the views of Australian innovators as

> Having a strong patent portfolio is not relevant to most SMEs . . . the cost of establishing and maintaining patents is high. For most, defending a patent is unthinkably expensive. Furthermore in a highly innovative environment, the lifetime of a patent is short. A more practical approach is to rely on industrial secrets.

Direct measures of innovation output such as surveying businesses about their innovative activity

The final measure of innovation is to directly survey businesses about their innovative activity. The advantage of such measures is that it is possible to avoid some of the 'size' biases evident in both R&D and patent measures of innovation. Surveying the individual business also allows for the identification of particular aspects of innovation. For example, the EU has a Community Innovation Survey (CIS 5) which asks the following questions of businesses:

Were any of your product innovations during the three-year period 2002–2004:

- New to your market? (Your enterprise introduced a new good or service onto your market before your competitors) No/Yes.

- Only new to your enterprise? (Your enterprise introduced a new good or service that was essentially the same as a product already available from your competitors in your market) No/Yes. (BERR 2008)

Such surveys as the CIS are also able to ask questions that examine a wider interpretation of innovation. For example, CIS 5 asks about four different measures:

1 implementation of a new or significantly changed corporate strategy;

2 implementation of advanced management techniques within your enterprise, e.g. knowledge management systems;

3 implementation of major changes to your organisational structure, e.g. introduction of cross-functional teams, outsourcing of major business functions;

4 implementation of changes in marketing concepts or strategies, e.g. packaging or presentational changes to a product to target new markets, new support services to open up new markets (BERR 2008).

The obvious disadvantage of these measures is that the results are subjective and, indeed, may be biased because business respondents are likely to remember their successes rather than their failures. There is also a risk that innovators are more likely to respond to such questions than non-innovators.

Overall, there is no easy way to measure innovation since each measure is likely to bring its own problems. However, any measure that seeks to uncover innovation needs to consider different types of innovation and the differences between small and large businesses (see section 5.4). In the next section, though, we will examine 'how' innovation occurs.

5.3 The context for innovation

The traditional economic view of how innovation develops is that technological change is 'manna from heaven' (Solow 1957). In other words, technological change seemed to be a chance, outside, event. It just occurs – what economists call an **exogenous** effect (i.e. it literally originates from 'outside'). However, this seems to be at variance with casual observation. Why, for example, should the US be so much luckier over a long period of time than Madagascar? More plausible is the argument that there are actions that individuals, businesses or governments can take so as to make themselves 'luckier'.

In practical terms, there appear two main ways of getting increases in output or quality. The first way is to simply increase inputs (capital and labour). For example, other things being equal, if a chef uses higher quality ingredients (the capital) or a better 'sous chef' to help them prepare the food (the labour), then their food should be better. The second way of increasing output is to be 'smart'. With the same ingredients, the clever chef can invent new combinations of ingredients and then 'innovate' such inventions by selling it to patrons. In other words, Romer (1990) has argued that what differentiates a good from a poor meal is not just the quality of the ingredients ('things') but the 'ideas' (knowledge) of the chef. In essence, therefore, technological change was not just an outside event (exogenous) but something that was caused by human activities: it was **endogenous**.

Illustration	'We both have a rich neighbour named Xerox': Apple vs Microsoft

Bill Gates and Microsoft argued that both he and Steve Jobs of Apple benefited from Xerox's innovation 'spill overs'.

Knowledge has a way of 'spilling over' to others because it is often intangible, can often be used by others (what is called non-rivalrous) and is easily imitated (what is called non-excludability). For example, Xerox set up the Palo Alto Research Center (PARC) in California. This produced very many of the fundamentals underlying personal computing: the ethernet, the graphical user interface (GUI), the mouse, the What You See Is What You Get (WYSIWYG) text editor and the laser printer. None of these were recognised by Xerox executives as having a business application. For example, prior to the development of the mouse and the GUI, all commands had to be typed. This obviously limited the usability of the computer. However, new start ups such as Apple and Microsoft did see the mouse and the GUI as resolutions to problems. This is evident from the following quote which is Bill Gates' response to Steve Jobs' accusation that Microsoft had 'borrowed' the GUI from Apple:

> No, Steve [Steve Jobs], I think its more like we both have a rich neighbor named Xerox, and you broke in to steal the TV set, and you found out I'd been there first, and you said, 'Hey that's not fair! I wanted to steal the TV set!'

Source: apple-history.com

Table 5.3	Successive waves of technological change					
Approximate timing	Kondratieff waves	Science technology education and training	Transport communication	Energy systems	Universal and cheap key factors	Key innovators
First 1780s–1840s	Industrial Revolution: Factory production for textiles	Apprenticeship, learning by doing, dissenting academies, scientific societies	Canals, carriage roads	Water power	Cotton	Richard Arkwright, Thomas Telford
Second 1840s–1890s	Age of steam power and railways	Professional mechanical and civil engineers, institutes of technology, mass primary education	Railways (iron), telegraph	Steam power	Coal, iron	Samuel Morse, George Hudson
Third 1890s–1940s	Age of electricity and steel	Industrial R&D labs, chemicals and electrical national labs	Railways (steel), telephone	Electricity	Steel	Thomas Edison, Andrew Carnegie
Fourth 1940s–1990s	Age of mass production of automobiles and synthetic materials	Large-scale industrial and government R&D, mass higher education	Motor highways, radio and TV, airlines	Oil	Oil, plastics	Carl Bosch, Sakichi Toyoda
Fifth 1990s–Present	Age of microelectronics and computer networks	Data networks, R&D global networks, lifetime education and training	Information highways, digital networks	Gas/oil	Microelectronics	Bill Gates

Source: Freeman and Soete (1997).
Note that the column 'key innovators' does not appear in Freeman and Soete (1997). This is a column we have added.

Schumpeter (1934) also argues that innovation does not occur in isolation. As we saw in section 5.2, he argues that innovation follows an evolutionary path punctuated by 'a gale of creative destruction'. A 'gale', however, is not the only way of characterising radical innovation. Freeman and Soete (1997) argue, '. . . successive industrial revolutions were based on the qualitative transformation of the economy by new technologies, rather than the simple quantitative growth of individual industries' (p. 20). Freeman and Soete suggest, therefore, that there have been a series of 'long waves' which have marked economic change. These are detailed in Table 5.3.

Table 5.3 suggests that there have been five waves. These are called 'Kondratieff waves' after the Russian economist Nikolai Kondratieff who suggested in the 1930s that economic development was marked by a series of long waves each lasting around 50 years. In developing this, Freeman and Soete (1997) argue that the first wave was the start of the industrial revolution. Central actors in this were Richard Arkwright who made a fortune from cotton and the road and canal engineer Thomas Telford.

The second wave (our 'age of steam power and railways') includes Samuel Morse – who invented and helped commercialise the telegraph – and George Hudson, the British railway entrepreneur. The third wave was the development of steel and electricity. Important here, were the American inventor Thomas Edison and the steel magnate Andrew Carnegie. Freeman and Soete (1997) suggest that the fourth wave lasted between the 1940s and the 1990s, reflecting the influence of the automotive (the Japanese industrialist Sakichi Toyoda (Toyota)) and synethetic materials (the German chemist Carl Bosch). Finally, the fifth wave suggests that Bill Gates is a symbolic example of a famous modern innovator.

Both Schumpeter (1939) and Freeman and Soete (1997) suggest that innovation is time and context specific. One of the first people to come up with the design for a helicopter was Leonardo da Vinci in the fifteenth century. Yet, the helicopter only became a 'reality' through engineers such as Igor Sikorsky in the twentieth century. There are also other examples. For instance, the 'cloned' sheep Dolly is reliant on prior understandings of DNA whilst it is impossible to think of a 'BlackBerry' without earlier developments in mobile phones and the internet. The suggestion is that innovation is path dependent. In other words, innovation activity cannot shake free of its history.

Dosi (1982) argues that what typifies innovation is that it follows a 'technological paradigm' which is a '. . . "model" or "pattern" of solution of *selected* technological problems, based on *selected* principles derived from natural sciences and on *selected* material technologies' (Dosi 1982: 152, *emphasis in original*). In other words, what Dosi suggests is that there are three main phases to innovation: a pre-paradigmatic phase; the emergence of a 'dominant design'; and a post-paradigmatic phase. The pre-paradigmatic phase is marked by uncertainty. The trouble faced by inventors and innovators is that it is often difficult to tell – particularly with radical innovations – which innovation is likely to become accepted in the marketplace. Rosenberg (2004) gives a number of examples of such uncertainty:

- The US phone company AT&T wanted to estimate the likely demand for 'mobile' phones in 1983. They knew that this new product was heavy, that the quality of voice transmission was limited and the price in 1983 was $3,000. They estimated that no more than 1 million people would use it by 1999. The actual uptake was 70 million in 1999.

- After a series of trials of 'television' in 1939, the *New York Times* declared: 'Television will never be a serious competitor for radio, because people must sit and keep their eyes glued on a screen; the average American family hasn't time for it.'

- The development of the laser was an example of 'blue sky' primary research if only because in the early 1960s it was difficult to foresee any commercial applications. Today, the laser is central to research in areas such as chemistry and surgical practice.

Faced with such uncertainty, Dosi (1982) and Tushman and Anderson (1986) argue that there are likely to be a range of radical competing designs each struggling to establish dominance in the marketplace. In the early stages of the technology life cycle, as Figure 5.1 shows, there is likely to have been a high rate of product innovation. An example of this is the early history

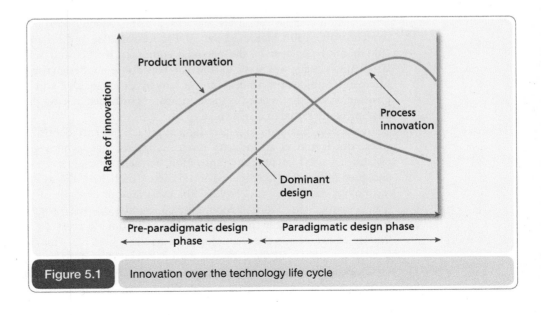

| Figure 5.1 | Innovation over the technology life cycle |

Table 5.4	Advantages and disadvantages of three ways of powering the early automotive engines	
	Advantages	**Disadvantages**
Steam	Proven technology (been around for 70 years), easy to maintain, fast	Short range (limited water boiler), potentially dangerous
Electricity	Quiet, smooth running, easy to maintain	Relied on batteries (short range), slow
Petrol	Potentially long range, fewer refuelling problems	New technology, few petrol stations, crank start made it potentially dangerous to driver

of the car industry. In 1900, there were three competing technologies for powering the car: steam, electricity and the internal petrol combustion engine. As Table 5.4 shows, each had advantages and disadvantages.

Teece (1986) argues that this pre-paradigmatic phase lasted until the petrol engine could be produced at a price that made it affordable to the US consumer. Following the introduction of the mass production methods by Henry Ford, this became possible. The petrol engine became the 'dominant design': 'A dominant design reflects the emergence of product-class standards and ends the period of technological ferment. Alternative designs are largely crowded out of the product class, and technological development focuses on elaborating a widely accepted product or process; the dominant design becomes a guidepost for further product or process change.' (Tushman and Anderson 1986: 441)

Subsequent to the emergence of a 'dominant design', Figure 5.1 shows that the rate of process innovations increases. This is evident in the car industry. Arguably, it is possible to discern particular international differences in these types of process innovations. For instance, European car manufacturers have tended to emphasise functional incremental innovations (e.g. front wheel drive, disc brakes, five-speed transmissions); American manufacturers incremental 'comfort' innovations (e.g. air conditioning, power steering, cruise control) and Japanese manufacturers 'quality' innovations (e.g. lean production systems, quality circles).

Dosi's (1982) technological paradigm approach can be applied to other industries. For example, the early personal computing industry was marked by a range of alternative designs (e.g. Altair 8800 (1975), Apple 1 (1976), Commodore Pet 2001, Apple II, TRS 80 Model 1 (1977), Atom, Apple II+, Atari 800 (1979), BBC Model (1981)). In 1981, however, IBM launched the 5150 which used the Intel processor 8088 and Microsoft's MS-DOS. By 1984, IBM had 40 per cent of the personal computer market and was the 'dominant design'. Unfortunately, and unknown to IBM, the 'real' dominant design was the software provided by Microsoft. Subsequent process innovations by Compaq, Dell and HP all meant that IBM's position was further eroded as these companies provided a better price/performance mix for customers interested in buying a PC.

In essence, the technology paradigm approach seeks to identify how it is that innovation works out largely at an industry level. It suggests that technology development has three phases: a period of product innovation 'ferment', the emergence of a dominant design and post-paradigmatic (process) innovation. Implicit in the approach is the sense that a technology has a 'life cycle'. Perhaps the most famous example of this is 'Moore's Law.' This 'Law' – named after Gordon Moore the co-founder of Intel – suggested that the number of transistors on a silicon chip would continue to double every 18 months. In other words, 'Moore's Law' follows the technology 'S' curve in Figure 5.2. This suggests that product performance increases in the early stages with increases in effort/resources spent. Performance increases in line with effort/resources until this relationship starts to break down as the technology matures. In terms of transistors, therefore, there were around 1,000 when the

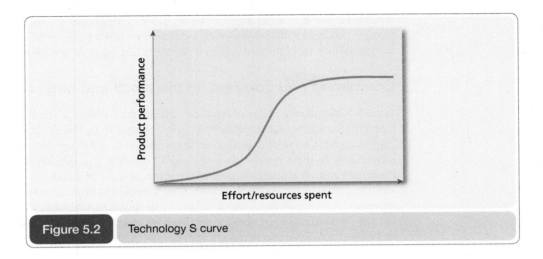

| Figure 5.2 | Technology S curve |

8008 silicon chip was introduced in 1972 but 100,000 transistors in 2000 when the Pentium 4 chip was launched.

One criticism of these approaches is that they do not pay enough attention to the social (demand) pressures that motivate the diffusion of a particular technology (Rogers 2003). Another criticism is that such approaches are often perhaps only useful tools in hindsight, and they apply only to technologies whose 'life cycle' has been long and full. Arguably, the most common fate of very many technologies/products is that their 'S' curve never really matures because the technology is never commercialised. A further issue with these approaches is that they may only apply to mass consumer markets. Teece (1986) suggests, for example, that the technology 'S' curve is not so applicable to smaller niche markets where there is less room for scale economies. Munir and Phillips (2005) also argue that such 'macro' views of innovation ignore the actions of businesses in favour of the activities of consumers. They argue, for example, that Kodak was largely responsible for shaping attitudes to photography from a past time of 'professional' photographers and 'artistic' amateurs to an activity that consumers saw as being essential for recording events in their life.

In summary, this section has identified 'macro' explanations of how innovation occurs. Each attempts to explain the historical evolution and diffusion of technology. Generally, it is fairly clear that a technological development follows an 'S' curve pattern and that there are identifiable periods such as a pre-paradigmatic phase (product innovation), the emergence of a 'dominant design', and a post-paradigmatic phase (process innovation). It is also clear that the diffusion of these technologies is shaped by social pressures. The main weakness of these explanations is that they are descriptive rather than predictive, and so cannot be used to say which innovation is likely to succeed.

5.4 Innovation in large and small businesses

The previous section discussed the context for innovation. In this section, we compare and contrast the importance of innovative large and small businesses. We start by highlighting some of the 'stylised' key differences between a small and a large business. We then return, again, to Schumpeter to examine whether these differences should result in larger businesses being 'more' innovative. We subsequently discuss the empirical evidence. This shows that large businesses, using static measures, are much more innovative than smaller businesses. This is because most small businesses do not set out to be innovative: at best, their key innovation is just to enter a given market. If small businesses are seen as dynamic 'agents of change' (Audretsch 2002*a*), however, a different picture emerges: one that suggests that small businesses play an important role in innovation and hence in economic and social welfare.

Comparing and contrasting the small and large business

Table 5.5 identifies a range of 'stylised' differences between a small and large business. In terms of management, the stereotypical view (Bommer and Jalajas 2004; Freeman and Engel 2007) suggests that smaller businesses are often run by a 'dynamic' entrepreneur who believes intrinsically in their innovation and seeks to develop it as quickly as possible. In contrast, the large business manager is potentially more nervous of the downsides of the innovation and the potential damage it can do to their 'career'. This risk-aversion may be at odds with the interests of the owners (shareholders) of the business who wish to see innovations in the business. Managers in large businesses, however, may be more 'objective' about an innovation and have the skills to commercially appraise the innovation.

Table 5.5 also identifies similar differences in terms of market position. A small business is often seen as being able to develop innovations that are 'closer' to the market. They may also be able to exploit smaller niches than a large business. Once commercialised, however, the small business is potentially at a disadvantage because it is more likely to be a price taker than a price maker. This affects its ability to influence the activities of suppliers and customers. Overall, however, a case can be made to suggest that smaller businesses enjoy behavioural advantages over larger businesses.

These behavioural advantages also apply to the organisation of the business. Smaller businesses may have flatter and less bureaucratic management structures, which may increase decision speed and ease the co-ordination of cross-functions in the business (e.g. engineers working directly with designers). However, this presumes that smaller businesses have the necessary skills and expertise to successfully develop an innovation. Indeed, the stereotypical view is that larger businesses are more likely to have greater numbers of specialist professional staff, because they have the resources to attract, recruit and retain skilled workers.

This resource advantage of the large business is most evident in terms of finance. Essentially, a small business is more reliant on internal sources of finance (e.g. owner's own savings) than external finance (e.g. bank or venture capital finance). Although they are more likely to use such finance 'efficiently', Ughetto (2008) shows that this places them at a disadvantage compared with larger businesses, which are likely to have greater pools of internal resources available to them, and enjoy greater access to external finance. This is important because – as we show in Chapter 18 on equity finance – financing the innovative business often requires more than one 'round' of finance to develop, commercialise and diffuse the innovation. Clearly, larger businesses enjoy a resource advantage because – if nothing else – outside investors are more likely to see them as a 'safer' investment than a smaller, less well known, business.

Overall, therefore, the 'stylised' result is that a small business enjoys a behavioural advantage whilst a large business has a resource advantage.

Schumpeter Mark I and Mark II

The big question is: are smaller businesses any more innovative than larger businesses? Before we turn to the empirical evidence on this, we suggest that there are two different theoretical approaches to understanding the question. Both of these approaches stem – yet again – from Schumpeter. In his early work, Schumpeter (1934) outlined a theory to explain why there were business cycles. As we suggested above in section 5.2, business cycles were marked by a 'gale of creative destruction'.

Schumpeter's (1934) starting point was that there was an initial equilibrium in a given market. This was characterised by routine behaviour. For example, one of his favourite examples was transport. In the early nineteenth century the most common and routine way to

Table 5.5 'Stylised' innovation advantages and disadvantages of small and large businesses

	Small businesses		Large businesses	
	Advantages	**Disadvantages**	**Advantages**	**Disadvantages**
Management	● Potentially run by dynamic managers ● Quicker decision making ● Often have a strong commitment to the innovation.	● Less professional ● Often emotionally linked to the innovation. ● Can be technically rather than market focused	● Likely to have qualified and 'professional' managers ● More likely to 'objectively' appraise an innovation.	● Managers may be risk averse (may fear failure) or lack dynamism ● Potential that 'managers' may not act in the interest of owners.
Market position	● Potentially 'closer' to the market ● Able to focus on small market niches.	● Lack market power – a price taker.	● Bargaining power with suppliers – potentially a price maker.	● Potentially 'distant' from the market (innovate from the 'top' down) ● More likely to focus on large market segments.
Organisation/People	● More informal communication ● Less bureaucracy ● Flatter management structures.	● Lack of highly skilled personnel ● Entrepreneurs may resent outside 'interference' from external financiers (e.g. business angels, venture capitalists).	● Able to call on specialist cross-functional resources (e.g. mix of marketing and technical professionals).	● Lack of internal flexibility ● More formal communication and bureaucracy ● May not welcome innovations developed by outsiders ('not invented here' syndrome).
Resourcing	● More likely to use R&D finance efficiently ● Fewer resources invested so less likely to 'fear' failure.	● Reliant on (usually limited) internal sources of finance ● Pay more for external finance ● Unable to gain from R&D scale economies ● 'Eggs' typically all in one basket so forced to go for growth.	● Financial resources necessary to conduct R&D ● Benefit from R&D scale economies ● Greater marketing resources. ● Can afford to wait	● Bureaucratic nature of the business may mean that it takes longer to introduce innovation.

get around was either by foot or by horse. However, from the mid 1830s onwards, a 'swarm' of innovations were brought to the transport market by entrepreneurs (e.g. Stephenson's steam locomotive, *The Rocket*). Schumpeter (1934) argued that such innovations were brought to the market by entrepreneurs who effectively destroyed the old 'routine' of using horses to travel around. These entrepreneurial endeavours eventually became the new routines as people adjusted to their introduction. In essence, a process of 'creative destruction' had occurred because the old routines had been destroyed whilst new routines had been created. **Schumpeter Mark I**, therefore, argues that central to innovation and economic development is the entrepreneur and their ability to radically and disruptively transform, undo and then remake routines.

The later Schumpeter (1950) argues, however, that: 'What we have got to accept is that it [the large business] has come to be the most powerful engine of that progress and in particular of the long-run expansion of total output . . .' (p. 106). This is often termed **Schumpeter Mark II**. Why did Schumpeter (1950) change his mind? One explanation is that central to Schumpeter's ideas was the notion that economic development was evolutionary (path dependent). He, therefore, believed that the earlier period of entrepreneurship was largely over. This was because, for example, he recognised that larger businesses had been able to develop R&D facilities and that they were able to devote considerable resources to R&D. This allowed them to 'routinise' innovation. Hence, his view was that: 'The romance of earlier commercial adventure is rapidly wearing away, because so many more things can be strictly calculated that had of old to be visualized in a flash of genius . . . Rationalized and specialized office work will eventually blot out personality, the calculable result, the "vision"' (p. 106). This was a view he shared with Alfred North Whitehead, another economist, who said: 'The greatest invention of the nineteenth century was the invention of the method of invention.'

Audretsch and Thurik (2000) argue that it was not surprising in the 1950s to 1970s to hold a Schumpeter Mark II opinion of innovation. This was a period of the 'managed economy' in which business ownership became concentrated, the emphasis was on the production of mass products, and governments, unions and businesses all sought to work together. However, they argue that since the 1980s the world's developed economies have shifted from a ' managed' to an 'entrepreneurial' economy. In other words, Schumpeter Mark I has become a better explanation of innovation activity.

Interestingly, the general empirical evidence on the amount of innovation carried out suggests that Schumpeter Mark II is a better explanation of innovatory activity. The EU (2007) showed that the smallest size of business in Europe's Community Innovation Survey (CIS 4) – 10–49 employees – was less likely to be innovative than larger businesses (250+ employees). It is also clear from Table 5.6 that larger businesses (250+ employees) in the UK are more likely to conduct R&D in their own organisation (intra mural), whilst at the same time contracting R&D to outside businesses (extra mural) and engaging in a range of innovation activities, from acquiring machinery to the market introduction of various innovations.

Robson and Haigh (2008) also identify that larger businesses are much more likely to be process, product, and managerial innovators than smaller businesses. Australian data confirms this picture. Table 5.7 shows that larger businesses are much more likely in general to be innovative businesses. They are also more likely to be involved in the creation of new products, processes or managerial innovations. What is also interesting is that the Australian data in Table 5.7 starts from a base of five employees. Arguably, as we showed in Chapter 3, this is 'unrepresentative' of small businesses – even at this low number – because the 'typical' small business is likely to employ only the owner of the business. The implication is that that if these were examined, the innovation rate differences between the very small business and 'large' business would be even starker.

So far, the evidence points to the comparative importance of large businesses (Schumpeter Mark II) rather than that of small businesses as sources of innovation (Schumpeter Mark I). It suggests that because innovation is a resource intensive activity, it is likely that the large business is better placed. Audretsch (2002*a*), however, argues that this is too static a picture of

Table 5.6	Innovation activities amongst UK businesses, 2004–6, in percentages		
	Employment size bands		
	10–49	**50–249**	**250+**
Intramural R&D	26	35	43
Extramural R&D	10	15	21
Acquisition of machinery, equipment and software	59	69	71
of which: Advanced machinery	18	25	31
Computer hardware	51	59	61
Computer software	52	62	65
Acquisition of external knowledge	14	16	20
Training	34	44	49
All forms of design	15	22	29
Market introduction of innovations *of which:*	35	45	51
Changes to product or service design	20	27	32
Market research	17	23	35
Changes to marketing methods	20	23	27
Launch advertising	18	22	28

Source: Robson and Haigh (2008).

Table 5.7	Innovation activities amongst Australian businesses, 2004–5, in percentages		
	Employment size bands		
	5–19	**20–99**	**100+**
Any new/significantly improved goods or services	15.8	29.2	28.9
Any new/significantly improved operational processes	16.9	34.4	34.7
Any new/significantly improved operational/managerial processes	20.7	35.6	40.0
Businesses innovating	28.4	46.6	51.5
Businesses which failed to complete/abandoned any innovative activity	10.1	17.2	21.4
Innovation-active businesses	29.8	47.9	54.8

Source: ABS (2005).

economic development. If, instead, innovation is seen as being marked by uncertainty, by dynamism and an analysis of sector and the life cycle of a technology, then a radically different picture emerges of the contribution of small businesses.

An early influential study by Acs and Audretsch (1988) examined two specific themes:

1 the influence of market structure on innovation;

2 the relationship between business size and innovation.

What they found was that in some market structures, innovation was less likely to occur because the market was highly concentrated (e.g. oligopolies or monopolies). The implication of this is that sectors which are highly concentrated are the ones that are more likely to be 'routinised' and, therefore, more conducive to innovation by large businesses. However, in newer, more uncertain, sectors – which were almost by definition less concentrated – there were greater opportunities for small businesses to act as 'agents of change'.

In terms of the second theme, Acs and Audretsch's (1988) results were surprising. Using an innovation measure (number of innovations/number of employees) they found that the extent to which small or large businesses dominate innovation was highly sector-specific: in some sectors they found that larger businesses dominate innovations whilst in other sectors smaller businesses were the dominant innovators. Indeed, arguably, Acs and Audretsch suggest that it is small, rather than large businesses that are more 'innovation fertile'.

Pavitt *et al.* (1987) also found that smaller businesses were more fertile than larger businesses. Again, Pavitt *et al.* (1987) found that if account was taken of different proportions of employment (innovation/employment) or R&D expenditure (innovation/R&D expenditure) then smaller businesses were more innovative than larger businesses. However, this result has been placed in doubt by Tether (1998) who shows that the Pavitt *et al.* research failed to distinguish adequately between small enterprises and small establishments.

Since this early research, there has been further evidence to suggest the importance of small businesses to innovation. Table 5.8 indicates that sales from new to market and new to the business innovation are a higher percentage of total turnover for the small business when compared with the larger business.

Santarelli and Piergiovanni (1996) also found that industry structure and size influenced innovation, with some sectors being more innovative than others, and that smaller businesses were – depending on the sector – more important than larger businesses. Dolfsma and van der Panne (2008) used Dutch data to attempt to replicate the findings of the initial Acs and Audretsch (1988) study. They found – again – that industry sector and the development of the sector along its 'life cycle' are important in explaining the relative importance of small and large businesses. Indeed, Syrneonidis's (1996) review of the evidence holds that: '. . . on the whole, there is little empirical support for the view that large firm size or high concentration are factors generally associated with a higher level of innovative activity. Moreover, even though there are circumstances where a positive association exists, this by no means implies the existence of a causal relationship.' (p. 59)

Overall, there is no clear cut general relationship between business size and innovation. What appears most likely is that larger sized businesses appear to be more innovative if the measure relates to the simple number of innovations. In essence, this suggests that resources

Table 5.8	Average distribution of total turnover from product innovation and novel innovation, 2006, in percentages		
	Employment size bands		
	10–49	**50–249**	**250+**
New to market	9	6	7
New to the firm	14	12	10
Significantly improved product	15	15	14
Unchanged product	62	67	69

Source: Robson and Haigh (2008).

are more important to innovation than any behavioural advantage. It also seems to vindicate Schumpeter Mark II that large businesses are more important to innovation. However, when we take a different innovation measure (e.g. innovation/employment), a different picture emerges which suggests that smaller rather than larger businesses are more 'fertile'. This suggests the importance of behavioural advantages and gives credence to Schumpeter Mark I.

In essence, however, the situation is much more complex than any simple contrast between Schumpeter Mark I and II. One of the points to emerge from section 5.3 is that innovation is path dependent. Indeed, Freeman and Soete (1997: 240) argue that 'Industry matters, technology matters and history matters'. This suggests that the relative innovation advantage of a small or large business is contingent upon sector, the development of that sector, the state of technology available and its historical development. Earlier on in section 5.3 we suggested that knowledge and how this 'spilled over' into other economic activities was arguably very important in explaining why it is that some businesses were more innovative than others. Indeed, Audretsch (2002a) argues that these spillover benefits are at the heart of a 'dynamic' interpretation of the pivotal innovatory role of smaller businesses. He argues that, because knowledge is difficult to get hold of or 'appropriate' (it is likely to be intangible, non-rivalrous and non-excludable), one of the ways individuals have been able to act as 'agents of change' is that they have been able to spin out a business from an existing large business. The classic example of this is to follow the lineage of the US business Fairchild Semiconductors. This was set up in 1957 by eight disaffected former employees of Shockley Transistors. Fairchild Semiconductors subsequently led to other spin-off businesses such as Intel and the venture capital business Kleiner Perkins.

| Illustration | From one small Acorn: how spin-out activity can have a lasting impact |

Garnsey and Heffernan (2005) argue that universities and research institutes are also likely to see high rates of spin-out activity. Examining spin-out activity at Cambridge University, they report that over 100 businesses were formed by members of the Computer Science Department of Cambridge University, with half of them being located in the Cambridge area. They also examine the spillover effects of Acorn Computers. Founded in 1979, Acorn Computers survived as an independent business for only five years until it was acquired by Olivetti. It was subsequently closed in 1989. Despite existing for only a decade, Garnsey and Heffernan show that more than 30 businesses were started by ex-Acorn employees. Similarly, their evidence also points to one individual, Hermann Hauser, who founded Acorn Computers and went on to found or co-found 17 businesses, including Amadeus Partners which has been a key provider of venture capital to many Cambridge technology businesses.

It would also be naïve to assume that small businesses are somehow separate from larger businesses. Indeed, arguably, one of the most pronounced changes in the activities of large businesses over the last 30 years is that they have tried to mimic the 'stylised' behavioural advantages of the small business. This is commonly called **intrapreneurship**. Intrapreneurship is said to occur when employees in a large organisation are able to act 'entrepreneurially'. Hence, they may be given a particular innovation project to work with or see that their business area is 'spun out' of the mainstream activities so that they can act entrepreneurially – although they have the resources and the safety net of a large organisation. For example, Xbox was a project that was developed and commercialised by a team of 'intrapreneurs' at Microsoft. An example of a 'spun out' company is the Internet bank Egg which was set up in 1998 by the Prudential bank which itself was set up in 1848. Because Egg was such a radical departure, Prudential set it up as an independent entity.

Summary

This chapter has examined the issue of innovation. It began by identifying that there was a marked difference between invention and innovation. Arguably, what distinguishes innovation from invention is that invention is about just one part of an innovatory process that seeks to create economic and social value. The chapter subsequently identified that there were a number of key terms in understanding innovation (radical, incremental, product and process) and that there were very real difficulties in quantifying the scale of innovation that actually takes place.

The chapter identified that the context for innovation was important. In particular, it described how technology seems to be path dependent.

The final section of the chapter assessed the evidence on the 'stylised' advantages and disadvantages of a 'large' and a 'small' business. Essentially, a small business has behavioural advantages whilst a large business has resource advantages. These resource advantages seemed important to the later Schumpeter (1950) (Schumpeter Mark II) because he believed that capitalism had evolved to the extent that the earlier advantages of the entrepreneur (Schumpeter Mark I) were no longer so marked. Empirically, it is the case that small businesses are – on many measures – much less innovative than larger businesses. This testifies to the resource advantages of larger businesses. However, this assumes a rather static picture of economic development. Audretsch (2002a) identifies that this ignores the dynamic nature of small businesses and the presence of uncertainty. Other empirical evidence suggests that once account is taken of sector, the life cycle of the technology and the innovation rate (e.g. innovations per employee), then small businesses emerge in particular sectors as key 'agents of change'.

Questions for discussion

1 Who is more innovative: large or small businesses? Discuss.

2 What do you think triggers the diffusion of products/services? Analyse a product/service to see if the pre-paradigm, dominant design and post-paradigm design phase fits. What does this tell you about how innovation works?

3 What is the difference between radical and incremental innovation? What role do small businesses play in these two types of innovation?

4 What is the best 'macro' explanation of innovation?

5 Can intellectual property rights be useful for the small business?

6 How should innovation be measured?

References

Acs, Z.J. and Audretsch, D.B. (1988) 'Innovation in Large and Small Firms: An Empirical Analysis', *American Economic Review*, 78(4), 678–90.

Agarwal, R. and Bayus, B.L. (2002) 'The Market Evolution and Sales Takeoff of Product Innovations', *Management Science*, 48(8), 1024–41.

Arundel, A. and Kabla, I. (1998) 'What Percentage of Innovations are Patented? Empirical Estimates for European Firms', *Research Policy*, 27(2), 127–41.

Åstebro, T. (2003) 'The Return to Independent Invention: Evidence of Unrealistic Optimism, Risk Seeking or Skewness Loving?', *Economic Journal*, 113(484), 226–39.

Audretsch, D.B. (2002a) 'The Dynamic Role of Small Firms: Evidence from the US', *Small Business Economics*, 18(1–3), 13–40.

Audretsch, D.B. (2002*b*) *Entrepreneurship: A Survey of the Literature.* Prepared for the European Commission, Enterprise Directorate General, EU: Brussels.

Audretsch, D.B. and Thurik, A.R. (2000) 'Capitalism and Democracy in the 21st Century: From the Managed to the Entrepreneurial Economy', *Journal of Evolutionary Economics*, 10(1–2), 17–34.

Australian Bureau of Statistics (ABS) (2005) *Innovation in Australian Business, 2005.* http://www.abs.gov.au/AUSSTATS/abs@.nsf/Lookup/8158.0Main+Features12005?OpenDocument (accessed 19 March 2009).

BERR (2008) *UK Innovation Survey.* http://www.berr.gov.uk/files/file44938.pdf (accessed 19 March 2009).

Bommer, M. and Jalajas, D.S. (2004) 'Innovation Sources of Large and Small Technology-Based Firms'. *IEEE Transactions on Engineering Management*, 51(1), 13–18.

Cameron, C. (1998) *Innovation and Growth: A Survey of the Empirical Evidence.* Oxford: Nuffield College.

Dolfsma, W. and van der Panne, G. (2008) 'Currents and Sub-currents in Innovation Flows: Explaining Innovativeness Using New-product Announcements', *Research Policy*, 37(10), 1706–16.

Dosi, G. (1982) 'Technological Paradigms and Technological Trajectories', *Research Policy*, 11, 147–62.

European Patent Office (2005) *Cost of a European Patent*, EPO: Munich. http://www.european-patent-office.org/epo/new/costs_ep_2005_en.pdf (accessed 20 March 2009).

European Union (2007) *Statistics in Focus: Community Innovation Statistics Is Europe Growing More Innovative?*, 61/2007. Brussels: EU.

Fagerberg, J. (2003) 'Innovation: A Guide to the Literature'. *Working Papers on Innovation Studies 20031012.* Centre for Technology, Innovation and Culture, University of Oslo.

Freeman, C. and Soete, L. (1997) *The Economics of Industrial Innovation*, 3rd edn. London: Pinter.

Freeman, J. and Engel, J.S. (2007) 'Models of Innovation: Startups and Mature Corporations', *California Management Review*, Fall, 94–119.

Garnsey, E. and Heffernan, P. (2004) 'Growth Setbacks in New Firms', *Futures*, 37(7), 675–97.

Hope, J. (1996) 'A Better Mousetrap', *American Heritage*, 47(6). http://www.americanheritage.com/articles/magazine/ah/1996/6/1996_6_90.shtml (accessed 19 March 2009).

Munir, K.A. and Phillips, N. (2005) 'The Birth of the "Kodak Moment": Institutional Entrepreneurship and the Adoption of New Technologies', *Organization Studies*, 26, 1665–87.

Pavitt, K., Robson, M. and Townsend, J. (1987) 'The Size Distribution of Innovating Firms in the UK 1945–1983', *Journal of Industrial Economics*, 35(3), 297–316.

Robson, M., Townsend, J. and Pavitt, K. (1988) 'Sectoral Patterns of Production and Use of Innovations in the UK, 1945–1983', *Research Policy*, 17(1), 1–14.

Robson, S. and Haigh, G. (2008) 'First findings from the UK Innovation Survey 2007', *Economic and Labour Market Review*, 2(4), 47–53.

Rogers, E.M. (2003) *Diffusion of Innovations*, 5th edn. New York: Free Press.

Romer, P. (1990) 'Endogenous Technological Change', *Journal of Political Economy*, 98, S71–102.

Roper, S. (1999) 'Under Reporting of R&D in Small Firms: The Impact on International R&D Comparisons', *Small Business Economics*, 12, 131–5.

Rosenberg, N. (2004) *Innovation and Economic Growth.* Paris: OECD.

Santarelli, E. and Piergiovanni, R. (1996) 'Analysing Literature-based Innovation Output Indicators', *Research Policy*, 25(5), 689–711.

Santarelli, E. and Sterlacchini, A. (1990) 'Innovation, Formal vs Informal R&D, and Firm Size: Some Evidence from Italian Manufacturing Firms', *Small Business Economics*, 2, 223–8.

Schumpeter, J.A. (1934) *The Theory of Economic Development.* Cambridge, MA: Harvard University Press.

Schumpeter, J.A. (1950) *Capitalism, Socialism and Democracy*. New York: Harper and Row.

Solow, R. (1957) 'Technological Change in an Aggregative Model of Economic Growth', *International Economic Review*, 6, 18–31.

Srinivasan, S., Pauwels, K., Silva-Risso, J. and Hanssens, D.M. (2009) 'Product Innovations, Advertising, and Stock Returns', *Journal of Marketing*, 73, 24–43.

Syrneonidis, G. (1996) 'Innovation, Firm Size and Market Structure: Schumpeterian Hypotheses and Some New Themes', *OECD Economic Studies*, 27.

Teece, D.J. (1986) 'Profiting from Technological Innovations', *Research Policy*, 15(6), 285–306.

Tether, B.S. (1998) 'Small and Large Firms: Sources of Unequal Innovations?', *Research Policy*, 27(7), 725–45.

Tushman, M.L. and Anderson, P. (1986) 'Technological Discontinuities and Organizational Environments', *Administrative Science Quarterly*, 31, 439–65.

Ughetto, E. (2008) 'Does Internal Finance Matter for R&D?: New Evidence from a Panel of Italian Firms', *Cambridge Journal of Economics*, 32(6), 907–25.

Ulku, H. (2004) *R&D, Innovation, and Economic Growth: An Empirical Analysis*, IMF Working Paper, WP/04/185. Washington, DC: IMF.

Vaona, A. and Pianta, M. (2008) 'Firm Size and Innovation in European Manufacturing', *Small Business Economics*, 30(3), 283–99.

Whitehead, A.N. (1931) *Science and the Modern World*. New York: Macmillan.

Yahaya, S.-Y. and Abu-Bakar, N. (2007) 'New Product Development Management Issues and Decision-making Approaches', *Management Decision*, 45(7), 1123–42.

Part 2 New Business Formation

In Part 2 we examine three main features of new businesses. In Chapter 6, the importance of new businesses is identified. Chapter 7 considers the types of factors that influence nascent entrepreneurship (people in the process of setting up a business) and the role played by social networks. In Chapter 8 we consider the economic treatment of new businesses.

Entrepreneurship in Action   FT

Go to the *Small Business and Entrepreneurship* companion website at www.pearsoned.co.uk/storeygreene to watch entrepreneurs and academics giving you their personal perspectives on some of these issues.

Nick Robertson, CEO of ASOS, talks about the economics of starting up his online fashion company.

6

Defining and measuring start ups

Key learning objectives

By the end of this chapter you should:

- Have an understanding of the role played by new businesses in economic growth

- Become aware of the issues involved in defining the new business

- Be able to identify the key issues involved in measuring the number of new businesses and computing a start-up rate.

6.1 Introduction

What would happen if there were no new businesses? Would the economy collapse? Would we even notice? The first task of this chapter is to identify why it is that new businesses are important. Three reasons are usually given: they are a productive outlet for people seeking an alternative to unemployment or working for someone else; they are a source of innovation; and, third, they bring competition to the market. In this chapter, our main focus is on the competitive aspects of new businesses. The evidence we present suggests that new businesses are economically important in replacing inefficient businesses and in pressuring existing businesses to consider and potentially change what they offer to customers. Their importance, however, is uneven. In terms of economic importance, larger new businesses are still more important than *all* new businesses. New businesses are also not a solution to all economic problems, particularly in disadvantaged areas.

This chapter also identifies the difficulties of defining and measuring the new business. Some of these difficulties are due to statistical and methodological issues but they also reflect conceptual problems. In Chapter 2, we identified two conceptually different approaches. In the economics approach, the primary concern is with the 'outcomes' of new business activity (e.g. contribution to economic growth). This is a concern shared by organisational theorists. However, organisational theorists more fully emphasise 'people and process'. Their focus is more upon individuals who are either considering or actually undertaking the entrepreneurial act and the factors that explain that decision. So, risking over-simplifying, economists are primarily interested in the economic consequences of new businesses, whereas organisational theorists are more concerned with the characteristics of those individuals who make the transition towards, and perhaps ultimately undertake, the entrepreneurial act – the 'process' of starting a new business.

This implies that there are evident differences in how new businesses are defined and measured. In this chapter, we will detail these differences and show that the number of new businesses created in a country can be twice or three times as high depending on how a new business is defined. We now examine why new businesses are important.

6.2 The importance of new businesses

There are three main reasons for regarding new businesses as being important. First, new businesses may act as an alternative way for someone to employ themselves. Individuals may feel that they are unsuited to being an employee and so gravitate towards self-employment. Setting up a new business, therefore, is an outlet for some people.

Others may perceive – or actually experience – difficulties in getting employment. This may be for a variety of reasons: because of their age; gender; ethnic background; youth or limited educational/work experience. Starting their own business may enable such individuals and groups to participate more fully in society. In essence, it empowers them (Blackburn and Ram 2006).

Another stated advantage of new businesses is that they are often seen as a mechanism for regenerating and revitalising disadvantaged communities. Perhaps the best expression of this is Porter (1995). He argued that new and existing businesses had the potential to radically reconfigure run-down urban areas. New and existing small businesses are suggested to be able to do this primarily because – as we showed in Chapter 4 – they create jobs. By contrast, Blackburn and Ram (2006) have argued that this overplays the role of new and existing businesses in run-down inner city areas. These areas, they argue, suffer from social as well as economic problems. This debate is really about the direction of government policies. Because of this we leave further discussion of the revitalising powers of new businesses to the public policy chapters (Chapters 19–21). Similarly, this chapter does not discuss the relationship between new businesses and innovation as this was discussed in Chapter 5.

A third reason why new businesses are important is that they are integral to the competitive process. This is apparent in two ways. First, new businesses replace existing less efficient businesses which have failed to meet customer needs. Second, the threat of entry, or the presence of an actual entrant, may discipline existing businesses to be more competitive in what they offer to customers. In this section, we look at the impact of new businesses in terms of replacing and disciplining existing businesses. We then consider other evidence on the contribution of new businesses to different economies.

New businesses replace existing less efficient businesses

Central to the competitive market process is that less effective or productive businesses disappear and their resources are used more efficiently by others. For example, suppose an inefficient printing business closes. As part of this, it is forced to sell its printing machinery. Another printing business is able to buy these second-hand assets – often at a much cheaper price – and use them in its business. Factors that prevent or slow that change – such as difficulties in starting or closing businesses – inhibit this process. A good example of this is the effect of the 'Loi Royer' (Royer's Law), introduced in France in the 1970s, which required new large-scale retail developments to gain a planning permit. Bertrand and Kramarz (2002) showed that the Loi Royer stopped the development of large retail stores. This was because large retailers had to obtain the necessary planning permit from the regional zoning board. This board was made up of consumers, local politicians and, crucially, owners of existing retail operations. The net result of this restriction of new businesses (however large) was limited job creation.

Disney *et al.* (2003) examined productivity (a measure of the efficiency by which inputs such as capital equipment or labour are used to produce outputs (goods or services)) increases in British manufacturing between 1980 and 1992. They found that *all* the productivity gains in independent businesses occurred because new entrants were more efficient than those that exited. There was no increase in the average output per worker (labour productivity) amongst *surviving* businesses. Foster *et al.*'s (2006) study of the US retail trade sector also found that productivity growth was driven by entrants being more productive than those that exited. The implication of this is that if productivity is to increase in an economy, the competitive process by which the inefficient businesses exit *and* new entrants emerge has to be facilitated and possibly even encouraged.

However, not all entrants are equal. Both Foster *et al.* (2006) and Disney *et al.* (2003) identify that it is larger entrants that are more likely to be sources of productivity gains. For example, Foster *et al.* (2006) found that entrants that were part of a large national chain were likely to be more productive than single entrants. The implication is that these larger chains, rather than single businesses, were largely responsible for much of the labour productivity growth.

New businesses 'threaten' existing businesses

A second key role of new businesses is to provide a credible threat to existing businesses. Existing businesses have to be aware that, if they fail to act efficiently, they may be replaced by new entrants or see a deterioration in their business prospects.

Again, however, it is not the *general* threat or presence of entrants that seems to discipline existing businesses. Geroski (1995) showed that existing businesses do not always react to the presence of new entrants. If they do, Geroski argued that it is mostly in terms of changing their marketing rather than their pricing strategy. The net effect is that new entrants potentially face an entry barrier because they may have to spend equivalent amounts on marketing (e.g. advertising) as the existing business in order to enter the market successfully.

Such decisions are obviously dependent on the structure of the sector. Existing businesses also know – as we will show in Chapter 9 – that one of the persistent features of new and small businesses is that they have high rates of closure. Most new entrants are undertaking risky gambles. These risky 'experiments', therefore, tend to under-invest (Baldwin *et al.* 2000). Indeed, Jensen *et al.*'s (2001) study of US manufacturers found that entrants had lower rates of productivity than the industry average (i.e. existing businesses). They argue that this was because of the presence of a large number of low productivity (under-investing) businesses who subsequently exited the industry. In other words, many entrants are gambling with a limited 'stake' and are hoping that their 'hunch' proves to be correct.

The implication of this is that many entrants come and go very quickly. However, those new entrants that do survive are likely to experience productivity gains (Jensen *et al.* 2001). It is also likely that the truly credible threat to existing businesses comes from these survivors rather than from short-lived new entrants.

It is not just in terms of productivity that the impact of the new business can be felt. Fritsch and Mueller (2004) examined the direct and indirect employment impact of new businesses. Figure 6.1 shows that in Germany new businesses had three employment effects. The first, shown as Phase I in Figure 6.1, is the immediate – one year – effect of starting the business. However, that immediate or direct effect soon becomes negative as the entry of the new business displaces existing businesses in Phase II. Finally, in Phase III there are 'supply-side' effects in which the performance of the surviving businesses is enhanced by the threat of the entrant.

The value of the Fritsch and Mueller contribution is that it shows there are both positive and negative (employment) consequences of new businesses and that these occur at different times. It also shows in the German case that, overall, the positive effects outweigh the negative effects – so that entry has positive employment consequences.

However, for the overall effect to be positive it is necessary for the Phase I and Phase III employment to exceed the losses in Phase II, and this is not always the case. This is illustrated in Figure 6.2 below taken from Mueller *et al.* (2008) using British data. It compares low-entrepreneurial regions with other regions. The low-entrepreneurial regions – those with low rates of new business formation – shown as dotted lines – have a larger and longer

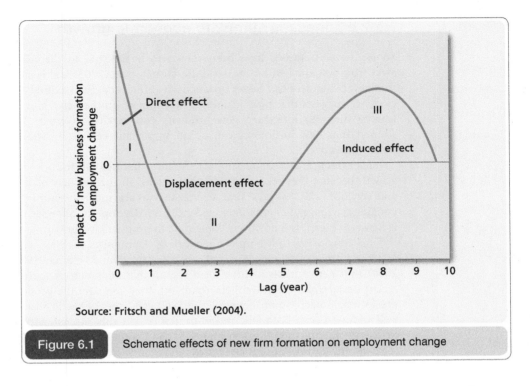

Source: Fritsch and Mueller (2004).

| Figure 6.1 | Schematic effects of new firm formation on employment change |

Phase II than the more entrepreneurial regions. They also have a smaller and shorter Phase III. The overall effect of this is that whilst new businesses in the 'other' regions have a positive long-term employment effect, this is not the case in the low-entrepreneurial regions. In simple terms, new businesses do not always lead to long-term job creation.

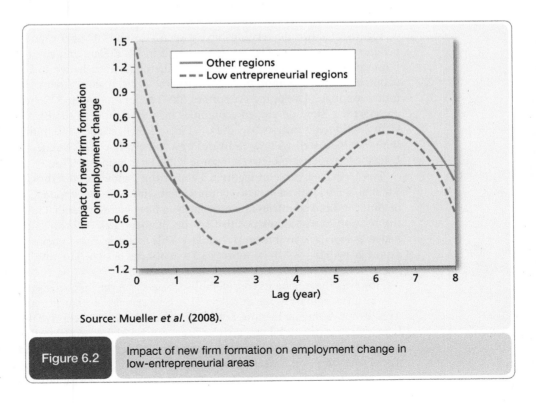

Source: Mueller et al. (2008).

| Figure 6.2 | Impact of new firm formation on employment change in low-entrepreneurial areas |

New businesses stimulate economic growth

So far, new businesses have been shown to be integral to the reallocation of resources away from less efficient businesses. Both Disney *et al.* (2003) and Foster *et al.* (2006) showed that new businesses had better productivity (efficiency) than exiting businesses. Equally, the evidence suggests that new businesses may impact on the behaviour of existing businesses, leading them to introduce new products and services (Geroski 1995). Chapter 5 also showed that new businesses can be an important vehicle by which economies become more innovative.

This evidence appears to support the idea that new businesses are central to economic growth because they lead to productivity gains. In their review of the evidence, van Praag and Versloot (2007) suggest that new businesses are, indeed, central to productivity growth. Looking at a range of international evidence from developed economies, their general conclusion is that new businesses positively contribute to productivity growth.

This conclusion draws upon the work of economists such as Acs and Audretsch. They argue in a range of articles (Acs *et al.* 1994; Audretsch and Feldman 1996; Acs and Armington 2004) that new businesses have been responsible for much of the economic growth over recent decades. To illustrate their argument, they compare the productivity of the US and the former Soviet Union between the 1960s and the 1990s. Whilst both economies were well endowed with both labour and capital (e.g. highly sophisticated technology), the rate of economic growth was much higher in the US than in the Soviet Union. This difference in economic performance is attributed by Acs and Audretsch, at least in part, to the presence of entrepreneurs in the US and their absence – at least from the formal or market economy – in the Soviet Union.

The relationship between new businesses and economic growth has also been extensively examined by the Global Entrepreneurship Monitor (GEM). This is an annual international survey which quantifies the number of people in the process of setting up a business (nascent entrepreneurs) and actual new business owners in an economy (see section 6.4). It calls this combined measure the Total Entrepreneurship Activity (TEA) rate. In 2007, it surveyed individuals in 42 countries.

Figure 6.3 shows the relationship between TEA and GDP per capita (a measure of income per inhabitant that in this case is expressed in US dollars and controls for the purchasing power parities – a measure that equalises differences in exchange and inflation rates between countries to give common prices). In general terms, it shows that the highest TEA rates are found amongst developing economies like Thailand, Peru and Columbia with lower rates amongst the more developed economies including most of the EU. However, amongst the most developed countries (e.g. the US, Finland, Switzerland) TEA rates are higher than those in more moderately wealthy countries from eastern Europe. The effect of this is to generate a U-shaped relationship between income (GDP) per head and TEA.

The U-shaped curve in Figure 6.3 shows that below the threshold of around $30,000 to $40,000, TEA rates are negatively associated with GDP per capita. This means that poorer income per head countries are more likely to have higher rates of TEA. Above this threshold, the relationship becomes positive so that higher rates of income per head go alongside increases in early entrepreneurial activity. This might lead us to believe that TEA causes economic growth in wealthy countries and that policies designed to raise TEA would then lead to higher levels of wealth.

However, there remains considerable debate about the link between economic growth and new business activity as measured by TEA. One criticism is that although new business activity rates may be higher in more developed economies, the direction of this causation is unclear. It may be that new business activity is caused by higher wealth rather than higher wealth being caused by early entrepreneurial activity. All else being equal, an individual is more likely to start a business in a wealthy area where there is higher demand than in a less prosperous area. Hence, whilst there is an *association* between income levels and new business formation, the direction of this *causation* is unclear. Thurik *et al.* (2008) seek to resolve these complexities

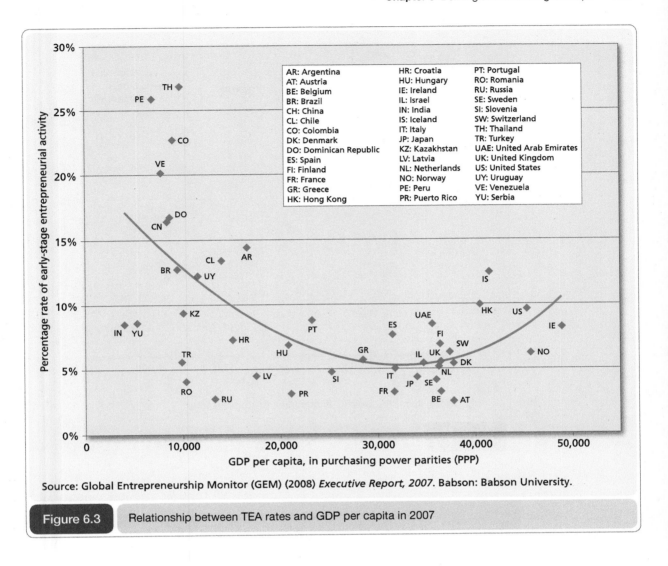

Source: Global Entrepreneurship Monitor (GEM) (2008) *Executive Report, 2007*. Babson: Babson University.

Figure 6.3   Relationship between TEA rates and GDP per capita in 2007

by examining the relationship between unemployment and self-employment. They conclude that there is evidence of the relationship working in both directions but that, on balance, the more powerful effect is of self-employment lowering unemployment.

A second criticism is that, as far as developed economies are concerned, the key element of the U-shape is that TEA is higher in the richer countries. However, an equally plausible interpretation of the data in Figure 6.3 is that the relationship is L-shaped rather than U-shaped. This makes a major difference. If it is L-shaped then the vertical element of the L implies that poor countries can have massive variations in TEA rates but no impacts on wealth. If true, then changing TEA rates, even if this were possible, would not have any influence on the income per head in such countries. The horizontal part of the L-shape relating to wealthy countries is also important. It would imply that differences in TEA rates are unrelated to wealth beyond a threshold of $25,000. On those grounds, there would be little merit in seeking to raise TEA rates in medium and rich income countries because they could not expect to see a wealth increase simply by raising rates of entrepreneurship.

To test this, Figures 6.4 and 6.5 split the 42 GEM countries into two sets. The 21 countries in Figure 6.4 all have a GDP level of less than $25,000 whilst the 21 countries in Figure 6.5 have GDP levels above $25,000. The debate is whether a linear (flat) or quadratic (U-shaped) line best fits the data: if it is the linear line there is little support for a ready association between

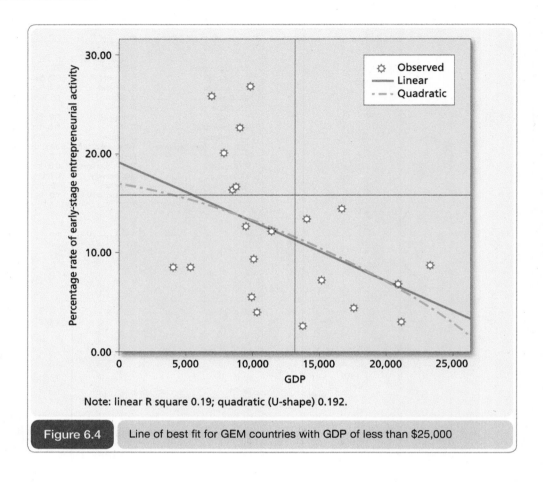

Note: linear R square 0.19; quadratic (U-shape) 0.192.

Figure 6.4   Line of best fit for GEM countries with GDP of less than $25,000

TEA and GDP; if it is U-shaped, there is more association found between TEA and GDP. In both Figures 6.4 and 6.5, the fit is very similar between the flat linear and U-shaped quadratic lines. At the very least, then, the link between TEA and GDP remains inconclusive.

Increasing levels of new business activity may also not always be desirable for some regional economies. As we have already seen, not all new entrants contribute equally to economic growth (Disney *et al.* 2003; Foster *et al.* 2006). Van Praag and Versloot (2007) argue that not all new businesses are productive. Very many new entrants may be unproductive because they are more likely to be started by individuals lacking entrepreneurial skills, lacking access to capital and seeking to sell products and services which are undifferentiated from those already existing in the marketplace. For instance, Greene *et al.* (2008) found no strong evidence to suggest that new business activity leads to regional economic benefits for disadvantaged regions. Van Stel and Storey (2004) and Mueller *et al.* (2008), as noted earlier, also showed that areas with low rates of new business formation also saw weaker job creation. In short, 'the wrong sort of entrepreneurship' is certainly possible.

Our final measure seeking to link entrepreneurship with economic development derives from Carree *et al.* (2002). They demonstrated the presence of a long-term equilibrium relationship between economic development and business ownership. They argued that there was evidence of this being U-shaped, the implication again being that the more developed countries had higher business ownership rates than 'middle-income countries'. As with the GEM analysis above, the 'easy' inference was that countries wishing to raise their incomes needed to raise business ownership. However, Caree *et al.* noted that a U-shaped could not be distinguished from an L-shaped function – implying that business ownership rates were *not*

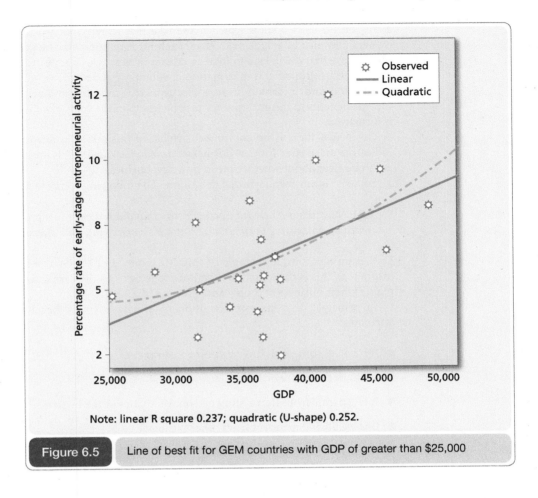

Note: linear R square 0.237; quadratic (U-shape) 0.252.

| Figure 6.5 | Line of best fit for GEM countries with GDP of greater than $25,000 |

a factor that distinguished middle from other income countries. Carree *et al.* (2007) continued to make the same point in their work using more recent data.

Overall, this section has shown that new businesses can play a very important role in the competitive process and in economic growth. Nevertheless, it has also shown that not all new businesses are equally productive and so, by implication, 'more is not always better'. We now turn to the tricky problem of defining a new business more precisely.

6.3 Defining the new business

In this section, we discuss the difficulties of reaching an appropriate definition of the new business. On the face of it, this seems a fairly simple task. A new business is surely a business that did not previously exist. By this definition, the number of new businesses can be quantified by comparing all businesses in existence now and excluding all businesses in existence last year, or last month or whenever the last enumeration took place. In practice, however, defining the new business and then estimating their number is fraught with both conceptual and statistical difficulties.

The statistical problem is that in no country in the world is there a complete list of all businesses. Nor, perhaps, is there ever likely to be. As noted in Chapter 2, many business activities – even in developed economies – are not recorded. This is partly because it imposes a cost on business owners which may make that activity not worth undertaking. Business owners may also be reluctant to share such information with the government because they may believe that it will lead to increased taxes or other business 'burdens'. Even if the government is able to collect this information, it still may not be worth doing so. Put simply, even if registration and information were electronically collected and recorded, the possible tax income benefits to the government may be less than the costs of collecting and recording the information.

Given that there is no comprehensive list of businesses in any country, then alternative indicators or 'proxies' for new businesses have to be sought. This means that it is very important to be clear about what we mean by a new business.

So, what is our own favoured definition? The following seems to reflect our objectives:

> *A new business is a new transacting entity that did **not** exist in a previous time period, is **not** owned by an existing business, and is **not** a simple change of ownership.*

Let's examine a simple example of this. Mr Storey and Mr Greene set up a business selling insurance. This is their first joint venture together and they are the only shareholders. They register their business as Storey and Greene Ltd.

In principle, this fits our definition of a 'new business' because it has the following attributes:

- It involves some activity (e.g. selling insurance).

- It did not exist previously.

- It is separate from the existing personal activities of the owners.

- It is legally independent from other businesses.

- It was not acquired from others.

- It has a unique name (in the UK limited companies have to have a name that is not the same or similar to other names).

What is distinctive about our definition is that we seek to exclude certain types of business which are outside our area of interest. So, what do we exclude and why? Below we identify a number of exclusions and ask you to think through the issues that they raise for defining a new business. Even using this definition, as we show below, conceptual and statistical issues arise that make it difficult to identify, and hence measure, the number of new businesses.

Separation of personal and business activities

We would argue that individuals creating a new business have to create some form of separation between themselves and their business activities: they must be able to recognise that the business has an identity that is separate from their own. One simple practical proxy for this would be obtaining a separate bank account or legal status for their business. Alternatively, individuals might make a separation between themselves as a worker and someone involved in business activities. Proxies for this include identifying for tax purposes work done for employment and work done for themselves. Creating a separate entity, though, is not sufficient to be a new business; it has to involve some form of transactional activity. Typically, this means making sales of a product or service but it may also include other forms of transactions such as bartering.

Illustration	Storey and Greene Ltd (Part 1)

Separating business interests from personal activities is a particularly important issue for partnerships.

Yes but: what about these two cases?

Case 1. Prior to setting up Storey and Greene Ltd, Mr Greene decided to register a separate business called Greene Ltd to sell sports goods. He also declared to the tax authorities that he had set up this business. Mr Greene subsequently found that other business issues took precedence and the net result was that he never spent the time to make any sales.

Case 2. Mr Storey is heavily involved in a voluntary mutual aid scheme. Mr Storey has building maintenance skills. He regularly exchanges his time and skill for the time and specialist skills of others in his local community. Because this is a bartering arrangement, Mr Storey does not see the need to register these activities.

● **Are either or both of these a new business?**
● **What do you think?**

A new branch or subsidiary of an existing enterprise

In our definition of a 'new business' we are interested in the creation of a business which is not owned by another organisation. We are not interested in one that is part of an existing business; only those that are new and independently owned business.

| Illustration | Storey and Greene Ltd (Part 2) |

Yes but: *Whilst we agree that we don't want to include every new outlet of a large business, what about this case?*

Storey and Greene Ltd operates from a single business location selling insurance. It decides to diversify into selling houses. It creates a new company called Storey and Greene (Housing) Ltd which is owned by exactly the same individuals that owned Storey and Greene Ltd, and it operates from the same premises. **Is this a new business?**

Yes it is: It is a new company, so it is a registered business which does not replace an existing company.

No it isn't: It still has the same owners as Storey and Greene Ltd and is still at the same location, so for economic purposes is merely a diversification of an existing business. Lots of businesses diversify by selling new products or services without them being called new businesses. After all, Mr Storey and Mr Greene might well have just continued to sell slightly different products to exactly the same group of customers.

● **What do you think? Is this a new business?**

A transfer of ownership, but no other change

We are also **not** interested in a business that is originally owned by one individual or group of individuals and is then sold to another. This is because the total number of businesses in the economy remains the same.

| Illustration | Storey and Greene Ltd (Part 3) |

Yes but: *what about the following two cases?*

Case 1. Storey and Greene Ltd is sold to new owners and both Mr Storey and Mr Greene resign and new director owners are appointed, but the name of the company and all other aspects remain the same.

Case 2. Storey and Greene Ltd is sold to new owners and both Mr Storey and Mr Greene resign and new director owners are appointed who are already owners and directors of Sykes, Mumby and Croft Ltd which has several other premises. The name Storey and Greene Ltd disappears and the business is now called Sykes, Mumby and Croft Ltd, but it continues to operate from its existing premises with the same employees.

● **Are either or both of these a new business?**
● **What do you think?**

A change of business name, but no other change

We are also **not** interested in a business which changes its name but continues to undertake the same economic activity. For example, solicitors, accountants and doctors may add new partners, so changing the name of the business, but the nature of that business remains unaltered, so it cannot be considered as new.

Insur2go

Yes but: *what about this case?*

Case 1. Mr Greene's daughter takes over the insurance business, Storey and Greene Ltd. She believes the name is boring and wants to revitalise and modernise its image. She registers a new company as Insur2go and closes Storey and Greene Ltd, but the share ownership is identical for both companies. Insur2go continues to trade at the same location providing a somewhat modernised service.

Is Insur2go a new business? What do you think?

A change of location, but no other change

Businesses do not always remain at the same location. A simple change of location cannot be considered as the closure of one business and the creation of a new business if all other aspects of the business remain unchanged.

Moving a business overseas

Yes but: *what about this case?*

Mr Storey and Mr Greene decide that England is too cold for them and they and their families will move to Spain and operate their business there. Is that a new business?

Yes it is: As far as Spain is concerned it is a new business, and as far as the UK is concerned it is a loss of a business.

No it isn't: It is no different in principle to the business moving to the next street since there is only a simple transfer of economic activity. The only difference is in terms of geographical units. It is a loss for England, but if the geographical unit were the European Union then it would be just a clear transfer.

- **Is the business in Spain new?**
- **What do you think?**

The above section highlights that there are very real issues in defining the concept of a new business. The above cases illustrate that there are a number of forms of economic activity which may be regarded by some, but not by others, as new businesses. The problem this creates is that varying definitions lead to different statistics being generated about new businesses, which may or may not coincide with each other. We address these issues in the next section.

6.4 Measuring new businesses

The previous section recognised there was no comprehensive census of businesses. So, whilst our favoured definition has its merits, converting it into a measure of the number of new business and estimating enterprise rates still involves a number of assumptions. The first is quantifying the number of new businesses. To show how problematic this is, we derive five separate measures that can be used to quantify the number of new businesses. Each of these measures has advantages and disadvantages. Unfortunately, they also produce very different estimates of the number of new businesses started in a given year.

The second task is to identify the *rate* of new business in a given year, as that is the basis for comparing business rates over time. This is important because, as we saw in Section 6.2, there is evidence to suggest that new businesses are important in reallocating resources away from inefficient businesses and 'disciplining' existing businesses. We, therefore, often want to know what is happening to business populations over time. As we will again see, arriving at a rate for new businesses (start-up rate) is also highly problematic.

Measuring the number of new businesses

Table 6.1 identifies five measures that can be used to quantify the number of new businesses or businesses in an economy. These five measures are:

1 individuals who say they have started a new business;

2 individuals who move into self-employment, who were not previously in self-employment;

3 the number of new enterprises registered;

4 the number of new companies registered; and

5 the number of new business bank accounts opened.

Table 6.1 details the advantages and disadvantages of these five measures. These largely stem from the unit of analysis that each adopts. The first of these – people who say they have started a new business – is derived from the Global Entrepreneurship Monitor (GEM) which concentrates on the business activities of adults in a population. It seeks to uncover how people are engaged in setting up or running a new business. As noted in Section 6.2, the principal advantage of this is that such survey evidence compares the scale of new business activities in different economies. What it may miss, however, is co-owned businesses. Table 6.1 also shows that it may over-estimate new business activity, since crucially not all of those who set out to create a business actually end up doing so. Also, many who actually start a business may have had a very short period in which they were 'nascents' (individuals in the process of setting up a business). This makes it difficult to identify if they are in the 'process' of starting a business.

The second measure – self-employment survey evidence which is usually derived from governmental agencies – again focuses on the individual. Whilst it gives a wider perspective on new business activity, it omits businesses created by individuals already in self-employment. As with GEM, it also makes no distinction between the economic value of these new business activities.

Table 6.1 shows three other measures that use the business, rather than the individual, as the unit of analysis. The first of these is based upon official sales tax registration data. This measure does not include businesses that fall below the specified sales tax registration threshold (although such businesses may choose to be included) and tends to ignore owner-ship or location changes. Official company registration data omits the bulk of the business population because, in the UK at least, only about one third of all registered businesses are companies. Company data is also potentially misleading because governments can offer tax incentives that favour incorporation over other ownership forms, leading to existing busi-nesses switching into or out of incorporation depending on the tax regime (see Chapter 20 for further information and Case study 8 on small business taxation). Also, businesses which have been trading for many years as sole proprietors or partnerships – and hence are not new businesses – can register as a company and hence appear as new. Arguably, the main advant-age of these two sources of business data is that concentrating on 'larger' new businesses

Table 6.1		Identifying the number of new businesses: advantages and disadvantages of different data sets		
Measure	**Unit of analysis**	**Source**	**Advantages**	**Disadvantages**
Individuals who say they have started a new business	People	Survey evidence (e.g. GEM estimates of 'baby' businesses)	• It is people who start up businesses. • Because GEM reports interviews with individuals it is likely to have much more comprehensive coverage of business activities and not be inhibited by official registration policies. • It tracks business owners and nascents (those in the process of starting a business). • GEM data is international and comparative.	• Individuals may already own a business and so this over-estimates the number of business owners. • Businesses may be started by more than one person so GEM can over-estimate the number of businesses. • Businesses set up are all treated equally. There is no distinction made between a part-time 'pin-money' business and one begun with 20 employees. • The prime focus of GEM is on people in the process of setting up a business. This is likely to over-estimate new business activity because not all of those involved in setting up a business – nascents – actually turn out to have economically active businesses. Van Stel (2005) shows that the number of individuals who convert from being a nascent to a 'baby' varies considerably internationally. • Reliable time series information is available for only for a small number of years.
Individuals who move into self-employment, who were not previously in self-employment	People	Survey evidence (e.g. Labour Force Survey evidence)	• It allows for the official identification of individuals entering self-employment who were previously employed, unemployed or economically inactive. • Self-employment data are available for many countries over long periods of time.	• It does not track businesses, only individuals. It gives an imperfect estimate of new businesses. • It may under-estimate the number of businesses. Westhead et al. (2005) report that about 1 in 4 new businesses are begun by individuals who already own a business. They would not be identified by statistics on the number of people entering self-employment since they are already in that category. • It may over-estimate the number of businesses. Very many are owned by more than a single person. They may be partnerships or companies in which there are multiple owners. Storey et al. (1987) report in their study of 146 manufacturing companies that these had 411 directors. Whilst most had only two directors, 13 companies had more than five, so the number of businesses would be expected to be less than the number of owners. • It may over-estimate the number of 'real' businesses since many self-employed are really employees, but classified as self-employed to minimise employer taxes (see Case study 2 on Dragonfly Consulting). Other self-employed are just people working part time for 'pin money'.

Table 6.1 continued

Measure	Unit of analysis	Source	Advantages	Disadvantages
The number of new enterprises registered	Business	Sales tax registration data Value Added Tax (VAT)	• This allows for the official identification of businesses. • It is likely to include all but the smallest new businesses. These have the greatest economic impact. Most tiny businesses matter little in aggregate terms, either to overall tax contributions or in the competitive process.	• Although only the very smallest businesses are excluded, the number of such businesses can be considerable. So, if the purpose is to estimate accurately the number of businesses the measure may be highly imperfect. • There is an incentive on the part of the business owner to have businesses with sales just below the registration threshold; or to create many businesses each of which is below the sales threshold; or perhaps to not register at all (Onji 2009). • The thresholds vary between countries and over time, making it difficult to make inter-country comparisons. This also impacts on individual countries because varying thresholds make comparisons over time difficult. • New businesses may be indistinguishable from mergers, acquisitions or subsidiaries.
The number of new companies registered	Business	Company incorporation data	• Data is generally available on new company registrations. • Creating a limited liability company reflects evidence of a serious business which is recognised across countries. • Whilst it may exclude many very tiny businesses, these are likely to have only very modest economic significance and so their exclusion is of limited aggregate economic value. • The vast majority of those businesses that do not start as companies transfer to this legal form once they become economically significant.	• Only a small proportion of new businesses are limited liability companies. • Tax incentives for incorporation may lead business owners to switch from a sole trader or a partnership into limited liability status. This just changes the proportions of incorporated and unincorporated businesses (see Case study 8 on small business taxation). • Some companies are created for tax avoidance or evasion purposes. • The cost of creating a limited company varies markedly between countries and so influences the extent to which it is valid to make international comparisons.
The number of new business bank accounts opened	Business	New business bank account registrations	• Most businesses in the world need banks to undertake financial transactions and banks have a commercial incentive to ensure the data are up to date and accurate. • It will include new businesses that are too small to be included in the official registration data.	• If the data are compiled by one bank, they have to be 'scaled up' based on their known market share. This market share may be inaccurate. • Businesses transferring from other banks are included and so will inflate the figures. There is potential, therefore, for 'double counting' small businesses (see Chapter 17). • Individuals may use their personal account as a business account without telling the bank. • International comparisons are difficult since banks may be unwilling to make such statistics publicly available.

better captures the bulk of economic activity in an economy. This is in contrast to GEM and self-employment data which may give a better measure of 'entrepreneurial activity' by the working population.

Finally, Table 6.1 identifies bank data as the fifth measure. The great merit of this data is that banks have a commercial incentive to ensure that their data is comprehensive and timely. The only, relatively minor, disadvantage of the data is that it may imperfectly measure businesses that switch between banks. However, survey evidence suggests that actual switching is only about 2–4 per cent annually in the UK (Fraser 2005; Cosh *et al.* 2009). On balance, therefore, for the UK, bank-based data is often superior to other sources.

Comparing the five measures

To demonstrate the differing results from each of these five measures, Figure 6.6 shows data for the UK. It takes the five measures – self-reported business start ups as used in GEM, new

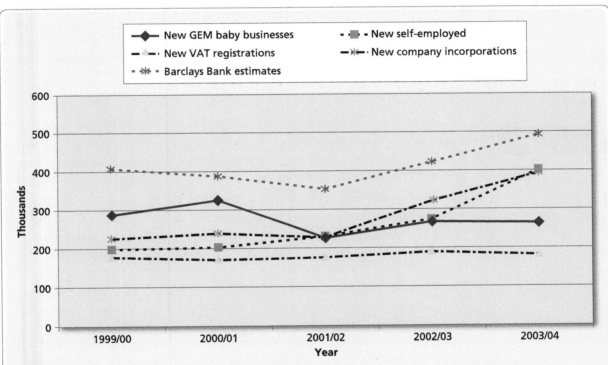

NOTES:
1   The GEM figures are based on our estimates. The 2004 GEM Report on p. 17 estimates 2,349,000 TEA participants. It also provides TEA rates for 2000–4. Paul Reynolds, in correspondence, estimates that about one third of TEA participants are baby businesses trading for between 3 and 42 months. Our assumption is that the baby start up was equally distributed over three years. No account is taken of GEM referring to UK and the other indicators of new business formation in Table 3.2 referring to GB.
    Hence, GEM TEA/3 = Babies and Babies/3 = Annual Start Ups/ New Business Formation.
2   The Barclays figures are for England and Wales. Based upon the VAT Registrations data, the figures are an approximately scaled-up number to also include Scotland and Northern Ireland to make them comparable with the other data sources.

Sources: Company incorporations data: Companies in 2003/4, Department of Trade and Industry; VAT new registrations: Small Business Service Statistics; Self-employment data from Labour Force Survey; GEM new/baby businesses data; and Barclays Bank.

| Figure 6.6 | The five measures compared, 1999–2004 |

entrants to self-employment, new business registrations, new company incorporations and new bank business bank account data from Barclays Bank. It then shows both the differences in the absolute numbers of businesses involved and how these varied over the relatively short period 1999/2000 to 2003/4.

The scale of the differences is reflected most clearly in the data for 2004. In that year Barclays Bank estimated there were 492,000 new businesses. The number of self-employed entrants was 401,000. There were also 390,000 company incorporations. In contrast, the GEM data suggests that there were 263,000 new businesses. The lowest figure is for new VAT registrations at 181,000.

The variation of the five measures over the five years is also striking. It seems to tell us fundamentally different stories about new business formation or new business creation over this period. In contrast with the broadly flat pattern on VAT registrations, and an almost continuous rise in company incorporations, the GEM data shows considerable year to year volatility but little overall change. The Barclays Bank estimates for 2001–2 onwards show a similar steep rise to that for company incorporations. However, in the 1999/2000 to 2001/2 period they declined at a time when company incorporations rose slightly.

The clear lesson is that, whilst all five measures are used to reflect new business formation, because they all measure different aspects of the phenomenon, none can claim to be definitive. As in all aspects of statistics, it is important to be clear what is the focus of interest, and to recognise that, in this case, there is no ideal measure of the *number* of new businesses created. Nevertheless, our judgement remains that, for the UK, the bank data best captures the scale of new business formation, but no international comparisons are possible.

Questions

One standardised approach to defining a new business was developed by Djankov *et al.* (2002). They used the following definition for comparing new businesses set up in developing and developed economies:

- Performs general industrial or commercial activities.
- It is a domestically owned limited liability company.
- Its capital is subscribed in cash (not in-kind contributions) and is the higher of (i) 10 times GDP per capita in 1999 or (ii) the minimum capital requirement for the particular type of business entity.
- It rents (i.e. does not own) land and business premises.
- It has between 5 and 50 employees one month after the commencement of operations, all of whom are nationals.
- It has turnover of up to 10 times its start-up capital, and it does not qualify for investment incentives.

They make these assumptions because they wish to make international comparisons between the costs and time it takes for a new business to be registered. What do you think about how useful this definition is? Does it help understand the nature of small business start ups in an economy?

Measuring the rate of start ups

Quantifying the number of new businesses is not the only issue involved in attempting to measure new business formation. A second important consideration is calculating the start-up *rate*. This is important because we need to need to 'normalise' new businesses to take account of regional and national differences so as to decide on whether Luxembourg or India is the more entrepreneurial.

Vale (2006) neatly identifies the problems in estimating the start-up rate for a given region or country. In order to identify the start-up rate, some measure of new businesses has to be taken. This subsequently has to be divided by some measure of population to arrive at a percentage rate. In other words, we need an appropriate numerator (measure of new businesses) and denominator (population). There are a range of factors that impact on the numerator, denominator and on both the numerator and denominator. In terms of the numerator, Vale (2006) identifies the following issues:

- **Timing** – at what point in the creation process is a start up measured?

- **Purity** – to what extent are 'pure' births distinguished from simple changes in ownership structure?

- **Periodicity** – over what period are start ups measured, and how does this affect the measurement of very short-lived businesses?

As we have already seen, such factors influence the estimate of the quantity of new start ups. Vale (2006) also shows that these can have dramatic impacts on the calculation of the start-up rate. To illustrate this, he shows French data from the Agence pour la Création d'Entreprises (APCE). These data separate out total creations (new business starts) from business start ups that have been created 'out of nothing' ('*ex nihilio*'). As Figure 6.7 shows, the impact can be significant with 'total creations' being around one-third greater than *ex nihilio* creations.

In terms of the denominator, Vale identified the following two issues:

- **Population** – business or people? Here there is a clear choice. If the comparison is between two areas, the favoured measure may be dividing new businesses by the working population (Anyadike-Danes *et al.* 2005) to normalise the number of new businesses. Alternatively, if the focus is on examining economic activity – such as prices, output, profitability, or productivity – then a sectoral analysis may be more appropriate, i.e. dividing new enterprises by the number of establishments or enterprises in the sector.

- **Temporal basis** – again the period of time during which the counting of businesses takes place will have an impact because populations vary over time.

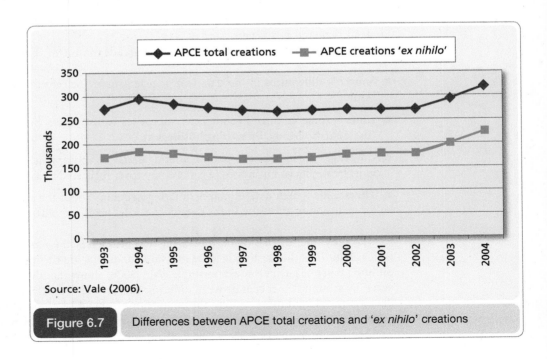

Source: Vale (2006).

| Figure 6.7 | Differences between APCE total creations and '*ex nihilo*' creations |

Table 6.2	UK stock and working population-based rates, 2007				
	VAT registrations in 2006	Stock of VAT registered businesses (start 2007)	Working-age population (16+)	Stock rate (new businesses/stock of businesses)	Population rate (new businesses/ 10,000 working-age population)
London	34,825	309,225	6,067,400	11.26	57
North West	17,920	186,045	5,531,000	9.63	32
North East	4,630	49,435	2,086,300	9.37	22
South East	28,680	306,920	6,656,300	9.34	43
Yorkshire and The Humber	12,900	139,970	4,163,200	9.22	31
East Midlands	12,320	134,195	3,544,800	9.18	35
West Midlands	14,800	164,810	4,309,200	8.98	34
East	17,495	196,480	4,528,800	8.90	39
Scotland	11,825	136,890	4,195,100	8.64	28
South West	15,745	183,420	4,201,800	8.58	37
Wales	6,625	84,995	2,404,700	7.79	28
Northern Ireland	4,445	64,365	1,361,500	6.91	33

Source: BERR (2008).

Table 6.2 illustrates these differences, particularly in relation to the differences in the measure of population. It shows the VAT registration rates, the stock of VAT-registered businesses and the populations for each of the nine English regions and Scotland, Wales and Northern Ireland. Table 6.2 shows the London region has the highest rates of business start up, both in terms of the stock and population rates. Other than in this region, there would seem to be little or no correlation between the stock and working population-based measures. For instance, the North East of England has the third highest business stock measure but the lowest working population-based measure. Northern Ireland, meanwhile, has the lowest stock-based measure but a working population-based measure higher than the North East of England, Scotland and Wales.

Vale also identified that both the numerator and denominator shared similar issues:

● **Source** – differences in the data (e.g. register, survey or census) may produce differing results.

● **Units** – some countries count new enterprises whilst others count new establishments (these can be created by existing businesses).

● **Coverage** – each dataset embodies differing decisions about what is included and excluded in its treatment of businesses (e.g. may only cover registered businesses).

● **Thresholds** – each dataset makes differing decisions about the acceptable size threshold for inclusion or exclusion in the dataset (e.g. sales tax thresholds).

As with the earlier discussion on measuring new businesses, these factors again raise further issues about how the start up is to be measured and what are the implications of excluding differing types of businesses. For example, Vale (2006) shows that the start-up rate in the US varies by around 10 per cent between differing data sets. He puts this down to how differing data sets treat 'new businesses' and the populations from which the start-up rates are drawn.

In summary, great care has to be taken with interpreting data which seeks to answer the apparently simple question 'How able is my region/country to "deliver" new businesses?' We have shown that very different answers emerge, which depend upon the measures of new business formation chosen and the population base upon which rates are calculated.

Summary

This chapter has examined three aspects of new businesses. First, it has assessed evidence which seeks to identify if new businesses are important for economic growth. Prior research has argued that new businesses are a source of innovation and a productive route for individuals to follow. It has suggested that new businesses replace inefficient businesses and provide discipline to existing businesses. There is good evidence that new businesses serve an important function in this competitive process. However, the chapter also identified that the picture was not uniform. It would appear that some entrants, particularly large ones, are more productive than the 'typical' small entrant. Equally, there is evidence that new businesses are not a panacea or 'cure all' for all the problems facing regional or national economies. This is primarily because there continues to be a lack of clarity about the actual direction of causality. Is it new businesses that cause economic growth or is it economic growth that causes new business activity? It is *not* justified to simply infer that creation of more enterprises makes a country more wealthy.

The second section of the chapter discussed the problems of defining a new business. Our favoured definition was:

*A new business is a new transacting entity that did **not** exist in a previous time period, is **not** owned by an existing business, and is **not** a simple change of ownership.*

Third, the chapter discussed the statistical and conceptual difficulties both in arriving at a measure of new businesses and computing an appropriate start-up rate measure. What emerges from this discussion is that, whether data are collected at local, regional, national or international levels, there is no uniformly accepted definition of a new business. That problem then increases when governments use data, which has often been collected for other purposes, to estimate the number of new businesses. Similarly, the computation of a rate of new business formation adds further uncertainty since the population used as the denominator in the ratio may also be imperfectly specified.

There is, therefore, no single, uniformly 'best' measure of new business activity that fits all situations. Instead, the strengths and limitations of the data have to be assessed and related to their requirements.

Questions for discussion

1 Assess the advantages and disadvantages of using data collected by government for tax purposes as a measure of the number of new businesses.

2 When measuring rates of new business formation, what is the appropriate denominator and why?

3 The UK has five main sources of data on new businesses. What are they and which do you think is the most valid?

4 What is the Global Entrepreneurship Monitor (GEM) and what contributions has it made to our understanding of entrepreneurship?

5 How enterprising is your country/region? What information would you use to decide and why?

References

Acs, Z.J. and Armington, C. (2004) 'Employment Growth and Entrepreneurial Activity in Cities', *Regional Studies,* 38(8), 911–27.

Acs, Z.J., Audretsch, D.B. and Feldman, M.P. (1994) 'R&D Spillovers and Recipient Firm Size', *Review of Economics and Statistics,* 76, 336–40.

Anyadike-Danes, M., Hart, M. and O'Reilly, M. (2005) 'Watch that Space!: The County Hierarchy of Firm Births and Deaths in the UK, 1980–1999', *Small Business Economics,* 25(3), 273–92.

Armington, C. and Acs, Z.J. (2004) 'Job Creation and Persistence in Services and Manufacturing', *Journal of Evolutionary Economics,* 14(3), 309–25.

Audretsch, D.B. and Feldman, M.P. (1996) 'R&D Spillovers and the Geography of Innovation and Production', *American Economic Review,* 86, 630–40.

Baldwin, J.R. (1998) 'Were Small Producers the Engines of Growth in the Canadian Manufacturing Sector in the 1980s?', *Small Business Economics,* 10(4), 349–64.

Baldwin, J., Bian, L., Dupuy, R. and Gellatly, G. (2000) *Failure Rates for New Canadian Firms: New Perspectives on Entry and Exit.* Ottawa: Statistics Canada.

BERR (2008) *SME Statistics.* http://stats.berr.gov.uk/ed/sme/.

Bertrand, M. and Kramarz, F. (2002) 'Does Entry Regulation Hinder Job Creation?: Evidence from the French Retail Industry', *Quarterly Journal of Economics,* 117(4), 1369–413.

Blackburn, R. and Ram, M. (2006) 'Fix or Fixation?: The Contributions and Limitations of Entrepreneurship and Small Firms to Combating Social Exclusion', *Entrepreneurship and Regional Development,* 18(1), 73–89.

Callejon, M. and Segarra, A. (1999) 'Business Dynamics and Efficiency in Industries and Regions: The Case of Spain', *Small Business Economics,* 13(4), 253–71.

Carree, M.A., van Stel, A.J., Thurik, A.R. and Wennekers, A.R.M. (2002) 'Economic Development and Business Ownership: An Analysis Using Data of 23 OECD Countries in the Period 1976–1996', *Small Business Economics,* 19(3), 271–90.

Carree, M.A., van Stel, A.J., Thurik, A.R. and Wennekers, A.R.M. (2007) 'The Relationship between Economic Development and Business Ownership Revisited', *Entrepreneurship and Regional Development,* 19(3), 281–91.

Cosh, A., Hughes, A. and Bullock, A. (2009) *SME Finance and Innovation in the Current Economic Crisis.* Cambridge: Centre for Business Research, University of Cambridge.

Djankov, S., La Porta, R., Lopez-de-Silanes, F. and Schleifer, A. (2002) 'The Regulation of Entry', *Quarterly Journal of Economics,* CXVII(1), 1–37.

Disney, R., Haskel, J. and Heden, Y. (2003) 'Restructuring and Productivity Growth in UK Manufacturing', *Economic Journal,* 113(489), 666–94.

Foster, L., Haltiwanger, J. and Krizan, C.J. (2006) 'Market Selection, Reallocation and Restructuring in the US Retail Trade Sector in the 1990s', *Review of Economics and Statistics,* 88(4), 748–58.

Fraser, S. (2005) *Finance for Small and Medium-sized Enterprises.* Coventry: Warwick Business School.

Fritsch, M., and Mueller, P. (2004) 'The Effects of New Business Formation on Regional Development over Time', *Regional Studies,* 38(8), 961–76.

Geroski, P.A. (1995) 'What Do We Know about Entry?', *International Journal of Industrial Organization,* 13(4), 421–40.

Greene, F.J., Mole, K.M. and Storey, D.J. (2008) *Three Decades of Enterprise Culture: Entrepreneurship, Economic Regeneration and Public Policy.* Basingstoke: Palgrave Macmillan.

Jensen, J.B., McGuckin, R.H. and Stiroh, K.J. (2001) 'The Impact of Vintage and Survival on Productivity: Evidence from Cohorts of US Manufacturing Plants', *Review of Economics and Statistics,* 83(2), 323–32.

Mueller, P., van Stel, A. and Storey, D.J. (2008) 'The Effects of New Firm Formation on Regional Development over Time: The Case of Great Britain', *Small Business Economics,* 30(1), 59–71.

Onji, K. (2009) 'The Response of Firms to Eligibility Thresholds: Evidence from the Japanese Value Added Tax', *Journal of Public Economics*, 93(5–6), 766–75.

Porter, M.E. (1995) 'The Competitive Advantage of the Inner City', *Harvard Business Review*, 73(3), 55–71.

Storey, D.J., Keasey, K., Watson, R. and Wynarczyk, P. (1987) *The Performance of Small Firms.* London: Croom Helm.

Thurik, A.R., Carree, M.A., van Stel, A. and Audretsch, D.B. (2008) 'Does Self-employment Reduce Unemployment?', *Journal of Business Venturing*, 23(6), 673–86.

Vale, S. (2006) *The International Comparability of Business Start-up Rates.* Paris: OECD.

van Praag, C.M., and Versloot, P.H. (2007) 'What is the Value of Entrepreneurship?: A Review of Recent Research', *Small Business Economics,* 29, 351–82.

van Stel, A. (2005) 'COMPENDIA: Harmonizing Business Ownership Data across Countries and over Time', *International Entrepreneurship and Management Journal*, 1(1), 105–23.

van Stel, A.J. and Storey, D.J. (2004) 'The Link between Firm Births and Job Creation: Is There a Upas Tree Effect?', *Regional Studies,* 38(8), 893–909.

Westhead, P., Ucbasaran, D. and Wright, M. (2005) 'Experience and Cognition: Do Novice, Serial and Portfolio Entrepreneurs Differ?', *International Small Business Journal*, 23(1), 72–98.

7 Nascent entrepreneurship and social networks

Key learning objectives

By the end of this chapter you should:

- Understand the importance of nascent entrepreneurship and social networks to the business start-up process
- Be able to critically evaluate nascent entrepreneurship and social networks.

> I wanted to be an editor or a journalist, I wasn't really interested in being an entrepreneur, but I soon found I had to become an entrepreneur in order to keep my magazine going.

Richard Branson, founder of Virgin

7.1 Introduction

In Chapter 6, we considered the importance of new businesses and the issues in defining and measuring such businesses. In this chapter, we will examine two approaches principally used by organisational theorists to explain the business start-up process (see also Chapter 2). The first approach is based upon identifying the role of nascent entrepreneurs in that process. These are individuals involved in an attempt to start up a business. The central question asked here is: *how* do individuals set up in business? To answer this question, we examine both the theoretical and empirical evidence on nascent entrepreneurship.

A second approach of organisational theorists is to examine the social processes involved in setting up a business. The focus here is on the social relationships (networks) that individuals make use of when establishing their business. In short, how do individuals use their social networks to help with business creation? We explore the basis of this issue and discuss the advantages and disadvantages of the social network approach.

7.2 Nascent entrepreneurship

The focus on nascent entrepreneurs (those in the process of setting up a business, usually for the first time) is the result of an interest in how organisations emerge. This is important because countries throughout the world are interested in easing the transition involved in turning a business from a 'dream' into a 'reality'. For this reason, many countries have programmes that directly seek to raise the awareness and skills of people thinking of setting up a business. Universities, too, nearly all now offer courses in setting up and running a new business. Katz (2003), for example, identified that the number of US university entrepreneurship courses had increased from around 300 in the early 1980s to around 2,200 courses 30 years later (see Chapters 19–21 on public policy for further information).

There are three questions that are typically asked in relation to nascent entrepreneurship. These are:

1 How do individuals go about creating a business?

2 What actually triggers them to go about starting a business?

3 How many individuals are actively involved?

This section examines each of these questions in turn.

Question 1 How do individuals go about creating a business?

The best known model for explaining organisational emergence is provided by Katz and Gartner (1988). This suggests four main 'properties' of emerging organisations:

- **Intentionality** – those seeking to set up a new business have to form some intentions towards explicitly setting up their business.

- **Resources** – resources (e.g. workers, finance) have to be identified, collected, assembled and used.

- **Boundary** – the creation of deliberate psychological (e.g. telling family or friends) or official (e.g. registering a business) boundaries.

- **Exchange** – making transactions (e.g. sales).

Katz and Gartner argue that successful organisational emergence is dependent on developing these four properties. Brush *et al.* (2008) have identified 26 'proxies' for these four properties. These are set out in Table 7.1. For example, an individual may follow a logical process. Hence, they may begin by having the intention to set up a business. They may, therefore,

Table 7.1	Proxies for Katz and Gartner's Four Properties of Emerging Organisations

Intentionality	Resources	Boundary	Exchange
Prepared business plan	Organised start-up team	Opened bank account	Started marketing efforts
Identified opportunity	Applied for a patent	Applied for a phone listing	Made sale
Prepared financials	Bought raw materials	Applied for a credit rating listing	Reached profit
Started working full-time	Bought equipment	Filed income tax	Paid salaries
Taken workshops	Saved money		Paid social security taxes
	Invested money		Paid insurance taxes
	Asked for funds		
	Applied for credit		
	Arranged for childcare		
	Hired employees		
	Developed product/service		

Source: Brush *et al.* (2008).

commit full time to the business and undertake some training. They may then decide to buy equipment and hire employees. Subsequently, they may open a bank account and seek out a phone listing. Finally, they may make sales and pay appropriate taxes.

The reality is that *how* organisations actually emerge is likely to be very different from one case to another. Reynolds and Miller (1992) examined 3,000 established businesses in the US. They found that the emergence or 'gestation' of these businesses showed substantial differences in the length and in the pattern of 'organisational emergence'. There was also no evident order to the sequencing of activities. Some people who had set up a new business had done so by first making sales (exchange) and then working 'backwards'. A good example of this is a hobbyist. Someone with a passion for making clothes may find that these prove popular with friends and family. They sell a limited number and subsequently decide to set up in business. The heterogeneity of the start-up process was confirmed by Carter *et al.* (1996) who looked at 71 nascent entrepreneurs. They, again, found no evident logical pattern to how organisations emerge.

Sarasvathy (2001) has argued that organisational emergence is not always a causal, logical process. To illustrate this she uses the analogy of how a chef cooks a meal. In a causal process, the chef follows a set recipe. If the chef does not have the necessary ingredients, she will go out and get them first so that she can follow the directions contained in the recipe. The alternative approach is to follow what Sarasvathy calls an 'effectuation' process. Here the key difference is that people take the ingredients that they have in their kitchen cupboard and then proceed to *imagine* how their meal should look given the ingredients they have. Once they have successfully realised how and what they are going to cook, they then proceed to cook the meal. This is rather like someone having resources (e.g. money or equipment) and wondering how to make use of them successfully.

Brush *et al.* (2008) confirm that there is a considerable variety of ways in which organisations emerge. They specifically test for organisational emergence using Katz and Gartner's (1988) model. They find that '. . . organizing a new venture is not a patterned or linear process but rather is simultaneous, messy and iterative' (p. 548). In other words, there might be a recipe but it may not be followed attentively or at all depending on the ingredients and the way that someone chooses to set up a business.

However, it may not be terribly complicated as the box below on Innocent Smoothies shows.

| Illustration | How Innocent Smoothies started up |

In the summer of 1998 when we had developed our first smoothie recipes but were still nervous about giving up our proper jobs, we bought £500 worth of fruit, turned it into smoothies and sold them from a stall at a little music festival in London. We put up a big sign saying 'Do you think we should give up our jobs to make these smoothies?' and put out a bin saying 'YES' and a bin saying 'NO' and asked people to put the empty bottle in the right bin. At the end of the weekend the 'YES' bin was full so we went in the next day and resigned.

http://www.innocentdrinks.co.uk/us/?Page=our_story (accessed 16 Sept. 2008).

The founders of Innocent Drinks let their first ever customers decide whether they should give up their day jobs.

Question 2 What actually triggers them to go about starting a business?

The second typical question asked is what triggers nascent entrepreneurship? Notice here that the unit of analysis shifts from the 'in-vitro', 'gestating' or 'emerging' organisation to that of the individual. The interest is in understanding why some people are actively involved in setting up a business and others are not.

The most common way of defining this is to use the following Global Entrepreneurship Monitor (GEM) survey question: 'Are you, alone or with others, currently trying to start a new business?' The advantage of this question is that it is easily understood by those asked it and, because of the prominence of GEM, widely accepted as a workable definition.

Studies specifically examining nascent entrepreneurship tend to look at two types of questions.

1) What distinguishes nascent entrepreneurs from the general population?

Delmar and Davidsson (2000) found that Swedish nascent entrepreneurs were more likely to be male, be young, have had prior self-employment experience, better education levels, more management experience and higher income levels compared with the general population. Davidsson and Honig (2003) found that parental self-employment background, encouragement by friends/family and having close friends/family in business lead to a higher incidence of nascent entrepreneurship activity.

Koellinger *et al.* (2007) found, in their cross-national study of 18 countries, that nascent entrepreneurs display overconfidence in their assessments of their skills, abilities and knowledge. Such optimism distinguishes them from those not involved in the start-up process. Carter *et al.* (2003), however, found it difficult to distinguish the reasons why US adults created a new business. They found little difference between nascents and the general population in terms of factors such as 'self-realisation' (e.g. the ability to lead and motivate others), financial success (e.g. size of income), innovation (e.g. the ability to develop an idea for a product) and independence.

In essence, this suggests there are differences between the general population and nascent entrepreneurs. However, these differences are similar to the differences between 'actual' new business founders and the general population. This begs the question of what is the economic value of studying nascent entrepreneurs? Since nascent entrepreneurs appear similar to actual new owners, is it not more appropriate to study people *actually* creating economic value than those *considering* creating economic value? From an economic perspective, it is unclear whether those who do not go on to set up a new business have any significance.

A second criticism of the study of nascent entrepreneurs is that the number of new businesses created is perhaps unrelated, or only weakly related, to economic development because only a tiny proportion of new businesses have a significant economic impact. Unless the study of nascent entrepreneurs can provide insights into the characteristics of these businesses, either at start up or early in their life, then studying nascent entrepreneurs does not add to our economic understanding. Indeed, it may be that focusing upon the number of businesses created, or even the businesses in gestation, only diverts attention away from the real role of entrepreneurship which is to enable businesses to grow quickly, enhance productivity and so transform the economic landscape.

2) Why is it that some nascent entrepreneurs make the transition into business and others do not?

The focus of this second question is on distinguishing those nascent entrepreneurs who go on to create a new business from those who abandon their attempt or are still trying to set up their business. van Gelderen *et al.* (2006) identifies Dutch nascent entrepreneurs who went on to actually start a business – compared with those who abandoned their nascent business idea – were more likely to be full-time in the business and be manufacturers. They also find that successful nascents used less money to set up the business and chose lower risk options. Parker and Belghitar (2006) report – using US data – that financial capital (e.g. established credit with suppliers, owning a home) is an important factor in explaining the transition into operating a business. Henley (2007) also points to UK differences between those who aspire to set up a business and those that actually make the transition. He finds that those that aspire to set up are more likely to come from an ethnic minority, are divorced and have lower education attainment levels.

Again, however, the criticism is that it would be a better use of time and resources to study those that actually start a new business. On balance, the differences between those that remain nascent, those that make the transition to new business status and those abandon their efforts are small. For example, Henley (2007) finds that both those that aspire and those that actually do make the transition into self-employment are similar. Again, this suggests the 'returns' to studying 'nascents' have been modest to date.

Question 3 How many individuals are actively involved?

The third reason for studying nascent entrepreneurship is that it gives a better understanding of the scale of entrepreneurial activity. It does so in three ways:

1 It is *people* who *do* business not businesses. Official statistics on entrepreneurial activity are based on businesses. This is likely to under-estimate entrepreneurial activity, if only because people may own more than one business.

2 Nascent entrepreneurship is a fundamental part of human activity. Reynolds *et al.* (2004) suggest that in the US 10.1 million people said they were attempting to set up a businesses. This means that nascent entrepreneurship is a more common phenomenon than birth or marriage in the US. Reynolds (2005) has further claimed that 'up to half a billion people in the world are actively involved in either the start-up process or in managing a new business' (p. 362).

3 Studying nascent entrepreneurship potentially gives a clearer understanding of how individuals make the transition to new business formation. This is important because, as we noted in Chapter 6, there is believed to be a relationship between new businesses and economic growth and development. So, by understanding nascent entrepreneurship, the hope may be that the barriers (e.g. regulation or finance) that prevent people from setting up their new business are either lowered or removed. Table 7.2 shows that there are

Table 7.2	What happens to nascent entrepreneurs after one year?			
Outcome	**PSED**	**Carter et al. (1996)**	**van Gelderen et al. (2001)**	**Diochon et al. (2003)**
Still nascent	159 (47%)	21 (30%)	89 (27%)	51 (39%)
Operating	112 (33%)	34 (48%)	155 (47%)	45 (34%)
Gave Up	69 (20%)	16 (22%)	86 (26%)	36 (27%)
Total	340 (100%)	71 (100%)	330 (100%)	132* (100%)
Country	US	US	Netherlands	Canada

Numbers of cases appear as the first cell entries, with sample percentages in parentheses.
Source: Parker and Belghitar (2006).

different outcomes for nascent entrepreneurial activity. These vary internationally (see also van Stel *et al.* 2005). The issue is what motivates these differences and how can they be changed.

A further criticism of the study of nascent entrepreneurship is that it fails to properly specify the transition into setting up a new business. At its simplest, the criticism is that intention is a poor proxy for behaviour. Parker and Belghitar (2006) suggest that amongst 'nascents' there are a number that might be better called 'dreamers'.

Mueller (2006) also provides an interesting perspective on nascent entrepreneurship status. Her data allowed her to ask German individuals to estimate how likely they were to become self-employed in the following year. Some people classified themselves as being 100 per cent likely to be self-employed in the following year whilst others classified themselves as being anything from 90 per cent to 0 per cent likely to be self-employed. She then found differing results depending on the level of intention. So, those with 100 per cent intentions were more likely to one year later become actual new business owners, compared with those with lower scores. The problem is that the GEM question is black and white: you are either intending to set up a business or you are not. This makes it hard to easily identify if someone is 'serious' or merely a dreamer.

But, even if nascent status was uniform, is it true that individuals have to form an intention prior to setting up a new business? The simple answer is no. Katz (1990) identified that some people who actually start up a new business had no intention of setting up a business. Henley (2007) confirms this. He finds, using longitudinal data from the British Household Panel Survey, that nearly half of people who become self-employed did not declare a year earlier their intention to become self-employed or embark on any formal training.

Mueller (2006) reported similar findings. She found that 66 per cent of those who actually become an entrepreneur never classified themselves as 'nascents'. In other words, the decision to become a business owner was taken 'at the last minute' and so such individuals never appeared as 'nascents'. The implication of this is that examining self-styled nascents could easily provide a biased understanding of how people come to create new businesses.

There is also the likelihood that there is always an underlying cultural bias in questioning intentions. Hayton *et al.*'s (2002) review of the relationship between different cultures and entrepreneurship suggests that there is a wide body of evidence that points to cultural differences. Therefore, it would be surprising if there were not major differences between respondents in different countries being willing to report to an outsider whether they were actually preparing to set up a business.

In summary, this section began by introducing Katz and Gartner's (1988) model of the four properties of organisational emergence. We also saw that there was no uniform pattern or sequence to how organisations emerge. Sarathasavy (2001) argues that this can be achieved by both linear (following a recipe) and non-linear (e.g. looking in the cupboard) processes.

We also asked what was distinctive about nascent entrepreneurs. The evidence suggested that there were differences between nascent entrepreneurs and the general population. These differences were, however, similar to the differences between new business founders and the general population. Evidence also identified that there were few differences between those nascent entrepreneurs who made the transition into setting up a new business and those who did not. The criticism here was that there was little point in studying nascent entrepreneurship because there was no guarantee that nascents generated economic value. The argument is that it is far better to concentrate on those individuals who actually had made the transition into enterprise and were growing quickly.

Finally, we identified that the scale of entrepreneurial activity is far greater if we examine nascent as well as actual entrepreneurship. This is, arguably, an important endeavour because new businesses are important to economic growth. The criticism of this is that nascent entrepreneurship is a poor proxy for the transition into setting up a new business. Some people have a doubtful intention to actually start up a new business and some never acknowledge that they were nascent entrepreneurs. The criticism, therefore, is that focusing on nascent entrepreneurship is an inexact mechanism for understanding the process of new business creation and of questionable economic value.

7.3 Social networks

In the last section, Table 7.2 showed that between one half and two thirds of nascent entrepreneurs had either abandoned their attempt to set up a business or were still in the process of actively attempting to set up their business two years later. One reason for these high percentages is that these 'failed' or 'failing' nascent entrepreneurs may lack the necessary human capital attributes. Human capital attributes typically refer to factors such as the education and background experiences of the individual. A second explanation is that individuals lack the financial resources necessary to buy capital equipment (e.g. machines), fund their day-to-day living costs or pay for market research. Organisational theorists recognise that these are important aspects of the new business formation 'process'.

However, organisational theorists suggest that there is a third type of capital that is important in explaining the new business activities. This is social capital. Social capital may be defined as '. . . the sum of the actual and potential resources embedded within, available through, and derived from the network of relationships possessed by an individual or social unit. Social capital thus comprises both the network and the assets that may be mobilised through that network' (Nahapiet and Ghoshal 1998: 243).

Organisational theorists hold that social capital and the networks that are the basis of such capital are important in explaining new business formation because, fundamentally, setting up a business is a social process. Besides the employment of human and financial capital, individuals access, and make use of, their social resources to establish the business. Drawing upon such resources enables a business to overcome the 'liability of newness' (Stinchcombe 1965) which reflects the lack of credibility to customers and suppliers of a business with no 'track record'. Nascent and new entrepreneurs, for example, have to be seen as being 'legitimate' before they can effectively trade (Aldrich and Fiol 1994). The iterative process that the new or nascent enterprise undergoes to overcome this lack of credibility is referred to as the 'credibility carousel' (Birley 2002). It is reproduced in Figure 7.1.

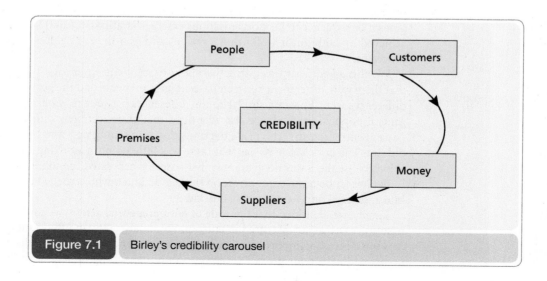

| Figure 7.1 | Birley's credibility carousel |

In essence, what Birley (2002) suggests is that individuals use their networks to gain 'legitim-ation' and resources for their nascent business. Without the benefit of such support, the implication is that very many nascent businesses would be stillborn.

Hoang and Antoncic (2003) provide a useful overview of the ways nascent and existing entrepreneurs use networks to support the development of their business. In their view: '. . . social networks are defined by a set of actors (individuals or organisations) and a set of linkages between the actors' (Hoang and Antoncic 2003: 168). They go on to identify three areas of networks that are particularly appropriate to entrepreneurship.

Network content. by this they mean how entrepreneurs access resources. This may be in terms of financial or physical resources but more typically it is intangible resources such as advice, information or emotional support. For example, because setting up a new business is often stressful, individuals may rely on their family and friends for emotional assurance and seek advice from banks and accountants on ways to properly store and account for their money.

Illustration	Birley's credibility carousel

Birley (2002) uses the example of Peter, who is a television producer who needs funding:

Peter is a producer of television programmes working for one of the major companies. He has a vision for a series about the development of the brain that he **knows** will work and is convinced that it could command major international sales. But he is tired of working for others and wants to use this as the foundation for a new, independent production company. He also knows that he will need £3 m because that is how much the series will cost to make. He has heard that there is no point in approaching venture capitalists since they are not interested in project financing and, anyway, he is not asking for enough money for them to be interested. So, he goes along to his bank manager and broaches the possibility of a loan. Of course, he is laughed 'out of court'. The bank manager says . . . 'That is much more than I can lend on the security of your house (assuming that your wife would agree) . . . and, anyway, who else is involved in this, . . . and, most important, your business plan is just a dream . . . where is the order?'

Undeterred, Peter approaches a couple of producers in other companies with his 'concept'. They express interest. They usually do. It is a way of keeping their options open! But they are not able to commit without a more detailed 'Proof of Concept', and a fully resourced plan. In other words, what is the evidence that this will syndicate worldwide, what is the technical team that Peter plans to use, who is going to 'front it', and who will provide the scientific support. So, he approaches the acknowledged world expert on the brain, the best animators, technicians and camera crew. To a person, they ask (or imply) 'What is in it for me, how do I know you can make this work, and where do you plan to set up the studio?' Still undeterred, he scours the available studio facilities, but the landlords are not interested in talking until Peter is prepared to sign a lease, produce guarantees, and pay a deposit. He also talks to camera and computer manufacturers that he has dealt with previously about the arrangements for leasing or buying equipment, but finds a very different reaction when they realise that this is a new venture. No longer can he negotiate special discounts and credit. Now they want full price and cash up front.

. . . In order to have a chance of moving forward, he needs to persuade someone to believe in him and to break the credibility carousel. For example, the world expert on the brain commits to the idea and begins to persuade others, his previous employers to agree to let him use an old studio, or a rich maiden aunt agrees to provide bank guarantees. Slowly, people begin to believe in him and the project gains credibility. It also gains more reliable data.

How did he do it? Almost certainly through his personal network, the people who know him personally or have been introduced to him by someone they trust. For example, the world brain expert just happens to play golf with his father! Now the dream is becoming a reality. More importantly, the business concept is becoming a business plan, with increasingly credible assumptions and costs.

Source: Birley (2002: 138–40).

Network governance. The key word here is trust. Instead of relationships being governed by money, organisational theorists hold that a far more prevalent and useful 'glue' is that of mutual trust. This 'allows both parties to assume that each will take actions that are predictable and mutually acceptable' (Hoang and Antoncic 2003: 170). The key benefit of a governance arrangement that relies on trust is that it makes it 'cheaper' for people to do business with each other because they do not have to monitor so closely the activities of others.

Network structure. This refers to the nature of ties that bind people together. There are strong ties and weak ties. Strong ties are close relationships that have been formed between people (e.g. family and friends) whilst weak ties are often more distant and perhaps infrequent (e.g. acquaintances). In examining these ties, organisational theorists also look at the size of the network, its density (the number of connections in relation to its potential number of connections), its diversity (mix of strong and weak ties) and where the individual sits in a network (centrality).

All of this implies that individuals use networks to reduce the cost, time and effort in setting up a business. Fundamentally, this is because individuals make use of 'socially embedded' ties with others who can provide support and guidance. Organisational theorists see this as being a more important feature of economic activity than 'market-based' interpretations. To illustrate this, the American sociologist Uzzi (1999) found that entrepreneurs who had a long-term account with a bank enjoyed favourable interest rates on their loans. He suggests that this benefit is due to the entrepreneur's close relationship with the bank manager.

From a network perspective, what is also key are the *networking* activities of individuals. Models of such processes (e.g. Larson and Starr 1993; Hite and Hesterly 2001) argue that organisational emergence is an evolutionary process. Individuals essentially move from a network of strong ties to one in which there is a greater mix of weak ties. What this involves is a process of adding ties, upgrading ties and dropping ties so that, in relation to the earlier example of Peter the television producer, there is a need for him to 'reconfigure' his network as he develops the new business (Elfring and Hulsink 2007).

Criticisms of the network approach

There are five main criticisms of the network approach: definitional issues; the compensation thesis; empirical evidence; the 'costs' of networking; and social embeddedness. We examine each of these in turn.

Definitional issues. One problem with network theory is that it ranges over differing units of analysis. The basic tension in network theory is between focusing on the individual and the business. To illustrate this, consider the three following definitions.

> '. . . social networks are defined by a set of actors (individuals or organisations) and a set of linkages between the actors' (Hoang and Antoncic 2003: 168)

> 'A network consists of single nodes (actors) and connections between these nodes (dyads), which as a whole form the structure of a network' (Witt 2004: 392)

> '. . . a firm's set of relationships with other organisations' (Perez and Sanchez 2002: 261)

These differences in focus between the individual and the business may seem to apply less to organisational emergence because the nascent business may be simply seen as an extension of the individual setting up the business. However, Witt (2004) suggests that they may not take full account of the socially embedded nature of start ups. Very many businesses are set up by more than one individual. This is not a perspective usually covered by the network approach. The reason for this is that it becomes increasingly difficult to first quantify and then disentangle the network of relationships between individual members of the entrepreneurial team.

This is largely because 'networks' or 'networking' are subjective. Chell and Baines (2000) suggest that 'networking does not have an objective existence independent of the person who is networking. It is a social construction that exists only so far as the individual understands and uses it' (p. 196). The implication is that the network content or structure may be prone to 'recall biases' by nascent or actual entrepreneurs. For example, one member of the start-up team may identify that a particular contact is a 'strong' tie whilst another may identify them as a 'weak' tie. This raises definitional issues, making it hard to appropriately capture the network relationships. If 'entrepreneurship' is a slippery concept, this is even truer for definitions of 'networking'.

Compensation thesis. Network theory usually focuses on the benefits of networking. Witt (2004) identifies that this may assume that all individuals start with the same human and financial capital. This is clearly not the case. Some people may be better able to process information perhaps because they are better educated. Some may also have larger pools of individual financial capital. Individuals who 'network' may only be doing so because they have to 'compensate' for their lack of human and financial capital. In this case, networking is not a positive choice but is forced upon individuals who recognise their resource constraints.

What is also clear is that some people are better 'networkers' than others. Networking 'talent' is unequally distributed across the population. It is, therefore, quite rational for some individuals, who recognise that they may be net-losers from networking, to avoid interacting with others, and seek to avoid those whom they view as effective networkers. As we shall show shortly, networks can be a 'two-way street' in which there are losers as well as gainers.

Empirical evidence. When entrepreneurs are asked about the reasons they set up in business, they typically list independence as a prime motive (Birley and Westhead 1994). Yet, network theory suggests that new entrepreneurs make use of extensive support and assistance. Similarly, networking often assumes that relationships with the outside world are voluntary. This is not always the case. Curran *et al.* (1993) identify that very many relationships are 'compulsory' in that in setting up or running a business individuals often have to speak to, and often be heavily reliant upon, an accountant, a bank manager or the tax authorities. Curran *et al.* also point out that individuals running their own businesses are notorious 'non-joiners' even of organisations where they might expect to meet others with whom they can network, such as trade associations.

The empirical evidence on whether 'strong' or 'weak' ties are important in starting up is also contradictory. Some have found a positive relationship between strong ties (e.g. Brüderl and Preisendörfer 1998; Jack 2005) whilst others have found weak ties to be more important (e.g. Greve and Salaff 2003). Part of the reason for the differences in findings may be the difficulty of actually identifying and quantifying the network (Johannisson 2000). In other words, it is difficult to identify the role played by networks in setting up a business.

Costs of networking. A further criticism of networking is that it appears to only consider the benefits of networking and to ignore any costs. One such cost is the 'returns to scale'. Network theory often seems to assume that the investment in networks (time, energy) results either in positive returns (increasing returns to scale) or constant returns to scale. So, the assumption is that if an individual invests 20 hours developing a relationship with a client then this is likely to reap equal (constant returns) or greater (increasing returns) returns than investing 10 hours with a client. However, in reality, it may, of course, be that such investments lead to diminishing returns. At some point, the time or energy invested – even if this could be easily matched with returns – is prone to tail off in value.

To illustrate this, Altinay (2005) found in his discussions with Turkish entrepreneurs that there was a 'darker' side to networking:

> I have been sharing business information with my friends for a long time, but to be honest with you I have never seen anything positive come out of it because every business is different.

> You should not share any information with Turkish friends. One day I was talking with my friend in the Turkish club and I told him that my café was doing very well and I will do even better in the future . . . the next thing I know . . . he bought the shop next door and opened a café.

The implication of this illustration that networks are a 'two-way street' is that for those individuals with superior networking skills the benefits may considerably outweigh the costs. For others, the reverse may be true. It is tempting to infer that individuals with strong networking skills will also have strong entrepreneurial skills but, to our knowledge, that has yet to be demonstrated.

Social embeddedness? Central to networks are trust, a willingness to respond positively to the positive actions of others (reciprocity) and the use of strong and weak ties to shorten and cheapen the cost of market participation. Earlier, to illustrate this we used the example of Uzzi (1999) who found that entrepreneurs who had a long-term account with a bank enjoyed favourable interest rates on their loans. Network theory explains this by suggesting that this is evidence of a strong tie, glued together by mutual trust built up over many years.

The alternative interpretation is that this is an *over-socialised* view of how people do business. What matters in relationships is their economic content. In the case of the entrepreneur and the bank, why the entrepreneur gets cheaper finance is because the monitoring costs of the bank are lower. Cheaper monitoring costs effectively lowers the cost of finance because the bank is confident it can judge borrower quality with accuracy. The potential borrower can clearly signal their quality by being prepared, for example, to offer collateral such as their house to the bank (Han *et al.* 2009). However, as we will show in Chapter 17, the bank also collects information from transactions and may be able to use that information for imposing a higher, rather than a lower, interest rate on the borrowing business.

In summary, the evidence suggests that network theory may be a powerful way of explaining organisational emergence. The advantage of the theory is that it provides an account of how some people use their social capital to overcome the 'liability of newness'. It is also aligned with many of the 'real-life' stories of new business foundation. The main disadvantage of the approach is that it can place too much emphasis on the positive benefits of networks. This may ignore the costs of networks and the economic basis of why it is people go into business.

Summary

This chapter examined two approaches that explain how businesses emerge. The first of these was nascent entrepreneurship. The second was social networks. The advantage of both these approaches is that they emphasise the importance of 'how' individuals work through the sometimes messy process of starting up a business. The main disadvantage of these approaches is that they provide an imprecise and incomplete understanding of such processes. They address the issue of the *process* of formation but offer only limited insights into the question of *who* starts a new business.

Questions for discussion

1 What insights does the concept of the nascent entrepreneur provide in improving our understanding of the process of new business creation?

2 Why do many nascent entrepreneurs never actually start a business?

3 Does it matter if so many nascent entrepreneurs never start a business?

4 What is the 'liability of newness?' How can social networks overcome this liability?

5 What key insights into the entrepreneurial process are illustrated by Birley's credibility carousel?

6 Is networking a 'two-way street'? Does this have implications for the willingness of individuals to share information with one another?

References

Acs, Z.J. and Audretsch, D.B. (1990) *Innovation and Small Firms*, Cambridge, MA: MIT Press.

Aldrich, H. and Fiol, M. (1994) 'Fools Rush In?: The Institutional Context of Industry Creation', *Academy of Management Review*, 19, 645–70.

Altinay, E. (2005) 'Ethnic Minority Entrepreneurship: Factors Influencing Business Growth. A Study of Turkish Community Businesses in London: Multivariate Analysis'. Thesis submitted for PhD, University of Reading.

Birley, S. (2002) 'Universities, Academics and Spinout Companies: Lessons from Imperial', *International Journal of Entrepreneurship Education*, 1(1), 133–54.

Birley, S. and Westhead, P. (1994) 'A Taxonomy of Business Start-up Reasons and their Impact on Firm Growth and Size', *Journal of Business Venturing*, 9(1), 7–31.

Brüderl, J. and Preisendörfer, P. (1998) 'Network Support and the Success of Newly Founded Businesses', *Small Business Economics*, 10(3), 213–25.

Brush, C.G., Manolova, T.S. and Edelman, L.F. (2008) 'Properties of Emerging Organizations: An Empirical Test', *Journal of Business Venturing*, 23(5), 547–66.

Carter, N.M., Gartner, W.B. and Reynolds, P.D. (1996) 'Exploring Start-up Event Sequences', *Journal of Business Venturing*, 11(3), 151–66.

Carter, N.M., Gartner, W.B., Shaver, K.G. and Gatewood, E.J. (2003) 'The Career Reasons of Nascent Entrepreneurs', *Journal of Business Venturing*, 18(1), 13–39.

Chell, E. and Baines, S. (2000) 'Networking, Entrepreneurship and Microbusiness Behaviour', *Entrepreneurship and Regional Development*, 12, 195–215.

Curran, J., Jarvis, R., Blackburn, R.A. and Black, S. (1993) 'Networks and Small Firms: Constructs, Methodological Strategies, and Some Findings', *International Small Business Journal*, 11(2), 13–25.

Davidsson, P. and Honig, B. (2003) 'The Role of Social and Human Capital among Nascent Entrepreneurs', *Journal of Business Venturing*, 18(3), 301–31.

Delmar, F. and Davidsson, P. (2000) 'Where Do They Come From?: Prevalence and Characteristics of Nascent Entrepreneurs', *Entrepreneurship and Regional Development*, 12, 1–23.

Diochon, M., Menzies, T.V. and Gasse, Y. (2003) 'Insight into the Dynamics of Canadian Nascent Entrepreneurs' Start-up Effort and the Role Individual Factors Play in the Process', *Proceedings of the 20th CCSBE/CCPME Conference*. Victoria, British Columbia, 11 November, 6–8.

Elfring, T. and Hulsink, W. (2007) 'Networking by Entrepreneurs: Patterns of Tie-formation in Emerging Organizations', *Organization Studies*, 28, 1849–72.

Greve, A. and Salaff, J.W. (2003) 'Social Networks and Entrepreneurship', *Entrepreneurship: Theory and Practice*, 28(1), 1–22.

Han, L., Fraser. S. and Storey. D.J. (2009) 'Are Good or Bad Borrowers Discouraged from Applying for Loans?: Evidence from US Small Business Credit Markets?', *Journal of Banking and Finance*, 36(4), 424–55.

Hayton, J.C., George, G. and Zahra, S. (2002) 'National Culture and Entrepreneurship: A Review of Behavioural Research', *Entrepreneurship: Theory and Practice*, 26(4), 33–52.

Henley, A. (2007) 'Entrepreneurial Aspiration and Transition into Self-employment: Evidence from British Longitudinal Data', *Entrepreneurship and Regional Development*, 19(3), 253–80.

Hite, J.M. and Hesterly, W.S. (2001) 'The Evolution of Firm Networks: From Emergence to Early Growth of the Firm', *Strategic Management Journal*, 22(3), 275–86.

Hoang, H. and Antoncic, B. (2003) 'Network-based Research in Entrepreneurship: A Critical Review', *Journal of Business Venturing*, 18(2), 165–87.

Jack, S.L. (2005) 'The Role, Use and Activation of Strong and Weak Network Ties: A Qualitative Analysis', *Journal of Management Studies*, 42(6), 1233–59.

Johannisson, B. (2000) 'Networking and Entrepreneurial Growth', in Sexton, D.L. and Landstrom, H. (eds), *The Blackwell Handbook of Entrepreneurship*. Oxford: Oxford University Press, 368–86.

Katz, J.A. (1990) 'Longitudinal Analysis of Self-employment Follow-through', *Entrepreneurship and Regional Development*, 2, 15–25.

Katz, J.A. (2003) 'The Chronology and Intellectual Trajectory of American Entrepreneurship Education, 1876–1999', *Journal of Business Venturing*, 18(2), 283–300.

Katz, J. and Gartner, W.B. (1988) 'Properties of Emerging Organizations', *Academy of Management Review*, 13, 429–41.

Koellinger, P., Minniti, M. and Schade, C. (2007). ' "I think I can, I think I can": Overconfidence and Entrepreneurial Behavior', *Journal of Economic Psychology*, 28(4), 502–27.

Larson, A. and Starr, J.A. (1993) 'A Network Model of Organization Formation', *Entrepreneurship: Theory and Practice*, 17(2), 5–16.

Mueller, P. (2006) 'Nascent Entrepreneurs: Why Do Only a Few Complete Their Journey and Become Self-Employed?', Paper presented at IECER Conference, 22–24 February 2006.

Nahapiet, J. and Ghoshal, S. (1998) 'Social Capital, Intellectual Capital and the Organizational Advantage', *Academy of Management Review*, 23(2), 242–66.

Parker, S.C., and Belghitar, Y. (2006) 'What Happens to Nascent Entrepreneurs?: An Econometric Analysis of the PSED', *Small Business Economics*, 27(1), 81–101.

Perez, M. and Sanchez, A. (2002) 'Lean Production and Technology Networks in the Spanish Automotive Supplier Industry', *Management International Review*, 42(3), 261–78.

Reynolds, P.D. (2005) 'Understanding Business Creation: Serendipity and Scope in Two Decades of Business Creation Studies', *Small Business Economics*, 24(4), 359–64.

Reynolds, P. and Miller, B. (1992) 'New Firm Gestation: Conception, Birth and Implications for Research', *Journal of Business Venturing*, 7(5), 405–17.

Reynolds, P.D., Carter, N.M., Gartner, W.B. and Greene, P.G. (2004) 'The Prevalence of Nascent Entrepreneurs in the US: Evidence from the Panel Study of Entrepreneurial Dynamics', *Small Business Economics*, 23(4), 263–84.

Sarasvathy, S.D. (2001) 'Causation and Effectuation: Toward a Theoretical Shift from Economic Inevitability to Entrepreneurial Contingency', *Academy of Management Review*, 26(2), 243–63.

Stinchcombe, A.L. (1965) 'Social Structure and Organizations', in March, J.G. (ed.), *Handbook of Organizations*. Chicago, IL: Rand McNally, 142–93.

Uzzi, B. (1999) 'Embeddedness in the Making of Financial Capital: How Social Relations and Networks Benefit Firms Seeking Finance', *American Sociological Review*, 64, 481–505.

van Gelderen, M., Bosma, N. and Thurik, A.R. (2001) 'Setting Up a Business in the Netherlands: Who Starts, Who Gives Up, Who Is Still Trying'. Unpublished report, EIM.

van Gelderen, M., Thurik, A.R. and Bosma, N. (2006) 'Success and Risk Factors in the Pre-Startup Phase', *Small Business Economics*, 26(4), 319–35.

van Stel, A., Carree, M. and Thurik, A.R. (2005) 'The Effect of Entrepreneurial Activity on National Economic Growth', *Small Business Economics*, 24(3), 311–21.

Witt, P. (2004) 'Entrepreneurs' Networks and the Success of Start-ups', *Entrepreneurship and Regional Development*, 16(5), 391–412.

Employee $\quad$ U = U(W): W = f(L, E)

Self-employed $\quad$ U = U(π): π = f(L, K, θ)

For both the employed and self-employed, the implication is that the greater the number of hours worked, the higher levels of capital or the better the entrepreneurial 'talent' of the individual, the more likely it is that they will earn higher wages or higher profits.

The extent to which they shift between these two states depends on relative, and not absolute, utility. In other words, if an employee expects to be relatively better off in self-employment, they are more likely to become self-employed.

We now identify five valid criticisms of this simple model.

1   In the model, individuals are able to switch from one state to another at zero cost. However, if there are positive costs, then an individual may choose to stay in a 'less preferred' state because the switching costs are high. Examples of switching costs into self-employment include the costs of registering the business and the costs of researching the viability of the business. But there may also be costs of switching from self-employment into employment. These may be the 'costs' (in time and energy required) of obtaining formal qualifications as well as those of searching for a job. These search costs may be part of the reason why Henley (2004) found that an individual who was self-employed a year previously was about 30 per cent more likely – once other factors have been controlled for – to be currently in self-employment. This indicates that employees will be less likely to become self-employed, whilst the self-employed are less likely to shift to becoming an employee. In practice, what is more plausible is that start-up costs are generally higher than the costs associated with closing down the business (unless there are debts to be paid).

2   It is unrealistic to assume that business owners are only interested in the income which they derive from their business. Both Morton and Podolny (2002) and Hamilton (2000) clearly demonstrate that business owners derive non-monetary utility from business ownership. Morton and Podolny show that very many Californian wine growers were people who had left a high pressure job often in the local high technology sector. They switched – even though it paid less – presumably because of the greater satisfaction they got from growing wine. Hamilton (2000) also found that the self-employed could, after 10 years, have been earning 35 per cent *more* as a waged employee. He attributes this to business ownership providing non-pecuniary benefits to the individual – such as the independence of choosing when and where to work or 'being one's own boss'. Blanchflower and Oswald (1998) also show that the self-employed have consistently higher levels of job satisfaction than employees. However, an equally plausible explanation is that business owners are prepared to work for low incomes in the short or medium term in the hope of eventually 'striking it rich'. Hurst and Lusardi (2004) provide indirect evidence of this by showing that it is *only* the top 10 per cent highest earners amongst the self-employed that actually earn more than employees.

3   A third weakness of the model is that it makes no reference to chance or luck, yet we know self-employment is riskier than paid employment and that individuals can be either lucky or unlucky, perhaps even over a prolonged period.

4   The model implicitly assumes that all individuals have similar motivations. However, later in this chapter, we show that the approach can be modified by recognising that the self-employed are more optimistic about their future (financial) prospects.

5   The final, and perhaps most contentious issue associated with the labour-market approach is the concept of entrepreneurial talent θ. The model assumes that profitability will be higher for individuals with higher entrepreneurial talent. The debate, however, is about the nature of this talent, with the leading author on this issue – Boyan Jovanovic – appearing to have two radically different approaches. In the first (Jovanovic, 1982), his assumption is that individuals do not know their level of entrepreneurial talent before they start a

business. It is only by being in business that they learn what that talent is. Crucially this does *not* imply that they enhance θ by being in business – merely that they are able to more accurately estimate their own level of θ. The second approach (Evans and Jovanovic 1989) assumes that the level of an individual's talent is known, not only to the individual themselves, but also to outsiders. They assume that the amount of capital that a business can raise is a multiple [K] of the individual's talent. We explore the implications of these issues more fully in Chapter 10.

In summary, a very basic interpretation of the economist's labour-market approach to business creation is that individuals exercise a choice between being a business owner and being an employee. The former is more risky than the latter, but the choice is based on expected utility in each state. This simple choice framework can be made more sophisticated by recognising that utility is only partially related to income and/or wealth; by recognising the stickiness or 'state dependence' of labour-market switching; and by acknowledging the key roles played by luck and optimism. Finally, the very different interpretations of the key concept of entrepreneurial talent have to be recognised.

The central tests of this theory are the insights that it generates, its ability to explain behaviour and, most importantly, its ability to predict outcomes. We now turn to a review of the evidence.

Questions

- How can entrepreneurial talent be observed?
- If you set up in business does this mean that you have entrepreneurial talent?
- Are the individuals who survive in business talented or are they just lucky?
- Can you learn to be talented?

8.3 Factors contributing to start up

This section reviews those factors that have been used to explain *whether* new businesses are started and *who* starts them. This evidence is based on large-scale surveys of self-employment and new business owners. One limitation of this approach, emphasised in Chapter 3, is that self-employment is an inexact measure of business ownership. A second limitation is that even large-scale surveys may still remain biased or unrepresentative.

Despite these limitations, our focus on the *whether* and *who* questions means that the results from large-scale surveys are an appropriate starting point. Surveys provide generalisations. The use of sophisticated statistical techniques can also help identify and isolate the impact of one specific factor *when all else is held constant*. However, the reality is that there is no identikit picture of what a new business founder looks like. For every general statement, there are many exceptions: this is why qualitative case study research is valuable (see also Case study 3 which examines a start up by two young entrepreneurs). To illustrate we examine a set of proxies for entrepreneurial talent that are identified in Table 8.1.

We now turn to examine in detail a range of factors that choice theory suggests might influence whether an individual chooses to become a business owner. The factors are grouped together under the broad headings of personal circumstances, labour-market experience, personality characteristics and resources.

Personal circumstances

Sex: In all countries, females are considerably less likely to enter self-employment than males. This is statistically evident from the studies reported in Table 8.1. Why is this? And what are the special characteristics (if any) of those females that *do* become business owners?

Table 8.1 Studies of self-employment

	Le (1999)	Carrasco (1999)	Blanchflower and Oswald (1998) Tables 3 and 4	Taylor (2004) Appendix Table A1 Men	Moore and Mueller (2002)	Giannetti and Simanov (2005)	Ekelund et al. (2005)	Ritsala and Tervo (2002)	Kolvereid and Isaken (2006)	Henley (2004)	Sleuwagen and Goedhuys (2002)	Lin et al. (2000)	Nykvist (2008)
Country	Review covering many countries	Spain	Great Britain	Great Britain	Canada	Sweden	Finland	Finland	Norway	Great Britain	Côte D'Ivoire	Canada	Sweden
Female			−	−	−	−	−	−	−	−		−	
Mid-age (30–45)	+	+		+	+	+			n.s.	n.s.	n.s.	−	+
Parental self-employment												−	
Father owned business	+	+	+				n.s.		n.s.		+		+
Education	?												
Some qualifications				n.s.	+	+	+	+	n.s.	+	+	n.s.	+
Degree or higher degree				−	+	+	−			+	+		+
Labour-market experience	?												
Prior managerial experience				+						+	+	+	+
Self-employment experience				+						+	+	+	+
Unemployed		+		+	+	n.s.	−	+				+	
Personality influences													
Anxiety acceptance score													
Risk-aversion index			−										
Married		n.s		n.s.	+	+	n.s.	+		n.s.			+
Spouse self-employed					+	+	n.s.	+		+		+	+
Children		−		+	+	+	n.s.	+		+		+	+
Financial capital	+												
House ownership				n.s.			+	+		+		+	
Wealth of household						+	+	+		+			
Windfall payments	+	+	+	+	n.s.	n.s					+		+
Ethnicity	?				n.s.					+			
Born abroad				+							+		−

Three explanations of why women are less likely than men to be self-employed are normally offered. The first focuses on women subjectively or objectively lacking the qualities necessary to successfully set up a new business. The second focuses upon discrimination faced by women in the labour market due to prevailing cultural attitudes or blocked access to employment. The third reason relates to women being more likely to have significant family responsibilities.

In terms of the first of these three explanations, if women 'objectively' lacked the necessary qualities to set up a new business, the expectation might be that there are obvious differences in the psychological profile of men and women. This assumes that any psychological differences can be readily attributed to starting a business. There is, however, a lack of evidence of a general direct link between 'objective' psychological traits (e.g. need for achievement, risk taking) and start up (see Chapter 2). Given this absence, there remains considerable doubt about the link between 'objective' traits and the start-up behaviour of women and men.

Langowitz and Minniti (2007) point to there being 'subjective' differences between male and female nascent entrepreneurs. Their study of 17 countries suggests that if women *perceive* that they have the necessary knowledge skills and abilities they are more likely to be nascent entrepreneurs. However, if they 'fear failure', they are less likely to pursue start-up opportunities. Verheul and Thurik (2001) also find in their study of Dutch entrepreneurs that women were more averse to risk. Cowling and Taylor (2001), however, argue that females with higher levels of education are more likely to enter self-employment relative to similarly educated males.

This leads on to the second explanation of why women are less likely to set up a new business. Marlow and Patton (2005) argue that women face discrimination in the workplace because the 'rules of the game' are made and ordered along masculine principles. One measure of this is the relative gender 'pay gap'. In the European Union (EU 15) in 2005, men had a median pay level that was 18 per cent higher than women (EFILWC 2006). Paradoxically, this might encourage women to favour self-employment over employment because of potentially greater earning opportunities in that state. It also opens up the possibility of less discrimination because, as a business owner, they have the ability to 'be their own boss'. Figure 8.1, however, shows that, across the OECD, female rates of self-employment are much lower than those of men. Indeed, there is not one country in the OECD which has comparable rates of male and female self-employment: the typical difference is more than 5 per cent.

These differences may be explained if the discrimination faced by women in paid employment is also present, or even higher, in self-employment (Coate and Tennyson 1992). Such discrimination, for example, may be reflected in women facing greater difficulties than males in accessing finance (Marlow and Patton 2005; Fraser 2005) but it may be also be related to difficulties in establishing relevant networks or accessing information (Morris *et al.* 2006).

The third explanation is that, on the one hand, having extra family responsibilities may also encourage self-employment entry because it may provide greater flexibility in balancing work and family concerns than in paid employment. For example, in the UK, around 30 per cent of women are not employed and half of those that are actually employed are in part-time employment. Wellington (2006) finds that self-employment is greater amongst women with very young children, amongst those with greater family responsibilities and amongst more educated females. This seems compatible with the choice focus. The alternative perspective is that having family responsibilities makes it harder to keep up their skills. If so, and if self-employment requires greater skills than employment, then women may feel that they are better off with employment. Both explanations are compatible with the choice framework.

An added factor in this is that the provision of a 'family-friendly' employment is likely to reduce the attractiveness of self-employment. This may explain why self-employment rates in the Nordic countries amongst women are low. However, this is not because of disinclination or discrimination. Instead, it is because the public service offers family-friendly employment that is more attractive than uncertain self-employment.

The evidence from Taylor (2004) in Table 8.1 and from other – more specialist – studies of male and female differences shows the following:

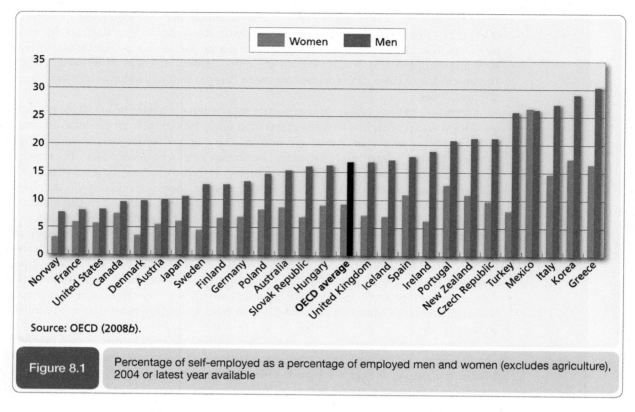

| Figure 8.1 | Percentage of self-employed as a percentage of employed men and women (excludes agriculture), 2004 or latest year available |

Source: OECD (2008b).

- Women were significantly more likely to enter self-employment from being economically inactive than men. These are often referred to as 'women returners'.

- Unmarried women were generally more likely to enter self-employment than married women. The exception is Pisani and Pagan's (2004) study of Nicaraguan self-employment which found that married women were more likely to enter self-employment.

- Women were more likely to enter self-employment if their spouse was employed. This is supported in studies by Bruce (1999) and Cowling and Taylor (2001) (not shown in Table 8.1).

- Women were more likely to enter self-employment if they had a higher qualification – but not a degree. This is in contrast to Cowling and Taylor (2001) who found that higher education did have a positive impact on female self-employment.

- As noted earlier, Wellington (2006) found that women were more likely to enter self-employment if they had three or more children. However, it is not clear if women choose self-employment because of its flexibility or because the self-employment allows them to have more children.

- Having parents with self-employment experience does not influence female entry to self-employment.

Questions

- Do women choose self-employment because its flexibility allows them to have children or does having children make self-employment more attractive?

- Is there anything that should or could be done to support women in setting up their own business?

- Would women benefit more if attention was instead directed towards addressing the sources of discrimination in employment?

- Should public-sector employment be made less family friendly in order to encourage more women to enter self-employment?

Age: The evidence on the impact of age on likelihood of starting a business is fairly clear. As Table 8.1 shows, those individuals who are 'middle aged' (30–50 years old) are much more likely to set up in business than those either less than 30 years of age or more than 50 years of age.

The choice framework explains this result in the following way: it sees self-employment as a choice in which there are different costs and benefits to different age groups.

For young people – perhaps under 30 years of age – the returns from business ownership may be modest because they lack business experience, credibility and/or access to capital. On the other hand, young people are likely to earn less than middle-aged or older workers as employees which may provide them with an incentive to view business ownership more favourably. They are also more likely to have the energy and commitment to work long hours for modest returns – possibly financially supported by their parents.

In contrast, older workers – perhaps aged 50 or more – have the advantages of experience and credibility. They are also more likely to be able to access their own sources of finance and be credible borrowers from the bank. However, such individuals may lack both the energy and commitment of younger workers and, if they are in employment, they may be earning relatively high incomes that it is difficult to match by starting a business.

Such logic implies that it is the middle-aged workers that are most likely to begin a business. Such individuals combine business experience with access to finance and the necessary energy and commitment to make a new venture successful. Their motivation may well be enhanced by also having dependent family commitments.

There are only a few specific studies that look at older and younger adult entry into self-employment. In terms of younger people, the evidence mirrors the key differences found in older populations: females and 'younger' people are much less likely to become business owners in the UK (Greene and Storey 2004), Australia (Blanchflower and Meyer 1994) and the US (Williams 2004). For older people, Zissimopoulos and Karoly (2007) found that US adults aged between 51–69 were more likely to become self-employed if they were not married (significant for women but not for men), had higher levels of education (men), had managerial experience (men and women), and had health issues (men and women). By contrast, Parker and Rougier's (2007) examination of UK retirees found that those with poor health were much *less* likely to move into self-employment.

For those over 50, the situation may be changing, as might be expected in accordance with choice theory (Weber and Shaper 2003). Primarily because of improved health, there is an expectation of individuals working later in life than was the case 10 or 20 years ago. Choice theory would imply that a higher proportion of today's older workers would have similar levels of energy to those of younger workers in the past. This is likely to give them the confidence to incur the costs of establishing a new business, the returns from which will not accrue immediately. Superimposed upon this development has been a deterioration of their employment prospects, with income for many employees either stagnating or declining once they reach 50–55 years, with this perhaps being accelerated by rapid technological change in the workplace. So, amongst such individuals, a combination of dissatisfaction with employment, higher energy levels and improved access to finance has led to a growth in self-employment. Chapter 3 reflects this, showing that the proportion of older male and females (50+) in self-employment has been increasing in the UK over the last 25 years (Kautonen *et al.* 2008).

Parental experience of self-employment. Three reasons have been put forward to explain why having a self-employed parent could increase the likelihood of a sibling also becoming self-employed. First, the son or daughter could inherit an existing family-owned business. Second, even if the family business is not transferred, the children of such parents will be more keenly aware of the entrepreneurial option than children whose parents were not business owners. They will have personal experience of what it is like to run a business and so be more able to accurately estimate whether they have the requisite personal qualities than someone without such a family background. Third, the children of entrepreneurs may have parents or relatives willing to provide finance and/or advice to make the transition to business ownership easier and hence more attractive. All the above elements are likely to increase the likelihood of self-employment entry.

In contrast, close experience of parental self-employment – particularly if it was an unhappy experience – may dissuade an individual from self-employment. Also, the children of parents made wealthy by business ownership may lack motivation. Table 8.1 shows that Le (1999), in his review of the evidence, found that individuals with a self-employed father were more likely to become a business owner than those without such a parental influence. The other studies also obtain the same result, although Ekelund *et al.* (2005) finds this to be insignificant. Overall, there is some modest evidence that a parent owning a business makes an individual more likely to start their own business or to be self-employed.

Marital status. All else being equal, choice theory predicts that individuals who are married are expected to be more likely to enter self-employment than unmarried individuals. Two main reasons for this are proposed. First, amongst males there is an 'incentive' effect where self-employment is seen as an opportunity for earning more money by choosing to work longer hours. Rees and Shah (1994) show that the married self-employed non-manual worker works about eight hours more per week than their non-married counterpart. On these grounds, an individual choosing self-employment – where income depends, more directly, on hours worked compared with paid employment where salary is fixed – may favour the former if income can be higher in self-employment.

A second argument is that many small businesses are only effective because of the often unpaid contributions of the 'staff'. Very many businesses are reliant on family support. Baines and Wheelock (1998) show that owners' spouses were a particularly significant source of labour, both paid and unpaid, and without which the marginal business would not survive. In those cases, only individuals with a spouse would regard starting a business as worthwhile. The findings of Clain (2000) are particularly interesting linking both gender and marital status. She finds that: '. . . in and of itself being married raises the likelihood of being self-employed for men. For women the effect of marriage works most strongly though the spouse's income: the greater the income the greater the likelihood of self-employment' (p. 507). Table 8.1 confirms this finding by showing a broadly positive relationship between being married and self-employment.

Children. Using choice theory, it might be argued that an individual with children is less likely to enter self-employment than an otherwise similar childless individual, because self-employment income is riskier. Choosing a risky form of income when responsibilities are high may be a difficult choice. On the other hand, children, especially when they are old enough to contribute to the business, may enhance the viability of a business and so make entry more likely. This is because they may be willing to forgo wages in the short to medium term so that the family business can develop. This is a form of 'sweat equity'. Also, self-employment is more likely to provide an opportunity to work additional hours and hence earn more money than someone who can only find a fixed hours wage contract as an employee. This may mean parents can earn more money for their children.

Table 8.1 shows that, all else being equal, most of the studies indicate that the self-employed are more likely to have children than be childless. Care, of course, has to be taken here because the variable 'children' may hide large differences. More detailed analyses have shown that the decision to enter self-employment is contingent on circumstances. Rees and Shah (1994) show that the second most powerful influence upon hours worked by the self-employed – after marital status – is the number of children. They find that working hours do fall upon the arrival of the first child, but that they increase upon the arrival of the second child. Bruce (1999) also shows that there are two key influences on females' transition to self-employment. First, it is made more likely by having a husband in self-employment and second by having children under the age of 18. Lin *et al.* (2000) using Canadian data also suggest that having children aged 0–4 makes self-employment entry more likely.

Education. Choice theory suggests the education level of the founder can exert either a positive or a negative influence on the likelihood of self-employment. The positive argument is that education provides the necessary skills to establish and manage a business. It is also plausible to argue that certain types of business – such as those using or developing new technologies – can only be established by those with advanced educational qualifications.

However, at the heart of choice theory is the notion that each individual faces a choice of whether starting a business is the best option for them. So, even if it were shown that educated individuals were always 'better' entrepreneurs than those with less education, it does not mean all educated individuals would start a business. This is because the educated individual is also likely to be able to earn more as an employee than the less educated individual.

Education may also have other, more subtle, effects. For example, the education system may encourage or discourage business entry. Encouragement may take the form of actively promoting business entry as a viable choice amongst students. Alternatively, education may explicitly or implicitly suggest that working for large corporations or in the public sector is more intellectually challenging, more prestigious and considerably less risky.

Illustration	Educational attainment and new hi-tech business start ups

Science parks have a strong association with high-tech business start ups.

One type of new enterprise clearly influenced by the educational attainment of the founder is the high-tech business. These are founded almost exclusively by those with the highest levels of educational attainment. For example, Lindelof and Lofsten (2002) show a strong association between having a postgraduate degree and opening a new business on a Swedish science park. Thirty-two per cent of those that opened up a new business on a science park had a postgraduate degree. This compares with only 5 per cent of new business founders having a postgraduate degree in 'off-science park' businesses.

The more general evidence on the role of education in self-employment is presented in Table 8.1. The evidence reviewed by Le (1999) covers a large number of independent studies in a wide variety of countries. He concluded, in line with choice theory, that education had no clear impact upon the likelihood of an individual starting a business. The other studies show an almost equally mixed picture. Perhaps the most comprehensive analysis of this relationship is provided by van der Sluis *et al.* (2005). They concluded that there is no relationship between an individual's level of schooling and their probability of business entry. The only slight exceptions to this, albeit based on only a very few studies, is that postgraduate education may enhance the likelihood of entry into certain types of high-tech business ownership.

The empirical evidence therefore reflects the expected outcome derived from choice theory. It is that, because education enhances the skill-set of the individual, it raises the earning potential of that individual in both 'states'. The extent to which it leads to individuals shifting from one to the other is less clear.

Questions

- Is there a minimum level of education that someone needs to set up a business?
- How does the type of business impact on the relationship between education and entrepreneurship?
- Should higher education be promoting entrepreneurship?

Ethnicity: Le's (1999) review of international studies in Table 8.1 makes the important point that there is probably greater diversity within ethnic groups than between ethnic and white groups in terms of enterprise creation. He finds evidence of striking diversity between different ethnic groups in terms of their likelihood of entering self-employment. This is evident from Clark and Drinkwater (2000) for the UK and Lunn and Steen (2005) for the US. Figure 8.2 also shows differences between different ethnic groups in the Netherlands (1999–2003). 'Native' Dutch self-employment is around 8–9 per cent whilst 'western foreigner' self-employment is lower at around 7 per cent. 'Non-western foreigner' is lower still at less than 5 per cent. However, as Figure 8.2 shows, this hides marked differences. Self-employment is particularly high amongst Egyptians, the Chinese and Indian/Pakistani individuals. It is much lower amongst those from Turkey, Surinam/Netherland Antilles and Morocco.

Similar differences are evident when UK data is considered. Figure 8.3 shows ethnic self-employment as a percentage of those in employment in 2004. It clearly shows that Pakistanis, the Chinese, the White Irish and Other Whites are much more likely to be in self-employment. By comparison, those characterised as Black Africans, Black Caribbeans or Mixed are much less likely to be in self-employment.

What Figures 8.2 and 8.3 may miss are the difficulties in defining 'ethnic' entrepreneurship. For example, Chaganti and Greene (2002) identify three different types of 'ethnic' entrepreneurship: businesses set up by recent immigrants to a country; an identifiable set of ethnic businesses (an 'ethnic enclave') set up to serve an ethnic market and employing 'ethnic' owners and workers; or a business set up to serve 'ethnic' products which may not be set up by someone from an ethnic minority.

Jones and Ram (2007) argue that the term 'ethnic' entrepreneur also tends to hide very real differences between different ethnic groups. They suggest that particular ethnic groups are treated as being isolated in some way from the other – usually 'White' or 'Western' – communities. This ignores the fact that all ethnic groups are subject to wider market and social forces that impact on all groups in society. The term may also hide differences between 'first' and 'second' or 'third' generation ethnic entrepreneurs.

When particular ethnic groups are examined, two types of explanation tend to be offered for ethnic self-employment. The first of these is culture; the second is discrimination.

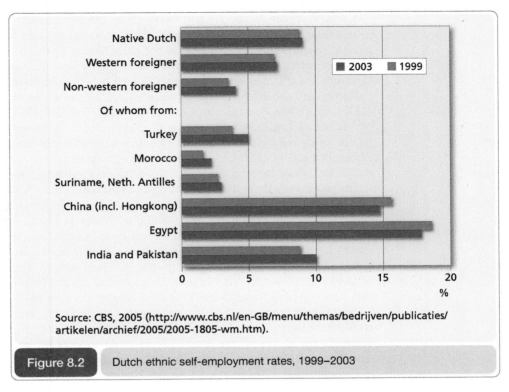

Source: CBS, 2005 (http://www.cbs.nl/en-GB/menu/themas/bedrijven/publicaties/artikelen/archief/2005/2005-1805-wm.htm).

| Figure 8.2 | Dutch ethnic self-employment rates, 1999–2003 |

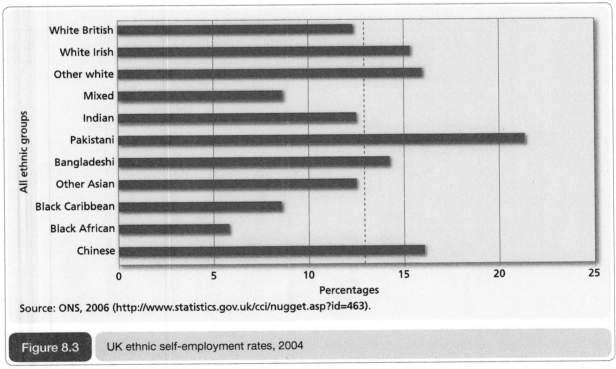

Source: ONS, 2006 (http://www.statistics.gov.uk/cci/nugget.asp?id=463).

| Figure 8.3 | UK ethnic self-employment rates, 2004 |

In terms of culture, the general argument is that '. . . some ethnic groups may have a cultural propensity towards entrepreneurship' (Basu and Altinay 2002: 373). For example, in the UK, Asians are said to have a cultural background that supports and promotes people setting up a business. Integral to this is a work ethic that supports what Jones and Ram (2007: 450) describe as '. . . hair shirt values of deferred gratification, thrift and industriousness . . .'.

Cultural influences also are said to impact on the prevalence of *ethnic resources* available to potential and actual business owners. Such resources are said to include wide and deep kinship relationships which allow for the employment of cheap but hard-working family members. Ethnic resources also include finance which, potentially, may be cheaper and better structured (e.g. longer term) than that offered by other equity or debt providers. Ethnic resources may also extend to wider resources available in the community. For example, Loebl (1978) has shown that the heavy concentration of sizable Jewish-owned businesses in the North East of England in the 1970s was, in part, due to the supportive nature of the wider Jewish community in this area. More broadly, a wider ethnic community potentially provides labour and acts as customers for ethnic-owned businesses. Hence, one explanation of why particular groups are more likely to set up a business is that they have a cultural background which predisposes them towards start up and that these groups have ethnic resources which ease the setting up of a business.

The second explanation has to do with discrimination and how particular ethnic groups in society respond to any perceived or real discrimination (Godley 2001). Hammarstedt (2006), using Swedish data, shows non-European immigrants face discrimination in the waged sector, and it is this that pushes them towards self-employment. These findings are supported by Clark and Drinkwater (2000). Further evidence by Clark and Drinkwater (2007) also indicates that Pakistanis and Bangladeshis in the UK continue to have high rates of self-employment because they face wider discrimination. Another symptom of this is the suggested difficulties ethnic entrepreneurs face in gaining credit from the banks (Ram *et al.* 2003). For example, Storey (2004) examined the availability of credit in Trinidad and Tobago. He found that Afro-Trinidadians were more likely to be denied credit compared to other ethnic groups.

One expectation, therefore, may be that, if discrimination in the formal labour market fell, then rates of self-employment amongst particular ethnic groups would also fall. One test of this is to examine differences between first- and second-generation ethnic entrepreneurs. The anticipation is that the self-employment rate amongst second-generation ethnic entrepreneurs would be lower because they are less likely – other things being equal – to experience discrimination. Figure 8.4 supports this for the UK using data from the 2001 Census. It shows that,

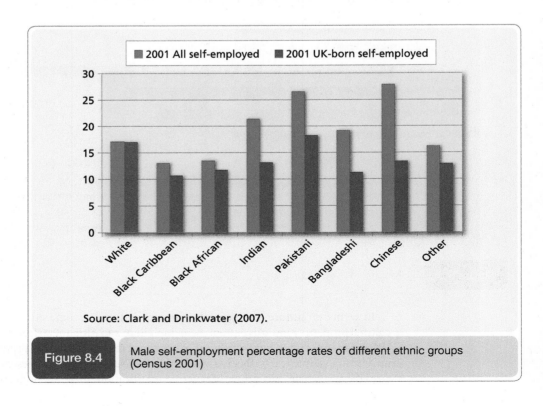

Source: Clark and Drinkwater (2007).

| Figure 8.4 | Male self-employment percentage rates of different ethnic groups (Census 2001) |

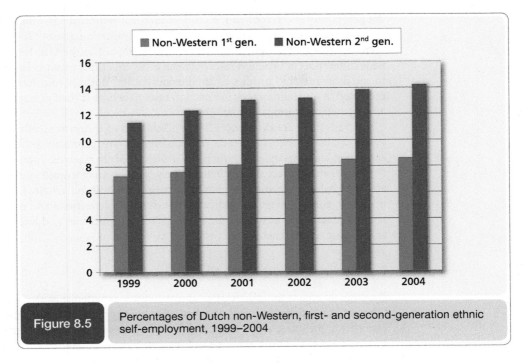

| Figure 8.5 | Percentages of Dutch non-Western, first- and second-generation ethnic self-employment, 1999–2004 |

all for all ethnic groups (except Whites), second-generation self-employment is lower than for first-generation in-migrants.

This finding, however, may be unique to the UK. Figure 8.5 shows similar data for the Netherlands split into first- and second-'non-Western' generations. It shows that self-employment rates are higher for second-generation ethnic entrepreneurs.

This evidence may suggest that cultural rather than discriminatory barriers are a better explanation of why it is that certain ethnic groups are predisposed to self-employment. Clark and Drinkwater (2007), however, find very little evidence to support the idea of 'ethnic enclaves'. Moreover, Ram and Jones (2008) also argue that there is a need to think more carefully about how culture, discriminatory barriers and entrepreneurial opportunities interact to produce different self-employment rates amongst ethnic groups (see Illustration below). For example, entrepreneurial opportunities are likely to be shaped by sectoral pressures.

| Illustration | Ethnic entrepreneurs and sectoral pressures |

It is no coincidence that the majority of ethnic entrepreneurs have traditionally found themselves in sectors such as convenience retailing, 'ethnic' restaurants and clothing production because these are relatively easy to enter sectors that require few financial resources. Jones and Ram (2007) argue that these sectors *require* cultural norms of long hours for little profit. What then looks like a cultural predisposition towards self-employment is, in fact, a response to sectoral pressures. Furthermore, Jones and Ram (2007) argue that although Asian retailers typically expect to work long hours, they find that they work the same hours as non-Asians.

Ram and Jones (2008) argue that self-employment is a transitional state for many individuals in ethnic communities. They subsequently point to evidence which suggests that ethnic entrepreneurship serves as a launching pad to more professional occupations for younger generations who are encouraged to become better educated. Moreover, Metcalfe *et al.* (1996) argue that one consequence of a culture of long hours and low pay is that ethnic entrepreneurs may seek to dissuade their sons and daughters from entering self-employment. Sons and daughters may also recognise the costs of such self-employment. Finally, there are differences between 'subjective' and 'objective' views of discrimination. Fraser (2006) examined the use of finance amongst different ethnic minority businesses in the UK. He found that there were wide differences in rejection rates between different ethnic groups. This he suggested was due to the different 'risk' profiles of the businesses and not due to discrimination. However, he proposed that the differences in rejection rates may have fuelled perceptions of discrimination amongst ethnic entrepreneurs.

Overall, there are differences in the likelihood of different ethnic groups being business owners. Choice theorists argue that differences are primarily explained by the different economic circumstances in which the groups find themselves. Typically, these factors, particularly if they reflect discrimination, may 'push' people towards self-employment. If there are more cultural reasons, this may 'pull' people towards self-employment. However, research on ethnic entrepreneurship indicates that different definitions and measures (e.g. first- and second-generation) as well as, for example, sector, education and location are likely to influence ethnic entrepreneurship.

Labour-market experience

Economists regard an individuals' labour-market experience as the second major influence (after personal circumstances) on whether or not they become self-employed. Labour-market experience includes: prior managerial experience, size of prior employer, prior business ownership, and experience of unemployment.

Labour-market experience influences the business ownership choice in two ways. First, it may enable the individual to better assess their abilities both as an employee and as a business owner. This is particularly important in business ownership since it is regarded as being more risky than being an employee. Second, relevant experience may mean that the learning period is shorter, as the individual can adapt more quickly. Labour-market experience is strongly linked to entrepreneurial talent. Choice theory would forecast that those with greater entrepreneurial talent would be most likely to enter self-employment and that elements of labour-market experience would influence their talent in either a positive or negative manner. These influences we discuss below.

Prior managerial experience. All else being equal, having prior managerial experience is likely to provide individuals with greater confidence in their ability to start a business. But, as with education, an individual with managerial experience is also likely to have higher earning potential as an employee than someone without that experience. The evidence from Le (1999) suggests the effect of these conflicting influences is ambiguous and may be also associated with access to finance issues.

This ambiguity has shifted the discussion away from the 'amount' of experience and more towards whether it is the 'type' of experience that influences the business creation choice. Lazear (2005) suggests there may be differences between those whose employment background is that of a 'generalist' – a 'jack of all trades' – compared with 'specialists' who have a narrower employment background. He found that, amongst his sample of US MBA graduates, those with more generalist experiences and roles were more likely to subsequently become self-employed. This result is confirmed by Wagner (2006) using German data.

Size of prior employer: Implicit in Lazear (2005) is also the argument that an individual who previously worked in a small business is more likely to have undertaken a greater variety of tasks than an individual working in a larger business. If such an individual found this to be to their liking, this might persuade them that they would be able to transfer this ability into their own enterprise. This may make them more likely to start their own business.

Lazear's finding was not new. Johnson and Cathcart (1979) found that if someone previously worked for a larger business they were less likely to subsequently become self-employed.

More recent research by Hyytinen and Maliranta (2008) for Finland confirms this finding. Individuals who worked in smaller businesses (0–19 employees) were much more likely to become self-employed than those who worked in larger businesses (50+ employees).

Prior business ownership or previous experience of being self-employed. Westhead *et al.* (2005) show that about one in five business owners in the UK were previously a business owner, and slightly more than one in five of businesses are owned by individuals who own more than a single business. Greene *et al.* (2008) find that 30 per cent of current business owners have previously owned a business. This raises the interesting question about whether an individual who has previously been a business owner is more likely to try again than someone with no prior experience (a novice).

Choice theory on this is again ambiguous. There are two reasons why a previous owner is less likely to start again. The first is that, if they failed, this may have been such a financially and emotionally chastening experience for them that they never wish to repeat it. This experience may have enabled them to accurately assess their own entrepreneurial talent, leading them to the view that they are unsuited to any further spells of self-employment. A second reason is that there may be financial penalties for business owners that 'fail', and this deters them from starting again.

In contrast, an individual who previously owned a business might be more willing to try to start another business for two very different reasons. First, they may feel the previous business provided them with clear lessons or pointers for future success – they may feel they have learnt from the experience. A second reason is that if business ownership is favoured by individuals of a particular personality type, and if an individual's personality type changes little over many years, then it seems likely that such individuals will continue to be attracted to business ownership – irrespective of whether or not they have failed in the past.

Henley (2004) and Lin *et al.* (2000) (Table 8.1) examine this relationship. Both find a positive association between prior business experience and business start up. This is in line with other evidence from Flores-Romero and Blackburn (2005). They asked 'failed' business owners if they were likely to start again and found that 'serial' owners were much more likely to say they planned to start again than novices.

Unemployment experience. In setting out choice theory at the start of this chapter, for purposes of simplicity, we identified the choice faced by an individual as being between self-employment and employment. However, this does not fit the circumstances faced by all adults. One particularly important other group is the unemployed.

In principle, the nature of the choice is identical. The unemployed individual chooses between the certainty of (any) income from the state and the uncertainty of income from self-employment. This choice is likely to be influenced by a range of factors. One is the scale of state benefits paid to the unemployed. All else being equal, if state benefits are high, fewer unemployed workers would make the transition from unemployment into self-employment than in an economy that provided lower levels of benefit.

A second influence on this choice is that, because unemployment is often geographically clustered, the unemployed individual is less likely to start a new business in an area where many other people are also unemployed. This is because local demand is depressed. Since most new businesses begin, at least initially, by selling locally, depressed local demand is likely to make starting a new business a less attractive option than in a more affluent area.

A third influence is that the unemployed may regard themselves as being unable to obtain employment as an employee and so feel 'pushed' towards self-employment. Alternatively, if being unemployed is a reflection that the individual lacks work-based skills – and perhaps lacks motivation – then they will be less likely to favour self-employment because there are fewer opportunities for 'shirking'. The unskilled unemployed individual may also have highly restricted access to capital. Choice theory, therefore, implies that the impact of unemployment has potentially very contradictory effects.

Turning now to the evidence, this broadly indicates that the unemployed are more likely than the employed to start a new business. Le (1999) reports the findings of Evans and Leighton (1989) for the US. They found a significant positive relationship for the 1980–1 period, although no significant relationship for earlier time periods. Four of the other studies reviewed in Table 8.1 point to a positive influence of unemployment upon entry into self-employment or business ownership.

Overall, choice theory is not able to predict unambiguously whether an unemployed individual is more or less likely to enter self-employment than an otherwise similar employed individual. The empirical evidence on the impact of unemployment on self-employment is mixed. However, most studies suggest that the unemployed are more, rather than less, likely to start a business than otherwise similar individuals who are employed.

Personality characteristics

Probably the single most important personality characteristic of the self-employed, identified by economists, is that of optimism. As reported in Chapter 1, the self-employed appear more optimistic about their future than the general population and appear to be at their most optimistic when they have least control over events.

Other important contributions by economists to the 'entrepreneurial personality' literature have been made by Blanchflower and Oswald (1998). They found evidence that those with higher levels of 'anxiety' as a child were less likely to be self-employed in later life. Ekelund *et al.* (2005) found that Finnish business owners are psychologically more pre-disposed to risk taking than those people who remain as employees. Taylor (2004) also points to personality differences amongst those entering self-employment, with those individuals who place less emphasis on job security being more likely to enter self-employment.

Blanchflower and Oswald (1998) also found that the self-employed are more likely than employees to report themselves as happy in their work. It is appropriate to be cautious about such associations since it may be that those of a happier disposition are attracted towards self-employment – rather than self-employment causing people to be happier.

Finally, Fairlie (2002) demonstrated a most interesting link between psychological characteristics as a young person and self-employment as an adult. He used US data from the National Longitudinal Survey of Youth. Individuals were interviewed in 1980 when they were between the ages of 15 and 23. In the survey, individuals are asked about their participation in 'illegal activities' – the most frequent form being drug dealing – during the previous year. Fairlie then tests whether dealing in drugs as a teenager influences whether on not that individual is in self-employment 16 years later. He finds that – even taking account of race, in-migration, wealth, any spells in prison, and years of schooling – those who reported participation in drug dealing in 1980 were between 11 per cent and 21 per cent more likely to enter self-employment in the next 16 years than those who did not. One inference from this finding is that those personality characteristics that imply some form of risk preference early in life are retained for many years. A second is that those with such preferences can and do shift from one form of entrepreneurship to another – making it compatible with Baumol's (1990) view that 'the entrepreneur is always with us' and that the task of society is to ensure that the 'rules of the game' favour 'productive' over unproductive or destructive forms of entrepreneurship (see Chapter 2).

Questions

- If the aim was to increase the number of new businesses amongst young people, would it be better to give 'real-world' experience of work to young people?
- If personality is important, is there any point in providing training to help people set up in business?
- Are people 'pushed' into self-employment because they lack choices?

In summary, there is evidence that some personality characteristics are associated with entry into self-employment. Amongst these are optimism and a willingness to take risks. What is equally clear is that these are one set of influences, among many, and that they interact with other influences such as age, education and economic context.

Financial capital

The single most valuable asset many individuals own is their home. A house can be used as security for borrowing from financial institutions, so easing access to start-up funds. Table 8.1 clearly shows that house ownership and access to funds have an important positive relationship with becoming self-employed.

This also applies to those with sources of funding other than housing. For example, Lindh and Ohlsson (1996) examined winners of the Swedish lottery. They found that winning the lottery made that individual much more likely to become self-employed. Similar results are apparent for the US (Dunn and Holtz-Eakin 2000) and for the UK (Taylor 2001).

The studies reviewed in Table 8.1 generally show that higher wealth – which facilitates access to finance – increases business formation. They also point to entry being higher amongst those experiencing a 'windfall gain' – defined as the unexpected arrival of wealth – such as a lottery win or an inheritance.

The key exception to this finding is from Hurst and Lusardi (2004). They examine US data and find the relationship between initial household wealth and propensity to start a business is highly non-linear, with a greater likelihood only being clearly characteristic of the extremely wealthy. To put it another way, for most people, having more wealth, or having an increase in wealth, does not mean they are more likely to start a business, unless they are or become exceptionally rich. Hurst and Lusardi reject the evidence based on 'lottery winners' or 'inheritors' on the grounds that these are not really 'windfall gains' since they are, in many cases, expected by the recipients.

Overall, the evidence suggests that lack of access to financial resources can clearly act as a constraint on whether an individual starts a new business. What is less clear is whether all, or just some, potential new business owners have problems accessing finance. We discuss this issue in depth in Chapters 16–18 on finance, but at this point it is important to note that much depends upon how much information the financier has on the business and the individual's wealth. If financiers have complete information, they are more likely to provide finance based on their fully-informed judgement of the prospects for the business. Alternatively, if their information is incomplete, an individual's wealth is likely to be a very important decision criterion since it is this that will be drawn upon if the business fails.

8.4 Criticisms of the economist approach

The labour-market approach used by economists to explain new business formation has its limitations. The favoured approach relies on large-scale data and uses statistical analysis. This means the typical focus is on the self-employed. As was shown in Chapter 6, this is an imprecise measure of new businesses. Businesses are often set up by teams and by families and these relationships may not always be fully considered.

In addition to being criticised for its empirical approach, choice theory is also criticised in the following ways:

1 Choice theory is based on the individual having (perfect) knowledge. However, many individuals often have very *imperfect* knowledge, so choice theory can't work.

2 Choice theory assumes rationality on the part of the individual whereas much of entrepreneurship is about 'hunches' or 'gut feelings'.

3 Choice theory may talk of utility but what it really means is income rather than a wider interpretation of what people get out of running their business (e.g. satisfaction, independence).

4 Choice theory fails to understand the diversity and subtlety of the entrepreneur's motivations. To capture these diverse motivations in a simple choice framework leads to highly imperfect – and probably misleading – insights.

5 Choice theory, whilst it does identify some factors that influence self-employment decision, is – in many cases – ambiguous in its predictions. This is particularly true for education and unemployment.

6 Fundamentally, choice theory suffers from a failure to address and understand the 'process' question; how do individuals go about identifying and then exploiting opportunities?

Question

● Taking each of the six criticisms outlined above, how would you expect the choice theorist to respond?

Summary

This chapter began by outlining the labour-market approach adopted by many economists to explain new business formation. This approach emphasises 'choice' and 'outcomes'. We then examined the key characteristics of those individuals who become self-employed. We reviewed the findings from large-scale studies that used (sometimes quite sophisticated) statistical techniques. The main disadvantage with this approach is that self-employment may be an imperfect measure of business ownership and may give an imprecise explanation of 'entrepreneurial talent' and the process of new business formation.

Nonetheless, the evidence suggested that the following factors are important in explaining self-employment decision:

● gender
● age
● optimism
● unemployment
● size of prior employer's business
● prior business ownership
● parents' occupation
● marital status
● access to wealth.

It might be tempting to use these findings to draw up a template or 'identikit' picture of what a typical business owner looks like. This would be extremely unwise for two reasons. First, the sheer numbers of people involved make it virtually impossible for there to be a single template or identikit picture for a (new) business owner. Indeed, the ability of particular factors (e.g. labour-market experience) to explain business ownership is modest. Second, the predictive power of the various factors is also likely to vary between different countries, across different time periods and be influenced by macroeconomic conditions. Also, central to this chapter has been the development of a choice framework to answer the question 'who becomes an entrepreneur'. This framework, however, does not always provide a clear and unambiguous theoretical stance on the likely impact of a particular factor (e.g. education). Hence, this perspective suggests that it may be difficult to construct a facsimile of an entrepreneur.

Questions for discussion

1 Outline the theoretical arguments surrounding whether highly educated individuals are more likely to start a business than those with low or medium educational qualifications. Does the evidence support the theory?

2 What role does entrepreneurial talent play in the choice of an individual to start a business? What proxies might be used for entrepreneurial talent?

3 Is there an 'enterprising personality'?

4 What more do we currently know about the factors influencing self-employment beyond those identified by Rees and Shah in 1986?

5 Why might the factors influencing new business formation differ between men and women?

6 Assess the merits and drawbacks of a policy seeking to convert juvenile drug dealers into entrepreneurs.

References

Baines, S. and Wheelock, J. (1998) 'Working for Each Other: Gender, the Household and Micro Business Survival and Growth', *International Small Business Journal*, 17(1), 16–35.

Basu, A. and Altinay, E. (2002) 'The Interaction between Culture and Entrepreneurship in London's Immigrant Businesses', *International Small Business Journal*, 20(4), 371–93.

Baumol, W.J. (1990) 'Entrepreneurship: Productive, Unproductive and Destructive', *Journal of Political Economy*, 98(5), 893–921.

Blanchflower, D.G., Levine, P.B and Zimmerman, D.J. (2003) 'Discrimination in the Small Business Credit Market', *Review of Economics and Statistics*, 85(4), 930–43.

Blanchflower, D.G., and Oswald, A.J. (1998) 'What Makes an Entrepreneur?' *Journal of Labor Economics*, 16(1), 26–60.

Blanchflower, D.G. and Meyer, B. D. (1994) 'A Longitudinal Analysis of the Young Self-employed in Australia and the United States', *Small Business Economics*, 6(1), 1–19.

Bruce, D. (1999) 'Do Husbands Matter?: Married Women Entering Self-employment', *Small Business Economics*, 13(4), 317–29.

Carrasco, R. (1999) 'Transitions to and from Self-employment in Spain: An Empirical Analysis', *Oxford Bulletin of Economics and Statistics*, 61(3), 315–41.

CBS (2005) *Dutch ethnic self-employment rates, 1999–2003*. http://www.cbs.nl/en-GB/menu/themas/bedrijven/publicaties/artikelen/archief/2005/2005-1805-wm.htm.

Chaganti, R. and Greene, P.G. (2002) 'Who Are Ethnic Entrepreneurs?: A Study of Entrepreneurs – Ethnic Involvement and Business Characteristics', *Journal of Small Business Management*, 40(2), 126–43.

Clain, S.H. (2000) 'Gender Differences in Full-time Self-employment', *Journal of Economics and Business*, 52(6), 499–513.

Clark, K. and Drinkwater, S. (2000) 'Pushed Out or Pulled In? Self-employment among Ethnic Minorities in England and Wales', *Labour Economics*, 7(5), 603–28.

Clark, K. and Drinkwater, S. (2007) *Ethnic Minorities in the Labour Market*. York: Joseph Rowntree Foundation.

Coate, S. and Tennyson, S. (1992) 'Labor-Market Discrimination, Imperfect Information and Self-employment', *Oxford Economic Papers, New Series*, 44(2), 272–88.

Cowling, M. and Taylor, M. (2001) 'Entrepreneurial Women and Men: Two Different Species?', *Small Business Economics*, 16(3), 167–75.

de Meza, D. (2002) 'Overlending', *Economic Journal*, 112(477), F17–31.

Dunn, T. and Holtz-Eakin, D. (2000) 'Financial Capital, Human Capital and the Transition to Self-employment: Evidence from Intergenerational Links', *Journal of Labor Economics*, 18, 282–305.

Ekelund, J., Johansson, E., Jarvelin, M.R. and Lichtermann, D. (2005) 'Self-employment and Risk Aversion: Evidence from Psychological Test Data', *Labour Economics*, 12(5), 649–59.

European Foundation for the Improvement of Living and Working Conditions (EFILWC) (2006) *The Gender Pay Gap*. Dublin: EFILWC.

Evans, D. and Jovanovic, B. (1989) 'An Estimated Model of Entrepreneurial Choice under Liquidity Constraints', *Journal of Political Economy*, 97, 808–27.

Evans, D. and Leighton, L. S. (1989) 'Some Empirical Aspects of Entrepreneurship', *American Economic Review*, 79, 519–35.

Fairlie, R.W. (2002) 'Drug-dealing and Legitimate Self-employment', *Journal of Labor Economics*, 20(3), 538–67.

Flores-Romero, M. and Blackburn, R. (2005) 'Is Entrepreneurship More About Sticking with a Firm or About Running Several of Them?: Evidence from Novice and Serial Entrepreneurs'. Lancaster University Management School (unpublished).

Fraser, S. (2005) *Finance for Small and Medium-sized Enterprises: A Report on the 2004 UK Survey of SME Finances*. Coventry: CSME, University of Warwick.

Fraser, S. (2006) *Finance for Small and Medium-sized Enterprises: Comparisons of Ethnic Minority and White-owned Businesses*. London: BERR.

Giannetti, M. and Simanov, A. (2005) *On the Determinants of Entrepreneurial Activity: Individual Characteristics, Economic Environment and Social Norms*. Stockholm: Stockholm School of Economics.

Godley, A. (2001) *Jewish Immigrant Entrepreneurship in New York and London, 1880–1914: Enterprise and Culture*. Basingstoke: Palgrave.

Greene, F.J. and Storey, D.J. (2004) 'An Assessment of a Venture Creation Programme: The Case of Shell Livewire', *Entrepreneurship and Regional Development*, 16(2), 145–59.

Greene, F.J., Mole, K.M. and Storey, D.J. (2008) *Three Decades of Enterprise Culture: Entrepreneurship, Economic Regeneration and Public Policy*. Basingstoke: Palgrave Macmillan.

Hamilton, B.H. (2000) 'Does Entrepreneurship Pay?: An Empirical Analysis of the Returns to Self-employment', *Journal of Political Economy*, 108(3), 604–31.

Hammarstedt, M. (2006) 'The Predicted Earnings Differential and Immigrant Self-employment in Sweden', *Applied Economics*, 38(6), 619–30.

Henley, A. (2004) 'Self-employment Status: The Role of State Dependence and Initial Circumstances', *Small Business Economics*, 22(1), 67–82.

Hurst, E. and Lusardi, A. (2004) 'Liquidity Constraints, Household Wealth and Entrepreneurship', *Journal of Political Economy*, 112(2), 319–47.

Hyytinen, A. and Maliranta, M. (2008) 'When Do Employees Leave Their Job for Entrepreneurship?', *Scandinavian Journal of Economics*, 110(1), 1–21.

Johnson, P.S. and Cathcart, D.G. (1979) 'The Founders of New Manufacturing Firms: A Note on the Size of Their "Incubator" Plants', *Journal of Industrial Economics*, 28(2), 219–24.

Jones, T. and Ram, M. (2007) 'Re-embedding the Ethnic Business Agenda', *Work, Employment and Society*, 21(3), 439–57.

Jovanovic, B. (1982) 'Selection and the Evolution of Industry', *Econometrica*, 50(3), 649–70.

Kautonen, T., Down, S. and South, L. (2008) 'Enterprise Support for Older Entrepreneurs: The Case of PRIME in the UK', *International Journal of Entrepreneurial Behaviour and Research*, 14(2), 85–101.

Kolvereid, L. and Isaksen, E. (2006) 'New Business Start Up and Subsequent Entry into Self-employment', *Journal of Business Venturing*, 21(6), 866–85.

Langowitz, N. and Minniti, M. (2007) 'The Entrepreneurial Propensity of Women', *Entrepreneurship Theory and Practice*, 31(3), 341–64.

Lazear, E.P. (2005) 'Entrepreneurship', *Journal of Labor Economics*, 23(4), 649–80.

Le, A.T. (1999) 'Empirical Studies of Self-employment', *Journal of Economic Surveys*, 13, 381–416.

Lin, Z.X., Picot, G. and Compton, J. (2000) 'The Entry and Exit Dynamics of Self-employment in Canada', *Small Business Economics*, 15(2), 105–25.

Lindelof, P. and Lofsten, H. (2002) 'Growth, Management and Financing of New Technology-based Firms: Assessing Value-added Contributions of Firms Located on and off Science Parks', *Omega-International Journal of Management Science*, 30(3), 143–54.

Lindh, T. and Ohlsson, H. (1996) 'Self-employment and Windfall Gains: Evidence from the Swedish Lottery', *Economic Journal*, 106(439), 1515–26.

Loebl, H. (1978) 'Government-financed Factories and the Establishment of Industries by Refugees in the Special Areas of the North of England, 1937–1961'. M Phil thesis, University of Durham.

Lunn, J. and Steen, T. (2005) 'The Heterogeneity of Self-employment: The Example of Asians in the US', *Small Business Economics*, 24(2), 143–58.

Marlow, S. and Patton, D. (2005) 'All Credit to Men: Entrepreneurship, Finance and Gender', *Entrepreneurship: Theory and Practice*, 29(6), 717–35.

Metcalf, H., Mohdood, T. and Virdee, S. (1996) *Asian Self-employment: The Interaction of Culture and Economics in England*. London: Policy Studies Institute.

Moore, C.S. and Mueller, R.E. (2002) 'The Transition from Paid to Self-employment in Canada: The Importance of Push Factors', *Applied Economics*, 34, 791–801.

Morris, M.H., Miyasaki, N.N., Watters, C.E. and Coombes, S.M. (2006) 'The Dilemma of Growth: Understanding Venture Size Choices of Women Entrepreneurs', *Journal of Small Business Management*, 44(2), 221–44.

Morton, F.M.S. and Podolny, J.M. (2002) 'Love or Money?: The Effects of Owner Motivation in the California Wine Industry', *Journal of Industrial Economics*, 50(4), 431–56.

Nykvist, J. (2008) 'Entrepreneurship and Liquidity Constraints', *Scandinavian Journal of Economics*, 110(1), 23–43.

OECD (2008a) *Measuring Entrepreneurship: A Digest of Indicators*. Paris: OECD.

OECD (2008b) *Women and Men in OECD Countries*. http://www.oecd.org/dataoecd/45/40/37964116.pdf.

ONS (2006) *UK ethnic self-employment rates, 2004*. http://www/statistics.gov.uk/cci/nugget.asp?id=463.

Parker, S.C. (2004) *The Economics of Self-employment and Entrepreneurship*. Cambridge: Cambridge University Press.

Parker, S.C. and Rougier, J.C. (2007) 'The Retirement Behaviour of the Self-employed in Britain', *Applied Economics*, 39(4–6), 697–713.

Pisani, M.J. and Pagan, J.A. (2004) 'Self-employment in the Era of the New Economic Model in Latin America: A Case Study from Nicaragua', *Entrepreneurship and Regional Development*, 16(4), 335–50.

Ram, M. and Jones, T. (2008) 'Ethnic-minority Businesses in the UK: A Review of Research and Policy Developments', *Environment and Planning C-Government and Policy*, 26(2), 352–74.

Ram, M., Smallbone, D., Deakins, D. and Jones, T. (2003) 'Banking on "Break-Out": Finance and the Development of Ethnic Minority Businesses', *Journal of Ethnic and Migration Studies*, 29(4), 663–81.

Rees, H. and Shah, A. (1986) 'An Empirical Analysis of Self-employment in the UK', *Journal of Applied Econometrics*, 1, 95–108.

Rees, H. and Shah, A. (1994) 'The Characteristics of the Self-employed: The Supply of Labour', in Atkinson, J. and Storey D.J. (eds), *Employment, The Small Firm and the Labour* Market, 317–27. London: Routledge.

Ritsila, J. and Tervo, H. (2002), 'Effects of New Firm Formation: Micro-level Panel Data Evidence from Finland', *Small Business Economics*, 19(1), 19–31.

Rosti, L. and Chelli, F. (2005) 'Gender Discrimination, Entrepreneurial Talent and Self-employment', *Small Business Economics*, 24(2), 131–42.

Sleuwaegen, L. and Goedhuys, M. (2002) 'Growth of Firms in Developing Countries, Evidence from Côte d'Ivoire,' *Journal of Development Economics*, 68(1), 117–35.

Storey, D.J. (2004) 'Racial and Gender Discrimination in the Micro Firms Credit Market: Evidence from Trinidad and Tobago', *Small Business Economics*, 25(5), 401–42.

Taylor, M.P. (2001) 'Self-employment and Windfall Gains in Britain: Evidence from Panel Data', *Economica*, 68(272), 539–65.

Taylor, M.P. (2004) 'Self-employment in Britain: When, Who and Why'. Paper presented at Economic Council of Sweden, March.

van der Sluis, J., van Praag, M. and Vijverberg, W. (2005) 'Entrepreneurship Selection and Performance: A Meta-analysis of the Impact of Education in Developing Economies', *World Bank Economic Review*, 19(2), 225–61.

Verheul, I. and Thurik, A.R. (2001) 'Start-up Capital: Does Gender Matter?' *Small Business Economics*, 16(4), 329–46.

Wagner, J. (2003) 'Are Nascent Entrepreneurs Jacks of all Trades?: A Test of Lazear's Theory of Entrepreneurship with German Data', *Applied Economics*, 38(20), 2415–19.

Weber, P. and Shaper M. (2003) 'Understanding the Grey Entrepreneur: A Review of the Literature'. Paper presented at the SEAANZ Conference, University of Ballarat, Australia.

Wellington, A.J. (2006) 'Self-employment: The New Solution for Balancing Family and Career?', *Labour Economics*, 13(3), 357–86.

Westhead, P., Ucbasaran, D., Wright, M. and Binks, M. (2005) 'Novice, Serial and Portfolio Entrepreneur Behaviour and Contributions', *Small Business Economics*, 25(2), 109–32.

Williams, D.R. (2004) 'Youth Self-employment: Its Nature and Consequences', *Small Business Economics*, 23(4), 323–36.

Zissimiopoulos, J.M., and Karoly, L.A. (2007) 'Transitions to Self-employment at Older Ages: The Role of Wealth, Health, Health Insurance and Other Factors', *Labour Economics*, 14(2), 269–95.

How and why businesses close is our subject in Part 3. Chapter 9 argues that business closure is a vital area of importance to anyone interested in small businesses – indeed that it is the ever-present threat of closure that is at the heart of 'smallness'. In Chapter 10, the focus is on presenting five approaches to business closure.

9 Defining and measuring business closure

10 Analysing business closure

Entrepreneurship in Action   FT

Go to the *Small Business and Entrepreneurship* companion website at www.pearsoned.co.uk/storeygreene to watch entrepreneurs and academics giving you their personal perspectives on some of these issues.

Don Sull, Professor of Management at London Business School, discusses the factors affecting business exit.

9 Defining and measuring business closure

Key learning objectives

By the end of this chapter you should:

- Understand why business closure is important

- Be aware of the issues involved in defining business closure

- Identify the key issues involved in measuring the number and rate of business closures.

9.1 Introduction

The following two chapters examine business closure. We have deliberately placed these chapters before those on business growth. This may seem odd. After all, the anticipation might be that businesses come into existence to develop rather than simply close. The truth is that, in practice, business entry is fairly easy, whereas rapid growth is highly unusual and business closure is all too frequent (Geroski 1995). Indeed, it is often forgotten that the *primary* aim of any business is to survive. Take the investment bank Lehman Brothers: this was the fourth largest investment bank in the world. Between 2003 and 2007, it enjoyed four years of record growth in its revenue, earnings and earnings per share for its shareholders. By September 2008, it no longer existed as a separate legal entity.

Lehman Brothers was not a small business, but it was a high profile case of business closure (see, however, Case studies 5 and 6 on business closure). We place business closure 'up front' in this book because it is the most likely fate of the average new or small business. To demonstrate this, let us look at VAT deregistration data from the UK. For every 100 VAT-registered businesses that were set up in 1995, only 32 of them were still registered by 2005 (BERR 2008). In the US, the evidence is even starker. Using a 'wider' definition of the business population (98 per cent of US businesses), Knaup (2005) shows that only 44 per cent of 1998 new starts were still in existence by 2002.

It is also the case that the smaller the business, the more likely it is to close. Australian data shows that around 46 out of every 100 businesses that began in 2003 with no employees had closed by 2006. However, if the business had between 1–4 employees in 2003, only 15 businesses out of 100 closed by 2006. This is also evident from Figure 9.1, which shows the 'death' rates by employee size categories for New Zealand businesses over the period 2005–7. It clearly shows that smaller businesses are much more likely to 'die' than larger-sized businesses. Hart and Oulton (1996) also showed, for the UK, that the doubling of company size lowered the death rate by 5 per cent, until 'flattening out' at 1,000 workers.

These central 'stylised facts' – that smaller and younger businesses are more prone to closure – are amongst the most important factors in distinguishing smaller from larger businesses. The obvious consequence is that small businesses are seen as risky endeavours, both for the owners and those that finance or sell to (suppliers) or buy from (customers) such businesses.

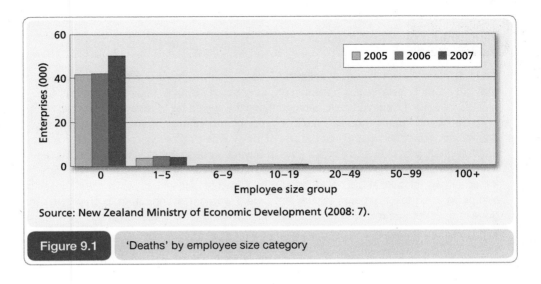

Source: New Zealand Ministry of Economic Development (2008: 7).

| Figure 9.1 | 'Deaths' by employee size category |

In this, the first of two chapters on business closure, we investigate why it is such an important aspect of understanding entrepreneurship and small business. We identify that one of the most common reasons for examining business closure is because of the devastating impact it can have on an individual and their family. Business closure can also impact heavily on those who are owed money (creditors) and those who are employed in the business. Despite the likely downsides of business closure, the chapter shows that there can also be some positive aspects to a business closing. It 'signals' to others – either thinking about entering the marketplace or who are already in the marketplace – that the resources used in the business were not being used effectively.

This chapter also highlights the very real problems in defining and measuring business closure. For example, besides the term 'closure', there are a range of alternatives: 'mortality', 'failure', 'death' and 'bankruptcy'. These are all negative terms. However, not all people close their business because their business has 'failed'. Some close their business because they have sold it, possibly for considerably more than its value when they began it. Others may close simply because they want to retire from work. A third, and very important, group simply close the business and move into employment (particularly those with zero employees). This chapter explores the issues in defining and measuring business closure. This mirrors the difficulties faced in defining and measuring new businesses that were identified in Chapter 6. In Chapter 10, we investigate why it is that smaller and younger businesses are more likely to close but, for now, we examine six reasons why business closure is important.

9.2 Why is business closure important?

The subject of business closure is an important one, particularly for small businesses. In this section, we examine six reasons why this is so, illustrated with real news stories from around the world.

Reason 1. The closure of a business is often associated with dire social and economic consequences. To illustrate this, consider the following two short cases.

The Times

Case 1. When Jeremy Harbour's first business, an amusement arcade and takeaway-food operation, failed after 18 months, swallowing his entire life savings of £60,000, he did not take it well. 'I stopped eating for weeks', he said. 'I went very pale and gaunt and my weight fell to about eight stone. I had to move back in with my parents and I pretty much stayed in my room for three months and didn't talk to anyone.' It was Harbour's first experience of failure and – at the age of 19 – it was a bitter lesson. He had run a market stall from the age of 14 and left school at 15 to make a living buying amusement machines for pubs, and up to that point had succeeded at every business venture he had attempted. But the amusement arcade proved a step too far. 'I made every mistake in the book', he said. 'I signed the lease in my own name, not through a limited liability company. I had taken on staff for the first time. I was promoting direct to customers for the first time. I had gone into something that was a complete unknown and I lost everything I had built up since I was 14.'

Source: Rachel Bridge, 'How to Cope When Your Business Goes Bust', *The Times*, 10 February 2008. © The Times, 10 February 2008/nisyndication.com.

Illustration   *China Daily*

Case 2. Two sisters from Hong Kong committed suicide in east China's Jiangxi province after their business failed, say police. The sisters released coal gas at their home in Zhangshu city at around 22:00 on March 23, local police officer Chen Yongping said. The younger sister, Zhan Miaoling, 52, died shortly after of gas poisoning. Zhan Meiling, 60, survived, but killed herself by lying on a railway track the next morning. The sisters started their wood product company in Zhangshu in 2005, after a similar factory in south China's Guangdong Province ran into difficulties. But the new company turned out to be another failure, said Chen.

Source: *China Daily*, 'HK Sisters Commit Suicide after Business Failure', 31 March 2007.

Reason 2. It is not just the individual or their family and friends that are likely to be impacted by a business closure. A business closure may mean the loss of employment to a significant number of people.

Reason 3. Business closure may have social and economic consequences for those that invested in the business or are owed money by the business. This may be no 'fault' of the business owners. However, some individuals set up a business to deliberately defraud investors and creditors. To illustrate these two related reasons, here are another two short cases.

Illustration   Gretna Football Club

Case 3. Gretna is a town on the Scottish/English border famous for allowing young people who had eloped from England to marry. Gretna was not famous, though, for its football team. Gretna Football Club spent most of the last century in the amateur football leagues. This all changed with the arrival of Brooks Mileson. Mileson was a millionaire entrepreneur who had made his fortune in insurance, construction and property. With Mileson's financial backing, Gretna FC's progress up the professional Scottish league ladder was rapid. Between 2005 and 2007, the team won the Division Three, Two and One Scottish titles. In 2006, they were runners up in the Scottish Cup and played in the UEFA cup. They won promotion to the Scottish Premier League (SPL) for the 2007–8 season.

Once in the highest league (the SPL), things started to go badly wrong. It emerged that the football club owed £4 million to its creditors. People owed included the tax authorities (HM Revenue). They were owed

£500,000. More than 100 local companies and organisations were also owed anything between £35 and £75,000. Brooks Mileson was in no position to pay. He had suffered a brain infection which left him seriously ill and unable to write the cheques to pay the bills. March 2008 also saw him £375,000 overdrawn at the bank.

One result of these debts was that 23 players, most of the coaching staff and Brook Mileson's son were made redundant. By June 2008, all of the other staff had been made redundant and Gretna Football Club was formally dissolved.

Illustration	Alan Bond

Case 4. Alan Bond, the Australian entrepreneur, started with almost nothing and went on to have interests in mining, property, brewing and manufacturing. Famously flamboyant, he bought Vincent van Gogh's 'Irises' at Sotheby's for US$53 m – the highest price that had ever been paid for a painting. He also had four jets and a yacht. After he bought the Australian TV 'Nine' network for A$1 billion, his businesses – the Bond Corporation – started to run into trouble. The result was that the Bond Corporation recorded the biggest loss in Australian corporate history. Bond himself ended up with personal debts calculated at A$1.8 billion.

In 1992, Bond was declared bankrupt. Out of the A$1.8 billion he owed, Bond paid A$12 million or about half a cent for every dollar to his creditors. He subsequently went on trial for deception in 1997. At his trial, Bond claimed that he had a kidney infection, was depressed and was suffering from memory loss. Bond served four years out of a seven year jail term. Out of prison, Bond subsequently rebuilt his business empire by investing in African oil and diamonds. He was able to do that because he had placed some of his earlier fortune in family trusts. These could not be accessed by his creditors. The *Australian Business Week Review* estimated his fortune in 2008 at A$265 million.

Reason 4. Business closure may not always be a negative event. As we shall see in section 9.4, some individuals close their business for positive reasons. These are termed 'successful closures'. This may be because they wish to retire or because they sell the assets of the business for a profit.

Reason 5. Business closure is also seen as a valuable learning experience for business owners. Take the earlier example of Jeremy Harbour, who lost his business, his life savings and was forced to go back home to his parents. This is what happened to him subsequently:

Illustration	*The Times*

Case 1 (continued). For Harbour, the collapse of his amusement arcade business was not to be his only experience of failure. After briefly going to work for someone else, he started up a telecoms company that he grew ambitiously for eight years. But the business was always undercapitalised and had to be rescued by an outside investor, with the result that Harbour lost £1 m. When this business failed, however, he was much better equipped to deal with it. 'I had a clearer head because I knew it doesn't hurt when you land and that gave me the clarity to constructively put together a deal to rescue the business and turn it round and not have to walk away with nothing', he said. 'It gives you clarity of thought when you have done it before.'

Proving the old adage that if at first you don't succeed, try, try, try again, Harbour did not give up on his dream of owning a successful company. He now runs a group called Unity Group, which, in a nice twist, helps to turn round other failing businesses. Primarily a telecoms company, Unity has a turnover of £8 m, employs 120 staff and also has a health club business. 'Failure taught me that the downside isn't actually as bad as the

A dismantled carousel on Coney Island.

thought of the downside, so the juice is probably worth the squeeze', said Harbour. 'Failure is all part of the journey of life. Life has its ups and downs but there is no way I'd want to wake up in the morning and do something safe. You're only on the planet for a finite amount of time and so you might as well spend it doing something you enjoy.' 'You have to quantify what failure really is. Emotionally it might tear you apart, but when you rationalise it, failure doesn't really mean anything. It's not tangible. It's not like you've lost a leg.'

Source: Rachel Bridge, 'How to Cope When Your Business Goes Bust', *The Times*, 10 February 2008.

Reason 6. The closure of a 'failed' business also has positive economic benefits. First, it represents a 'signal' to others that the customer does not want what the business offers. This lesson may be 'picked up' by potential or actual business owners who recognise that they cannot afford to repeat these 'mistakes'. The closure of a business may also lead to learning, and a change in behaviour on the part of existing or potential business owners. They recognise that they will have to do something different from the business that failed, or else they will simply repeat the experience.

Second, the closure of a business is likely to reflect the inability of the combination of those resources – managerial and financial – to profitably deliver a given product or service. Closure means that those resources then become available to be used elsewhere in the economy, for a higher economic return. The business owner and the workforce are free to try to earn a living in another way, rather than their labour being utilised inefficiently.

In summary, business closure may equate to an economic and social disaster for those involved in, and associated with, the business (including its clients). Business closure is often associated with suicide (Weyerer and Brenner 1996), and can also place huge financial and psychological stress on the business owner and their families. It can also lead to the loss of employment and personal savings built up by investors over many years. But, it can also have positive impacts. First, it allows for the reallocation of resources away from inefficient operations. Second, it has the potential to provide 'lessons' to the business owner and 'signals' to other potential and actual business owners.

Questions

- Look back at Illustration, Case 4 (Alan Bond). Whom should the law favour? Should legislation protect creditors and employees, or give better support for the entrepreneur?
- Should we care if a business fails? Is it not part of the competitive process?

9.3 Defining business closure

We saw in Chapter 6 the very real difficulties in defining the new business. This section mirrors those difficulties in its attempt to define a closed business. It begins by outlining the wide variety of terms that can be used to formally describe business closure. It then considers some tangible problems in deciding whether or not a business has closed. Finally, it differentiates between 'successful' and 'unsuccessful' closures.

Terms used to describe business closure

As we showed in Chapter 6, no country has a fully comprehensive list or census of *all* its businesses. In essence, we know only imperfectly how many businesses come into existence or close in any given period of time. Hence, a number of proxies for describing business closure are often used. These are identified in Table 9.1, and are grouped in three ways: by individual, by type of business, and by plant/workplace/establishment. The following description is necessarily complex, reflecting the real differences in terminology both within and between countries.

Table 9.1	The terminology of business closure		
Individual	**Business/Enterprise**	**Business/Enterprise**	**Plant/Workplace/ Establishment**
	Limited companies	*Unincorporated businesses*	
Bankruptcies	Bankruptcies	Bankruptcies	
	Insolvencies		
	Liquidations		
Exit	Exit	Exit	Exit
	Deregister	Deregister	
	Failure	Failure	
	Death	Death	
	Mortality	Mortality	

Bankruptcy

The first term identified in Table 9.1 is bankruptcy. In the UK, this applies just to the individual. In other countries it also applies to businesses, both incorporated (limited and public limited companies) and unincorporated (sole traders and partnerships). Notable examples here are the Netherlands, Canada and the US. Bankruptcy is a formal legal procedure for people (UK) and people and businesses (most other countries) that can no longer pay their creditors. The advantage for the individual and the businesses is that they are relieved of their financial obligations. This allows them to make a fresh start. The downside is that bankrupts often lose control of their assets, face real difficulties in gaining future credit, and may be denied rights such as becoming a company director (for a period of time).

Insolvency and liquidation

The next terms in Table 9.1 are insolvency and liquidation. These refer solely to limited companies. Again, these are situations where companies are no longer able to pay their debt. This can be a decision reached by the business owners (voluntary insolvency), a decision reached by creditors (involuntary insolvency) or forced on them (compulsory insolvency). Liquidation occurs when the assets of the business are distributed amongst the creditors of the business.

'Exit'

Table 9.1 also identifies that 'exit' is used to define business closure. For the individual, this is used to describe someone who has left self-employment for an alternative labour-market activity (e.g. employment, unemployment). For the business, 'exit' usually means the closure of an enterprise. Plant/Workplace/Establishment exit is different. Earlier, in Chapter 3, we showed that there were differences between enterprises and establishments. Enterprises are businesses, whereas establishments are parts of a business. These may be stores, manufacturing 'plants', or offices that are part of a broader business or retail chain.

When a plant/establishment/workplace closes or exits, this does not necessarily mean that the enterprise itself closes. For example, a supermarket chain may close one of its local branches, but this does not mean that the chain has ceased as a business.

Deregistration

A further term which is often synonymous with business closure is deregistration. This refers to a business deregistering from its inclusion in a register, such as sales tax or a trade directory. However, as we will show, deregistration is an imperfect measure of business closure, since many businesses are never registered for tax purposes whilst some businesses continue to trade even though they de-register.

'Exit' versus 'Failure'

As we have shown, there are a wide range of terms that can be used as synonyms for business closure. Some relate to people, others to enterprises and some to plants or establishments, but none are ideal as a measure of business closure. Sten (1998) makes an interesting attempt to resolve some of the ambiguity surrounding these terms. He concentrates on the distinction between 'exit' and 'failure', and argues that 'failure' should be reserved for those cases where the business owner had no choice but to close a business. By contrast, 'exit' should be used for all other forms of closure.

Watson and Everett (1993) make a similar distinction. First, they identify that there is a continuum of business closure terms. At one end is business 'discontinuance'. This may be itself split into discontinuance of ownership or discontinuance of the business. At the other end is a narrow definition which sees closure as being associated with bankruptcy or to prevent further losses to creditors. Watson and Everett (1993) believe that a more appropriate measure of business 'failure' is a 'failure to make a go of it'. The advantage of such a definition is that it relies on business owners' views about whether or not they have earned an appropriate return from their business. The disadvantage of this term is that it is subjective. What is an appropriate return for one business owner may be inappropriate for another. This makes it difficult to construct meaningful comparative data using this definition.

Business closure: a definition

So, what is our favoured definition? We return to the objectives we identified in Chapter 6 when we were considering a definition of a new business. We now adapt this definition to reflect business closure. Again, our definition is motivated by an interest in excluding certain types of business which are outside our area of interest. Our favoured definition is:

> **A business closure occurs when a transacting entity stops its activities and does not transfer its ownership to another business and is independent of an existing business.**

To illustrate, we make use of the fictitious company, Storey and Greene Ltd, which we introduced in Chapter 6. We saw that this business was created 'out of nothing' – reflecting our interest in wholly new businesses. In terms of 'closing' this business, we want to reflect the following:

- it involved some activity (e.g. selling or bartering);
- it was separate from the existing personal activities of the owners;
- it was legally independent from other businesses;
- it was not acquired by others; and
- closure does not involve a simple name change.

Notice that we do not make any judgement about whether this was a successful or unsuccessful closure. Instead, we will outline a number of scenarios and ask you to think through the issues that they raise for defining business closure.

Separation of personal and business activities

Individuals closing a business have to bring to an end the separation between their own activities and their business activities. A 'proxy' for this is closing a business bank account, winding up the business or deregistering the business for sales tax purposes. At the individual level, it may mean ending the separation for tax purposes of work done for employment and work done for themselves, although ending the separation between the individual and the entity is usually not sufficient to identify all of the dimensions of business closure.

| Illustration | Storey and Greene Ltd (Part 1) |

Yes but: what about these two cases?

Case 1. Mr Greene had decided to register a separate business called Greene Ltd to sell sports goods. He also declared to the tax authorities that he had set up this business. Mr Greene subsequently found that other business issues took precedence and the net result was that he never spent the time to make any sales. He subsequently deregistered the business for tax and legal purposes.

Case 2. Mr Storey was heavily involved in a voluntary mutual aid scheme. He no longer feels that he can keep up the commitment to provide his specialist building maintenance skills. Since there was never any registration needed for the scheme, there is no requirement to deregister his interest.

- **Are either or both of these a closed business?**
- **What do you think?**

A new branch or subsidiary of an existing enterprise

We are only interested in the closure of businesses that were independently owned.

| Illustration | Storey and Greene Ltd (Part 2) |

Storey and Greene Ltd operated from a single business location, selling insurance. They decided to diversify into selling houses and created a new company called Storey and Greene (Housing) Ltd, but deregistered Storey and Greene Ltd. Storey and Greene (Housing) Ltd is owned by exactly the same individuals and it operates from the same premises.

Is Storey and Greene Ltd an example of a closed business?

Yes it is: A company, Storey and Greene Ltd, has been closed.

No it isn't: It still has the same owners and is still at the same location. Lots of businesses diversify by selling new products or services. After all, Mr Storey and Mr Greene might well have just continued to sell slightly different products to exactly the same group of customers.

- **What do you think?**
- **Is this a closed business?**

A transfer of ownership, but no other change

We are also *not* interested in a business that is originally owned by one individual or group of individuals and is then sold to another. This is because the total number of businesses in the economy remains the same.

| Illustration | Storey and Greene Ltd (Part 3) |

Yes but: what about the following two cases?

Case 1. Storey and Greene Ltd is sold to new owners and both Mr Storey and Mr Greene resign and new director-owners are appointed, but the name of the company and all other aspects remain the same.

Case 2. Storey and Greene Ltd is sold to new owners and both Mr Storey and Mr Greene resign. The new owners appoint new directors. The name Storey and Greene Ltd disappears and the business is now called Sykes, Mumby and Croft Ltd, but it continues to operate from its existing premises with the same employees.

- **Are either or both of these closed businesses?**
- **What do you think?**

A change of business name, but no other change

We are also *not* interested in a business which changes its name but continues to undertake the same economic activity. For example, solicitors, accountants and doctors may lose one or more of their partners, so changing the name of the business, but the nature of that business remains unaltered, so it cannot be considered as new.

Illustration	Storey and Greene Ltd (Part 4)

Yes but: what about this case?

Case 1. Mr Greene's daughter takes over the insurance business, Storey and Greene Ltd. She believes the name is boring and wants to revitalise and modernise its image. She registers a new company as Insur2go and closes Storey and Greene Ltd, but the share ownership is identical for both companies. Insur2go continues to trade at the same location providing a somewhat modernised service.

● **Has Storey and Greene Ltd actually been closed?**

● **What do you think?**

A change of location, but no other change

Businesses do not always remain at the same location. A simple change of location cannot be considered as the closure of one business and the creation of a new business if all other aspects of the business remain unchanged.

Illustration	Storey and Greene Ltd (Part 5)

Yes but: what about this case?

Mr Storey and Mr Greene decide that England is too cold for them and they and their families will move to Spain. Is this a closed business?

Yes it is: For the UK it is a loss of business.

No it isn't: It is no different in principle to the business moving to the next street since there is only a simple transfer of economic activity. The only difference is in terms of geographical units. It is a loss for England, but if the geographical unit were the European Union then it would be just a clear transfer.

● **Has the UK business actually been closed?**

● **What do you think?**

This section highlighted the very real issues in defining business closure. The above cases also illustrate that there are a number of forms of economic activity which may be regarded by some, but not by others, as examples of business closure, just as there were with business openings. It emphasises that business closures can, in many respects, be viewed as the 'mirror image' of business openings. The problem that this creates is that varying definitions lead to different statistics being generated about business closure, which may or may not coincide. We address these issues in the next section.

9.4 Measuring business closure

Generally, the definition of failure used has, to a large extent, depended on the nature of the data available.

(Everett and Watson, 1998: 374).

Without a comprehensive census of economic activity, it remains difficult to identify the number of business closures. As the quote above suggests, definitions are often dependent on how business closure is measured. This section details six main ways of measuring business closure. Each has advantages and disadvantages, and each leads to differing assessments of the scale of business closure. Supplementary to this is the issue of identifying – for a given year – the closure or exit rate. This – as with the start-up rate – is important, because we would like to know what is happening to the business population over time because, if nothing else, it helps us makes judgements about the entrepreneurial performance of a region or country. This section shows that there are very real problems in measuring both the number and rate of business closures.

Measuring the number of business closures

Table 9.2 identifies six measures that have been used to quantify business closure. These six measures are:

1 individuals who say they have closed a business;

2 individuals who move out of self-employment;

3 the number of bankruptcies, insolvencies or liquidations;

4 the number of enterprises deregistering;

5 the number of companies deregistering; and

6 the number of business bank accounts that are closed.

Table 9.2 details the advantages and disadvantages of these six measures.

The advantage of asking people if they have closed a business is that this can offer insights into why people choose to close a business. It re-emphasises that closure is not synonymous with failure. Bates (2005), using the US Census Bureau's CBO database (1989–1996), asked the following question: 'Which item below best describes the status of this business at the time the decision was made to cease operations?' The two options were: 'successful' or 'unsuccessful'. Of those that had closed, 38 per cent of the businesses claimed they were successful. This may be surprisingly high because the common conception is that closure is likely to be for negative (e.g. bankruptcy) reasons.

Everett and Watson's (1998) survey of Australian managed shopping centres also identified that there were diverse reasons for the closure of a business. The most common reason was 'to realise a profit' (35 per cent). The other main reasons were bankruptcy (7 per cent), 'to avoid further losses' (16 per cent), 'did not make "a go of it"' (10 per cent) and retirement or ill health (5 per cent). In other words, four out of 10 business closures were, arguably, 'successful' at the time of closure which is similar to the findings of Bates (2005) for the US noted above.

Further evidence of the value of surveys is provided by Taylor (1999) for the UK and Harada (2007) for Japan. Taylor highlights (Table 9.3) that there are different reasons why people exit self-employment, and that this is influenced by the period of time the individual has been in self-employment. The first column shows that those individuals with only a very short experience of self-employment were the most likely to move to becoming an employee. There is a striking contrast with those who had been self-employed for more than a decade. These individuals are likely to be much older, and more likely to retire than become an employee. Table 9.3 also shows that a comparatively small proportion of those exiting self-employment did so because their business went bankrupt. For those with only a short experience of self-employment, 15 per cent of individuals were in this category, compared with 11 per cent for individuals in self-employment for a decade or more.

Harada (2007) also looks at the links between the age of the Japanese business owner and the reasons given for business closure (Table 9.4). He compares the reasons for business

| Table 9.2 | Identifying the number of business closures: advantages and disadvantages of different measures |

Measure	Unit of analysis	Source	Advantages	Disadvantages
Individuals who say they have closed a new business	People/ business	Survey evidence (e.g. business surveys or self-employment data)	• Can tease out differences between successful and unsuccessful business closures.	• Relies on subjective interpretations. • Difficult to make national and international comparisons.
Individuals who move out of self-employment into employment, or who exit from the labour market	People	Survey evidence (e.g. Labour Force Survey)	• It allows for the official identification of individuals leaving self-employment and traces their subsequent labour-market status (e.g. un/employed).	• It only tracks individuals, not businesses, and gives an imperfect estimate of closures. • It may under-estimate the number of business closures because some people may own more than one business. • It may over-estimate the number of businesses because more than one person may own a business. • It may over-estimate the number of closures since many self-employed are really employees, but classified as self-employed to minimise employer taxes. Some self-employed are also just people working part-time for 'pin money'.
Bankruptcy, insolvency and liquidations	People/ business	Official data on bankruptcies, insolvencies and liquidations	• Provides data on those who have 'failed'. • International comparative data potentially available.	• Provides a narrow interpretation of business closure. • Does not explain why it is that individuals/businesses have failed. • Potentially difficult to establish standardised national or international comparative data.
The number of enterprises deregistering	Business	Sales tax registration data	• This allows for the official identification of business closure. • It is likely to include most large businesses. These have the greatest economic impact. Most tiny businesses matter little in aggregate terms, either to overall tax income or to the competitive process.	• It is often the case that only businesses with a (relatively) high sales threshold appear in official statistics. • The thresholds vary between countries and over time, making it difficult to make inter-country comparisons. This also impacts on individual countries because varying thresholds make comparisons over time difficult. • Closures may be indistinguishable from mergers, acquisitions or the closure of subsidiaries. • Business activity is often informal in very many countries and so there is only weak data on closures.

Table 9.2 continued

Measure	Unit of analysis	Source	Advantages	Disadvantages
The number of companies deregistering	Business	Company incorporation data	• Data is generally available on deregistrations. • Closure of a company reflects evidence of a change in economic value in a country. • Whilst it may exclude many very tiny businesses, these are likely to have only very modest economic significance and so their exclusion is of limited aggregate economic value.	• Only a small proportion of new businesses are limited liability companies. • Some closures are not 'real' businesses – instead they are 'shell' companies that never trade. • Differences in threshold levels and costs vary markedly between countries and so influence the extent to which it is valid to make international comparisons.
The number of business bank accounts closing	Business	Bank accounts	• Most businesses in the world need banks to undertake financial transactions and banks have a commercial incentive to ensure the data are up to date and accurate. • It will include closures that are too small to be included in the official registration data.	• If the data are compiled by one bank, they have to be 'scaled up', based on their known market share. This market share may be inaccurate. • Businesses transferring from other banks are included and so will inflate the figures. Bank switching, however, is fairly rare in many countries. • Individuals may close their business account but use their personal account to run their business. Banks are able to monitor payments. This may allow them to impose a clear distinction between personal and business payments.

Table 9.3	Reasons for exiting from self-employment (in percentages)	
	Less than 1 year's duration	**Greater than 10 years' duration**
Better/Different job	70	29
Bankruptcy	15	11
Retirement	0	35
Health	4	9
Family care/House move/Education	2	5
Not specified	9	10

Source: Taylor (1999).

Table 9.4	Reasons for closing a business (in percentages)			
	Main reason for exit	**Total**	**Manager under 65**	**Manager over 65**
1	To take life easy	3.1	3.3	2.9
2	To take a new job or start a new business	3.1	4.9	0.8
3	Ageing of the manager	20.0	5.4	38.7
4	Ageing of employees	0.8	0.4	1.2
5	Illness or injury of the manager	14.5	13.0	16.4
6	Illness or injury of the manager's relatives	2.7	2.4	3.1
7	Family issues, such as marriage or relocation (issues not covered by 6)	0.9	1.4	0.1
8	Disaster (except for 5–7)	0.3	0.4	0.1
9	Diminished motivation for the business	6.9	8.6	4.7
10	Despairing perception of further business (except for 3–8)	37.9	49.2	23.4
11	Bankruptcy	2.3	2.8	1.7
12	Others	7.6	8.3	6.8

Source: Harada (2007).

closure for those business owners under and over 65 years old. Those over 65 are much more likely to close their business because of age, and are much less likely to consider a new job. Illness and injury are also important. Nonetheless, a 'despairing perception of further business' like Watson and Everett's (1999) 'failure to make a go of it' is also an important reason for business closure.

The other main advantage of such survey information is that it can allow for distinctions to be drawn between successful and unsuccessful closures. This is important because it gives insights into how valuable assets are successfully reallocated by business owners. It also focuses on the characteristics of those businesses and individuals that failed. This may be an important signal to potential and existing entrepreneurs, and may also help guide public policy.

Watson and Everett (1998) – in their study of Australian retail centres – argued that the impact of macro-economic factors (e.g. interest rates, unemployment) differed depending on the type of business closure. For example, they found an association between interest rates and bankruptcy which (they suggested) reflected the costs incurred in setting up and

Table 9.5	Three studies of 'successful' closure		
	Harada (2007)	**Bates (2005)**	**Taylor (1999)**
Country	Japan	US	UK
Definition	Unforced exit	Successful closure	Voluntary terminations
Human capital attributes			
Being older	+	−	ns
Age^2		+	ns
Coming from an ethnic minority		−	ns
Being male	−	−	
Education		+	+
Prior sectoral experience		+	
Prior managerial experience	−		
Parents in self-employment			ns
Self-employment experience			−
Smaller businesses	ns		
Younger businesses		ns	
Limited company	ns		
Manufacturing		+	
Construction	ns	ns	−
Wholesale/Retail	+		
Business services	ns		+
Other	+		
Having assets/capital		−	
Use of a bank loan	−		
Sales decreasing	−		
Deficits	−		

operating a retail centre. Interest rates, however, were not so important for other classes of business closure. Instead, what mattered for those failing to 'make a go of it' or 'discontinuing ownership' was the level of retail sales.

Further differences are identified in Table 9.5, which shows the findings from three studies of 'successful' closure. Harada (2007) associates successful closure with 'unforced economic exit'; Bates (2005) uses a self-reported measure ('successful closure'); and Taylor (1999) uses voluntary terminations from self-employment. Table 9.5 shows whether a particular factor (when it is examined in the study) has a positive influence (+), a negative influence (−) or no influence (n.s.). It shows there is a negative association between males and success. In other words, males are much less likely, in both Bates (2005) and Harada (2007), to have 'successful' business closures. It would also appear that age of the individual is important. Harada reports that older people are more likely to have a successful business closure. Bates, however, specifies that this is a 'U'-shaped association: the likelihood of a successful closure falls, then plateaus before rising as people age. In other words, the closer the individual is to retirement the stronger the influence this has on the closure decision.

There also appears to be some evidence that education is positively associated with successful closure. This is evident in both Bates (2005) and Taylor (1999), and may imply support for choice theory (Chapter 8). Here, the educated entrepreneur is more likely to quit self-employment, even when obtaining a reasonable income, because of greater earning opportunities elsewhere as an employee. In this sense, the business is successful when the owner quits. There is also evidence from each of the three studies of the differential impact that sector has on a successful closure. The role of finance is also interesting. Harada (2007) identifies that those who used a loan are less likely to be a successful closure. Bates (2005) identifies a similar association between use of capital and closure. Harada (2007) suggests that poor sales and increasing deficits are more likely to lead to a forced economic exit. Finally, there are no significant differences (n.s.) found in terms of the age, size or legal form of the business. This is interesting because – as with the evidence on business entry (Chapter 8) – it may have been expected that younger people, smaller businesses and non-incorporated businesses would be more likely to experience 'unsuccessful' closure of the business.

Whilst survey evidence enables the respondent to distinguish between 'successful and unsuccessful' business closures, the responses are subjective. They are likely to be influenced by particular cultural and social conceptions of 'failure'. There is also no unified approach or set of questions – however imperfect – that would allow for the construction of national or international comparative data. It is, therefore, difficult to gain widespread and reliable information on the number and rate of successful business closures. The cultural differences and the unwillingness of respondents to admit business failure – even if they can blame others for it – and the difficulty of tracking such individuals present real problems for enumerators. As was seen in the cases of Jeremy Harbour or Alan Bond, it is much easier for such individuals to come forward when they are successful than when they 'pretty much stayed in my room and didn't speak to anyone for three months', as Harbour retrospectively admitted.

The second approach identified in Table 9.2 is to use self-employment 'exit' data. The advantage of such data is that it allows for a wider interpretation of business closure. The problem – like much other survey data – is that no distinction is made between the economic value of business closures.

Table 9.2 identifies three further measures that use the business as a unit of analysis. The advantage of the first of these – data on company insolvencies – is that, potentially, it might be called a 'common sense' interpretation of business 'failure'. The other advantage – despite differences in the unit of analysis (individual or business) – is that it is possible to use such data to examine national and international data on bankruptcies. Its disadvantage is that it uses a very narrow interpretation of business closure, as insolvency is only one reason for business closure. Additionally, insolvency data in relation to smaller businesses is often difficult to interpret. Business owners often mix their personal finances with business finance (Fraser 2005). This makes it difficult to know if insolvency was due to business difficulties or, for example, gambling on horses by the individual. Finally, even within a single area such as the UK, it is difficult to produce consistent statistics: only England and Wales identify if a bankrupt was self-employed – the Scottish and Northern Irish services do not collect such information.

Enterprise and company deregistration data have the advantage that they allow for a wider definition of business closure, since it is likely to represent the 'discontinuance' of the business. Such data are also available, usually at a national and international level. The other main advantage of this type of measure is that it is more likely to record deregistration by larger businesses. Arguably, these data are more reflective of economic value and, by assessing these businesses, we are more likely to gain an accurate aggregate understanding of economic change. The problem with such data is that they are also imperfect measures of business closure, because deregistration may only mean the business no longer fits the criteria set down by those compiling the register: it does not necessarily mean the business has ceased trading.

For example, take the hypothetical case of Business A. In year 1, it makes its first sales but these are not sufficient for it to have to register for VAT. In year 2, it obtains a large order, and registers – this means registration takes place some time after trading begins. Then, in year 3, sales return to the level of year 1 and the business deregisters. This might be taken to be a sign of business failure/closure, yet the business does continue to trade, with sales which are the same as year 1. There is, therefore, a problem in interpreting exits based on sales tax data records, particularly for very small businesses.

The last measure of business closure identified in Table 9.2 is the closure of a bank account. Banks have a commercial incentive to ensure that their data is accurate, but, as noted in Chapter 5, some businesses may simply have chosen to switch banks, so account closure cannot be treated as a wholly reliable indicator of whether a business has closed.

Comparing measures of business closure

Ideally, we would like to be able to compare the six measures identified above. Unfortunately, the first measure (survey evidence from individuals) does not readily allow us to make comparisons. Such data tends to be idiosyncratic, using different definitions, and may not examine trends over time. We would also like to have available to us self-employment exit data but, unfortunately, these are not publicly available and, in any event, only count those exits that meet official taxation thresholds. Figure 9.2 makes use of UK data for five other measures of business closure: company insolvencies, business de-registrations, company dissolutions (removal from the business register), self-employed bankrupts (only for England and Wales) and closed bank account data. It shows both the differences in the absolute numbers of businesses involved and how these vary over the relatively short period 1998 to 2007.

The scale of differences is wide. Figure 9.2 shows that the number of self-employed bankrupts in 2006 was around 12,000 per annum. This compares to around 29,000 company insolvencies, 140,000 VAT deregistrations, 240,000 removals from the company register and 460,000 bank account closures in 2006. It is not just in terms of scale that there are evident differences. Figure 9.2 shows that the number of self-employed bankrupts and VAT registrations were broadly flat between 1998–2006. However, company insolvencies rose from around 18,000 in 1998 to 29,000 in 2006. Removals from the company register also increased markedly, effectively doubling from around 120,000 to more than 240,000. Finally, bank data shows that around 320,000 accounts were closed in 1998. This increases to around 460,000 in 2006.

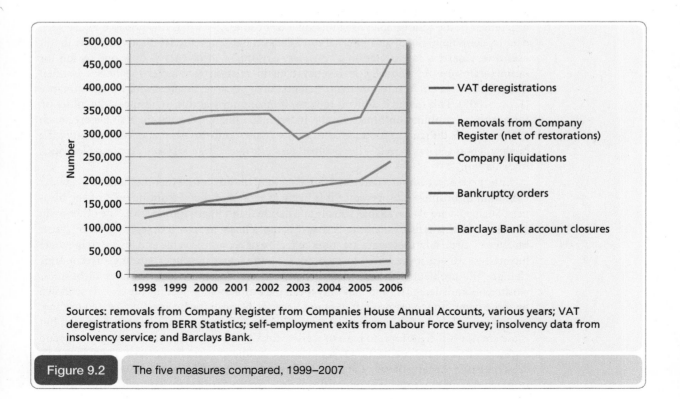

Sources: removals from Company Register from Companies House Annual Accounts, various years; VAT deregistrations from BERR Statistics; self-employment exits from Labour Force Survey; insolvency data from insolvency service; and Barclays Bank.

Figure 9.2   The five measures compared, 1999–2007

The clear lesson is that, whilst all five measures are used to reflect business closure, none can claim to be definitive because they all measure different aspects of the phenomenon. As in all aspects of statistics, it is important to be clear what the focus of interest is, and to recognise that, in this case, there is no ideal measure of the *number* of business closures.

Measuring the rate of business closures

Measuring the number of business closures is not the only challenge. A second problem is assessing the business closure **rate**. This is difficult because of the issues involved with the numerator and the denominator (see Chapter 6, where similar issues were raised in measuring business birth rates). Some measure of business closure (numerator) has to be taken and divided by an appropriate measure of the population (denominator), then multiplied to give a percentage figure for the rate of business closure. The problems with the numerator are that timing issues (e.g. when is closure measured, and how often is closure measured?) and purity of 'closure' (e.g. is it just a change of business ownership?) constitute real measurement issues. Likewise, measurement of the denominator is affected by issues such as the appropriate population measure (e.g. labour-market population, or stock of businesses?).

A fundamental problem is that data sources share biases. These may range from differences in the unit of measurement (enterprises or establishments) and coverage (e.g. threshold levels). These issues produce differing interpretations of business closure rates. The net result is that the measurement of closure rates can produce wide variations.

Table 9.6 illustrates these differences, with particular reference to the differences in the measure of population. It shows the VAT deregistration rates, the stock of VAT businesses and the adult populations for each of the nine English regions and Scotland, Wales and Northern Ireland. Table 9.6 shows that London has the lowest rate of business deregistration (by stock measure), and that Northern Ireland is the region with the highest deregistration rate by stock. If, however, adult population is used as the denominator, London has the lowest rate of VAT deregistrations, whilst the North East of England has the highest rate. Again, as with start up rates, Table 9.6 simply illustrates the impact that differing measurement criteria can have on our understanding of business closure.

Table 9.6	Stock and working population based rates, 2007				
	VAT deregistrations in 2006	Stock of VAT registered businesses (start 2007)	Working-age population (16+)	Stock rate (new businesses/stock of businesses)	Population rate (new businesses/ 10,000 working-age population)
London	27,575	309,225	6,067,400	11.2	22.0
South East	22,665	306,920	6,656,300	13.5	29.4
North West	13,670	186,045	5,531,000	13.6	40.5
Yorkshire and the Humber	10,125	139,970	4,163,200	13.8	41.1
West Midlands	11,855	164,810	4,309,200	13.9	36.3
East	14,020	196,480	4,528,800	14.0	32.3
North East	3,475	49,435	2,086,300	14.2	60.0
East Midlands	9,180	134,195	3,544,800	14.6	38.6
Scotland	9,230	136,890	4,195,100	14.8	45.5
South West	12,095	183,420	4,201,800	15.2	34.7
Wales	5,320	84,995	2,404,700	16.0	45.2
Northern Ireland	3,865	64,365	1,361,500	16.7	35.2

Summary

This chapter has tried to combine 'real' stories with large-scale international comparisons. The real stories are intended to bring home the impact a business closure can have upon an individual and their family. It means if their business fails the owner may be so traumatised that they lock themselves away in their room – sometimes for a prolonged period.

Drawing upon these stories, this chapter has examined three features of business closure. First, it has identified that business closure can have direct economic and social effects for those intimately involved in the ownership of the business. These effects may be negative for former employees, investors or creditors. The chapter has also shown that business failure has potentially important benefits in re-allocating resources away from inefficient uses.

We also saw that there are a wide range of terms used to describe business closure. Most of these are negative, indicating the failure of the business. Our favoured definition sought to exclude very many instances so that we could arrive at a 'purer' understanding of business closure. Our favoured definition was:

> A business closure occurs when a transacting entity stops its activities and does not transfer its ownership to another business and is independent of an existing business.

The remainder of the chapter was devoted to the very real difficulties of arriving at a purer measurement of either the number, or the rate, of business closure. The chapter identified that an important part of understanding business closure was to recognise that some closures were successful, with perhaps two fifths being viewed as successful by the business owners. Empirical evidence pointed to there being some differences between successful and unsuccessful closures. However, it is clear that further research in this area is needed.

Five other measures of business closure were identified. Each of these has advantages and disadvantages, and each gives rise to differing numbers and rates of business closure. As with business formation rates, there is no single, uniformly 'best' measure of business closure activity that fits all circumstances. Instead, the strengths and limitations of the data have to be assessed and related to their requirements.

Questions for discussion

1 How is business closure best defined?
2 Which measure of business closure is the most appropriate?
3 What issues are involved in quantifying a rate of business closure for a country?
4 Does a high rate of business closure indicate a region/country is 'entrepreneurial'?
5 Evaluate the economic and social consequences of business closure.

References

Bates, T. (2005) 'Analysis of Young, Small Firms that Have Closed: Delineating Successful from Unsuccessful Closures', *Journal of Business Venturing*, 20(3), 343–58.

BERR (2008) *Enterprise Directorate: Small and Medium Enterprise Statistics for the UK and Regions*. http://stats.berr.gov.uk/ed/sme/ (accessed 1 February 2009).

Everett, J. and Watson, J. (1998) 'Small Business Failure and External Risk Factors', *Small Business Economics*, 11(4), 371–90.

Fraser, S. (2005) *Finance for Small and Medium-sized Enterprises*. Coventry: Warwick Business School.

Geroski, P.A. (1995) 'What Do We Know about Entry?', *International Journal of Industrial Organisation*, 13, 421–40.

Harada, N. (2007) 'Which Firms Exit and Why?: An Analysis of Small Firm Exits in Japan', *Small Business Economics*, 29, 401–14.

Hart, P.E. and Oulton N. (1996) 'Growth and Size of Firms', *Economic Journal*, 106(438), 1242–52.

Knaup, E.E. (2005) 'Survival and Longevity in the Business Employment Dynamics Data', *Monthly Labor Review*, May, 50–6.

New Zealand Ministry of Economic Development (2008) *SMEs in New Zealand: Structure and Dynamics 2008*. Wellington: Ministry of Economic Development.

Sten, J. (1998) 'Exit – Success or Failure'. Paper presented at International Council of Small Business, Stockholm, Sweden.

Taylor, M.P. (1999) 'Survival of the Fittest?: An Analysis of Self-employment Duration in Britain', *Economic Journal*, 109(454), C140–55.

Watson, J. and Everett, J. (1993) 'Defining Small Business Failure', *International Small Business Journal*, 11(3), 35–48.

Watson, J. and Everett, J. (1999) 'Small Business Failure Rates: Choice of Definition and Industry Effects', *International Small Business Journal*, 17(2), 31–47.

Weyerer, S. and Brenner, M.H. (1996) 'Determinants of Suicide Rates in Middle-Age in Western Germany between 1955–1989', *European Psychiatry*, 11(4), 359s.

10 Analysing business closure

Key learning objectives

By the end of this chapter you should:

- Be able to compare and contrast the five approaches to business closure

- Be able to critically evaluate the empirical evidence on business closure.

In 1922, Walt Disney founded his first company Laugh-O-gram Films. He was 20 years old. He had raised $15,000 [around $191,000 now] from investors to fund a new animation business based in Kansas. With the capital, he employed staff and rented space in a new development. He won a contract from another small company called Pictorial Clubs to distribute his cartoons. The contract was worth $11,100. Disney took a $100 down payment for the cartoons. Six months later, Pictorial Clubs went bankrupt. Disney could no longer afford to pay the rent nor his staff. He borrowed another $2000 against his film equipment and materials from one of his original investors. He still ended up a year later bankrupt owing money to his former employees and investors. By the time Disney was declared a bankrupt, he had already left for Los Angeles.

Source: Adapted from Barrier (2007)

10.1 Introduction

This chapter discusses five approaches that are used to explain why it is that businesses such as Walt Disney's first venture close. The first approach – *gambler's ruin* – emphasises the role of chance. It suggests that businesses closure is similar to gambling. Business owners 'gamble' their resources in the hope that they will be successful. If they are unlucky, they are 'ruined', just as Disney was by the bankruptcy of the distributor Pictorial Clubs. The second approach – *population ecology* – suggests that business closure is an inevitable part of the evolution of industries. A feature of new industries like the animation industry in the 1920s, or railways in Britain in the 1840s, is that there are a lot of entrants and exits, so it should come as no surprise that there are a lot of short-lived businesses.

Resource-based theory is the third approach. It implies that business closure is down to the type and use made of business resources. *Utility* is the fourth theory. This identifies that the closure of the business occurs because the business owner recognises that she or he would get greater utility if they chose to do something else. The final theory argues that business closure is the outcome of *entrepreneurial learning*. In essence, entrepreneurs learn that they have insufficient skills or ability to successfully run their own business and so decide to close. Crucially, however, they may learn from this experience and go on to subsequently form a new, perhaps more successful, business.

We will discuss each of the five approaches in turn. In discussing these five approaches, we present the theory underpinning each approach and empirical evidence on its validity. The chapter concludes that, although they are presented independently, the approaches are not mutually exclusive. Each shares a concern with the riskiness of running a small business and each seeks to identify why it is that younger and smaller businesses close.

10.2 'Gambler's ruin'

At its core, 'gambler's ruin' emphasises the importance of chance (Cressy 2006). It is called gambler's ruin because it suggests that running a business is like being at a roulette table. The gambler (business owner) is faced by a risky proposition and has to make a decision. They can either use their chips (resources) to gamble on getting a successful outcome (staying or growing the business) or take these chips away from the roulette table (close the business). If the business owner decides to gamble, they have to decide how much to gamble and when. Having made this decision they may be lucky and win, so enhancing their stock of wealth, and possibly making them more confident/optimistic about the accuracy of their own judgement. If they lose, this reduces their stock of wealth. This may make them leave the table but, if they continue to gamble and continue to lose, they will be eventually be 'ruined' because they have no chips or can access no further credit to purchase more chips.

The similarities with the business owner are clear. The owner is continually making risky decisions. Examples of such decisions would be taking on new workers, investing in new equipment, switching premises, developing new products or selling abroad. Such decisions, if successful, will lead to additional profits which may, in turn, increase their wealth. If unsuccessful this leads to business losses, draining existing resources or causing the owner to access resources from outside borrowing.

It is not just current or past conditions that influence the decision to stay or quit: future expectations are also important. If the owner believes they have hit a losing streak, this is likely to influence their decision to close the business. Alternatively, the business owner may believe they have 'turned the corner', remain at the table, and lose heavily. Pivotal to the gambler's ruin theory are how lucky the owner is, and how lucky they feel they are going to be.

This simple version of gambler's ruin is very abstract and, therefore, of limited use. To make it more realistic, four modifications can be made:

1 Vary the level of wealth held by the owners. Those owners with greater wealth are more likely to 'survive' a run of bad luck. Those with less wealth may be forced to close their business.

2 Vary the access to finance. Again, those with greater access – other things being equal – are less likely to close their business.

3 The simple version of gambler's ruin above assumes that all businesses owners are at the mercy of chance. However, some may be better 'gamblers' because they have learnt from past experiences. Indeed, the longer they stay at the table the less likely it is that they will be ruined by chance.

4 The simple version assumes that gambling is the only option available to the business owner. Some gamblers leave when they have reached a 'threshold' of winnings or losses, rather than when they are ruined.

Yet, even the simple version of the gambler's ruin model offers four insights into understanding business closure. First, it highlights the important role of chance. Second, it emphasises that the current performance of the business is only one of a number of factors influencing whether the business continues to trade. Third, it recognises that access to resources, as well as performance, is important. Finally, it conjectures that entrepreneurs may learn by being in business.

Gambler's ruin makes three key predictions about business closure:

1 In its simplest version, chance is pivotal.

2 Nonetheless, observable patterns will be apparent. Those with fewer resources or less access to credit are more likely to see their business close. In other words, 'smaller' (e.g. those with fewer employees) or under-capitalised businesses are more likely to close.

3 Likewise, there will be an evident timeline to business closure. The assumption is that at the start everyone has resources. Subsequently, even if the business owner is unlucky, they keep hold of enough resources to allow them to carry on gambling if they so choose. Closure rates are modest at this initial stage. However, if bad luck continues, the result will be that more owners will close their businesses. This may be because they are 'ruined' or because they have reached their 'threshold'. The minority that stay – perhaps because they have learnt to gamble, have greater resources, or are just luckier – are more likely to stay in business. In essence, closure rates should follow an inverted 'U'-shaped pattern: low rates at the start, then high rates, before returning to low rates as time goes on.

The key prediction of gambler's ruin is that smaller and younger businesses have higher closure rates. This is clearly supported by the evidence presented in Table 10.1, which summarises 34 studies that examine business closure. The studies are drawn from all over the world. They all use statistical techniques to examine the determinants of business closure, so enabling the impact of particular individual factors (e.g. age and size of the business) to be isolated. There are three possible outcomes: a study may show a positive (+), negative (−) or non-significant (n.s.) association between the factor and business closure.

In Table 10.1, there are 16 studies that include the age of the business. Thirteen of these studies show that younger businesses are more likely to close, with the other three showing this to be a non-significant association. The association between the size of the business and closure is just as clear. Twenty-three studies investigate this association: 20 of them find that smaller businesses are more prone to closure. Only three show a non-significant relationship. There are also a further 12 studies that look at the assets/capital of the business. Again, eight of these studies show that assets/capital promotes business survival, with four showing a non-significant relationship. The overall evidence, then, is pretty clear: smaller and younger businesses are statistically more likely to close. These results also emerged from earlier reviews (e.g. Geroski 1995; Caves 1998).

The gambler's ruin approach sees 'luck' as pivotal in explaining business closure. One proxy for this may be the state of the macro economy. In the UK, there were two major periods of recession: the early 1980s and the 1990s. In between these periods and up until the late 2000s, the UK experienced a positive macro-economic environment. The expectation is that business closures will increase in periods of 'bad' luck. This is evident from Figure 10.1, which shows insolvent companies and self-employed bankrupts as a percentage of the stock of UK businesses. These rates rose in the early 1980s and 1990s, but fell away at other times.

The second prediction made by the gambler's ruin theory is that there will be temporal differences in closure patterns. The specific prediction is that closure rates will follow an inverted 'U' shape: start off modest (period 1), rise (period 2), before falling away (period 3). The accuracy of the prediction is clearly shown in Figure 10.2. The data are taken from business bank accounts and show the proportion of accounts that are closed within the following six months. The figure shows that at the end of the first six months, 8 per cent of new businesses had closed. This rose to a peak of about 12 per cent when businesses were

Table 10.1	Review of 34 survival studies

Human capital attributes	(+)	(−)	n.s.
Being older	2, 3, 6, 9, 10, 11, 16, 19, 20, 22, 25		4, 21, 28, 29
Age squared		9, 16, 25	3, 4, 20, 22,
Coming from an ethnic minority			21, 22, 25
Having prior entrepreneurial experience	21, 22, 33, 34		3, 9, 10, 26
Previously unemployed		3	21, 22
Males	3, 4, 6, 29, 34		10, 21, 22, 25, 28
Education	6, 9, 10, 20, 21, 25, 27, 28, 34	2, 19	3, 4, 22, 29
Having children		6	4
Having a spouse		6	25
Prior sectoral experience	3, 10, 20		27, 33
Prior managerial experience	22, 34		10, 20, 25
Being disabled			21
Being indigenous to an area (born and bred)	2		10, 19
Parental experience of entrepreneurship	20, 24		9
Team entrepreneurship	34	26	
Business characteristics			
Smaller businesses		1, 2, 5, 7, 8, 10, 11, 12, 13, 14, 16, 17, 20, 21, 25, 29, 30, 31, 32, 34	27, 28, 29
Younger businesses		1, 2, 5, 7, 8, 14, 16, 19, 21, 25, 29, 30, 32	12, 24, 27
Conducted research and development	1		
Sub-contracting business	1		
Single-plant business		2, 13, 15, 31	
Business has scale economies	7		
Limited company	9, 10, 11		28, 30, 33
Franchise business		25	
Strategy			
Business planning	33		
Product range of business	14		
Networking by businesses	10, 30		
Internationalisation	4, 10		24
Low-cost strategy		24, 28	
Niche strategy			24
Quality strategy			24
Finance			
Business has difficulty in accessing finance	28		
Having assets/capital	5, 10, 12, 17, 20, 21, 25, 29		3, 19, 24, 27

Table 10.1 continued

Human capital attributes	(+)	(−)	n.s.
Being a home owner			4
Cost of finance to business		4	
Use of a bank loan	28	8	4
Sector			
Agriculture	3	2	11
Manufacture	10		3, 28
Construction	10	11, 22	3, 9, 28
Wholesale/Retail	11	2, 4, 9, 22	3
Hotels	2		3
Transport		2, 9	3, 10, 28
Financial			2, 3
Business	2, 3	11	28
Public	2		3
Other		2	3, 10
Industry's prior growth	13, 15	16	17, 33, 34
Industry's level of R&D	14	15	12, 16
Industry's capital/labour ratio	13, 14, 16	12	
Industry's minimum efficient scale		12, 15, 18, 34	16
Industry's demand for goods/services	23		
Macro-economy			
Unemployment rate			3, 6
Employment growth	18		
Entry rate of businesses		13, 16, 18, 24, 29, 31, 32, 34	
Population density/growth		18	
Business failure rate		3, 23	

Note: Numbers refer to studies – see appendix key to Table 10.1 on p. 204.

12–18 months old. Rates then fall away to around 6 per cent after four years. Assuming, therefore, that the rate of bank switching is consistent across these time periods, the evidence confirms the inverted 'U'-shaped pattern to business closure as predicted by gambler's ruin.

A very similar pattern has been found in other countries. In a study of businesses in Germany, Brüderl and Schusler (1990) report a peak closure rate of 12 months. Mahmood (2000) and Baldwin *et al.* (2000) find similar inverted 'U'-shaped patterns using US and Canadian data, respectively.

In summary, the gambler's ruin problem – which predicts that chance, combined with gamblers having different resourcing levels, will lead to the gambler with fewer resources going broke – appears to be compatible with the evidence of an initial 'honeymoon' before rates rise and then tail away.

The main criticism of the theory is that it overplays the role of chance. Other theories suggest – as we shall see – that the business owner plays an important role, and it is not just chance but their skills and abilities that determine the fate of the business. This is a debate that we will return to later in the chapter. For now, we turn to population ecology.

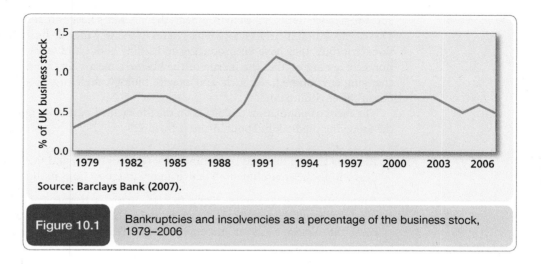

Source: Barclays Bank (2007).

| Figure 10.1 | Bankruptcies and insolvencies as a percentage of the business stock, 1979–2006 |

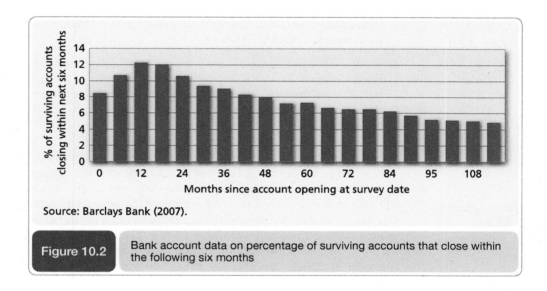

Source: Barclays Bank (2007).

| Figure 10.2 | Bank account data on percentage of surviving accounts that close within the following six months |

10.3 Population ecology

The unit of analysis in population ecology is organisations rather than the individual business or business owner. It was principally developed by the American sociologists Hannan and Freeman (1977). Its central focus is to explain why whole 'populations' of organisations emerge, develop and eventually 'die'. The theory suggests that organisational emergence is due to the nature of resources in the environment (e.g. how rich, or munificent, the environment is) and the level of competition in that environment. Other things being equal, rich environments with little competition for resources are likely attract new organisations to take advantage of these resources. Organisations that can successfully adapt to this environment are more likely to experience growth.

However, there are two factors that may particularly push individual organisations to close. First, if competition is intense, then, other things being equal, only some organisations will be able to fit in with the prevailing environmental conditions. Second, even if an organisation is able to establish itself in the environment, their 'Achilles heel' is that they all carry with them a set of 'structural inertia' factors. This relates to the way they *do* business (e.g. the 'organisational routines' they have for producing and selling goods and services). Over time, population ecology argues that the inertia of the business means that it no longer fits in with the changing environment. As such, and as with biology, these organisations become 'selected' out of the environment.

The focus of population ecology is on the life cycle of particular industries. It gives rise to the following predictions about business closure:

1 Business closure depends on the industry (environment) and the nature of competitiveness within the environment in which an organisation finds itself.

2 Young businesses are more likely to close. This is because new businesses have not yet fully established routines (ways of doing business) or management structures to meet the requirements of the environment. This is sometimes called the 'liability of newness'.

3 As with gambler's ruin, the pattern of business closure is likely to follow an inverted 'U' shape. Again, this is because new businesses begin with some initial resources but these soon became dissipated, making it difficult for the new business to meet the challenges of competing in a particular industry.

4 Finally, although business closure is less dramatic as a business ages, cumulative 'structural inertia' means that older organisations may not fit with environmental conditions. Indeed, over time the expectation is that very many older businesses will close because their particular chosen environment disappears (e.g. manufacturing manual typewriters, camera film).

These predictions may be modified to take account of chance. As in the natural world, unexpected events can occur. For example, Christensen (1997) argued that even in situations where managers and organisations are successfully meeting current customer needs, they may still be overtaken by new forms of 'disruptive technologies' which cause their mortality (see Chapter 5). To illustrate this, he examined the fortunes of the hard-disk-drive industry. He showed that there had been successive waves of 'disruptive' technologies introduced into the industry. First, there was the 14-inch disk drive, designed to meet the needs of 'mainframe' computer manufacturers. This disk drive, however, was replaced by the 8-inch disk drive because it offered superior performance. None of the 14-inch disk-drive manufacturers survived, despite meeting their customers' needs. This same disruptive process continued in the disk-drive industry. Eight-inch drives were replaced by $5^1/_4$-inch drives (desktops), then by $3^1/_2$-inch drives (portables), and $2^1/_2$-inch drives (notebooks).

Population ecology would also seem to fit with much empirical evidence. One measure of this is the expectation that industry sector influences business closure. It is clear from the large number of studies in Table 10.1 – which are not specific population ecology studies – that industry and sector play a positive (+) or negative (−) role in closure. Second, it might be expected that entry rates (density dependence) would impact on closure. The general sense from Table 10.1 is that this is the case. Also, as we have already seen, there is strong evidence that younger and smaller businesses are more likely to close. This also fits with population ecology models.

What the evidence in Table 10.1 does not chart are the dynamics of organisations over time. Specific population ecology studies have identified that there is a particular pattern to the evolution of many industries. Studies of such diverse industries as newspapers in San Francisco (Hannan and Freeman 1987), the US bicycle industry (Dowell and Swaminathan 2000) and UK Railways (Tether and Storey 1998) indicate that sectors with high entry rates and with smaller and younger businesses are all more prone to closure. To illustrate this more

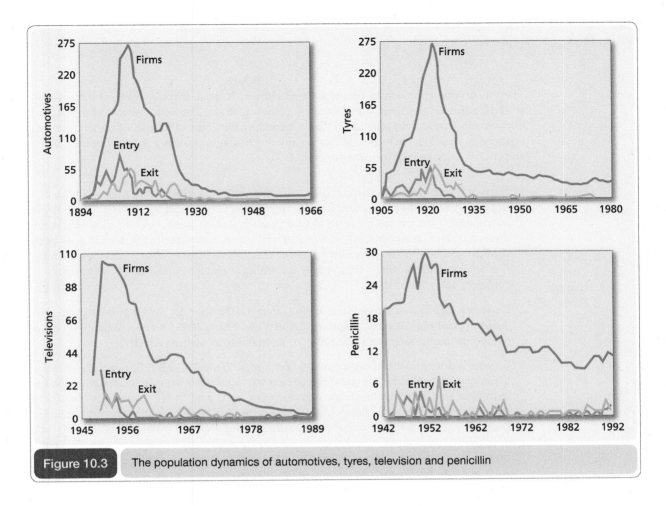

| Figure 10.3 | The population dynamics of automotives, tyres, television and penicillin |

fully, Klepper (2002) has considered the dynamics of four US industries: automobiles, televisions, tyres and penicillin. For each industry, he looks at the entry and exit rates and the number of businesses that survive over time. Figure 10.3 shows a common pattern. There are lots of entrants and exits in the automotive, tyre and television industries but fewer in the penicillin industry (as can be seen by comparing the vertical axes). Klepper then argues that after a number of entrants have arrived in a new market, there is a period of high closures (a 'shakeout') caused by technological changes. Subsequently, the number of businesses tends to fall away (even in a comparatively small industry like penicillin), to the point where there are only a few businesses left.

In summary, population ecology, like gambler's ruin, can be fruitfully used to explain why it is that newer and smaller businesses are more likely to close. It also suggests that entry rates are important determinants of closure rates. Further, it provides useful insights into the long-run organisational dynamics of a particular industry.

The main criticism of the theory is that it focuses almost exclusively on the environment. The individual business is largely absent from population ecology. What determines closure are industry structure and environmental change. Whilst there is evidence to support this, the approach may be criticised because it places minimal focus on the business closure decision made by the business owner, or upon the qualities of the business owner. It is as if there is an inevitable fatalism about population ecology. We now turn to explanations of business closure where the owner, more realistically, does play a role.

10.4 Resource-based closure

There is no one approach to resource-based closure. Instead, there appear to be numerous strands, but what ties them together is a common focus on the entrepreneur as the unit of analysis. Here we set out four illustrative approaches. However, although we present them as separate approaches, we recognise that, in any one business closure, almost all permutations and combinations of the four are possible.

1 Closure is due to a lack of financial controls and resources (Burns 2002). This may be due to poor levels of financial record keeping in small businesses (Nayak and Greenfield 1994) or situations where a business fails to recognise that the business is **overtrading** (has more business than it can adequately fund). Business owners may take too much money out of the business, because they are either inept or fraudulent. Businesses may also close because – as with gambler's ruin – they simply do not have enough resources in the business or sufficient access to finance.

2 Closure is due to deficiencies in available managerial resources. This may be expressed in terms of poor management planning (Delmar and Shane 2003), an over-reliance on price competitiveness (Saridakis *et al.* 2008), or an inability to manage effectively.

3 Closure is due to a lack of organisational resources. Central to this is Stinchombe's (1965) 'liability of newness'. He argued that younger businesses lack knowledge, for example, on individual roles and functions, and about how to 'legitimate' their business with outsiders (e.g. customers, suppliers, financiers). Gaining specific knowledge about how to organise the business and deal with outsiders is costly and not acquired instantaneously. This lack of organisational resources may be too great to stave off early business closure. This concept relates to the network approach to understanding business closure, since if networks are integral to setting up a business (see Chapter 6), then it is to be expected that they are also integral to its survival.

4 A fourth theory – more often applied to business development – can also be used to reflect business closure. The 'Resource-Based View' of business growth argues that central to business performance (survival) is internal resources rather than the wider environment. 'Resources' are usually divided into two: stocks of available factors such as 'land, labour, and capital that are owned or controlled by the firm' (Amit and Schoemaker 1993: 35) and capabilities. The latter are 'information-based, tangible or intangible processes that are firm-specific and are developed over time through complex interactions among the firm's resources' (Amit and Schoemaker 1993: 35). The resource-based view of the business suggests that where resources and capabilities are valuable, rare, imperfectly imitable and not easily substitutable, there is a basis for competitive advantage (Barney 1991). In terms of business closure, the lack of these 'idiosyncratic, hard to imitate resources and capabilities' (Thornhill and Amit 2003: 498) may explain rates of business closure. In other words, the survival of a business is dependent on whether its resources/capabilities are unique and incapable of being copied. If they are unique and cannot easily be copied, then business closure is less likely.

In addition to the usual predictions about smaller and younger businesses being more likely to close, further predictions are derived from these approaches:

1 As with gambler's ruin, business closure is more likely amongst those with fewer financial resources or access to such resources.

2   Regardless of their age or size, businesses that have more appropriate management structures and routines (ways of doing business) are less likely to close. Evidence of this could
include having stronger planning systems in place and better networking capability.

3   Businesses that have more unique or less imitable processes, products or services would be
less likely to close. Evidence of this is that the strategy and technologies of the businesses
would be in some way distinguishable from others.

We have already seen from Table 10.1 that businesses with better access to financial resources
are less likely to close.

However, it is much more difficult to link managerial or finance resource deficiencies
with business closure. One reason for this is the difficulty of reliably measuring their scale.
The traditional approach was to examine business closure from a financial perspective by
examining key accounting ratios (e.g. liquidity, solvency or profitability). Beaver (1966)
showed that the business that closed had lower ratios than those that survived. Whilst this was
an interesting and important finding, its predictive powers were modest. The problem is that
these ratios can be computed in very many ways, leading to different results and differing
indicators of who was at 'risk' of closure. A second problem is that the data on which such
ratios are calculated can often be 'out of date'. This meant that by the time evidence of 'ratio
deterioration' became available there was insufficient time left to take action to avert closure.
The ratios were, therefore, a 'symptom' rather than a 'cause' of failure (Storey *et al.* 1987).

Measurement issues also emerge when managerial based explanations for closures are
tested. Put simply, if you ask liquidators why businesses have closed, they tend to put the
blame for business closure squarely on the shoulders of the business owners. Ask business
owners, however, and they will say it was the fault of the bank or other financiers, or that it
was simply due to bad luck (Brough 1970).

Nonetheless, Baldwin *et al.* (1997) concluded that internal managerial factors were important in explaining business closure. Using data from a survey of Canadian bankruptcy trustees
(people appointed to look after the 'failing' business), they found that the most common
internal reasons for bankruptcy were general and financial management problems. Figure 10.4
shows that more than 70 per cent of bankrupt businesses were held to have these problems.

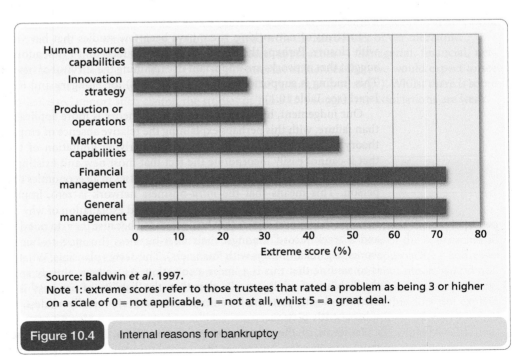

Source: Baldwin *et al.* 1997.
Note 1: extreme scores refer to those trustees that rated a problem as being 3 or higher
on a scale of 0 = not applicable, 1 = not at all, whilst 5 = a great deal.

| Figure 10.4 | Internal reasons for bankruptcy |

This important issue is left to the standard economic treatment of relative earnings.[1] This assumes that relative earnings are a proxy for the utility that an individual derives from pursuing a particular activity. It *assumes* that the stay/quit decision faced by the business owner is the mirror image of the entry decision (see Chapter 8). The individual quits business when their utility is less than the utility of another labour-market state (being an employee, being unemployed or exiting the labour force).

Three predictions emerge from this:

1 The decision to stay/quit the business depends not only on the performance of the business, but also on the alternative income from wages. All else being equal, businesses could be closed even if profits rose. This might be because wages in paid employment rose faster, making becoming an employee much more attractive.

2 Even if profitability is maintained – so that income from business ownership remains unchanged – there may be exits. This may be because of alternative employment opportunities as an employee, but it may also be because of higher state benefits from being unemployed or because the individual chooses to exit from the labour force – possibly by retiring or for other family-related reasons.

3 There is an increased likelihood that the individual will quit business ownership when income from that activity declines. This reflects the conventional economic view that unprofitable businesses will exit the industry.

This simple model can be supplemented by adding 'switching' costs such as the costs of the self-employed seeking qualifications to make them more attractive to employers or the employed incurring the costs of undertaking market research to start their business. Such costs are realistic: Taylor (1999) showed that there was a much lower rate of 'switching' into employment amongst those who had been self-employed for a decade, when compared with those who had been self-employed only for a year (see Chapter 8).

A second complexity is the extension of the concept of utility to cover both pecuniary (earnings) and non-pecuniary factors (e.g. attitudes towards 'being your own boss', choice of when and who to work for). Hamilton (2000) demonstrated the value of this wider conceptualisation of utility. His key finding was that those in self-employment continue in business even though they could earn on average about 35 per cent more as an employee. This emphasises that non-monetary factors may powerfully influence the stay/quit decision, so that the term 'utility' is only appropriate if it includes non-monetary as well as monetary elements.

A third extension of utility theory is to see it in terms of 'thresholds'. The 'classic' article outlining this approach is Gimeno *et al.* (1997). They show that the choice of whether or not to stay in business is influenced not only by the income earnings of the business, but also by alternative earning opportunities. Quite simply, it is not always the lowest performing organisations that close.

---

[1] An alternative economic approach is called the industrial economist approach. The unit of analysis is the business rather than the individual. It examines why it is that businesses exit a market. The standard equation used to explain exit (the mirror of entry) is: $EXIT_i = f(\Pi_i, G_i, BAR_i, CONC_i)$ (see Chapter 7). We note, however, that Audretsch and Mahmood (1995) and Mata and Portugal (1994) report very little support for this industrial economic approach to understanding business closure. Audretsch and Mahmood, for example, show that exit rates are *higher* in more profitable sectors. This they attribute to these sectors having powerful businesses able to dispose of new entrants. Both studies agree that industry growth rates are associated with *higher* exit rates. This is presumably because rapidly growing sectors attract more entrants and it is this that explains the higher closure rate. The evidence provided by the two studies on the impact of entry barriers and concentration is mixed. Mata and Portugal find competition intensity to be unrelated to exit, whilst Audretsch and Mahmood find capital intensity – a measure of entry barriers – associated with higher exits. Overall, the 'standard' industrial economics approach to exit does not seem to perform well as an explanatory model.

Classic research	Gimeno, J., Folta, T.B., Cooper, A.C. and Woo, C.Y. (1997) 'Survival of the Fittest? Entrepreneurial Human Capital and the Persistence of Underperforming Businesses', *Administrative Science Quarterly*, 42(4), 750–83.

Why Gimeno *et al.*'s (1997) article may be considered a classic is that it sets out and subsequently provides an answer to the simple question: 'Why is it that some businesses continue to trade when others, despite making higher profits, exit?'

Their key insight is to highlight the importance of wider aspects of utility, not only in terms of non-pecuniary motivations but also in terms of the alternatives open to the business owner. It is valuable in that it gives insights into why it is that – if two businesses have exactly the same profitability – one may close while the other stays open.

It also points to the importance of human capital attributes (e.g. gender, education and ethnicity) in determining the business closure decision. Although human capital attributes are obviously important in many if not all approaches, and particularly so in resource-based approaches, they have formed the mainstay of the utility approach.

They show that the choice of whether or not to stay in business is influenced not only by the income earnings of the business, but also by alternative earning opportunities. Quite simply, it is not always the lowest performing organisations that close. Instead, they find that:

- The answer is that different businesses have different 'thresholds' of economic performance.
- The threshold depends on alternative earning performance and 'psychic' income from self-employment.
- So, where the individuals can easily switch to alternative paid or self-employment they are more likely to quit.
- But if they really love being self-employed they stay.
- Psychic income may be 'being own boss', 'love the job', 'fits in with personal life'.

In Table 10.1, we showed that human capital characteristics influence income as an employee, as well as income as a business owner. We also showed that younger, smaller and more weakly capitalised businesses were more likely to close. There was also some evidence that the strategic orientation of the business could be important in explaining closure.

In terms of human capital attributes, Table 10.1 identifies a range of possible proxies. It shows that older individuals are more likely to stay in business than younger individuals. This is apparent from 11 studies, with a further four studies indicating that it has no significant impact on closure. None of the studies suggest a negative impact. The age effect, however, may have an inverted 'U' shape: younger and older individuals are more likely to see their business close. Three studies suggest that the impact of age (age squared) is negative and a further four suggest non-significance. Overall, it appears that young business owners are more likely to close their business. A more mixed picture emerges when 'prime age' and 'older' individuals are compared.

There is less clear-cut evidence for gender. Although five studies indicate that males are more likely to stay in business, a further five indicate a non-significant effect. Mixed evidence is also apparent for prior experience in running a business, in a relevant sector, managerial experience and having parents with prior experience of self-employment. Having a spouse or being indigenous to an area was also found to have a mixed impact. Indeed, the only other clear factor besides age would appear to be education. Although there are some studies that point to either a negative or non-significant association, there are nine studies in Table 10.1 pointing to a positive relationship between education and staying in business.

To summarise, the simple utility approach offers a limited but crude interpretation of which owners close, and which continue, their businesses. It does not seek to offer explanations for such decisions. It also implies that people make 'free' choices, when in fact circumstances may dictate their actions. But neither of these is its purpose: instead, the utility approach assumes that people shift when their utility is greater in one state than in another. *Why* that should be is not of particular interest. Nevertheless, its key advantage is that it can be used to examine who shifts and who does not, and under what circumstances the shift occurs.

10.6 Entrepreneurial learning

The findings on human capital outlined above in Table 10.1 are a puzzle. We might have anticipated that there would be clear evidence that specific knowledge of starting and running a business would clearly reduce the likelihood of business closure. Table 10.1, however, makes it clear that this assumption is *not* supported by the evidence.

This finding is important because one of the fundamental assumptions of the entrepreneurial learning approach is that prior experience has a direct impact on the performance (business survival) of the business. There is a clear logic to this. At the start of the chapter, we saw that Walt Disney's first business failed, leaving employees and investors stranded. However, Disney went on to create one of the biggest and most successful businesses in the world. We also saw in Chapter 9 how Jeremy Harbour went on to run a successful business after an early failure. Hence, entrepreneurial learning theorists like Mezirow (1991) and Harvey and Evans (1995) have argued that entrepreneurship is path-dependent. Cope (2005) has also argued that aspiring entrepreneurs need to consider the stock of their accumulated knowledge, whilst Minniti and Bygrave (2001) suggest that '. . . knowledge is cumulative. What is learned in one period builds upon what was learned in an earlier period' (p. 7). In short, business closure leads to learning effects and, by implication, those that have closed more businesses will have learnt more.

Illustration	How multiple failures launched Chefs on the Run

Chefs in a restaurant kitchen.

An Aussie-style restaurant with a giant neon sign of a kangaroo and a grizzly bear shaking hands, Foster's and prawns being served to cold and hungry Americans. How could it fail? Surely the appetite of Americans for all things Australian, combined with their love affair with tacky neon signs, would create some bizarre winning recipe. But fail it did. Five times. The dream that Stephen Scrogings had from his childhood days lay in tatters on an icy street corner in Alaska.

But those dark chapters of failure, some 20 years ago, spawned another dream, one that created a wonderful success story. Returning from the frontier state with his tail between his legs, Scrogings couldn't face his Brisbane friends. 'I failed miserably and I couldn't come back to Brisbane and be confronted by anyone so I went to Melbourne and lost it on the streets for 12 months', he says. 'An American friend came over and belted me in the face one day and told me I was wasting my life and the talents I had. I woke up the next morning with $10.82 in my back pocket. I was a qualified chef and I thought, well, let's just get back into it. I started scrubbing pots and pans again before I went back cooking, as I had no confidence in myself.'

After months grinding his elbows in sinks, the budding entrepreneur found a hole in the market that he could exploit. 'After a while I thought: there's a market here because there are always people complaining about staffing agencies', he says. 'I thought if people wanted a chef they should deal directly with chefs. I put myself in a shirt and tie, cut my hair, became more professional and set up the business.' He dubbed his new company Chefs on the Run – a collection of trained chefs and catering staff hired out for events or to fill staff shortages at restaurants. The company now has 800 chefs on its books, offices in Sydney, Melbourne and Brisbane and annual turnover of $25 million.

Source: *Sunday Telegraph* (Australia), 22 February 2009.

Question:

Do you think that his previous failings had a positive impact on his subsequent success or was he just lucky?

An alternative theoretical basis for entrepreneurial learning comes from Jovanovic (1982). His 'classic article' is outlined in the box below and the crucial assumption is assumption 4.

Classic research	Jovanovic, B. (1982) 'Selection and the Evolution of Industry', *Econometrica*, 50(3), 649–70.

Jovanovic's article is a classic because it is one the main theories that have been used to explain the performance of small businesses. It makes four basic assumptions:

1 He assumes that prior to entry into business, people do not know their level of entrepreneurial talent. They only become aware of their talent by actually being in business. If their talent is less than they envisaged they stop running their business.

2 Even if an individual has high levels of entrepreneurial skill they may still find that they have to close their business. This is because they may experience random shocks (unlucky draws) which mean that they close their business. Less talented individuals might, however, get lucky.

3 Over time, luck is cancelled out and the talented win out.

4 Jovanovic does NOT assume the individual adds to their level of skills whilst being in business . . . only that they get a better understanding of what those skills are and how to use them effectively. In other words, Jovanovic suggests that entrepreneurs learn passively.

There have been two main modifications to Jovanovic's approach. The first is by Frank (1988). He pointed out that the initial size of business entry varied. He put this down to differences in the optimism of the business owner. In other words, whilst agreeing with Jovanovic that owners do not know how talented they are before they start their business, their perceptions of their talent are influenced by their optimism.

The second variation of the Jovanovic model is to alter the type of learning undertaken by the business owner. For Jovanovic, owners are passive learners in that they do not learn new skills, they only learn about their own abilities and it is this learning that enables them to assess whether they should stay in business. However, it is just as feasible that owners are active learners. Ericson and Pakes's (1995) model suggests that owners can learn about their own business and those of their competitors. This allows them to adjust the size of their business in response to external conditions. In other words, they are able to develop new strategies to cope with their changing perceptions and information about the market.

Entrepreneurial learning gives rise to the following predictions about business closure:

1 Younger businesses are more likely to close because owners are able to learn quickly that they are unsuited to running a business. They recognise that their time and labour would be better served in alternative employment.

2 Smaller businesses are more likely to close. Frank (1988) suggests that prior optimism impacts on initial size, so more optimistic owners that start larger are more likely to remain in business. Even if they start small, Ericson and Pakes (1995) suggest that those that are 'active' learners are able to quickly adjust their size to meet the conditions they face.

3 This implies that the strategic orientation and the behaviour of the owner are important.

4 Chance is still important. Although entrepreneurial talent is likely to be the ultimate determinant of business performance, entrepreneurial learning still recognises that even talented people may be unlucky and 'talent-free' individuals can be lucky.

In essence, entrepreneurial learning looks to have the greatest potential of all the theoretical approaches that we have discussed. It combines elements of chance (gambler's ruin), a recognition of the importance of fit with the external environment (population ecology), strategy (resource-based approaches) and utility (people switching behaviour). It also fits in with policy perceptions about the advantages of business closure.

In the US, in particular, there appear to be many cases, like Walt Disney, of individuals who ultimately ran highly successful business, but who previously owned a business that failed. The inference is that, because they are currently now successful, failure must have been 'a learning experience' for them. This has led to the suggestion that Europe (and other places where bankruptcy legislation penalises failure heavily) should become more like the US in being 'tolerant' if it wishes to become more entrepreneurial and hence more wealthy.

| Illustration | A debate between European and American policy makers on business closure |

One of the most contentious issues in entrepreneurship and small business is over the balance of emphasis between the interests of the business owner and those of the creditors and employees. In the US, the balance is towards the business owner. It may be claimed that the US is the most entrepreneurial society in the world, and that a direct reason for this is it allows owners to restart without the stigma of failure. Other countries wishing to mimic this success need to address the issue of stigma by allowing owners to restart more easily. We seek to reflect the debate in the following fictional 'spat' between a European and US policy maker.

US: You Europeans really have not grasped the concept of entrepreneurship. You seem to think it is about penalising people who try to start a business, when it is about encouraging them.

Europe: Our task is to strike a balance between the interests of the business owner and the creditors. What we cannot have is people irresponsibly starting a business with the purpose of defrauding suppliers and misleading customers.

US: That is typical 'Euro-speak'. It is always focusing on the downside of everything. People should be given the freedom to follow their own interests. That way you don't just focus narrowly upon creditors, but upon the economy more widely. By allowing businesses to start easily – and to fail – the people who run those businesses learn from their mistakes. It may take them several attempts but many of our most successful businesses have been established by people who have had several previous failures. Look at Walt Disney and a whole host of famous entrepreneurs like him. They are precisely the sort of people that would never have been given a second . . . never mind a fourth or fifth chance . . . in Europe. As a result, Europe has lost out on having rapid growth businesses which make such a major contribution to the long-term high rates of growth achieved in the US.

Europe: So, let me understand the case you are making: you are saying that it doesn't matter that business owners can act irresponsibly by leaving behind them debts after a business closes . . . even though they may have extravagantly purchased yachts, helicopters and sports cars using money from the business. Are you saying we should encourage people like the Australian entrepreneur Alan Bond?

US: Again, this is the wrong focus. Sure there will be people who will do that and it is the task of creditors to ensure that funds are spent on the purposes for which they are provided. That is for the stakeholders in the venture to make sure that the business is properly managed and accountable. But the purpose of legislation is to get the philosophy right. Most people who run businesses do so for legitimate purposes. If their business fails it may because they made a mistake or because of matters beyond their control. We don't believe that, because they made a mistake, they should be penalised. In fact the reverse, we believe they will most likely have learnt from that mistake and that, if they choose to start again, they will not repeat the error. After all, entrepreneurs learn from their own experience and if you don't give them the chance to put that experience into practice then that is a loss to the economy.

Europe: Let me get this right. You are claiming that if you give people a second or any number of chances – no matter what havoc they cause on the way – this will lead to successful businesses. So, where is your actual evidence? All you have done is point to anecdotal 'war' stories about this or that entrepreneur. How do we actually know that entrepreneurs actually learn anything?

US: Who is the more successful economy? Who has the biggest businesses in the world? I am telling you that Europe lags in economic development. You need to change your attitudes to closure or else you will fall further behind.

● *Which of these two approaches do you back? Why do you back them?*

However, critics of the entrepreneurial learning approach point out that the evidence is much less robust than it appears at first sight. In essence, the assumption seems to be that 'of course everyone learns – so why should business owners be any different?' Entrepreneurial learning is taken as a given. Where there is 'evidence' this typically relies 'self-report' data from the entrepreneurs themselves, although this is often open to question (Harrison and Leitch 2005). After all, who would ever admit they have never learnt?

Other forms of evidence looking directly at the influence of prior entrepreneurial experience suggest there is little evidence to support the predictions of entrepreneurial learning. For example, Parker (2006) shows that the self-employed adjust their behaviour only very marginally in the face of recent evidence. Instead, they are much more strongly driven by their 'priors' which, in this context, we take as their long-term experience and personality characteristics.

Metzger's (2007) German study is also illuminating. He examines two types of business owners – those who were bankrupts and those who voluntarily closed their business. He found that individuals who had voluntarily closed their previous business were no more or less likely to survive in their next business compared to novices. His most interesting result, though, is that bankrupts were *more* likely to subsequently experience business closure than both the other groups. This is directly contrary to the predictions of entrepreneurial learning. It implies that performance in an individual's first business is broadly indicative of how they will perform in later businesses.

Metzger's view is broadly compatible with what we will call the 'lottery' theory. Suppose starting a business is like buying tickets for a lottery. Everyone recognises that it is chancy but that the prize is substantial. One strategy for increasing the chance of a win is to buy more tickets. In other words, the owner is more likely to be 'lucky', other things being equal, if they have more attempts at running a business. It does not follow, though, that they have 'learnt' how to 'play the lottery'. What is clear – following the US/EU discussion – is that the price of a lottery ticket is lower in the US and this is perhaps the reason more 'tickets' are bought. The price is higher in the EU because of the higher 'stigma' associated with failure.

Two final factors are also important. First, we saw in Chapter 1 that business owners have clear cognitive biases. One of these is that they are 'super-optimists', particularly about events outside their control (de Meza 2002). Hence, in the context of the lottery analogy, optimists buy more tickets. If optimism is equated with starting a business, the fact that, in such a risky environment, individuals continue to buy more tickets (start more businesses) reflects their optimistic personality, rather than their ability to learn. Second, the reason why the lottery analogy is valid is that no two business situations are identical. The individual who has been in business before may have not experienced, and thus be no more able to deal with, certain business situations than the novice. One analogy is with parenting. Given that every child is unique, the notion that a parent with eight children is significantly more knowledgeable in dealing with their ninth child, compared with a 'novice' parent, seems a little fanciful.

In summary, whilst entrepreneurship books and magazines provide numerous examples of individuals who claim to have learnt from the experience of business failure to go on to ultimately succeed, the empirical support for this is weak. Equally, if not more, plausible is the proposition that business survival is strongly influenced by chance, endowments of entrepreneurial talent, and optimism on the part of the business owner. It is these factors which best explain the willingness of individuals whose business has failed to seek to try again and perhaps, ultimately, be successful. Whether, of course, such lottery playing should be subsidised by creditors or consumers is a more open question – one we return to in later chapters.

Summary

This chapter has examined five approaches to business closure. These are 'gambler's ruin', population ecology, resource-based approaches, utility and entrepreneurial learning. Each approach provides an explanation of why smaller and younger businesses are more prone to business closure and each has its advantages and disadvantages, which are summarised in Table 10.2.

Empirically, besides the key 'stylised facts' that younger and smaller businesses are more likely to close, the only other solid finding from the range of international multivariate studies identified in Table 10.1 was that older owners and those with higher levels of education were less likely to experience business closure. Outside of these findings, there would appear to be few other guides to identifying who is more likely to close. In part, this reflects the wide heterogeneity and appropriateness of variables used in business closure studies.

As the 'poor cousin' to business growth, such studies have suffered because they have not been able to fully identify why it is that some people, or some strategies, may be more likely to lead to business survival. There is a clear need, therefore, for more and better research in this area. It is fairly clear that smaller and younger businesses are more likely to close. The question is why, and what factors explain the closure of businesses that are neither very small nor very young?

	Unit of analysis	Key focus	Key advantage	Key disadvantage
Table 10.2		Summary of the five approaches		
Gambler's ruin	Business owners	Chance	Able to explain 'liability of adolescence'	Leaves little room for the entrepreneur
Population ecology	Populations of businesses	Population dynamics	Explanation of organisational life cycle	Leaves little room for the entrepreneur
Resource-based approaches	Businesses/ Business owners	Internal resources of the business	Focus on business and entrepreneur	Limited empirical evidence
Utility	Business owners	Decision-making process of owner	Decision thresholds of the entrepreneur	Weak coverage of entrepreneurial motivations/behaviours
Entrepreneurial learning	Business owners	Role of learning	Focus on positives of business closure	Limited empirical evidence other than that based on self-report data

This chapter has also shown that there is a need to be cautious about any calls to culturally redefine attitudes towards business closure. There appears little robust evidence that would suggest a direct link between prior entrepreneurial learning and business survival.

Questions for discussion

1 What is meant by 'the liability of newness?' To what extent does it explain the high closure rates of new businesses?
2 What are the strengths and weaknesses of 'gamblers ruin' as an explanation of new business failure?
3 What is Resource Based View (RBV) Theory? What insights does it provide for explaining new business closure?
4 Is a 'networked business' less likely to fail? Give reasons for your answer.
5 'The lesson I have learnt is to recognise when I have made a reasonable return, to sell leaving something on the table for the next guy, and move on swiftly to another opportunity. This denotes the difference between an entrepreneur and a gambler (James Caan, entrepreneur, in the *Sunday Times*, 15 June 2008). Is Mr Caan correct? Is 'gambler's ruin' a better explanation of failure or has it more to do with a lack of entrepreneurial talent?
6 Take an industry of your choice and show, as it has evolved, how business birth and deaths interact.
7 What do you think are the three main causes of small business closure?
8 Review briefly the theories of business closure. Provide a justification for identifying the theory that you feel is, overall, most plausible.
9 Review the contribution of Jovanovic (1982) to the subject of entrepreneurial learning. Do you think entrepreneurs learn and, if so, how?
10 In the Chefs on the Run case, Mr Scrogings failed five times to successfully set up a business. Subsequently, he did succeed. Do you think that his previous failings had a positive impact on his subsequent success or was he just lucky? Discuss your answer in relation to the arguments for and against entrepreneurial learning.

References

Agarwal, R. (1996) 'Technological Activity and Survival of Firms', *Economic Letters*, 52(1), 101–8.

Amit, R. and Schoemaker, P.J.H. (1993) 'Strategic Assets and Organizational Rent', *Strategic Management Journal*, 14, 33–46.

Aspelund, A., Berg-Utby, T. and Skjevdal, R. (2005) 'Initial Resources Influence on New Venture Survival: A Longitudinal Study of New Technology-based Firms', *Technovation*, 25(11), 1337–47.

Audretsch, D.B. (1995) 'Innovation, Growth and Survival', *International Journal of Industrial Organization*, 13(4), 441–57.

Audretsch, D.B., Houweling, P. and Thurik, A.R. (2000) 'Firm Survival in the Netherlands', *Review of Industrial Organization*, 16(1), 1–11.

Audretsch, D.B. and Mahmood, T. (1995) 'New Firm Survival: New Results Using a Hazard Function', *Review of Economics and Statistics*, 77(1), 97–103.

Azoulay, P. and Shane, S. (2001) 'Entrepreneurs, Contracts and the Failure of Young Firms', *Management Science*, 47(3), 337–58.

Baldwin, J., Bian, L., Dupuy, R. and Gellatly, G. (2000) *Failure Rates for New Canadian Firms: New Perspectives on Entry and Exit*. Ottawa: Ministry of Industry.

Baldwin, J., Gray, T., Johnson, J., Proctor, J., Rafiquzzaman, M. and Sabourin, D. (1997) *Failing Concerns: Business Bankruptcy in Canada*. Ottawa: Ministry of Industry.

Baptista, R., Karaöz, M. and Mendonça, J. (2007) 'Entrepreneurial Backgrounds, Human Capital and Start-up Success'. *Jena Economic Research Papers* 2007-045. Jena: Max Planck Institute.

Barclays Bank (2007) *Small Firms in Britain, 2007*. London: Barclays Bank.

Barney, J.B. (1991) 'Firm Resources and Sustained Competitive Advantage', *Journal of Management* 17(1), 99–120.

Barrier, J.M. (2007) *The Animated Man: A Life of Walt Disney*. Berkeley and Los Angeles, CA: University of California Press.

Bates, T. (1995) 'Analysis of Survival Rates among Franchise and Independent Small Business Startups', *Journal of Small Business Management*, 33(2), 26–36.

Beaver, W.H. (1967) 'Financial Ratios as Predictors of Failure: Empirical Studies in Accounting, Selected Studies', *Journal of Accounting Research*, 5(Supplement), 77–111.

Brough, R. (1970) 'Business Failures in England and Wales', *Business Ratios*, 8–11.

Brüderl, J. and Preisendörfer, P. (1998) 'Network Support and the Success of Newly Founded Businesses', *Small Business Economics*, 10(3), 213–25.

Brüderl, J., Preisendörfer, P. and Ziegler, R. (1992) 'Survival Chances of Newly Founded Business Organizations', *American Sociological Review*, 227–42.

Brüderl, J. and Schussler, R. (1990) 'Organizational Mortality: The Liabilities of Newness and Adolescence', *Administrative Science Quarterly*, 35(3), 530–47.

Burns, P. (2002) *Entrepreneurship and Small Business*. London: Palgrave.

Caves, R.E. (1998) 'Industrial Organization and New Findings on the Turnover and Mobility of Firms', *Journal of Economic Literature*, 36(4), 1947–82.

Cefis, E. and Marsili, O. (2006) 'Survivor: The Role of Innovation in Firms' Survival', *Research Policy*, 35(5), 626–41.

Christensen, C.M. (1997) *The Innovator's Dilemma*. Cambridge, MA: Harvard Business School Press.

Cope, J. (2005) 'Toward a Dynamic Learning Perspective on Entrepreneurship', *Entrepreneurship: Theory and Practice*, 29(4), 373–97.

Cressy, R. (1995) 'Business Borrowing and Control: A Theory of Entrepreneurial Types', *Small Business Economics*, 7(4), 291–300.

Cressy, R. (1996) 'Small Firm Failure: Failure to Fund or Failure to Learn by Doing'. CSME University of Warwick Discussion Paper.

de Meza, D. (2002) 'Overlending', *Economic Journal*, 112(477), F17–F31.

Delmar, F. and Shane, S. (2003) 'Does Business Planning Facilitate the Development of New Ventures?', *Strategic Management Journal*, 24(12), 1165–85.

Doms, M., Dunne, T. and Roberts, M.J. (1995) 'The Role of Technology Use in the Survival and Growth of Manufacturing Plants', *International Journal of Industrial Organization*, 13(4), 523–42.

Dowell, G. and Swaminathan, A. (2000) 'Racing and Back-Pedalling into the Future: New Product Introduction and Organizational Mortality in the US Bicycle Industry, 1880–1918', *Organization Studies*, 21(2), 405–31.

Ericson, R. and Pakes, A. (1995) 'Markov-Perfect Industry Dynamics: A Framework for Empirical Work', *Review of Economic Studies*, 62(1), 53–82.

Esteve-Perez, S. and Manez-Castillejo, J.A. (2008) 'The Resource-based Theory of the Firm and Firm Survival', *Small Business Economics*, 30(3), 231–49.

Frank, M.Z. (1988) 'An Intertemporal Model of Industrial Exit', *Quarterly Journal of Economics*, 103(2), 333–44.

Fotopoulos, G. and Louri, H. (2000) 'Location and Survival of New Entry', *Small Business Economics*, 14(4), 311–21.

Fritsch, M., Brixy, U. and Falck, O. (2006) 'The Effect of Industry, Region, and Time on New Business Survival: A Multi-dimensional Analysis', *Review of Industrial Organization*, 28(3), 285–306.

Geroski, P.A. (1995) 'What Do We Know About Entry?', *International Journal of Industrial Organization*, 13(4), 421–40.

Greene, F.J., Mole, K.F. and Storey, D.J. (2008) *Three Decades of Enterprise Culture: Entrepreneurship, Economic Regeneration and Public Policy*. London: Macmillan/ Palgrave.

Gimeno, J., Folta, T.B., Cooper, A.C. and Woo, C.Y. (1997) 'Survival of the Fittest? Entrepreneurial Human Capital and the Persistence of Underperforming Firms', *Administrative Science Quarterly*, 42(4), 750–83.

Hamilton, B.H. (2000) 'Does Entrepreneurship Pay?: An Empirical Analysis of the Returns to Self-employment', *Journal of Political Economy*, 108(3), 604–31.

Hannan, M.T. and Freeman, J. (1977) 'Population Ecology of Organizations', *American Journal of Sociology*, 82(5), 929–64.

Hannan, S. and Freeman, J. (1987) 'The Ecology of Organizational Founding: American Labor Unions, 1836–1985', *American Journal of Sociology*, 92, 910–43.

Harrison, R. and Leitch, C.M. (2005) 'Entrepreneurial Learning: Researching the Interface between Learning and the Entrepreneurial Context', *Entrepreneurship: Theory and Practice*, 29(4), 351–71.

Harvey, M. and Evans, R. (1995) 'Strategic Windows in the Entrepreneurial Process', *Journal of Business Venturing*, 10(5), 331–47.

Henley, A. (2004) 'Self-employment Status: The Role of State Dependence and Initial Circumstances', *Small Business Economics*, 22(1), 67–82.

Jovanovic, B. (1982) 'Selection and the Evolution of Industry', *Econometrica*, 50(3), 649–70.

Klepper, S. (2002) 'Firm Survival and the Evolution of Oligopoly', *Rand Journal of Economics*, 33(1), 37–61.

Lin, P.C. and Huang, D.S. (2008) 'Technological Regimes and Firm Survival: Evidence Across Sectors and Over Time', *Small Business Economics*, 30(2), 175–86.

Lin, Z.X., Picot, G. and Compton, J. (2000) 'The Entry and Exit Dynamics of Self-employment in Canada', *Small Business Economics*, 15(2), 105–25.

Lyles, M.A., Saxton, T. and Watson, K. (2004) 'Venture Survival in a Transitional Economy', *Journal of Management*, 30(3), 351–75.

Mahmood, T. (2000) 'Survival of Newly Founded Businesses: A Log-Logistic Model Approach', *Small Business Economics*, 14(3), 223–37.

Mata, J. and Portugal, P. (1994) 'Life Duration of New Firms', *Journal of Industrial Economics*, 42, 227–46.

Mata, J., Portugal, P. and Guimaraes, P. (1995) 'The Survival of New Plants: Start-up Conditions and Post-entry Evolution', *International Journal of Industrial Organisation*, 13(4), 459–81.

Meager, N., Bates, P. and Cowling, M. (2003) 'An Evaluation of Business Start-up Support for Young People', *National Institute Economic Review*, 186, 70–83.

Metzger, G. (2007) *Personal Experience: A Most Vicious and Limited Circle!? On the Role of Entrepreneurial Experience for Firm Survival*. Discussion Paper 07-046. Baden-Württemberg: Centre for European Economic Research.

Mezirow, J. (1991) *Transformative Dimensions of Adult Learning*, San Francisco, CA: Jossey-Bass.

Minniti, M. and Bygrave, W. (2001) 'A Dynamic Model of Entrepreneurial Learning', *Entrepreneurship: Theory and Practice*, 25(3), 5–16.

Nafziger, W.E. and Terrell, D. (1996) 'Entrepreneurial Human Capital and the Long-run Survival of Firms in India', *World Development*, 24, 689–96.

Nayak, A. and Greenfield, S. (1994) 'The Use of Management Accounting Information for Managing Micro-business', in Storey, D.J. and Hughes, A. (eds), *Finance and the Small Firm*. London: Routledge, 182–231.

Nziramasanga, M. and Lee, M. (2002) 'On the Duration of Self-employment: The Impact of Macroeconomic Conditions', *Journal of Development Studies*, 39(1), 46–73.

Parker, S.C. (2006) 'Learning about the Unknown: How Fast Do Entrepreneurs Adjust Their Beliefs?', *Journal of Business Venturing*, 21(1), 1–26.

Persson, H. (2004) 'The Survival and Growth of New Establishments in Sweden, 1987–1995', *Small Business Economics*, 23(5), 423–40.

Priem, R.L. and Butler, J.E. (2001) 'Tautology in the Resource-based View and Implications of Externally Determined Resource Value: Further Comments', *Academy of Management Review*, 26(1), 57–66.

Raz, O. and Gloor, P.A. (2007) 'Size Really Matters: New Insights for Start-ups' Survival', *Management Science*, 53(2), 169–77.

Reid, G.C. (1999) 'Complex Actions and Simple Outcomes: How New Entrepreneurs Stay in Business', *Small Business Economics*, 13(4), 303–15.

Robson, M.T. (1996) 'Macroeconomic Factors in the Birth and Death of UK Firms: Evidence from Quarterly VAT Registrations', *Manchester School of Economic and Social Studies*, LXIV(2), 170–88.

Saridakis, G., Mole, K.F. and Storey, D.J. (2008) 'New Small Firm Survival in England', *Empirica*, 35, 25–39.

Stearns, T.M., Carter, N.M., Reynolds, P.D. and Williams, M.L. (1995) 'New Firm Survival: Industry, Strategy, and Location', *Journal of Business Venturing*, 10(1), 23–42.

Stinchcombe, A.L. (1965) 'Social Structures and Organizations', in March, J.G. (ed.), *Handbook of Organizations*. Chicago, IL: Rand McNally.

Storey, D.J., Keasey, K., Watson, R. and Wynarczyk, P. (1987) *The Performance of Small Firms*. London: Croom Helm.

Storey, D.J. and Wynarczyk, P. (1996) 'The Survival and Non-survival of Micro Firms in the UK', *Review of Industrial Organization*, 11(2), 211–29.

Strotmann, H. (2007) 'Entrepreneurial Survival', *Small Business Economics*, 28(1), 87–104.

Taylor, M.P. (1999) 'Survival of the Fittest?: An Analysis of Self-employment Duration in Britain', *Economic Journal*, 109(454), C140–55.

Thornhill, S. and Amit, R. (2003) 'Learning About Failure: Bankruptcy, Firm Age, and the Resource-based View', *Organization Science*, 14(5), 497–509.

Tsionas, E.G. and Papadogonas, T.A. (2006) 'Firm Exit and Technical Inefficiency', *Empirical Economics*, 31(2), 535–48.

van Praag, C.M. (2003) 'Business Survival and Success of Young Small Business Owners', *Small Business Economics*, 21(1), 1–17.

Wagner, J. (1999) 'The Life History of Cohorts of Exits from German Manufacturing', *Small Business Economics,* 13(1), 71–19.

Yasuda, T. (2005) 'Firm Growth, Size, Age and Behaviour in Japanese Manufacturing', *Small Business Economics*, 24(1), 1–15.

Key to Table 10.1

No. in Table 10.1	Study author, year and place	Binary (B) or hazard (H) approach	Unit of analysis	Table no.	Years studied
1	Yasuda (2005) Japan	B	Fifty or more employee businesses	2	1992–5
2	Persson (2004) Sweden	B	All new establishments	6	1987–8
3	van Praag (2003) US	H	Young self-employed	4	1979–89
4	Nziramasanga and Lee (2002) Zimbabwe	H	Self-employed	2	1989–96
5	Fotopoulos and Louri (2001) Greece	H	All plc and ltd companies	3	early 1980s–92
6	Lin *et al.* (2000) Canada	B	Self-employment	7	1981–95
7	Wagner (1999) Germany	B	Manufacturing units	3	1990–2
8	Reid (1999) Scotland	B	New business starts	3	1994–5
9	Brüderl *et al.* (1992) Germany	B	New business closures	3	1985–90
10	Brüderl and Preisendörfer (1998) Germany	B	New business closures	3	1985–90
11	Cressy (1996) UK	B	Bank start ups	3	1988
12	Tsionas and Papadogonas (2006) Greece	H	All private businesses of corporate forms	1	1995–9
13	Mata *et al.* (1995) Portugal	B	New plants	7	1983–90
14	Doms *et al.* (1995) US	B	Manufacturing plants	2	1987–91
15	Audretsch (1995) US	B	New businesses in manufacturing	3	1976–86
16	Storey and Wynarczyk (1996) UK	B	New business owners	7	1985–94
17	Audretsch *et al.* (2000) Netherlands	H	Manufacturing businesses	2	1978–92
18	Fritsch *et al.* (2006) Germany	H	New businesses	6	1984–2000
19	Nafziger and Terrell (1996) India	H	New entrepreneurs	2	1971–93
20	Gimeno *et al.* (1997) US	B	New businesses	3	1985–7
21	Meager *et al.* (2003) UK	B	Young self-employed	3	2000–1
22	Taylor (1999) UK	B	Self-employment	5	1991–5
23	Robson (1996) UK	B	VAT registrations	2	1973–90
24	Lyles *et al.* (2004) Hungary	B	New businesses	3	1991–6
25	Bates (1995) US	B	New and franchise businesses	2	1984–7
26	Aspelund *et al.* (2005) Sweden	H	New technology businesses	3	1995–2000
27	Azoulay and Shane (2001) US	H	Franchises	5	1992–5
28	Saridakis *et al.* (2008) UK	H	New businesses	6	1990–9
29	Honjo (2000) Japan	H	New businesses	5	1986–94
30	Raz and Gloor (2007) Israel	B	Software start ups	2	1997–2000
31	Strotmann (2007) Germany	H	Manufacturing businesses	1	1980–99
32	Lin and Huang (2008) Taiwan	B	Businesses	5	1981–96
33	Delmar and Shane, 2003 (Sweden)	H	New businesses	3	1998–2000
34	Baptista *et al.* (2007) Portugal	B	New businesses	2	1986–94

Source: Greene *et al.* (2008).

Part 4 Business Growth

Part 4 looks at the important issue of business growth. Chapter 11 examines why fast growth businesses are important, how they have been defined and measured, and what 'stylised facts' have been developed out of our understanding of business growth. Chapter 12 introduces six approaches to business growth. Chapters 13 to 15 examine the empirical evidence for the factors that have been used to explain fast growth. This is done by examining entrepreneurial characteristics ('pre' start up factors), business characteristics ('at' start up) and business strategy factors ('post' start up).

11 Defining business growth

12 Analysing and measuring business growth

13 Growing the business: pre start-up factors

14 Growing the business: at start-up factors

15 Growing the business: post start-up factors

Entrepreneurship in Action   FT

Go to the *Small Business and Entrepreneurship* companion website at www.pearsoned.co.uk/storeygreene to watch entrepreneurs and academics giving you their personal perspectives on some of these issues.

Stuart Roberts, founder of Two Seasons, the specialist skiing and board-riding retailer, talks about the challenges of growing a retail business beyond its first outlet store.

11 Defining business growth

Key learning objectives

By the end of this chapter you should:

● Understand six different approaches to business growth

● Be able to identify the difficulties in defining and measuring fast-growth businesses

● Critically evaluate four 'stylised facts' of business growth.

Congratulations!

Simply by opening up this copy of **How to be a Billionaire**, you have taken an important step forward on the journey to extraordinary wealth. In fact, you are already far off where the self-made billionaires stood when they began their careers. Unlike you, they had no road map. There was no manual that systematically and objectively analyzed the methods of the individuals that preceded them.

How to be a Billionaire: Proven Strategies from the Titans of Wealth, *Fridson (2000: 3)*.

11.1 Introduction

This excerpt from a 'practical' self-help management book suggests that there are secrets that we can learn from existing billionaires so that we, too, can become successful entrepreneurs. This book is not alone. Other books suggest that we have to change our thinking (*Think Like a Billionaire, Become a Billionaire*), develop the appropriate 'strategy' (*Billionaire in Training*) or learn from famous entrepreneurs (*Billionaire Secrets to Success*).

Our view is the polar opposite. We do not think that there is a magic 'bullet' to guarantee business success. After more than two decades of careful empirical research in a variety of different countries, over different macro-economic conditions, using both quantitative and qualitative methods, a 'guaranteed' story about small fast-growth businesses has failed to emerge.

Indeed, as this chapter will later show, we really only know four 'stylised facts' about small business growth.

1 Businesses that grow – even at a modest level – are more likely to survive.

2 Fast-growth businesses are highly unusual. Typically, they make up no more than 5 per cent of any business population.

3   Growth is 'spotty'. Just because a business has grown in one period it is no guarantee that it will grow at the same rate in a second period.

4   Smaller and younger businesses tend to grow more quickly than larger businesses.

However, all these 'facts' apply to the business population in general. Individual businesses can, and do, constitute very important exceptions.

Other than these four 'facts', no owner characteristics or ways of doing business have been shown to guarantee success. This may mean that we have failed to identify the 'DNA' of success in growing a business. Alternatively, it could be that part and parcel of business growth is luck.

Our chapters on business growth are concerned with what we mean by growth, why it is important, what theories we can use to explain growth and what is the actual evidence on business growth. In this chapter, our interest is in identifying why small fast-growth businesses are so pivotal to economic prosperity. We then consider why it is difficult to measure growth. For example, growth may be seen by some entrepreneurs as merely surviving. Others might see it as no more than providing personal satisfaction for themselves, meeting social and environmental needs or simply looking after their family. Other, more 'objective' measures (e.g. sales, profits, market share) also bring problems – most notably that of deciding what constitutes fast or rapid growth. These are important issues because if there were any 'magic bullets' to explain growth then we have to sure what we mean by 'growth'.

We subsequently identify evidence to support our four 'stylised facts' about small business growth.

Illustration	boo.com

The internet retailer boo.com was set up by three Swedish entrepreneurs in 1998. Their initial forecast was that they needed 30 people and £20 million to set up the business. By October 1999 they employed 400 people and had attracted £125 million of venture capital. Over a very short period of time, employment growth was more than 1,300 per cent. By May 2000, however, the company had collapsed, leaving it with no employees. The name was taken over by fashionmail.com and subsequently re-launched with a team of 10 people.

Having read this example, how would you characterise performance? How would you measure it, and over how long?

11.2 The importance of fast-growth businesses

Small, fast-growth businesses are central to economic prosperity. Jovanovic (2001) reported that four of the largest US companies in terms of market capitalisation in August 1999 were less than 20 years old. These four companies were Microsoft, Cisco Systems, MCI and Dell. Their total company valuation was equivalent to 13 per cent of US GDP. This is a huge economic contribution and emphasises the role which rapidly growing, but initially small, businesses can play over a short period of time.

In some senses, the significance of these four companies is inflated by Jovanovic's choice of August 1999 since this was the height of the US dot-com boom. Nonetheless, since then the US has produced other international 'names' to be added to this list – such as Google and Facebook.

But it is not only in the US that rapidly growing new and small businesses have played an important role. Nokia, the Finnish telecommunications company, was a small enterprise in

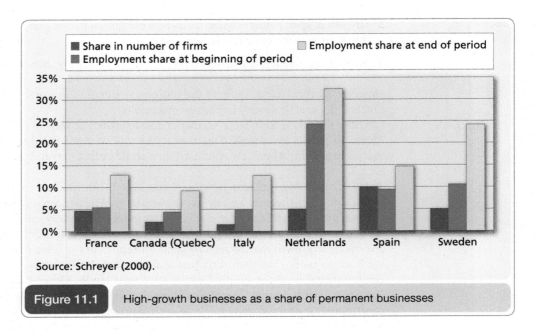

Source: Schreyer (2000).

Figure 11.1 High-growth businesses as a share of permanent businesses

the early 1980s. It subsequently grew so rapidly that it (virtually single-handedly) pulled the Finnish economy out of recession during the mid-1990s. Indeed, Autio *et al.* (1999) report that Nokia, by the end of the 1990s, was responsible for about one-third of Finland's GDP growth.

Schreyer (2000) also sought to identify for the Organisation for Economic Co-operation and Development (OECD) the employment contribution of fast-growth businesses. His findings are detailed in Figure 11.1. This shows that fast-growth businesses in six countries (France, Canada, Italy, The Netherlands, Spain and Sweden) represented less than 10 per cent of all businesses, but were responsible for a high proportion of employment generation in these countries.

It is not just individual small businesses that are important for economic development, but also groups of small businesses. This phenomenon was first noted by Piore and Sabel (1984), whose research on the 'Third Italy' (i.e. the areas around Bologna, Modena and Florence) showed that this area had achieved considerable prosperity based upon an economy comprising groups of small businesses in sectors such as clothing, footwear and musical instruments.

Since then, a whole range of important 'clusters' of small businesses have been identified. Perhaps the most famous of these is Silicon Valley in California (Saxenian 1994). This has led to the identification of 'spin-off' 'silicon' clusters: Silicon Glen in Scotland; Silicon Fen in Cambridgeshire, England and Silicon Wadi in Israel. Van der Linde (2004) claims that these groupings of businesses – he identifies 833 worldwide – are central to world economic prosperity.

The importance of new fast-growth business is hardly a recent phenomenon. Schumpeter (1934) argued that the fundamental role of the entrepreneur was as an agent of economic change (see Chapter 5). Entrepreneurs brought with them a 'gale of creative destruction' which tore up existing ways of doing businesses and replaced them with new ways that radically transformed economic and social behaviour.

Overall, there is little doubt that small businesses that become middle-sized and ultimately large businesses, over a comparatively short period of time, are central to economic prosperity. It is because of this power to create wealth that fast-growth small businesses are of huge interest to those in the business community and to politicians seeking to create the conditions for prosperity. Ultimately, the ability of a country to nurture the growth of such businesses is probably *the* most important element in enterprise development.

| Illustration | The fast growth of Britain's railways |

Arguably the world's most famous tour operator, Thomas Cook's first organised trips in the 1840s utilised Britain's growing rail network.

Prior to the coming of the railways, it took about 100 hours to get from London to Edinburgh by stagecoach. With the development of the railways, it took about 12 hours. In the 1840s, there was about 1,500 miles of rail track. By 1850, it had quadrupled to 6,000 miles. Investment in the railways ran at nearly 7 per cent of national income or, expressed alternatively, about two-thirds of total UK domestic exports. Central to the development of the railways was George Hudson, the 'Railway King'. Through clever acquisitions, Hudson grew his railway business so that by the late 1840s, he controlled one quarter of all the railways.

The development of railways led to the creation of other industries. Mass tourism, for example, began with the first 'excursion' organised by Thomas Cook in 1841 when he took 'temperance' (anti-alcohol) supporters to a rally by rail. Equally, because the railways were so capital intensive (requiring rails, buildings, locomotives), there was a need to properly account for its capital equipment. This led to the development of accountancy as a recognised profession.

11.3 Defining the fast-growth business

Although '. . . growth is the very essence of entrepreneurship' (Sexton 1997: 97), defining and measuring precisely what is meant by growth businesses is difficult. In this section, we consider the variety of definitions that can be used to identify 'growth'. We then consider what is meant by 'fast' growth. Finally, we put these two elements together to identify 'fast-growth' businesses.

Growth measures

Table 11.1 identifies eight measures of growth: sales, profits, financial ratios, employment, market share, the income of the entrepreneur, subjective measures (e.g. entrepreneur's satisfaction) and multiple measures of growth. Of these measures, reviews of business growth studies (e.g. Murphy *et al.* 1996; Weinzimmer *et al.* 1998; Wiklund and Shepherd 2005) have tended to conclude that the measures most commonly used by researchers are, first, sales and then employment. Sales is the most commonly used measure because the data are relatively easy to obtain and would appear to be used as a growth measure by entrepreneurs themselves (Barkham *et al.* 1996).

Employment data are also favoured by researchers because they are fairly easy to collect and give an indication of the resource base of the business. However, Table 11.1 identifies that employment and sales have disadvantages as growth measures. For example, sales growth may be influenced by price changes (inflation) over time whilst employment growth is influenced by the structure of sectors. For example, a cleaning business typically needs far more employees to generate revenue than a consultancy business.

Table 11.1 also shows the advantages and disadvantages of other growth measures. The common problem with these measures is that they often have to rely upon the discretion and knowledge of the business owner. If owners/managers are unwilling or unable to provide accurate information on the growth of the business, it is difficult to see how reliable and robust growth measures can be established. This is because small businesses are often not obliged to disclose their performance publicly (Dess and Robinson 1984). Also, the information used by secondary data sources may be inaccurate or out of date (Birley *et al.* 1995).

Table 11.1	Growth measures and their advantages and disadvantages	
Growth measure	**Advantages**	**Disadvantages**
Sales/ Revenue	● Measure most likely to be used by entrepreneurs to assess growth (Barkham *et al.* 1996). ● Insensitive to capital intensity. ● Applies to virtually all businesses. ● Sales are necessary for the growth of other assets (e.g. employment). ● Relatively simple to identify and compute.	● Price changes (inflation) over time may make comparisons difficult. ● Entrepreneurs may withhold sales data because they believe it is confidential to them. ● May be subject to selection (entrepreneurs over-estimating their success) and hindsight bias (failure to accurately remember). ● Some businesses (e.g. biotechnology) may have products that take several years to develop and subsequently sell.
Profits	● Potential goal of entrepreneurs. ● Relatively easily understood by entrepreneurs. ● Applies to virtually all businesses.	● Entrepreneurs may withhold profit data because they believe it is confidential. ● May be subject to selection and hindsight bias. ● Open to interpretation (e.g. gross profits, profits after tax, normalised by sales?). ● Some businesses (e.g. biotechnology) may have products that take several years to develop and subsequently sell.
Financial ratios	● Potential goal of entrepreneurs. ● Applies to virtually all businesses.	● Open to interpretation (e.g. return on assets, investments, equity?). ● May not be readily understood by the small business owner (Nayak and Greenfield 1994). ● May be subject to selection and hindsight bias. ● May be sensitive to sectoral differences. ● Some businesses (e.g. biotechnology) may have products that take several years to develop and subsequently sell.

Table 11.1 continued

Growth measure	Advantages	Disadvantages
Employment	• Easy to measure because entrepreneurs do not normally see it as confidential information. • Gives an indication of the resources of the business. • Not so readily subject to selection or hindsight bias (Fraser *et al.* 2006). • Important to policy makers because they often see small businesses as a source of employment generation. • Often a correlation between sales and employment growth.	• Business owners do not see this as a growth measure (Wiklund 1998; Robson and Bennett 2000). • Fast-growth businesses may outsource employment (Delmar *et al.* 2003). • Employment may vary widely across industries.
Market share	• Provides an indication of the acceptance of the product/service in the market. • May be a better indicator of the value of the business' strategy because it gives an indicator of the business' viability in the marketplace. • Information often available from secondary data sets.	• Not seen as a prime goal of entrepreneurs • Small businesses are price *takers* not price *makers* so the concept of market share may be meaningless. • Difficult to verify with entrepreneurs (selection and hindsight bias). • Market share growth may due to a competitor choosing no longer to compete in the marketplace. • Comparing shares across industries may be meaningless for very small businesses where market share is miniscule.
Income of entrepreneur	• Potential goal of entrepreneurs. • Applies to virtually all businesses.	• Entrepreneurs may not wish to share such information. • Open to hindsight and selection bias. • Can be difficult to separate out personal and business assets. • Difficult to make sectoral comparisons.
Subjective measures (e.g. owner satisfaction)	• May reflect more accurately the objectives of a business owner. • Applies to virtually all businesses.	• Subjective measures of growth may not be correlated with actual growth (McMullan *et al.* 2001). • Potentially difficult to compare between sectors or between different areas. • Potentially likely to be prone to selection/hindsight bias. • Fast-growth businesses should surely be judged in terms of pecuniary outcomes (e.g. actual sales).
Multiple measures of growth	• May capture/control for the 'latent' (underlying) features of growth because it is unlikely that one measure will fully capture the performance of the business (e.g. a business may experience sales growth but see a downturn in employment growth).	• Tends to be constructed based on the subjective opinions of entrepreneurs. These may have little correlation with actual growth. • Any index has to decide on weights and it is not clear what these should be. • Index may not be any better at identifying dimensions of growth. • Difficult to control for spatial and sectoral differences. • Ultimately, makes the concept more complex and may generate little insight.

Another issue to consider is how adequately the measure reflects the goals of the entrepreneur. It is difficult, for example, to see how employment growth would ever be a primary goal of a business owner. As small businesses tend to be price takers, increased market share would also seem an unlikely goal. Sales, financial ratios measures (e.g. return on equity, assets) and increases in the income of entrepreneur would all seem better measures. However, there are measurement problems with each of these measures (see Table 11.1).

Many entrepreneurs claim not to be motivated wholly in terms of financial gain (see Chapter 2). Birley and Westhead (1990) identify that there are five typical reasons why people set up in business. These are: 'freedom', 'to take advantage of an opportunity', 'to control their time', it 'made sense at the time' and for 'security'. It would seem then that businesses are often vehicles for meeting family, personal, social or environmental objectives. Wiklund and Shepherd (2003) call for more subjective measures of performance, as these are more likely to reflect the growth intentions of entrepreneurs. Unfortunately, the problem is that growth intentions may fail to correspond with actual outcomes (Chandler and Hanks 1993).

A second problem is that subjective measures may be more appropriate to businesses whose growth is, in practice, modest. This occurs when business owners tell researchers that they never intended to have a rapidly growing business. Whether this *was* their actual intention when the business began is much more difficult to establish. Fast-growth businesses are those that do not just *think* that they have grown quicker but *actually* grow quicker.

Debates over the use of a single measure of growth have led to the use of multiple measures of growth. The advantage of multiple measures is that they seek to provide a more complete assessment of the growth trajectory of a business. The extent to which this is achieved depends upon how the index is constructed and, again, how well it actually reflects the growth of a business.

In essence, Table 11.1 makes three points. The first is that '. . . there is no way of measuring an amount of expansion, or even the size of a business, that is not open to serious conceptual objections' (Penrose 1959: 199). Second, as Cooper (1993) argued, 'Research to date has tended to focus upon variables that are relatively easy to gather information about or to measure' (p. 249). Finally, Table 11.1 indicates that a common source of bias is from the business owners themselves. One way of limiting this is to examine businesses over long periods of time (Fraser *et al.* 2006).

This, though, is not the only consideration. So far, we have assumed that growth is 'organic' in that businesses grow from *within* themselves. Growth may, however, be by acquisition. Davidsson and Wiklund (2000) show that this distinction is important. They report that, whilst amongst young businesses growth was primarily organic, the reverse was the case for longer-established businesses, whose primary means of growth was by merger or acquisition.

None of this would matter if the different metrics of growth were strongly correlated with each other. But sadly they are not. As Shepherd and Wiklund (2009) show in their evocatively titled article 'Are we comparing Apples with Apples or Apples with Oranges?', growth in sales, employment, assets, equity and profit – for Swedish businesses – are only weakly correlated with each other. The choice of metric, therefore, makes a difference since a choice based on fast growth in employment identifies different businesses from one based on profits or assets.

Measuring the rapidity of growth

It may also seem pretty straightforward at first to identify the rapidity of growth: take a sample or population of businesses, identify a growth criterion (e.g. sales, employment), rank them in order and then focus on the top end of the distribution. This tends to be the approach adopted in very many lists of fast-growth companies. For example, the UK's *Sunday Times* 'Fast Track' 100 orders businesses in terms of their sales growth over the previous three years.

But, how do you know that a piece of fruit is really a 'plum' rather than a 'lemon'? What looks in the very short term to be a 'plum' may turn out to be a 'lemon'. So, over what time period should growth be measured: if too short a time span is taken, it may not allow growth to emerge; too long, and the factor driving growth may be missed.

A second difficulty is actually working out how to measure any growth. There are four main ways:

1 annualised growth (take explicit account of year-to-year variation);

2 absolute growth (measure actual increase e.g. an increase in the number of employees);

3 relative growth (measure percentage changes); and

4 log transform growth measure (e.g. transform the data so that it growth is 'normally' distributed across the business population).

Why these measures matter is because it is relatively easy for some businesses to appear like fast-growth businesses using one measure whilst appearing as 'trundlers' using another measure. For example, if a business has 10 employees but grows to 100 employees we can say it has grown either by 90 employees (absolute measure) or 1,000 per cent. Relative measures, therefore, tend to favour smaller-sized businesses. Absolute measures, though, tend to favour larger-sized businesses. Because of these issues, Almus (2002) argues that, to limit the biases that come from just using an absolute or relative measure, it is more appropriate to combine the two approaches.

To illustrate these issues more fully, consider Table 11.2, which is from Delmar *et al.* (2003). They focus on all Swedish businesses with more than 20 employees in 1996, and trace their development back to 1987. They define fast-growing businesses as those in the top 10 per cent of all businesses, in terms of an annual average in one or more of the following six categories:

- absolute total employment growth;

- absolute organic employment growth;

- absolute sales growth;

- relative (i.e., percentage) total employment growth;

- relative organic employment growth; and

- relative sales growth.

In total, they identified that around 13 per cent of Swedish businesses can be considered to be high growth. However, the novelty of their study is that they are able to cluster their businesses into seven different patterns. Amongst the cluster of growers it is interesting that the erratic one-shot growers – defined as those that exhibit an unsustained burst of growth – are numerically dominant. Businesses growing by acquisition are also important. The implication then from Table 11.2 is that how you measure growth is pivotal in understanding fast growth.

Fast-growth businesses (gazelles)

Despite Delmar *et al.*'s evidence that there is no such thing as a typical fast-growth business, there has certainly been no weakening of interest in defining and measuring fast-growth businesses. Indeed, such fast-growth businesses have been given the name **gazelles**. According to Birch *et al.* (1995), a gazelle is a business that had a 20 per cent increase in sales and started with a base of at least $100,000. This is in contrast to **elephants** (large businesses) that employ lots of people but do not generate many new jobs, and **mice** (small businesses) that start out small and only contribute marginally to employment growth.

The OECD (2008) also sought to distinguish between fast-growth businesses and gazelles. Fast-growth businesses, which they define as 'high-growth' as measured by employment (or

Table 11.2		Patterns of fast growth amongst Swedish businesses		
Cluster	**Percentage of all growers**	**Name**	**Growth pattern**	**Demographic characteristic**
1	13.5%	Super absolute growers	Exhibited high absolute growth both in sales and employment.	Dominated by small and medium-sized businesses. Found in knowledge intensive manufacturing industries.
2	12.8%	Steady sales growers	Rapid growth in sales and negative development in employment.	Almost totally dominated by large businesses. Found in traditional industries such as pulp, steel, and other manufacturing. Dominated by businesses affiliated with company groups.
3	10%	Acquisition growers	Resembles Cluster 1 but has negative organic employment growth. Growth is achieved by acquiring other businesses.	Large businesses are over represented. Dominated by older businesses (i.e., businesses created before 1987). Found in traditional industries such as pulp, steel, and manufacturing. Dominated by businesses affiliated with company groups.
4	16.3%	Super relative growers	Has a very strong but somewhat erratic development of both sales and employment.	Dominated by small and medium-sized businesses. Seventy-one percent of the businesses created during the period of observation. Found in knowledge intensive service industries. A high representation of independent businesses.
5	16.7%	Erratic one-shot growers	Has on average negative size development, with the exception of one, single, very strong growth year.	Dominated by small and medium-sized businesses. Found in low-technology service industries.
6	16%	Employment growers	Growth is relatively stronger in employment than in sales.	Dominated by small and medium-sized businesses. Found in low-tech service industries.
7	14.8%	Steady overall growers	Resembles Cluster 1, but has weaker development.	Larger businesses are over represented. Found in manufacturing industries. Dominated by businesses affiliated with company group.

Source: Delmar *et al.* (2003).

by turnover), are 'all enterprises with average annualised growth in employees (or turnover) greater than 20 per cent a year, over a three-year period, and with ten or more employees at the beginning of the observation period' (p. 18). However, the OECD (2008) argues that gazelles are a subset of fast-growth businesses, and are distinguished by their relative youth. Hence, it defines gazelles as:

> . . . high-growth enterprises born five years or less before the end of the three-year observation period. In other words, measured in terms of employment (or of turnover) gazelles are enterprises which have been employers for a period of up to five years, with average annualised growth in employees (or in turnover) greater than 20 per cent a year over a three-year period and with ten or more employees at the beginning of the observation period (p. 20).

Overall, there is no consistently accepted way of measuring fast growth. Equally, no measure would appear ideal for all circumstances. Much depends upon the period of time over which growth is to be measured, whether it is absolute or relative growth which is of interest, and whether growth by acquisition is seen to be as valid as organic growth.

Recognising these limitations, we now consider four 'stylised facts' about business growth.

11.4 Four 'stylised facts' about business growth

1 **Businesses that have grown are more likely subsequently to survive.** One of the main 'stylised facts' from Chapters 9 and 10 was that bigger businesses were more likely to survive than smaller businesses. Even modest growth can be important. Phillips and Kirchhoff (1989) showed that if a business failed to grow then only 26 per cent of such businesses (1–4 employees) survived for six years. However, if just one employee was added, the survival rate increased to 65 per cent.

2 **Fast business growth is highly unusual.** To demonstrate this, consider Figure 11.2. This is based on official New Zealand data on business activity, covering 442,000 businesses. Hull and Arnold (2008) track the changes in sales for all of these businesses over the period 2000–5. Figure 11.2 shows – for the purposes of comparison – that all businesses had their sales/turnover band set at 0 in 2000. It then shows what happens over the next five years. The first panel to the right shows what happens one year later. Clearly, the vast majority of businesses continue to be in the same size band but, where there is movement, it is to the left rather than the right – implying that businesses move into smaller size bands. By the fifth

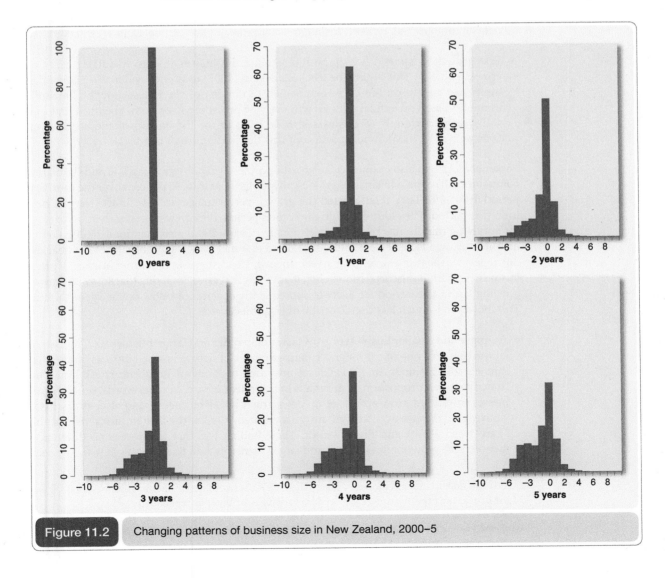

Figure 11.2 Changing patterns of business size in New Zealand, 2000–5

year (2005), only about 30 per cent of businesses are still in their original sales/turnover size band. The vast bulk of businesses had slipped to the left – reflecting a reduction in their sales/turnover. Only a tiny percentage of businesses had actually shifted to the right over the period. In other words, high growth is again highly unusual, and decline is the norm.

Such a finding is confirmed by other evidence. Cosh and Hughes (2000), for example, showed that only about 1 per cent of UK businesses that started off as 50–99 employee-sized businesses ended up in the 200–499 size category.

The OECD (2008) also found that gazelles made up between less than 1 per cent (measured in terms of employment) and less than 2 per cent (sales) of all businesses. Henrekson and Johansson (2010) reviewed more than 20 international studies across different time periods, using different measures of growth (e.g. absolute, relative, multiple) and different definitions of fast growth. Their review also identified different types of growth (e.g. organic, acquired) and used data on different business types and industries. They confirm the conclusions above: generally less than 5 per cent of businesses can be construed as fast-growth businesse, although these fast-growth businesses are responsible for a disproportionate contribution to economic development.

Whilst fast growth is unusual, it is also important. Statistical analysis of new businesses has persistently pointed towards evidence that, amongst every 100 start ups, the largest four survivors provide half of all jobs after a decade. In essence, 4 per cent of start ups provide 50 per cent of jobs (Storey 1994; Anyadike-Danes et al. 2008; Schindele and Weyh 2009).

3 **Fast growth is 'spotty'.** It may be thought that businesses that grow quickly carry on growing quickly. This is not true. Nicholls-Nixon (2005) examines evidence on how many businesses appear on the US's Fortune 500 (a ranking of the fastest-growth companies in the US based on annual sales growth over the preceding five years). She finds that over a 22-year period, only 69 businesses made it on to the list on two or more occasions. Delmar et al.'s (2003) Swedish data confirms this finding (see Table 11.2).

Parker et al. (2010) also examined the growth profiles of rapidly growing UK middle-market companies. All of these businesses grew by an average of at least 30 per cent over the four-year period 1991–5/6. They then charted the growth performance of this cohort over the next four-year period. They found that, in the second period, they grew no faster than the average for surviving middle-market companies. Finally, Coad (2007) also examined 10,000 French manufacturing businesses. He found that those that had grown substantially over a year did not repeat this feat in the following year. Indeed, Coad suggests that other studies of small businesses point to the correlation being, if anything, negative, implying that small businesses growing fast in one period are likely to subsequently experience below average growth rates. This, however, is much less characteristic of large businesses.

4 **Younger and smaller businesses grow faster than older and larger businesses.** This issue is at the centre of one of the longest running sources of debate in small business and entre-preneurship research. In 1931, Gibrat proposed the 'Law of Proportionate Effect'. This stated that that proportionate growth is independent of size. In other words, smaller businesses would not grow any faster or slower than larger businesses and also, as discussed above, growth rates would be serially uncorrelated.[1] One of the first empirical tests of this 'Law' was by Hart and Prais (1956).[2] Their finding was that there were no differences between the growth rates of small and large businesses, and that Gibrat's Law was upheld.

---

[1] Formally stated, Gibrat's Law is $S_{it} = \varepsilon_t S_{it-1}$ Where: S_{it} is the size of the businesses at time t, S_{it-1} is the size of the firm at the previous time, ε is a random variable distributed independently of S_{it-1}.

[2] Gibrat's Law is tested by taking logs of both sides: Log $S_{it} = a + \beta \log S_{it-1} + \varepsilon_t$. Hence, Gibrat's Law is confirmed where $\beta = 1$. Alternatively, where $\beta = <1$ smaller businesses grow faster and where $\beta = >1$ larger businesses grow faster.

However, Hart and Prais (1956) only examined surviving businesses. This is a problem since smaller businesses are more likely to close and the closures are more likely to have had lower growth rates. So, by examining only survivors, there is upward bias on small businesses' growth rates, because large businesses are much less likely to close. Another problem is that, as we noted in Chapter 10, some businesses do not close because of 'failure', but because of acquisition/merger activity. For example, smaller businesses are more likely to be acquired, whilst larger businesses are more likely to acquire other businesses.

A study of limited companies by Dunne and Hughes (1994) addressed both these issues. They found that, taking account of survivor bias, smaller companies grew faster than large, and that age is negatively related to growth. In this respect, Gibrat's Law, for small businesses, is not upheld.

Further work by a range of researchers is detailed in Table 11.3. It is an adaptation and extension of Lotti *et al.*'s (2003) helpful review of the evidence and shows that, on the whole,

Table 11.3	Selected empirical studies on Gibrat's Law	
Study	**Data**	**Results**
Wagner (1992)	About 7,000 West German manufacturing plants over 1978–89 (only incumbents).	Gibrat's Law fails to hold, but no evidence that small businesses grow faster.
Dunne and Hughes (1994)	2,149 UK companies over 1980–85 (only incumbents).	Smaller businesses grow faster.
Mata (1994)	3,308 Portuguese manufacturing businesses over 1983–87 (only entrants).	Smaller businesses grow faster.
Hart and Oulton (1996)	87,109 UK companies over 1989–93 (only entrants).	Smaller businesses grow faster.
Harhoff *et al.* (1998)	10,902 West German businesses over 1989–94 (only incumbents).	Smaller businesses grow faster.
Almus (2000)	Persistent 39,355 West German manufacturing businesses over 1989–96 (only entrants).	Smaller businesses grow faster.
Weiss (1998)	40,000 farm households in Upper Austria (1979–90).	Smaller businesses grow faster.
Heshmati (2001)	5,913 Swedish businesses with fewer than 10 employees (1993–8).	Results very sensitive with respect to the method of estimation.
Lotti *et al.* (2001)	129 micro-businesses >5 employees and 85 businesses >5 employees in the Italian Instruments industry (1987–93) (only entrants).	Initially, smaller businesses grow faster. A few years after entry, a Gibrat-like pattern of growth is detected.
Fotopoulos and Louri (2001)	2,640 Greek manufacturing businesses operating (1992–7).	Business size is found to have a negative effect on business growth, particularly in the case of fast-growing businesses.
Becchetti and Trovato (2002)	1,144 businesses with <50 employees, 1,427 businesses with <100 employees, and 462 businesses with >100 employees in Italy.	Gibrat's Law is not rejected for large businesses; rejected for small and medium-sized businesses under financial constraints.
Lotti *et al.* (2003)	1,570 new manufacturing businesses in Italy (1987–93).	Small businesses grow faster but, as entrants age, growth of small businesses is not significantly different from large businesses.
Rodriguez *et al.* (2003)	1,092 businesses operating in the Canaries, Spain (1990–6).	Smaller businesses grow faster.
Audretsch *et al.* (2004)	1,170 Dutch hospitality businesses (1987–91).	Acceptance of Gibrat's Law.
Ward and McKillop (2005)	866 credit unions in the UK (1994–2000).	Smaller credit unions grow faster.
Lotti *et al.* (2009)	Radio, TV and communication equipment sectors in Italy, 1987–94.	Smaller businesses grow faster, but 'core' surviving businesses behave according to Gibrat's Law.

smaller businesses are more likely to grow than larger businesses. This seems a rejection of Gibrat's Law. However, there are interesting nuances. Hart and Oulton (1996), for example, point to a 'break point' of around eight employees. Businesses smaller than this were more likely to grow but once businesses have more than eight employees, size and growth are unrelated. Hart (2000) also emphasised that younger businesses grow faster than long-established businesses whilst Audretsch *et al.* (2004) argue that smaller service businesses in hospitality are no more likely to grow quickly when compared to larger businesses. Finally, Lotti *et al.* (2009) argue that whilst Gibrat may not apply to all businesses, it does apply to a 'core' of surviving businesses.

In summary, the very smallest and the very youngest businesses are more likely to grow faster than older and large businesses. However, Gibrat's Law does appear to be broadly valid for the rest of the population of businesses, and the focus of the debate is upon the proportion and economic importance of businesses to which it does *not* apply. The significance of this is that Gibrat's Law assumes that growth is a random variable – implying the powerful role of chance/luck.

Summary

This chapter has examined the difficulties of defining and measuring business growth. These difficulties arise because of the variety of available measures for growth (e.g. sales, employment) and the ways that these measures can be interpreted (e.g. relative, absolute growth). The evidence from Delmar *et al.* (2003) suggests that further complicating any measurement is whether growth is organic or through acquisition. As Penrose (1959) indicates, there is unlikely to be a completely satisfactory resolution of such measurement issues.

Although hampered by these definitional issues, this chapter has shown the importance of fast-growth businesses to economic development. The chapter argues that they are pivotal to explaining the importance of particular regions and particular sectors. Although their importance is evident for Silicon Valley this is, by no means, an exclusively modern phenomenon. An equally powerful illustration is the pivotal role of the railways in the economic development of Victorian England.

Despite their importance, this chapter argues that there are only four 'stylised' facts' that we know about fast-growth businesses and even then they do not apply to every business. The first is that even modest growth promotes business survival. Second, fast-growth businesses and new fast-growth businesses (gazelles) are highly unusual. Typically, they represent a tiny proportion of all businesses. Third, just because a business grows in one period does not mean that it becomes more likely to continue to grow in the next period. Finally, the smallest and youngest businesses would seem to grow more quickly, but this effect fades as the business size and age increases. For businesses other than the very smallest and the very youngest, Gibrat's Law is broadly upheld, implying that growth is a random variable.

Questions for discussion

1 What is the best way of defining fast-growth businesses?

2 What are the four stylised features of fast growth? Explain what this has to say about the study of such businesses.

3 Does Gibrat's Law hold for small businesses?

References

Almus, M. (2000) 'Testing "Gibrat's Law" for Young Businesses: Empirical Results for West Germany', *Small Business Economics*, 15(1), 1–12.

Almus, M. (2002) 'What Characterizes a Fast-growing Firm?' *Applied Economics*, 34(12), 1497–508.

Anderson, S. (2006) *Think Like a Billionaire, Become a Billionaire*. Mesa, AZ: Winword.

Anyadike-Danes, M., Bonner, K., Hart, M. and Symington, D. (2008) *Escaping the Dead Hand of the Past: The Direct Employment Effects of New Firm Formation and the Dynamics of Job Growth in Northern Ireland, 1995–2005*. ERINI, Monograph 33. Belfast: Economic Research Institute of Northern Ireland.

Audretsch, D.B., Klomp, L., Santarelli, E. and Thurik, A.R. (2004) 'Gibrat's Law: Are the Services Different?', *Review of Industrial Organization*, 24(3), 301–24.

Autio, E., Wallenius, H. and Arenius, P. (1999) 'Finnish Gazelles: Origins and Impacts'. Paper presented at ICSB Conference, Naples, 20–23 June.

Barkham, R., Gudgin, G., Hart, M. and Hanvey, E. (1996) *The Determinants of Small Firm Growth*. Gateshead: Athenaeum.

Bartman, B. (2005) *Billionaire Secrets to Success*. Dallas, TX: Brown Books Publishing Group.

Becchetti, L. and Trovato, G. (2002) 'The Determinants of Growth for Small and Medium-sized Businesses. The Role of the Availability of External Finance', *Small Business Economics*, 19(4), 291–306.

Birch, D.L., Haggerty, A. and Parsons, W. (1995) *Who's Creating Jobs?* Boston: Cognetics Inc.

Birley, S. and Westhead, P. (1990) 'Growth and Performance Contrasts between "Types" of Small Firms', *Strategic Management Journal*, 11(7), 535–57.

Birley, S., Muzyka, D., Dove, C. and Russel, G. (1995) 'Finding the High-flying Entrepreneurs: A Cautionary Tale', *Entrepreneurship: Theory and Practice*, 19(4), 105–12.

Chandler, G.N. and Hanks, S.H. (1993) 'Measuring the Performance of Emerging Businesses: a Validation Study', *Journal of Business Venturing*, 8(5), 391–408.

Coad, A. (2007) 'A Closer Look at Serial Growth Rate Correlation', *Review of Industrial Organization*, 31(1), 69–82.

Cooper, A.C. (1993) 'Challenges in Predicting New Firm Performance', *Journal of Business Venturing*, 8, 241–53.

Cosh, A. and Hughes, A. (eds) (2000) *British Enterprise in Transition*. Cambridge: Centre for Business Research, University of Cambridge.

Davidsson, P. and Delmar, F. (2003) 'Hunting for New Employment: The Role of High-growth Businesses', in Kirby, D.A. and Watson, A. (eds), *Small Businesses and Economic Development in Developed and Transition Economies: A Reader*. Aldershot: Ashgate Publishing, 7–19.

Davidsson, P. and Delmar, F. (2006) 'High-growth Businesses and their Contribution to Employment: The Case of Sweden', in Davidsson, P., Delmar, F. and Wiklund, J. (eds), *Entrepreneurship and the Growth of Businesses*. Cheltenham, UK and Northampton, MA: Edward Elgar, 156–78.

Davidsson, P. and Wiklund, J. (2000) 'Conceptual and Empirical Challenges in the Study of Firm Growth', in Sexton, D.L. and Landstrom, H. (eds), *The Blackwell Handbook of Entrepreneurship*. London: Blackwell, 26–44.

Davidsson, P., Achtenhagen, L. and Naldi, L. (2004) 'Research on Small Firm Growth: A Review,' in *Proceedings European Institute of Small Business*. Paper presented at ESIB Conference, Barcelona.

Delmar F., Davidsson, P. and Gartner, W.B. (2003) 'Arriving at the High-growth Firm', *Journal of Business Venturing*, 18, 89–216.

Dess, G. and Robinson, R.B. (1984) 'Measuring Organizational Performance in the Absence of Objective Measures: The Case of the Privately Held Firm and Conglomerate Business Unit', *Strategic Management Journal*, 5(3), 265–73.

Dunne, P. and Hughes, A. (1994) 'Age, Growth and Survival: UK Companies in the 1980s', *Journal of Industrial Economics*, 42(2), 115–40.

Fotopoulos G. and Louri, H. (2001) *Corporate Growth and FDI: Are Multinationals Stimulating Local Industrial Development?* Discussion Paper No. 3128. London: Centre for Economic Policy Research.

Fraser, S., Greene, F.J. and Mole, K.F. (2006) 'Systematic Biases in Self-reported Data: The Role of "Anchoring" and "Impression Management"', *British Journal of Management*, 18(2), 192–208.

Fridson, M.S. (2000) *How to Be a Billionaire: Proven Strategies from the Titans of Wealth*. New York: Wiley.

Harhoff, D., Stahl, K. and Woywode, M. (1998) 'Legal Form, Growth And Exit of West German Businesses: Empirical Results From Manufacturing, Construction, Trade and Service Industries', *Journal of Industrial Economics*, 66(4), 453–88.

Hart, P.E. (2000) 'Theories of Businesses' Growth and the Generation of Jobs', *Review of Industrial Organization*, 17(3), 229–48.

Hart, P.E. and Prais, S.J. (1956) 'The Analysis of Business Concentration: A Statistical Approach', *Journal of the Royal Statistical Society*, Series A, 119, 150–90.

Hart, P.E. and Oulton, N. (1996) 'Growth and Size of Businesses', *Economic Journal*, 106(438), 1242–52.

Henrekson, M. and Johansson, D. (2010) 'Gazelles as Job Creators: A Survey and Interpretation of the Evidence', *Small Business Economics* (forthcoming).

Heshmati, A. (2001) 'On the Growth of Micro and Small Businesses: Evidence from Sweden', *Small Business Economics*, 17(3), 213–28.

Hull, L. and Arnold, R. (2008) *New Zealand Firm Growth as Change in Turnover*. Wellington: Ministry of Economic Development.

Jovanovic, B. (2001) 'New Technology and the Small Firm', *Small Business Economics*, 16(1), 53–5.

Lotti, F., Santarelli, E. and Vivarelli, M. (2001) 'The Relationship between Size and Growth: The Case of Italian New-born Firms', *Applied Economics Letters*, 8(7), 451–54.

Lotti, F., Santarelli, E. and Vivarelli, M. (2003) 'Does Gibrat's Law Hold among Young, Small Businesses?', *Journal of Evolutionary Economics*, 13(3), 213–35.

Lotti, F., Santarelli, E. and Vivarelli, M. (2009) 'Defending Gibrat's Law as a Long-run Regularity', *Small Business Economics*, 32(1), 31–44.

Mata, J. (1994) 'Firm Growth During Infancy', *Small Business Economics*, 6(1), 27–39.

McMullan, W.E., Chrisman, J.J. and Vesper, K.H. (2001) 'Some Problems in Using Subjective Measures of Effectiveness to Evaluate Entrepreneurial Assistance Programs', *Entrepreneurship: Theory and Practice*, 26(1), 37–54.

Murphy, G.B., Trailer, J.W. and Hill, R.C. (1996) 'Measuring Performance in Entrepreneurship', *Journal of Business Research*, 36, 15–23.

Nayak, A. and Greenfield, S. (1994) 'The Use of Management Accounting Information for Managing Micro-business', in Storey, D.J. and Hughes, A. (eds), *Finance and the Small Firm*. London: Routledge, 182–231.

Nicholls-Nixon, C.L. (2005) 'Rapid Growth and High Performance: The Entrepreneur's "Impossible Dream"?', *Academy of Management Executive*, 19(1), 77–89.

OECD (2008) *Measuring Entrepreneurship: A Digest of Indicators*. Paris: OECD.

Parker, S., Storey, D.J. and van Witteloostuijn, A. (2010) 'What Happens to Gazelles?', *Small Business Economics* (forthcoming).

Penrose, E.T. (1959) *The Theory of the Growth of the Firm*. London: Blackwell.

Phillips, B.D. and Kirchhoff, B.A. (1989) 'Formation, Growth and Survival: Small Firm Dynamics in the US Economy', *Small Business Economics*, 1(1), 65–74.

Piore, M. and Sabel, C. (1984) *The Second Industrial Divide*. New York: Basic Books.

Robson, P.J.A. and Bennett, R.J. (2000) 'SME growth: The Relationship with Business Advice and External Collaboration', *Small Business Economics*, 15(3), 193–208.

Rodriguez, A.C., Molina, M.A., Perez, A.L.G. and Hernandez, U.M. (2003) 'Size, Age and Activity Sector on the Growth of the Small and Medium-size Firm', *Small Business Economics*, 21(3), 289–307.

Saxenian, A. (1994) *Regional Advantage: Culture and Competition in Silicon Valley and Route 128*. Cambridge, MA: Harvard University Press.

Saxenian, A. and Hsu, J.-Y. (2001) 'The Silicon Valley–Hsinchu Connection: Technical Communities and Industrial Upgrading', *Industrial and Corporate Change*, 10, 893–920.

Schindele, Y. and Weyh, A. (2009) 'The Direct Employment Effects of New Businesses in Germany Revisited: An Empirical Investigation for 1976–2004', *Small Business Economics*, published online 8 July.

Schreyer, P. (2000) *High-Growth Businesses and Employment*, OECD Science, Technology and Industry Working Papers, 2000/3. Paris: OECD.

Schumpeter, J.A. (1934) *The Theory of Economic Development: An Inquiry into Profits, Capital, Credit, Interest and the Business Cycle* (Opie, R., trans.). Cambridge, MA: Harvard University Press (1968).

Sexton, D.L. (1997) 'Entrepreneurship Research Needs and Issues', in Sexton, D.L. and Smilor, R.W. (eds), *Entrepreneurship 2000*. Chicago, IL: Upstart Publishing, 401–8.

Shepherd, D. and Wiklund, J. (2009) 'Are We Comparing Apples with Apples or Apples with Oranges?: Appropriateness of Knowledge Accumulation across Growth Studies', *Entrepreneurship: Theory and Practice*, 33(1), 105–23.

Storey, D.J. (1994) *Understanding the Small Business Sector*. London: Routledge.

van der Linde, C. (2004) *Findings from the Cluster Meta Study*. www.isc.hbs.edu.

Wagner, J. (1992) 'Firm Size, Firm Growth, and Persistence of Chance: Testing Gibrat's Law with Establishment Data from Lower Saxony, 1978–1989', *Small Business Economics*, 4(2), 125–31.

Ward, A.M. and McKillop, D.G. (2005) 'The Law of Proportionate Effect: The Growth of the UK Credit Union Movement at National and Regional Level', *Journal of Business Finance and Accounting*, 32(9–10), 1827–59.

Weinzimmer, L.G., Nystrom, P.C. and Freeman S.J. (1998) 'Measuring Organizational Growth: Issues, Consequences and Guidelines', *Journal of Management*, 24(2), 235–62.

Weiss, C.R. (1998) 'Size, Growth, and Survival in the Upper Austrian Farm Sector', *Small Business Economics*, 10(4), 305–12.

Wiklund, J. (1998) 'Small Firm Growth and Performance: Entrepreneurship and Beyond'. Doctoral dissertation. Jönköping International Business School.

Wiklund, J. and Shepherd, D. (2003) 'Aspiring for, and Achieving Growth: The Moderating Role of Resources and Opportunities', *Journal of Management Studies*, 40(8), 1919–41.

Wiklund, J. and Shepherd, D. (2005) 'Entrepreneurial Orientation and Small Business Performance: A Configurational Approach', *Journal of Business Venturing*, 20(1), 71–91.

12 Analysing and measuring business growth

Key learning objectives

By the end of this chapter you should:

- Understand the six different approaches to business growth
- Be able to compare and contrast these different approaches to business growth
- Begin to develop your own opinions on fast-growth businesses

12.1 Introduction

Why is it that some businesses grow much faster than others? For example, how can we explain the phenomenal growth of peer-to-peer websites such as Facebook, MySpace and YouTube? Were they just lucky? Let's take a look at some of the stories behind the start up of each of these businesses.

- The three founders of YouTube – Chad Hurley, Steven Chen and Jawed Karim – all met when they worked at PayPal. PayPal was subsequently sold to eBay for $1.5 billion. As employees, each of them was given a bonus when PayPal was sold. These bonuses provided the money to fund the early development of YouTube.

- MySpace grew out of a company called eUniverse whose executives had strong internet experience. Did they need to have the appropriate capabilities to exploit the opportunity?

- Mark Zuckerman set up Facebook at Harvard to support the social networking of his fellow students. He subsequently moved to California. Was this because there was a mature venture capital industry in California that had supported new internet businesses?

One potential explanation is that these individuals and businesses had the necessary managerial ability to identify and exploit their markets. Or was it, instead, the strategies of these businesses that made them grow so quickly? Both MySpace and YouTube brought forward innovative marketing strategies. MySpace initially promoted growth from within by encouraging competition amongst its eUniverse employees to see who could sign up the most users. YouTube used the same strategy, giving away free iPod Nanos to those who introduced new users.

In this chapter, we examine six approaches that have been used to explain why some businesses grow quickly.

1 **Evolutionary approaches.** These come in two basic forms: 'life-cycle' models, which focus on the organic growth of *individual* businesses, and the population ecology approach, which focuses on the dynamics of business *populations.*

2 **Social network approaches.** This, again, comes in two forms: the use of social networks by individual businesses to grow their own businesses; and how 'clusters' of businesses benefit from being geographically close to each other.

3 **Resource-based view (RBV) of the business.** This approach has a greater focus on the internal resources of the business, rather than how the external environment shapes growth. RBV argues that business growth arises because the resources of the business are in some way unique and hard to imitate.

4 **Managerial approaches.** These suggest that business growth is the result of the psychological profile, management style or orientations of the entrepreneur and their business.

5 **Economic approaches.** These approaches assume that growth is strongly influenced by an industry's cost structure.

6 **Random approaches.** Are Facebook, MySpace and YouTube typical fast-growth businesses? Were they just lucky, appearing in the right place at the right time?

We discuss the advantages and limitations of each of these approaches. Our overall view is that the role of chance is extremely important, and has to date been given too small a role in the research on small businesses and entrepreneurship.

12.2 Evolutionary approaches to growth

One of the oldest approaches to explaining fast growth is to see it as organic: businesses come into existence, grow, mature and then eventually 'die'. This section identifies two evolutionary approaches: stage models and population ecology.

Stage models

Stage models characterise business growth as happening (as the name suggests) in clearly defined stages. There have been numerous studies that have used some form of stage model to explain business growth. As Phelps *et al.*'s (2007) review of these studies suggests, stage approaches are appealing because entrepreneurs often talk about 'moving the business on to the next stage'. They also seem to fit with business behaviour. Businesses are born, experience transitions (which are often traumatic) and, eventually, mature or pass away.

The classic example of a stage model is Greiner's (1972), reproduced in Figure 12.1. It shows that businesses pass through five stages as they age and grow. Each transition between stages is marked by a crisis in a particular area, such as leadership, autonomy or control. By successfully navigating their way through these crises, the entrepreneur is able to reach the next stage. For example, stage 1 identifies that growth is achieved by the entrepreneur creating new products and opening up new markets. As the business continues to grow, though, there comes a turning point – a 'crisis' of leadership – where the established reliance on informal communication between the entrepreneur and their staff begins to break down. To resolve this, the entrepreneur has to establish a more formal leadership role.

Alternatively, if the interest is in the business as the unit of analysis it may be defined as:

> . . . a firm's set of relationships with other organisations

(Perez and Sanchez 2002: 261).

We now examine two approaches to business growth using social capital/network approaches. The first takes as its unit of analysis the individual business. Here business growth is dependent on access to, and the position of, the entrepreneur within a network. The second approach takes groups of businesses as the unit of analysis. These are often called 'clusters'. The cluster approach is interested in explaining why communities of businesses, rather than individual businesses, grow.

Networking for growth

Networking tends to explain business growth by suggesting it is associated with the use of external resources. Typically, these external resources are divided into two types: 'formal' (e.g. the use of external advisers) and 'informal' sources of support (e.g. contacts with other business owners). These two types often correspond closely with what Granovetter (1973) called 'weak' and 'strong' ties. By this, Granovetter meant the degree of association entrepreneurs have with others. Some 'ties' are 'strong' (e.g. family and friends) whilst other ties are weak (e.g. business acquaintances, customers).

The network approach has most commonly been used to explain why businesses start (see Chapter 7). The interest has, therefore, been on what types of support are used, how 'strong' and 'weak' ties actually are, and how these serve to support the development of the business. Very few studies have specifically examined the association between business growth and networking (Watson 2007).

Nonetheless, three main approaches to analysing how networking is related to growth have been identified:

1 **The 'network magnitude' approach.** This suggests that the greater the size or 'magnitude' of an entrepreneur's network, the greater the opportunity for business growth. In other words, the emphasis is on entrepreneurs extending their network – perhaps by attending conferences, going to trade fairs, joining business, charitable or sporting clubs. The implication is that entrepreneurs with larger networks will have, other things being equal, more 'network' resources to call upon.

2 **The 'network closure' approach.** Coleman (1988) argued that social capital is maximised when people make use of a pre-existing network based on strong ties. Hence, what matters for growth is not the size or magnitude of the network, but how close or 'closed' is the network. Entrepreneurs within strong and stable networks are able to closely observe the actions of others in the network. This reduces the cost of monitoring the activities of others in the network. It also reduces the likelihood of others acting 'opportunistically' (following their own ends rather than following mutually agreed ends). In essence, a reliance on a closed network reduces the costs faced by the entrepreneur which, in turn, if all other things are equal, might give them a competitive advantage. For example, Oprah Winfrey's company Harpo Inc. is 90 per cent owned by her and 10 per cent by her long-time lawyer and business 'mentor' Jeff Jacobs. Employees of Harpo Inc. are also barred from talking about her private or business life for the rest of their own lives. The implication is that a few 'strong' ties are important determinants of business success.

3 **The 'network position' approach.** In contrast, Burt (1995) argues that growth is more likely to occur when networks are porous and open-ended. This allows for the easy transfer of knowledge about opportunities. To be successful, the entrepreneur needs to 'position'

themselves to find what Burt calls the 'structural holes' between networks. In simple terms, having access to structural holes is similar to being a 'gatekeeper' between two networks. For example, suppose one network is made up of 'strong' ties between friends, all of whom run a business. Unknown to this network is another network – again bound together by 'strong' ties – of entrepreneurs. Burt (1995) argues that an entrepreneur who acts as a bridge between these networks brings two benefits for themselves. First, it increases their ability to bargain between different actors in the networks. Second, it gives them privileged information which they can use to identify and exploit opportunities. Indeed, Burt (1995) argues that if entrepreneurs can effectively exploit structural holes in networks, they are more likely to see their business grow.

There are a number of criticisms that can be made of networking in general and of the three variants in particular (network magnitude, closure and position):

1 There are difficulties in measuring the degree of any association between networking and business growth. This stems from the fact that networks are '. . . a social construction that exists only so far as the individual understands and uses it' (Chell and Baines 2000: 196). In essence, measurement of the network (size, shape or density) is dependent on the recall of the entrepreneur. We saw in Chapter 11 that subjective assessments of growth were not often closely correlated with actual performance. Hence, entrepreneurs may not only fail to recall their 'network', but also potentially inaccurately estimate its contribution to business growth.

2 'Trust' is often seen as being beneficial. The suggestion is that entrepreneurs seek to 'trust' others and use this – rather than market-based mechanisms such as the price of a good – to make decisions. The alternative argument is that entrepreneurs do not use 'trust' because this would involve giving away information, which may negatively impact on their competitive position.

3 The evidence of a positive association between business growth and networking is weak or non-existent. Havnes and Senneseth (2001), for example, found no clear link between networking intensity and business performance in terms of sales or employment growth. Equally, Watson (2007) found only a very limited association between business growth (measured in sales) and networking but none when growth was measured in terms of the return on equity. He, however, empirically suggests that any benefits of networking follow an inverted 'U'-shaped pattern: there are benefits in using networks up to some level and after this expending time and money on networks becomes counter-productive to business growth. Quite what this level is, or should be, for the individual business remains unclear, but this suggests that there are likely to be limits to the value of networking.

4 Zaheer and Bell (2005) specifically tested for the importance of network 'closure' as opposed to network 'position' in their Canadian study of mutual fund companies. They found that businesses that used 'structural holes' were more likely to grow than those who used network closure. The problem however, as Shaw (2006) suggests, is that each social network is in some way unique. Even if networking can be dynamically associated with business growth, it is difficult to provide entrepreneurs with concrete advice as to the best way to configure their network. Arguably, network 'position' may help with identifying opportunities, but these opportunities may only be realised through support of 'strong' ties. In short, despite considerable theorising, the practical assistance to individual business owners is thin because the term 'network' is so slippery.

Cluster approaches to growth

Networking approaches seek to explain business growth by examining its relationship with the *individual's* network. An alternative approach is to examine what advantages businesses receive from being *grouped* together. Marshall (1890) long ago recognised that there were three advantages – or spillover benefits – from business that located close to each other:

1   Businesses located close to each other were likely to have large pools of specialist labour. Other things being equal, this means businesses are less likely to face skill shortages.

2   Business located close together are likely to gain a cost advantage because they are able to economise on transport costs if their suppliers and customers are in easy reach, or able to operate with lower stock levels because suppliers are nearby.

3   There is the potential of knowledge spillovers by which businesses gain advantages in terms of information ('know how' and 'know who') from other businesses, which may improve their ability to exploit price and non-price advantages.

The cluster approach is based upon these three advantages. Porter (2003) defines clusters as: '. . . a geographically proximate group of interconnected companies, suppliers, service providers and associated institutions in a particular field, linked by externalities of various types' (p. 562). The approach emphasises the advantages of costs savings and having pools of specialist labour. However, the cluster approach tends to place more emphasis on the third advantage: the role and importance of networks in developing knowledge spillovers. Porter (1998) argues that 'Clusters offer a new way of exploring the mechanisms by which networks, social capital and civic engagement affect competition' (p. 227). In other words, what is important for business growth is having privileged 'knowledge' which is often intangible (i.e. not written down). This, in turn, is dependent upon being part of a network that provides access to privileged knowledge. Also, the network is not only confined to other businesses but extends to the relationships the business has with other specialist services and sources of support.

For example, Porter and Ketels (2003) use the example of the Boston 'life science' cluster (Figure 12.2). In part, they explain the development and growth of this cluster as being based on traditional customer–supplier relationships. Figure 12.2, therefore, shows that Surgical Instruments and Supplies are a key input to Biological/Pharmaceutical products. However, Figure 12.2 also shows that the 'cluster' has relationships with universities, research institutions and the wider regional/national government bodies. But, even these are not the only external resources. Also important are specialist business service provision (e.g. banking, accountancy) and the provision of specialist risk capital (e.g. venture capitalists). The argument here – as with businesses located in Silicon Valley – is that the provision of these external resources is pivotal to business growth. Hence, if an individual entrepreneur wishes to see their business grow, an important aspect of their approach should be to ensure that they are integrated within a 'cluster' of associated businesses and support providers. This improves the opportunities for knowledge 'spillovers' and potentially provides opportunities to reduce their cost base.

Although (or perhaps because) the cluster approach has been widely favoured by policy makers in many countries, it has also been the subject of influential criticism. These are best captured in the classic article by Martin and Sunley (2003), summarised below. The reason for choosing this as a classic article is that it is a very good example of how to critique a particular position. The paper first identifies the basis of the cluster approach and then forcefully, but coherently, attempts to provide a full critique of the approach.

This section has focused on two types of networking approach to explaining business growth. The first focused on the individual business and how it uses outside resources. We suggest there are three varieties of this approach. One is network 'magnitude' which implies that the use of networks is directly associated with business growth. The second version was network 'closure'. This argued that business growth was based upon having a close and stable network of 'trusted' support. This lowered the costs of monitoring the activities of others and potentially limited them from acting opportunistically. In contrast, the third variant – the network 'position' – emphasised the need for openness. This gave entrepreneurs control and information advantages.

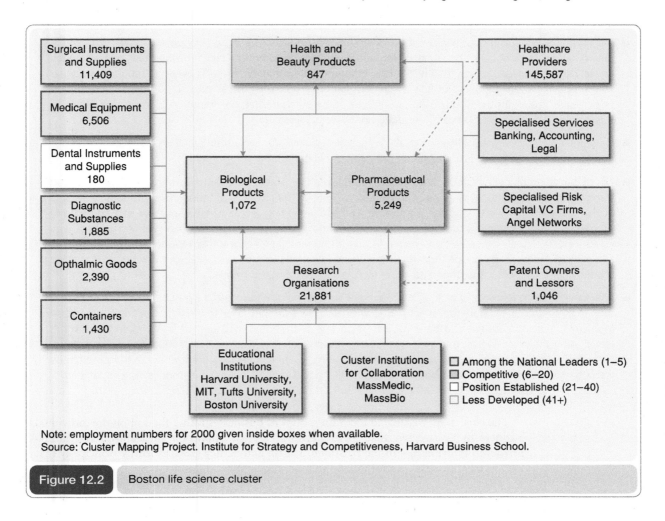

Note: employment numbers for 2000 given inside boxes when available.
Source: Cluster Mapping Project. Institute for Strategy and Competitiveness, Harvard Business School.

Figure 12.2   Boston life science cluster

Classic research   Martin, R. and Sunley, P. (2003) 'Deconstructing Clusters: Chaotic Concept or Policy Panacea?', *Journal of Economic Geography*, 3, 5–35.

- There essentially is nothing new in the cluster approach. Economic geographers identified around 100 years ago that if a business is spatially close to other businesses and does similar activities, then there are likely to be externalities. (For example, port wine from Oporto in northern Portugal has been produced for more than 200 years. In other words, the cluster approach is 'old' wine in 'new' bottles.)

- The cluster approach has a vague definition of what actually constitutes a cluster. The 'space' across which a cluster can range is extremely elastic: it can range from a very precise locality to one that spans different countries. Martin and Sunley identify ten different definitions of the approach.

- Because there is no one way of defining the cluster, the empirical identification of clusters is open to question. Because they can be variously interpreted, it follows that the number, size, shape and dynamics of clusters can also vary.

- Economic locations and the activities that occur within them are likely to be highly heterogeneous. The cluster approach assumes, however, that business activity conforms to particular generalisable patterns.

- Martin and Sunley claim that social networks are 'under-theorised' because they do not explain how these networks use knowledge for business advantage. For example, although 'tacit' knowledge is given primacy in the cluster approach, how this is actually different from other types of knowledge, such as codified (written down) knowledge, is not fully explained. Other evidence by Turok *et al.* (2004) for Scotland, and Boddy *et al.* (2004) for the South West of England, suggests that trust, co-operation or 'reprocity' between businesses did little to explain any interaction between businesses.

- Clusters also appear hermetically sealed from their locality and the other types of economic or social activity that may be going on outside the prescribed 'cluster'.

- There is little empirical evidence that clusters are the premier source of growth. Lewis *et al.* (2002) charted the sources of US productivity gains over the period 1995–9. They found that the six most productive sectors of the US economy were: wholesale trade, retail trade (including restaurants), securities and commodity brokerage, semiconductors, computer manufacture and telecommunications. This 'Wal-Mart' effect was not driven principally by knowledge gains, but by managerial innovations that emphasised economies of scale (bigger stores) and scope (non-retail lines), and lower cost structures ('everyday low prices'). In other words, it was tangible rather than intangible factors that explained growth.

- There are costs to following a cluster approach because it 'locks in' an area to a particular economic trajectory. In other words, clusters represent a 'one-way bet'. For example, prior to the financial crisis that began in 2007/8, London was seen to benefit from being one of the main 'clusters' of financial services in the world. After the crisis began, this over reliance on financial services was seen as a source of disadvantage. Historically there appear to have been numerous examples of former clusters that exhibited precipitous decline – textiles in Lancashire, coal in the Ruhr Valley and the petro-chemical sector on Teesside.

The cluster approach is to focus on groups of businesses rather than upon the individual business. It also argues that social networks are an important mechanism for gaining privileged information. In their critique, Martin and Sunley (2003) identify principally that the cluster approach is definitionally 'chaotic' and empirically weak.

12.4 Resource-based views and learning approaches

Central to the approaches in this section is that it is the resources and capabilities of the business that explain their growth. Rumelt (1984) argued that businesses have bundles of resources; that these vary between businesses; and that some of these resources act as 'isolating mechanisms' protecting the business from competition. Rumelt (1991) went on to argue that the 'acid test' of this view is whether business growth is more likely to be explained by internal factors (what a business does) rather than external (the influence of the environment) factors.

Rumelt's own evidence implied that the theory passed the acid test. These findings are consistent with the resource based view (RBV) of the business that emerged in the 1980s and 1990s (e.g. Wenerfelt 1984; Barney 1986, 1991). The RBV approach can be summarised as follows:

1 Businesses are administrative units that link up bundles of resources. This is a view derived from Penrose (1959).

2 Penrose also argued that these bundles of resources are heterogeneous. This means that each and every business combines and uses resources that are in some way unique.

3 Resources are also in some way likely to be immobile. This means it is difficult for businesses to easily switch resources from one use to another. For example, some workers might find it difficult to switch from working in the 'factory' to subsequently working in the 'office'.

4 Because resources are relatively immobile, the use and exploitation of resources is likely to be path-dependent. This means that how the resources were used in the past is likely to influence how they are used in the future.

The RBV argues that variance in business growth occurs because some businesses have resources that are:

● Valuable;

● Rare;

● Imperfectly imitable;

● Non-substitutable.

These are called the VRIN attributes. Essentially, these attributes suggest that a high growth business is likely to have unique resources that are difficult and costly to copy. Because of this, businesses with these resources are more likely to enjoy a competitive advantage over other businesses, both in the short and long term.

What, though, is meant by 'resources'? Essentially, resources come in two forms. First there are physical tangible resources. These include the business' physical, financial and human capital. A second form of resources is capabilities – a term which refers to a business' capacity for performing an activity. These capabilities are often intangible: they refer to 'how' a business goes about using its tangible assets.

| Illustration | 'Mission accomplished'? Ryanair courts controversy |

Ryanair's controversial 'charge for everything' approach has been designed to generate not just profits, but also publicity.

The Irish airline company Ryanair has proved remarkably willing to use its marketing campaigns to push the idea that it will do virtually anything – including charging for the use of toilet facilities on its airplanes – to reduce its cost base. No other low-cost airline has found it easy to replicate this marketing focus on cost reduction. Ryanair's chief executive, Michael O'Leary, suggested: 'If you can generate PR and controversy, it means more seat sales for Ryanair and that's mission accomplished.'

Source: *The Guardian*, 'No-Frills Boss Who Keeps One Foot on the Ground', 10 October 2008.

RBV theorists and other organisational theorists have, however, tended to focus upon the intangible capabilities of a business. This has led to a huge volume of research into how businesses use 'knowledge' to grow the business. For example, there has been an interest in the **dynamic capabilities** of a business. Zahra *et al.* (2006) define these as '... the abilities to reconfigure a business's resources and routines in the manner envisioned and deemed appropriate by its principal decision-maker(s)' (p. 918). By this, they draw attention to the ways in which a business learns and suggest that businesses have existing 'substantive capabilities' (e.g. people, management structures and routines) which allow them to solve problems they face. However, all businesses face change and in order to cope with this change and stay competitive, there is a need to develop 'dynamic capabilities' by improvising (making up strategies there and then) or adopting a 'trial and error' approach.

A related concept is **absorptive capacity** which was originally developed by Cohen and Levinthal (1989). Again, this seeks to explain business growth by how well a business is able to learn. Lane *et al.* (2006) suggest that '... absorptive capacity refers to one of a firm's fundamental learning processes: its ability to identify, assimilate, and exploit knowledge from the environment' (p. 833). In other words, absorptive capacity defines the limits of a business' ability to manage current circumstances and its ability to learn so that it can predict future developments. Absorptive capacity suggests that what matters is how 'smart' the business is, rather than the resources available to it.

In essence, what RBV, dynamic capabilities and absorptive capacity suggest is that businesses develop knowledge about 'how' to identify and exploit opportunities. They then use these resources to make a 'prediction' of what the market needs. If this prediction is correct – if it fits with the environment – then, because they have superior knowledge, they are more likely to grow. If they are wrong or if they cannot change what they do (absorptive capacity or dynamic capabilities), then they will either fail to grow or will grow at a much slower pace.

There remain, however, question marks over these approaches:

1 Priem and Butler (2001) question the very validity of RBV. They argue that it is tautological. By this they mean that it follows a circular logic: VRIN attributes lead to business growth, but business growth is dependent on having VRIN attributes.

2 How do businesses realise they have the necessary VRIN attributes? Is it because they have particular tangible or intangible resources? If they are intangible, how is it possible to easily measure this? How is it that researchers achieve this, yet competitors find it so difficult? Surely competitors should be able to identify the attributes of a particular business? After all, it is in their economic interest to work out what successful businesses are doing.

3 The RBV approach implies that businesses that learn to successfully combine their resources will continue to do so. However, the statistical evidence from Chapter 11 shows that decline is more typical than growth, and that 'one shot' growth is the most typical form of growth. What RBV fails to address is why the VRIN attributes are normally so transitory.

4 Are approaches such as RBV, dynamic capabilities or absorptive capacity really just explanations for being in the right place at the right time? Entrepreneurs are potentially unreliable witnesses to their own good fortune so how reliable are their accounts of their success?

Overall, the approaches in this section explain fast growth as the result of unique and hard to copy resources and capabilities held by the business. They are appealing because they identify that businesses are potentially responsible for their own growth, and not at the whim of chance or the external environment. Learning approaches also identify that, even if a business is facing particular issues, it can still improvise or rely on trial and error to successfully achieve growth. The problem is that it is very difficult to actually show that businesses are responsible for their own growth. Growth is spotty and normally very short term and, almost by definition, it is difficult to measure intangible capabilities.

12.5 Entrepreneurial management approaches

This section examines three entrepreneurial management approaches. The first emphasises that business success is rooted in the entrepreneur's psychological profile. The second approach is to examine the particular managerial style of the entrepreneur. As with the trait-based approach, the conjecture is that those who have the appropriate managerial style and structure are more likely to own a business that grows rapidly. The third approach is to consider entrepreneurial 'orientations' of both the entrepreneur and their business.

Central to the first approach (rooting business success in the entrepreneur's psychological profile) is the assumption that those entrepreneurs with the 'right stuff' will be successful in growing their business quickly. Hence, the interest has been on whether entrepreneurs who run fast-growth businesses have particular traits such as risk taking, a need for achievement, a strong locus of control (see Chapter 2). Unfortunately, the evidence of a direct relationship between entrepreneurial traits and growth is extremely thin. Gartner (1988) concluded that no particular trait could be found that was consistently associated with growth, and that examining traits was not a helpful field of enquiry.

The second approach has been to consider the managerial style of the entrepreneur or small business manager, and his or her relationship with business development. Typical of this is Scott and Bruce's (1987) model of the stages of small business management. This is shown in Table 12.1, which emphasises that there are five stages in a business' life cycle. Growth is the third of these stages, and Scott and Bruce emphasise a need to delegate/co-ordinate and have an organisational structure that is split into various functional areas (e.g. finance, sales, production), but remains under the control of the entrepreneur. They predict that the successful manager (and the successful business) is one that adopts the most appropriate managerial style. However, as we showed in Section 12.2, stage models were conceptually weak and the empirical support for them is very limited. Moreover, if the focus is just on management styles as being the cause of fast growth, it potentially ignores the contribution of other resources, the wider environment and chance.

A third managerial approach has been to focus on intentions. We can, for example, look at the growth intentions of the individual entrepreneur. The argument is that business growth is associated with the entrepreneur's intention to grow the business. There would appear to be some evidence to support such a view. For example, Hakim (1989) identified – out of a survey of approximately 750,000 UK businesses – that 55 per cent had no plans for growth even though wider economic growth was strong at the time. Presented with the opportunity for growth, then, the suggestion is that most business owners will turn it down.

Wiklund and Shepherd (2003) also examined the relationship between the growth intentions of the entrepreneur and growth amongst Swedish businesses. They found these growth

Table 12.1	Scott and Bruce's (1987) managerial stages model		
Stage	**Management role**	**Management style**	**Organisation structure**
1 Inception	Direct supervision	Entrepreneurial, individualistic	Unstructured
2 Survival	Supervised supervision	Entrepreneurial, administrative	Simple
3 Growth	Delegation/Co-ordination	Entrepreneurial, co-ordinated	Functional, centralised
4 Expansion	Decentralisation	Professional, administrative	Functional, decentralised
5 Maturity	Decentralisation	Watchdog	Decentralised/Functional/Product

Source: Scott and Bruce (1987).

intentions are positively associated with growth, but they also suggest that this relationship is not direct. Instead, they argued that it is influenced by the education of the entrepreneur, their experience and the dynamism of the environment. Wiklund *et al.* (2003) also argue that what shapes the orientation towards growth are 'non-economic' concerns (e.g. the well-being of employees, need for independence) rather than economic concerns (e.g. profitability). Finally, Delmar and Wiklund (2008) also find some evidence to support the relationship in terms of employment growth but not in terms of sales growth.

Unfortunately, these studies rely upon self-reported measures of growth. These may be inexact because they assume that entrepreneurs are the best judges of their own and competitors' performance. Also, the studies do not focus on fast-growth businesses. Even if they did, it may be that the other influences that the studies point to, as well as the business's management team, would be shown to be even more important. Hence, there may be little value in examining the entrepreneur's growth intentions unless a range of other factors are taken into account. However, what does seem intuitively sensible is that few owners of very fast-growth businesses never had *any* intention of growing their business. Much more questionable is whether those with 'intentions' ultimately succeeded in having a fast-growth business. Intentionality may be a necessary condition for growth, but is certainly not sufficient in itself.

The second version of intentions takes the business as the unit of analysis and examines its **entrepreneurial orientation (E-O)**. Wiklund and Shepherd (2005) argue that this is a '. . . strategic orientation, capturing specific entrepreneurial aspects of decision-making styles, methods, and practices' (p. 74). This orientation rests on three aspects derived from Miller (1983): innovativeness, proactiveness, and risk taking. By this Miller (1983) meant 'An entrepreneurial firm is one that engages in product market innovation, undertakes somewhat risky ventures, and is first to come up with innovations, beating competitors to the punch' (p. 771). Lumpkin and Dess (1996) subsequently argued that two further constructs should be added: competitive aggressiveness and autonomy (independence of activity).

Wiklund, Patzelt and Shepherd (2009) conclude, based on 413 small Swedish businesses, that E-O – capturing self-report statements from business owners on matters such as risk taking, proactiveness and innovativeness – is a powerful factor explaining growth. Indeed they argue that resources had only an indirect effect on growth – much more important was how those resources were used.

E-O has been studied across different environmental conditions such as environments that are dynamic or stable and those that are 'hostile' or 'benign' (e.g. Covin *et al.* 2000). Rausch *et al.*'s (2004) review of these studies indicates some positive relationship between 'entrepreneurial orientation' and business performance. This is mostly in terms of 'objective' rather than 'subjective' measures of performance. They also argue that some of the constructs of E-O apply (innovativeness, proactiveness, autonomy) whilst others (risk taking, competitive aggressiveness) show less association with growth. Finally, they suggest that the causal relationship may work the other way. Instead of E-O causing growth, it may be growth that causes E-O.

Two other criticisms also apply. First, E-O takes what are essentially psychological traits and applies them to the business. However, it is people who *do* business, not organisations. Perhaps the best that can be said about the influence of psychological traits on business performance is that its role is indirect. Second, and most powerfully, E-O traits are likely to be broadly stable over time – businesses don't change their character radically over six months – yet small business performance, as we have seen, is extremely volatile in the short run.

This section has examined three managerial approaches to business growth: traits, management styles and orientations. The trait-based approach argues that the psychological profile of an individual directly explains growth. The management style approach suggests that there is some fit between which style is adopted and business growth. A further approach argues that the growth orientation of the individual entrepreneur affects growth. An alternative version of this approach – the business' entrepreneurial orientation – argues that this is important in explaining growth.

The problem with all these approaches is that they have, at best, an indirect impact on business growth. Partly this is because, as the business develops, it is arguably the case that the direction and control of the entrepreneur weaken. A second criticism is that it has proved very difficult to disentangle traits, styles and orientations from other explanations that may influence the growth pattern of a business. The third criticism is that because traits, styles and orientations are likely to be long-term characteristics of individuals or organisations they are unlikely to explain the massive short-term variations in the growth rates of small businesses.

12.6 Economic approaches

The fifth approach we consider derives from economics. Perhaps the best summary of these approaches is the review by Hart (2000). He identified eight approaches which are detailed in Table 12.2. This table also indicates their likely advantages and disadvantages. Table 12.2 shows that there are strong links between the various economic approaches and the earlier approaches identified in this chapter. For example, economists are also interested in how the goals of the owner impact on business growth. The evolutionary growth perspective in economics equally suggests that growth is path dependent so that growth in one period leads to growth in another period.

Similarly, the economist's interest in economies of scale links in with other explanations of growth. For instance, Table 12.2 shows that the cluster approach is rooted in the economist's interest in external economies of scale (i.e. externalities or spillovers) whilst dynamic economies of scale share an interest in how experience and learning shape the competitive advantage enjoyed by a business. This is similar to the interest in dynamic capabilities or the absorptive capacity of the business.

Where economic approaches differ somewhat from the other approaches is that they tend to emphasise cost advantages that derive from being a bigger business (technical scale economies) or bigger businesses having access to cheaper finance (pecuniary scale economies). For example, the neo-classical theory assumes that businesses face a U-shaped cost curve, which implies they need to achieve a minimum efficient scale (MES) to avoid having a cost structure that makes them uncompetitive. This is compatible with the first of our four 'stylised facts' in Chapter 11 – that new businesses that grow are considerably more likely to survive than those that do not grow.

However, the economic approaches also have their limitations. For example, the imperfect competition model treats businesses as essentially 'black boxes' since it does not explain why some businesses reach MES and others do not. It also assumes the cost structure facing businesses is given, whereas it is clear that businesses can shape and influence the industry cost structure. Finally, Table 12.2 identifies – in common with learning-based approaches to growth – that there is little actual evidence that fast growth in one period leads to similar fast growth in the next period.

12.7 'Random' approaches

Hart (2000) also considered one other economics-based approach – random growth. In this section, we consider two approaches that emphasise the random or lucky nature of business growth. The first is based upon Jovanovic's (1982) model of 'noisy selection' and the second suggests growth is primarily about being lucky.

Table 12.2	Economics based approaches to business growth		
Approach	**Explanation of approach**	**Observations**	**Disadvantages**
Neoclassical theory of the business	Single product businesses face a U-shaped average cost curve so businesses grow until they reach the minimum point on the curve but do not grow beyond this point.	Mental model for explaining relationship between costs and growth.	Unrealistic: U-shaped cost curves unlikely, as are single product businesses. Mental model that prefers simple errors to complex truths.
Imperfect competition	Assumes L-shaped curve so growth is possible whilst costs are falling. Most businesses operate at minimum efficient scale. Most growth is due to demand conditions (demand curve is downward sloping).	More realistic assumptions. Businesses have different minimum efficient scales and are influenced by demand conditions.	Assumes single products but that these can be shifted into new sectors. Still treats businesses as 'black boxes'.
Technical economies of scale	Scale economies are said to exist when increases in inputs induce a more than proportionate change in output (increasing returns to scale).	Provides an explanation of differences in growth e.g. large businesses are more likely to fund and afford up-to-date machinery.	No real evidence that large businesses are more likely to grow faster than smaller businesses.
Pecuniary economies of scale	Assumes that larger businesses are more likely to be able to access finance.	Larger businesses typically find finance cheaper and easier to access and so have a lower cost base.	No real evidence that large businesses are more likely to grow faster than smaller businesses.
External economies of scale	There are externalities or spillovers from being located close to other businesses (e.g. specialist labour, transportation cost savings, learning from other businesses).	Essentially, this is the economic root of the 'cluster approach' to business growth. Businesses that have better labour, cheaper costs and superior knowledge are more likely to grow.	Not clear which type of business will necessarily grow more quickly (see van Praag and Versloot 2007) because smaller businesses may benefit most from spillovers but large businesses may be able to exploit their own 'network' just as well.
Dynamic economies of scale	This is really 'learning by doing'. Businesses with greater experience are more likely to grow.	Focus on learning is shared with other approaches (e.g. absorptive capacity). Explains why it is that some businesses are more likely to grow.	No evidence that age of business (outside of the very young) has an impact on growth rates. Larger and older businesses are no more likely to grow once the very youngest and the very smallest are excluded.
Goals of the business	Suggests that business growth is a function of the goals of the business.	Expectation is that those businesses with more pecuniary orientated goals (e.g. profit maximisers) are more likely to grow than those with non-pecuniary (e.g. desire for independence) motives.	Difficult to identify how the goals impact on the growth of the business. No necessary link between growth and profit maximisation.
Evolutionary growth	Suggests that growth in one period is associated with growth in a later period: success breeds success, failure breeds failure.	Basis of growth is the 'routines' of the business. Businesses with better/more adaptable routines experience growth.	No powerful evidence of serial correlation – so that businesses growing fast in one period are not more likely to grow faster in a later period.

The basis of Jovanovic's (1982) 'noisy selection' model is that people, prior to entry, do not know their level of entrepreneurial talent. They only find this out by running the business. If they find that their talent is low, they close the business. If their talent is high, they are able to expand their business. What makes this process random is that the entrepreneur may experience random shocks (unlucky draws) which mean that they may not be able to grow their business or, in the event of really bad luck, be forced to close the business (see also its implications for business closure in Chapter 10). Growth, therefore, is 'noisy' because of the presence of unforeseen events.

Growth is also selective, however, because over time entrepreneurial talent wins out and the element of luck is cancelled out. Selection is made possible as the entrepreneur realises their own entrepreneurial talent. In Jovanovic's model they can do little to change their level of talent. Ericson and Pakes (1995) modify this 'passive' model so that entrepreneurs are able not only to learn about their own business and that of their competitors, but actually change their strategy in line with changing external conditions. In other words, learning is 'active', allowing for new strategies to emerge.

There are obvious links here with RBV and the other learning approaches discussed earlier. Noisy selection suggests that growth – although bounded by chance – can be something that the business owner can directly influence, if they can realise their talent. A business with only limited entrepreneurial talent might get lucky initially, but will eventually be 'caught out' by its lack of talent.

Illustration	'I was in the right place – believe it or not, Luton – at the right time'

Sir Stelios Haji-Ioannou (founder of easyJet):

'If you want a quote, I was just lucky with easyJet', he says. 'I mean the unbelievable thing with easyJet is I took an enormous risk with my family's fortune back in the 90s and I was lucky to have been in the right place, which believe it or not was Luton, and at the right time – mid-90s when the European airline industry was deregulating – and with the right father, to give me a lot of money to bet on new aircraft. And it worked.'

Source: *The Guardian*, 28 November 2008.

The more extreme stochastic approach is to say that growth is largely random. The justification for this approach is that there are so many factors which influence the performance of an individual business that growth essentially becomes a matter of chance. Even if a business has experienced growth in an earlier period, the factors which influence its subsequent growth will be radically different during a later period. For example, macroeconomic conditions might be very different, the business might lose key personnel, it may choose to enter markets which are more challenging, or perhaps the growth in the earlier period was purely to do with luck.

Earlier we showed that RBV argued that each individual business had a set of unique resources. It argued that these resources were the source of competitive advantage and, potentially, business growth. The alternative explanation is that each business is akin to someone buying a lottery ticket. Each has their own unique set of numbers and if these come up, they will get a prize (business growth). Those with more resources or with more optimistic owners may also choose to buy more lottery tickets by opening new businesses or targeting new sectors. These attempts may lead them to *believe* that any likely success they have is down to their ability to 'predict' the right numbers. The reality may be that they are just lucky. To illustrate this, consider the short case in the box below:

> **Illustration** Derren Brown's foolproof system for beating the odds
>
> There is a British entertainer called Derren Brown. He suggested that he could devise a system that would win any lottery. To show how it worked, he told a 'random' woman that he could correctly identify the winners of five horse races for her. The odds of getting the winners of these five horse races correct were very low. To show how confident in his system he was, Derren Brown agreed to pay for the first of her five bets. After the first bet, if she won, it was her own money at stake. She won the first race. She subsequently went on to win all five horse races. She believed that the system worked and Derren Brown had devised a system that could beat 'luck'.
>
> What was the secret of the scheme? Was it that Derren Brown had an intimate knowledge of the horses in each of the races? Was it that he is a statistical genius? Was it that he had a special intuitive talent denied to the rest of us?
>
> No. What he did was to get a large population of people together that did not know each other. He agreed to pay for all of the bets for everyone in the first race. If they lost the first race, each of the losers was told that it was part of a 'con' on his part. If they won the first race, they were told they were kept in the 'system' but were asked to stake their own money. A similar procedure was followed for each of the following four races. Those that lost a race were told sorry but it was a 'con'. Winners were kept in and were told nothing. Eventually, after the fifth and final race, the only person left was the 'random' woman. She was the 'winner' and went away believing that Derren Brown had devised a foolproof system for beating chance.

There are three main pieces of evidence to support the importance of chance:

1 As we showed in Chapter 11, growth in one period does not often lead to growth in another period: success doesn't often breed success. This is important because if growth was more deterministic than random, we would expect a stronger link between growth in one period and the next.

2 The anticipation is that older and bigger businesses would grow more quickly than younger and smaller businesses. Older, bigger businesses have more experience, more 'know-how' and greater resources. Yet, Chapter 11 showed that there was little association between growth and size or age once the smallest sized and youngest businesses were discounted.

3 Our final piece of evidence is a review of growth studies by Coad (2007). He found that studies were largely unable to explain why it is that businesses grew. Indeed, he found that most studies were unable to explain more than 10 per cent of why it was that businesses grew. In other words, 90 per cent was 'unexplained'. Coad, however, only covered economics-based studies of growth and it might be assumed that the inclusion of RBV and learning factors might have increased the ability of these studies to explain business growth. Yet, the fact that Coad reveals a fairly stable pattern suggests that growth is primarily influenced by chance.

The idea of being 'lucky' applies to more than just being in the right place at the right time. The argument is that having the 'right stuff' is also related to being lucky: you can have the right stuff for one business but these very same talents prove unhelpful for another business or the same business in different circumstances.

Emphasising the importance of the part played by luck or chance may seem dismal. It denies the human agency of individuals, puts limits on the choices of entrepreneurs, and says that we either lack the tools to adequately explain business growth or that there is very little that anyone can do to promote growth in a business.

It also runs counter to our expectation of how businesses grow and develop – especially those influenced by the 'war stories' of successful entrepreneurs. Such individuals rarely place any emphasis upon luck or chance, unless their previously highly successful business collapses.

Our prediction may be that luck is important but that people with the 'right stuff' – as Jovanovic (1982) suggests – will win through. Our view, though, is that this may have a modest influence. In the next chapter we examine the types of factors that influence business performance. However, because chance is so important, it remains the case that we cannot predict, with any satisfactory accuracy, those businesses which will grow rapidly from those that will not.

Summary

In this chapter, we have provided six theoretical approaches to business growth:

1 evolutionary approaches to growth

2 social network approaches to business growth

3 resource-based views and learning approaches

4 managerial approaches

5 economic approaches

6 stochastic approaches.

Table 12.3 summarises their advantages and disadvantages. It shows a spectrum of reasons why some businesses grow. This spectrum ranges from 'deterministic' to 'lucky' approaches. Towards the deterministic end of the spectrum this chapter showed that there were approaches such as stage models and population ecology. These tend to suggest that the external environment is likely to play an overriding role in the growth of the business. The external environment is also important for a 'cluster'

Table 12.3	Approaches to business growth

	Advantages	Disadvantages
Evolutionary approaches to growth		
Stage models	• Intuitively appealing use of an 'organic' approach (businesses are born, grow and die). • Seems to fit in with business behaviour.	• Businesses are actually more likely to close than grow. • Assumes a one-size-fits-all approach. • Businesses never go back down the 'growth' curve. • Unclear how many stages or 'crises' there are.
Population ecology	• Intuitively appealing use of an 'organic' approach to business populations. • Offers an explanation of why businesses are 'selected' by the environment, how resources in the environment are important, how competition helps select out businesses and why 'structural inertia' (organisation habits) can limit growth.	• Traditional focus has been on business growth and closure. • Gives little room for strategy or human agency. Appears that individuals and businesses are just at the mercy of the external environment.
Social network approaches to business growth		
Social network theory	• Offers an explanation why social capital/networks are important to individual businesses. • Gives a rationale why 'trust' and 'reprocity' are important. • Structural holes theory can be used to explain how entrepreneurial opportunities arise.	• Methodological difficulties in identifying if social capital/networks should be focused on business or the entrepreneur. • Trust and reprocity may be overplayed: competition may offer a better explanation. • Weak empirical evidence of an association between growth and networking.

▶

Table 12.3 continued

	Advantages	Disadvantages
Cluster approach	• Offers an explanation of why positive externalities can benefit businesses. • Fits in with prevailing theory that suggests social capital/networks explain business growth.	• Essentially nothing new in cluster approach. • Methodologically weak approach (Martin and Sunley 2003). • Even if 'clusters' can be identified and are successful, they represent a 'one way bet'.

Resource based views (RBV) and learning approaches

	• RBV suggests that the business strategy is more important than external environment. Argues that businesses with unique hard to imitate resources are likely to be more successful. • Identifies the importance of non-tangible resources (e.g. business strategy). • Offers an explanation of why some businesses are more successful than others. • RBV – along with dynamic capabilities and core competencies – offers a mechanism to understand how businesses learn.	• Seems more applicable to large business 'strategic management' practices than small entrepreneurial businesses. • Potentially tautological i.e. a learning business is successful because it is learning. • What is more important: tangible or intangible assets? • How are researchers able to identify the keys to success but competitors are not?

Managerial approaches

Trait-based approach	• Intuitively appealing focus on the importance of the 'personality' of the entrepreneur and how this drives business growth.	• Gartner (1988) argues that such an approach is a dead end because there is little evidence linking growth to traits.
Managerial styles	• Intuitively appealing identification of the managerial styles that the entrepreneur has to adopt to grow the business.	• Shares the same weaknesses as stage theories.
Entrepreneurial orientations	• Provides a more plausible account of how the intentions of the entrepreneur and/or the orientation of the business impact on growth. • Arguably the case that business growth can only occur if the entrepreneur/business intends it.	• At best, an indirect explanation of business growth. • Difficult to methodologically and empirically disentangle the growth orientations of the entrepreneur and/or the business.

Economic approaches

	• Tends to be a focus on 'outcomes' (i.e. business growth). • Range of approaches seeking to account for the importance of external/internal factors.	• More focused on questions of 'what' rather than 'how'.

Stochastic approaches

	• Jovanovic's theory of 'noisy selection' suggests that some business performance can, at least in part, be explained by chance events. • Lottery approach suggests that growth is largely independent of the activities of the entrepreneur. • Argues that most entrepreneurs tend to 'forget' that luck was important in business growth.	• Dismal view of human agency. • Offers little in the way of comfort to policy makers, academics, students or consultants seeking to help a business grow.

approach because it shows that externalities (i.e. benefits derived from being close to other businesses – access to labour, cost savings and knowledge spillovers) – are important in business growth. Social network approaches also emphasise the importance of social capital as an explanation of business growth. Other approaches, however, give primacy to internal factors rather than external factors. For example, the managerial approaches highlight the qualities of the entrepreneur, how they manage and what their intentions are, and imply these are important determinants of business success. A more stochastic and wider version of this is, arguably, the resource-based view (RBV) suggests that some businesses may be lucky in how they achieve success but, typically, RBV argues that business success is a product of it having rare and hard to copy resources (e.g. a particular business strategy). More stochastic approaches are Jovanovic's (1982) theory of 'noisy selection' or that business growth is a lottery.

Each of these approaches can be used to explain the development of internet businesses such as YouTube, Facebook and MySpace. For example, YouTube, Facebook and MySpace all relied on social networks for their development. The Californian venture capital industry also obviously supported each of these three businesses and, arguably, each of these businesses had resources that, in some sense, uniquely 'fitted' the environment. Alternatively, however, a large part of the success of such businesses may be just luck: the founders of YouTube, Facebook and MySpace were in the right place at the right time, and were founded by lucky people. These are issues that we return to in the following three empirical chapters on business growth.

Questions for discussion

1 Do stage models such as Greiner (1972) and Scott and Bruce (1987) provide insights into business growth?

2 Is a network position approach better than the network magnitude or network closure approaches in explaining the role of networks in the growth of a small business?

3 What is meant by the term 'social network'? What role do such networks play in explaining growth businesses?

4 Does the cluster approach provide anything new in understanding business growth?

5 What are the VRIN attributes? Are these sources of business growth?

6 'Small business growth is primarily a matter of chance.' Do you think this is true? Justify your response.

References

Barney, J.B. (1986) 'Strategic Factor Markets: Expectations, Luck and Business Strategy', *Management Science*, 32(10), 1231–41.

Barney, J.B. (1991) 'Firm Resources and Sustained Competitive Advantage', *Journal of Management*, 17(1), 99–120.

Baum, J.A. (1996) 'Organizational Ecology', in Clegg, S.R., Hardy, C. and Nord, W.R. (eds), *Handbook of Organizational Study*. London: Sage Publications, 77–115.

Boddy, M., Bassett, K., French, S., Griffiths, R., Lambert, C., Leyshon, A., Simth, I., Stewart, M. and Thrift, M. (2004) 'Competitiveness and Cohesion in a Prosperous City Region: The

Case of Bristol', in Boddy, M. and Parkinson, M. (eds) *City Matters: Competitiveness, Cohesion and Urban Governance*. Bristol: Policy Press, 51–70.

Burt, R.S. (1995) *Structural Holes: The Social Structure of Competition*. Cambridge, MA: Harvard University Press.

Carroll, G.R. (1985) 'Concentration and Specialization: Dynamics of Niche Width in Populations of Organizations', *American Journal of Sociology*, 90(6), 1262–83.

Chell, E. and Baines, S. (2000) 'Networking, Entrepreneurship and Microbusiness Behaviour', *Entrepreneurship and Regional Development*, 12, 195–215.

Coad, A. (2007) *Firm Growth: A Survey*. CES Working Papers, 24. Paris: Sorbonne University.

Cohen, W.M. and Levinthal, D.A. (1989) 'Innovation and Learning: The 2 Faces of R&D', *Economic Journal*, 99(397), 569–96.

Coleman, J.S. (1988) 'Social Capital in the Creation of Human Capital', *The American Journal of Sociology*, 94, S95–120.

Covin, J.G., Slevin, D.P. and Heeley, M.B. (2000) 'Pioneers and Followers: Competitive Tactics, Environment and Firm Growth', *Journal of Business Venturing*, 15(2), 175–210.

Davidsson, P., Achtenhagen, L. and Naldi, L. (2004) 'Research on Small Firm Growth: A Review', in *Proceedings European Institute of Small Business*. Paper presented at ESIB Conference, Barcelona.

Delmar, F. and Wiklund, J. (2008) 'The Effect of Small Business Managers' Growth Motivation on Firm Growth: A Longitudinal Study', *Entrepreneurship: Theory and Practice*, 32(3), 437–57.

Ericson, R. and Pakes, A. (1995) 'Markov Perfect Industry Dynamics: A Framework for Empirical Work', *Review of Economic Studies*, 62(1), 53–82.

Gartner, W.B. (1988) ' "Who Is an Entrepreneur?" Is the Wrong Question', *American Journal of Small Business*, 12(1), 11–32.

Granovetter, M.S. (1973) 'The Strength of Weak Ties', *American Journal of Sociology*, 78(6), 1360–80.

Greiner, L.E. (1972) 'Evolution and Revolution as Organizations Grow', *Harvard Business Review*, 50(4), 37–46.

Hakim, C. (1989) 'Identifying Fast Growth Small Firms', *Employment Gazette*, 97, 29–41.

Hart, P.E. (2000) 'Theories of Firms' Growth and the Generation of Jobs', *Review of Industrial Organization*, 17(3), 229–48.

Havnes, P.A. and Senneseth, K. (2001) 'A Panel Study of Firm Growth among SMEs in Networks', *Small Business Economics*, 16(4), 293–302.

Hoang, H. and Antoncic, B. (2003) 'Network-Based Research in Entrepreneurship: A Critical Review', *Journal of Business Venturing*, 18(2), 165–87.

Jovanovic, B. (1982) 'Selection and the Evolution of Industry', *Econometrica*, 50(3), 649–70.

Lane, P.J., Koka, B.R. and Pathak, S. (2006) 'The Reification of Absorptive Capacity: A Critical Review and Rejuvenation of the Construct', *Academy of Management Review*, 31(4), 833–63.

Lawson, C. (1999) 'Towards a Competence Theory of the Region', *Cambridge Journal of Economics*, 23, 151–66.

Lewis, W.W., Palmade, V., Regout, B. and Webb, A.P. (2002) 'What's Right with the US Economy', *Mckinsey Quarterly*, 1, 31–40.

Lumpkin, G.T. and Dess, G.G. (1996) 'Clarifying the Entrepreneurial Orientation Construct and Linking it to Performance', *Academy of Management Review*, 21(1), 135–72.

Marshall, A. (1890) *Principles of Economics*. London: Macmillan and Co., Ltd.

Martin, R. and Sunley, P. (2003) 'Deconstructing Clusters: Chaotic Concept or Policy Panacea?', *Journal of Economic Geography*, 3, 5–35.

McPherson, M.A. (1996) 'Growth of Micro and Small Enterprises in Southern Africa', *Journal of Development Economics*, 48(2), 253–77.

Miller, D. (1983) 'The Correlates of Entrepreneurship in Three Types of Firms', *Management Science*, 29(7), 770–91.

Nahapiet, J. and Ghoshal, S. (1998) 'Social Capital, Intellectual Capital and the Organizational Advantage', *Academy of Management Review*, 23(2), 242–66.

Penrose, E.T. (1959) *The Theory of the Growth of the Firm*. London: Blackwell.

Perez, M. and Sanchez, A. (2002) 'Lean Production and Technology Networks in the Spanish Automotive Supplier Industry', *Management International Review*, 42(3), 261.

Phelps, R., Adams, R. and Bessant, J. (2007) 'Life Cycles of Growing Organizations: A Review with Implications for Knowledge and Learning', *International Journal of Management Reviews*, 9(1), 1–30.

Porter, M.E. (1998) 'Clusters and the New Economics of Competition', *Harvard Business Review*, 76(6), 77–90.

Porter, M.E. (2003) 'The Economic Performance of Regions', *Regional Studies*, 37(6–7), 549–78.

Porter, M.E. and Ketels, C.H.M. (2003) *UK Competitiveness: Moving to the Next Stage*. DTI Economics Paper No. 3. London: DTI.

Priem, R.L. and Butler, J.E. (2001) 'Tautology in the Resource-based View and Implications of Externally Determined Resource Value: Further Comments', *Academy of Management Review*, 26(1), 57–66.

Rauch, A., Wiklund, J., Frese, M. and Lumpkin, G.T. (2004) *Frontiers of Entrepreneurship Research 2004*. Babson Park, MA: Babson College.

Rumelt, R.P. (1984) 'Towards a Strategic Theory of the Firm', in Lamb, R.B. (ed.), *Competitive Strategic Management*. Englewood Cliffs, NJ: Prentice-Hall, 566–70.

Rumelt, R.P. (1991) 'How Much Does Industry Matter?', *Strategic Management Journal*, 12(3), 167–85.

Saxenian, A. (1994) *Regional Advantage: Culture and Competition in Silicon Valley and Route 128*. Cambridge, MA: Harvard University Press.

Scott, M. and Bruce, R. (1987) 'Five Stages of Growth in Small Businesses', *Long Range Planning*, 20(3), 40–52.

Shaw, E. (2006) 'Small Firm Networking: An Insight into Contents and Motivating Factors', *International Small Business Journal*, 24(1), 5–29.

Turok, I., Bailey, N., Atkinson, R., Bramley, G., Docherty, I., Gibb, K., Goodlad, R., Hastings, A., Kintrea, K., Kirk, K., Leibovitz, J., Lever, B., Morgan, J. and Paddison, R. (2004) 'Sources of City Prosperity and Cohesion: The Case of Glasgow and Edinburgh', in Boddy, M. and Parkinson, M. (eds) *City Matters: Competitiveness, Cohesion and Urban Governance*. Bristol: Policy Press, 13–33.

van der Linde, C. (2004) *Findings from the Cluster Meta Study*. www.isc.hbs.edu.

van Praag, C.M. and Versloot, P.H. (2007) 'What is the Value of Entrepreneurship? A Review of Recent Research', *Small Business Economics*, 29, 351–82.

Watson, J. (2007) 'Modeling the Relationship between Networking and Firm Performance', *Journal of Business Venturing*, 22(6), 852–74.

Wernerfelt, B. (1984) 'The Resource-based View of the Firm', *Strategic Management Journal*, 5(2), 171–80.

Wiklund, J. and Shepherd, D. (2003) 'Aspiring for, and Achieving Growth: The Moderating Role of Resources and Opportunities', *Journal of Management Studies*, 40(8), 1919–41.

Wiklund, J. and Shepherd, D. (2005) 'Entrepreneurial Orientation and Small Business Performance: A Configurational Approach', *Journal of Business Venturing*, 20(1), 71–91.

Wiklund, J. and Shepherd, D. (2009) 'Are We Comparing Apples with Apples or Apples with Oranges?: Appropriateness of Knowledge Accumulation across Growth Studies', *Entrepreneurship: Theory and Practice*, 33(1), 105–23.

Wiklund, J., Davidsson, P. and Delmar, F. (2003) 'What Do They Think and Feel about Growth?: An Expectancy Value Approach to Small Business Managers' Attitudes toward Growth', *Entrepreneurship Theory and Practice*, 27, 247–70.

Wiklund, J., Patzelt, H. and Shepherd, D. (2009) 'Building an Integrative Model of Small Business Growth', *Small Business Economics*, 32(4), 351–74.

Zaheer, A. and Bell, G.G. (2005) 'Benefiting from Network Position: Firm Capabilities, Structural Holes, and Performance', *Strategic Management Journal*, 26(9), 809–25.

Zahra, S.A., Sapienza, H.J. and Davidsson, P. (2006) 'Entrepreneurship and Dynamic Capabilities: A Review, Model and Research Agenda', *Journal of Management Studies* 43(4), 917–55.

13 Growing the business – pre start-up factors

Mini contents list

Key learning objectives

By the end of this chapter you should:

- Understand the range of pre start-up factors commonly associated with business growth
- Be able to compare and contrast pre start-up factors
- Critically evaluate the importance of pre start-up factors.

13.1 Introduction

As we have already seen in Chapter 12, one central problem in understanding business growth is the huge number of theories and factors that have been proposed to explain why some (small) businesses grow faster than others.

To make this literature manageable, this chapter begins by introducing how we intend to examine the empirical evidence on business growth over the next three chapters. We make use of Storey's (1994a) analytical distinction between **'pre' start-up** (the entrepreneur and their resources), **'at' start-up** (business-level factors such as legal form, sector and location), and **'post' start-up** (strategy) of the business.

The merit of grouping variables in this way is that the three factors relate directly to the process of start up. This makes it possible to address the question of whether the key influential decisions that affect new/small business growth are made before it begins (pre start), when it begins (at start) or once the business has begun (post start). This generates insights into the question of whether the performance of a new business is influenced by its founding conditions, and if the entrepreneur can undertake actions that significantly influence that growth once the business has begun to trade.

However, even at this early stage, we issue a key 'health warning'. By separating out and grouping the variables into these three factors, this does not imply that the variables are necessarily independent of each other. It may be that related variables found at *pre*, *at* and *post* start up are all associated with business growth. It may also be that fundamental influences straddle all three groups. A simple example illustrates this. We might argue that the educational attainment of the founder (a pre-start factor) influences the growth of the business. However, individuals with a degree are much more likely to start a business in a high-tech sector (sector is an 'at-start-up' variable), and perhaps high-tech businesses grow faster than businesses in low-tech sectors. We might then also observe that businesses in the high-tech sectors are more likely to train their workers (a post-start-up factor), and that those businesses that provide more training are more likely to experience faster growth. In this way, the same basic influence – in this case, education – can straddle the groupings.

Nevertheless, our approach is to focus on a range of 'core' variables which have commonly appeared in growth studies. These are grouped as to whether they appear at the *pre* (e.g. age, gender, ethnicity and education), *at* (e.g. legal form, sector) or *post* (e.g. innovation) start-up stage. We then assess the evidence for whether or not empirical studies support their link with new/small business growth.

Our focus is on studies that adopt a multivariate approach to understanding business growth, and have examined at least 100 businesses. One disadvantage of this approach is that it excludes potentially valuable qualitative research using case studies or small samples of business. To ignore such evidence where it has merit would be very unwise, so – where there are insightful studies that do not comply with our overall approach – we do report their findings. A second potential disadvantage of our approach is that some readers may find the results from large-scale quantitative studies difficult to interpret and understand. However, one of the critical advantages of such studies is that they are able to control for very many of the factors that may influence growth. Such studies may also provide greater levels of generalisability than relying solely on a few, possibly atypical, businesses. In the chapters that follow, we adopt the following simple way of describing the impact of a variable on business growth:

- **+** this means that there was a statistically significant *positive* association with growth;
- **−** this means that there was a statistically significant *negative* association with growth;
- **n.s.** this means that there was no statistically significant association with growth; and
- **blank** this means that the particular study did not include this variable.

The approach clearly shows, for example, if male entrepreneurs are more likely to have faster-growing businesses than female entrepreneurs, having controlled for other variables. The focus is on statistically significant differences, so the term (n.s.) is also important, because it points to where there is no clear impact. We believe this can be just as important as a positive or negative finding. Similarly, the fact that some variables are 'blank' points to the potential for 'omitted variable bias'. By this we mean the absence of a variable is potentially important because its absence may 'bias' the other variables, and so provide an imprecise understanding of business growth.

It is important then to consider Table 13.1. The 36 studies reviewed cover small businesses in Africa, Europe, Asia and the Americas. These 36 studies cover 50 different measures of growth: employment growth (E) (18 studies); sales growth (S) (13); mixed measures (M) (9); profitability growth (P) (6); income (I) (3); and assets (A) (1). Besides its breadth of international studies, Table 13.1 also shows a wide variation of different units of analysis from illegal entrepreneurs through to venture-capital-backed initial public offerings (IPOs). Table 13.1 is also important because we will be referring to it continually throughout the following three chapters on growth.

Arguably, for the sake of consistency, this chapter might do better to focus on only one measure of growth (such as employment or sales) and on one type of business. The advantage of such an approach would be that it would make it more likely that we are comparing 'apples with apples' (Shepherd and Wiklund 2009). However, our view is that if a variable is important, it should be so almost regardless of the growth measure or the type of business used in the particular study. Our compromise is that, for presentation purposes, we group the

Table 13.1 Growth studies, dependent variables and business age

Study	Dependent variable	Business age	Code
Cooper et al. (1994) US	Relative employment growth	Not given	E
Storey (1994b) UK	Employment size per year of life	Mean of four years	E
Honjo (2004) Japan	Change in log of sales growth 1997–9	Businesses up to seven years old	S
Schutjens and Wever (2002) Netherlands	Employment Growth = 1; No Employment Growth = 0	New businesses	E
Brüderl and Preisendörfer (2000) Germany	Employment growth	New businesses	E
Mata (1994) Portugal	Log of start-up size	Not given	E
Almus and Nerlinger (1999) Germany	$G_i = E_{tl2} - E_{tl1}/(t_{l2} - t_{l1})$ where E is employment and t_i is time	Businesses up to seven years old	E
Basu and Goswami (1999) UK	Log $y_i = (Y_t/Y_s)^{1/(t-s)} - 1$ where Y_t is the ith business's sales turnover in period t and Y_s is the sales turnover in the first year after start up	Mean of 19 years	S
Brixy and Kohaut (1999) East Germany	Log of 1996 employment less employment when first registered	Up to six years old	E
Brüderl and Preisendörfer (2000) Germany	Fastest growing 4% of start ups. Growth is >100% and at least five jobs	Four years	M
Pffeifer and Reize (2000) Germany	Employment growth	Between two and three years old	M
Reid and Smith (2000) UK	Three clusters of businesses reflecting performance in profitability, productivity and employment change	Mean of two years	M
Almus (2002) Germany	Businesses in the upper 10% of employment growth distribution, businesses in the upper 10% of the Birch Index distribution	Between six and nine years old	M
Dahlqvist et al. (2000) Sweden	Sample classified into marginal survivors and high performance	New businesses up to five years old	M
Wiklund and Shepherd (2003) Sweden	An index composed of four variables (relative change in sales and employment, self-reported rate of sales and employment growth compared to competitors)	Not given	M
Box et al. (1994) (US)	Employment growth per annum	All less than ten years old	E
Bonaccorsi and Giannangeli (2005) Italy	Growing at least by 30% and by at least two workers	Average of two years old	M
Bosma et al. (2004) Netherlands	Profit in 1997 Cumulative employment (1994–7)	New businesses 1994–7	P E
Brüderl and Preisendörfer (1998) Germany	Increase in employment Average sales growth 10% per annum	New founders	E S
Baum and Wally (2003) US	Percentage change in annual sales and percentage change in year-end employment (1996–2000)		M
	Average annual pre-tax net profit % of assets (1998–2000)	CEOs (age not given)	P
Honig (1998) Jamaica	Average monthly earnings	Informal micro-entrepreneurs (average business age is 14 years)	I
Aidis and van Praag (2007) Lithuania	Log of employment Turnover Income relative to expenses	Illegal business owners (age not given)	E S I

Table 13.1 continued

Study	Dependent variable	Business age	Code
Altinay and Altinay (2006) UK	Compound employment growth since start up	Turkish business owners (age not given)	E
Koeller and Lechler (2006) Germany	Absolute employment change	New technology businesses under six years old	E
Roper (1999) Ireland	Real sales growth Return on assets Assets to turnover	Small businesses (trading for at least four years)	S A S
McPherson (1996) African countries	Average annual growth of employment	Micro and small enterprises (average age, six to eight years old)	E
Robson and Bennett (2000) UK	Percentage rate of employment growth Percentage rate of turnover growth	SMEs (Table V) (median age 13 years)	E S
Coleman (2007) US	Return on sales Growth in sales	Women-only businesses (average age 11 years)	S S
Persson (2004) Sweden	Average annual employment growth	New establishments	E
Shrader and Siegel (2007) US	Profitability Sales growth	IPO ventures (less than six years old)	P S
Sleuwaegen and Goedhuys (2002) Ivory Coast	Average annual employment growth Average annual sales growth	Ivorian manufacturers (anything up to 77 years)	E S
Foreman-Peck *et al.* (2006) Wales	Profit–turnover ratio	Welsh SMEs (age not given)	P
Freel and Robson (2004) UK	Growth in profitability/No. of employees Growth in turnover/No. of employees	Scottish and northern England manufacturing SMEs (age not given)	P S
Harada (2003) Japan	Profitability Sales greater than expected before start up Income greater than at start up	New businesses	P S I
Capelleras and Greene (2008) Spain	Logarithmic change in employment	New businesses	E
Baum *et al.* (2001) US	Composite of employment, profit and sales	Aged between two and eight years	M

Code: E = employment-based growth study; P = profitability growth study; S = sales-based growth study; M = mixed-measure-based growth study; A = assets-based growth study; and I = income-based growth study.

36 studies in three ways: employment growth-based measures, sales-based measures and other measures (e.g. income, profit and mixed/multiple measures).

Finally, the 36 studies are all relatively recent studies. Storey (1994*a*) showed (using the same *pre*, *at* and *post* start-up approach) that, for example, education, age, incorporation, team entrepreneurship were all important in explaining business growth in the 1980s and early 1990s. The expectation – particularly if growth is deterministic rather than stochastic – is that these same variables will continue to be important influences in the late 1990s and 2000s.

Having explained the basis of our approach, our second aim in this chapter is to examine 'at-start-up' factors. We ask questions such as: do businesses grow because there is something special about the entrepreneur and how they do business?

The popular press seems to think that there is a photo-fit of the entrepreneur – what Casson (1982) would call a 'Jack Brash' figure. Typically, such an entrepreneur – according to the press – would consist of a he (but more occasionally she), who is likely to have started off his entrepreneurial career whilst at school. The 'true' entrepreneur, though, shuns further and higher education. Instead, the values of his immigrant family and the 'university of life' soon teach him the value of spotting and exploiting opportunities. His self-obsessed personality drives him on to early success. However, it is not long before he tastes failure. Temporarily brought low, the entrepreneur has time to reflect on his mistakes. Suitably invigorated, the entrepreneur rebuilds his fortune.

The question addressed in this chapter is: how true is the stereotype? We examine a range of 'pre-start' characteristics of the owner that are commonly associated with business growth. These are:

- age
- gender
- ethnicity
- education
- prior managerial experience
- prior business ownership
- partners
- unemployment
- personality.

We ask questions such as does the gender, education or ethnicity of the entrepreneur make much of a difference to growth? Should entrepreneurs have prior experience of managing a business to begin a fast-growth business? Is the experience of prior business ownership more likely to lead to subsequent business growth in the next business? Does a particular personality lead to business growth?

To see if there is any value in the popular photo-fit of the entrepreneur, we present empirical evidence for each of the pre start-up factors in turn. To achieve this, we make use of the 36 growth studies that we introduced earlier. We organise the 36 studies in terms of employment (Table 13.2a), sales (Table 13.2b) and mixed growth measures (Table 13.2c). Our interest here is in what are the 'entrepreneurial' factors that are associated with growth rather than – as in Chapter 8 – with the entrepreneurial factors associated with business start up.

13.2 Age and (Age)^2

This section examines whether the age of the founder influences business growth. There are two contrasting arguments. The first says that young people are best placed to run growth businesses because they are more likely than older entrepreneurs to have the necessary energy and enthusiasm to both seek and achieve growth. They are also likely to be 'closer' to new emerging technologies that are likely to take off and grow.

The counter-argument is that these are unusual examples that have been 'hyped' up by the media, purely because such individuals are so exceptional. More typically, young people lack the requisite business experience, have limited pools of available capital, and have few of the essential social and professional contacts to successfully grow a business. The general expectation, however, is that 'prime age' individuals (35–50 years old) are more likely to grow a business, and that age should be positive (+) in Tables 13.2a, 13.2b and 13.2c.

Table 13.2a 'Pre-start' variables: employment growth

Study	Age/Age²	Male	Ethnicity	Education	Sector-specific experience	Prior managerial experience	In business before	Partners	Unemployed	Personality
Cooper et al. (1994) US		+	–	+		n.s.	n.s.	n.s.		
Storey (1994b) UK	+/–			+		n.s.	n.s.	+	–	
Schutjens and Wever (2002) Netherlands	n.s.			n.s.		n.s.	n.s.	+		
Brüderl and Preisendörfer (2000) Germany		+		n.s.	+	n.s.	n.s.			
Mata (1996) Portugal	+	+		+						
Almus and Nerlinger (1999) Germany		+								
Box et al. (1994) US	–			n.s.		+	n.s.			
Bosma et al. (2004) (Holland)	n.s./n.s.	+		n.s.	+	–	n.s.			
Brüderl and Preisendörfer (1998) Germany	+	+	n.s.[1]	+	+	n.s.	n.s.			
Aidis and van Praag (2007) Lithuania	+/–	+	n.s.			–				
Altinay and Altinay (2006) UK	n.s.			n.s.		n.s.[3]				
Koeller and Lechler (2006) Germany						+				n.s.[4]
McPherson (1996) African countries	+	+	–[2]	+						
Persson (2004) Sweden	+			+				–		
Capelleras and Greene (2008) Spain	–	n.s.		n.s.			n.s.	n.s.		

Notes: 1 = non-German; 2 = non-Nordic countries; 3 = family tradition; 4 = nAch, locus of control.

| Table 13.2b | 'Pre-start' variables: sales growth[1] |

Study	Age/Age[2]	Male	Ethnicity	Education	Sector-specific experience	Prior managerial experience	In business before	Partners
Honjo (2004) Japan	+/−	n.s.		+				
Basu and Goswami (1999) UK			n.s.	+		n.s.		
Brüderl and Preisendörfer (1998) Germany		+	n.s.[2]	+	+	n.s.	n.s.	
Aidis and van Praag (2007) Lithuania	n.s./n.s.	+	+			n.s.		
Coleman (2007) US	n.s.			n.s.			+	n.s.[3]
Coleman (2007) US	n.s.			n.s.			−	n.s.
Shrader and Siegel (2007) US					−		n.s.	
Harada (2003) Japan	−/n.s.	+				n.s.		

Notes: 1 = no measures of unemployment or personality; 2 = non-German; 3 = family.

Table 13.2c 'Pre-start' variables: other measures

Study	Age/Age²	Male	Ethnicity	Education	Sector-specific experience	Prior managerial experience	In business before	Partners	Unemployed	Personality
Honig (1998) Jamaica (I)		+		+		+²				
Aidis and van Praag (2007) Lithuania (I)	n.s./n.s.	+	+			n.s.				
Harada (2003) Japan (I)	–/–	+				–				
Brüderl and Preisendörfer (2000) Germany (M)	n.s./n.s.	n.s.	n.s.	n.s.		+	n.s.			
Pfeifer and Reize (2000) Germany (M)	n.s./n.s.	n.s.							n.s.	
Reid and Smith (2000) UK (M)				n.s.					–	
Almus (2002) Germany (M)				+						
Dahlqvist et al. (2000) Sweden (M)		+	–¹							
Wiklund and Sheperd (2003) Sweden (M)				n.s.		+				
Bonaccorsi and Giannangeli (2005) Italy (M)	n.s./n.s.			n.s.		n.s.	n.s.		n.s.	–³
Baum et al. (2001) US (P)										+⁴
Bosma et al. (2004) Netherlands (P)	n.s.	+		+	+	n.s.	n.s.			+⁵
Shrader and Siegel (2007) US (P)					–		n.s.			
Harada (2003) Japan (P)	–	+				+				
Roper (1999) Ireland (A)	–							n.s.		

Notes: 1 = immigrant; 2 = experience squared; 3 = set up for independence reasons; 4 = traits (tenacity, passion for work); motivation (vision, self-efficacy, growth goals); 5 = higher income motive.

Illustration	Bright young things

Do you recognise this young entrepreneur? Clue: imagine him wearing a beard.

It has been suggested that young people are likely to be closer to new and emerging technologies. Bill Gates, for example, was only 20 when he set up Microsoft, whilst Sergey Brin and Larry Page were 23 when they set up Google. Another striking example is the Indian web company Directi. This was set up by two brothers – Bhavin and Divyank Turakhia – in 1998. Bhavin was 19 and Divyank was 16 at the time. By 2008, Directi's web products had been used by more than 1 million customers and the business employed over 500 people.

A similar set of arguments can be put forward for Age² (age squared) which is often taken as a measure of 'general experience'. Older people (over 55 years of age) are more likely to have the necessary access to capital, more business experience and appropriate contacts – all factors which facilitate growth. Greater experience (Age²) should be positively associated with growth.

The counter-argument is that older people lack the enthusiasm and energy necessary to run a growth business. They may be thinking more about retirement, or may already have access to a pension and so their business may be more of a hobby or a source of 'pin money'. Finally, older people may be more prone to ill-health which may inhibit the growth of their business. If those founding a business above the age of 55 are likely to have slower growing businesses, for the above reasons, then the Age^2 term will be negative.

Combining these arguments the inference is that the entrepreneur's age has an inverted U-shaped relationship with business performance, initially rising with age – because the very young lack capital and experience. However, the old lack energy so their businesses are also less likely to grow, implying that it is the middle-aged entrepreneur who combines energy with experience that is most likely to start a business that grows quickly.

The evidence from the studies in Tables 13.2a, 13.2b and 13.2c suggests that Age is positive whilst Age^2 is negative, particularly in terms of employment growth. This indicates that there is a 'prime age' that is associated with business growth. This relationship is less robust when alternative measures such as sales or other/mixed measures of business growth are used. Here the typical pattern is that neither Age nor Age^2 is significant. However, when Age and Age^2 are considered together, Age tends to be positive whilst Age^2 (experience) appears more likely to be negative. Unfortunately, many studies do not include an Age^2 variable, so throwing doubt on the sign on the Age variable where this is included.

Our overall view is that the owner's age when starting a business does influence the growth of the business. Prime age business owners are more likely to have fast-growing businesses than those from either the younger or the older age group.

13.3 Gender

Our tables clearly show that businesses owned by males are much more likely to grow than businesses owned by females. Out of the 21 studies that examine gender, 17 show that males are more likely to be involved in growth businesses, whilst the remaining 4 show a non-significant relationship. There are no studies that show businesses owned by females to be significantly more likely to grow than businesses owned by males.

This poses the question: why do female-owned businesses grow more slowly than male-owned businesses? Four main explanations have been offered:

1   *Women do not have the requisite abilities to successfully run a growth business.* Verheul and Thurik (2001) found that women were more risk averse, had less financial management experience and spent less time networking. Cliff's (1998) qualitative study of Canadian entrepreneurs also argued that women, compared with men, were more likely to want to grow their business to a certain size and no further. They were also more likely to adopt a more cautious approach to such growth.

2   *Women face discrimination.* Gender theory (Oakley 1973) argues that an individual's gender is socially constructed. One consequence of this suggested 'gendered' socialisation is that there are 'male' activities (e.g. running a business) and a range of social norms or stereotypes surrounding such activities (Marlow and Patton 2005) which serve to limit the chances of women running growth businesses. Hence, it is not that women lack the necessary abilities to successfully run a business: instead it is more likely that they have to behave like 'honorary men'. Also, because there are fewer females running a business (see Chapter 8), there also are fewer female entrepreneurial 'role models', particularly in the 'high-tech' industries.

Women may also experience problems accessing resources as a result of discrimination. They may be excluded from influential networks because they are 'not one of the boys'. Morris *et al.* (2006) argue that females face real barriers in trying to sell their products/services. This, they suggest, stems from imperfect access to key networks of customers and suppliers. Another potential example of discrimination is access to finance. Brush *et al.* (2001) argue that women perceived that the US venture-capital businesses were less likely to back their growth propositions. Carter *et al.*'s (2007) study of UK bank-loan officers also found gender differences. They reported that females' commitment to loans was also more likely to be questioned. Fraser (2005) also found that women were more likely to pay more for term loans. If so, this has obvious implications for the female entrepreneur seeking sources of finance.

Coleman's (2007) study of US female entrepreneurs, however, found that growth in female businesses was not constrained by inadequate access to finance. Instead, she argued that it was more to do with women's education and experience levels. Greater education, in particular, was more likely to lead to growth. Storey (2004) reports very similar results from his study of female business owners in Trinidad and Tobago. He finds that neither application rates nor denial rates for funding vary by gender. Becker-Blease and Sohl (2007) also argue that women are just as likely to receive business angel-based finance as men. Blanchflower *at al.* (2003) equally find no evidence that female-owned businesses suffer from discrimination.

3   *Women are more likely to have family responsibilities.* Marlow (2002) argues that women are much more likely to have 'caring' responsibilities than men. As such, they are more likely to choose part-time, rather than full-time, business ownership. This is likely to limit their ability or willingness to successfully grow their business.

4   *Female entrepreneurs find themselves located in particular sectors which generally have fewer rapidly growing businesses.* Munoz and Perez (2007) examined female Spanish entrepreneurs in the nineteenth and twentieth centuries. They found that women tended to work in 'dead end' service sectors, such as cleaning and personal care. They also found that women were, at least until the 1970s, largely denied the opportunity to work in other sectors and, if they did, this was usually only as part of a wider family business. They were often not recorded as business owners or paid. Potentially, therefore, the contribution to business growth by women is under-recorded. Menzies *et al.* (2004) also argued that women were less likely to have backgrounds in engineering and computing, which effectively excluded them from starting businesses in these sectors.

Our view is that there is no question that female entrepreneurs have shown slower growth than male entrepreneurs. Issues of family, potential discrimination and the choice of sector all seem to play important roles in explaining this finding.

13.4 Ethnicity

We observed in Chapter 8 that there were difficulties in defining and measuring 'ethnic' entrepreneurship. Nonetheless, the available data point to sharp differences in self-employment rates between different ethnic groups. For example, in both the Netherlands and the UK, self-employment was higher amongst Indian/Pakistani and Chinese groups, but relatively low amongst those of African origin. We also saw that self-employment rates were likely to differ between the first and second generations of a particular ethnic group. Jones and Ram (2007) argued that there was a need to take account not only of cultural differences, but also of discriminatory barriers and the nature of the entrepreneurial opportunities taken up by ethnic entrepreneurs.

In terms of business growth, we may expect that those ethnic groups with higher rates of self-employment would also be more likely to have fast-growth businesses. One reason for this might be that successful entrepreneurs from a particular ethnic community act as 'role models' for others in the community. Particular ethnic communities may also have denser cultural ties that promote business growth. For example, Jones and Ram (2007) have pointed to the presence of a 'moral economy' amongst some ethnic groups which promotes entrepreneurial hard work and forbearance. Being in a supportive environment may also allow for particular ethnic resources to be made available. Family and friends may offer finance to support the business, or may be willing to forego a 'market' salary until the business grows.

Such ethnic ties and resources may prove invaluable for growth purposes. Saxenian (2000) shows that one quarter of all high-tech businesses in Silicon Valley have chief executives who were from India or China and who came to the US to study. She concludes that:

> The new immigrant entrepreneurs thus foster economic development directly, by creating new jobs and wealth, as well as indirectly, by coordinating the information flows and providing the linguistic and cultural know-how that promote trade and investment flows with their home countries. *(p. 24).*

However, the example above in fact combines two, possibly quite separate, influences. The first is ethnicity and the second is immigration. The reason for examining them separately is that immigrants may be either a self-selecting, or selected (see Illustration below), group of individuals, albeit having the same ethnic origin. The reason why such individuals are self-selecting is that, as economic migrants, they are perhaps more entrepreneurial than those that remain behind in their original country. If migrants establish fast-growth businesses in their host country, this can only partly be attributed to their 'ethnicity', because those individuals that choose to migrate are a self-selected (non-random) sample of the ethnic group.

Illustration   The case of Jewish migrants from Germany in the 1930s

Between 1933 and 1938, 11,000 Jewish refugees from Germany, Czechoslovakia and Hungary were admitted into Britain. By 1939, these individuals had established more than 200 new enterprises, employing more than 15,000 people.

Loebl (1978) describes a number of these cases in detail. Two important points emerge:

- The first is that in the northern region of England, Loebl identifies 54 manufacturing businesses established by Jews who left Nazi Germany between 1933 and 1938. By 1974, these businesses employed 16,932 workers, demonstrating an exceptional growth performance in England's most economically deprived region.

- Loebl also demonstrates that these were not a 'random sample' of German Jews. He shows that the only immigrants that were granted entry rights were those able to show they and their parents owned a business, had access to capital and were prepared to commit to starting a business in northern England, where unemployment rates were high. The immigration selection that took place can be seen as the precursor of current procedures that operate in many countries where individuals are given 'points' for having desirable economic qualities.

However, there are also reasons why the ethnicity of the owner may inhibit the growth of their business. First, many ethnic businesses are set up to serve their particular community, so growth is ultimately constrained by the size of that marketplace. Also, as Casson (1982) observes, many ethnic businesses rely heavily upon those of similar ethnicity for labour, but this strategy has its costs. Although members of an ethnic 'network' may share similar values, it does not necessarily follow that people from this network are necessarily as talented at managing the business as 'outsiders'. This may limit the growth of the business.

Second, ethnic entrepreneurs can face discrimination. One reason why entrepreneurs turn to their own ethnic community is that they are perhaps denied resources (e.g. access to customers/suppliers) by other groups in society. There may also be real or perceived difficulties because of language or cultural barriers. Finally, there may be institutional barriers: for example Blanchflower *et al.* (2003) found that, in the US, Black-owned small businesses are twice as likely to be denied credit as otherwise similar White-owned businesses.

A third limitation on any growth is the choice of sector – a topic which we address in more detail in the next chapter. Most first generation immigrants to an economy, lacking access to capital, have to start businesses in sectors which require only modest capital (Basu and Altinay 2002), have low skill requirements and low entry barriers. Unfortunately, they also generally have low growth potential. Typically, therefore, ethnic entrepreneurs have tended to enter retailing, textiles and catering. Jones and Ram (2007) argue that these sectoral choices have a major impact on subsequent growth prospects. They argue that entrepreneurs in these sectors have to work long hours for very little profit just to survive. This is particularly the case in 'sunset' industries like textiles which are subject to competitive pressures from foreign sources and small-scale retailing which cannot cope with the economies of scale and scope of larger businesses. Finally, even in the catering industry, competition is severe, limiting the growth potential of restaurants and those supplying such restaurants. Their conclusion – which they believe applies to the majority of ethnic entrepreneurs – is starkly different from the earlier quote from Saxenian (2000):

> As a general rule we would argue that immigrant origin entrepreneurs are heavily over-concentrated in a small range of inherently poorly remunerated, labour-intensive activities, some of which are sunset industries on their last legs, which would be problematic for any entrepreneur of whatever origin.
>
> *Jones and Ram (2007: 451)*

Curiously, ethnicity is imperfectly covered in multivariate studies. Tables 13.2a, 13.2b and 13.2c show, in total, that there are nine studies that include some 'ethnicity' measure, but the measures themselves have important limitations. First, ethnicity is often reduced to just a binary measure of whether or not someone has a form of 'ethnicity'. A second problem is that several studies combine 'immigration' with ethnicity. In essence, 'ethnicity' has tended to be used in a fairly unsophisticated and limited way.

Nevertheless, some ethnic groups – most notably Blacks in the US – do have businesses that under-perform: Fairlie and Robb (2007) showed that Black-owned businesses in the US are less successful on virtually all dimensions than comparable White-owned businesses. They attribute this to Black individuals being much less likely to have had parents who were self-employed.

Our overall conclusion is that ethnicity has a mixed influence on business growth, but that there are clear instances – most notably blacks in the US – of some ethnic groups performing less well than others. A more positive picture emerges from observing immigrants. Here there is rather stronger evidence that immigrant groups, especially when they bring with them human and financial capital, do establish some notably successful businesses if and when they break out of the narrow 'ethnic' market.

13.5 Education

One view of entrepreneurship is that qualifications are pointless if the aim is to grow a business. For example, the British entrepreneur Sir Alan Sugar said:

> They [qualifications] are meaningless in the world of business. They are a badge that shows a person is at a certain level of intelligence – it doesn't demonstrate that they are an expert in anything. The learning starts when you come into industry.
>
> *The Times (26 March 2008) © The Times 26 March 2008/nisyndication.com*

In support of his argument, Alan Sugar might have pointed to Bill Gates, Steve Jobs and Michael Dell, who all dropped out of university. Others, such as Richard Branson, did not even attend university. These cases might imply that education channels individuals into conventional forms of employment and encourages conformity. This does not sit easily with the 'personality' of the entrepreneur who sees opportunities where others see only conformity and so is inevitably 'uncomfortable' within formal education.

However, five justifications have been offered for the alternative argument, which is that the educational level of the entrepreneur enhances new/small business growth.

1 Education enhances the skill base of an individual, enabling them to address and overcome the problems associated with running a rapidly growing enterprise.

2 Education may be a 'selection mechanism' which 'sorts' the able from the less able. If it is the ability of the entrepreneur that influences business performance, then education is likely to be associated positively with business performance.

3 Education influences the sectors in which the individual begins a business, and a lack of formal educational qualifications can effectively be a barrier to entry. This is particularly relevant in a knowledge-based economy where faster growing businesses are more likely to be concentrated. Examples include the high-tech sectors where virtually all entrepreneurs have a degree and a majority have a doctorate (Lindelof and Lofsten 2002).

4 All else being equal, educated individuals are more likely to be able to access resources from a financial institution than those with low educational attainment (Storey 2005).

5 Economic choice theory (Chapter 8) predicts that educated individuals have, on balance, higher earning opportunities as an employee than those with low or no educational qualifications. Hence, if their business fails to achieve a level of income which they can earn as an employee, then they will switch into employment. Since the income generated by the business is likely to be broadly related to its size and growth, the expectations of growth by the educated entrepreneur will be greater than of those with lower educational qualifications.

The findings in Tables 13.2a, 13.2b and 13.2c are split almost evenly. Eleven of the 23 studies indicate a positive relationship between education and business growth. The other 12 studies indicate that there is a non-significant relationship between growth and education. However, not one study points to a negative relationship. The clarity of these findings parallels the only truly 'meta study' of this topic by van der Sluis *et al.* (2005). They identified 86 studies that linked education to some measure of entrepreneurial performance such as survival or growth. In terms of growth, they showed that years of schooling are positively related to earnings as an entrepreneur. For example, they calculated for the US that entrepreneurs increased their income by 6.1 per cent for each year of schooling – although this return is less than for employees where it is in the region of 7–9 per cent.

Our view is that the findings on education are clear and wholly at variance with those of Sir Alan Sugar quoted at the start of this section. They point to education being clearly linked to higher earnings in entrepreneurship.

13.6 Specific sectoral experience

Having an understanding of how a sector 'operates' may be thought to be useful to an individual starting their own business in that sector. It seems plausible that those with prior sector experience would be more likely to start a business that grows than an individual with no knowledge of the sector. At a simple level, having detailed knowledge of a sector allows an individual to develop a range of strong and weak ties that serve to legitimise the business and help identify 'structural' holes (Burt 1995).

For example, the Norwegian, John Fredriksen, began his career as a ship broker transporting cargoes of fish from Iceland to Germany. Following that, he moved to the Lebanon in the late 1960s where he developed his expertise in shipping oil out of Saudi Arabia and Iraq. In 1973, following the Arab–Israeli war, oil prices rose considerably leading to a fall in demand for oil. This then led to a collapse in the demand for long haul oil tankers. Fredriksen sensed an opportunity and subsequently managed to lease ships at very cheap rates. Fredriksen subsequently went on to have the largest oil-tanker fleet in the world.

In contrast, a random approach would suggest that no two opportunities in a given sector are identical and knowledge of a sector is a poor guide to likely success. Indeed, it may be that the truly original ideas that underpin a growth business come from those entrepreneurs who approach a sector and are able to 'think outside the box'. The case in the Illustration below (Halborg *et al.*, 1998) emphasises both the role of chance and the idea that prior sectoral experience may be irrelevant.

Illustration	'Mr X'

'Mr X' loved pop music and sought some form of employment that would generate an income for him, whilst enabling him to be involved in some way in popular music.

Initially, he played in various unsuccessful bands until he realised that he lacked the musical talent to earn a living from playing. His first dabble into a music-related business was in music publishing. This earned him enough to stay alive – but only just.

So, to supplement his income he began to work for a friend in a music shop selling instruments and music. His friend lost interest in the shop and asked X if he would buy the shop. Recognising that it was the only way he would continue to have a job, X agreed.

The shop proved to be about as successful as the music publishing but X, desperate to do something that would encourage repeat customers, agreed one day to book a mini-bus for a group of his customers and himself to go to a local pop concert.

The idea seemed to catch on amongst his customers and gradually more and more bookings were arranged for different groups of customers to go to different concerts, and the mini-buses became coaches.

This was, however, a sideline for the music shop – merely a way of ensuring that he got more customers returning though the door. One day this changed when a customer asked him to organise the tickets as well as the transport. X found both that he could buy the tickets in bulk at reduced prices and that he had a detailed knowledge of the music tastes of large numbers of customers and potential customers.

Despite having no background whatever in computers or ticketing, today X runs one of the largest ticket agencies in the UK. Sales rose from £1.5 m to £20 m in seven years. He no longer needs to run his music shop.

In our tables only three studies investigate specific sectoral experience and the picture is mixed. Shrader and Siegel (2007) find a negative relationship for both in terms of profits and sales. Bosma *et al.* (2004) and Brüderl and Preisendörfer (1998) find a positive relationship using employment (both studies), sales (Brüderl and Preisendörfer, 1998) and profits (Bosma *et al.* 2004).

Evidence of whether businesses founded by an owner who has prior sectoral experience grow faster than businesses where the owner does not have this experience is too limited to draw a definitive conclusion.

13.7 Prior managerial experience

Whilst the majority of new businesses may not employ others, those that grow would normally do so by taking on workers. Hence, the ability of a small business owner to satisfactorily manage others might be viewed as a pre-condition for a growing business. Prior managerial experience may, therefore, be thought to be a key quality. For example, Emily Trail and Jacquie Craus set up their Australian cleaning business, Maid My Day, after working in corporate managerial roles. Their approach was to take their experience of using a 'systems approach' and apply it to their cleaning business. Their aim was to use '. . . the critical importance of systems and processes to enable scalability. Every action, from taking leads, to billing, to recruitment; all has to be a process to allow us to work on growing the business.' (*The Australian*, 27 September 2008)

The alternative argument is that prior management experience is of limited value since managing others in someone else's business is fundamentally different from managing them in your own business. This is because of the greater commitment of the business owner, compared with the 'professional' manager, or because the managerial situations are likely to differ markedly.

Our tables show that there are 22 measures of prior managerial experience. Of these, three studies find a negative relationship, six a positive relationship, and thirteen a non-significant relationship.

The reasonable inference from this evidence is that, whilst prior managerial experience of the business owner might play a modest role in explaining business growth, its impact is not clear. We attribute this to managing as a business owner being very different from managing a business as an employee.

13.8 Prior business ownership

One hotly disputed issue in small business and entrepreneurship research is the nature and extent of entrepreneurial learning. In Chapter 10, we saw that there are two contrasting views of the importance of entrepreneurial learning. The first asserts that entrepreneurs learn from both their successes and their mistakes. By having been in business before, the entrepreneur accumulates experience and knowledge, so businesses established by such individuals will out-perform businesses begun by novices. Prior business ownership experience, therefore, enhances the entrepreneurial talent of the individual. Support for this is provided by

Delmar and Shane (2006) and some mixed support is provided for some groups of starters by Taylor (1999).

The alternative argument is that prior business experience as an owner is unrelated to entrepreneurial talent. This reasoning was first outlined by Jovanovic (1982), who argued that what changed as a result of the experience of being a business owner was the ability of the individual to accurately assess their own entrepreneurial talent. Central to this approach was that a novice has very little idea of how good they are as an entrepreneur when they start up a business. They obtain a much clearer idea only through being in business. In other words, what business experience does is reduce the *variance* of their estimate of their own entrepreneurial talent. This is valuable information for the individual, since it helps them decide whether or not to stay in business and perhaps, even if they fail, whether or not to start another business. It does *not* mean, though, that their entrepreneurial talent increases with each business that they open.

A more extreme version of this argument is that an individual who has tried to be successful as a business owner, yet never succeeded, lacks the necessary entrepreneurial talent. The fact that they keep trying is more a reflection of their optimistic personality than of their entrepreneurial talent. According to this argument, those who have been in business before will be less likely to be successful than novices.

In the ten studies that examined previous business ownership, reported in Tables 13.2a, 13.2b and 13.2c, only Coleman (2007) points to a positive relationship between prior ownership and business growth. Furthermore, this finding is only for the 'return on sales' measure and is reversed for the 'sales growth' measure. For the other nine studies – all of which use different measures of business growth – being in business before is not significant. These results are in line with Ucbasaran *et al.* (2006), whose research specifically examines performance differences between novice (no business experience), serial (been in business before) and portfolio (currently running another business) entrepreneurs. They find there are differences between the performance of novice, serial and portfolio entrepreneurs if these variables are examined in isolation. However, when other human capital variables (like age and gender) are included, these differences disappear, indicating that prior business ownership is not a significant determinant of business growth.

Such findings raise important issues about the value of entrepreneurial learning. The assumption is that entrepreneurial learning takes place. Parker (2006), however, shows that the self-employed adjust their behaviour only very marginally in the face of recent evidence. Instead, they are much more strongly driven by their 'priors', which in this context we can take to be their long-term experience and personality characteristics.

Our view is that prior business experience as an owner does not influence business growth, either positively or negatively. It points to the need to review the evidence on the extent to which entrepreneurial learning takes place and whether it influences business performance.

13.9 Family

Do family-owned/controlled businesses grow more strongly? A positive link is normally proposed on two grounds. First, family businesses may have fewer 'principal–agent' problems. In other words, the family who owns the business (principal) are also workers (agents) in the business. Such a unified governance structure means that – compared with non-family businesses – there are likely to be fewer monitoring costs (Westhead and Howarth 2006).

The second basis for a positive link derives from stewardship theory. This argues that people are rarely motivated by the short-term economic factors stressed by economic theories that assume individuals maximise their own utilities (the principal agent–approach). Instead, stewardship theory emphasises that what marks behaviour is collectivism, altruism and trust (amongst those who are responsible for the business). This behaviour is said to be more prevalent amongst family businesses because of close family bonds which allow the family to 'steward' the business to achieve stronger business growth (Corbetta and Salvato 2004).

There are, however, difficulties with both of these approaches. First, it is not necessarily the case that owners (principals) and workers (agents) in non-family businesses may have divergent motives. Equally, non-family members may prove just as able in providing effective stewardship of the business as family members.

In contrast, there are a number of powerful reasons why family businesses may underperform. Perez-Gonzalez (2006) suggests that there may be contradictions between family goals and business objectives, which may harm the economic performance of the business. Families do not necessarily share the same objectives. Even if they do, the very altruism of the family business may mean that it is more focused on a 'family' agenda than a 'business' agenda. Another example is that if it relies on the talents of the family, it may be denying itself access to the superior abilities of non-family members. As the famous investor Warren Buffet suggested, picking managers by relying on them being family members was akin to '. . . choosing the 2020 Olympic team by picking the eldest sons of the gold-medal winners of the 2000 Olympics' (quoted in Perez-Gonzalez 2006: 1560).

In our tables, only one study looks explicitly at family ownership. Coleman (2007) finds a non-significant relationship. This is reflective of the wider doubts about the influence of family on business growth. Dyer's (2006) review of family businesses suggests that the empirical evidence on the relationship between performance and family ownership is mixed. Part of this ambiguity stems from the absence of a single and simple definition of a 'family business' (Westhead and Cowling 1998). Another reason is that much of the evidence is on businesses that have evolved 'corporate' structures. This may not relate closely to the experiences of most small businesses although, arguably, fast-growth businesses are more likely to make use of corporate structures.

The third reason is that – besides the focus on performance differences between family and non-family businesses – prior research has been interested in the performance of different generations of a family business. Westhead and Cowling (1997, 1998) concluded that it is difficult to attribute a performance impact based purely upon family ownership. The evidence on the relationship between business 'succession' and performance, however, is less opaque. Cucculelli and Micucci (2008) using Italian data, Bennedsen et al. (2007) using Danish data, and Perez-Gonzalez (2006) using US data all find that those businesses that employed second-generation family members under-perform relative to those businesses that elected to employ non-family members.

Our overall view is that it is difficult to disentangle the extent to which family-owned businesses have faster or slower growth rates compared with otherwise similar businesses that are not family owned. The topic is beset by definitional issues but, where the matter is addressed, studies largely fail to identify a performance effect of family ownership.

13.10 Partners

Similar issues also apply to the influence of the number of partners on business performance. The evidence reviewed by Storey (1994) suggested that businesses started and owned by more than one individual – a team – were more likely to grow than businesses started by a single owner. This is partly because a growing business requires a wider range of skills and talents than is likely to be possessed by a single individual. To achieve this range, individuals have to 'team up'. A second supportive argument is that, almost by definition, team businesses have greater resources to draw upon in the pursuit of business growth. Both Harper (2008) and Cooney (2005) argue that these insights are often lost because of the prevailing dominance of research that examines just the individual entrepreneur. Cooney (2005) argues, for example, that the success of the Apple computer was not just down to Steve Jobs but also due to Steve Wozniack inventing the first PC model and Mike Markkula's business expertise and contacts with venture capitalists. A third argument is that a business with two or more 'mouths to feed' is likely to have to grow quickly in order to survive.

Tables 13.2a, 13.2b and 13.2c suggest the evidence on whether more partners are associated with faster new business growth is mixed. Of the seven studies that looked at the influence of team businesses, one finds a negative relationship, two a positive relationship and four others a non-significant relationship with growth. This evidence is supplemented by some specific studies.

Davidsson *et al.*'s (2004) review argues that the skills of individuals in team businesses are often more likely to be similar rather than diverse. If that is the case, the 'skill diversity' argument outlined above is invalid, and would explain the non-significant relationship between teams and business performance. Stam and Schutjens (2005) specifically tried to distinguish performance differences between solo and team starts. They also found a fairly mixed picture: in their early years of life the 'team businesses' performs better, but, subsequently, teams seemed to have more difficulty in achieving further growth.

It would appear, therefore, that there are a number of problems in understanding the influence of partners on business performance. First, there is no common definition of team entrepreneurship (Cooney 2005): for example, are families an example of team entrepreneurship? Second, there is an implicit assumption that the team members share goals and objectives that spur on business development. As with families, this may not in fact be the case. Third, isolating the impact of teams on business performance is difficult because such businesses are much more likely to choose incorporation as a legal form. Being incorporated – as the next chapter will show – brings the benefits of providing both limited liability and 'credibility'. Hence, even if there is an association between business performance and multiple owners, it is not clear to what extent this merely reflects the 'standard' benefits of incorporation.

A final problem relates to research methods. Some businesses begin with a single owner and then, after they have grown, acquire one – or more – new owners. Simply observing that (current) team-owned businesses have grown faster than sole-owned businesses might give the misleading impression that they had grown *because* they were team owned. Instead, the correct interpretation is that, because they grew, they *became* team owned. Stam and Schutjens (2005) specifically focus on the performance of start-up teams and so we are more confident in its findings – there may be initially be faster growth in 'team-starts' – but that this growth evaporates in the medium term.

Our view is that the evidence is mixed as to the actual impact of teams on business growth. As with family businesses, there is a need for greater conceptual clarity and further research in this area before a firm conclusion can be reached. On balance, because it adopts the most methodologically sound approach, we favour the Stam and Schutjens result of an initially faster growth amongst team-starts, but no medium to long-term effect.

13.11 Unemployment

There are two reasons why new businesses might grow more slowly if begun by individuals who were unemployed. The first is that unemployment may so scar an individual that they make sure, if they do start a new business, that they take fewer risks. This may mean they avoid high-risk, but also high-return, projects and so may forgo any growth opportunities that arise.

Second, instead of unemployment signalling 'bad luck' or an adverse economic climate, unemployed individuals, on balance, may have lower levels of skills and abilities than the employed. If such individuals find it difficult to gain employment, they may also lack the skills and abilities to successfully grow a business.

The contrasting argument is that a period of unemployment may allow an individual the time to develop a business concept, so that when the business begins it has been thoroughly researched and hence is more likely to grow. For example, following the stock market crash of 1929, Charles Darrow developed and commercialised the game of Monopoly, which eventually made him a millionaire.

Furthermore, many individuals made unemployed also receive a redundancy payment. This can give them sufficient capital to start a business. However, there is little evidence pointing to the impact of redundancy payments on business growth. Perhaps the nearest proxy is the work of Burke *et al.* (2000) that shows that those who receive an inheritance, and Lindh and Ohlsson (1996) who show that Swedish lottery winners – which like redundancy payments are another form of 'windfall' payments – are more likely to achieve higher self-employment income.

Four studies in our tables examined the influence of the previous unemployment of the entrepreneur on business growth. Two found a negative relationship and the other two found a non-significant relationship.

Unfortunately, none of these studies include the possible impacts of alternative labour states such as being 'inactive' (e.g. being sick) as opposed to being in work or unemployed. Andersson and Wadensjo (2007) specifically control for these different labour-market states but still find that those who are employed are more likely to have greater levels of income as business owners than either the unemployed or the inactive.

There is a need for further research in this area to disentangle the influence of different labour-market states and 'windfalls' (redundancy payments) on business growth. However, what evidence there is suggests that a business founded by an unemployed individual is less likely to grow than one founded by an employed individual.

13.12 Personality characteristics

In Chapter 2, we reviewed the evidence on the personality profile of the entrepreneur. We concluded, like Gartner (1988), that there was little evidence of particular personality traits (e.g. risk taking, need for achievement) being directly associated with setting up a business. There might, however, be expected to be a clearer relationship between business growth and the 'entrepreneurial personality'. So, individuals who start businesses and have characteristics such as being dynamic, determined, confident, resourceful, thrusting or insightful might be more likely to grow their businesses than individuals without these characteristics.

There are, however, three possible objections to the suggested influence of personality on business growth. One is ideological: some people might consider the successful entrepreneur as confident or dynamic, whilst others see the same person as arrogant or exploitative. Also, simply asking entrepreneurs what they think caused their success is likely to lead to recall biases (e.g. a willingness to ascribe success to their own actions or personality). Second, as we have seen, many businesses comprise a team of individuals, so it might be the collective characteristics of a group of people, rather than those of a single entrepreneurial 'hero', that explain business success. Gartner (1988) also argued that there was little evidence to suggest that 'traditional' personality traits (e.g. risk taking, locus of control) were related to business success. For example, the Box *et al.* (1994) study finds a non-significant relationship between the need for achievement and any locus of control with employment growth. In short, until recently, examining such traits had become a dead end: the evidence was very weak, and it was likely that other factors (e.g. luck, human capital or strategy) were far more important in explaining business growth.

However, some interesting research has subsequently emerged. Baum and Locke (2004), for instance, examined 'passion' and 'tenacity' and found – like the earlier Baum *et al.* (2001) study – that such traits had an indirect effect on business performance. There has also been a move towards considering cognitive aspects (like self-efficacy), and a wider concern with the impact of motivations on entrepreneurial performance (see Table 13.2c).

Cassar (2007) investigated the role of motivations by asking potential business owners, before they started in business, about their aspirations and then tracking the businesses over time. This has the considerable advantage that it is less likely to be subject to recall bias. Cassar (2007) finds that the most common motivation is a desire for independence. Like Bonaccorsi and Giannangeli (2005) in Table 13.2c, Cassar (2007) finds that those with a desire to be independent are less likely to experience business growth. Cassar also finds that those entrepreneurs who claimed – prior to start up – that their desire was to make money were the ones most likely to start businesses that grew faster. Delmar and Wiklund (2008) find similar results for Sweden. They show that motivations are related positively to employment growth and, to some extent, to sales growth.

Other research, however, shows that motivations may have only an indirect impact on business growth. For example, Wiklund and Shepherd's (2003) Swedish study argues that whilst motivations may have positive impacts on growth, the relationship is made more complex by the influence that education, experience and the dynamic nature of the external environment has on motivations. Another Swedish study (Wiklund *et al.* 2003) argues, instead, that non-economic concerns – particularly revolving around employee well-being – were more important than financial outcomes in determining growth motivations.

Our view is that recently there have been some useful developments in seeking to better understand the role of 'personality' in business growth. These studies emphasise the importance of indirect impacts and the importance of motivations. The problem, however, is that the research base in this area remains largely confined to Swedish or US data. If motivations do have an indirect influence on business growth, such motivations are also likely to be influenced by the particular culture of that country.

Summary

The aim of this chapter has been first to introduce our method for reviewing the vast range of 'growth' studies. Our focus has been on using 36 international multivariate studies to guide the discussion of pre, at and post start-up variables that are commonly associated with business growth. We again emphasise that these variables are likely to be interlinked. Our second aim has been to review the evidence on the 'pre' start-up factors commonly associated with business growth. Our evidence is that, for example, educational attainment is positively associated with business growth. We also found strong evidence that being older, or at least middle-aged, is also associated with business growth. Third, we confirmed that businesses owned by men are much more likely to experience growth than businesses owned by women. Finally, business founders who were unemployed prior to starting their business are less likely to have a growing business. These are the four 'stand out' results of this review. This, therefore, may be taken as the beginnings of a profile of a growth business.

However, despite the wide range of evidence we reviewed, this chapter has also shown that a number of pre start-up factors are not so easily associated with business growth. For example, there is weak evidence on the importance of ethnicity and the specific sectoral experience of the business owner on business growth. Storey (1994a) argued that prior managerial experience was associated with business growth but results from more recent research have been less clear-cut. Another revision of the Storey (1994) conclusions relates to the role of multiple owners – team starts. The more careful research in this area (Stam and Schutjens, 2005) suggests this relationship between team starts and growth is more ambiguous than was previously assumed.

Finally there are, to us, two surprises. First, we were surprised about the absence of robust evidence linking prior business ownership with employment growth. Given that learning is argued by many to be fundamental to entrepreneurial performance, and one element of learning is having been in business before (through its contribution to the 'stock' of knowledge upon which the entrepreneur draws), the absence of a relationship points to a need to re-think the issue of entrepreneurial learning.

Our review also points to a re-emergence – of sorts – of personality factors as an influence on business growth. In recent years, studies in this area have matured so that, instead of examining traits that almost have a genetic basis to them, the focus has shifted towards an examination of how cognitive factors link directly and indirectly with business growth. The results imply that a clear commitment to growth when the business begins is likely to enhance the likelihood of achieving such growth.

Our overall conclusion is that, perhaps with the exception of the education, age, gender and employment status of the founder, the links between pre start-up factors and new/small business performance are difficult to identify. Furthermore, even these four factors provide only a modest insight into the performance of the new/small business.

Questions for discussion

1 Carefully review the evidence and decide whether or not entrepreneurs learn.

2 What pre start-up factors are likely to influence new business growth? Of these factors, which do you think is most influential and why?

3 Assess the strengths and weaknesses of existing research which links the personality characteristics of entrepreneurs to business growth.

4 What do you think explains lower growth amongst businesses owned by women?

5 Why is there no clear evidence on the role of 'ethnicity' in explaining fast business growth?

6 Are family-owned businesses more likely to grow?

7 Evaluate the importance of team-based entrepreneurship to understanding business growth.

References

Aidis, R. and van Praag, M. (2007) 'Illegal Entrepreneurship Experience: Does It Make a Difference for Business Performance and Motivation?', *Journal of Business Venturing*, 22(2), 283–310.

Almus, M. (2002) 'What Characterizes a Fast-growing Firm?', *Applied Economics*, 34, 1497–508.

Almus, M. and Nerlinger, E.A. (1999) 'Growth of New Technology-based Firms: Which Factors Matter?', *Small Business Economics*, 13(2), 141–54.

Altinay, L. and Altinay, E. (2006) 'Determinants of Ethnic Minority Entrepreneurial Growth in the Catering Sector', *Service Industries Journal*, 26(2), 203–21.

Andersson, P. and Wadensjo, E. (2007) 'Do the Unemployed Become Successful Entrepreneurs?', *International Journal of Manpower*, 28(7), 604–26.

Basu, A. and Altinay, E. (2002) 'The Interaction between Culture and Entrepreneurship in London's Immigrant Business', *International Small Business Journal*, 20(4), 371–94.

Basu, A. and Goswami, A. (1999) 'Determinants of South Asian Entrepreneurial Growth in Britain: A Multivariate Analysis', *Small Business Economics*, 13(1), 57–70.

Baum, J.R. and Locke, E.A. (2004) 'The Relationship of Entrepreneurial Traits, Skill, and Motivation to Subsequent Venture Growth', *Journal of Applied Psychology*, 89(4), 587–98.

Baum, J.R. and Wally, S. (2003) 'Strategic Decision Speed and Firm Performance', *Strategic Management Journal*, 24(11), 1107–29.

Baum, J.R., Locke, E.A. and Smith, K.G. (2001) 'A Multidimensional Model of Venture Growth', *Academy of Management Journal*, 44(2), 292–303.

Becker-Blease, J.R. and Sohl, J.E. (2007) 'Do Women-owned Businesses Have Equal Access to Angel Capital?', *Journal of Business Venturing*, 22(4), 503–21.

Bennedsen, M., Nielsen, K.M., Perez-Gonzalez, F. and Wolfenzon, D. (2007) 'Inside the Family Firm: The Role of Families in Succession Decisions and Performance', *Quarterly Journal of Economics*, 122(2), 647–91.

Blanchflower, D.G., Levine, P.B. and Zimmerman, D.J. (2003) 'Discrimination in the Small Business Credit Market', *Review of Economics and Statistics*, 85(4), 930–43.

Bonaccorsi, A. and Giannangeli, S. (2005) *Why New Firms Never Get Large? Evidence on Post-entry Growth of Italian New Firms*. Rome: Institute for Studies and Economic Analyses.

Bosma, N., van Praag, M., Thurik, A.R. and De Wit, G. (2004) 'The Value of Human and Social Capital Investments for the Business Performance of Startups', *Small Business Economics*, 23(3), 227–36.

Box, T.M., Watts, L.R. and Hisrich, R.D. (1994) 'Manufacturing Entrepreneurs: An Empirical Study of the Correlates of Employment Growth in the Tulsa MSA and Rural East Texas', *Journal of Business Venturing*, 9(3), 261–70.

Brixy, U. and Kohaut, S. (1999) 'Employment Growth Determinants in New Firms in Eastern Germany', *Small Business Economics*, 13(2), 155–70.

Brüderl, J. and Preisendörfer, P. (1998) 'Network Support and the Success of Newly Founded Businesses', *Small Business Economics*, 10(3), 213–25.

Brüderl, J. and Preisendörfer, P. (2000) 'Fast-growing Businesses: Empirical Evidence From a German Study', *International Journal of Sociology*, 30(3), 45–70.

Brush, C., Carter, N., Gatewood, E., Green, P. and Hart, M. (2001) *'The Diana Project', Women Business Owners and Equity Capital: The Myths Dispelled*. Insight Report. Kansas City, MO: Kauffman Center for Entrepreneurial Leadership.

Burke, A.E., Fitzroy, F.R. and Nolan, M.A. (2000) 'When Less is More: Distinguishing between Entrepreneurial Choice and Performance', *Oxford Bulletin of Economics and Statistics*, 62(5), 565–87.

Burt, R.S. (1995) *Structural Holes: The Social Structure of Competition*. Cambridge, MA: Harvard University Press.

Capelleras, J.L. and Greene, F.J. (2008) 'The Determinants and Growth Implications of Venture Creation Speed', *Entrepreneurship and Regional Development*, 20(4), 317–43.

Carter, S., Shaw, E., Lam, W. and Wilson, F. (2007) 'Gender, Entrepreneurship, and Bank Lending: The Criteria and Processes Used by Bank Loan Officers in Assessing Applications', *Entrepreneurship Theory and Practice*, 31(3), 427–44.

Cassar, G. (2007) 'Money, Money, Money?: A Longitudinal Investigation of Entrepreneur Career Reasons, Growth Preferences and Achieved Growth', *Entrepreneurship and Regional Development*, 19(1), 89–107.

Casson, M. (1982) *The Entrepreneur*. Oxford: Martin Robertson.

Cliff, J.E. (1998) 'Does One Size Fit All?: Exploring the Relationship between Attitudes towards Growth, Gender, and Business Size', *Journal of Business Venturing*, 13(6), 523–42.

Coleman, S. (2007) 'The Role of Human and Financial Capital in the Profitability and Growth of Women-owned Small Firms', *Journal of Small Business Management*, 45(3), 303–19.

Cooney, T.M. (2005) 'Editorial: What is an Entrepreneurial Team?', *International Small Business Journal*, 23(3), 226–35.

Cooper, A.C., Gimeno-Gascon, F.J. and Woo, C.Y. (1994) 'Initial Human and Financial Capital as Predictors of New Venture Performance', *Journal of Business Venturing*, 9(5), 371–95.

Corbetta, G. and Salvato, C. (2004) 'Self-serving or Self-actualizing? Models of Man and Agency Costs in Different Types of Family Firms: A Commentary on "Comparing the Agency Costs of Family and Non-Family Firms: Conceptual Issues and Exploratory Evidence"', *Entrepreneurship: Theory and Practice*, 28(4), 355–62.

Cucculelli, M. and Micucci, G. (2008) 'Family Succession and Firm Performance: Evidence from Italian Family Firms', *Journal of Corporate Finance*, 14(1), 17–31.

Dahlqvist, J., Davidsson, P. and Wiklund, J. (2000) 'Initial Conditions as Predictors of New Venture Performance: A Replication and Extension of the Cooper *et al.* Study', *Enterprise and Innovation Management Studies*, 1(1), 1–17.

Davidsson, P., Achtenhagen, L. and Naldi, L. (2004) 'Research on Small Firm Growth: A Review', in *Proceedings of the European Institute of Small Business*. Paper Presented at ESIB Conference, Barcelona.

Delmar, F. and Wiklund, J. (2008) 'The Effect of Small Business Managers' Growth Motivation on Firm Growth: A Longitudinal Study', *Entrepreneurship: Theory and Practice*, 32(3), 437–57.

Delmar, F. and Shane, S. (2006) 'Does Experience Matter?: The Effect of Founding Team Experience on the Survival and Sales of Newly Founded Ventures', *Strategic Organization*, 4, 215–47.

Dyer, W.G. (2006) 'Examining the "Family Effect" on Firm Performance', *Family Business Review*, 19(4), 253–73.

Fairlie, R.W. and Robb, A.M. (2007) 'Why Are Black-owned Businesses Less Successful than White-owned Businesses?: The Role of Families, Inheritances, and Business Human Capital', *Journal of Labor Economics*, 25, 289–323.

Foreman-Peck, J., Makepeace, G. and Morgan, B. (2006) 'Growth and Profitability of Small and Medium-sized Enterprises: Some Welsh Evidence', *Regional Studies*, 40(4), 307–19.

Fraser, S. (2005) *Finance for Small and Medium-sized Enterprises: A Report on the 2004 UK Survey of SME Finances*. Coventry: CSME, University of Warwick.

Freel, M.S. and Robson, P.J.A. (2004) 'Small Firm Innovation, Growth and Performance: Evidence from Scotland and Northern England', *International Small Business Journal*, 22(6), 561–75.

Gartner, W.B. (1988) ' "Who is an Entrepreneur?" Is the Wrong Question', *American Journal of Small Business*, 12(1), 11–32.

Halborg, A., McPhie, D. and Storey, D.J. (1998) *Marketing Success in Fast Growth SMEs*. Warwick SME Marketing Case studies. The Marketing Council.

Harada, N. (2003) 'Who Succeeds as an Entrepreneur? An Analysis of the Post-entry Performance of New Firms in Japan', *Japan and the World Economy*, 15(2), 211–22.

Harper, D.A. (2008) 'Towards a Theory of Entrepreneurial Teams', *Journal of Business Venturing*, 23(6), 613–26.

Honig, B. (1998) 'What Determines Success? Examining the Human, Financial, and Social Capital of Jamaican Micro-entrepreneurs', *Journal of Business Venturing*, 13(5), 371–94.

Honjo, Y. (2004) 'Growth of New Start-up Firms: Evidence from the Japanese Manufacturing Industry', *Applied Economics Letters*, 11(1), 21–32.

Jones, T. and Ram, M. (2007) 'Re-embedding the Ethnic Business Agenda', *Work Employment and Society*, 21(3), 439–57.

Jovanovic, B. (1982) 'Selection and the Evolution of Industry', *Econometrica*, 50(3), 649–70.

Koeller, C.T. and Lechler, T.G. (2006) 'Employment Growth in High-tech New Ventures', *Journal of Labor Research*, 27(2), 135–47.

Lindelof, P. and Lofsten, H. (2002) 'Growth, Management and Financing of New Technology-based Firms: Assessing Value-added Contributions of Firms Located on and off Science Parks', *Omega-International Journal of Management Science*, 30(3), 143–54.

Lindh, T. and Ohlsson, H. (1996) 'Self-employment and Windfall Gains: Evidence from the Swedish Lottery', *Economic Journal*, 106, 1515–26.

Loebl, H. (1978) *Government Financed Factories and the Establishment of Industries by Refugees in the Special Areas of the North of England 1937–1961*. M Phil., Durham University.

McPherson, M.A. (1996) 'Growth of Micro and Small Enterprises in Southern Africa', *Journal of Development Economics*, 48(2), 253–77.

Marlow, S. and Patton, D. (2005) 'All Credit to Men? Entrepreneurship, Finance, and Gender', *Entrepreneurship: Theory and Practice*, 29(6), 717–35.

Marlow, S. (2002) 'Self-employed Women: Apart of, or Apart from, Feminist Theory?', *Entrepreneurship and Innovation*, 2(2), 83–91.

Mata, J. (1994) 'Firm Growth during Infancy', *Small Business Economics*, 6(1), 27–39.

Menzies, T.V., Diochon, M. and Gasse, Y. (2004) 'Examining Venture-related Myths Concerning Women Entrepreneurs', *Journal of Developmental Entrepreneurship*, 9, 89–107.

Morris, M.H., Miyasaki, N.N., Watters, C.E. and Coombes, S.M. (2006) 'The Dilemma of Growth: Understanding Venture Size Choices of Women Entrepreneurs', *Journal of Small Business Management*, 44(2), 221–44.

Munoz, L.G. and Perez, P.F. (2007) 'Female Entrepreneurship in Spain during the Nineteenth and Twentieth Centuries', *Business History Review*, 81(3), 495–515.

Oakley, A. (1973) *Sex, Gender and Society*. London: Temple Smith.

Parker, S.C. (2006) 'Learning about the Unknown: How Fast do Entrepreneurs Adjust Their Beliefs?', *Journal of Business Venturing*, 21(1), 1–26.

Perez-Gonzalez, F. (2006) 'Inherited Control and Firm Performance', *American Economic Review*, 96(5), 1559–88.

Persson, H. (2004) 'The Survival and Growth of New Establishments in Sweden, 1987–1995', *Small Business Economics*, 23(5), 423–40.

Pfeiffer, F. and Reize, F. (2000) 'Business Start Ups by the Unemployed: An Econometric Analysis Based on Firm Data', *Labour Economics*, 7(5), 629–63.

Ram, M. and Jones, T. (2008) 'Ethnic-minority Businesses in the UK: A Review of Research and Policy Developments', *Environment and Planning C-Government and Policy*, 26(2), 352–74.

Reid, G.C. and Smith, J.A. (2000) 'What Makes a New Business Start-up Successful?', *Small Business Economics*, 14(3), 165–82.

Robson, P.J.A. and Bennett, R.J. (2000) 'SME Growth: The Relationship with Business Advice and External Collaboration', *Small Business Economics*, 15(3), 193–208.

Roper, S. (1999) 'Modelling Small Business Growth and Profitability', *Small Business Economics*, 13(3), 235–52.

Saxenian, A. (2000) *Silicon Valley's New Immigrant Entrepreneurs*. Working Paper 15. San Diego, CA: Center for Comparative Immigration Studies University of California.

Schutjens, V.A.J.M. and Wever, E. (2002) 'Determinants of New Firm Success', *Papers in Regional Science*, 79, 135–59.

Shepherd, D. and Wiklund, J. (2009) 'Are We Comparing Apples with Apples or Apples with Oranges? Appropriateness of Knowledge Accumulation across Growth Studies', *Entrepreneurship: Theory and Practice*, 33(1), 105–23.

Shrader, R. and Siegel, D.S. (2007) 'Assessing the Relationship between Human Capital and Firm Performance: Evidence from Technology–based New Ventures', *Entrepreneurship Theory and Practice*, 31, 893–908.

Sleuwaegen, L. and Goedhuys, M. (2002) 'Growth of Firms in Developing Countries, Evidence from Côte d'Ivoire', *Journal of Development Economics*, 68(1), 117–35.

Stam, E. and Schutjens, V.A.J.M. (2005) 'The Fragile Success of Team Start Ups'. Papers on Entrepreneurship. Growth and Public Policy, Paper 1705. Jena: Max Planck Institute.

Storey, D.J. (1994a) *Understanding the Small Business Secto*r. London: Routledge.

Storey, D.J. (1994b) 'The Role of Legal Status in Influencing Bank Financing and New Firm Growth', *Applied Economics*, 26, 129–36.

Storey, D.J. (2004) 'Racial and Gender Discrimination in the Micro Firms Credit Market?: Evidence from Trinidad and Tobago', *Small Business Economics*, 23(5), 401–22.

Storey, D.J. (2005) *The Competitive Experience of UK SMEs: Fair and Unfair*. Report to the Competition Commission. London: OFT.

Taylor, M.P. (1999) 'Survival of the Fittest?: An Analysis of Self-employment Duration in Britain', *Economic Journal*, 109(454), C140–C155.

The Times (2008) *Sir Alan Sugar: Talking Tough*. http://entertainment.timesonline.co.uk/tol/arts_and_entertainment/tv_and_radio/article3618754.ece (accessed 26 March 2008).

Ucbasaran, D., Westhead, P. and Wright M. (2006) 'Habitual Entrepeneurs', in Casson, M., Yeung, B., Basu, A. and Wadeson, N. (eds), *The Oxford Handbook of Entrepreneurship*. Oxford: Oxford University Press, 461–83.

van der Sluis, J., van Praag, M. and Vijverberg, W. (2005) 'Entrepreneurship Selection and Performance: A Meta-Analysis of the Impact of Education in Developing Economies', *World Bank Economic Review*, 19(2), 225–61.

Verheul, I. and Thurik, R. (2001) 'Start-up Capital: "Does Gender Matter?"', *Small Business Economics*, 16(4), 329–45.

Westhead, P. and Cowling, M. (1997) 'Performance Contrasts between Family and Non-family Non-quoted Companies in the United Kingdom', *International Journal of Entrepreneurial Behaviour and Research*, 3(1), 30–52.

Westhead, P. and Cowling, M. (1998) 'Family Firm Research: The Need for a Methodological Re-think', *Entrepreneurship: Theory and Practice*, 23(1), 31–56.

Westhead, P. and Howorth, C. (2006) 'Ownership and Management Issues Associated with Family Firm Performance and Company Objectives', *Family Business Review*, 19(4), 301–16.

Wiklund, J., Davidsson, P. and Delmar, F. (2003) 'What Do They Think and Feel about Growth?: An Expectancy Value Approach to Small Business Managers' Attitudes toward Growth', *Entrepreneurship: Theory and Practice*, 27 (Spring), 247–70.

Wiklund, J. and Shepherd, D. (2003) 'Aspiring for, and Achieving Growth: The Moderating Role of Resources and Opportunities', *Journal of Management Studies*, 40(8), 1919–41.

14 Growing the business – at start-up factors

Key learning objectives

By the end of this chapter you should:

- Understand the range of 'at start-up' factors commonly associated with business growth
- Be able to compare and contrast 'at start-up' factors
- Critically evaluate the importance of 'at start-up' factors.

14.1 Introduction

Anyone setting up a business has many decisions to make when they begin. One of the first decisions is the level of resources that they are going to devote to exploit the perceived opportunity. For example, should they devote modest resources to 'test pilot' their idea? Or do they believe that the nature of the opportunity demands that they have to enter the market aggressively to exploit the opportunity? The origins of the French company L'Oréal followed the first pattern. The founder of L'Oréal was the chemist Eugène Schueller, who developed a hair dye called Auréole and sold it to Parisian hairdressers. He later expanded into shampoos and soaps. By contrast, Fred Smith required huge amounts of venture capital funding to set up FedEx. This is because FedEx was set up to deliver cargo overnight throughout the US. To do that, Smith needed lots of airplanes and workers if he was to have 'a freight service company with 550-mile-per-hour delivery trucks'.

Another choice is the legal form of the business. The business owner can either elect to incorporate their business or they can choose to be unincorporated. This choice is dependent upon what value they place upon limited liability, the ease in terms of speed and cost of establishing a limited company, any tax advantages that accrue and the costs of compliance with the legal responsibilities. These are all very important considerations. For example, Germany in 2008 introduced a new law because it realised that its own form of limited liability – GmbH – was losing ground to the UK's 'Ltd'. The perception was that it was it was easier and cheaper to set up using 'Ltd', easier to change the corporate structure of a 'Ltd', and that 'Ltd' had a better international 'brand' name.

A third choice to be made is what the business is going to sell. The choice of sector is, therefore, important. In a recession, for example, consumers are more likely to cut back on non-food items such as electrical goods. They may also be more price-conscious and be more likely to use discount food retailers. This may have implications for a business proposing to offer high quality or expensive goods.

A final choice is the location of the business. Should the owner begin the business at home, where rental costs are either low or nil, or would a home-based business lack credibility and lead to lower sales? If the decision is made to seek formal business premises, then should these be close to the entrepreneur's home to enable easy access, or should they be in a place where networking with other businesses is easier?

This chapter looks at these four common choices – initial size, legal form, sector, and location – and how they impact on business growth. We begin by examining the influence of initial size, before considering the influence of legal form, sector and location. To examine the role of each, we return to the 36 growth studies identified in Chapter 13. Again, these multivariate studies are used to identify if the four factors have a positive (+), negative (−) or non-significant (n.s.) impact on business growth. The chapter examines the importance of these four choices in relation to business growth.

14.2 Initial size

Chapter 11 identified that a key topic in growth studies was the validity of 'Gibrat's Law'. This 'Law' suggested that growth was independent of the size of the business. In other words, smaller businesses do not grow any faster or slower than larger businesses. Despite this prediction, two alternative and competing theories suggest that initial size at start up is important in explaining subsequent growth.

The first of these is that businesses which initially begin small will grow faster. This is because, to survive, they have to reach the minimum efficient scale (MES) of production. If they do not, they are likely to face closure because their costs are too high. In order to survive, therefore, they must grow to the MES level. The alternative approach is to suggest that larger businesses are the most likely to grow. This is because such businesses have sufficient human and financial capital to immediately overcome any inefficiency problems and are able to 'hit the ground running'.

It is possible to reconcile these two approaches to size. This relies on there being two types of start up. The first are those that wish to grow just enough to survive. The second are those that wish to achieve longer-term, but more substantial, growth. The first group grow quickly initially to achieve MES, but seek no further growth. The second group start large and continue to grow. Almus and Nerlinger (1999), in their study of German start ups, found a U-shaped relationship between initial size and subsequent growth which is compatible with both theories.

Chapter 11, however, identified that a 'stylised fact' of business growth was that younger and smaller businesses were more likely to grow. In the tables that we use in this chapter (see description of the studies used in Chapter 13), there are 21 measures of initial size. In overall terms, the evidence on initial size is mixed: five measures of growth indicate a negative relationship (−), nine a positive relationship (+), and a further six indicate that the relationship between initial size and business growth is non-significant. There is also no clear pattern dependent upon the type of measure used. For example, various studies using an employment measure have found a positive, negative and non-significant relationship. This reflects the nature of the conflicting theories and examples outlined above.

Our view is that there is support for the idea that new businesses need to grow quickly if are to survive. What seems less clear is whether starting relatively large (or small) subsequent growth.

14.3 Legal form

A second key choice is legal form. If the entrepreneur or incorporation, they obtain some advantages over unincorpor means that a company becomes a separate legal identity independ

of this, owners have limited liability. This means that if the business is liquidated, personal assets cannot be required as payments for business debt. Instead, it is the assets *in* the business that are liable. Being incorporated also allows businesses to 'trade' equity shares to increase the capital base of the company, eases the selling of the business, and potentially offers tax advantages.

Chittenden and Sloan (2006) demonstrate how incorporation can provide financial advantages. In 2002, the UK government introduced a zero per cent rate of corporation tax (taxes paid on a company's profits or incomes) to increase the likelihood of them retaining profits, increasing investments and, thereby, growing faster. One consequence of this was it created a tax 'loophole' where business owners could gain favourable tax treatment if they incorporated. The net result was a 43 per cent increase in new incorporations and a loss of more than £1 billion in tax revenues. In 2004, the UK government 'reformed' corporation tax.

However, incorporation also has disadvantages for the business owner. First, it may be a 'fiction' to presume that business owners enjoy limited liability. Often collateral – usually in the form of the business owner's own house – is required by external financiers such as banks as 'security' against a business loan. This collateral is often sought irrespective of the legal form of the business. Second, with limited liability there are more regulatory checks and balances in place. For example, German incorporated businesses still need a minimum share capital of €25,000. There is also a requirement to file audited financial accounts to the authorities. Incorporation, therefore, increases the regulation and compliance costs for the business.

Business owners that choose not to be incorporated can gain tax advantages over the average employed individual. Chittenden and Sloan (2006) examine the differential tax treatments between the self-employed and the employed. They find that people choose non-incorporation (self-employment) because it means that they have to pay less tax and avoid some of the burden of employment legislation. Being 'under the radar' may also more easily allow the unincorporated business to take cash payments for work and avoid tax on these payments.

It is not only the risks or potential rewards that determine the choice of legal form. Earlier on, we identified that one advantage of limited liability was that it was akin to a 'brand'. Arguably, being a limited company reassures suppliers and customers about the 'credibility' of the business. Freedman and Godwin (1994) report that credibility was the second most important reason – after limited liability – for businesses choosing to incorporate. In terms of business growth, the subsequent suggestion is that those businesses that incorporate are more likely to grow. This is because credibility with customers and suppliers is more important to such businesses, encouraging them to accept the reporting arrangements of incorporation, such as producing audited public accounts.

The evidence of the impact of incorporation is shown in Tables 14.1a, 14.1b and 14.1c. Here there are 15 studies, using 20 measures of business growth. Only one study finds a negative relationship between incorporation and growth. A further six find a non-significant relationship, but 13 find a positive relationship. This pattern is found using several measures of growth (including employment and sales measures). It also appears to hold in very different countries (e.g. Lithuania, the Ivory Coast and Wales). Indeed, of the variables influencing the growth of small businesses, choice of legal form is one of the most consistently influential.

What underpins this powerful association? One interpretation is that it is a proxy for 'team' entrepreneurship. In Chapter 13, we discussed the importance of teams in explaining business growth. We noted that one of the difficulties in understanding whether teams are important is that team entrepreneurship is strongly correlated with incorporation, since incorporation generally requires the involvement of more than one individual in the business. It is difficult, therefore, to separate out whether growth is due to incorporation or team entrepreneurship.

However, incorporation may also be driven by the underlying motivations of the business owner – so that the business owner who expects the business to grow will seek to enhance

Table 14.1a	'At-start' variables: employment growth			
Study	**Initial size**	**Legal form**	**Sector**	**Location**
Cooper *et al.* (1994) US			Retail and personal services –	
Storey (1994) UK		+	Manufacturing +	
Schutjens and Wever (2000) Netherlands	+	n.s.	Manufacturing, construction, business services +	
Brüderl and Preisendörfer (2000) Germany	+	+		
Mata (1994) Portugal	Log of industry size +, log of MES +, Suboptimal scale –			
Almus and Nerlinger (1999) Germany	+	+	High tech +	U-shaped relationship with population density
Brixy and Kohaut (1999) East Germany	–	+	Energy/mining, manufacturing, construction, transportation, business services +	Positive growth if located close to the border with West Germany
Brüderl and Preisendörfer (1998) Germany	n.s.	+	n.s.	
Aidis and van Praag (2007) Lithuania		+	Construction, manufacturing +, business and personal services –	
Altinay and Altinay (2006) UK		n.s.	n.s.	
McPherson (1995) African countries			Construction, chemicals, services +, real estate –	+
Robson and Bennett (2000) UK	+			
Persson (2004) Sweden	–		Mining +	n.s.
Sleuwaegen and Goedhuys (2002) Ivory Coast		+	Textiles +	n.s.
Capelleras and Greene (2008) Spain	–		n.s.	n.s.

its credibility by choosing a prestigious legal form. Business owners choose incorporation because it is in line with their motivation to grow their business. Finally, incorporation is chosen because it is a 'brand'. Again, it is difficult to separate out any 'brand' advantage from the other practical reasons for electing to become incorporated. All we can say is that, as our German example at the start of the chapter indicates, the international resonance of the t' 'Ltd' should not be under-estimated.

There remains a need for further research in this area. For example, Chittend qualitative research indicates that there is a need for more conceptual clarity evidence on why individuals choose a particular legal form. We judge tha* the pioneering Freedman and Godwin's (1994) findings that taxation, ° expectations of growth will continue to be the dominant influence* between incorporation and new business growth points to the stand whether this link reflects owner motivation, the brand or evading tax (see Chapter 20).

Table 14.1b	'At-start' variables: sales growth			
Study	**Initial size**	**Legal form**	**Sector**	**Location**
Honjo (2004) Japan			Growing sectors +	Tokyo CBD +
Basu and Goswami (1999) UK			Wholesale –	
Brüderl and Preisendörfer, 1998 (Germany)	n.s.	n.s.	n.s.	
Aidis and van Praag (2007) Lithuania		+	hotel/catering, business and personal services –	
Roper (1999) Ireland	n.s.			
Roper (1999) Ireland			n.s.	
Robson and Bennett (2000) UK	n.s.			
Coleman (2007) US		–		
Coleman (2007) US		n.s.		
Sleuwaegen and Goedhuys (2002) Ivory Coast		+	n.s.	–
Harada (2003) Japan	+		food –, business services, construction +	

Table 14.1c	'At-start' variables: other measures			
Study	**Initial size**	**Legal form**	**Sector**	**Location**
Roper (1999) Ireland	+	n.s.		
Aidis and van Praag (2007) Lithuania		n.s.	n.s.	
Harada (2003) Japan	n.s.		Food –, business services, construction +	
Pffeifer and Reize (2000) Germany		+	Data processing +	Bremen has fast growth concentration
Almus (2002) Germany	–	+	Construction, transport and communication, bus. services (not knowledge-based) +	n.s.
Dahlqvist et al. (2000) Sweden	–	+	Retail and private service +	Rural –
Wiklund and Shepherd (2003) Sweden	n.s.		n.s.	
Bonaccorsi and Giannangeli (2005) Italy	+		Manufacturing, construction +	
Foreman-Peck et al. (2006) Wales	–	+	Professions +, other –	
Harada, 2003 (Japan)	+		n.s.	

Our view is that the statistical relationship between the choice of the incorporated legal form and new/small business growth is robust. Indeed, it is probably more consistently strong than any other relationship we identify across all the pre start-up, at start-up and post start-up factors. What is less clear is the underlying cause: does it reflect the tax regime, minimising down-side losses, teams, motivation or 'brand'?

14.4 Sector

Figure 14.1 shows the profound changes in the sectoral composition of employment in three selected countries – Netherlands, the UK and the US – over the last 300 years. Agriculture was dominant in the UK and the US as a proportion of employment in 1700. In the Netherlands, it represented 40 per cent of employment. By 2002, agriculture represented less than 5 per cent of employment in all three countries. Figure 14.1 also shows that manufacturing represented a bigger share of employment in the UK in 1890 than in either the US or the Netherlands. This reflects that the UK was the 'workshop of the world' during this period. By the twenty-first century, services had come to dominate sectoral composition in the US, UK and the Netherlands.

Figure 14.1 also shows that demand – and how businesses respond to demand – does change over time. The most marked changes have been the switch from agriculture to manufacturing and into services. This is an ongoing trend. Illustrative of this has been the increase in the number of Real Estate, Renting and Business Activities sector businesses in the UK. In 1994, there were 607,132 such businesses. By 2007, there were 1,130,890 such businesses. This represents an increase of 54 per cent over the period (source: BERR, 2008a). This is not unique to the UK. Bryson *et al.* (1997) have argued that small service businesses have intangible, competitive advantages: '... for small business service businesses the most important competitive advantages are "personal attention to client needs", "specialised expertise or products" and "established reputation"' (Bryson *et al.*, 1997: 352).

The way business is conducted has also changed since the era of mass production and standardised goods. The minimum efficient scale (MES) has fallen in many industries, allowing smaller businesses to become much more competitive, as they do not necessarily face a cost disadvantage. An example of this is the Spanish fashion retailer Zara (see Illustration overleaf).

How a business selects its sector and how it tries to protect itself from competition are pivotal to business success. This is the essential point behind Porter's (1980) five forces framework. This framework is shown in Figure 14.2, which suggests that an understanding of how sectors or industries operate is integral to business success. There is a need to consider the

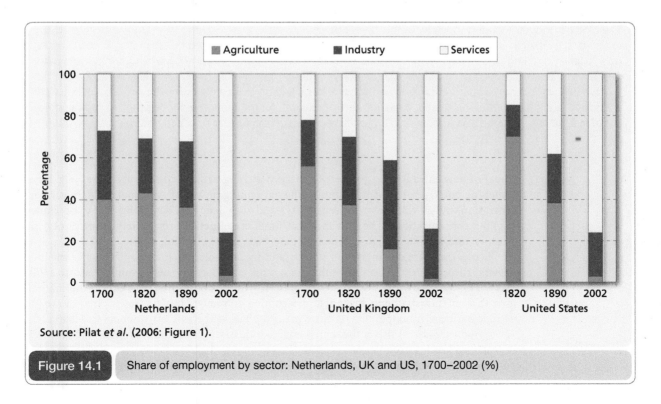

Source: Pilat *et al.* (2006: Figure 1).

Figure 14.1   Share of employment by sector: Netherlands, UK and US, 1700–2002 (%)

Illustration	Zara

Tightly controlled costs have helped Zara to grow worldwide, across 68 countries.

Zara was originally set up by Amancio Ortega in 1975 to offer cheaper versions of popular high-end clothing. The clothing industry tended to follow at this time a business model that had long lead times and little ability to respond quickly to changes in fashion. Arguably, this process was exacerbated by the shift of production to Asia to take advantage of lower costs. What Zara did was to vastly reduce the time between producing its own designs and the distribution of its ranges, by locating production closer to its markets. This allowed Zara to be much more responsive to customer needs and cut the stock tied up in its stores. Smaller production batches and lower stock levels free up valuable cash (its working capital) for the business. Since opening its first store in 1975, Zara has expanded so that, by 2007, it operated in 68 countries and had 3,691 stores (Inditex, 2009).

threat of new entrants (e.g. barriers to entry, switching or sunk costs), substitutes (e.g. buyer switching costs, pricing of substitutes), the bargaining power of customers (e.g. buyer concentration, buyer volume, price sensitivity) and suppliers (e.g. switching costs, substitutes, supplier concentration). The fifth and final 'force' is competitive rivalry (e.g. number of competitors, rate of industry growth, exit barriers, economies of scale).

Clearly, there are advantages in understanding how such factors may influence business growth. Klepper (2002) has shown that for a range of industries there would appear to a 'life-cycle'. This generally follows a standard pattern with business entry and exit in the infancy/growth of an industry being high, before becoming dominated by a few (oligopoly) or even by a single business (monopoly) in its more 'mature' phase as the 'sun sets' upon it (see Chapter 5).

A good example of this is the search engine industry. Early pioneers in this industry were websites such as Infoseek (launched 1994), Lycos (1994), Alta Vista (1995). None of these search engines have a significant presence today. In 1998, Google was launched, to be followed

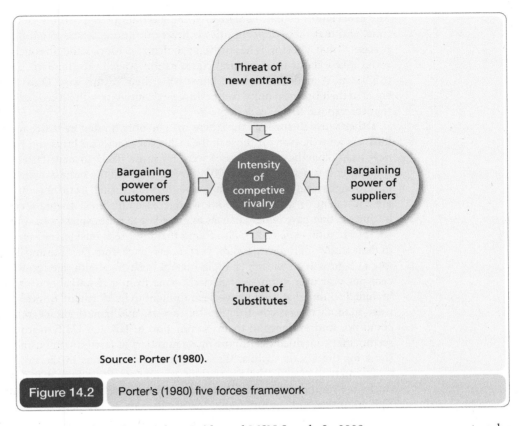

Source: Porter (1980).

| Figure 14.2 | Porter's (1980) five forces framework |

by other search engines such as Baidu and MSN Search. In 2008, a new company, set up by former employees of Google, was launched. This search engine – Cuil (pronounced cool) – initially had around 0.4 per cent of internet traffic (according to the website Alexa). By January 2009, this had slipped to 0.0055 per cent, suggesting that there was little room for new (small) entrants to grow in this industry: Google holds the monopoly, to the extent that 'to Google' someone or something has become synonymous with 'searching the web'.

Subsequent research has focused on whether particular sectors are more likely to grow than others. The expectation is that 'sunrise' rather 'sunset' industries are more likely to experience growth. Typical of sunrise industries are 'high-tech' manufacturing industries such as air- and spacecraft, pharmaceuticals, telecommunications and precision, medical and optical instruments. In terms of service sectors, equivalent high-tech businesses include software, management consultancy, tourism, post and communications, and research and development.

| Illustration | Growth in the UK's creative industries |

The UK has a number of 'creative industries' (e.g. advertising, architecture, fashion, leisure software, film and video, radio and TV, music and the performing arts, and publishing). DCMS (2009) suggest that these industries are pivotal to the UK economy in terms of exports (£16 billion in 2006) and in terms of gross value added (6.4 per cent in 2006). DCMS (2009) also shows that the 'creative industries' grew by an average of 4 per cent per annum between 1997 and 2006. By comparison, the rest of the economy, over the same period, grew by only 3 per cent. Part of this was the strong growth of two industries: software, computer games and electronic publishing (10 per cent per annum), and radio and TV (8 per cent per annum). Creative industries also had a higher average employment growth rate (2 per cent) than the rest of the UK economy (1 per cent) and two sectors – software, computer games and electronic publishing, and the design and designer fashion sectors – saw employment grow by 5 per cent.

The expectation is that the nature of these economic opportunities is likely to change over time, and that these opportunities will vary from one sector to another. However, defining precisely what a 'sector' is has proven problematic. Mezias and Starbuck (2003) reported that when asked about their sectoral classification (called the standard industrial classification (SIC)), most managers did not know what their 'sector' was: 'Only 5 of our 70 managers equated their business units' competitive environments with SIC codes or used industry labels that correspond to SIC codes' (p. 8).

Other research suggests that there may be only limited evidence to associate sector with business growth, even for those in the technology sectors. Almus and Nerlinger (1999) found new technology-based businesses were no more likely to have faster employment growth than other businesses. Almus (2002) further analysed the same dataset and found that 'There are no signs that technology-intensive manufacturing branches [in Germany, 'branches' are equivalent to 'sectors'] and knowledge-based business related service sectors consist of businesses that have better chances to grow fast than (businesses in) other economic sectors' (p. 1507). Autio *et al.* (2000) also found that high-tech businesses were not over-represented in their study of Finnish 'gazelles'. Further evidence from Deloitte and Touche (1998) showed that fast-growth businesses (middle-market businesses with sales growing faster than 30 per cent per year over a four-year period) came from a remarkable diversity of sectors. These included sectors that might have been thought to be 'dormant' or even in 'decline' (e.g. footwear manufacturers, construction businesses, mechanical engineers). BERR (2008b) also could not find evidence in their examination of UK and US fast-growth businesses of any sectors that contained disproportionate numbers of fast-growth businesses. Acs *et al.* (2008) show for the US that whilst there are sectoral variations in the proportion of businesses achieving high growth, these variations are modest. For example, in a high-tech sector such 'Instruments and Related' 3.89 per cent of businesses were classed as high impact in 2006. This compares with a more traditional sector such as 'Leather Products' where 2.57 per cent of businesses were 'high impact'. On these grounds, Acs *et al.* say:

> High-impact firms exist in all industries. While some industries have a higher percentage of these firms, they are not limited to high-technology industries.
>
> *(p. 1)*

Our view is that whilst it is the case that fast-growth businesses are more likely to be concentrated in some sectors than others, it is also true that an examination of 'growth sectors' alone would lead to the exclusion of many – and perhaps the majority – of fast-growth businesses.

14.5 Location

Where an owner chooses to locate their business *ought* to be associated with business growth. As we saw in Chapter 12, there are three main theoretical grounds for believing that there are advantages (positive externalities) in businesses 'co-locating' with other businesses. These are: access to pools of labour; cost advantages; and the possibility of knowledge spillovers.

Having other businesses around them makes it more likely that individual businesses will be able to exploit price and quality advantages. A ready stock of workers opens up the possibility of employing specialist workers. Such workers may increase the quality of what a business has to offer. Being close to suppliers also means that they are likely to save – at the very least – on transport costs. Finally, because knowledge is often 'tacit', there are likely to be informational benefits from being close to other businesses. In other words, businesses can get the opportunity to understand business practices much more clearly ('know-how') and develop their existing contacts ('know-who').

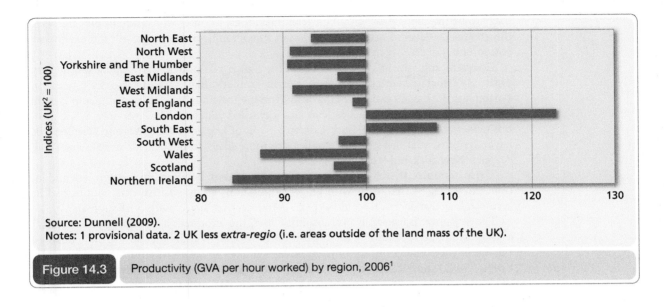

Source: Dunnell (2009).
Notes: 1 provisional data. 2 UK less *extra-regio* (i.e. areas outside of the land mass of the UK).

| Figure 14.3 | Productivity (GVA per hour worked) by region, 2006[1] |

These three externalities suggest that any individual is likely to gain benefits from being 'co-located' with other businesses. These advantages are called agglomeration advantages because they either allow individual businesses to save or benefit from the presence of other businesses.

The expectation, therefore, is that fast-growth businesses are more likely to be found in urban areas and, more particularly, in large urban conurbations. There is evidence to suggest just such an association between location and business growth. First, at a general level, some regions in the world are more 'productive' than other regions. Figure 14.3, for example, shows an index of Gross Value Added (a measure of productivity) where the average = 100 on the horizontal axis. It shows that the southern regions of England (i.e. London and the South East) have higher rates of gross value added – are more productive – than all the other regions of England as well as Wales, Scotland and Northern Ireland.

Martin and Cambridge Econometrics (1999) also show that Europe's most productive regions are found in the 'hot banana' (the area between Milan and London, containing northern Italy, southern Germany, south-east France, the Ruhr area, Île de France, Belgium, the Netherlands and south-east England) and that these are the very same regions that are most likely to possess exporting, innovative or high-tech businesses. These regional differences are also evident in North America. Greene *et al.*'s (2007) review of regional competitiveness points out that the evidence tends to show that the East Coast (e.g. New York) and the West Coast states (e.g. California) of the US perform more strongly than other states.

Another general indicator of the importance of location is the association between labour and location. The argument is that areas with businesses that have access to specialist workers are more likely to host fast-growth businesses. Von Hipple (1994) suggested that knowledge can often be costly to acquire and difficult to transfer and use between people. In other words, knowledge tends to be 'sticky'. So, entrepreneurs are more likely to gain benefits from know-ledge spillovers if they are located close to the people that hold relevant 'knowledge'. Audia and Rider (2005) also argue that proximity provides a 'blueprint' for new entrepreneurs by, first, providing access to pre-existing 'role models', and second by giving them the necessary experi-ence and contacts to successfully exploit ideas. Florida (2002) has also argued that there is a more subtle association between labour and business growth. His interest is in 'bohemians', whom he classifies as those in particular creative occupations such as authors, painters and performers. He finds that those geographical areas with higher levels of 'bohemians' are more likely to be the same areas with high-tech businesses. In other words, the implication is that the greater the level of artistic 'creativity' in a geographic area, the greater the likelihood of entrepreneurial activity in that area.

Hoogstra and van Dikjk (2004) show, for Dutch businesses, that population density is positively associated with employment growth. Similarly, Baptista and Preto (2007) examined Portuguese businesses and found that employment growth is likely to be stronger in 'dynamic' metropolitan areas. BERR (2008b) has also identified that, in the UK, very many fast-growth businesses are located in the south-eastern regions of England, whilst Acs and Mueller (2008) have identified that fast-growth 'gazelles' are more likely to be located in cities such as Los Angeles, New York and Houston.

These examples, therefore, imply a positive association between business growth and location. They suggest that areas with bigger populations enjoy positive externalities and have access to bigger markets. It would appear, therefore, that 'space matters' (Krugman 1995).

The evidence, however, is not absolute. First, the 'productivity' of a region is clearly an average of the performance of all its businesses: very many individual fast-growth businesses can be located and grow in 'unfavourable' regions, or in more rural areas. Vaessen and Keeble (1995) showed that 'how' a business did business was more important than 'where' it did business. Acs *et al.* (2008) also argue that in the US 'High-impact businesses exist in almost all regions, states, metropolitan statistical areas (MSAs) and counties' (p. 1).

The influence of location on business growth is also unclear if we consider four specific 'tests' of this relationship. These tests are:

- universities;
- science parks;
- 'born globals'; and
- the location decisions of individual business owners.

We might expect, because of the intellectual capital housed within them, that universities are more likely to host fast-growth businesses. The obvious examples of these include Palo Alto in California (Stanford University) and Boston (MIT). The early work by Jaffe (1989) documented the close link between university research and business patent usage. Association with particular universities, however, does not necessarily guarantee growth. Lawson (1999) points out that none of the businesses located around Cambridge, UK, became a large multinational enterprise, although subsequently Autonomy achieved that status.

Second, it might be anticipated that businesses located on **science parks** are more likely to grow than otherwise comparable businesses, since a science park provides an environment in which the co-locating of knowledge workers occurs. Westhead and Cowling (1995) conducted a study matching businesses located on UK science parks with similar businesses that were not located on a science park. They found no statistically significant differences between these two types of business in terms of business growth. Lindelof and Lofsten (2002) also conducted a similar 'matched-pairs' analysis of Swedish science park and off-park businesses. They found no significant differences in terms of patenting and new products. However, Yang *et al.* (2009) found the productivity of R&D of technology-based businesses on science parks in Taiwan was greater than that of the off-park businesses, whilst Squicciarini (2009) finds that patenting is enhanced by a science park location. This is discussed further in Chapter 21.

A third test is to consider the growth of **'born globals'**. Oviatt and McDougall (1994) define these as '. . . a business organization that, from inception, seeks to derive significant competitive advantage from the use of resources and the sale of outputs in multiple countries. The distinguishing feature of these start-ups is that their origins are international, as demonstrated by observable and significant commitments of resources (e.g. material, people, financing, time) in more than one nation' (p. 49).

Illustration	Logitech, born global

An example of this is the development of Logitech, the computer peripheral company. Set up in Switzerland in 1981, one of its first actions was to open an office in California close to the developing personal computer market. By 1986, it had opened up a manufacturing facility in Taiwan. Businesses such as Logitech are examples of enterprises that have 'escaped' their location. In other words, such enterprises leapt over the steady and sequential movement from a 'home' location to 'export' markets by quickly moving to operate at a global scale.

'Born globals', therefore, appear to 'break the rules', because their location at start up exerts no influence on their growth. However, whilst they are interesting curiosities, their significance should not be over-estimated for four reasons:

1 Agglomeration advantages continue to evolve and persist. It is no accident, for example, that Logitech sought to site its first office in California. Indeed, its move to California can be argued to reflect the persistence of, rather than the disappearance of, location factors.

2 The 'born global' concept has been operationalised in a wide range of ways so definitions are highly diverse (Gabrielsson *et al.* 2008). This means that we may often be comparing 'apples' with 'pears'.

3 Fan and Phan (2007) argue that the shape of the 'home' market may be just as important in explaining being 'born global' as the external market. This is an important point because 'born globals' remain largely a phenomenon of small open economies such as those found in Scandinavia and Australasia. In countries such as New Zealand, Finland or Australia the 'size' of the home market is usually modest, making it perhaps inevitable that exporting becomes important.

4 It has to be recognised that, perhaps because they are so rare, 'born globals' have been the focus of more attention than is justified given their economic contribution.

The final test is to examine what motivates **the location decisions of individual business owners**. For new and smaller businesses, the evidence suggests that it is based heavily on 'lifestyle' choices (e.g. freedom, being in control) (Birley and Westhead 1994).

Illustration	Grand Theft Auto's Scottish roots

The production of the Grand Theft Auto series of games was led by Leslie Benzies. Benzies could have gone to the US to develop Grand Theft Auto III and IV. Instead, he chose to stay in Scotland, 'For the weather,' says Benzies. 'There is no sun. If I am abroad I can sit in the sun for a whole day and do nothing and feel great. If I sit outside here, I'm fidgeting after a couple of minutes. There are a lot of us here. This is our home. I love Scotland. I like the people.'

Source: *Sunday Times*, 27 April 2008. © Sunday Times, 27 April 2008/nisyndication.com.

Figueiredo *et al.* (2002) also identify 'home' as a pivotal explanation of where Portuguese entrepreneurs choose to locate their business. They suggest this is because the location decision is often influenced by personal business contacts and family networks. Indeed, 'home'-based businesses account for a high percentage of all businesses: 67 per cent of the self-employed in the US (BLS 2005), and 46 per cent of all businesses in the UK (Enterprise Nation 2007). Arguably, such home-based businesses have little potential to become growers because they typically involve a part-time activity and are marked by high rates of business closure (Brodie *et al.*, 2002). However, it is not always the case that such enterprises have limited growth potential or that their owners lack ambition. Perhaps the most frequently quoted exception was the setting up of Hewlett-Packard by William Hewlett and David Packard in 1938. They began their business using a garage in Palo Alto, California. Working from home may also mean that business overheads are lower which can provide a cost advantage to the small business. Equally, because of the internet, arguably it has become easier and more accepted that businesses can be successful run from someone's home.

However, it has proven difficult to determine the extent to which initial location decisions influence the growth of a new business. Stam (2007) argues that it is unsurprising that so many businesses are set up at, or near to, the home of the entrepreneur, because most economic opportunities that are seen as exploitable are found in local markets. The choice to locate a business at home is a rational economic one as well as being compatible with a lifestyle choice. Stam (2007) also argues that when new businesses begin, there is a great deal of uncertainty about future profits. Choosing to locate the business at home reduces this risk by having a lower cost base, and so, again, the choice of a home location reflects economic as well as 'lifestyle' influences.

In terms of actual fast-growth businesses, Greene *et al.*'s (2008) study of new businesses in England found that the businesses that moved most frequently were more likely to have grown faster than non-movers but this again is likely to be an outcome, rather than a cause, of growth. Stam's (2007) more qualitative evidence suggests that fast-growth businesses – what he calls 'butterflies' – are likely to be radically different from start ups ('caterpillars'). He indicates, however, that when business do experience fast growth it is still likely that they will stay within their 'home' region or country. In other words, fast-growth businesses often tend to stay close to where they were initially set up. He argues that this is largely due to economic costs already sunk into the business.

Our view is that the evidence suggests the location of a new business does influence its performance. All else equal, new businesses grow faster if they are located in and sell into buoyant prosperous markets. However, the evidence is not as clear as we might expect. Fast-growing small businesses are found in many 'unfavourable' locations. Our four 'tests' of the relationship between location and business performance – universities, science parks, 'born globals' and individual location decisions – produced mixed results which, if anything, suggest that an unfavourable location was not a major hindrance to business growth.

Summary

This chapter has considered four basic choices that are made by the owner(s) when starting their business: initial size, legal form, sector and location.

The evidence on the impact of initial size on subsequent growth is mixed. It suggests that smaller and younger businesses grow more quickly than larger and older businesses, but that these effects are only clear for very young and very small businesses.

A second potential influence upon new and small business growth is that of legal form. The frequency with which this link with fast growth occurs in studies, and its robustness across countries, is remarkable, with limited companies consistently being more likely to exhibit faster growth than those businesses choosing other legal forms. Research has yet to satisfactorily resolve the reason for this: is it the taxation advantages? Is it the credibility advantages? Is it the importance of teams? What is clear is that it is not based on lower costs or administrative simplicity, since these are both higher in limited companies than for other legal forms.

Our review of the impact of sector demonstrated the error of assuming fast-growing businesses were heavily concentrated in a narrow range of sectors – particularly those characterised as 'sunrise' or 'high-technology' sectors. Whilst these sectors were more likely to have faster-growing businesses than those in more traditional sectors, two points need emphasising. First, fast-growing businesses were found even in declining sectors. Second, focusing exclusively upon the 'sunrise' sectors only identifies a tiny proportion of 'fast growers'. The message to the aspiring business owner is that there is the potential for growth in all sectors.

Finally, the choice of location can influence business growth. The chapter shows that business growth is not evenly distributed across space, and that growth is more likely in businesses located in, and selling into, buoyant local markets. Beyond that, the impact of location is less clear, with, for example, favoured locations such as science parks failing to consistently demonstrate that they host an especially disproportionate number of fast-growth businesses.

Questions for discussion

1 What factors should the new business owner take into account when deciding where to locate their enterprise?

2 Review the case for, and against, starting a new business from home.

3 What explains why it is that new businesses that begin as limited companies grow faster than those choosing other legal forms?

4 What is 'minimum efficient scale'? What insights does the concept provide into the early growth of a new enterprise?

5 What are 'born global' enterprises? Does their presence imply that, in a globalised world, location is unimportant?

6 Why is it that fast-growth businesses are found in sectors which are often in terminal decline?

References

Acs, Z.J. and Mueller, P. (2008) 'Employment Effects of Business Dynamics: Mice, Gazelles and Elephants', *Small Business Economics*, 30(1), 85–100.

Acs, Z.J., Parsons, W. and Tracy, S. (2008) *High-impact Firms: Gazelles Revisited*. Washington, DC: SBA.

Aidis, R. and van Praag, M. (2007) 'Illegal Entrepreneurial Experience: Does It Make a Difference for Business Performance and Motivation?', *Journal of Business Venturing*, 22(2), 283–310.

Almus, M. (2002) 'What Characterizes a Fast-growing Firm', *Applied Economics*, 34, 1497–508.

Almus, M. and Nerlinger, E.A. (1999) 'Growth of New Technology-based Firms: Which Factors Matter?', *Small Business Economics*, 13(2), 141–54.

Altinay, L. and Altinay, E. (2006) 'Determinants of Ethnic Minority Entrepreneurial Growth in the Catering Sector', *Service Industries Journal*, 26(2), 203–21.

Audia, P.G. and Rider, C.I. (2005) 'A Garage and an Idea: What More Does an Entrepreneur Need?', *California Management Review*, 48(1), 6–28.

Autio, E., Arenius, P. and Wallenius, H. (2000) *Economic Impact of Gazelle Businesses in Finland*. Working Papers Series 2000:3. Helsinki: Helsinki University of Technology, Institute of Strategy and International Business.

Basu, A. and Goswami, A. (1999) 'Determinants of South Asian Entrepreneurial Growth in Britain: A Multivariate Analysis', *Small Business Economics*, 13(1), 57–70.

BERR (2008*a*) *Enterprise Directorate: Small and Medium Enterprise Statistics for the UK and Regions*. http://stats.berr.gov.uk/ed/sme/ (accessed 1 February 2009).

BERR (2008*b*) *High-growth Firms in the UK: Lessons from an Analysis of Comparative UK Performance*. BERR Economics Paper 3. London: BERR.

Baptista, R. and Preto, M.T. (2007) 'New Firm Formation and Employment Growth: Differences across Regions and Start-ups'. Paper presented at European Regional Science Association Conference, Paris.

Baum, J.R. and Wally, S. (2003) 'Strategic decision speed and firm performance', *Strategic Management Journal*, 24(11), 1107–29.

Birley, S. and Westhead, P. (1994) 'A Taxonomy of Business Start-up Reasons and their Impact on Firm Growth and Size', *Journal of Business Venturing*, 9(1), 7–31.

BLS (US Bureau of Labor Statistics) (2005) *Table 5. Self-employed Persons with Home-based Businesses by Selected Characteristics, May 2004*. Washington: BLS.

Bonaccorsi, A. and Giannangeli, S. (2005) *Why New Firms Never Get Large?: Evidence on Post-entry Growth of Italian New Firms*. Rome: Institute for Studies and Economic Analyses.

Bosma, N., van Praag, M., Thurik, A.R. and de Wit, G. (2004) 'The Value of Human and Social Capital Investments for the Business Performance of Start Ups', *Small Business Economics*, 27(3), 227–36.

Box, T.M., Watts, L.R. and Hisrich, R.D. (1994) 'Manufacturing Entrepreneurs: An Empirical Study of the Correlates of Employment Growth in the Tulsa MSA and Rural East Texas', *Journal of Business Venturing*, 9(3), 261–70.

Brixy, U. and Kohaut, S. (1999) 'Employment Growth Determinants in New Firms in Eastern Germany', *Small Business Economics*, 13(2), 155–70.

Brodie, S., Stanworth, J. and Wotruba, T.R. (2002) 'Direct Sales Franchises in the UK: A Self-employment Grey Area', *International Small Business Journal*, 20(1), 53–76.

Brüderl, J. and Preisendörfer, P. (1998) 'Network Support and the Success of Newly Founded Businesses', *Small Business Economics*, 10(3), 213–25.

Brüderl, J. and Preisendörfer, P. (2000) 'Fast-growing Businesses: Empirical Evidence from a German Study', *International Journal of Sociology*, 30(3), 45–70.

Bryson, J.R., Keeble, D. and Wood, P. (1997) 'The Creation and Growth of Small Business Service Firms in Post-industrial Britain', *Small Business Economics*, 9(4), 345–60.

Capelleras, J.L. and Greene, F.J. (2008) 'The Determinants and Growth Implications of Venture Creation Speed', *Entrepreneurship and Regional Development*, 20(4), 317–43.

Chittenden, F. and Sloan, B. (2006) 'Fiscal Policy and Self-employment: Targeting Business Growth', *Environment and Planning C: Government and Policy*, 24(1), 83–98.

Chittenden, F. and Sloan, B. (2007) 'Quantifying Inequity in the Taxation of Individuals and Small Firms', *British Tax Review*, 1, 58–72.

Coleman, S. (2007) 'The Role of Human and Financial Capital in the Profitability and Growth of Women-owned Businesses', *Journal of Small Business Management*, 45(3), 303–19.

Cooper, A.C., Gimeno-Gascon, F.J. and Woo, C.Y. (1994) 'Initial Human and Financial Capital as Predictors of New Venture Performance', *Journal of Business Venturing*, 9(5), 371–95.

Dahlqvist, J., Davidsson, P. and Wiklund, J. (2000) 'Initial Conditions as Predictors of New Venture Performance: A Replication and Extension of the Cooper *et al.* Study', *Enterprise and Innovation Management Studies*, 1(1), 1–17.

DCMS (2009) *Creative Industries Economic Estimates Statistical Bulletin*. London: DCMS.

Dunnell, K. (2009) 'National Statistician's Article: Measuring Regional Economic Performance', *Economic and Labour Market Review*, 3(1), 18–30.

Enterprise Nation (2007) *Home Business Report*. London: Enterprise Nation.

Eurostat (2008) *Eurostat Regional Yearbook 2008*. Luxembourg: Eurostat.

Fan, T. and Phan, P. (2007) 'International New Ventures: Revisiting the Influences behind the "Born-Global" Firm', *Journal of International Business Studies*, 38(1), 13–31.

Figueiredo, O., Guimaraes, P. and Woodward, D. (2002) 'Home-field Advantage: Location Decisions of Portuguese Entrepreneurs', *Journal of Urban Economics*, 52(2), 341–61.

Florida, R. (2002) *The Rise of the Creative Class, and How It's Transforming Work, Leisure, Community and Everyday Life*. New York: Basic Books.

Foreman-Peck, J., Makepeace, G. and Morgan, B. (2006) 'Growth and Profitability of Small and Medium-sized Enterprises: Some Welsh Evidence', *Regional Studies*, 40(4), 307–19.

Freedman, J. and Godwin, M. (1994) 'Incorporating the Micro-business: Perceptions and Misperceptions', in Hughes, A. and Storey, D.J. (eds), *Finance and the Small Firm*. London: Routledge.

Freel, M.S. and Robson, P.J.A. (2000) 'Small Firm Innovation, Growth and Performance', *International Small Business Journal*, 22(6), 561–75.

Gabrielsson, M., Kirpalani, V.H.M., Dimitratos, P., Solberg, C.A. and Zucchella, A. (2008) 'Born Globals: Propositions to Help Advance the Theory', *International Business Review*, 17(4), 385–401.

Greene, F.J., Mole, K.F. and Storey, D.J. (2008) *Three Decades of Enterprise Culture: Entrepreneurship, Economic Regeneration and Public Policy*. London: Macmillan/Palgrave.

Greene, F.J., Tracey, P. and Cowling, M. (2007) 'Re-casting the City into City Regions: Place Promotion, Competitiveness Benchmarking and the Quest for Urban Supremacy', *Growth and Change*, 38, 1–22.

Harada, N. (2003) 'Who Succeeds as an Entrepreneur?: An Analysis of the Post-entry Performance of New Firms in Japan', *Japan and the World Economy*, 15(2), 211–22.

Honig, B. (1998) 'What Determines Success?: Examining the Human, Financial and Social Capital of Jamaican Micro-entrepreneurs', *Journal of Business Venturing*, 13(5), 371–94.

Honjo, Y. (2004) 'Growth of New Start Up Firms: Evidence from the Japanese Manufacturing Industry', *Applied Economics Letters*, 11(1), 21–32.

Hoogstra, G.J. and Van Dijk, J. (2004) 'Explaining Firm Employment Growth: Does Location Matter?', *Small Business Economics*, 22(3–4), 179–92.

Inditex (2009) *Our Group*. http://www.inditex.com/en/who_we_are/our_group (accessed 1 February 2009).

Jaffe, A. (1989) 'Real Effects of Academic Research', *American Economic Review*, 79(5), 957–70.

Klepper, S. (2002) 'Firm Survival and the Evolution of Oligopoly', *Rand Journal of Economics*, 33(1), 37–61.

Koeller, C.T. and Lechler, T.G. (2006) 'Economic and Managerial Perspectives on New Venture Growth: An Integrated Analysis', *Small Business Economics*, 26(5), 427–37.

Krugman, P. (1995) *Development, Geography and Economic Theory*. Cambridge, MA: MIT Press.

Lawson, C. (1999) 'Towards a Competence Theory of the Region', *Cambridge Journal of Economics*, 23, 151–66.

Lindelof, P. and Lofsten, H. (2002) 'Growth, Management and Financing of New Technology-based Firms: Assessing Value-added Contributions of Firms Located on and off Science Parks', *Omega-International Journal of Management Science*, 30(3), 143–54.

Martin, R. and Cambridge Econometrics (1999) *A Study on the Factors of Regional Competitiveness*. Cambridge: Cambridge Econometrics.

Mata, J. (1994) 'Firm Growth during Infancy', *Small Business Economics*, 6(1), 27–39.

McPherson, M.A. (1995) 'The Hazards of Small Firm Growth in Southern Africa', *Journal of Development Studies*, 32(1), 31–54.

Mezias, J.M. and Starbuck, W.H. (2003) 'Studying the Accuracy of Managers' Perceptions: A Research Odyssey', *British Journal of Management*, 14, 3–17.

Oviatt, B.M. and McDougall, P.P. (1994) 'Toward a Theory of International New Ventures', *Journal of International Business Studies*, 25(1), 45–64.

Persson, H. (2004) 'The Survival and Growth of New Establishments in Sweden, 1987–1995', *Small Business Economics*, 23(5), 423–40.

Pfeiffer, F. and Reize, F. (2000) 'Business Start Ups by the Unemployed: An Econometric Analysis Based on Firm Data', *Labour Economics*, 7(5), 629–63.

Pilat, D., Cimper, A., Olsen, K. and Webb, C. (2006) *The Changing Nature of Manufacturing in OECD Economies.* STI working paper 2006/9. Paris: OECD.

Porter, M.E. (1980) *Competitive Strategy: Techniques for Analysing Industries and Competitors.* London: MacMillan.

Reid, G.C. and Smith, J.A. (2000) 'What Makes a New Business Start-up Successful?', *Small Business Economics*, 14(3), 165–82.

Robson, P.J.A. and Bennett, R.J. (2000) 'SME Growth: The Relationship with Business Advice and External Collaboration', *Small Business Economics*, 15(3), 193–208.

Roper, S. (1999) 'Modelling Small Business Growth and Profitability', *Small Business Economics*, 13(3), 235–52.

Schutjens, V.A.J.M. and Wever, E. (2002) 'Determinants of New Firm Success', *Papers in Regional Science*, 79, 135–59.

Shrader, R. and Siegel, D. (2007) 'Assessing the Relationship between Human Capital and Firm Performance: Evidence from Technology-based New Ventures', *Entrepreneurship Theory and Practice*, 31(6), 893–908.

Sleuwaegen, L. and Goedhuys, M. (2002) 'Growth of Firms in Developing Countries, Evidence from Côte d'Ivoire', *Journal of Development Economics*, 68(1), 117–35.

Sorenson, O. and Audia, P.G. (2003) 'The Social Structure of Entrepreneurial Activity: Geographic Concentration of Footwear Production in the US, 1940–1989', *American Journal of Sociology*, 106/2, 424–62.

Squicciarini, M. (2009) 'Science Parks: Seedbeds of Innovation? A Duration Analysis of Firms' Patenting Activity', *Small Business Economics*, 32(2), 169–90.

Stam, E. (2007) 'Why Butterflies Don't Leave: Locational Behavior of Entrepreneurial Firms', *Economic Geography*, 83(1), 27–50.

Storey, D.J. (1994) 'The Role of Legal Status in Influencing Bank Financing and New Firm Growth', *Applied Economics*, 26(2), 129–36.

Vaessen, P. and Keeble, D. (1995) 'Growth-oriented SMEs in Unfavorable Regional Environments', *Regional Studies*, 29(6), 489–505.

von Hipple, E. (1994) 'Sticky Information and the Locus of Problem Solving: Implications for Innovation', *Management Science*, 40, 429–39.

Westhead, P. and Cowling, M. (1995) 'Employment Change in Independent Owner-managed High-technology Firms in Great Britain', *Small Business Economics*, 7(2), 111–40.

Yang, C.-H., Motohashi, K., Chen, J.-R. (2009) 'Are New Technology-based Firms Located on Science Parks More Innovative? Evidence from Taiwan', *Research Policy* 38(1), 77–85.

Wiklund, J. and Shepherd, D. (2003) 'Aspiring for, and Achieving Growth: The Moderating Role of Resources and Opportunities', *Journal of Management Studies*, 40(8), 1919–41.

15 Growing the business – post start-up factors

Key learning objectives

By the end of this chapter you should:

- Understand the range of post start-up factors commonly associated with business growth
- Be able to compare and contrast post start-up factors
- Critically evaluate the importance of post start-up factors
- Provide a reasoned critique of factors that are associated with growth.

15.1 Introduction

Chapter 13 examined the association between a range of 'pre' start-up factors and business growth, whilst Chapter 14 investigated 'at' start-up factors. In this chapter, we examine the importance of 'post' start-up factors to business growth. Our focus is on examining a range of strategic factors that may influence the performance of a new and small business. For instance, does writing a business plan lead to superior performance? Is training positively associated with business growth? Is growth, instead, just down to the entrepreneur's skills or the strategy they use? Finally, what role does innovation play in business growth?

Our prime evidence base is the 36 international multivariate studies that we used in Chapters 13 and 14. These are detailed in Tables 15.1a, 15.1b and 15.1c. But, as previously, we complement this evidence in each of the sections by examining a wider range of studies. We also reiterate that each of the factors we examine should not be seen as existing in isolation. It is combinations of factors that are likely to exert a strong influence on business performance. The chapter begins by examining formal planning. Subsequent sections examine the following core 'strategic' issues, such as workforce training, sources of finance and entrepreneurial skills and innovation.

The chapter concludes by reviewing all of the evidence on business growth that we have examined in this chapter and earlier on in Chapters 13 and 14. This is important because we began our discussion of growth in Chapter 11 by arguing that there exists a range of books whose aim is to identify the 'timeless principles' and reveal the 'secrets' of how to develop a successful growth business. For example, the typical claim is that 'Just about anyone can be a key protagonist in building an extraordinary business institution. The lessons of these companies can be learned and applied by the vast majority of managers at all levels' (Collins and Porras 2001, quoted in Rosenzweig 2007: 12). In the final section, therefore, we summarise the evidence on business growth and conclude that, with some notable exceptions (e.g. limited liability status), the link between the factors identified here and actual new/small business growth is surprisingly weak.

Table 15.1a	'Post start-up' variables: employment growth						
Study	New products	Formal planning	Workforce training	Finance	External environment	Strategy
Box et al. (1994) US		Scanning environment +				
Bosma et al. (2004) Netherlands				–		
Brüderl and Preisendörfer (1998) Germany				Initial finance +		
Altinay and Altinay (2006) UK			Formal recruitment +, training, incentives for employees n.s.			
Koeller and Lechler (2006) Germany	Technological capacity n.s.				Customer concentration n.s., industry growth n.s.	Owners' skills +
McPherson (1995) African countries			+			Exporting +
Robson and Bennett (2000) UK	n.s		Skills of workforce n.s.		Competitive intensity n.s.	Exporting, design +, price, marketing, speed of service, cost, quality, expertise n.s., reputation –
Capelleras and Greene (2008) Spain		n.s.		Personal finances +		
Honig (1998) Jamaica				Starting capital, received a loan +		

Table 15.1b	'Post start-up' variables: sales growth					
Study	**New products**	**Formal planning**	**Workforce training**	**Finance**	**External environment**	**Strategy**
Brüderl and Preisendörfer (1998) Germany				Initial finance +		
Roper (1999) Ireland	–			Finance shortages +	Product focus +	
Robson and Bennett (2000) UK	+		Skills of workforce n.s.		Competitive intensity n.s.	Exporting, design +, marketing, speed of service, cost, quality, expertise n.s., price, reputation –
Coleman (2007) US				Have a loan –, inheritance n.s.		
Coleman (2007) US				n.s.		
Shrader and Siegel (2007) US					Competitive intensity, industry growth +	Breadth, low cost +, aggressiveness, differentiation n.s.
Freel and Robson (2004) UK	Novel process, incremental process, incremental product n.s., novel product innovation –		Type of worker n.s.		Large competitors +, customer concentration n.s.	Exporting n.s.

Table 15.1c	'Post start-up' variables: other measures						
Study	**New products**	**Formal planning**	**Workforce training**	**Finance**	**External environment**	**Strategy**
Roper (1999) Ireland				Finance shortages n.s.	Market focus, exporting +	Centralised power +
Honig (1998) Jamaica				Starting capital, received a loan +		
Bonaccorsi and Giannangeli (2005) Italy		n.s.		Initial finance +		
Bosma et al. (2004) Netherlands				–		
Baum and Wally (2003) US					Munificence +, dynamism n.s.	Centralisation of strategy, decentralisation of operations, formalisation of routines, informalisation of non-routines +
Shrader and Siegel (2007) US		Marketing plan +			Competitive intensity n.s., industry growth +	Breadth, aggressiveness, low cost, differentiation n.s.
Foreman-Peck et al. (2006) Wales			Type of worker n.s.			
Freel and Robson (2004) UK	Novel process, incremental process, incremental product n.s., novel product innovation –				Large competitors +, customer concentration n.s.	Exporting n.s.

15.2 Formal plans

One of the essential questions in strategic management is how businesses come to adopt particular strategies. Are strategies analytically thought out so that goals are set, processes decided on and formal plans realised? Alternatively, are 'strategies' actually just what people report they do in response to external events and circumstances? Entrepreneurs might say it was 'their' strategy but, in reality, was their strategic decision actually shaped by wider changes in the economy or society?

This begs the question: how should the entrepreneur plan? Should the emphasis be on a written formal business plan, on the basis that such plans are a good precursor to action? This is the view promoted by Ansoff (1991), who argued that planning provides a framework for subsequent actions. Or is it better to adopt a 'learning' approach, as suggested by Mintzberg? Mintzberg (1990) argued that, alongside intentions, entrepreneurs need to 'improvise' a strategy by 'trial and error' until it fits in with the environment.

There has been no ready resolution of the debate between Mintzberg (1990) and Ansoff (1991) as to the merits of formal planning. We do know that, worldwide, an estimated 10 million business plans are written annually (Gumpert 2002). We will now detail the reasons why entrepreneurs may or may not use formal business plans.

There are two potential benefits to writing a plan. The first of these is that it improves the ability of the entrepreneur to take a 'strategic' view of their business. This might be particularly important if the entrepreneur is inexperienced. Making mistakes on paper is less costly than actually spending money on the business. In addition, if entrepreneurs are inclined to be overly optimistic, a written business plan may act as a 'reality check' and keep them 'grounded'.

Delmar and Shane (2003) propose that written business plans actively help the strategic direction of the business. They argue that planning increases the speed of decision making, helps manage the efficient supply and demand of resources, and allows for clear goal-setting: '. . . by setting concrete objectives for the future, planning helps people develop specific steps for the achievement of their goals' (p. 1167). These may be judged critical, as entrepreneurs have to make numerous strategic adjustments (North and Smallbone 1995) such as whether to introduce new products/staff or develop new markets. Arguably, such decisions require timely information of the kind that is best captured in a business plan.

The second main advantage of a written business plan is that it might increase the likelihood of the business receiving extra resources. This is because business plans can be used to 'signal' the quality of the business to third parties such as financiers (who may be banks, government agencies, or business angels). By setting down the goals of the business, establishing how these goals are to be realised, and what will be the benefits to any potential investor, the written business plan can explicitly 'legitimise' the business. In so doing, the business plan can serve as a mechanism for gaining external funding.

Written business plans, however, require a cost and time input from the business owner, and whether they actually enhance the competencies of the entrepreneur or their business is not clear. One argument says that entrepreneurs only have a limited time to prosecute their business. They are often faced by a trade-off: spend time writing plans on *how* to pursue the business opportunity, or time *pursuing* the business opportunity. Bhide (2000) also suggests that a key to this trade-off is the experience or ability of the entrepreneur. He argues that experienced/able entrepreneurs are much better off pursuing the business opportunity than writing a plan for its exploitation. Also critical to the value of business plans is that smaller businesses are much more prone to external uncertainty (see Chapter 1). Hence, even if enough information is available to make seemingly robust and reliable plans about the future, an unexpected event may still occur which completely destroys the strategic direction adopted by the business. Bhide (2000) argues that most entrepreneurs know this and realise that their time is better spent pursuing the business idea.

A second argument against written business plans is that they provide little direct value to the business itself. Honig and Karlsson (2004) suggested that written business plans are largely 'mimetic', 'coercive' or 'normative' devices. By normative, they mean that there are a set of norms surrounding the business plans. For instance, Honig (2004) details that business planning is taught in the majority of the world's universities. He notes, however, that 'Notably, neither the teaching of business plans, nor the plans themselves, are sufficiently justified on the basis of theoretical or empirical literature' (p. 258). Honig's argument is that business plans are implicitly taken as the 'best' model for understanding how to set up and run a successful business, without there actually being much evidence to suggest that such teaching actually 'improves' entrepreneurial outcomes.

Honig and Karlsson (2004) argue that there are also 'mimetic' forces underlying the use of business plans. In order to be legitimate, part of what a business has to do is act like other businesses in their industry, so one element of being similar to other businesses is writing a business plan.

Finally, business plans may be 'coercive', in that funding in the form of a government grant or a private financier could be dependent on presentation of a business plan. In essence, Honig and Karlsson (2004) argue that there are dubious benefits to presuming, expecting, or forcing businesses to write business plans. In other words, their view is that would-be entrepreneurs do not necessarily see intrinsic value in writing a business plan. Instead, the reason why they write business plans is because they are simply following what everyone expects them to do.

Although Gumpert (2002), as we identified earlier, estimates that as many as 10 million business plans are written across the world each year, particular studies have identified that not all businesses write plans. Honig and Karlsson (2004) found that only 23 per cent of nascent entrepreneurs wrote a formal business plan, whilst Burke *et al.* (2009) identified that 56 per cent of new entrepreneurs wrote a business plan. Businesses that are fast growth would appear even less likely to write a plan: Bhide's (2000) study of 500 Inc. start ups (a US measure of fast-growth businesses) found that only 28 per cent of them had a fully developed, written business plan. Most (41 per cent) had no plan whatsoever, 26 per cent had a 'rudi-mentary' plan, and a final 5 per cent had a pro forma that was used to satisfy external financiers.

Based on this, the view might be that there is little value in written business plans. One reason for this is that very many new and existing businesses have little need for external advice (see Chapters 19–21 on public policy). Another reason might be that written business plans do not promote business growth. The actual empirical evidence, however, is mixed. Some studies point to a positive impact (e.g. Perry (2001), Delmar and Shane (2003), and Liao and Gartner (2006)) whilst others cannot identify a positive relationship (e.g. Bhide (2000), Tornikoski and Newbert (2007), Bygrave *et al.* (2007), Haber and Reichel (2007), and Honig and Karlsson (2004)).

Burke *et al.* (2009) argue that these mixed findings are due to what they call the 'multiple effects' of business plans on performance. Their argument is that the value of a written business plan is likely to be dependent upon the context in which it is written and the 'profile' of the business. These are likely to be very different for each individual business. For example, some businesses will choose to write a business plan and others will not, depending on whether they need external finance or have to conform to 'mimetic' pressures. They also argue that there are likely to be big differences between a business context (which is highly uncertain and innovative) and a context in which a business is 'reproducing' or mimicking other businesses (such as setting up a small-scale retail business). Taking these multiple effects of written business plans into account, Burke *et al.* find that those UK businesses that wrote business plans had faster employment growth than those that did not write business plans.

Probably because of this mixture of motivations for producing a written plan, the evidence on the association between business plans and growth in Tables 15.1a, 15.1b and 15.1c is mixed. Two of the four studies that look at this issue find a positive association, whilst the other two find no relationship. This ambiguity may point to the role of external 'pressures'. For example, Mason and Stark (2004) emphasise that different types of investors look to different aspects

We begin by reviewing an approach which, although frequently found in the literature, has important limitations. It is the favoured approach of observing the managerial practices of (currently) highly successful businesses and inferring that if such practices are copied, others will achieve similar success.

Rosenzweig (2007) calls this the 'halo' effect. To illustrate it he shows that, every ten years or so, a management book is produced that clearly associates fast growth with identifiable superior management and successful strategies. In the 1980s, there was Peters and Waterman's *In Search of Excellence* (1984). In the 1990s, there was *Built to Last* (Collins and Porras, 1994) whilst in the 2000s there was *Why Some Companies Make the Leap . . . and Others Don't* (Collins 2001).

Each of these very influential books shows how successful companies grow and develop. Peters and Waterman (1984) examined 43 businesses, Collins and Porras (1994) 18 businesses, and Collins just 11 businesses in the US. Typical of these approaches is the identification of 'core' skills and strategies. For example, Peters and Waterman (1984) identified that successful businesses had 'a bias for action', stayed 'close to the customer', considered employees to be key ('productivity through people') and the businesses were 'hands-on, value driven', but stuck to what they were good at ('stick to their knitting').

Rosenzweig's retrospective review of these texts, however, shows just how fickle success can prove to be. Only five businesses in the Peters and Waterman's (1984) study had improved their profitability by 1989. The other 30 businesses for which data are available saw a decline in profitability. Rosenzweig also shows that a similar fate befell the 18 'successful' businesses of the 1990s (Collins and Porras 1994): five years later, only five had improved their profitability, whilst the other 11 had seen their profitability decline. In the 2000s, the picture is much the same. One of the 'chosen' 11 was Fannie Mae, which was effectively nationalised by the US government following the sub-prime crisis that began in 2008. In essence, Rosenzweig highlights the pitfalls of taking managers' interpretations of 'their' success at face value.

Parker *et al.* (2010) explore this more formally. They identify five groups of managerial strategies: human resource management; innovation and technology: administration and governance; marketing and sales; and corporate strategy. As this chapter shows, all have been argued to positively enhance business growth. To test whether these strategies exert a consistent impact on business performance, Parker *et al.* first identify a group of exceptionally fast-growing businesses and examine the extent to which the five strategies 'explain' that growth. Then they observe the same group of businesses in a later time period, when the businesses grew no faster than the industry average, to see whether the same strategies that explained exceptional performance in the growth period continued to explain performance in the later period. The simple answer is that they did not. The strategies that explained good performance in the first period were not the same ones that enhanced performance in the second period.

Parker *et al.* point to two possible explanations for this finding. The first is compatible with Gibrat's Law, in which growth is a random walk, meaning growth in one period will be unrelated to growth in the second period. The factors 'explaining' the performance differences will also change. The second explanation is that, because the circumstances facing the business have changed by the second period, it is to be expected that the strategies would also have to differ. The key to success is the extent to which the business is able to 'fit' its strategies to the circumstances it faces.

In practice, it is difficult to distinguish between these explanations. Nevertheless, what is clear is that it is methodologically unjustifiable to observe only success, to rely for an explanation on the views of the managers, or to identify some common factors and then assume these constitute 'golden rules' that can be consistently applied by others to achieve growth in their businesses. What is also open to question is to seek the views of current owners of businesses and ask them about their 'attitudes' since their answers will have been shaped by their performance to date.

What does seem plausible is that managerial skills and strategies are likely – as is suggested by 'organic' theories of business growth – to vary across the 'life-cycle' of the business.

Businesses, therefore, need managers with very different sets of experience and abilities to aid business development. One essential question, therefore, is 'in order to grow, must the founder go?' (Willard *et al.* 1992).

The argument 'for' is that – as Hellmann and Puri (2002), in observing changes in high-tech companies in Silicon Valley, suggest – 'While founders may be very suited to the initial phases, not all founders can make the transition from entrepreneur to manager' (p. 181). Hence, few founders have the 'bandwidth' of skills to effectively manage the business from its entrepreneurial origins through to creating a complex administrative business. Wasserman (2003: 153) reports the perspective of a venture capitalist:

> The toughest time to change CEOs is when the CEO has been really successful at developing the company. But those fast-growth companies outstrip the CEO's skills the fastest, and that's when we have to push the hardest for a change . . . With a good 'story', it is best to add a professional CEO *before* the scale of operations might logically justify it. You must stay ahead of the curve to drive momentum.

The alternative argument is that founders are *more* likely to be better placed to run a successful growth business. For a start, it is their 'baby' and so they may be prepared to 'go the extra mile'. They are also likely to own a significant share of the business, reducing the potential conflict between the objectives of the owners and the managers. Thirdly, the reason why the business has actually grown is that the founders genuinely have superior managerial and entrepreneurial skills. One example of this is Michael Dell. He stepped down in 2004 as the CEO (chief executive officer) of Dell. He was replaced by Kevin Rollins, but in 2007, because of 'poor' performance, Dell resumed the CEO role and replaced Rollins.

One reason why the relationship between owner skills and performance is so obscure is that as the business grows, it also adds additional administrative structures. For example, Michael Dell was still the chairman of the board when he resigned as CEO in 2004. The board of directors may exert a powerful influence on the strategy of the business. Equally, it may be the team of managers that runs the business – rather than one director – who effectively influence growth. Such influences may dilute the relationship between founders and performance. A further influence is the presence of outside influences such as venture capitalists. Jain and Tabak (2008) argue that venture capitalists are often pivotal in making judgements about whether founders should stay or go.

Our overall view is closely aligned with that of Covin and Slevin (1989), who argue that there is no 'one-size-fits-all' managerial strategy. They clearly show that the managerial strategies associated with successful performance in 'hostile' marketplaces seemed to differ radically from those that worked well in more 'benign' environments. Put simply, Covin and Slevin found that procedural managerial strategies worked well in benign environments, whereas being 'light on your feet' was associated with good performance in a hostile environment. This finding chimes with simple intuition, but still highlights the point that if the external environment changes for reasons beyond the control of the business – for example, it becomes more hostile as a result of the entry of a new business – then the ideal managerial skill set also changes. In short, a good manager in one context may prove a bad manager in another.

This is clearly evident from Tables 15.1a, 15.1b and 15.1c, which show that a whole range of strategic and external environmental factors have been seen to influence business growth. These include the intensity of competition, how dynamic the industry is, and how munificent (generous) the environment is. Equally, our tables identify a whole range of possible business strategies that have been examined in relation to business growth. Again, Covin and Slevin's basic point seems to hold: there would not appear to be a simple 'one-size-fits-all' approach to business growth.

However, Zhou and De Wit's (2009) Dutch study appears to refute this assertion. It groups the factors influencing small business growth into three: those relating to the individual, those relating to the organisation and those relating to the environment. They conclude that the environmental influences are the weakest and that growth motivation and Need for Achievement (NAch – see Chapter 2) are dominant. However, it appears that the motivation questions were asked only after the performance was assessed.

The Zhou and De Wit study findings also seem to conflict with the studies of the 'ten percenters', described in the Illustration below. These imply that external factors exert the dominant influence on small business growth – with some businesses responding and others not.

Illustration	Water-based analogies of small-business growth, the 'ten percenters'

In observing the characteristics of rapidly growing middle-market companies – defined as 'ten percenters' (those with <30 per cent per annum sales growth over a four-year period and sales of between £10 m and £100 m) – the following two analogies may be drawn:

1 The current and the crew.

2 The ocean liner and the surfboarder.

In terms of the 'current and the crew', the analogy is that the business is like a boat moving quickly down a river. The boat has two strategies:

● A big strong co-ordinated crew all pulling in the same direction.

● Locate the boat in a current which enables it to move quickly.

In a business context, the first strategy can be considered to be 'big business management', involving ensuring clearly specified procedures, controls and systems. The second strategy is comparable to opportunity identification – seeing a market opportunity and then initiating and developing the niche.

Peter Morgan of Deloitte and Touche commented: 'Our observation is that the "ten percenters" place much more emphasis upon locating the boat correctly in the current than on the quality of the crew.'

In terms of the second analogy – the ocean liner and the surfboarder – the assumption is that the entrepreneur's skills are different from those of the professional manager of a large business. As we saw in Chapter 1, the large business (the ocean liner) is likely to have some power to shape markets – and in this sense it has the *power to set, and keep to, a course even in choppy seas.*

In contrast, the small business owner has no such power. Their skill is to be in a position to take advantage of an opportunity when it presents itself. The analogy is with the surfboarder. The latter succeeds by staying on the surfboard for a relatively short period of time; the surfer does not seek to control or influence the direction of the waves, but rather to roll with them.

This resonates with the evidence of small business growth which we saw as characterised by short bursts of growth, often followed by periods of much slower growth or decline.

So, at any one time the sea (the market) comprises some surfboarders that are on top of a wave, others having toppled off their boards, others going backwards as the tide retreats and the bulk of surfers waiting for something to happen.

If the analogy is valid, it implies that the skills of the surfboarder are very different from those of the ocean-liner captain.

To summarise, the skills and strategies required to successfully manage a large business are likely to differ from those required to manage a new or small business. It is also clear that, if a business grows, these skills and strategies are likely to change, and that changes in external circumstances are also likely to place a different premium upon different skills and strategies.

15.6 Innovation

When we discussed innovation in Chapter 5, we saw the very real difficulties there were in defining and measuring the innovative activity of businesses. Despite these difficulties, we expect to see a close association between business innovation and growth. Indeed, businesses are constantly being reminded by the press, and by their local, regional or national governments, of the importance of innovation to success.

Illustration	Glasses Direct

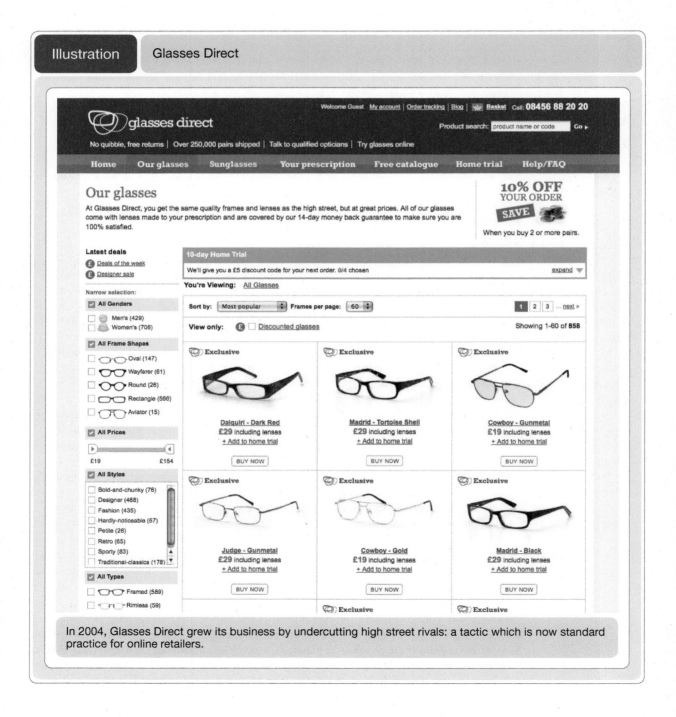

In 2004, Glasses Direct grew its business by undercutting high street rivals: a tactic which is now standard practice for online retailers.

In the business world, there are few more evocative metaphors than that of David and Goliath; the single entrepreneur versus the might of the high street chains. Usually, the idealistic entrepreneur comes a cropper because he is mercilessly undercut by the superior buying power of the big boys – but not always. Aged 21, James Murray-Wells is pitting himself against some of the best-known names in retailing. Running his company from a disued stable block in his parents' south Gloucestershire farmyard, the English graduate believes his mail order and internet company will revolutionise the way the British buy their spectacles. By selling glasses at a fraction of the conventional price, Murray-Wells's fledgling company, Glasses Direct, is competing head-to-head with such high-profile names as Specsavers, Vision Express and Dollond & Aitchison.

'People generally can't believe our Glasses Direct prices, but that's because the high street shops are maintaining retail prices at 10–20 times the cost price of the spectacles', he says. It comes as no surprise to learn that most first-time visitors to Murray-Wells's website are astonished at the prices. All standard glasses cost £15, including frame, prescription lenses, case, delivery and guarantee. Rimless glasses are £25 and the charge for bendable titanium frames, again including lens and delivery, is £35 – compared with £150 in many high street opticians.

'What I'm giving people is choice, and so far it looks as though they are delighted', he says. 'An average pair of glasses is manufactured for less than £7, so I charge just over double. Even with advertising and overheads, I still make a profit.'

Source: 'One in the Eye for the Big Boys', *Daily Telegraph*, 18 August 2004.

Support for the importance of innovation is provided by Geroski and Machin (1992). They examined large UK businesses with the aim of establishing if innovators outperformed non-innovators. The answer was clear. They found a virtuous circle: innovation enhanced sales and profitability which, in turn, provided funding for further innovation, leading to further sales and profitability growth. Of course, there were recognised to be lags in this process, because innovations were unlikely to come 'on stream' immediately, and competition was likely to erode the profits from innovation. Nonetheless, the broad link between innovation and large business performance was confirmed.

Other studies have tested the association between growth and innovation. Some of these studies show a positive association. Roper (1999) shows that innovators in Germany, the UK and Ireland are more likely to experience growth than non-innovators. Calvo (2006), for Spain, found similar results. The evidence provided by Freel (2000) is more ambiguous. His sample of innovators and non-innovators shows overall no significant difference in growth rates between the two on metrics such as sales or profits. However, he does find significantly faster sales growth amongst the innovators and that the distribution of this growth is heavily skewed. His key finding is that, amongst businesses that grow their sales fast, innovative businesses are heavily represented.

This suggests that integral to fast growth is an ability to innovate. The advice to the business owner, therefore, might be to innovate. Hoffman *et al.*'s (1998) review, however, concluded that: '. . . the mixture of available research results suggests that though innovation appears to be widespread [amongst small businesses] this does not translate directly into improved business performance and ultimately greater profitability' (p. 44).

Such a finding is reflected in our tables in terms of new products: there does not seem to be a ready association between business performance and new products. There are several reasons why this link between innovation and small business growth appears to be less robust than for large businesses. The first relates to the greater external uncertainty faced by the small business. There may be uncertainty about whether a product or process will work. Second, even if products or processes do successfully pass through the research and development phase, there remains the risk that the product or process will be impossible to commercialise. Third, even if a product or process can be commercialised, the return from investment may be inadequate to justify continuing production. Fourth, there are often considerable costs – in terms of both time and money – in licensing innovations: this may place great pressure on the cashflow of the new business. In all cases, the 'downside risk' of the innovation stalling or failing is generally greater for the small business, which lacks the portfolio of ideas (and diverse income streams) that a larger business is likely to be able to draw upon (see Case study 3).

One such example is the 'Segway'. This was designed as an individual 'human transportation' device. Sales were expected to be $1 billion and its inventor, Dean Kamen, prophesised in 2001 that: 'I would stake my reputation, my money and my time on the fact that 10 years from now [2011], this [the Segway] will be the way many people in many places get around'. (*Time* 2001). It is difficult to see how this prediction will ever be realised, never mind by 2011.

Any link between innovation and business performance is likely to be 'lagged'. Typically, it may take many years for the financial returns from an innovation to feed back to the business, and the variance in the lag is likely to be greater for small businesses. Indeed, Cosh and Hughes (2007) suggest that one of the main features of UK innovative businesses is that innovation is positively associated with employment, but not with the profitability of the business.

A second difficulty in linking performance and innovation is that the latter may not be a persistent feature of (small) business activity. For example, Cefis (2003) and Geroski *et al.* (1997) find that businesses that were 'innovative' in one period had stopped innovating a short time later – although Roper and Hewitt-Dundas (2008) show that Irish businesses were generally 'persistent' innovators over a three-year period. The effect of this spotty innovation activity – which is quite understandable from the perspective of the individual business – is to make the link between innovation and performance very difficult to identify. A second example of innovation 'spottiness' is that there are also large differences between sectors and subsectors (see Chapter 5).

Freel (2000) highlights a third difficulty with linking innovation to small business growth. He argues that:

> The returns to innovation are, at least in part, contingent upon the size of the firm . . . whilst small innovators in aggregate grow faster than non-innovators this is not to suggest that innovation is a necessary, nor less a sufficient condition for growth or superior performance.
>
> (pp. 207–8)

Coad and Rao (2008) provide support for this view. They found no general relationship between innovation and growth amongst smaller businesses. Their important exception was observing a link between innovation and exceptionally fast-growing businesses. This is plausible, since to achieve exceptionally rapid growth – even for a short period of time – a business requires something innovative to differentiate it from the competition. However, even this is not supported by the study from O'Reagan *et al.* (2006) who examine fast-growing manufacturing businesses in the electronic and electrical engineering sectors. Their study also could not find any association between fast growth and innovation.

There are also measurement issues that make it difficult to assess the association between performance and innovation. There are two main reasons for this. First, if the growth measure is employment then, arguably, a 'productive' innovation may mean that employment actually falls if the innovation replaces the workforce. This occurred – to some extent – when robots began to replace humans in car production assembly in the 1980s and 1990s. Second, as we saw in Chapter 5, very many of the measures of innovation are fairly crude and may mask why a businesses innovates. For example, Tether and Storey (1998) argued that many of the 'innovative' new small businesses actually came into existence because larger businesses found research and development either too costly or risky. Rather than conduct R&D 'in-house', large businesses sought to outsource R&D to smaller businesses.

In summary, the association between very fast-growth businesses and innovation has some empirical support. More open to question is whether there is support, across a wide range of small businesses, for innovation being a key factor influencing business performance. In part, this is due to the difficulties with measuring innovation, but it also reflects the fact that small businesses are inconsistent innovators and suffer considerable external uncertainty. This means a general link between innovation and small business performance is often difficult to identify.

15.7 Summarising business growth

In this section, we seek to summarise the overall empirical evidence on business growth. We have seen in Chapter 11 that there are a variety of methodological challenges that make this difficult. For example, what is the appropriate measure of growth (e.g. sales, employment, profits etc.)? Should growth be measured using an absolute or a relative measure? What is the 'best' timeframe to judge the performance of a business – one year, two years, five years? What should be done in terms of organic versus acquisition growth? The conclusion from this is that studies of fast-growth businesses are often hard to compare. As often as not, studies are comparing 'apples' with 'pears'.

We also identified that there are very real issues in associating particular variables with growth. One obvious example we identified in Chapter 14 was the use of 'ethnicity'. We showed that this was often taken as a 'binary' (yes/no) variable in most studies, although it disguises the very real differences between different ethnic groups and between 'immigrants' and ethnic groups. Moreover, even when the status of a variable is clear – incorporation – there are very real difficulties in identifying what interpretation should be given to positive results (e.g. does it reflect a 'brand', team entrepreneurship, tax avoidance, etc.?).

A further problem is that – as we showed in Chapter 12 – the actual success of studies in explaining business growth is extremely modest. Coad (2007) identified that the variation explained by very many studies generally did not go much above 10 per cent – meaning that 90 per cent remains unexplained. One possible reason for such a poor level of explanation is that many studies of business growth are extremely partial in what they examine. For instance, our review of 36 international growth studies identified a number of 'common' variables normally associated with business growth. It is fairly clear from these studies that they tended to focus on particular parts of growth. Hence, some studies examined 'pre' start-up influences whilst others examined 'at' or 'post' start-up influences. Whilst this is understandable because the focus of researchers differs, it means most studies suffer from omitted variable bias.

A final issue makes us uncomfortable with research on this topic and prevents us from being able to offer, with any accuracy, *predictions* of which (small) businesses will grow fast and which will not. It is that almost all research engages in 'back-casting' rather than 'forecasting'. It generally takes a group of businesses where the performance is known and then asks what factors, or groups of factors, explained that performance. It informs us about what the significant factors are but, in most cases, does not highlight the overall explanatory power of the model. As far as we are aware, there has yet to be a study which then takes the model and uses it to forecast which businesses will grow in a subsequent time period.

There are, therefore, huge methodological challenges to those seeking a better understanding of business growth. For this reason we have identified, in the box below, an example of a 'classic' article, and then ask you to speculate on how the authors might respond to the points we have raised.

Despite the methodological issues, two questions still remain. First, what are the factors associated with business growth? Second, which of the six theoretical approaches that we identified in Chapter 12 provides the 'best' explanation of business growth? Does growth follow a prescribed path? Alternatively, at the other extreme, is it just a stochastic event – what is called a random walk?

To gain a clearer picture, we have investigated a range of 'pre', 'at' and 'post' start-up factors. To reiterate, these three groups of factors are all likely to be interrelated and it is only one method for examining the variables associated with business growth.

A summary of the overall findings for these chapters is presented in Table 15.2, which has three columns. The first column includes the factors where there was some positive evidence of a significant association with new business growth. Column 2 indentifies negative associations whilst column 3 identifies those factors where the evidence was generally indeterminate.

Classic research	Baum, J.R., Locke, E.A. and Smith, K.G. (2001) 'A Multidimensional Model of Business Growth', *Academy of Management Journal*, 44(2), 292–303.

This is a study that examined businesses in the architectural woodworking sector that were between two and eight years old in 1993. These were surveyed in 1994 and re-surveyed in 1995.

The reason why we consider this to be a 'classic' article is that:

- It adopts a holistic approach that looks at a range of factors:
  - traits: passion for work, tenacity;
  - general competencies: opportunity and organisation skills;
  - specific competencies: industry specific and technical skills;
  - motivation: vision, growth goals, etc.;
  - competitive strategies: low cost, differentiation, etc.;
  - external environment: munificence, concentration;
  - size: in terms of sales or employment.

This is appealing since it is evident that very few studies try, or are able, to examine a wide spectrum of influences on business growth. We think this is important because it seems unlikely that a single explanation will capture the multiplicity of factors at work.

It also seems intuitively sensible that combinations of factors acting together, rather than being measured separately, would offer more powerful explanations.

The key conclusions of the study were that:

- the personal traits and specific competency characteristics, when taken by themselves, provide only a weak explanation of growth;
- however, it is when the interactions between the characteristics are taken into account that the explanations become more powerful; and
- overall, strategic choice, leadership and entrepreneurship – factors internal to the business – are more important than external environmental factors.

They summarise their findings in the following way:

The story begins with a hard-working pro-active entrepreneur with a strong set of technical, organisational and industry skills. The entrepreneur is highly motivated, which is reflected in clear organisational vision, together with high-growth goals and confidence in achieving these goals. Perhaps because of tenacity and pro-activity, organisational skills or high motivation, this entrepreneur is capable of delineating an effective differentiation strategy that works to generate high growth.

(p. 299)

If you were to be critical of this study, do you think that the following are suitable grounds for the critique?

- Study asks entrepreneurs what they think – so you are bound to get a 'halo effect'.
- Explains prior growth rather than predicts future growth.
- Study only looks at one industry over a short period.
- Study does not look at 'brand' new businesses.

Table 15.2 shows six factors that we could readily associate with new and small business growth. Growing businesses had entrepreneurs who were male, 'prime age' and had higher education experience. There was also some indirect evidence that personality factors (e.g. cognitive biases such as over-optimism, self-efficacy) had an impact on business growth. There was also evidence that incorporation and location were positively linked to business growth.

Table 15.2	Summary of pre, at and post start-up factors		
	Positive	**Negative**	**Unclear impact**
Pre start-up factors	Prime age	Unemployment	Team entrepreneurship
	Higher education		Prior managerial experiences
	Males		Prior sectoral experience
	Personality (indirect impacts)		In business before
			Family
At start-up factors	Limited company		Initial size
	Location		Sector
Post start-up factors			Formal business plans
			Entrepreneurial skills
			Strategy
			External environment
			Equity financing
			Innovation

Our judgement, based on our review of the evidence, also indicated that previously unemployed people were less likely to run a growth business. Table 15.2 also shows a range of factors where there was no discernable impact. We, for example, could find little consistent convincing evidence that team entrepreneurship, prior sectoral or managerial experience, prior business ownership or family ownership had much of an impact on business growth.

Similarly, although sector *ought* to have a positive impact on business growth, we judged that businesses could still grow in 'unfavourable' sectors. There was also a range of post start-up factors where the evidence was unclear. The anticipation is that businesses that have better business plans, stronger management, a better 'strategy', a more favourable external environment, greater equity finance or that were more innovative *ought*, again, to experience faster growth. The problem was that we could not find simple 'lessons' that would readily identify which was the optimal path to follow.

There is, therefore, some evidence that growth is 'deterministic', with six factors being readily associated with business growth. If we look back to Storey (1994) we can see that some of these factors appear on a consistent basis, such as 'prime age', education, and incorporation. This suggests that there is, at least, some consistency over time. Potentially, it is also evident that businesses in the 'right' sector, with the right management, financing, planning, strategy and innovation are more likely to succeed than other businesses. This may indicate, therefore, a general level of support for non-stochastic approaches.

The trouble is that we – like Rosenzweig (2007) – find it difficult to identify which are the 'timeless' factors other than, for example, being a limited company or being educated. This is for three main reasons. First, although there is some evidence of continuity, there are a range of other factors that Storey (1994) found to be positive (e.g. prior managerial experience, niche specialisation, team entrepreneurship) which appear in our chapters not to be so important. Arguably, some of these differences may be due to the availability of data or a better understanding of factors. However, we had expected – given the huge number of studies that have investigated growth – that there would have been a clearer, more definitive, understanding of the factors underlying growth. For many variables, this is just not apparent.

Second, very many of the non-stochastic approaches specifically identify that there ought to be an evident relationship between a particular variable and business growth. For example, population ecology suggests that sector should be pivotal whilst cluster analysis suggests that sector and location are important. Managerial, stage theory, RBV and social networking approaches all identify that entrepreneurial skills, strategy and plans are important explanations of business success. Learning-based approaches also identify the importance of prior experience either in the sector, in management or in running a business. Whilst there is some evidence to suggest that all of these factors can have some importance, the overall impression is that they are not clearly and identifiably associated with business growth.

Our third and final argument suggests that the absence of strong and consistent associations indicates that luck plays an important – if not pivotal role – in business growth. One reason for this is that growth is spotty: entrepreneurs might tell us what their 'secrets' are, but there is no guarantee that these 'secrets' are portable to another sector or time period. Even if entrepreneurs tell us that they have the 'right stuff', there is no evidence to suggest that they are able to carry this forward into their next business. Also, even if a strategy works in a particular environment, it is unclear if it will work in a different environment. Finally, whisper it, but not all entrepreneurs tell us the truth: the problem is that we cannot easily distinguish between those that do and those that do not.

Essentially, there are few factors or 'timeless lessons' that are consistently linked to new/small business growth. Furthermore, even if a business exhibited all of these factors, it would not reliably guarantee that growth would be achieved.

Summary

This chapter has examined a range of strategic factors that are often commonly associated with (small/new) business growth. These are: formal planning, workforce training, entrepreneurial skills, finance and innovation.

What emerges from our review of the evidence, both in our tables and from the specialist studies, is the contingent nature of 'post' start-up factors. For example, there are both costs and benefits to business planning. The actual evidence on its importance in enhancing growth is mixed. Indeed, on balance, we just about side with those taking the view that formal planning can in the right circumstances modestly enhance the growth of a new enterprise.

Similarly, it ought to be the case that workforce training, innovation and entrepreneurial skills are pivotal to business growth. The expectation is that businesses that are innovative, employ the best and most creative workers, and have the strongest entrepreneurial skill base are most likely to grow. This is the message – as Rosenzweig (2007) suggests – of some of the biggest-selling business books. However, like Rosenzweig, we struggle to find compelling evidence to support such assertions.

Instead, what seems more plausible is that the entrepreneurial skill base of the enterprise has to 'fit' the circumstances faced by the business. In the simple terms of Covin and Slevin (1989), the skill base required of a business facing hostile conditions is likely to be very different from one facing benign conditions. The smaller the business, the more it has to accept its market conditions – and perhaps the more likely it is that these conditions may change very quickly. This implies that it is only the very unusual business that is able to exploit the range of circumstances it may face. Most businesses may experience spurts of growth when their entrepreneurial skill base is aligned to the external environment, but once these circumstances change, they return to more 'normal' performance. In short, it is the circumstances that change, rather than the entrepreneurial skill base.

In overall terms, the chapter also concluded that there was very little general evidence to suggest that there was a ready-made formula or recipe that entrepreneurs followed to grow their business. Instead, except for a few factors – age, being male, being a limited company – our exhaustive review of the empirical evidence suggests that much business growth remains unexplained. This does not imply that business performance is purely a random walk, but it does imply that chance has a major role to play.

Questions for discussion

1 Should growth-oriented entrepreneurs write business plans?
2 Does training provide growth benefits to the small business? Discuss the evidence.
3 What role does equity finance play in fast-growth businesses?
4 Are innovative businesses likely to be growing businesses?
5 'In order to grow, the founder must go.' How true is this statement?
6 'What is important for the fast-growth business is locating the right current rather than having a capable crew.' Discuss.
7 Why are there so few factors associated with small business growth?
8 Identify the factors associated with fast-growth businesses. Does this evidence support a particular approach to understanding business growth?
9 'Growing a business is a matter of luck rather than choices: it is all about having the "right stuff" at the "right time" and in the "right place".' Discuss.

References

Altinay, L. and Altinay, E. (2006) 'Determinants of Ethnic Minority Entrepreneurial Growth in the Catering Sector', *Service Industries Journal*, 26(2), 203–21.

Ansoff, H.I. (1991) 'Critique of Henry Mintzberg's "The Design School: Reconsidering the Basic Premises of Strategic Management" ', *Strategic Management Journal*, 12(6), 449–61.

Beck, T. and Demirguc-Kunt, A. (2006) 'Small and Medium-sized Enterprises: Access to Finance as a Growth Constraint', *Journal of Banking and Finance*, 30(11), 2931–43.

Betcherman, G., Leckie, N. and McMullen, K. (1997) *Developing Skills in the Canadian Workplace*. CPRN Study W02. Ottawa: Renouf Publishing.

Bhide, A.V. (2000) *The Origin and Evolution of New Businesses*. New York: Oxford University Press.

Birley, S. and Westhead, P. (1990) 'Growth and Performance Contrasts between "Types" of Small Firms', *Strategic Management Journal*, 11(7), 535–57.

Bonaccorsi, A. and Giannangeli, S. (2005) *Why New Firms Never Get Large? Evidence on Post-entry Growth of Italian New Firms*. Rome: Institute for Studies and Economic Analyses.

Bosma, N., van Praag, M., Thurik, R. and de Wit, G. (2004) 'The Value of Human and Social Capital Investments for the Business Performance of Start Ups', *Small Business Economics*, 27(3), 227–36.

Box, T.M., Watts, L.R. and Hisrich, R.D. (1994) 'Manufacturing Entrepreneurs: An Empirical Study of the Correlates of Employment Growth in the Tulsa MSA and Rural East Texas', *Journal of Business Venturing*, 9(3), 261–70.

Brüderl, J. and Preisendörfer, P. (1998) 'Network Support and the Success of Newly Founded Businesses', *Small Business Economics*, 10(3), 213–25.

Bullock, A., Cosh, A.D., Hughes, A. and Milner, I. (2008) *United Kingdom Survey of Small and Medium-sized Enterprises' Finances, 2007*. October 2008. SN: 6049. Colchester, Essex: UK Data Archive.

Burke, A., Fraser, S., and Greene F.J. (2009) 'The Multiple Impacts of Business Planning on New Venture Performance', *Journal of Management Studies*, early view, September.

Bygrave, W.D. and Hunt, S.A. (2007) 'More for Love than Money?: Financial Returns on Informal Investments'. Paper presented at the 4th AGSE International Entrepreneurship Research Conference, Brisbane, February.

Calvo, J.L. (2006) 'Testing Gibrat's Law for Small, Young and Innovating Firms', *Small Business Economics*, 26(2), 117–23.

Capelleras, J.L. and Greene, F.J. (2008) 'The Determinants and Growth Implications of Venture Creation Speed', *Entrepreneurship and Regional Development*, 20(4), 317–43.

Carter, N., Gartner, W. and Reynolds, P. (1996) 'Exploring Startup Event Sequences', *Journal of Business Venturing*, 11, 151–66.

Cefis, E. (2003) 'Is There Persistence in Innovative Activities?', *International Journal of Industrial Organization*, 21(4), 489–515.

Certo, S.T., Covin, J.G., Daily, C.M. and Dalton, D.R. (2001) 'Wealth and the Effects of Founder Management among IPO-Stage New Ventures', *Strategic Management Journal*, 22(6–7), 641–58.

Coad, A. (2007) *Firm Growth: A Survey*. CES Working Paper 24. University of Paris, Sorbonne.

Coad, A. and Rao, R. (2008) 'Innovation and Firm Growth in High-tech Sectors: A Quantile Regression Approach', *Research Policy*, 37(4), 633–48.

Coleman, S. (2007) 'The Role of Human and Financial Capital in the Profitability and Growth of Women-owned Businesses', *Journal of Small Business Management*, 45(3), 303–19.

Collins, J.C. (2001) *Good to Great: Why Some Companies Make the Leap . . . and Others Don't*. New York: Random House Business Books.

Collins, J.C. and Porras, J.I. (1994) *Built to Last: Successful Habits of Visionary Companies*. New York: HarperBusiness.

Cosh, A., Hughes, A., Bullock, A. and Milner, I. (2009), *SME Finance and Innovation in the Current Economic Crisis*. Cambridge: Centre for Business Research, University of Cambridge.

Cosh, A.D. and Hughes, A. (eds) (2007) *British Enterprise: Thriving or Surviving?* Cambridge: Centre for Business Research, University of Cambridge.

Cosh, A., Hughes, A. and Weeks, M. (2000) *The Relationship between Training and Employment Growth in Small and Medium Enterprises*. Report RR.245. Cambridge: Department for Education and Employment Research.

Covin, J.G. and Slevin, D.P. (1989) 'Strategic Management of Small Firms in Hostile and Benign Environments', *Strategic Management Journal*, 10(1), 75–87.

Daily, C.M. and Dalton, D.R. (1992) 'Financial Performance of Founder-Managed vs. Professionally Managed Small Corporations', *Journal of Small Business Management*, 30, 25–34.

Davila, A., Foster, G. and Gupta, M. (2003) 'Venture Capital Financing and the Growth of Startup Firms', *Journal of Business Venturing*, 18(6), 689–708.

Delmar, F. and Shane, S. (2003) 'Does Business Planning Facilitate the Development of New Ventures?', *Strategic Management Journal*, 24(12), 1165–85.

Foreman-Peck, J., Makepeace, G. and Morgan, B. (2006) 'Growth and Profitability of Small and Medium-sized Enterprises: Some Welsh Evidence', *Regional Studies*, 40(4), 307–19.

Fraser, S. (2003) 'The Impact of Investors in People on Small Business Growth: Who Benefits?', *Environment and Planning C-Government and Policy*, 21(6), 793–812.

Fraser, S., Storey, D., Frankish, J. and Roberts, R. (2002) 'The Relationship between Training and Small Business Performance: An Analysis of the Barclays Bank Small Firms Training Loans Scheme', *Environment and Planning C-Government and Policy*, 20(2), 211–33.

Freel, M.S. (2000) 'Do Small Innovating Firms Outperform Non-innovators?', *Small Business Economics*, 14(3), 195–210.

Freel, M.S. and Robson, P.J.A. (2000) 'Small Firm Innovation, Growth and Performance', *International Small Business Journal*, 22(6), 561–75.

Geroski, P. and Machin, S. (1992) 'Do Innovating Firms Outperform Non-Innovators?', *Business Strategy Review*, Summer, 79–90.

Geroski, P.A., Machin, S.J. and Walters, C.F. (1997) 'Corporate Growth and Profitability', *Journal of Industrial Economics*, 45(2), 171–89.

Gumpert, D.E. (2002) *Burn Your Business Plan*. Needham: Lauson Publishing.

Haber, S. and Reichel, A. (2007) 'The Cumulative Nature of the Entrepreneurial Process: The Contribution of Human Capital, Planning and Environment Resources to Small Venture Performance', *Journal of Business Venturing*, 22(1), 119–45.

Harada, N. (2003) 'Who Succeeds as an Entrepreneur? An Analysis of the Post-entry Performance of New Firms in Japan', *Japan and the World Economy*, 15(2), 211–22.

Hellmann, T. and Puri, M. (2002) 'Venture Capital and the Professionalization of Start Up Firms: Emprirical Evidence', *Journal of Finance*, 57(1), 169–97.

Hoffman, K., Milady, P., Bessant, J. and Perren, L. (1998) 'Small Firms, R&D, Technology and Innovation in the UK: A Literature Review', *Technovation*, 18(1), 39–55.

Honig, B. (1998) 'What Determines Success?: Examining the Human, Financial and Social Capital of Jamaican Micro-Entrepreneurs', *Journal of Business Venturing*, 13(5), 371–94.

Honig, B. (2004) 'Entrepreneurship Education: Toward a Model of Contingency-based Business Planning', *Academy of Management Learning and Education*, 3(3), 258–73.

Honig, B. and Karlsson, T. (2004) 'Institutional Forces and the Written Business Plan', *Journal of Management*, 30(1), 29–48.

Huselid, M.A. (1995) 'The Impact of Human Resource Management Practices on Turnover, Productivity and Corporate Financial Performance', *Academy of Management Journal*, 38(3), 635–72.

Inchniowski, C., Shaw, K. and Prennuski, G. (1997) 'The Effects of Human Resource Management Practices on Productivity: A Study of Steel Finishing Lines', *American Economic Review*, 87(3), 291–313.

Jain, B.A. and Tabak, F. (2008) 'Factors Influencing the Choice between Founder versus Non-founder CEOs for IPO Firms', *Journal of Business Venturing*, 23(1), 21–45.

Karlsson, T. and Honig, B. (2009) 'Judging a Business by Its Cover: An Institutional Perspective on New Ventures and the Business Plan', *Journal of Business Venturing*, 24, 27–45.

Kitching, J. and Blackburn, R. (2002) *The Nature of Training and Motivation to Train in Small Firms*. Research Report RR 330. Sheffield: Department for Education and Skills.

Koeller, C.T. and Lechler, T.G. (2006) 'Economic and Managerial Perspectives on New Venture Growth: An Integrated Analysis', *Small Business Economics*, 26(5), 427–37.

Liao, J. and Gartner, W.B. (2006) 'The Effects of Pre-venture Plan Timing and Perceived Environmental Uncertainty on the Persistence of Emerging Firms', *Small Business Economics*, 27, 23–40.

Mason, C. and Stark, M. (2004) 'What Do Investors Look for in a Business Plan? A Comparison of the Investment Criteria of Bankers, Venture Capitalists and Business Angels', *International Small Business Journal*, 22(3), 227–48.

McPherson, M.A. (1995) 'The Hazards of Small Firm Growth in Southern Africa', *Journal of Development Studies*, 32(1), 31–54.

Mintzberg, H. (1990) 'The Design School: Reconsidering the Basic Premises of Strategic Management', *Strategic Management Journal*, 11(3), 171–95.

Moreno, A.M. and Casillas, J.C. (2007) 'High-growth SMEs versus Non-high-growth SMEs: A Discriminant Analysis', *Entrepreneurship and Regional Development*, 19(1), 69–88.

North, D. and Smallbone, D. (1995) 'The Employment Generation Potential of Mature SMEs in Different Geographical Environments', *Urban Studies*, 32(9), 1517–36.

O'Reagan, N., Ghobadian, A. and Gallear, D. (2006) 'In Search of the Drivers of High Growth in Manufacturing SMEs', *Technovation*, 26(1), 30–41.

Parker, S.C., Storey, D.J. and van Witteloostuijn, A. (2010) 'What Happens to Gazelles?' (forthcoming).

Patterson, M.G., West, M.A., Lawthom, R. and Nickel, S. (1997) 'Impact of People Management Practices on Buisness Performance', *Issues in People Management*, 22. London: Institute of Personnel and Development.

Patton, D., Marlow, S. and Hannon, P. (2000) 'Frameworks and Lost Quests: The Relationship between Training and Small Firm Performance', *International Small Business Journal*, 19(1), 11–27.

Perry, S.C. (2001) 'The Relationship between Written Business Plans and the Failure of Small Businesses in the US', *Journal of Small Business Management*, 39(3), 201–08.

Persson, H. (2004) 'The Survival and Growth of New Establishments in Sweden, 1987–1995', *Small Business Economics*, 23(5), 423–40.

Peters, T.J. and Waterman, R.H. (1984) *In Search of Excellence: Lessons from America's Best-run Companies*. New York: Warner Books.

Robson , P.J.A. and Bennett, R.J. (2000) 'SME Growth: The Relationship with Business Advice and External Collaboration', *Small Business Economics*, 15(3), 193–208.

Roper, S. (1999) 'Modelling Small Business Growth and Profitability', *Small Business Economics*, 13(3), 235–52.

Roper, S. and Hewitt-Dundas, N. (2008) 'Innovation Persistence: Survey and Case Study Evidence', *Research Policy*, 37(1), 149–62.

Rosenzweig, P. (2007) 'Misunderstanding the Nature of Company Performance: The Halo Effect and Other Business Delusions', *California Management Review*, 49(4), 6–20.

Shrader, R. and Siegel, D. (2007) 'Assessing the Relationship between Human Capital and Firm Performance: Evidence from Technology-based New Ventures', *Entrepreneurship: Theory and Practice*, 31(6), 893–908.

Sleuwaegen, L. and Goedhuys, M. (2002) 'Growth of Firms in Developing Countries, Evidence from Côte d'Ivoire', *Journal of Development Economics*, 68(1), 117–35.

Storey, D.J. (1994) *Understanding the Small Business Sector*. London: Routledge.

Storey, D.J. (2004) 'Exploring the Link, among Small Firms, between Management Training and Firm Performance: A Comparison between the UK and Other OECD Countries', *International Journal of Human Resource Management*, 15(1), 112–30.

Storey, D.J. and Westhead, P. (1997) 'Management Training in Small Firms: A Case of Market Failure?', *Human Resource Management Journal*, 7(2), 61–71.

Tether, B.S. and Storey, D.J. (1998) 'Smaller Firms and Europe's High Technology Sectors: A Framework for Analysis and Some Statistical Evidence', *Research Policy*, 26(9), 947–71.

Time (2001) *Reinventing the Wheel*. http://www.time.com/time/business/article/0,8599,186660-4,00.html (accessed 2 December 2001).

Tornikoski, E.T. and Newbert, S.L. (2007) 'Exploring the Determinants of Organizational Emergence: A Legitimacy Perspective', *Journal of Business Venturing*, 22(2), 311–35.

Wasserman, N. (2003) 'Founder-CEO Succession and the Paradox of Entrepreneurial Success', *Organization Science*, 14(2), 149–72.

Willard, G.E., Krueger, D.A. and Feeser, H. R. (1992) 'In Order to Grow, Must the Founder Go?: A Comparison of Performance between Founder and Non-founder Managed High-growth Manufacturing Firms', *Journal of Business Venturing*, 7(3), 181–94.

Winborg, J. and Landstrom, H. (2001) 'Financial Bootstrapping in Small Businesses: Examining Small Business Managers' Resource Acquisition Behaviours', *Journal of Business Venturing* 16(3), 235–54.

Zhou, H. and de Wit, G. (2009) *Determinants and Dimensions of Firm Growth*. SCALES Working Paper H200903. Zoetermeer: EIM.

Part 5

Finance and the Small Business

In Part 5 we turn to the important topic of finance. Chapter 16 describes the basic forms of finance available to the new and established business. In Chapter 17, we present theories of entrepreneurial finance. We, therefore, examine the range of 'signals' available to both the lender (the bank) and the borrower (small business) and the evidence on finance gaps, discrimination and any financial constraints in debt finance. Chapter 18 considers equity finance. That chapter examines the role and activities of two types of equity financiers: 'business angels' and 'venture capitalists'.

16
17
18

Theories of entrepreneurial finance

Debt finance for small businesses

Equity finance for small businesses

Entrepreneurship in Action   FT

Go to the *Small Business and Entrepreneurship* companion website at www.pearsoned.co.uk/storeygreene to watch entrepreneurs and academics giving you their personal perspectives on some of these issues.

Andrew Rickman, investor and entrepreneur, discusses the differences between business angels, 'super angels', and venture capitalists.

Paul Stanyer, CEO of Holidaytaxis.com, talks about his decision to use equity finance to fund his business.

16 Theories of entrepreneurial finance

Key learning objectives

By the end of this chapter you should:

- Understand the key sources of finance for small businesses

- Understand how these sources differ between businesses of different size

- Understand how these sources vary in different macro-economic circumstances.

16.1 Introduction

Finance is a crucial lubricant for small businesses. Without finance – the life blood of a business – it is difficult to see how a business can start, grow or survive. Businesses typically need finance to pay for assets (e.g. plant, machinery and vehicles), to fund the operation of the business (working capital) and to grow the business. For example, Cosh *et al.* (2008) estimated that the median amount of finance used in the UK to start up a business was £7,500.

Growing businesses also need funding. Innocent, the UK 'smoothie' drink maker, announced in 2009 that it had sold between 10 and 20 per cent of the business to Coca-Cola for £30 million. Innocent's rationale was:

> We raised money to make the most of the opportunity we have in Europe. We are on sale in several countries on the continent, and there is a lot of demand for our healthy drinks, but we have been coming under increasing pressure from big brands such as Chiquita and Tropicana (owned by Pepsi) who have launched against us. Without the funds to invest in these markets, we would simply lose the fight. And then that would leave us open to those brands coming after us in our home market of the UK. We want to move forward as a business and the funds raised will allow us to do so.
>
> *Innocent (2009)*

In this chapter, our first aim is to define, describe and quantify the sources of finance available to the small business. In doing so, we draw an important distinction between sources of funds that are used to start a business and the sources of funding used to operate an existing small business.

A second aim of this chapter is to compare – at a general level – the differences between 'small' and 'large' business finance. What we show is that small businesses are more heavily reliant upon their own resources, whilst larger businesses have greater access to, and make greater use of, external finance.

Finally, this chapter shows that the sources used are heavily dependent upon macro-economic conditions and evolve over time. We, therefore, trace some of the changes in how finance has been used by small businesses and compare 'buoyant' 2004 with 'credit-constrained' 2008.

The ultimate purpose of the chapter is to provide an introduction to the factors influencing behaviour in the marketplace for small business finance. As we shall see in Chapters 17 and 18, these basic understandings are developed when we more closely examine debt (e.g. bank) and equity (e.g. venture capital) finance.

16.2 Sources of finance for new and small businesses

This section provides a broad picture of the variety of different sources that a small business may draw upon for funding. We begin by describing and defining each type of funding source available to the small business. We then show how these typically vary between different types of small business and different sizes of small business. Below is a description of 12 main sources of finance available to a small business.

Overdrafts. An overdraft is a facility or option to borrow, provided by a bank, which is flexible in the sense of being able to borrow up to an agreed limit whenever required. The borrower only pays interest when the overdraft facility is used, and not for the availability of the overdraft. The overdraft is expected to fund operational needs (working capital) and to even out fluctuations in cashflow. Its disadvantages are that it is immediately repayable on demand from a bank and that the interest rate payable – if the limit is exceeded without permission – may be punitive.

Grants or subsidised loans. A grant is generally a non-repayable payment that is usually provided by a public organisation. Subsidised loans are repayable, but at an interest rate which is often below commercial rates. The balance is typically funded from public money. Grants and subsidised loans are often only available in certain geographical areas – often those suffering high unemployment, or are made only to businesses in certain sectors such as 'high-tech' or 'creative' sectors.

Term loans. Term loans are made by banks or other financial institutions for a fixed period of time, normally not exceeding three years. In return, repayment is required – of both the amount borrowed and the interest – at agreed regular intervals. Term loans are normally used for the purchase of 'fixed assets' such as plant and machinery.

Asset finance. Besides using a term loan, a business wishing to acquire the use of an asset – such as a machine – can finance this in two main ways: 1) hire purchase – here the business makes regular payments for a fixed time period to the owner of the asset to cover its purchase price, the interest charges and a profit margin – once all payments are complete, the business *owns* the asset; 2) leasing – this is effectively identical to hire purchase except that the ownership of the asset always remains with the owner (lessor) rather than the business (lesee).

Credit cards. This may provide the opportunity to purchase assets or to smooth variations in operational needs (working capital) by providing access to cash. Credit cards are, therefore, often quick and convenient forms of finance. If repaid quickly, the funding also incurs no interest charge, but if the funds are not repaid within that time, the interest rates are punitive.

Equity finance. Equity is a stake or share of the ownership of a business. The owner of a business may choose to sell (normally part) ownership of their business to an outside person or organisation in return for a cash sum. This provides a cash boost to the business upon which there are no interest charges. The 'downside' from the business owner's perspective is that by selling a share of the business, the owner can no longer assume that he or she is in full control of the business.

Equity financiers provides these funds on the expectation that their ownership stake will rise in value as the company grows and that they will be able to recoup their funds in the medium term by selling their ownership. In other words, they are seeking a capital 'gain' from buying equity in a business at a low price and, as the business develops, subsequently selling their equity (share) in the business at a higher price. Normally, a distinction is drawn between formal and informal equity financiers. Formal equity finance is provided by established, and normally specialist, financial institutions. Typically, these financial institutions are called venture capitalists. Venture capitalists' funding is often provided by pension funds or other financial institutions. In contrast, informal equity finance is often provided by 'business angels' – normally very wealthy individuals or groups of individuals looking to diversify their wealth portfolio. Both formal and informal equity financiers seek to purchase ownership with a view to realising at some future point a capital gain.

Personal savings. Cash or other assets of the owner.

Mortgage on home. Funds borrowed based on the collateral value of property. Normally, this is the business owner's own house.

Gifts from friends and family. Gifts are normally assumed to be non-repayable.

Loans from friends and family. Loans are assumed to be repayable. In the case of family and/ or friends, sometimes these will incur some interest charges, but rarely at 'commercial' rates. More frequently, there will be zero or very nominal interest charges.

Asset-based finance. There are three basic types of such financing. First, there is factoring which involves a business *selling* its invoices (its sales not yet paid) to a third party (a 'factor') in return for a proportion of the yet unpaid invoices. Invoice discounting involves the business *borrowing* against its unpaid invoices, again for a fixed proportion of the invoices. Finally, there is stock finance which raises finance *against* the stock a business holds. Such forms of asset-based finance can make a valuable contribution to the cashflow of a small business (working capital) but the cash payment made to, for example, a 'factor' is less than the 'face' value of the invoices/stock.

Other. Trade credit might be an example of another source of finance. Here the business owner may be able to acquire the use of an asset – such as a machine – without having to pay for it until some point in the future.

We now turn to examine the sources of finance used at start up, and for an established business (of two years or more) in the UK.

Sources of start-up finance

Figure 16.1 uses the diagram format of Deakins and Freel (2009) to show a breakdown of the major reported sources of funding amongst UK small businesses. The top row of Figure 16.1 shows that only about 4 per cent of businesses begin without any source of funding.

Of those using some form of finance, Figure 16.1 first distinguishes between internal and external sources of finance. These are not independent of each other. As we will show in Chapter 17, the external resources available to entrepreneurs at start up – the extent to which they can borrow – also depends upon their own wealth or that of their immediate family/ friends. However, for the moment, we discuss them separately simply to provide a basic understanding of their usage.

Illustration	How a business may start up without finance

Hire purchase and deferred costs can help small businesses to start manufacturing and selling their products *before* paying out for plant and equipment.

Although rare, it quite plausible for businesses to begin without any finance. For example, a 'hat maker' may already own a machine and the materials necessary to make an initial batch of hats. Alternatively, they may be able to lease or hire purchase a machine for which the initial payment is not due for three months. They may also be able to convince a material supplier to provide them with materials, payment for which is not due, again, for three months. Using their own stock or a mix of hire purchase (machinery) and trade credit (material supply), the owner subsequently uses the material and the machine to produce hats. The payment for these hats is received before the bills for the materials and the machine have to be settled. When paid, the providers of the material and the machine are likely to be willing to make future supplies. The hat maker may also have enough funds of his/her own (retained profits from the selling of the hats) to be in a position to expand and develop the business.

Internal sources comprise primarily the personal wealth of the business owner and that of his or her immediate family. These are shown in the left-hand side of Figure 16.1. It shows that 85 per cent of new businesses are funded, to some degree, from these internal sources with the most common source being personal savings (91 per cent of all internal sources). This highlights the extent to which new businesses are funded from the personal wealth of the business owner. Two other internal sources are also important: loans and gifts from friends and relations (13 per cent); and house mortgages (4 per cent). The reason why a mortgage is regarded as an internal rather than an external source of funds is that it is directly linked to the wealth of the individual (although the mortgage is, in practice, provided by an external

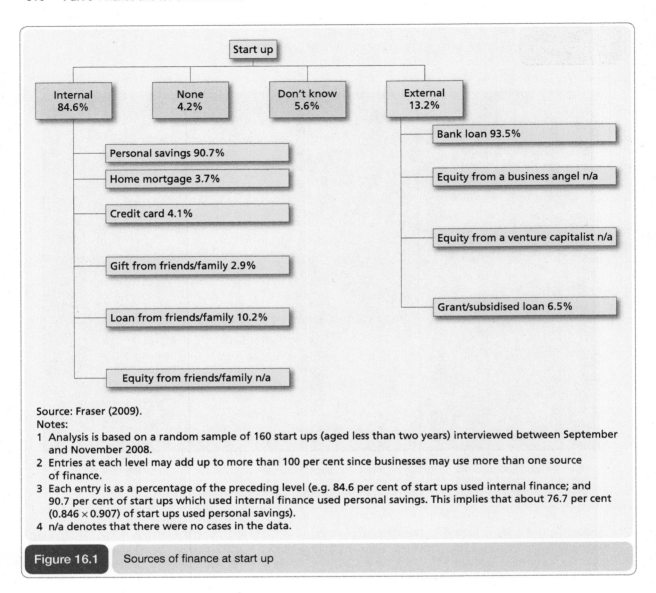

Source: Fraser (2009).
Notes:
1 Analysis is based on a random sample of 160 start ups (aged less than two years) interviewed between September and November 2008.
2 Entries at each level may add up to more than 100 per cent since businesses may use more than one source of finance.
3 Each entry is as a percentage of the preceding level (e.g. 84.6 per cent of start ups used internal finance; and 90.7 per cent of start ups which used internal finance used personal savings. This implies that about 76.7 per cent (0.846 × 0.907) of start ups used personal savings).
4 n/a denotes that there were no cases in the data.

Figure 16.1   Sources of finance at start up

financial institution). The only other internal source identified is credit cards, which are used by 4 per cent of those using internal sources. Again, as with mortgages, this is really an external source, since the credit is provided by an external party, but again we view it as internal because of its close link to a person's financial status/viability. Overall, Figure 16.1 clearly shows the importance of 'internal' sources of finance to the start up. Berger and Udell (1998), for the US, and Cassar (2004), for Australia, also find internal sources to be pivotal.

In contrast, external resources are provided by public and private organisations. These are shown on the right-hand side of Figure 16.1. This figure shows that only 13 per cent of UK start ups are funded from external sources.

Figure 16.1 clearly shows that the most common source of external funding for a new business is a bank loan. Of businesses using external funding sources, more than 90 per cent used a bank loan, and the remainder used some form of public loan or grant. In contrast, the involvement in new businesses of external equity providers – whether formal (venture capitalists) or informal (business angels) – is extremely rare. However, because equity finance is judged to be of central importance to fast-growth businesses, we discuss equity finance more fully in Chapter 18.

Sources of finance for established small businesses

Figure 16.2 examines the sources of funding used by established (more than two years old) UK small businesses over a three-year period (2005–8). Figure 16.2 shows two main differences between established and start-up businesses. First, established businesses make use of a wider range of finance sources that are often easier to access once a business begins trading. Hence, there is greater use of asset finance (leasing and hire purchase), asset-based finance (invoice discounting, factoring and stock finance), term loans and trade credit. Another major difference is that established businesses are much more likely to make use of credit cards. Indeed, credit cards are the source of finance most commonly used (54 per cent) by established businesses. However, both start ups and established small businesses share one major similarity: both are extremely shy of using equity finance. Equity finance is also largely irrelevant – as a proportion of external finance – in other countries such as the US (Berger and Udell, 1998).

Question | Credit cards often attract penal interest rates if a payment is late or if the balance is not fully paid off. Why is it that established businesses use credit cards as a source of finance?

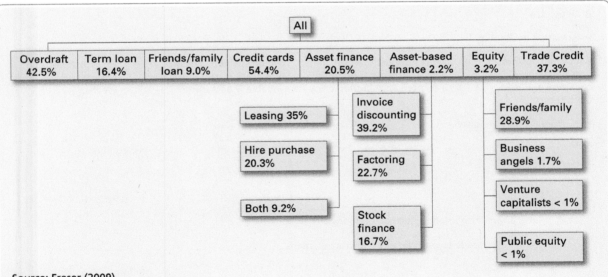

Source: Fraser (2009).

Notes:
1 Analysis is based on a random sample of 2,500 SMEs (fewer than 250 employees) interviewed between September and November 2008.
2 Entries at each level may add up to more than 100 per cent since businesses may use more than one source of finance.
3 Each entry is as a percentage of the preceding level.
4 35 per cent of businesses which had used asset finance in the last three years were no longer using it at the time they were interviewed.
5 27.3 per cent of businesses which had used asset-based finance in the last three years were no longer using it at the time they were interviewed.

Figure 16.2 | Sources of finance used in the last three years: all firms

16.3 Differences between small and large businesses

To demonstrate how large and small businesses utilise very different sources of finance, we draw upon the diagram first formulated by Berger and Udell (1998) and shown as Figure 16.3. The diagram assumes that businesses lie on a stylised age/size continuum, with older, large businesses on the right side and younger, newer businesses on the left. It shows that the sources of funds used vary along that continuum. So, young businesses rely heavily upon internal sources of finance (e.g. personal savings, retained profits) but, as they mature and increase in size, they are increasingly able to draw upon trade credit and the short- to medium-term loan market.

However, Figure 16.3 also makes it clear that smaller businesses do not have access to the same sources of finance used by large businesses. For example, it is difficult to see how a small or new business can sell 'commercial paper' (a promise to pay at a date in the future the face amount of the loan) to fund its short-term working capital needs (e.g. paying wages) because commercial paper often requires an excellent and long-established track record with a credit rating agency. Similarly, very many small businesses have difficulties making 'private placings' (issue of equity to a restricted number of institutions or high net worth individuals) because the market for small business equity is often illiquid (see Chapter 17) and because very many small businesses lack the assets (e.g. capital equipment) that are often required as collateral by funders (see Case study 3).

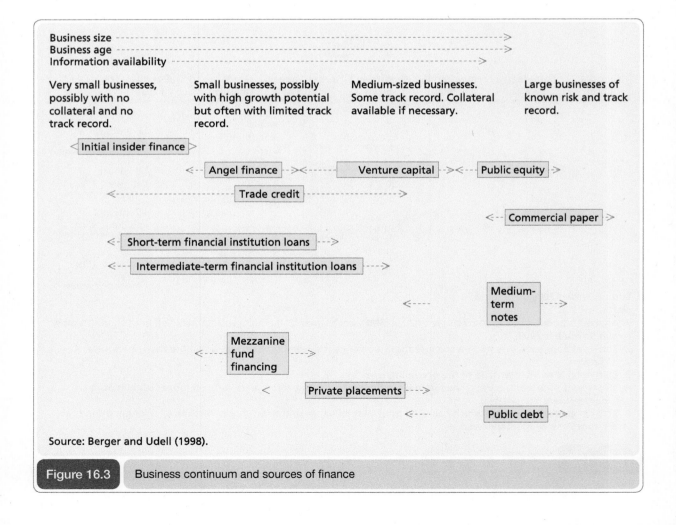

Source: Berger and Udell (1998).

Figure 16.3 Business continuum and sources of finance

Table 16.1	Sources of funds used to finance small businesses (by business size in 2004)				
Type of business	**All (% using)**	**0 Employees (% using)**	**1–9 Employees (% using)**	**10–49 Employees (% using)**	**50–249 Employees (% using)**
Type of finance					
Overdrafts	53	46	63	70	81
Grants	6	4	10	12	21
Term loans	24	17	35	40	58
Asset finance	27	17	38	61	75
Asset-based finance	3	2	3	11	24
Credit cards	55	50	62	70	74
Equity finance	3	1	5	6	12

Source: Fraser (2005).

Table 16.1 further illustrates the differences between smaller and larger businesses. It illustrates four main points:

1 The smallest businesses – those without employees – are the least likely to use any of the external sources of funds. Instead, their funding is heavily dependent upon internal sources (e.g. retained profits).

2 Where external sources are used by these smallest businesses, by far the two most frequently used are credit cards and overdrafts. Such business, though, make little use of asset-based finance (e.g. factoring). In contrast, medium-sized businesses – those with between 50 and 249 employees – make extensive use of asset funding (e.g. leasing), with it being used by a similar proportion to those using credit cards and overdrafts.

3 The medium-sized businesses are much more likely to use multiple sources of finance than the smaller businesses. Mach and Wolken (2006) found similar results for the US.

4 Only 3 per cent of businesses make any use of equity finance – this reflects that it is virtually irrelevant to most smaller businesses. However, equity finance is much more likely to be used by medium-sized businesses. Table 16.1 shows that 12 per cent of businesses with 50 or more employees have made some use of equity in the past three years, compared with only 1 per cent of businesses without any employees. Nevertheless, even for those using some form of external equity, it was the least likely source of finance to be used.

Burns (2007) also suggests that small businesses, in comparison with large businesses, over-invest in debtors (literally people in *debt* to you) and stock, but under-invest in fixed assets (e.g. machinery and equipment). He also finds that small businesses are more reliant on trade credit and on short-term finance (e.g. overdrafts and term loans). Compared with large businesses they are under-capitalised. In other words, small businesses often do not have enough funds to support their activities and investments. We explore the reasons for this in Chapter 17.

16.4 Changes over time

In this final section, we examine how the use of finance has changed over time. We present four pieces of evidence. First, we examine the evolution of finance for new businesses. We then compare how established businesses' use of finance has changed between 1991 and 2004.

Finally, we compare and contrast the situation in 'buoyant' 2004 with that of 'credit-constrained' 2008.

Table 16.2 uses data on financing new businesses in Teesside in northern England (Greene *et al.*, 2008). Table 16.2 is useful because it shows the monetary importance of a particular type of finance. In other words, it provides information on which sources of finance are important, rather on how frequently a source of finance is used. The patterns in the table are clear and seem to vary only modestly over time. The single most important source of finance used to start a new business, in monetary terms, is the personal savings of the business owner. The second most important source is funding from banks, in the form of loans and overdrafts. The only other major source is that of friends and family, although in the 1980s extending the house mortgage was also quite important, perhaps because in the UK house ownership became more prevalent.

The evidence from Table 16.2 suggests that, at least for new businesses, the most important (monetary value) sources of finance have remained broadly similar over a 30-year period. However, it is clear from the earlier Figures 16.1 and 16.2 that there exists today a wider range of finance sources available to the new and existing small business. Perhaps the most striking example of this is the credit card but there have also been developments in the use of finance (e.g. leasing) and asset-based finance (e.g. factoring).

These changes are reflected in Table 16.3 which compares sources of finance used by UK SME business service and manufacturing businesses. It compares the recessionary conditions

Table 16.2	Most important sources of funding for new businesses in Teesside					
Source of finance	**1970s**	**Rank**	**1980s**	**Rank**	**1990s**	**Rank**
Personal savings	32.4	2	45.8	1	58.0	1
House mortgage	2.9	5	11.9	3	1.7	4
Bank	44.1	1	37.3	2	16.6	2
Finance company	5.9	4	5.1	4	1.7	4
Friends and family	14.7	3	0.0	5	10.5	3

Source: Greene *et al.* (2008): 156.

Table 16.3	Sources of external finance for businesses that raised finance (% of total finance raised)	
Source of finance	**1991**	**2004**
Banks	61.5	55.0
HP/Leasing	18.5	16.4
Partners/Shareholders	6.7	6.4
Other sources	4.6	7.2
Venture capital	2.8	5.1
Invoice finance	2.4	6.1
Trade credit	2.3	0.7
Private individuals	1.2	3.1

Source: Centre for Business Research (2007), exhibit 9.16.

of 1991 with buoyant 2004. Over that time there remain some similarities, but some differences also appear. The key similarity is the dominant role of the banks as suppliers of the bulk of SME external finance – confirming the finding in Figure 16.1. The second most important source of funding – asset funding (leasing, hire purchase) – continues to be almost equally important in 2004. The key differences are the growth, albeit from low bases, of invoice financing and venture capital.

In general, therefore, the evidence indicates that access to finance, until the 2008 recession, had become less problematic for small businesses. Greene *et al.* (2008) examine changes in new business finance over three decades in North East England. Their conclusion is compatible with that shown in Table 16.3. They find:

> In buoyant macro-economic conditions access to finance is significantly less of a problem than was the case two decades ago. In part, this is because of greater competition amongst suppliers of finance and in part because those suppliers are better informed due to technological changes and the ease of processing customer information.

This position changed radically with the onset of the 2008 recession. Figure 16.4 shows how the usage of particular sources of external finance altered between 2004 and 2008. It shows that, whilst there are many different sources of finance used by established small businesses, in practice three are dominant. For operational businesses, more than half of small businesses in buoyant 2004 had used an overdraft in the last three years, and a similar proportion used credit cards. In 2004, about one in four used a term loan and almost one in three used some form of asset financing. However, in credit-constrained 2008, virtually all sources of finance were used less – although the use of credit cards was reduced only very marginally.

Table 16.4 further illustrates the changes that have taken place over the same four-year period. It shows that rejection rates for those SMEs seeking bank finance more than doubled over the period. This is the case for both term loans and overdrafts. Yet, even this statistic

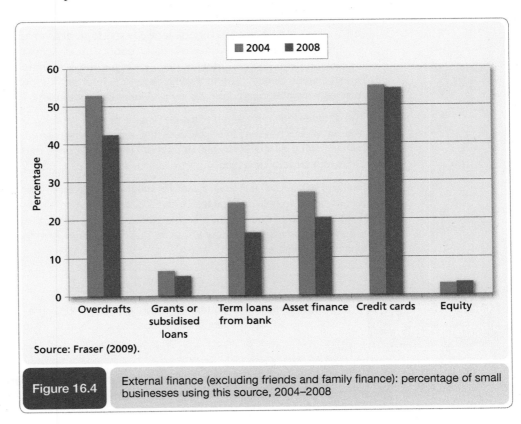

Source: Fraser (2009).

| Figure 16.4 | External finance (excluding friends and family finance): percentage of small businesses using this source, 2004–2008 |

Table 16.4	Rejection and discouragement rates, 2004–2008			
	Rejection rate in 2004	**Rejection rate in 2008**	**Percentage discouraged in 2004**	**Percentage discouraged in 2008**
Term loans	7.4	16.3	3.9	9.8
Overdrafts	7.2	15.3	n.a	n.a

Source: Fraser (2009).

under-estimates the tightening of the credit market, since, to be rejected, businesses must have applied for funds in the first place. If businesses feel that it is pointless applying for funds because they believe they will be rejected, then they are defined as 'discouraged' (Kon and Storey 2004). The table shows that the proportion of SMEs that were discouraged rose even faster than those rejected, from 3.9 per cent to 9.8 per cent. Finally, we can estimate the total number of businesses denied access to funds by combining the numbers of both rejections and the discouraged. This implies that the proportion of businesses denied access to funds rose from about 11 per cent to about 25 per cent over the four-year period.

In essence, therefore, this section has shown that there has been a steady maturing and a wider range of external finance used by smaller businesses. However, access to such finance remains contingent on macroeconomic conditions.

Summary

This chapter has identified and defined the key sources of finance used by small businesses. It has made a distinction between the sources used when the business starts and those used once the small business is established. It concluded that, when they begin, small businesses draw heavily upon the wealth of the founder, and that about one in five obtain bank funding, generally in the form of term loans. Once they reach a 'steady state', small businesses draw upon a much greater variety of sources, including retained profits, credit cards, term loans and overdrafts from the bank. Asset-based finance is also important. What was not important for the vast majority of small businesses was funding from equity providers like venture capitalists.

The chapter then contrasted – at a general level – the sources of finance used by large and small businesses. It concluded that small businesses are much more heavily reliant upon their own (internal) resources, whereas access to the capital market was critical for large businesses.

Finally, the chapter suggested that for much of the period from the early 1990s until recent times, small businesses in the UK were able to draw upon an increasingly diverse source of funds. However, the 2008 recession abruptly halted that trend, to the extent that perhaps one in four UK small businesses were unable to access the funding which they required.

Questions for discussion

1 What are the prime sources of finance used in starting a small business? How and why do these change as the business develops?

2 What is meant by factoring? Describe the role that it might play in financing a small business.

3 Describe the various forms of asset finance. What advice would you provide to a small business seeking to choose between them?

References

Berger, A.N. and Udell, G.F. (1998) 'The Economics of Small Business Finance: The Roles of Private Equity and Debt Markets in the Financial Growth Cycle', *Journal of Banking and Finance*, 22(6–8), 613–73.

Burns, P. (2007) *Entrepreneurship and Small Business*. Basingstoke: Palgrave.

Cassar, G. (2004) 'The Financing of Business Start-ups', *Journal of Business Venturing*, 19(2), 261–83.

Cosh, A. and Hughes, A. (2007) *British Enterprise: Thriving or Surviving?* Cambridge: Centre for Business Research, University of Cambridge.

Cosh, A., Hughes, A., Bullock, A. and Milner, I. (2009) *SME Finance and Innovation in the Current Economic Crisis*. Cambridge: Centre for Business Research, University of Cambridge.

Deakins, D. and Freel, M. (2009) *Entrepreneurship and Small Firms*. London: McGraw-Hill.

Fraser, S. (2005) *Finance for Small and Medium-sized Enterprises*. London: Bank of England.

Fraser, S. (2009) *How Have SME Finances Been Affected by the Credit Crisis?* London: BERR/ESRC Seminar.

Greene, F.J., Mole, K.M. and Storey, D.J. (2008) *Three Decades of Enterprise Culture*. Basingstoke: Palgrave.

Innocent (2009) *Why Did You Raise Funds, Couldn't You Have Stayed as You Are?*. http://www.innocentdrinks.co.uk (accessed 25 June 2009).

Kon, Y. and Storey, D.J. (2003) 'A Theory of Discouraged Borrowers', *Small Business Economics*, 21(1), 37–49.

Mach, T.L. and Wolken, J.D. (2006) 'Financial Services Used by Small Businesses: Evidence from the 2003 Survey of Small Business Finances', *Federal Reserve Bulletin*, 92, A167–95.

17 Debt finance

Mini contents list

Key learning objectives

By the end of this chapter you should:

- Clearly distinguish entrepreneurial from corporate finance
- Recognise that the key characteristic of the entrepreneurial finance marketplace is its opacity
- Identify the responses of both the small business and the finance suppliers to this opacity
- Reach a judgement about whether the market opacity means that too many 'good' small businesses are denied access to credit and if there is discrimination in the credit market.

17.1 Introduction

The central purpose of this chapter is to provide an understanding of *why* some small businesses successfully access the funds they require, and others do not. We will see that funds for small businesses are provided in a marketplace, meaning that lack of access could be a reflection of supply and demand factors. If the marketplace works well, the 'good' borrowers will get the money and the 'bad' borrowers will be rejected. If the market works less well then some good borrowers will not be funded and some bad borrowers will be funded. We will assess the extent to which the small business finance marketplace works well, and the extent to which it is imperfect.

In Chapter 16, we saw that the sources of finance used by large and small businesses were very different. This implies that the small business finance marketplace is very different from the large business finance marketplace. This chapter identifies the three key reasons for this (Han *et al.* 2009a):

1 The entrepreneur's personal characteristics play a much more pivotal role in financing small, than large, businesses. For example, the personal wealth of the owner is frequently used to access bank loans and so is closely linked with the assets of the business (Ang *et al.* 1995). Because of this, a distinction is often made between 'entrepreneurial finance' and 'corporate finance'.

2 Compared with 'corporate finance', 'entrepreneurial finance' places greater emphasis on the risks associated with business closure (this risk is often called 'downside risk') as smaller businesses have a higher likelihood of defaulting on their loan. This is because business closure is far more characteristic of new and small businesses than it is of large and mature businesses (see Chapter 9).

3   The market for entrepreneurial finance is marked by a lack of information. For example, in comparison with large businesses, very little information about small businesses or their owners is in the public domain (e.g. there is virtually no public information on sole traders or partnerships and limited companies often only have to provide abbreviated financial accounts). Collecting such information is, therefore, costly for the finance provider, particularly in proportion to the amounts borrowed. The term that is used to describe the marketplace for entrepreneurial finance, reflecting these information imperfections, is 'opaque'. So, although information gaps also exist in public corporations between insiders and outsiders, the gaps are argued to be less likely to materially affect the decisions of external financiers than is the case for small businesses.

The key themes of the chapter reflect these three characteristics. In Chapter 16, we identified that the most common form of external finance used by a small business was debt finance (e.g. term loans), usually provided by a bank. In this chapter, we examine how a supplier of funds – which we will call the bank – knows that small business customers are both more diverse and more risky than large business customers. By 'more risky', we mean that the proportion of 'bad' to 'good' customers is higher, and a good customer is defined from the lender's perspective as one making full and timely repayment of outstanding debt. The bank also knows that, whilst some small business customers are good and others are not, it does not know which customers are which. Hence, there is imperfect knowledge. Faced with an opaque marketplace, the bank collects information in order to be able to identify the good from the bad businesses. For its part, the good business will send 'signals' to the bank which aim to show that it is a good business. The bad business will try to send the same signals, in the hope that the bank is not able to decode them accurately.

17.2 Financing large and small businesses: key concepts

Chapter 1 identified a number of aspects which emphasised that smaller businesses were not simply 'scaled down versions' of larger businesses. In finance, these 'stylised' differences were set out by Ang (1991):

- A large business has access to capital markets for debt and equity. Their shareholders have limited liabilities and own diversified portfolios.

- A small business has no publicly traded securities. Owners have undiversified personal portfolios. Limited liability is absent or ineffective. Owners could be risk lovers.

In Chapter 16, we noted that small businesses are funded primarily from personal savings, retained profits and the banks. As Ang notes, the capital or stock markets, so crucial to larger businesses as a source of funding, are irrelevant to the vast bulk of small businesses, because they are often unincorporated so cannot easily 'trade' equity.

Both large and small businesses, therefore, can find funding in the marketplace, but the nature of these marketplaces is very different. We now review two dimensions in which small and large businesses differ. Both are key influences on entrepreneurial finance: information and performance diversity.

Information

Markets work efficiently when there is accurate information available to both buyers and sellers. It is primarily to inform stock markets that large businesses make quarterly statements

Illustration	Bernard Madoff

The finance market is prone to abuse, as the high-profile case of Bernard Madoff showed.

Bernard Madoff was the former chairman of the NASDAQ stock exchange and had run his business for more than 40 years. His clients included the rich and famous as well as established and reputable banks. Unknown to these clients, Madoff was actually running a giant $50 billion 'Ponzi' scheme, which is a pyramid scheme that 'robs' Peter (the new investor) to 'pay' Paul (the original investor). He eventually confessed that 'it's all just one big lie'.

about their financial performance. It is for the same reason that an information 'industry' has developed around stock markets – comprising the financial press, specialist media and financial brokers. The task of that industry is to provide information about current and expected future financial performance of listed businesses. For this reason, boardroom disputes in listed companies are viewed as 'newsworthy'. For example, take the dispute between the founder of the easyJet airline, Stelios Haji-Ioannou, and the management board of easyJet over its strategy. This 'spat' led to a fall in the share price of easyJet shares by 14 per cent (*Europe Airline Daily*, 2008). Equally, the retirement, or departure, of a highly regarded chief executive is news on the grounds that this may lead to poorer future performance. For example, Aer Lingus, the Irish airline, saw its chief executive, Dermot Mannion, leave '. . . to bring fresh thinking and new ideas to the business' (*Guardian*, 2009).

The contrast with small businesses could not be starker. Whilst many large businesses make daily appearances in the financial press, small businesses rarely appear. To illustrate this difference, take the example of the *Financial Times*. Its UK edition generally has about 50 pages per day (excluding supplements). Over a six-day week there will be perhaps three pages devoted to smaller businesses, whilst more than 150 pages are devoted to large businesses – the remainder of the newspaper providing more general economic news and comment. Yet, as Chapter 2 showed, this 50:1 ratio does not reflect the economic contribution of small and large businesses. If, for example, the 'coverage' ratio were based upon employment then it would be about 1:1 (see Chapter 3). If coverage reflected contribution to GDP, it might be nearly 2:1 – but nothing like 50:1. Instead, the ratio reflects the demand for information on large businesses that oils the operation of financial markets.

The demand for information about small businesses is much more limited, primarily because their shares are not normally traded. The consequence is that the owner of a small business has vastly greater knowledge about the current and expected future performance of their business than anyone else, particularly those outside the business. Information available to outsiders is said to be *imperfect*.

Also, in contrast to large businesses, external organisations such as banks or providers of trade credit often have highly imperfect information about the performance of individual small businesses. Banks, faced with a decision of whether or not to lend to a small business, cannot pick up the papers and expect to read about the business. Nor can they get a broker's report on the business, or expect to see the chief executive on television and form their own impression of his or her competence.

They cannot even assume that, because the sector in which the business trades is either prospering or, conversely, facing difficulties, this means that an individual small business reflects such trends. For example, a small business may occupy a profitable niche in an otherwise troubled sector or may find itself 'shut out' of a generally booming market. In contrast, large businesses, or market leaders, are much more likely to reflect market trends, simply because of their large market share.

In most countries, the amount of publicly available information on small businesses is very modest indeed. In most cases, the small company is only legally required to provide publicly available audited accounts information on an annual basis – and very often that information refers to a period some considerable time in the past. Because of this, even recently published accounts are a very imperfect guide if a bank is seeking guidance today on whether a loan application should be granted. Furthermore, the information required is generally only at an aggregate level. In the UK, for example, small companies are required only to submit 'modified' accounts which, for the smallest size of company, does not even require a statement on total value of sales in the year. A detailed picture of the business is, therefore, not easily available to outsiders. Yet, even this level of public disclosure is only required for smaller businesses that choose limited liability status (see Chapter 14). For those small businesses choosing to remain as sole proprietors, or as partnerships, there is no requirement for information about their business to be made public.

Berger and Udell (1998) refer to the small business financing marketplace as characterised by '*information opacity*'. By this they mean that, whilst some information is available to outsiders, it can be very imperfect. One analogy is that the external provider of finance to a small business is peering into a fog, through which only a somewhat blurred picture emerges.

We will use this 'fog' analogy several times in the chapter, since the response of an individual caught in fog is to 'signal'. As we noted earlier, it is the ability of the small business to send signals that are positively received by the bank that ensures that the negative effects of 'information opacity' are minimised. Equally, it is the role of the suppliers of finance both to correctly interpret the signals received, and to send out their own positive signals. It is this which determines their success in lending to those with the strongest likelihood of repaying. We discuss signalling later on in the chapter.

Question

Below are the financial profiles of two British companies (Table 17.1). One is W.H. Smith, which is a plc and retails books, newspapers and stationery. The other is W.H. Smith (Harborne) Ltd, which is a small investment company. Because of its size, W.H. Smith (Harborne) is not legally required to provide full accounts. Suppose that you were interested in owning shares in these companies. What sorts of financial information might you require to make such a decision? In the case of W.H. Smith (Harborne), how could you go about collecting extra information to inform your decision?

Table 17.1	Comparison of the financial profile of two UK companies	
	W.H. Smith plc	**W.H. Smith (Harborne) Limited**
	31/08/08	31/03/08
	12 months	12 months
	mil GBP	mil GBP
Financial profile		
Turnover	1,352	
Profit (Loss) before taxation	76	
Net tangible assets (Liabilities)	130	0.10
Shareholders funds	161	0.10
Profit margin (%)	5.62	
Return on shareholders funds (%)	47.20	
Return on capital employed (%)	41.08	
Liquidity ratio	0.31	1.88
Gearing ratio (%)	32.92	
Number of employees	17891	

Source: FAME (2009).

Performance variance

Chapters 9 and 10 showed that small businesses are more likely to fail than large businesses. As a group, they are, therefore, viewed as risky, since the lender is less likely to be repaid in full. Even if small businesses survive, their performance is more variable than that of larger businesses. The variance of (sales) growth, both positive and negative, is larger for small businesses. For example, Dunne and Hughes (1994) showed, for a sample of quoted and unquoted UK companies, that the standard deviation of growth rates of companies with net assets of less than £1 m is approximately five times that of companies with net assets exceeding £64 m. More recent work by Sutton (1997) also found a similar relationship, but of a much smaller magnitude. In other words, there is greater variation in the performance of smaller businesses.

This is likely to reflect the diverse motivations of small business owners. As we noted in Chapter 1, some small business owners see their business as a route to considerable personal wealth, some see it as a temporary activity, others as a hobby and still others as a desirable way of providing an income for themselves and their family. A final, unscrupulous, group may view it as a means of defrauding the government of tax revenue, finance providers of repayments, and customers and suppliers of their payments. This performance variability makes the provider of finance to a small business nervous, and further encourages the collection of (expensive) information to seek to identify the good from the bad borrower.

All this contrasts with the assumptions of classical economic theory in which enterprises operate in a perfectly informed marketplace, and are assumed to maximise shareholder value. In reality, small businesses frequently operate in local product niches where competition is modest and where the business owner can survive without necessarily seeking to maximise either profitability or their own income derived from the business.

These clear differences between large and small business justify the use of a radically different theoretical framework to provide a real understanding of the market for entrepreneurial finance. Let us now examine the key building blocks of this theory.

17.3 Entrepreneurial finance theory

Small business or entrepreneurial finance theory draws upon the following: agency theory; information asymmetries and imperfections; failure costs; and pecking order (or bootstrapping).

Agency theory

Agency theory is applied in contexts where there is an arm's-length relationship between two parties – the *principal* and the *agent*. The principal takes some action which benefits the agent, but from which the principal expects a payback. A second assumption of the theory is that the principal has imperfect control over, and/or knowledge of, the actions of the agent, and that the agent has objectives that differ from those of the principal. Finally, the theory assumes that it is costly for the principal to monitor the agent to ensure perfect compliance.

This theory is highly relevant to understanding the relationship between the small business and its bank. The central problem for the bank – the principal – is how to ensure that the small business – the agent – uses its finance in a manner likely to lead to repayment of a loan, with interest, in full and on time. Agency theory assumes that to achieve this, the lender specifies, and is able to enforce, a contract in which any agent behaviour that is regarded as unacceptable to the principal is discouraged. For example, a small business borrowing money from the bank will normally have a contract which requires repayment at regular intervals and, in the event of non-repayment, the bank has the option of either imposing financial penalties or claiming ownership of some or all of the business's assets. There may also be restrictions on how the business may use the monies lent. For example, monies lent by the bank for the purpose of purchasing new plant and machinery may be clearly specified in the contract – preventing them from being spent, for example, on a new Porsche.

However, the extent to which the lender is able to monitor the actions and efforts of the borrower is variable, and is likely to be less in the case of smaller businesses, compared with larger businesses. This is because the bank may have many small business customers who borrow modest sums of money, making it difficult to keep detailed track of these customers, except by monitoring repayment or non-payment. From the bank's perspective, it is clearly uneconomic to spend considerable sums of money monitoring small loans. However, it may be much more rational for the bank to spend heavily on monitoring a small number of its largest loans.

The contract, therefore, is a vital mechanism which the principal (the bank) uses to specify the terms and conditions of the loan, and then uses it to monitor and control its agent (the small business). The contract means that the principal incurs agency costs, in addition to those of any loss in the event of a default. These agency costs are:

- drawing up and managing the contract;
- setting performance standards;
- setting in place a mechanism for enforcing repayment in some form in the event of a default.

Specifying the small business–bank relationship in terms of principal–agent offers the following insights:

1 Several agency costs are fixed – such as the drawing up of the contract and the requirement to establish a monitoring system – irrespective of the sum of money borrowed. This means that the agency costs – per pound, euro or dollar borrowed – will be higher for smaller, rather than for larger, sums. Since small businesses are more likely to borrow smaller sums, they would be expected to pay higher costs per pound, euro or dollar borrowed.

2 The principal's access to monitoring information on small businesses is likely to be relatively expensive to obtain, compared with larger businesses. Unlike small businesses, large businesses are required to provide detailed, publicly available, information. And, as we noted earlier, there is an active market for information about large businesses which does not exist for small businesses.

3 Principal–agent theory provides one explanation for the complexity of bank lending contracts, as the principal seeks to ensure that the agent is excluded from taking any action which might jeopardise its interests.

Information asymmetries

Besides information being imperfect, it is also often unequally shared amongst the parties. Such informational 'asymmetries' usually favour the smaller business. As we have seen, they, rather than the bank, are more likely to be better informed about their business. Although the bank may have access to a business' financial transactions, it is likely that the owner will know immediately whether there is good news – such as acquiring a new contract – or bad news, such as non- or late payment from a major customer. In contrast, the bank may know something about developments in the sector, but will only become aware of any problems in that particular business once either the business informs them, or when there is a default on repayments. This asymmetry is of course even greater for potential lenders who do not have access to banking records.

Illustration	Moral hazard and adverse selection

There are two key consequences of asymmetric information – adverse selection and moral hazard. Adverse selection occurs because the party with poor information – the lender – is unable to distinguish the good from the bad borrower and therefore makes poor lending decisions. It risks lending to the bad borrower and so not being repaid. It also denies funding to the good borrower who would have repaid in full and with interest.

The second consequence is moral hazard. This we discuss in more detail in Chapter 18 but for current purposes it is sufficient to note that the contract designed to overcome asymmetric information can influence the behaviour of the borrowing party. A simple example of this is car insurance. If someone insures a car, they usually have to pay an 'excess'. If this excess is high then – other things being equal – they are more likely to make sure they do not damage the car because they have to pay the high excess before they receive an insurance payout. Suppose, though, that the excess is close to zero. The car owner is less likely to worry about damaging the car.

Perhaps the only exception to asymmetric in
perhaps before, the business starts. At that tim
plete idea of their own entrepreneurial talent
ceed. In contrast, the lender may have many ye
This experience is often shaped by their und
businesses are in particular locations and th
business borrowers and the previous credit w
words, it is able to accurately credit score a nev

Illustration	Credit scoring

This is what the British Bankers Association has to say about credit scoring.

Credit scoring takes into account information banks may hold about you, and any information they may obtain from other organisations, such as credit reference or fraud prevention agencies. Where they use information from other organisations, they will tell you who they are. In this objective process, information regarding race, gender disability, colour and religion is not used . . . The credit scoring system allocates points for each piece of relevant information and adds these up to produce a score. When your score reaches a certain level then banks may agree to your application. If your score does not reach this level, they may not. Additionally, banks may have policy rules to determine what sort of financial products they are prepared to offer and at what price. These reflect their commercial experience and requirements . . . The points allocated are based on many factors such as, for example, thorough analysis of large numbers of repayment histories over many years of providing credit. This statistical analysis enables banks to identify characteristics that predict a likelihood of future performance. Credit scoring is designed to ensure all applicants are treated fairly. Every credit application involves a certain level of repayment risk for the lender, no matter how reliable or responsible an applicant is. Credit scoring is one of the ways that lenders use to calculate the level of risk associated with lending money, based on the information obtained. If the level of acceptable risk is exceeded, the lender may refuse the application or offer the applicant a more appropriate alternative.

Source: British Bankers Association, 14 December 2005.

The bank can use this information to make an informed judgement of the likelihood of success of the new venture – a judgement which may be better informed than that made by the business owner. In this case, the information is again asymmetric, but here the information of the owner is more imperfect than that available to the lender.

Specifying the bank – small business relationship in terms of asymmetric information offers the following insights:

● The bank, because of its information disadvantages, seeks to compensate by collecting and processing information about its client base.

● It uses that information both to compensate for its disadvantage in dealing with individual small businesses, but also to gain a comparative advantage over rival lenders who may be even more disadvantaged. The informed bank will be able to make more loans to good borrowers and fewer loans to bad borrowers than the ill-informed bank. Indeed, it is this skill which determines the bank's success in the lending marketplace.

Failure costs

In the most simple of cases, where the assets of the business are less than the liabilities, there would be an equal proportionate payout to all creditors in the event of a business 'failing'.

it is rarely the case that all the creditors are deemed to be 'equal'. In most instances, are **preferred creditors** who are either repaid in full, or who take priority over other, called **unsecured creditors**. In most countries, the government – in the form of unpaid tax bills – is normally a preferred creditor. A second priority creditor may be a financial institution which has lent money to the business and where this is linked to an identifiable asset (e.g. a house). In the event of a default, the lender may have priority access to that resource. It is also the case that the amount of money retained by the business owner in the event of failure also influences the amount available for distribution amongst the creditors. In some countries, most notably the US, this proportion varies quite markedly between individual states, leading to access to finance being more difficult in those states where bankrupts are able to retain a high proportion of their former assets than where the allowance is less generous (Gropp *et al.* 1997).

The implication is that those organisations or individuals that are low in priority are understandably more nervous about lending to small enterprises than high priority lenders. Two main options are open to the lender:

1 Charge higher rates of interest on the money they lend.

2 Ensure that their lending is secured – ideally on a specific asset upon which they can claim ownership in the event of default. However, 'perfect' assets rarely exist. Even the house of the business owner is an imperfect asset in four respects.

   (a) Valuations are notoriously subjective and imperfect. This generally means the bank will have a much lower valuation of the property than does its owner, but each may be able to justify their own valuation.

   (b) There are transaction costs to the bank in selling the house.

   (c) House prices often fall sharply in recession conditions when the number of failed businesses increases. So, the bank will be more likely to be selling in conditions when sales are low and prices are falling.

   (d) There is the opportunity for considerable negative publicity if the bank is seeking to sell the house of a business owner whose family may have been unaware of the debts of the business, or that the house in which they lived was secured against those debts. Media coverage of banks putting children 'out on the street' is unlikely to be welcome publicity.

Pecking order or bootstrapping

The central plank of the Pecking Order Hypothesis (POH) is that business owners prefer one source of finance over another – even if they are 'priced' similarly. POH, as originally developed by Myers (1984) and Myers and Majluf (1984), applied to large businesses. It argued that a company with good prospects would avoid selling shares (equity) to outsiders, since this would dilute their ownership. Instead, shareholders would seek alternative sources of funds. The most favoured source – highest in the 'pecking order' – would be internally generated profits, on the grounds that this involved no repayment commitment.

Chapter 16 has already shown the extensive use of personal savings and retained profits in the financing of small businesses. Second in the pecking order was debt finance. Here there was a repayment commitment, but not one in which they were required to share ownership. Chapter 16, again, showed that debt finance was the most frequently used external source of finance.

Watson and Wilson (2002) argue that, although developed to explain the behaviour of large public companies, POH is highly relevant to small business because owners also seemed to prefer internally generated sources of funds over external sources. Vanacker and Manigart (2008) show, for instance, that Belgian growth businesses are more likely to prefer using retained profits (internal source of finance) rather than debt or equity finance. Equally, debt finance seems to be preferred to equity finance by these growth businesses. This meant that businesses owned by individuals who expected their business would grow (and hence become more valuable) would seek to avoid diluting their shareholding – selling equity – at almost any cost. Their response to financial constraints is to become highly creative in finding alternative ways to fund their enterprise. These ways were collectively described as 'bootstrapping' (Winborg and Landstrom (2001); Ebben and Johnson (2006)). Examples of bootstrapping include business owners delaying making payments, forgoing salary, buying second-hand equipment, or using the owner's credit card despite the risks involved, rather than seeking external funding.

17.4 Operating in an opaque marketplace

The preceding sections have emphasised that the entrepreneurial finance marketplace is characterised by high risk, and by imperfect and asymmetric information. The market is opaque or 'foggy' but the bank and the small business can send 'signals' to one another (Blumberg and Letterie 2007).

What does the small business do?

The small business has to persuade the bank that they are good, in the sense of being prepared to repay in full any loans. Their task is to send positive signals to the bank to persuade them of their 'quality'. The small business can generally do this in six ways. The first five are individual approaches – defined as actions taken by individual businesses. The sixth is a 'collective' approach which will be described in more depth:

1 The small business may point to their creditworthiness, possibly with the same bank. This is called 'the relationship factor': it means that small business owners who have banked with the same institution for a number of years and have an unblemished credit history are more likely to obtain loans, possibly at a lower rate, than individuals who have moved banks (Petersen and Rajan 1994). In these cases, the bank can consult its own records to confirm the credit history of the individual.

2 The bank may collect additional information that will allow it to evaluate a small business borrower. The task of the small business may, therefore, be to produce a plausible business plan, or emphasise those aspects of his or her background that will reassure the bank.

3 The business may provide collateral to cover the value of the loan in the case of a default. The bank may view this as a positive signal, reflecting the confidence of the entrepreneur that the business will succeed.

4 The business may provide third-party cover in the event of a loan default. Again this may reassure the bank that any losses would be limited.

5 The most difficult to demonstrate to the lender is the entrepreneurial talent (θ) of the borrower. It is to be expected that those individuals with greater entrepreneurial talent would be more likely to be funded, but persuading the lender of this is tricky.

6 The final approach to addressing the collateral shortage problem is a collective one in which small enterprises collaborate with each other to reduce the risk to lenders (Wydick 1999; Zeller 2003). The clearest example of this is the establishment of a mutual guarantee scheme or group lending. Here, groups of people or businesses come together to create a

fund. Each individual or business makes a payment into the fund, which is then used to act as collateral for a loan from a financial institution. Such activities are argued to have good signalling properties for two reasons. The first is that the financial institution is provided with collateral from the fund and so is guaranteed not to lose in the event of a default. Second, in addressing the moral hazard issue, the owners of individual enterprises are assumed to only be prepared to join with other individuals whom they trust. Since they are likely to have considerably greater insight into the trustworthiness of individuals than a conventional bank, they can exclude any individuals about whom they have doubts and so groups generally comprise individuals who have known one another, either socially or through business, for many years. Group members are strongly incentivised by the fear of losing their own money in the event of a default. Group lending, therefore, means that, for reliable but low wealth borrowers, there can be better access to funds since such individuals could not provide sufficient collateral on the same scale from their own resources. It also means that any profits from the fund can be re-invested and used for re-lending, and that the bank will be prepared to lend in the future to those funds with a track record of repayment.

However, there are problems with group lending. Group success is judged primarily on whether or not its members repay in full and punctually. Lorenzo (2007) argues that this depends upon four factors.

1 Peer selection – defined as the ability to accurately assess those who are allowed to join the group. The qualities sought from a potential new member will be reliability and responsibility. This is assessed most accurately when individuals are known to one another either through family, business or social contacts.

2 Peer monitoring – as with a bank, it is important to keep records of who is repaying and who is not. The quality of record keeping is likely to influence the overall performance of the group, since only when it is clear that individuals are in arrears can any action be considered.

3 Peer pressure – this is the response of the rest of the group when faced by individuals or a business that is not repaying on time. The group may respond in several ways. It may begin simply by making the late-payer aware that they are in arrears. Depending on how the individual responds, and his or her previous history, the group may allow a temporary repayment 'holiday', or provide other forms of assistance. Alternatively and ultimately, it may threaten to, or actually, expel the individual from the group.

4 Nature of social capital – common bonds such as membership of churches or clubs are argued to be of considerable importance.

Of these four influences, peer selection and social capital are likely to dominate since mutual trust amongst members is central to the group. Quite simply, the best strategy for the group is to be extremely careful about whom it allows to join because the sanctions it is able to exert upon a rogue member are modest. Indeed, the ultimate sanction – that of expulsion from the group – actually damages the group more than it damages the individual, since the remaining group members have to accept responsibility for the debt.

What does the bank do?

The bank can respond to opacity in the following ways:

● Require collateral.

● It can see if borrowers offer collateral. If they do then the bank may view this as a positive signal, reflecting the confidence of the borrower to repay the loan.

Table 17.2 — Reaction of lenders to problems in financing small businesses

Problems with lending to small businesses	Reaction of the lender
High default rates.	• Minimise downside risk by taking collateral. • Charge higher interest rates to small businesses. • Collect information.
Difficult to distinguish good from bad borrowers.	• Collect information. • Encourage borrower to give 'positive' signals such as collateral provision.
Expensive to collect good information.	• Provide a 'bonus' to good businesses to self-identify – in the form of guaranteed access to funds or lower interest rates.
Expensive to realise collateral.	• Specify priority access to collateral in lending contract.
Charging higher interest rates attracts small businesses with high-risk but high-return pay-offs.	• Requiring collateral should address the 'downside' risk problem.
Requiring collateral means good projects which are not backed by collateral are denied funds, and the lender loses a potential source of income.	• Collect information to better distinguish good from bad borrowers.

- It can collect information about the borrower (from credit histories, public accounts and other public documents).
- It can offer more attractive terms to those it views as low risk in the hope of attracting other low-risk borrowers.

Table 17.2 summarises the reaction of the lender – assumed to be a bank – to lending to small businesses. Table 17.3 shows the reaction of the borrower – making a distinction between good and bad borrowers.

Table 17.3 — Reaction of businesses – good and bad – to problems of lending

Problems for small businesses seeking funding	Reaction of the good business	Reaction of the bad business
Lender is suspicious, as some small businesses have a reputation for not repaying in full.	• Signal that it is a good business, perhaps by offering collateral. • Reduce the need to borrow by 'bootstrapping'.	• Pretend it is a good business, perhaps by over-estimating the expected profits of the project.
The bank may require collateral which the business owner does not have.	• Seek to obtain that collateral from personal resources, friends or family.	• Emphasise that the bank is missing an 'opportunity'.
The bank may require considerable documentation to verify the project and this may be time-consuming.	• Take this into account in planning the business.	• Emphasise there is only a short 'window of opportunity'.
The bank may seek reassurance of the creditworthiness of the individual.	• The business may be able to point to a track record of loan repayments with that bank.	• The business may seek loans from a bank that does not have access to its credit history.

17.5 What would we expect to see in an opaque marketplace?

The previous section identified that there were potentially very real challenges faced in the supply and demand for finance where the market is opaque. In this section, we identify five potential characteristics of this opaque marketplace. We then take each of these five features and identify if, indeed, the market for small business finance exhibits these features:

1 Some good borrowers would be denied access to funds and some bad borrowers would obtain funds. Some borrowers or potential borrowers are, therefore, 'credit constrained'.

2 Evidence of discrimination.

3 Higher interest rates.

4 Better terms.

5 Collateral.

Credit constrained

We begin by making the case that credit constraints do not exist, and that the entrepreneurial finance market works well. We then make the case for the presence of credit constraints.

The case for the absence of credit constraints is based on evidence from Chapter 16. It showed that the vast majority of small businesses that seek funding are successful in their application. In the UK, 89 per cent of applications for loans made by small businesses are successful (Fraser 2005). In New Zealand, the success rate on loan applications is 90 per cent (Ministry of Economic Development 2005). Even in the less developed economy of Trinidad and Tobago, where opacity might be expected to be greater because of lower literacy levels, Storey (2004) finds that 85 per cent of small businesses seeking bank funding were successful. In the US, however, denial rates are higher. Cavalluzzo and Wolken (2005) report that, for US small businesses overall, 28 per cent reported being denied credit.

As we showed in Chapter 16, these low rejection rates partly reflect the relatively buoyant macro-economic conditions when these surveys were undertaken. The world recession that began in 2008 provided an opportunity to examine how the small business finance market operated in a tougher economic climate. As a valid comparator, Chapter 16 showed that whilst rejections for term loans were 7.4 per cent in buoyant 2004, rejection rates were 16.3 per cent for those same businesses applying in 2008. Whilst this is a sharp increase, it is also important to recognise that, even in those difficult macro-economic circumstances, the vast bulk of applicants were successful.

Nevertheless, even if most applicants get funded, it does not necessarily imply that the market is working efficiently. It might be that, although most applications are successful, there are many small businesses that would like to obtain credit but which did not apply because they expected to be rejected. 'Discouraged borrowers' (see Chapter 16) might, for example, be expected to be found in opaque marketplaces, since their 'discouragement' stems from their inability to correctly interpret 'signals' that funding is possible.

However, Han *et al.* (2009*a*) show that, in the US market, discouraged borrowers have two characteristics. First, good borrowers are less likely to be discouraged, implying that the borrowers know the bank will be able to identify correctly a bad borrower. Second, the discouraged borrower is more likely to have had a lengthy relationship with the bank. This implies that the bad borrower knows the bank can reasonably assess their reliability. So, the bad business does not apply for funds – even though they would like to – because they know the bank will reject them. Both these findings lead Han *et al*. to conclude that in the US, although there are discouraged borrowers, this reflects a market in which both parties are well informed.

The case for the presence of financial constraints in the entrepreneurial finance market is both theoretical and empirical. The theoretical case is based on Evans and Jovanovic (1989) shown in the 'Classic research', below. Broadly they argue that more entrepreneurially talented individuals are more likely to seek larger sums to initially fund their businesses than less talented individuals. In contrast, banks are likely to restrict lending to a multiple of the wealth of the individual because this is likely to reflect the maximum amount of collateral that the business can provide. So, in Evans and Jovanovic's model, the untalented yet wealthy individual is unlikely to be financially constrained from starting a business. In contrast, the poor but entrepreneurially talented individual is more likely to be constrained, and so prevented from starting a business. This is clearly an undesirable outcome.

Using this theoretical framework, Evans and Jovanovic then found that an increase in family assets was associated with a higher probability of entrepreneurship and they inferred that financial constraints existed and so lowered the rate of business start ups.

Classic research	Evans, D. and Jovanovic, B. (1989) 'An Estimated Model of Entrepreneurial Choice under Liquidity Constraints', *Journal of Political Economy*, 97, 808–27.

Evans and Jovanovic assume that aspiring entrepreneurs have two sources of funds:

1 Their own personal wealth (W).
2 Money they can borrow from the bank. However, the bank will only lend a multiple (k) of their own wealth.
3 So total access to finance is W (1 + k). (Amount that can be accessed is their own wealth W and a multiple k of their wealth.)

Evans and Jovanovic also assume that:

1 Individual X is a talented entrepreneur – with higher θ – who requires more capital to start a business than the less talented individual Y.
2 Unfortunately, the bank cannot observe θ, and only allocates loans on the W(1 + k) formula above.
3 Financial constraints occur when individuals are unable to acquire the funding they seek.

Evans and Jovanovic then infer that:

1 Low θ individuals are less likely to be financially constrained than high θ individuals, because they seek less funding.
2 Financial constraints bind on the talented individuals – who may then not start a business.

Evans and Jovanovic then show that:

An increase in family assets (their own assets (wealth) and what they can beg, borrow or 'steal' from their family) enhances the likelihood of entering entrepreneurship.

The original article generated, and continues to generate, a stream of work very briefly summarised in the bulleted list below.

- Blanchflower and Oswald (1998) criticise Evans and Jovanovic (1989) by pointing out that the reason why wealthier individuals are more likely to make this shift may be either because the individual wishing to start a business accumulates wealth through saving and then starts a business, or because children inherit businesses. For Blanchflower and Oswald, the valid test is whether those individuals who obtain gifts and inheritances – 'windfall gains' – are subsequently more likely to enter self-employment. They find evidence to support this and conclude that credit constraints do exist.

- Hurst and Lusardi (2004) take issue with this conclusion. They accept there is a positive association between propensity to start a business and wealth. However, they show this is primarily because the very rich are very much more likely to start a business. For most families across the wealth spectrum, increases in wealth are unrelated to the likelihood of starting a business.

- Cressy (1996) also argues that it is human capital that influences access to bank credit, and that the findings both of Evans and Jovanovic, and of Blanchflower and Oswald, reflect their failure to include a sufficient range of human capital variables.

- Finally, Parker (2002) makes a distinction between Type I and Type II constraints. Type I constraints relate to receiving a smaller loan than they desired. Type II is when businesses are denied access to loans even though they appear identical to businesses that receive loans. Parker concludes that the evidence for either type of constraint is weak.

However, the extent to which access to finance prevents individuals becoming a business owner remains an empirically open question.

Overall, there continues to be a debate about the scale of financial constraints and their effect on the market for entrepreneurial finance. Some evidence – based on 'self-report' evidence – suggests such constraints are real, particularly in tight macro-economic conditions. However, the view of most economists – summarised by Cressy (2002) – is that whilst the quantity of lending may be less than in a perfectly informed marketplace, most interventions by governments to address these market imperfections have a limited success record (see Chapter 21).

Evidence of discrimination

Discrimination in the credit market is more likely in an opaque marketplace. But even if the market is generally competitive and there are few wide-ranging credit constraints, specific groups might still experience discrimination. The two groups most frequently viewed as being likely to experience this are ethnic minorities and females.

However, conducting a reliable test for the presence of discrimination is difficult. For example, it is *not* sufficient to show that some ethnic minorities or females are more frequently rejected for bank loans than Whites or males. It is also *not* sufficient to show that ethnic minorities or females pay higher rates of interest than white males. Instead, demonstrating the presence of discrimination requires showing that, taking account of all factors relevant to the loan decision, females or those from ethnic minorities continue to be disadvantaged.

Three examples of the factors that have to be taken into account in confirming the presence or absence of discrimination are:

1   Ethnic minorities or females may have higher default rates than Whites or males, for reasons unrelated to their gender or ethnicity. For example, they may be much more likely to operate businesses in high-risk sectors or in high-risk locations or have weak repayment records. For all these reasons they are likely to be (and so are deemed to be) more risky. If they are more risky, they would expect to incur higher rejection rates and/or higher interest rates whatever their ethnicity or gender. The rejection rate reflects these characteristics, rather than their ethnicity or their gender.

2 Ethnic minorities or females may have less human capital or entrepreneurial talent than Whites or males. On these grounds, they also might be expected to incur higher loan rejection rates and/or higher interest rates.

3 Rejection rates are only one potential measure of discrimination. Others might be higher interest rates on loans provided or if ethnic minorities or females are discouraged for applying for a loan because they feel they will be rejected.

Evidence of discrimination against ethnic minorities

There is evidence of some ethnic minorities having a higher than expected likelihood of credit denial. Cavalluzzo and Wolken (2005) show that in the US, there are striking differences between ethnic groups in terms of the denial of credit (Table 17.4). The first column of Table 17.4 shows that whilst 24 per cent of White small business owners were denied credit, denial rates were 62 per cent for African-Americans, 50 per cent for Hispanics and 52 per cent for Asians. All of the latter are statistically significantly higher than for Whites.

The last two columns of Table 17.4 show that such differences continue even after taking account of whether the business owner owns his or her own home. Understandably, since the home may be offered as collateral and also perhaps can be used as a measure of wealth, individuals not owning their own home have a denial rate of 59 per cent, which is more than twice that of homeowners (24 per cent).

Nevertheless, differences continue, even for homeowners, depending upon their ethnicity. Table 17.4 shows that, whilst there are no differences between White and Hispanic owners, when homeownership is taken into account, it continues to be the case that African-Americans and Asian homeowners are more likely to be denied access to credit than their White counterparts.

The final column shows that, for those not owning their own home, African-Americans and Hispanics are more likely to be denied credit than Whites. So, whether or not they own their own home, African-Americans have higher credit-denial rates.

The evidence provided by Cavalluzzo and Wolken is that ethnicity does influence the likelihood of a small business owner being turned down for a loan, even when a range of other factors are also included – such as their credit history, their personal wealth, their education, the sector of the business, and whether they have a lengthy relationship with a financial institution.

There is also some, albeit more mixed, evidence of racial discrimination in credit markets from other studies reviewed in the box below. This appears to provide support for the important Cavalluzzo and Wolken findings that racial discrimination is present in these markets (see Illustration, below).

Table 17.4	Small business loan turndowns, personal wealth and discrimination (%)		
	Denied credit	**Denied credit that owned own home**	**Denied credit not owning their own home**
All	28	24	59
White	24	21	53
African-American	62*	58*	100*
Hispanic	50*	35	87*
Asian	52*	48*	65

* Denotes significant at 1%.

| Illustration | Ethnic discrimination in the credit market: the evidence |

UK evidence

- Fraser (2005) shows that ethnic minority businesses were more likely to be rejected for bank loans than White-owned businesses. He also finds that ethnic minority-owned businesses have lower overdraft limits than White-owned businesses, but that after controlling for a range of business and loan characteristics ethnic minority businesses pay *lower* interest rates.

- Qualitative evidence supporting the Fraser finding of higher rates of bank rejection amongst ethnic minority-owned business was provided by Smallbone *et al.* (2003).

- Basu and Parker (2001) find no evidence that the greater use of loans from family amongst South Asian-owned businesses in the UK reflects credit rationing by banks. It is better explained by the motives of the business owners and the finance suppliers.

US evidence

- Bates (1973) undertook the pioneering work on this subject demonstrating lower repayment rates for Black borrowers.

- Blanchflower *et al.* (2003) find, using the US Survey of Small Business Finance for both 1993 and 1998, that Black-owned small businesses are about twice as likely to be denied access to credit even after taking account of differences in personal creditworthiness and other factors.

- Cavalluzzo and Wolken (2005): see main text, above.

Other countries

- Trinidad and Tobago: Storey (2004) finds that all else being equal, Afro-Trinidadians are more likely to be rejected for loans than those from other ethnic groups.

- Zimbabwe: Raturi and Swamy (1999) find differences both in application and rejection rates amongst different ethic groups.

Gender discrimination

In terms of the impact of gender issues on the market for entrepreneurial finance, three questions dominate:

1 Are (small) businesses owned by females less likely to apply for loan finance from a bank (application rate)?

2 Are (small) businesses owned by females more likely to be rejected for a bank loan than businesses owned by males (rejection rate)?

3 Are (small) businesses owned by females more likely to be charged a higher interest rate than businesses owned by males (interest rate charged), or be otherwise constrained?

Fundamental to addressing these questions is the ability to isolate the contribution of gender, and to be persuaded that the evidence provided is reliable and generalisable. The evidence on these questions is now reviewed.

Are (small) businesses owned by females less likely to apply for loan finance from a bank (application rate)?

The evidence from Madill *et al.* (2006), for Canada, and from Zimmerman-Treichel and Scott (2006), for the US is that, even taking account of many other factors, businesses owned by women are less likely to apply for bank loans than those owned by men. However, Storey (2004), for Trinidad and Tobago, finds that whilst there are differences in application rates between males and females, these disappear when account is taken of a range of other business characteristics. The extent to which gender influences application rates may well differ between countries, but it may also depend on the extent to which non-gender factors are taken into account in the analysis.

In their review of these and other findings, Leitch and Hill (2006) suggest that women are more likely than men to be discouraged – defined as a creditworthy individual who does not apply for finance for fear of rejection. They regard this as plausible because of, in their words, '. . . the widespread belief that banks discriminate against females' (p. 10).

Are (small) businesses owned by females more likely to be rejected for a bank loan than businesses owned by males (rejection rate)?

A number of multivariate studies examining the factors influencing the accept/reject decision for bank loans are reviewed in Table 17.5. These cover a wide range of different countries but point to several common elements. First, the positive influences upon loan acceptance are business size and age, as well as lengthy and positive relationships with the bank. There is no evidence from any of the studies that gender exercises any significant influence on loan acceptance, and this is also confirmed by Blumberg and Letterie's (2008) findings. In this sense '. . . the widespread belief that banks discriminate against females', referred to by Leitch and Hill above, may be the reported view of potential applicants. The evidence to support it, however, is weak.

Are small businesses owned by females more likely to be charged a higher interest rate than businesses owned by males (interest rate charged), or be otherwise constrained?

Discrimination against females may not necessarily be captured only by examining rejection rates. It could also occur by the application being accepted, but the terms and conditions imposed being more onerous than those required of the identical male-owned business. The clearest example of this would be if businesses owned by females were charged a higher interest rate than that for an otherwise identical male-owned business.

Evidence on this seems to be collected much more infrequently. Nevertheless, Fraser (2005) suggests that there is an interest rate premium paid by females in the UK. He finds that females pay a 1 per cent premium on loans compared with the otherwise identical male-owned business. It should be emphasised that Fraser also found no evidence that gender was a factor influencing the accept/reject decision of banks.

The Norwegian evidence provided by Alsos *et al.* (2006) finds that female-owned businesses obtain significantly less financial capital to develop their new business than those owned by men. However, this clearly interacts with the lower growth rate of female-owned businesses, implying that it is difficult to separate cause from effect. Finally, Muravyev *et al.* (2009) do find evidence, across a wide range of countries, that females experience discrimination in the sense of being less likely to obtain a bank loan and being charged higher interest rates. However, this appears more clearly characteristic of less developed countries than of developed countries.

Overall, the evidence on discrimination in the credit market seems significantly more robust on ethnicity than on gender. If the entrepreneurial finance market is competitive, then any form of discrimination is surprising since financial institutions that discriminate are forgoing potentially profitable opportunities to lend. Creating a competitive lending market is crucial for minimising any incentive for discrimination. So, the findings that rejection rates are not identical for all ethnic groups and that there may also be contractual differences between males and females, even when a wide range of factors are taken into account, point to some evidence of opacity.

Higher interest rates

In an opaque market, lenders would view all borrowers as equally risky. Interest rates would be high for good as well as bad borrowers, since the bank would be unable to differentiate between them.

Table 17.5	Factors influencing accept/reject decision				
	Blanchflower et al. (2003)	**Fraser (2005)**	**Storey (2004)**	**Madill et al. (2006)**	**Zimmerman et al. (2006)**
Country	US	United Kingdom	Trinidad and Tobago	Canada	US
1 Amount sought				No impact	
2 Collateral provided				No impact	
3 Relationship measure		Longer relationship reduces likelihood of rejection		Longer relationship reduces likelihood of rejection	Banking with lender reduces likelihood of rejection
4 Credit history	Included but no coefficient shown				
5 Education of owner	Included but no coefficient shown		Highly educated individuals are less likely to be rejected		
6 Gender of owner	No impact	No impact	No impact	No impact	No impact
7 Ethnicity of owner	Black-owned businesses 28–38% more likely to be rejected		African-owned businesses more likely to be rejected		
8 Finance professional in business		Lowers rejection rate			
9 Legal form				No impact	Corporations less likely to be rejected
10 Business age			No impact	No impact	Young businesses more likely to be rejected
11 Business growth		No impact	No impact	No impact	
12 Business size			Rejection initially falls with business size but then rises	Larger businesses less likely to be rejected	Larger businesses less likely to be rejected
13 Multiple banking supplier		Increases likelihood of rejection			
14 Sector/Region	Included but no coefficients shown		Some sectoral effects	No impact	Location and sector influence rejection

The evidence, summarised in Table 17.6, is that the interest rates charged to small businesses are in the range of 1–3 per cent above base or prime rate in several countries. Furthermore, although the US has small business interest rates that appear to be much higher than those in other countries, there is a wide variation which appears to link to the risk profile of the business. This implies that, whilst the market may not be transparent, neither is it heavily opaque.

Table 17.6	Interest rates charged to small businesses: some international comparisons

Country	Author	Margin over base
UK	Fraser (2005)	1–3%
UK	Cressy (1996)	2–4%
US	US Survey of Small Business Finance (1998)	Mean and median interest rates are 9%, ranging from 0.9 to 25%
Belgium	Degryse and van Cayseele (2000)	Mean interest rate is 8.1, ranging from 1.6 to 22.4%. Interest rates on a Belgian government security – the risk-free rate – varied from 3% to 8%
Japan	Ono and Uesugi (2005)	1–3%

Better terms

The rationale for this test is that, in a well-informed marketplace, the bank that fails to offer 'better terms' risks losing customers, who will switch to a bank prepared to offer terms that accurately reflect the level of risk. 'Switching' is, therefore, a key concept. We define better terms to include both access to, and the price of, finance.

Petersen and Rajan (1994) argued that the development of 'relationships' between the lender and the borrower was the mechanism for transmitting reliable information between the two parties, thereby overcoming opacity. In practice, the strength of these relationships was measured by the length of time that the business had been a customer, on the grounds that the finance provider is more able to gauge reliability over time. Petersen and Rajan found that businesses borrowing from institutions with which they had a long relationship were more likely to be able to access credit. However, they also found that, whilst relationships enhanced *access* to finance, they did not appear to influence the *price* – the interest rate charged on the loan by the provider.

In contrast, subsequent work by Berger and Udell (1995) found that the longer the duration of the relationship between a bank and a business, the more likely the business was to benefit from lower interest rates (cheaper finance). The reason for this difference, according to Berger and Udell, is that they focus only on lines of credit (overdraft facilities). This is important because overdraft facilities are not secured against an asset. Hence, the bank has to make a 'judgement'. Berger and Udell (1995) suggest that the interest rate charged on a line of credit is, therefore, likely to be influenced by the nature of the bank's relationship with the business. This differs from loans which were examined by Petersen and Rajan. Essentially, loans are likely to be for assets against which the bank may have some claim. Hence, such loans are more likely to be transaction, rather than relationship, driven.

As we have emphasised throughout this chapter, relationships are a two-way street. So, it may be that (small) businesses with a long relationship with the bank may be at a disadvantage if they feel that the bank is fully informed about their reliability, but is under no competitive obligation to offer them better terms. In short, in such conditions, the asymmetric information advantages of the business have disappeared.

To induce the bank to offer better terms, the business must have the option of switching to another bank. Shifting is not costless: if they are to get a better deal, the small business must overcome any initial suspicion on the part of the new bank as to why they wish to shift. Memorably demonstrating the scale of these suspicions, the Chairman of Barclays Bank once said:

> We find as a matter of experience, something like half of our bad debts are from customers we have taken on from other banks in the last year or two, so . . . if you get offered business from another bank look at it hard, once, twice or three times, before you take it.

Reported in Storey (1994: 238)

Other factors discouraging bank switching include the administrative costs of completing forms and the risk of an interrupted banking service. Given these real costs of transferring, the small business may be prepared to pay a premium in excess of their risk profile to stay with the same bank, especially if a new bank, because of its suspicions of new customers, is unprepared to offer attractive terms. Of course, in buoyant macro-economic conditions, when individual banks are seeking to raise their market shares, switchers may be welcomed, but the reverse is likely to be the case in a downturn.

It is also important to recognise that the Anglo-American model of business–bank relationships is not the same as that in Continental Europe. As Lehmann and Neuberger (2001) emphasise, business and bank relationships are much closer in Germany than in what they refer to as the 'short-term or arm's length lending', characteristic of the Anglo-American model. They illustrate this by showing that both access to, and the price of, credit is heavily influenced by the 'quality' of the relationship – most notably the two-way trust between the banker and the business owner. In contrast with the US findings, relationship duration is not significant in influencing access to credit in Germany.

A second aspect in which the Anglo-American model differs from Continental Europe is in the role of **multiple banking** (using more than one bank). This is traditional in many European countries, and particularly characteristic of Italy, where all sizes of business use more than one bank for finance. Cosci and Meliciani (2002) in their review of multiple banking in Italy report findings from an earlier review by Ongena and Smith (2000). The latter found that Italian businesses had an average of 15 banking relationships, and that this was the highest in Europe. Nevertheless, 'monogamy' was the exception rather than the rule elsewhere in Europe – with the average number of bank relationships per business being 11 in Portugal, France and Belgium, and 8 in Germany. Whilst these figures are derived from large businesses, multiple banking is also a characteristic of small businesses. Detragiache *et al.* (2000) show that 55 per cent of small businesses in the US have more than one banking relationship, compared with 89 per cent in Italy.

If multiple banking relationships are the norm, then, what are the implications for the earlier theory that implied that good but externally opaque small businesses benefited from a relationship with a bank as a way of signalling their quality? These issues are examined by Detragiache *et al.* (2000) who conclude that the single/multiple banking relationship is influenced primarily by the factors shown in Table 17.7. The benefits of monogamy to the good business are that the bank is confident that they have full information. In return, the business expects the bank to make 'good' decisions: essentially, it will be funded, and the bad businesses will be rejected. The bank will also incur lower monitoring costs, which could be passed on to the business in the form of lower interest rates.

Table 17.7	Issues relating to single and multiple banking for good and bad small businesses	
	Single bank	**Multiple bank**
Good business	• By demonstrating their quality, this leads to better terms and conditions. • The information transmitted to the bank might lead to the business being exploited by paying higher rates or charges.	• Bank has only partial information so it may be suspicious of the business. • Business may need specialist financial services not provided by all banks. • If banks are risky, it is prudent for the business to use multiple banks. • Businesses can get banks to compete for service. • Businesses are not so reliant on financing decisions of a single bank – 'eggs in one basket'.
Bad business	• No opportunity to disguise credit record.	• Can ensure that some banks are unaware of defaults on loans at other banks.

However, this theory makes several implicit assumptions: first, that all banks offer identical services; second, all banks are equally risk-free in the sense of being able to repay depositors in full; and third, banks are competitive and so have to pass on lower costs to good customers in order to keep those customers.

In practice, these assumptions are only partly valid. All banks do not offer identical services, some may be regarded as more reliable than others, and the extent to which they are disciplined by competition also varies.

Hence, the good small business which, for example, wishes to use a financial service not conveniently available at its main bank may choose to look elsewhere but, in doing so, runs the risk that it will be viewed as a 'lemon' (see earlier quote by Barclays Bank chairman). However, as shown in Table 17.7, multiple banking does provide the opportunity for businesses that find switching costly to obtain financial services at competitive rates.

Neuberger and Ratke (2006) examine multiple bank relationships for German professional service micro businesses. They find that, on average, these micro businesses have two banking relationships, and that these increase with business size and age. They attribute this finding to an increased demand for a greater diversity of services. They also find that micro businesses choose multiple banking because their main bank imposes credit restrictions upon them. But they obtain no clear picture of whether it is the more risky businesses that are more likely to have multiple relationships. One explanation for this is that, whilst the 'bad' business may choose to have multiple relationships in order to avoid being tracked, the bank is predisposed to be highly suspicious of such businesses.

In summary, relationships are a potentially valuable way in which 'good' small businesses signal their quality to a financial institution. In Anglo-American countries where 'arm's length' lending is traditional, this generally takes place monogamously, with businesses being customers of a single bank. In that way signals are clear, since the bank has full information on the performance of the business and its loan repayments. An opaque marketplace with high switching costs, therefore, would be expected to be characterised by low switching rates.

However, monogamy is not universal and multiple banking relationships are very common, particularly in Continental Europe. Having more than a single bank may give the business access to a wider range of services. It may also mean it is less financially constrained since, even if its proposal is rejected by one bank, it may be accepted by another. Third, even without switching banks, the business may be able to 'shop around' to get the best deal. These advantages have to be offset against the strong suspicion on the part of banks when they have incomplete information on the business. In these circumstances, they are likely to either reject the application, charge a high price or demand identifiable security.

Collateral

In a perfectly informed marketplace there would be no need for collateral. This is because the bank would be able to judge the entrepreneurial talent of the borrower and their likelihood of repayment. Any use of collateral, therefore, reflects opacity, and the greater the use made of it, the more likely it is that the market is opaque.

We have seen that offering collateral (collateral pledging) can act as a positive signal in an opaque marketplace. A borrower willing to pledge collateral – the value of which if resold would considerably exceed the sum borrowed – is likely to be viewed by the lender as demonstrating confidence in their ability to repay. Where the lender has no other way of judging the likely success of a project – where the market is opaque – then collateral-based lending is likely to be important. Not only does this compensate the lender in the event of default, it also provides reassurance that the borrower is committed to the success of the project and is likely to offer it their full commitment.

This addresses the issue in agency theory where the lender seeks to ensure that the borrower was using the funds for which they were intended, and not, for example, for the purchase of a Porsche. It also overcomes the moral hazard issues in which the recipient of the loan changes his or her behaviour as a result of obtaining the loan.

Illustration	Some examples of moral hazard

In the context of small firm–banking relationships, moral hazard issues emerge when the nature of the contract influences the behaviour of the borrower. Assume the borrower has a choice of projects, one of which is high-risk and high-return and the other is low-risk and low-return, yet both have the same expected value. If the lending contract specifies that the borrower repays when the project is successful, but does not have to cover the full 'downside losses' if the project is unsuccessful, then this changes the behaviour of the borrower to favour the high-risk return project. This is because if the project is successful then the borrower keeps all the 'upside gains', but if it is unsuccessful losses are 'capped' at the amount borrowed.

Moral hazard therefore encourages risky behaviour. Other examples abound: below we give two from financial, and one from everyday life.

1 The world's banking system was said to exhibit moral hazard in 2008/9 when, having benefited from under-taking high-risk speculation in the previous decade it was then, in many countries 'bailed out' by tax payers when these speculations catastrophically failed. It was argued by many that banks should have had to suffer the downside loss consequences of their risk taking, otherwise their behaviour would remain unchanged and they would see high-risk and high-return projects as desirable in the future.

2 A second area where the term moral hazard is common relates to international debt in less developed countries. Here it is argued that some extremely poor countries devote so much of their resources to debt repayment that they are unable to deliver adequate public services to their people. A practical and simple way of helping such countries is for international lenders such as the World Bank to write off such loans, enabling the countries to use this funding for service provision and investment.

   However, this has moral hazard consequences because it signals to other, perhaps equally poor, countries which have repaid their debt, that there is a reward for non-payment so therefore encourages risk-taking and behavioural change which is undesirable.

3 A more homely example is requiring cyclists to wear helmets. In principle this seems like a good idea since there are many serious accidents caused by head injuries to cyclists which could have been prevented if the cyclists had been wearing a helment. However, mandating cyclists to wear helmets has moral hazard consequences because it encourages them to take risks which they otherwise would not have taken – since they now view themselves as 'safe'. It therefore changes their behaviour since they believe they do not have to suffer the downside loss consequences of their actions. Whether, on balance, the wearing of helmets has been a benefit to both the cycling and the non-cycling community is, therefore, unclear.

The problem is that, in a perfectly informed marketplace, it would be the merit of the project – reflected in the likelihood of repayment – that would influence the willingness of the lender to provide funding, rather than the willingness to provide collateral. However, since that information is not available to the lender, collateral pledging, which is an improvement on chance, is used.

The problem from the viewpoint of the economy is that, if access to collateral is used as the basis for lending decisions, as Evans and Jovanovic (1989) argued, then the best projects are not always selected for funding – but rather those that have collateral backing. Since collateral backing is more likely to be available to the rich rather than the poor it means that the identical project from a poor person is less likely to be funded. Alternatively it may be that a bad project from a rich person is more likely to be funded than a good project from a poor person.

The evidence on the role of collateral as a signalling mechanism was initially provided by Berger and Udell (1995), but subsequently examined by Han *et al.* (2009*a*). Using the 1998 US Survey of Small Business Finance, they found that 63 per cent of loans are collateralised. The likelihood of the loan being collateralised increases with the value and duration of the loan. It is also, as expected, higher when the borrower has a business in a risky sector. The human capital of the owner also influences the likelihood of a collateralised loan – with educated founders being less likely to have collateral-backed loans. In contrast, those with a poor credit history were more likely to have such loans. The effect of collateral is to lower the interest rate charged.

This implies that, even in a relatively well-informed finance market such as the US, collateral is seen by the bank as a positive signal of borrower quality.

In summary, there is evidence that the small business finance market is characterised by opacity. To address this, banks respond in the following ways:

1 They offer incentives in the form of lower interest rates to those borrowers that provide collateral.

2 They offer lower interest rates to borrowers with good characteristics which the bank is able to verify (e.g. have a 'high' credit score). So, businesses with long bank relationships are able to obtain better access and lower interest rates than those where the bank is less able to verify past performance.

3 However, if banks operate in markets that are not competitive, then there is less pressure to pass on the benefits to good customers. Effectively, banks will make high profits by over-charging these good customers.

Summary

This chapter has sought to provide a deeper understanding of the factors at work in the small business or entrepreneurial finance market. It provides explanations of why in Chapter 15 we found such a diversity of finance sources were used by small businesses, and why there were high rejection rates.

The key theme of the chapter is that the entrepreneurial finance market is radically different from that of the corporate finance market. Fundamental to this difference is the issue of information: the entrepreneurial finance market is characterised by opacity and asymmetry. So, there is less information (greater opacity), and generally the lender is less well informed than the borrower (informational asymmetry). It is, therefore, more difficult to assess the good from the bad borrower in this marketplace.

The chapter has set out how both parties respond to this opacity. Each does so by sending signals to the other party which reflect their quality. The most powerful signal sent by the borrower is a willingness/ability to provide collateral for loans. In contrast, the most powerful signal sent by a lender is to provide finance, and to do so at favourable rates.

The problem created by opacity is that it means that some good borrowers may be unable to access funds and, by implication, some bad borrowers obtain funding (adverse selection). We, therefore, looked for evidence of opacity, and found some, but it was not wholly consistent. So, for example, we would expect to find evidence that individuals with lower wealth were less likely to become a business owner than more wealthy individuals – on the grounds that the wealthy are more able to offer collateral. The evidence suggests this is broadly, but not consistently, the case. A second indicator of opacity might be discrimination against certain groups. Here we also find mixed evidence – the case is robust for some ethnic groups, but weak for females.

Questions for discussion

1 What role does collateral play in facilitating lending in an opaque marketplace? What limitations does it have?

2 What is meant by 'relationship lending'? Under what circumstances does it benefit the bank and under what circumstances does it benefit the small business?

3 What is a discouraged borrower? Under what circumstances might there be many discouraged borrowers?

4 Review the evidence that discrimination exists in the small business finance market. How might discrimination be rectified?

5 In what respects, and why, does the financing of small and large businesses differ?

6 What is meant by 'financially constrained'? Show the value of the concept in providing an understanding of the choice facing an individual whether or not to become a business owner.

7 What are the advantages and disadvantages to the small business of multiple banking?

References

Alsos, G.A., Isaksen, E.J. and Ljunggren, E. (2006) 'New Venture Financing and Subsequent Business Growth in Men- and Women-led Businesses', *Entrepreneurship Theory and Practice*, 30(5), 667–86.

Ang, J.S. (1991) 'Small Business Uniqueness and the Theory of Financial Management', *Journal of Small Business Finance*, 1(1), 1–13.

Ang, J.S., Lyn, W. and Tyler, F. (1995) 'Evidence on the Lack of Separation between Business and Personal Risk amongst Small Businesses', *Journal of Small Business Finance*, 4, 197–210.

Basu, A. and Parker, S.C. (2001) 'Family Finance and New Business Start Ups', *Oxford Bulletin of Economics and Statistics*, 63(3), 333–58.

Bates, T. (1973) 'An Econometric Analysis of Lending to Black Businessmen', *Review of Economics and Statistics*, 55(3), 272–83.

Berger, A.N. and Udell, G.F. (1995) 'Relationship Lending and Lines of Credit in Small Business Finance', *Journal of Business*, 68(3), 351–81.

Berger, A.N. and Udell, G.F. (1998) 'The Economics of Small Business Finance: The Roles of Private Equity and Debt Markets in the Financial Growth Cycle', *Journal of Banking and Finance*, 22(6–8), 613–73.

Blanchflower, D.G. and Oswald, A.J. (1998) 'What Makes an Entrepreneur?' *Journal of Labor Economics*, 16(1), 26–60.

Blanchflower, D.G., Levine, P.B. and Zimmerman, D.J. (2003) 'Discrimination in the Small-business Credit Market', *Review of Economics and Statistics*, 85(4), 930–43.

Blumberg, B.F. and Letterie, W.A. (2007) 'Business Starters and Credit Rationing', *Small Business Economics*, 30(2), 187–200.

Carter, S., Shaw, E., Wilson F. and Lam, W. (2006) 'Gender Entrepreneurship and Business Finance: Investigating the Relationship between Banks and Entrepreneurs in the UK', in Brush, C.G., Carter, N.M., Gatewood, E.J., Greene, P.G. and Hart, M.M. (eds) *Growth-orientated Entrepreneurs and their Businesses*. Cheltenham: Edward Elgar, 373–92.

Cavalluzzo, K. and Wolken, J. (2005) 'Small Business Loan Turndowns, Personal Wealth, and Discrimination', *Journal of Business*, 78, 2153–78.

Cosci, S. and Meliciani, V. (2002) 'Multiple Banking Relationships: Evidence from the Italian Experience', *Manchester School*, 70(Supplement), 37–54.

Cosh, A.D. and Hughes, A. (eds) (2007) *British Enterprise: Thriving or Surviving?* Cambridge: Centre for Business Research, Cambridge University.

Cressy, R.C. (1996) 'Are Business Start Ups Debt Rationed?', *Economic Journal*, 106(438), 1253–70.

Cressy, R.C. (2002) 'Funding Gaps: A Symposium', *Economic Journal*, 112, F1–F16.

Degryse, H. and van Cayseele, P. (2000) 'Relationship Lending within a Bank-based System: Evidence from European Small Business Data', *Journal of Financial Intermediation*, 9(1), 90–109.

Detragiache, E., Garella, P. and Guiso, L. (2000) 'Multiple versus Single Banking Relationships: Evidence from the Italian Experience', *Journal of Finance*, 55(3), 1133–61.

Dunne, P. and Hughes, A. (1994) 'Age, Size, Growth and Survival', *Journal of Industrial Economics*, 42(2) 115–40.

Ebben, J. and Johnson, A. (2006) 'Bootstrapping in Small Businesss: An Empirical Analysis of Change over Time', *Journal of Business Venturing* 21, 851–65.

Europe Airline Daily (2008) 'easyJet. Just as Things Were Looking Good, Along Comes Stelios . . .', 19 November.

Evans, D. and Jovanovic, B. (1989) 'An Estimated Model of Entrepreneurial Choice under Liquidity Constraints', *Journal of Political Economy*, 97, 808–27.

FAME (2009) *FAME Dataset on UK Businesses*. fame.bvdep.com/.

Fraser, S. (2005) *Finance for Small and Medium-sized Enterprises: A report on the 2004 UK Survey of SME Finances – ESRC UK Data Archive: SN 5326*. London: Bank of England.

Fraser, S. (2009) 'How Have SME Finances Been Affected by the Credit Crisis?' BERR/ESRC Seminar, March.

Greene, F.J., Mole, K.M. and Storey, D.J. (2008) *Three Decades of Enterprise Culture*. Palgrave, p. 156.

Gropp, R., Scholz, J.-K. and White, M.J. (1997) 'Personal Bankruptcy and Credit Supply and Demand', *Quarterly Journal of Economics*, 112(1), 217–51.

Guardian (2009) 'Aer Lingus Chief Quits', 6 April.

Han, L., Fraser, S. and Storey, D.J. (2009a) 'The Role of Collateral in Entrepreneurial Finance', *Journal of Business Finance and Accounting*, 36(3–4), 424–55.

Han, L., Fraser, S. and Storey, D.J. (2009b) 'Are Good or Bad Borrowers Discouraged from Applying for Loans? Evidence from US Credit Markets', *Journal of Banking and Finance*, 33(2), 415–24.

Hurst, E. and Lusardi, A. (2004) 'Liquidity Constraints, Household Wealth and Entrepreneurship', *Journal of Political Economy*, 112(2), 319–47.

Lehmann, E. and Neuberger, D. (2001) 'Do Lending Relationships Matter?: Evidence from Bank Survey Data in Germany', *Journal of Economic Behaviour and Organisation*, 45(4), 339–59.

Leitch, C. and Hill, F. (2006) 'Guest Editorial: Women and the Financing of Entrepreneurial Ventures: More Pieces for the Jigsaw', *Venture Capital*, 8(1), 1–14.

Lorenzo, R. (2007) 'Micro Enterprise Group Credits in Mexico: Do They Work?', PhD Dissertation, University of Warwick.

Madill, J.J., Riding, A.L. and Haines, G.H. (2006) 'Women Entrepreneurs: Debt Financing and Banking Relationships', *Journal of Small Business and Entrepreneurship*, 19(2), 121–42.

Marlow, S. and Patton, D. (2005) 'All Credit to Men?: Entrepreneurship Finance and Gender', *Entrepreneurship Theory and Practice*, 29(6), 717–35.

Ministry of Economic Development (2003) *Bank Lending Practices to Small and Medium-sized Enterprises*. Wellington.

Muravyev, A., Talavera, O. and Schafer, D. (2009) 'Entrepreneurs' Gender and Financial Constraints: Evidence from International Data', *Journal of Comparative Economics*, 37(2), 270–86.

Myers, S.C. (1984) 'The Capital Structure Puzzle', *Journal of Finance* 39(3), 575–92.

Myers, S.C. and Majluf, N.S. (1984) *Corporate Financing and Investment Decisions When Businesss Have Information that Investors Do Not Have*. NBER Working Paper 1396. Cambridge, MA: NBER.

Neuberger, D. and Ratke, S. (2006) 'Microenterprises and Multiple Bank Relationships: Evidence from a Survey amongst Professionals'. Paper presented at International Comparisons in the Financing of SMEs in Developed Countries, 4–5 April, University of Warwick.

Ongena, S. and Smith, D.C. (2000) 'What Determines the Number of Bank Relationships?: Cross-Country Evidence', *Journal of Financial Intermediation*, 9(1), 26–56.

Ono, A. and Uesugi, I. (2005) *The Role of Collateral and Personal Guarantees in Relationship Lending: Evidence from Japan's Small Business Loan Market*. Mizuho Research Institute, RIETI Discussion Paper Series 05-E-027. Tokyo: RIETI.

Parker, S.C. (2002) 'Do Banks Ration Credit to New Enterprises?: And Should Governments Intervene?', *Scottish Journal of Political Economy*, 49(2), 162–95.

Petersen, M.A. and Rajan, R.G (1994) 'The Benefits of Lending Relationships: Evidence from Small Business Data', *Journal of Finance*, 49(1), 3–37.

Raturi, M. and Swamy, A.V. (1999) 'Explaining Ethnic Differentials in Credit Market Outcomes in Zimbabwe', *Economic Development and Cultural Change*, 47(3) 585–604.

Sharpe, S.A. (1990) 'Asymmetric Information, Bank Lending, and Implicit Contracts: A Stylised Model of Customer Relationships', *Journal of Finance*, 45(4), 1069–87.

Smallbone, D., Ram, M., Deakins, D. and Baldock, R. (2003) 'Access to Finance by Ethnic-minority Businesses in the UK', *International Small Business Journal*, 21(3), 291–314.

Storey, D.J. (1994) *Understanding the Small Business Sector*. London: Routledge/ITP.

Storey, D.J. (2004) 'Racial and Gender Discrimination in the Micro Firms Credit Market: Evidence from Trinidad and Tobago', *Small Business Economics*, 25(5), 401–42.

Survey of Small Business Finance (1998) *Survey*. Washington, DC: Federal Reserve Bank.

Sutton, J. (1997) 'Gibrats Legacy', *Journal of Economic Literature*, 35(1), 40–59.

Vanacker, T.R. and Manigart, S. (2009) 'Pecking Order and Debt Capacity Considerations for High-growth Companies Seeking Financing', *Small Business Economics*, published online October 2008.

Watson, R. and Wilson, N. (2002) 'Small and Medium-sized Enterprise Financing: A Note on Some of the Empirical Implications of a Pecking Order', *Journal of Business. Finance and Accounting*, 29, 557–78.

Winborg, J. and Landstrom, H. (2001) 'Financial Bootstrapping in Small Businesses: Examining Small Business Managers' Resource Acquisition Behaviors', *Journal of Business Venturing*, 16, 235–54.

Wydick, B. (1999) 'Can Social Cohesion Be Harnessed to Repair Market Failures?: Evidence from Group Lending in Guatamala', *Economic Journal*, 109, 463–75.

Zeller, M. (2003) 'Models of Rural Finance Institutions'. Paper presented to the International Conference on Best Practices in Rural Finance Institutions, 2–4 June, Washington, DC.

Zimmerman-Treichel, M. and Scott, J.A. (2006) 'Women-owned Businesses and Access to Bank Credit: Evidence from Three Surveys since 1987', *Venture Capital*, 8(1), 51–67.

18 Equity finance

Key learning objectives

By the end of this chapter you should:

- Understand the role of venture capital funding in entrepreneurial finance markets
- Recognise the different roles played by formal and informal venture capital
- Understand how these suppliers of venture capital address the twin problems of adverse selection and moral hazard
- Have a clear appreciation of the similarities and differences between debt and equity capital.

18.1 Introduction

Equity is the ownership of a business, normally in the form of shares. Where a young, growth-orientated business wishes to expand, but wishes to do so in a way where formal external borrowing in the form of loans – and the associated interest costs of this – are not incurred, it can obtain monies from external organisations or individuals. These providers of equity are normally referred to as *venture capitalists* (VCs). Such groups or individuals provide funds in return for (normally) *part* ownership of a business, with a view to facilitating the long-term growth of such a business. The VC expects to sell this ownership at some point in the future when, because of its growth, the valuation of the business will be considerably higher than when the shares were purchased (Landstrom 2007).

Two initial distinctions are important. The first is between VC and private equity. The latter is equity provided to more established businesses involved in, for example, management buy-outs and 'turnarounds'. Private equity is not the focus of this chapter. Instead, our focus is on venture capital, which is provided to young businesses with growth potential.

A second further distinction is between formal and informal equity – both of which are examined in this chapter. Formal VC is generally provided by specialist VC funds. In contrast, informal VCs are investments made by high net worth (rich) individuals directly. Such individuals are commonly referred to as *business angels*.

To repeat, the objective of the venture capitalist – both formal and informal – is to purchase ownership in a new or very young business that has the potential to grow. The VC will seek to sell shares (exit) some years later when their share valuation has risen. Dividends, or other income from the shares, is not the prime factor influencing the decision of the VC to invest.

In this chapter, we begin by providing an overview of the evolution of VC finance. We then consider the structure of a 'typical' fund before explaining how VCs deal with the problems of adverse selection and moral hazard in an opaque entrepreneurial finance marketplace. The chapter then considers the issues faced by business angels before, finally, comparing equity with loan finance.

18.2 The history and evolution of venture capital

Although often portrayed as a post-1945 financial device pioneered in the US, in reality venture capital has been in operation for centuries. By no means the first, but certainly a highly influential, venture capitalist was Queen Isabella of Spain who, in 1492, funded the exploits of Christopher Columbus.

Nevertheless, venture capital in its current form is strongly influenced by its development in the US. This is because many of the most successful young businesses that evolved into household names were part funded by venture capital. These include Google, Dell and Facebook.

The US has maintained that leadership over many decades, with both Europe and Asia Pacific lagging significantly. Cumming *et al.* (2007) show that, over the period from 1968 to 2005, VC investment in all European countries never exceeded 50 per cent of the US level, and in most years was below 30 per cent of the US level. The role of VC in Asia Pacific countries was even smaller.

It is clear that the scale and success of the US venture capital sector is closely aligned to young businesses in the high-tech sectors. Lockett *et al.* (2002) show that there has recently been a shift in Europe towards a greater focus on technology-based investments, with about 25 per cent (by value) of all European VC deals being in technology businesses. This compares with 12 per cent in 1995. However, the comparable proportion for the US is consistently above 75 per cent, implying that the US and the EU continue to differ markedly.

Murray (2007) captured this sentiment by reporting the remarks of a senior UK venture capitalist when asked if his fund invested in high-tech start ups: 'If it has got coloured wires and a plug, we won't touch it'.

Instead, the VC sector in the UK has favoured investment in private equity, particularly *management buy outs* (MBOs), where the existing managers of established businesses seek to purchase the business from the current owners. Usually, the managers seek external capital because they are unable to raise it from their own resources. The UK VC industry has found this a consistently more profitable use of funds than investing in high-tech businesses. Murray and Dimov (2007) report that early stage VC investments over a 20-year period yielded a return of 4.7 per cent, compared with a 16.4 per cent return on MBOs. Several reasons have been put forward to explain these differences. The first is that it is relatively easy to assess the viability of an established business, with a track record and with an experienced management team. It is much harder to assess an early-stage technology business, where the technology may be complex, imperfectly developed and where the developer of the technology often has unproven managerial skills (see Case study 3).

More difficult to explain, however, is why early-stage investments in the US obtained returns that were virtually five times that of MBOs. Lockett *et al.* (2002) argue that successful VC investment in new and small businesses in the US is primarily a reflection of the availability of viable proposals from the technology sector, rather than the low attractiveness of MBOs. By implication, UK and EU technology proposals are weaker than those in the US.

18.3 The structure of venture capital funds

The structure of a typical venture capital fund is shown in Figure 18.1. Three main parties are involved: a venture capital firm (the VC), investors and entrepreneurs. The left-hand side of Figure 18.1 shows the venture capital firm which comprises individuals with expertise and a track record in managing venture capital funds. These are often referred to as 'general partners'. Usually, the firm is focused on a particular sector (e.g. biotechnology, software), a particular type of business (e.g. start ups or university spin-outs) and/or particular geographic areas (e.g. Silicon Valley). These interests often reflect the experience and expertise of the venture capital firm. Part of the core skills of the venture capital firm, therefore, is having the ability to attract funding to support the fund (Walske and Zacharakis 2009).

Income for the 'general' partners (the venture capital firm) comes from two sources. First, they charge a management fee for managing the fund. This is often around 2–3 per cent of the fund. Second, they derive income from the appreciation of the fund. Typically, they expect to retain between 20 to 30 per cent of the capital gains made by the fund.

In return, venture capital firms provide a range of services. They are responsible for:

- finding prospective entrepreneurs to invest in (deal generation);
- screening the entrepreneurs (what is called due diligence);
- negotiating the 'deal' with entrepreneurs;
- monitoring and advising the entrepreneur; and
- 'harvesting' the investment through the sale of venture capital funds invested in the entrepreneurial business.

After funding has been raised, the VC may typically anticipate that, over the course of a ten-year period, they will spend 2–3 years generating, screening and negotiating any deals

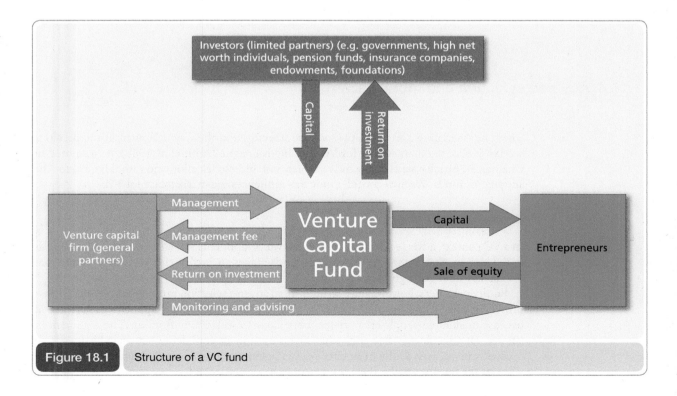

| **Figure 18.1** | Structure of a VC fund |

with prospective entrepreneurial businesses. Subsequently, they might anticipate working with the entrepreneurial business (monitoring and advising) for a further 4–5 years before seeking to 'harvest' their investment in the final years of the fund.

Figure 18.1 shows that the key investors in a venture capital fund are pension funds (both public and private), insurance companies, governments, endowment funds, high net worth individuals and charitable foundations. These are shown at the top of Figure 18.1. These investors are typically seeking to diversify their investment portfolio by investing in high-risk/high-return businesses. Therefore, investing in a venture capital fund tends to be part of a portfolio of investments that mix relatively safe investments which provide reasonable returns with riskier investments, such as venture capital funds, that offer the potential of greater returns.

Their investment is also likely to be 'patient' in the sense that investors realise that the typical VC fund runs for around ten years. They may also choose to invest in more than one VC fund. This diversifies their investment portfolio (reduces their risk). They may choose to invest, therefore, in a range of VC funds, perhaps managed by several VC firms. Typically, investors are seeking to realise between 70 and 80 per cent of the appreciation of the venture capital fund to reflect the risks involved in investing in high-risk businesses.

The third party – shown on the right of Figure 18.1 – is the entrepreneurial business. This receives a capital injection into the business. The advantage of this, as we have seen, is that it typically carries no debt implications. Normally, this is in return for some equity stake taken by the VC. However, besides taking ordinary shares (which carry voting rights), the venture capital fund (through the venture capital firm) may also choose a mix of different types of equity such as preference shares. Preference shares may be an option because – although they do not carry voting rights – preference shareholders receive dividends before ordinary shareholders. They are also ahead of ordinary shares and debtors in receiving payment in the event of a liquidation of the business. Finally, the last advantage of preference shares is that they can be converted into ordinary shares later on.

Besides receiving finance, the entrepreneurial business also receives a range of 'soft' support from the venture capitalist. Because of their expertise in a given sector, the VC may be able to offer particular skills, expertise and 'networks' that will improve the core businesses. For example, this may be in terms of putting the business in touch with key external contacts within the industry who can add 'legitimacy' to the business.

18.4 Adverse selection and moral hazard

The fundamental reason why VC funds are structured in the way described in the previous section is that the marketplace for VC funding is opaque (Amit *et al.* 1988). As we noted in Chapter 17, opacity leads to the twin problems of adverse selection and moral hazard for the supplier of funds. We now consider how this influences the marketplace for VC.

Adverse selection

In a VC context, adverse selection comprises two components. The first, which is the same as in the loan market, is that the provider of funds makes an 'incorrect choice', in the sense that it mistakes a bad for a good investment.

Equity providers, however, face an additional adverse selection problem not faced by those providing loans. For equity providers, the risk of selecting the wrong applicant is heightened because unsuitable people are perhaps more likely to seek equity funding. The argument in support of this view is that individuals who are totally confident that their business will succeed will not seek equity from outside, on the grounds that they will then have to share the value of the business with others if it becomes highly successful. As we argued in Chapter 17, these business owners will, instead, seek a range of other sources of finance – often called bootstrapping – to ensure the project succeeds without the need to share equity. In contrast, those that are less confident of the project will seek equity, since they then can share the risk with others. In other words, at the 'deal generation' stage, VCs may be faced by a range of prospective entrepreneurial businesses that are seeking to, at least, 'pool' the risks of the business with the VC and, at worst, shift their risks entirely over to the VC.

Table 18.1 shows that the VC has two possible responses to this dual adverse selection problem. Initially, it will seek to 'screen' prospective businesses. VCs do this by typically suggesting that they have a particular investment focus. For example, this may be by investment stage: hence, they may exclusively focus on 'early-stage' or 'seed' funding rather than focusing on private equity for MBOs. A second focus may be on geography. Again, a VC may only choose to look at potential investments that are in a particular country or a particular region of a country. VCs may also elect to focus on particular sectors.

Table 18.1	Addressing the problems of adverse selection and moral hazard		
Problem	**Problem description**	**VC strategies**	**Actions**
Adverse selection	• The VC picks the wrong businesses in which to invest. • Only the businesses that have doubts about their success seek funding.	• Due diligence • Syndication	• Spends considerable sums to investigate the market and the entrepreneur's track record. • Syndicates the deal so that risk is shared with others.
Moral hazard	• The businesses, once they receive the money, feel that they do not need to grow.	• Monitoring • Staging • Legal contract	• Appoint a non-executive director. • Invest funds in stages so that additional funding reflects performance. • Managers/entrepreneurs are remunerated via share options rather than salary. • Share options only accumulate value over time.

Illustration	Venture capitalists

Here are three examples of particular VCs and their particular focus.

1 **Viking Venture.** 'Viking Venture has 200 million USD (NOK 1,1 billion) capital under management. The fund invests in companies originating in the Nordic countries. Viking Venture focuses on technology companies within electronics, software, oil and gas, materials and clean technology. Viking Venture will typically invest after the seed phase and will be a proactive owner with a significant shareholding in its portfolio companies. Typical investment period of 3–5 years.'

Source: Viking Venture (2009) 'Investment Focus', http://www.vikingventure.com/index.asp?menuid=3353 (accessed 29 June 2009).

2 **SPARK Ventures.** 'Sector focus – primarily the high-growth sectors of information and communication technology, healthcare and life sciences. But we won't miss the opportunity to invest in exciting technology outside these broad areas. Geographic focus – We invest primarily in Europe, and worldwide alongside local venture capital firms. Stage of investment – We are early stage investors . . . but we will also consider investing in more developed businesses at pre-IPO stage. Size of investment – we take significant minority stakes, investing between £0.5 m and £2.0 m in the first round, and in subsequent funding rounds for companies successfully executing their business plans.'

Source: SPARK (2009) 'Investment Focus', http://www.quester.co.uk/Home/About_SPARK/Investment_focus/default.aspx (accessed 29 June 2009).

3 CVC Group. 'The CVC Renewable Energy Equity Fund is a venture capital fund established to increase Australian private investment in renewable energy and enabling technologies through the provision of equity finance. Approximately A\$18 million of the available funding is provided under the Australian Greenhouse Office's REEF licence and approximately A\$9 million is from private sources. CVC REEF invests in high growth, emerging Australian companies with domestic and global market potential in the renewable energy industry.'

Source: CVC Group (2009) 'About CVC REEF' http://www.cvc.com.au/cvcr/index.php (accessed 29 June 2009).

However, for businesses that meet their 'criteria' and look promising, the main activity conducted by VCs at this stage is to follow a 'due diligence' process. This is designed to identify only those businesses with outstanding growth potential. It requires a careful assessment of the marketplace for the product/service to see if the business has the potential to deliver significant capital gains.

It also requires an assessment on the part of the VC of whether the entrepreneur(s) have the entrepreneurial talent (θ) to deliver exceptional growth. Assessing precisely what constitutes θ, and precisely how it influences the growth of new and small businesses, has been reviewed in Chapters 13–15. It will be recalled that the key lesson emerging from these chapters is that forecasting exceptional success is extremely difficult. Nevertheless, it has long been the case (Macmillan *et al.* 1985), in spite of the evidence we reviewed in those chapters, that the VC is strongly influenced by what they perceive to be the track record of the individual.

Illustration	The views of two VCs on the due diligence process

'In my opinion, due diligence is:

- A process designed to get a 360-degree view of the business.
- An evaluation of an entrepreneur's ability to ascertain strength AND weakness.
- An opportunity to validate true customer demand.
- The beginning foundation of trust and partnership.'

Source, 'An Interview with Mr. Ziad K. Abdelnour – President and CEO of Blackhawk Partners', Inc. http://westernhq.com/blog/archives/16 (accessed 28 June 2009).

'As active early-stage investors, SPARK has wide experience of the issues facing growing technology companies, and detailed knowledge of our specialist sectors. Our experience blends ambition with the strategic, financial and commercial skills to enable us to maximise returns.

Key criteria –

- Strong management teams
- Identifiable and addressable markets with strong growth potential
- Market-ready technology
- Demonstrable route to profitability
- Clear exit strategy.'

Source: SPARK (2009) 'Investment Focus'. http://www.quester.co.uk/Home/About_SPARK/Investment_focus/default.aspx (accessed 29 June 2009).

One debate surrounding this process is which is more important: the *horse* (the market – what we called in Chapter 15 the fast-flowing current) or the *jockey* (the management – what we called the capable crew in Chapter 15)? Kaplan *et al.* (2009) suggest that two opposing views are held by VCs:

Illustration   The opposing views of VCs

A combination of management and market knowledge has put Apple's products on top.

Tom Perkins of Kleiner Perkins (a prominent VC) looked at a company's technological position and asked whether the technology was superior to alternatives and proprietary. Don Valentine of Sequoia (a prominent VC) assessed the market for the product or service and considered whether the market was large and growing. For example, many VCs declined to invest in Cisco because the team was considered weak. Valentine invested in Cisco anyway because he saw a huge market.

Alternatively, Arthur Rock, a prominent VC and early investor in Apple Computers, emphasized the quality, integrity, and commitment of management. According to Rock, a great management team can find a good opportunity even if they have to make a huge leap from the market they currently occupy. In their *Venture Capital Handbook*, Gladstone and Gladstone (2002) also take this perspective, quoting an old saying: 'You can have a good idea and poor management and lose every time. You can have a poor idea and good management and win every time' (pp. 91–2).

Source: Kaplan *et al.* (2009: 72).

One test for assessing which of these two – the management or the opportunity presented in the market – is more important to the VC is to assess how long the founder of the venture stays as the 'CEO' of the business post VC funding. The general finding from Kaplan *et al.* (2009) and Hellmann and Puri (2002) for the US, Cressy and Hall (2006) for the UK and Heger and Tykvova (2006) for Germany is that founders of VC funded business typically find themselves quickly replaced post-VC funding. Cressy and Hall (2006), for example, found that 32 per cent of founders were replaced when the businesses moved into the initial commercialising of the product/service. Whilst this may be explained by the need for different 'skill sets' to develop and subsequently commercialise a product/service, Kaplan *et al.* (2009: 79) agree with Warren Buffett: 'When a management team with a reputation for brilliance tackles a business with a reputation for bad economics, it is the reputation of the business that remains intact'.

Zacharakis and Meyer (1998), however, argue that VCs are susceptible to cognitive biases (see Chapter 2). They report, for example, that 'VCs do not have a strong grasp on their decision-making process' (p. 72) whilst Zacharakis and Shepherd (2001) argue that VCs are over-confident and rely on an 'availability bias' (the influence of recent successes or failures on the current decision) in making their decisions. In essence, the sense is that VCs are not much different from entrepreneurs in that they are likely to be over-optimistic and prone to cognitive biases.

Nonetheless, the consequence of both the expectation of high growth and the due diligence is that, unlike banks that provide loan capital, relatively few applications for VC are accepted. If nine out of every ten applications for loan capital from banks are likely to be funded in 'buoyant' macro-economic conditions (see Chapter 16), probably fewer than two per cent of applications to VCs are successful (gain funding) in the same conditions. For example, the Regional Venture Capital Funds in the UK in 2004 reported that 48 investments had been made from 2,680 applications. This is a 'success' rate of 1.8 per cent.

A second approach to addressing adverse selection is for a VC to offer other VCs the same opportunity. This is referred to as 'syndication'. It means that VCs do not always act individually and independently, but frequently do so as part of a group. There are four prime benefits of syndication to the VC. The first is that VC_1 may feel more confident about making an investment if VC_2 – which may have an expertise or skill set in an area where VC_1 knows they are weak – is also prepared to make an investment. Second, a formal syndication agreement means the costs of due diligence are shared amongst the syndicate – although, arguably, the actual costs are likely to be borne, either explicitly or implicitly, by the entrepreneurial business. The third benefit is that syndication means smaller sums are invested per project by each VC, which means the risks are more evenly spread. Finally, if the project does fail, then the losses are also proportionately smaller.

Of course, if the investment turns out to be very successful, then the returns have to be shared by the group.

In practice, syndication is also open to 'game playing'. VC_1, when offered the 'opportunity' to invest in company X by VC_2, may be suspicious of the latter's motives. VC_1 may ask, 'Why, if this is such a good prospect, does VC_2 not wish to make all the investment itself, since if the company succeeds VC_2 will have to share the value?' This may be further complicated if VC_2 indicates that it will only consider investing if there is also a commitment from VC_1. Trust is, therefore, a critical success factor.

Moral hazard

Table 18.1 shows that the second problem facing a VC is that of moral hazard. As we showed in Chapter 17, moral hazard occurs when the behaviour of an agent is unfavourably changed by the, often desirable, behaviour of the principal (Reid 1998). Take the example of the car driver with a low 'excess' on their insurance policy. Because of the low excess (only liable to pay a small amount in the event of an accident), there may be moral hazard consequences: such drivers may think that they are 'better' protected and, therefore, may be more prone to carelessly drive their car and endanger their car, those in the car or road users.

In a VC context, moral hazard comes into play when the VC, after undertaking due diligence, decides to invest in a business. Making that decision is intended to galvanise the growth of the business and to motivate the entrepreneur. However, what the VC fears is that the money is used to fund plush offices and a champagne lifestyle for the entrepreneurs, rather than for business development. The ability of enterprises to 'consume' VC funding is clearly illustrated in the high-profile Boo.com illustration (below).

Illustration	Boo.com

Boo.com was an internet start up that sought to sell fashionable sports and clothing brands via the internet. As Amazon.com had succeeded in books, Boo.com was expected to prosper in the branded sports and clothing markets.

Boo.com was established by Ernst Malmsten, Patrik Hedelin and Kajsa Leander in 1998 in London, launched its website in the autumn of 1999, had a peak valuation of $390 m, and yet was in receivership by May 2000.

When subsequently it was liquidated it is reported to have lost $US135 m or about £100 m. Funding for Boo.com was provided by Bernard Arnault, the chairman of luxury group LVMH, investment banks JP Morgan and Goldman Sachs. The other major loser was Omnia, a Middle Eastern Fund which alone is reported to have lost more than $US30 m.

Boo.com failed primarily because its website was slow to come online. Costs, though, also spiralled in a 'party' atmosphere. To demonstrate the 'champagne' lifestyle of the owners during this period, Leander reported ruefully after the collapse – as if to demonstrate her frugality – that she only travelled on Concorde [at the time the fastest but also the most expensive way of flying between Europe and the US] when it was on special offer.

The Boo.com business plan – which forecast that it would need £20 m, 30 people and three months to launch – was largely a work of fiction. In reality, it employed 400 people in eight offices, with headquarters on Carnaby Street – one of the most expensive areas in London. Some months later, in addition to the London offices, Boo.com also had accommodation in Munich, New York, Paris and Stockholm.

To compare this with the story of ASOS, another online clothes retailer – go online to www.pearsoned.co.uk/storeygreene to watch an FT video.

Table 18.1 shows that the VC has three strategies designed to minimise the effects of moral hazard. These are: monitoring, staging and contracting.

The prime monitoring information sought by the VC is the standard monthly financial reporting data. This enables the VC to assess whether or not the business is on track in terms of, for example, following its business plan.

However, monitoring provides very little insight into future prospects of the enterprise, and does not enable the VC to influence key strategic decisions. In order to play a more positive role, many VCs will identify an individual whose task is to add value to the business, but also to guard the interests of the VC. Such an individual normally becomes a non-executive director, who is a member of the board of the company, sees all relevant papers and is aware of news, both good and bad. However, this 'spy in the cab' will only be accepted by the entrepreneur(s) if the non-executive director provides a range of skills that enhance the performance of the business and so add value.

There is some evidence that VCs do add value to a business, over and above the finance they provide. By 'value' we mean the services/expertise which they provide, and which serves to 'professionalise' the companies in which they invest. Specifically, this guidance may be in the form of contacts, specialist industry knowledge and expertise. Hellman and Puri (2002) find evidence for this amongst businesses in Silicon Valley in the US. They find that VCs formalise and enhance staff recruitment, get rid of inappropriate chief executive officers (CEOs) and choose the best time for the VC to sell.

A second strategy adopted by the VC to overcome moral hazard is to provide funding in stages, rather than all at once. The benefit to the VC in this is the option to increase ownership at a later point in time, when the progress of the company has become clearer. In this case, the VC may initially only purchase 20 per cent of shares, at an agreed valuation, but may, for example, have the option to buy a further 10 per cent within three years, depending upon performance. This provides the VC with a reduced exposure to risk in the early stages, but the opportunity to increase ownership at a later date. It also means that funds which were not initially invested by the VC can perhaps be used in syndicated ventures with other VCs in order to further reduce risk. However, since staging is performance-related, it means the VC has to monitor the business very carefully and, as we saw in Chapter 17, such monitoring is costly.

From the perspective of the business, staged contracts have advantages and disadvantages. Their key disadvantage is that the risk clearly lies with the business – if it does well in its early years it automatically loses ownership, but if it does badly it absorbs all the costs. However, without staged contracts the VC might walk away from a deal because they fear over-exposure to moral hazard problems. Staging is a frequently used strategy, particularly for successful investments. Gompers and Lerner (2003) report that successful investments receive up to four 'rounds' of investment.

A third strategy to address moral hazard relates to contract formulation and compliance. The VC has to ensure that the entrepreneur only benefits from future success. This incentive is formalised in a contract in which the prime source of remuneration for the entrepreneur is share options which have future value, rather than a salary which is of immediate value. The VC, therefore, favours a restriction on a salary by effectively placing the entrepreneur in the same boat as the VC, who only benefits when the business is sold at a high valuation. The fear of the VC is that, if the entrepreneur starts to benefit prior to the business being sold, this will discourage effort. In the VC's mind, prior benefits will encourage the entrepreneur to 'shirk'. The contract, therefore, specifies that the options only become valuable x years in the future. Here the VC is seeking to ensure that entrepreneurs – or other critical employees – do not 'walk away' from the business before it achieves its full potential. Essentially, the idea of leaving today has to be penalised, whereas the prospect of leaving some years from now has to be made highly attractive. In this way, the VC expects to generate from the entrepreneur the extra effort and dedication needed to make the business successful.

18.5 The demand for equity

The previous section essentially suggested that, faced with adverse selection and moral hazard problems, the VC attempts to minimise their 'downside' risks (e.g. entrepreneur not being fully committed to the business) and maximise their 'upside' benefits (e.g. stock options). What, though, are the advantages of the entrepreneur in accessing equity finance? There are five main advantages:

1 Equity finance does not incur interest payments. Hence, other things being equal, this improves the cashflow position (working capital) of the business.

2 The business might not be able to access other funds. The bulk of VC finance is in high-tech sectors (e.g. software, biotechnology) and very many of these businesses only have intangible assets (e.g. a patent). Hence, they may find it difficult – without collateral – to raise funding from anywhere else but the VC.

3 The additional equity can then be used to lever additional borrowing in the form of loans from banks or other financial institutions if required. This is important to very many high-tech businesses because they often require successive rounds of finance to successfully develop and commercialise their product.

4 The VC may provide information and advice to help the business, since it is in the joint interest of both the entrepreneur(s) and the VC that the business increases in scale and value.

5 The money provided is 'patient' in the sense that the VC will not be seeking a return – in terms of selling the shares – generally for at least 3–5 years and probably longer.

The disadvantages of VC, from the perspective of the entrepreneur are:

- The requirement to share ownership with the VC. This may create a psychological disaffection on the part of the entrepreneur, from 'not being in control', or from having to consult others before making decisions. It may also reflect a reluctance on the part of the entrepreneur, who is wholly confident that the business will grow rapidly, to share the increased valuation with a third party. Entrepreneurs may judge that the VC has made little contribution to the growth of the business and has, indeed, acted as a 'free rider'.

- Equally, if successive rounds of financing are required to grow the business, the entrepreneur is likely to end up with a tiny proportion of the 'cake' (equity) when the equity is sold. The entrepreneur might be unhappy with this dilution of their equity share, particularly if they believe that it is they, rather than the VC, that is more likely to see their equity diluted.

- Although VC funding is 'patient', the entrepreneur may find that they are too hastily 'pushed' into selling the business or bringing the business to flotation (Initial Public Offering).

These issues are reflected in discussions about the appropriate valuation of the business and the proportion of these shares to be owned by the VC, which we now discuss.

18.6 'Clearing the market'

The central feature of any market is that buyers and sellers come together, and the market is said to clear at a particular price and quantity. To illustrate, we examine the market for venture capital in the context of the television programme, 'Dragons' Den'. Here, those seeking VC for their business 'pitch' in a 'den' to the 'dragons' (VC suppliers). There are two typical outcomes from the pitch. The first is that the dragons show no interest, and no transaction takes place. The second is that the market clears, in the sense that the dragons acquire x per cent of the business (quantity) in return for an investment of y (price).

Assume, for example, that $x = 20$ and the dragon is prepared to invest 200,000: then the value of the business is 1 million euros, dollars or pounds.

But how is this valuation reached? In principle, the answer is that, as with any investment decision, a Net Present Value (NPV) can be calculated based upon the flow of profits from the business over time. This yields an NPV figure that can then be linked to the investment being sought.

However, valuing a new business is extremely problematic. The central problem is the uncertainty over the cash flows in a new business, since these are dependent upon expected future performance of a business often with a limited or even non-existent 'track record' on which to base such a forecast.

Inevitably, the business entrepreneur(s) will argue that, because of the unique growth prospects of the business, the valuation should be high. In contrast, the VC will argue that the risk of the investment is high and the shares should be priced accordingly. The outcome of these negotiations is unclear, with the entrepreneur, on occasion, walking away from the deal, and, in other cases, the VC viewing the entrepreneur's assessments as being unrealistic.

A second key influence on the market for external equity is the presence of a well-established 'exit route' or marketplace. For this purpose, an initial public offering (IPO) – in which shares are floated on the Stock Exchange – is ideal, because this creates a formal marketplace in which all financial institutions may bid for shares. Other, but less ideal, exit routes by which entrepreneurs and VCs may sell some or all of their equity also exist. Of these, the most important are trade sales, whereby the business is sold in full or in part to another enterprise. The central disadvantage of this exit route is that there are likely to be a very limited number of purchasers who will also perhaps be in a strong position to ensure the valuation is low.

18.7 The venture capitalist's portfolio

We now examine the outcomes of the VC marketplace by taking, as an illustration, the portfolio of a hypothetical venture capital fund. This is shown in Table 18.2. We make a number of assumptions for the sake of simplification.

Table 18.2	A venture capital portfolio					
Business/ Investment	Amount invested (£ m)	Share (%)	Outcome	Final value	Return (%)	Category
1	4	20	Fail	0	0	F
2	7	20	None	7	0	LD
3	10	30	None	13	30	T
4	1	10	Trade sale	3	300	T
5	6	30	None	3	−50	LD
6	5	20	Flotation	50	1,000	W
7	3	20	None	3	0	LD
8	10	30	Trade sale	70	700	W
9	1	10	None	1	0	LD
10	8	30	Fail	0	0	F
11	2	20	Trade sale	10	500	T
12	8	30	None	10	25	LD
13	2	20	None	2	0	LD
14	6	30	Fail	0	0	F
15	4	30	Fail	0	0	F
16	2	10	Flotation	20	1,000	W
17	5	30	None	8	60	T
18	6	20	Fail	0	0	F
19	8	40	Fail	0	0	F
20	2	10	Flotation	50	2,500	W
Total	**100**	–	–	**250**	**250**	

First, we assume the fund has £100 million for investment purposes, and that it invests all of it immediately in 20 enterprises. There is no staging and no syndication. Column 2 of Table 18.2 shows that the VC invests different sums of money in the ventures, with the amounts varying from £1 m to £10 m.

Column 3 shows that the VC is a minority shareholder in each business, with its ownership share varying from 10 per cent to 40 per cent. In only one case is the ownership as high as 40 per cent. As we saw above, the monetary investment by the VC, and the percentage owned, can then be used to calculate the value of the business at the time the VC makes the investments. So, for example, in Business 1, the value of the business at the time of the investment is £20 m ($4 \times 1/0.2$). Some businesses are more highly valued at the time of the investment. For example, Business 3 has an implied value of £33 m ($10 \times 1/0.3$), whilst Businesses 9, 11 and 13 each have a valuation of only £10 m.

The fourth column of Table 18.2 shows the outcome of the investment. We have seen that several options are possible. The first, and most desirable from the viewpoint of the VC, is a flotation. Flotations are, however, quite rare: the table shows that only Businesses 6, 16 and 20 have this desirable outcome. A second 'exit route' for the VC is the sale of the business to another, generally larger, business. This is referred to as a 'trade sale'. In Table 18.2 this occurs in the case of Businesses 4, 8 and 11. The lower returns from a trade sale, compared with flotation, are apparent from columns 5 and 6. Column 5 shows the 'final' valuation of the 20 investments and column 6 shows the return on the investment. In essence, column 6 shows that the percentage return for trade sales varies from 300 to 600 per cent, compared with those for a flotation which vary from 1,000 to 2,500 per cent. A third outcome, shown in column 4 of Table 18.2, is that there are eight businesses which report 'None' as their outcome. This means that they remain as private companies and the VC has therefore not 'exited' – although in some cases the VC's shares may have been purchased by the majority shareholders. The valuation of such businesses is particularly difficult because these businesses have probably not been even offered for sale. The valuation is, therefore, highly subjective, and may have to be estimated using only the tangible assets of the business, its goodwill, and/or benchmarked against any broadly comparable recent trade sales (see Case studies 3 and 4).

The final outcome in column 4 is 'Fail'. In this case the business has ceased trading. There are assumed to be six cases out of the 20 when this has occurred. This is 30 per cent failure rate over a seven-year period, and is broadly in line with the findings of Kaiser *et al.* (2007). This, as we know from Chapters 9 and 10, is a lower failure rate than is typical for small businesses, but is nevertheless a high rate given that these businesses were selected for their growth potential. We assume that, in all these 'fail' cases, the VC lost all of their investment. In practice, when the business is liquidated, there may be some modest return to the shareholders.

Column 5 of Table 18.2 shows the final value of the business seven years after the VC initially made their investment. As we noted above, some of the valuations – such as those business from flotations or trade sales – are reliable, and the VC will have the money. In other cases, particularly where there has been no sale or exit, the valuations are more subjective. Reflecting these points, the column shows that there are four businesses – Businesses 6, 8, 16 and 20 – which have increased in value considerably since the VC investment. Of these, the most spectacular growth is in Business 20. This was originally valued at £20 m when the investment was made. However, when it was floated it was valued at £500 m, yielding the VC a 2,500 per cent return on investment.

The percentage return for all investments is shown in column 6, and it demonstrates the considerable spread of returns. They range from 2,500 per cent for Business 20 to −50 per cent for Business 5. In this case, the negative valuation occurs because, although the business has not ceased trading, a realistic valuation implies that it is now worth less than when the VC investment was initially made.

The final column of Table 18.2 shows how the investments might be grouped or classified. We give these four labels. The first and most desirable from the viewpoint of the VC are the 'Winners' (W). These are businesses that have grown substantially in value, and where the VC has also been able to exit and recoup the investment.

Table 18.3	Outcomes from a VC portfolio				
	Winners	**Failures**	**Living Dead**	**Trundlers**	**Total**
Number	4	6	5	5	20
Amount invested (£ m)	19	36	27	18	100
Valuation (£ m)	190	0	26	34	250
Contribution to fund value (%)	76	0	10.4	13.6	100

The second group are referred to as 'Trundlers' (T). These are businesses which, although they were expected to grow rapidly, in fact performed little better than many other small businesses. They showed modest growth, but not the scale of growth expected by the VC when the investment was made.

The third group are often unflatteringly referred to by VCs as the 'Living Dead' (LD). These are businesses that survive, but exhibit very low or perhaps even no growth. In many cases, their performance is broadly similar to that of small businesses more widely but, since they were selected for their growth potential, such businesses are a disappointment to the VC.

The fourth and final group are those that have ceased to trade or 'Failures' (F).

We now turn to Table 18.3 and examine the composition of the VC's portfolio, distinguishing between the four groups. We know from Table 18.2 that the overall value of the portfolio has risen from £100 m to £250 m over seven years. However, Table 18.3 shows that the contribution from the various groups varies markedly. The four Winners constitute 20 per cent of the portfolio and 19 per cent of the initial investment. Seven years later, however, they provide 76 per cent of the value of the fund. The success of the VC fund is, therefore, heavily dependent upon a low proportion of the total investment. The heavy dependence upon a small number of winners in our hypothetical example is closely mirrored by the performance of most VC funds. For example, American Research and Development (ARD) was supposedly the first formal VC fund in the US. It was established in 1946 and existed for 26 years. Gompers and Lerner (2001) report that almost half of ARD's profits came from a single $70,000 investment in Digital Equipment Corporation (DEC). This investment eventually realised $355 million.

The second and third groups are the numerically dominant 'Trundlers' and 'Living Dead'. These businesses provide 24 per cent of the value of the fund, but their growth rates are nowhere near large enough to be attractive to the VC. The final group is the 'Failures'. There were six businesses in this group, and the VC invested more in them than in the 'Winners'.

Two main lessons emerge from this hypothetical, yet realistic example:

- The contribution of a small number of spectacular performers is the key to the overall success of the fund. This is illustrated by reflecting on the consequences for the fund had it decided *not* to invest in their 'superstar' (Business 20) because it was thought to be too risky. This error would have cost the fund £50 m – which is more than the total valuation of 15 of the businesses in which investments were made. To put it another way, we can say that a single business adds more to the fund than three quarters of all of the other businesses. The converse is that, if the fund had been able to add another superstar, this alone would have added 20 per cent to the value of the fund and, as we will show, almost 50 per cent to the overall return on the fund.

- This is a portfolio of high risk and high return. The implication is that if the VC sees an investment as offering the real possibility of an upside gain, then it would be extremely foolish to ignore such a business on the grounds that it also has a high risk of failure. In short, the real risk to the fund is that of losing a 'Winner' rather than acquiring a 'Failure'.

Table 18.4	Return to a VC fund over seven years	
Funds invested at time t_3		£100 million
Costs of management of funds including bonus over seven years		£50 million
Value of fund in t_{10}		£250 million
Return on funds		£100 million
Average annual rate		8 per cent

Assumptions:
1 All investments are made at t_3.
2 Constant prices.

Finally, let us assess the overall profitability or 'return' to the fund. We shall assume the funding is provided by a financial institution or consortia of financial institutions. Some broad calculations on the return to the fund are provided in Table 18.4.

Table 18.4 shows, once again, that the value of the fund increased from £100 million to £250 million over the seven-year period. This gross increase of £150 million is, however, achieved at the cost of £50 million shown in the table as the management funds. We assume that these costs include the management fee charged by the VC (2–3 per cent) as well as staff costs (e.g. general partners costs, costs of analysts, lawyers, and accountants) and costs of providing services, such as non-executive directors (NEDs).

Also, as we have already seen, the success rate of applicants to a VC fund is very much lower than the success rate for those seeking other forms of finance. So, perhaps 19 businesses are rejected for each that receives funding. This means that VCs spend a considerable amount of time making assessments of applications in which ultimately they choose not to invest. In our hypothetical example, if the fund invests in 20 businesses, it implies that it received around 1,000 applicants, all of which incur some costs in the assessment process.

We have also seen that the overall success of the fund depends crucially upon not rejecting a 'winner'. So, for that reason, even though few are accepted, the due diligence has to be under-taken thoroughly.

Overall, Table 18.4 shows that the return on this hypothetical fund is a respectable 8 per cent per annum, but that the three key influences upon this return are:

- the ability to select winners;
- the ability to sell investments – the exit route;
- the cost structure of the fund.

18.8 Business angels

Thus far we have implicitly assumed that the venture capital is provided by professional VC firms and managed by their staff. This is referred to as formal VC. However, the uncertain, but potentially high, returns for those taking an equity stake in new businesses with high growth potential also provide an opportunity for wealthy *individuals* to provide equity capital for new businesses. This is called **informal venture capital** and is provided by so-called **'business angels'**. The term 'angels' is believed to derive from wealthy individuals who supported theatre productions in the West End of London. They were regarded as angels by theatre

Table 18.5	Venture capital: comparing formal and informal sources	
	Angels	**Formal venture capital**
1 Status	(Rich) individuals	Corporate
2 Type of investment	Start up or very early stage	Start ups to development capital, but generally more mature projects
3 Amounts invested in individual projects	Range from £0.02 m to £0.3 m	Range from £0.4 m to £5 m
4 Total invested	$30 billion in US	$30–35 billion in US
5 Time horizon	Four to six years	Six to nine years
6 Speed of decision	Weeks	Months
7 Selection criteria	Commercial but also 'interesting' projects	Strictly commercial
8 Addressing adverse selection	• Local, even personal, knowledge of sector • Can afford to be patient when selecting where to invest	• Seeking expert views • Specialise in sectors
9 Addressing moral hazard	Personal involvement with the company	• Appoint NEDs • Staging of investment • Linking returns for the entrepreneur to business performance
10 Staging	Less likely	Very likely
11 Syndication	Yes	Yes
12 Management costs	Low	Higher

owners and producers because they were prepared to fund the cost of preparing for and rehearsing for the production, prior to the first night, in return for sharing in any profits made after that time. The term angel was a combination of 'theatre-speak' and the fact that since so few productions were profitable, such individuals *must* have had angelic qualities.

However, knowledge about such individuals is sparse, primarily because their investments are the financial affairs of rich individuals who generally seek to keep this information confidential. Nevertheless, the pioneering work of Wetzel (1983) in the US, subsequently developed by Mason and Harrison (2002) in the UK, Riding *et al.* (2007) in Canada, and Maula *et al.* (2005) on a global scale, have provided a knowledge-base for making broad comparisons between angels and the formal VC industry. The essential differences between business angels and the formal VC sector are summarised in Table 18.5 (see also the views of Andrew Rickman, investor and entrepreneur, who discusses the differences between business angels, what he calls 'super angels' and venture capitalists: www.pearsoned.co.uk/storeygreene).

1 Angels are individuals rather than formal financial institutions. The individual who becomes an angel is wealthy and generally has accumulated this wealth through business experience, often by selling their own business. Angels favour taking an equity stake in a business sector in which they have direct personal experience, because they have valuable knowledge which may not be easily available to the 'outsider'.

2 Angels are much more likely to make investments in either start-up or fledgling businesses. In contrast, whilst some formal VC funds do make investments in young businesses, the bulk of their funding is focused on young, but nevertheless established, businesses.

3 The individual sums provided by angels for a project are generally much smaller than the sums provided from formal VC.

4 Although they only invest relatively small sums, angels are ubiquitous in countries such as North America and the UK. This explains why the most recent estimates by Sohl (2003) imply that the total funding pool provided by angels is broadly similar to that of the VC.

5 The time horizons of angels are broadly similar, if a little shorter, than that of a formal VC.

6 It appears that angels reach a decision on whether or not to invest more quickly than a VC.

7 Angels may feel less constrained than VCs in selecting only those investments which they feel will yield the highest commercial returns. This is not to imply that angels generally act 'un-commercially', but rather that some of their portfolio contains investments that are chosen out of their 'interest' rather than the expectation of high return.

We now ask how angels differ from VCs in their response to both adverse selection and moral hazard. These differences are summarised in Table 18.5.

● Angels believe they can better address the issue of adverse selection than the VC sector for several reasons. First, often their own personal experience of operating a business in a sector gives them a unique insight into the nature of the marketplace, the personal skills required and the necessary contact network for a new business in that sector. In essence, they believe their experience gives them unique insights not easily available to the professional outsider. It is very likely that angel investors have, themselves, successfully run their own business whilst the VC experience may be more in raising finance (VC funds) and in assessing potential business propositions (Walske and Zacharakis 2009). Second, they may either be more motivated to select only the best projects since they are using their own – as opposed to someone else's – money. Alternatively, as we noted above, they may explicitly select some projects for their 'interest' – but they do so in an informed and explicit manner. Third, whilst the formal VC sector may be under pressure to make investments in order to use the funds with which they are provided, there is no such pressure on the angel.

In contrast, as we saw earlier, the formal VC sector generally addresses this issue by seeking the views of specialists – perhaps by making use of individuals who are also angel investors in their own right.

● Moral hazard issues also tend to be addressed very differently by angels and VCs. As we saw above, the key to overcoming moral hazard is to seek to align the interest of the entrepreneur with those of the external equity provider. For both angels and VCs, knowing what is going on – monitoring – is vital, but for the formal VC sector this frequently involves the appointment of a non-executive director (NED) to sit on the board. Although that person can add value, he or she is more likely to be seen as a 'spy in the cab' rather than as 'one of the family'. In contrast, the angel, whose own money is clearly 'on the line', can make a more plausible case for sitting on the board on the grounds that 'we are all in this together'. Second, the evidence of Kelly and Hay (2003) seems to imply that, whilst the formal sector favours the 'tight contract' approach to avoiding moral hazard, a less legalistic approach is adopted by the angel. This is feasible if the angel is able to demonstrate the same level of energy, interest and commitment to the venture as the entrepreneur.

These different approaches to overcoming adverse selection and moral hazard explain the remaining differences between angels and the VC sector shown in Table 18.5.

● Staging is a key response of the VC to moral hazard, on the grounds that the business only gets injections of equity if performance is 'on track'. This approach is less important to the angel for two reasons: the first is because the sums of money provided by angels are relatively small, and so it is not very practical for them to be staged. The second is that the close involvement of the angel with the business means that the moral hazard problem is less likely to exist (the interests of the angel and the entrepreneur are naturally aligned), and so there is less need to stage investments.

● Syndication – involving other VCs as partners in the investment – is a characteristic of both angels and the formal sector, but for different reasons. The prime motive for syndication in the formal sector is to spread the risk of making a bad investment. It also reflects acknowledged information imperfections, and recognition by the VC that its investment partners bring additional information or insights. It may also reflect the need of the VC to provide reassurance that similar 'like-minded' financiers are prepared to take the same risk. These are less important motivations for the angel who believes they have better insights and information. Instead, the attraction of a syndicate (referred to as a *business angel network*) is being able to make investments in more businesses for the same sum of money.

● Finally, we noted earlier in Table 18.4 that formal VC funds incurred substantial management costs. In addition, there is an expectation that there will be appropriate (expensive) office accommodation. This is very different for angels, who will have lower costs. For example, the investment(s) can be managed from home, there is less need to pay for the views of others, and more modest salaries and bonuses will be sought.

On balance, the comparisons between the formal and informal VC providers shown in Table 18.5 imply that angels would be expected to 'outperform' the formal VC industry. Evidence for this is, however, difficult to obtain. Mason and Harrison (2002) report on a study of UK angels. They find that, as with the formal VC investments, the distribution is negatively skewed, with about one third of investments incurring a total loss and only 10 per cent obtaining a return in excess of 100 per cent. Insofar as it is possible to compare this with the formal sector returns, Mason and Harrison conclude that on average the returns differ little between the formal and the informal sectors. One significant difference, though, is that the angels are less likely to have exits, but more likely to have only modestly performing investments. Mason and Harrison attribute this to angels having 'pet' projects, where they made an investment choice based on partly on financial return expectations, and at least in part on 'finding the project interesting'.

Summary

To conclude the finance section of this book, Table 18.6 summarises the similarities and differences between equity and loans, along eight separate dimensions.

Table 18.6 Loans and equity: a summary comparison

	Equity	Loan
Objective of supplier	Growth leading to increased business valuation	Repayment of the loan and interest in full and on time
Collateral	No	Yes
Duration	Medium term – about seven years	Short to medium
Interest charged	No	Yes
Ownership	Yes	No
'Soft' assistance	Sometimes	Rarely
Monitoring	Yes	Yes
Chances of obtaining it	Very low	High

Table 18.6 shows, first, that the objectives of the loan and the equity provider differ. The loan provider seeks a business owner that will repay a loan in full. Whether or not the business expands or contracts is a secondary consideration, so the loan provider's ideal client is a low-risk business that may seek just to 'trundle' along making modest profits, drawing upon modest amounts of external finance but, crucially, paying on time and in full.

Such a client is of no value to the VC or the business angel, who only wants a business that will grow rapidly and where it can exit easily and recoup the return on its investment. The VC focuses on maximising upside gains, whereas the loan provider seeks to minimise downside losses.

A second difference is that equity providers do not normally require collateral, primarily because the businesses in which they invest have little of re-saleable value. In contrast, the loan provider seeks to minimise downside losses, and collateral to be drawn upon in the event of default is often crucial. Differences are also apparent in terms of the duration of the finance. Essentially, loans tend to be of short to medium term, whilst equity providers, as we have seen in this chapter, are likely to be much more 'patient'.

Chapter 17 also identified that a key reason for banks providing loans is that the profits mainly accrue from interest payments. This is absent from equity finance. However, equity provision is about taking some (part) ownership in the business. As often as not, the loan provider studiously avoids this involvement except when, in the event of a default, business assets or the personal assets of the owner may be acquired. Concomitant with this is that, as we have seen, equity providers are proactive providers of information, guidance and advice to the business. It does this because it believes that such support – as we have seen in this chapter – will help the business to grow and, thereby, benefit both the entrepreneur and their own equity interests.

Such 'soft' assistance is rarely provided by loan providers. Because of the transaction costs of providing loans, and that those loans are likely to be relatively small, there is little incentive for banks to provide such assistance. Instead, they prefer an 'arm's-length' relationship. Finally, as Table 18.6 shows, there are huge differences in the likelihood of obtaining equity and loan funding. Broadly, the vast majority – perhaps even nine out of ten applications – of loan applications are successful, compared with less than two per cent of venture capital applications.

Questions for discussion

1 What are business angels? In what respects do they differ from the formal venture capital industry?

2 Compare and contrast the use of loans and equity amongst small businesses.

3 Do venture capitalist add value? Justify your answer.

4 How does the response to moral hazard and adverse selection differ between formal and informal providers of venture capital?

5 What factors are likely to influence the decision of a new business seeking venture capital?

6 What is a non-executive director (NED)? Does a NED act in the interests of the business or in the interests of the VC?

References

Amit, R., Brander, J. and Zott, C. (1988) 'Why Do Venture Capital Firms Exist?: Theory and Canadian Evidence', *Journal of Business Venturing*, 13(3), 441–66.

Cressy, R. and Hall, T. (2006) *'When Should a Venture Capitalist Replace an Owner-Manager?: Theory and Empirics'.* London: Cass Business School.

Cumming, D., Fleming, G. and Schwienbacher, A. (2007) 'The Structure of Venture Capital Businesses', in Landstrom, H. (ed.), *Handbook of Venture Capital Research*. Cheltenham: Edward Elgar, 155–76.

Gompers, P. and Lerner, J. (2001) 'The Venture Capital Revolution', *Journal of Economic Perspectives,* 15(2), 145–68.

Gompers, P. and Lerner, J. (2003) 'Equity Financing', in Acs, Z.J. and Audretsch, D.B. (eds) *Handbook of Entrepreneurship Research: An Interdisciplinary Survey and Introduction.* Dordrecht: Springer, 267–98.

Heger, D. and Tykova, T. (2006) 'Kick It Like Beckham: The Impact of Venture Capitalists on Management Turnover'. Paper presented to the DRUID Summer Conference, Copenhagen.

Hellmann, T. and Puri, M. (2002) 'Venture Capital and the Professionalization of Start Up Firms: Empirical Evidence', *Journal of Finance*, 57(1), 169–97.

Kaiser, D.G., Lauterbach, R. and Schweizer, D. (2007) 'Total Loss Risk in European versus US-based Venture Capital Investments', in Gregoriou, G.N., Kooli, M. and Kraeussi, R. (eds), *Venture Capital in Europe*. Amsterdam: Elsevier, 371–88.

Kaplan, S.N., Sensoy, B.A. and Stromberg, P. (2009) 'Should Investors Bet on the Jockey or the Horse?: Evidence from the Evolution of Firms from Early Business Plans to Public Companies', *Journal of Finance*, 64(1), 75–115.

Kelly, P. and Hay, M. (2003) 'Deal Makers, Reputation Attracts Quality', *Venture Capital*, 2(3), 183–202.

Landstrom, H. (2007) *Handbook of Research on Venture Capital*. Cheltenham: Edward Elgar, 3–65.

Lockett, A., Murray, G. and Wright, M. (2002) 'Do UK Venture Capitalists Still Have a Bias against Investment in New Technology Businesses?', *Research Policy*, 31(6), 1009–30.

Macmillan, I.C., Siegel, R. and Subba Narasimha, P.N. (1985) 'Criteria Used by Venture Capitalists to Evaluate New Venture Proposals', *Journal of Business Venturing*, 1(1), 119–18.

Madill, J.J., Haines, G.H. and Riding, A. (2005) 'The Role of Angels in Technology SMEs', *Venture Capital*, 7(2), 107–29.

Mason, C.M. and Harrison, R.T. (2002) 'Barriers to Investment in the Informal Venture Capital Sector', *Entrepreneurship and Regional Development*, 14(3), 271–87.

Maula, M., Autio, E. and Arenius, P. (2005) 'What Drives Micro-Angel Investments?', *Small Business Economics*, 25(5), 459–75.

Murray, G. and Dimov, D. (2007) 'Through a Glass Darkly: New Perspectives on the Equity Gap', in Clarysse, B., Ruore, J. and Schamp, T. (eds) *Entrepreneurship and the Financial Community: Starting Up and Growing New Businesses*. Cheltenham: Edward Elgar, 161–74.

Murray, G.C. (2007) 'Venture Capital and Government Policy', in Landstrom, H. (ed.), *Handbook of Research on Venture Capital*. Aldershot: Edward Elgar, 113–51.

Reid, G.C. (1998) *Venture Capital Investment: An Agency Analysis of Practice*. London and New York: Routledge.

Riding, A., Madill, J.J. and Haines, G.H. (2007) 'Investment Decision Making by Business Angels', in Landstrom, H. (ed.) *Handbook of Research on Venture Capital*. Cheltenham: Edward Elgar, 332–46.

Sohl, J.E. (2003) 'The Private Equity Market in the US: Lessons from Volatility', *Venture Capital*, 5(1), 29–46.

Walske, J.M. and Zacharakis, A. (2009) 'Genetically Engineered: Why Some Venture Capital Firms Are More Successful than Others', *Entrepreneurship Theory and Practice*, 33(1), 297–318.

Wetzel, W.E. (1983) 'Angels and Informal Risk Capital', *Sloan Management Review*, 24(4), 23–4.

Zacharakis, A. and Meyer, G. (1998) 'A Lack of Insight: Do Venture Capitalists Really Understand Their Own Decision Process?', *Journal of Business Venturing*, 13(1), 57–76.

Zacharakis, A.L. and Shepherd, D.A. (2001) 'The Nature of Information and Overconfidence on Venture Capitalists Decision Making', *Journal of Business Venturing*, 16(4), 311–32.

Part 6

Public Policy and the Small Business

In Part 6 we explore the role that policy makers and government play in the life of the entrepreneur or small business owner. Chapter 19 provides an overview of the main issues involved in public policy. This chapter covers why policy makers are typically attracted to supporting entrepreneurs and small businesses and what justifications are used to legitimate such support. Chapter 20 considers the impact that 'macro' influences (e.g. economic conditions, taxation, regulation) have on the development of entrepreneurship and small business policies. Finally, Chapter 21 examines the impact of policies targeted at entrepreneurs and small businesses. The chapter reviews five main areas of public support – enterprise culture, finance, advice and assistance, supporting technology and innovation and the development of particular groups (e.g. women, ethnic minorities).

19   Public policy, small businesses and entrepreneurs

20   Macro policies towards small businesses and entrepreneurs

21   Policy in practice

Entrepreneurship in Action   **FT**

Go to the *Small Business and Entrepreneurship* companion website at www.pearsoned.co.uk/storeygreene to watch entrepreneurs and academics giving you their personal perspectives on some of these issues.

Paul Kesterman, Chief Executive of the National Endowment for Science, Technology and the Arts (NESTA), talks about the role the public sector can play in start ups.

19 Public policy, small businesses and entrepreneurs

Mini contents list

Key learning objectives

By the end of this chapter you should:

- Understand the different ways public policy seeks to support entrepreneurs and SMEs and why taxpayers' money is used for this purpose

- Be able to identify and distinguish between the justifications offered for this support

- Be able to critically compare and contrast different policy 'regimes' in different countries

- Be able to categorise these policy regimes and evaluate the general arguments for and against such support

- Be able to identify the range of choices open to policy makers in designing and implementing enterprise policy.

19.1 Introduction

Almost every government in the world provides support for SMEs (small and medium-sized enterprises) and entrepreneurs (Hoffman 2007). The OECD (2008a) suggests that there are six main areas – what it calls 'determinants of entrepreneurship' – that public policy may seek to influence. These determinants are: the regulatory framework; R&D and technology; entrepreneurial capabilities; enterprise 'culture'; access to finance; and market conditions. In the first section of this chapter, we identify how the OECD believes these six determinants can impact on entrepreneurial performance and, subsequently, on the wider economy and society.

This is important because public support for SMEs and entrepreneurs involves significant taxpayer expenditure. For example, in 2003/4 the UK government estimated that about £10 billion was spent supporting SMEs (DTI 2002). In other words, the UK taxpayer spent more on funding SMEs than on either its universities or its police force.

The second section of this chapter asks: what are the motivations for such expenditure? We identify four stimuli: SMEs and entrepreneurs create jobs, aid economic development, provide sustainability benefits (e.g. provide a productive outlet for people) and represent a core political constituency.

However, just because SMEs and entrepreneurs are 'valuable' is not a sufficient reason why taxpayer funds should be used for such support. In the third section of this chapter, we identify that the main justification for public intervention to support entrepreneurs and small businesses is that there is evidence of **market failure**. This means that the 'market' has failed to provide goods/services at a socially optimal level. We explain the reasons for this shortfall in Section 19.4.

This means that what policy makers should be asking is 'What can SMEs and entrepreneurs do for us?' rather than asking the more usual question: 'What can we do to help SMEs and entrepreneurs?' This, again, is important because it is public funds and, hence, a judgement on their effective use has to be based on the public benefits that they generate. Funds used for supporting SMEs and entrepreneurs could be spent in a variety of other ways that might benefit society – such as on hospitals, schools and roads. Alternatively, the expenditure could be saved and so enable taxes to be lowered. Hence, if public funds are used for supporting SMEs and entrepreneurs they have to be at least as effective for society as other possible uses of public funds.

The third section, however, also shows that market failure is not the only justification used by policy makers to support SMEs and entrepreneurs. Instead, a second approach is termed the 'political economy' approach. Here policies are often justified because some groups or individuals may experience unequal outcomes. We also show that politicians, civil servants and lobby groups also have their own vested interests. This makes 'communication' between policy makers and small businesses difficult.

The chapter recognises, in the fourth section, that different countries provide support for small businesses often in very different ways. For this reason, we explore the policy regimes adopted by different countries and the choices that underpin them. To illustrate this we make use of Dennis' (2004) typology of international policy regimes. We show – using the US and UK as examples – that politicians evolve over time. This is important because, central to understanding any policy regime, is information on the costs of support and its place within the overall framework of government activities.

The fifth section of this chapter examines the segmentation of policies. We use Lundstrom and Stevenson's (2007) distinction between entrepreneurship (focused on raising individual entrepreneurial capacities and propensities) and SME policies (focused on existing small businesses). We then show that there are general arguments for and against supporting such policies.

In the chapter's final section, we identify the range of choices faced by policy makers interested in designing and implementing support. Using the Mole and Bramley (2006) framework, we show that these choices involve difficult decisions for the policy maker.

19.2 The OECD framework

This section provides examples of the forms of public support for entrepreneurs and SMEs within the context of the formal model provided by OECD (2008). The OECD model is in three parts (Figure 19.1). First, it assumes there are a range of 'Determinants of Entrepreneurship' that public policy can influence. It then assumes that these influence entrepreneurial performance, which then determines the impact of entrepreneurship policy.

Figure 19.2 presents the elements of that framework in more detail. It shows the OECD has six key determinants over which they believe policy makers have an influence: the regulatory framework; R&D and technology; entrepreneurial capabilities; 'culture'; access to finance; and market conditions. Figure 19.2 suggests that these six determinants can be further broken

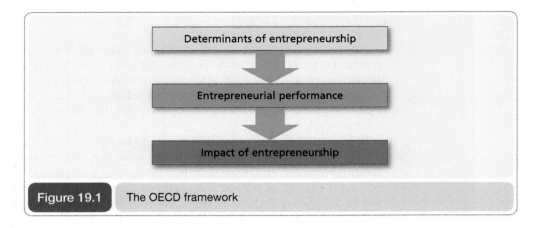

Figure 19.1   The OECD framework

Determinants					
Regulatory framework	R & D and technology	Entrepreneurial capabilities	Culture	Access to finance	Market conditions
Administrative burdens for entry	R & D investment	Training and experience of entrepreneurs	Risk attitude in society	Access to debt financing	Anti-trust laws
Administrative burdens for growth	University/industry interface	Business and entrepreneurship education (skills)	Attitudes towards entrepreneurs	Business angels	Competition
Bankruptcy regulations	Technological co-operation between firms	Entrepreneurship infrastructure	Desire for business ownership	Access to VC	Access to the domestic market
Safety, health and environmental regulations	Technology diffusion	Immigration	Entrepreneurship education (mindset)	Access to other types of equity	Access to foreign markets
Product and labour-market regulation	Broadband access			Stock markets	Degree of public involvement
Court and legal framework	Patent system; standards				Public procurement
Social and health security					
Income, wealth, business and capital taxes					

Figure 19.2   Entrepreneurship determinants: policy areas

down into a range of policy areas. For example, Figure 19.2 shows that if a government decided that the country lacks an 'enterprise culture', it might seek to influence attitudes to risk and how entrepreneurs are viewed in society. A government may also decide that its R&D and technology need improving. If so, it could seek to develop policies/programmes that aim to

Entrepreneurial performance		
Firm-based	**Employment-based**	**Other**
Employer firm birth rate	High-growth firm rate by employment	High-growth firm rate by turnover
Employer firm death rate	'Gazelle' rate by employment	'Gazelle' rate by turnover
Business churn	Ownership rate start ups	Value added by young firms
Net business population growth	Ownership rate business population	Productivity contribution by young firms
Survival rate, three and five years	Employment: three- and five-year-old firms	Innovation performance, young or small firms
Proportion three- and five-year survival rates	Average firm size after three and five years	Export performance, small firms

Figure 19.3   Framework indicators

strengthen the university/industry interface, technology co-operation between businesses or how technology is diffused. The central point of these determinants is that they highlight the range of policy choices available. In other words, we can see that there are many ways to improve culture or R&D/technology.

A second value of the framework identified in Figure 19.1 is that it highlights that these choices can be linked to three measures of entrepreneurial performance: firm, employment and other measures. These are shown in Figure 19.3. For each of these three areas, the OECD (2008a) identifies a number of indicators. For example, in terms of firm-based measures, Figure 19.3 identifies indicators of business 'birth' and 'deaths'. Employment- and 'other'-based measures also identify indicators that seek to identify the growth, employment and innovatory performance of businesses.

The logic of this framework is that it can be seen to operate 'in reverse'. For example, if it is decided that the problem facing an economy – in terms of Figure 19.3 – is low business birth rates or a shortage of 'gazelles', then policies to address these issues (Figure 19.2) can be implemented. This implies that targets based on Figure 19.3 are chosen by politicians and their advisors to maximise, in the most cost-effective way, the interests of the taxpayer.

The final element of Figures 19.1 to 19.3 is that the determinants of entrepreneurship and entrepreneurial performance are linked to the impact of entrepreneurship. The OECD (2008) indicates that there are three broad areas where policy makers may see SMEs and entrepreneurs making a valuable contribution to society:

1 job creation (see Chapter 4);

2 economic growth (see Chapters 11–15 on growth and Chapter 5 on innovation);

3 poverty reduction.

Again, there is a wide choice open to the policy maker. So, for example, when unemployment is high policy makers might place greater emphasis upon indicators that reflect job creation; when the economy is in a steady-state there might be a greater focus on raising productivity, innovation or the growth rates of businesses.

The fundamental value of the OECD framework is to emphasise to policy makers the ranges of choice open to them and that it provides some help to countries seeking to identify their level of entrepreneurship.

19.3 Why should taxpayers provide support for entrepreneurs and SMEs?

The previous section outlined the range of policies open to public policy makers seeking to enhance entrepreneurship and small businesses in their country. As we will show, some combination of these policies exist in almost all developed countries. However, just because these policies are commonplace, it does not detract from the need to examine the rationale for such policies. In essence, this section asks: why have these policies?

Answering this question requires some historical context. Prior to the 1980s, Audretsch and Thurik (2004) argue 'enterprise' policy in almost every country in the world meant satisfying the interests of large businesses. They gave two reasons for this:

- Mass production of standardised goods. Consumer needs were most likely to be met by large businesses with the economies of scale to meet these needs (e.g. the 1950s and 1960s was the first time that consumers really had the opportunity to own fridges and washing machines).

- Close co-operation between large businesses, unions and government (Galbraith 1957). This gave workers the opportunity for life-time employment (e.g. it was not uncommon for some workers up until the end of the 1970s to routinely believe that their whole working life would be with one large business and that they would be part of the 'union').

In contrast small businesses were seen as backward and old fashioned:

- The contribution of small businesses to employment and to the total enterprise population seemed to be falling in the 1960s and 1970s in many developed economies (see Chapter 3).

- Small businesses paid their workers less, offered less favourable conditions of employment (see our discussion of working conditions in Chapter 4) and were seen as '. . . inimical to progress and professionalism' (Boswell 1973: 19). They frequently were run by individuals at the 'margins of society' (Stanworth and Curran 1976). In other words, entrepreneurs were largely seen as 'spivs' or people who did not readily conform to the norms of society.

- Small businesses were seen as being inefficient. Many operated at below minimum efficient scale and were, hence, less productive than larger businesses. The standard of living was likely to fall in an economy that relied heavily on small businesses (Audretsch 2002).

- Small businesses were marginally involved in innovation. The consensus was that Schumpeter Mark II (large businesses were the main source of innovation) was the better explanation of innovatory activity (Chapter 5).

Prior to the 1980s, then, there were two policy challenges. For the US, the issue was to ensure that it remained the richest and most productive nation. For all other countries, particularly in Europe, the policy challenge was equally straightforward:

> The first problem for an industrial policy for Europe consists in choosing 50 to 100 businesses which, once they are large enough, would become the most likely to become world leaders of modern technology in their field. At the moment we are simply letting industry be destroyed by the superior power of American corporations.
>
> *Servan-Schreiber, 1968 quoted in Audretsch (2002: 46)*

Enterprise policy in European countries like the UK, therefore, sought to 'pick winners' from amongst their large businesses. Edgerton (1996) suggests that this involved picking 'bridge-head industries' (e.g. aircraft production, automotives, nuclear power) and merging and reforming businesses in these industries to ensure that they could effectively compete with US corporations.

Matters, however, changed radically in the 1980s and since then governments have seen entrepreneurs and SMEs as playing an important economic and social role and so being worthy of financial support from the taxpayer. Four reasons for supporting SMEs and entrepreneurs are usually provided by governments:

1 contribute disproportionately to job creation;

2 are central to economic development;

3 provide sustainability benefits;

4 represent a core political constituency.

We now examine each of these arguments in more detail.

Contribute disproportionately to job creation

Several economic changes meant that the focus on large businesses became a 'busted flush' by the 1970s (Greene 2002). The 1970s saw a doubling of the real price of oil, high international interest rates, high rates of inflation, and unemployment in developed economies not seen since before the Second World War. Large businesses in both the US and Europe began suffering from competition, particularly from Japan, but also from businesses in other Asian countries.

Perhaps in response to these difficult economic conditions, the US and the UK elected governments of the political right. Ronald Reagan became US president and Margaret Thatcher became the British prime minister, and it was this receptive audience that grasped the research by Birch (1979) on the dynamic importance of small businesses to employment creation. His work showed that new and small businesses were major contributors to job creation in the US. As we showed in Chapter 4, this research was at the time, and continues to be, a subject of controversy but it was unquestionably highly influential. It provided the intellectual 'muscle' underpinning the views of both Thatcher and Reagan that overcoming the economic difficulties faced by their respective countries required them to become more 'enterprising'. This meant rejecting the notion of 'big' government picking 'big' businesses to succeed on the 'big' international stage. In place of 'bigness', the concept of 'enterprise' was developed.

Contributions to economic development

A decade later, by the end of the 1980s, Brock and Evans (1989) argued that the following structural changes to economies had occurred:

● Technological advances (e.g. the introduction of computers and robots) meant a reduction in the minimum efficient scale of enterprises. This allowed small businesses to compete more effectively with larger businesses.

● Increased globalisation and competition led to greater volatility amongst large businesses. Shutt and Whittington (1987) and Harrison (1994) argued that this led to the fragmentation of large businesses, with the latter seeking to pass their risks on to (new) smaller businesses.

● Changes in workforce composition meant that, for example, women became more likely to work. This increased the need for greater flexibility amongst employers so making small businesses more attractive to employees. Also, women and younger workers are likely to be paid less (Chapter 4), again allowing small businesses to compete more effectively.

● Consumers increasingly demanded tailored and personalised products rather than those that were mass produced. This disadvantaged large businesses which obtained their cost advantages from the scale of their production.

- There was a greater focus on innovation due to a shortening of product life-cycles and competitive pressures.

Three other reasons added to the belief that SMEs and entrepreneurs had become pivotal to economic development:

- Romer (1986, 1990) had shown that a fundamental mechanism for economic growth was the presence of knowledge 'spillovers'. Audretsch and Thurik (2004) argued that entrepreneurship was an important transmission mechanism in diffusing innovations. In other words, entrepreneurs were critical to innovation because they have behaviourial characteristics – creativity, originality, independence, autonomy and openness – that are potentially more suited to modern economic conditions. In contrast, large businesses are seen as bureaucratic, rule-bound, hierarchical and conformist (Audretsch and Beckman 2007). Being closer to the market and having greater flexibility allows entrepreneurs to be potentially more dynamic than larger, more stable, businesses.

- Chapter 6 identified that there were two principal economic benefits of new businesses: first, they replace inefficient businesses and second, they 'threaten' existing businesses which have to improve their offer in order to survive. In other words, new businesses increase the level of competition in an economy and, thereby, potentially enhance economic growth (Disney *et al.* 2003).

- Chapter 11 showed that new industries and fast-growth businesses were integral to economic development. Recall, for example, that Jovanovic (2001) reported four of the largest US companies in terms of market capitalisation in August 1999 were less than 20 years old. Autio *et al.* (1999) also reported that Nokia, by the end of the 1990s, was responsible for about one third of the growth of GDP in Finland.

So, for all these reasons, SMEs and entrepreneurship were seen as central to economic development in the modern world.

Sustainability benefits

A third reason for valuing SMEs and entrepreneurs is that they may provide sustainability benefits. These advantages are:

(a) SMEs and entrepreneurs provide choice and variety to consumers.

(b) They support local communities because of the personalised way that owners run their business.

(c) They represent an alternative productive outlet for people that may perceive that they are unsuited to employment. This may encourage them to become more self-reliant and help them to shift from a 'dependency' to an 'enterprise' culture.

(d) They offer a productive outlet for an individual or groups in society who are disadvantaged, either because of limited labour-market experience (e.g. young people) or because of real or perceived discrimination (e.g. women, minorities).

(e) They can act as agents of social change by integrating social and environmental concerns into their business operations (Tracey and Jarvis 2007). Hence, they may reflect the local indigenous culture of an area (e.g. farmers' markets) but also the importance of other cultures (e.g. fair-trade goods).

A core political constituency

A final set of factors explaining the scale and focus of enterprise policy is that entrepreneurs and SMEs constitute a large group of voters in democratic countries. As we showed in Chapter 3, at least 95 per cent of all businesses in any economy are SMEs. There are also large numbers of self-employed in very many countries. In Mexico, the OECD (2007) estimated that in 2005, self-employment stood at 35.6 per cent of total civilian population. In Greece it was even higher at 36.4 per cent whilst in Italy it was 27 per cent. From a political perspective, the sheer number of people employed in SMEs and the large numbers of owner-managers/self-employed individuals mean that they represent a very sizeable constituency for any democratically elected politician.

19.4 Justifications for intervention

The above section made the case that entrepreneurs and SMEs make vitally important economic, social and political contributions in a modern developed economy. This section reviews two approaches to making the decision to support or promote such activity. The first approach is the market failure approach, the second we shall refer to as the political economy approach.

Market failure

Although SMEs and entrepreneurs provide jobs, contribute to economic growth and offer sustainability benefits, these advantages, of themselves, do not justify using tax-payers' money for their support. This is because many, or perhaps even most, of these benefits would accrue even if no taxpayer funds were provided.

It is well established that, subject to certain key assumptions, goods and services are allocated optimally through the price or market mechanism. These key assumptions are:

- competition in the goods market;
- fully informed customers and suppliers;
- an absence of externalities; and
- willingness to pay reflecting demand.

Where these assumptions are not met there is said to be **market failure**. Here there is a case for government 'intervention' – a term used to reflect government intervening in the market mechanism so as to make it work better.

In terms of SME and entrepreneurship policy, Storey (1982: 205) identified the basis of market failure. He argued:

> Government intervention is justified only where the private and social costs and benefits diverge, or where the existing distribution of income significantly distorts the extent to which willingness to pay reflects an individual's or a group's demand for goods and services.

Intervention is, therefore, justified on four grounds:

- First, as argued by Johnson (2005), there may be grounds for intervention if there is evidence of barriers to entry and exit and the presence of oligopoly or monopoly businesses because these may contravene the assumption of 'competition in the goods market'. This may unfairly disadvantage the small business because the competition between businesses is not on a 'level playing field'. Governments may, therefore, seek

London's eighteenth-century 'thief-takers' – private citizens who claimed money for making arrests – were a response to market forces.

A classic example of a market failure would be the provision of a 'public good' like a police force. Although it is in (almost) everyone's interest to have a police force, it can be quite difficult to identify who is likely to use the police service and who, therefore, should pay for the police. If left to the market, the police service might be similar to the 'thief-takers' of eighteenth-century London, who were paid by subscription to identify and catch thieves. The result was that very many thieves were able to 'work' effectively in areas that were not covered by these thief-takers. This produced a socially sub-optimal level of welfare.

to 'level the playing field' to ensure that there is adequate competition. For example, the European Union fined Microsoft because it felt that it had abused its 'dominant' position by not allowing other businesses access to its operating system. (See also Case study 1, Competition at the crematorium, on the nature of market 'power' in terms of two funeral directors.)

- A second justification for intervention is the presence of information imperfections, contravening the assumption of 'fully informed customers and suppliers'. For example, some individuals may be ignorant of the benefits of starting a business. Alternatively, existing business owners may also not realise the benefits of obtaining expert advice from outside specialists. Similarly, financial institutions may not be competitive with one another and, therefore, have little incentive to accurately assess the viability of small businesses. This may mean that they are likely to over-estimate the risks of lending to this group, leading to rationing of debt finance (Chapter 17). Policies to address these imperfections are, therefore, in principle justified under the market failure approach.

- A third justification for intervention is the presence of externalities. In terms of enterprise policy, there are argued to be advantages in supporting small businesses if they either generate, or benefit from, spillovers. Audretsch (2002) suggests three versions of these spillovers:

  - *Demonstration or learning externalities.* For example, in a deprived area of the economy, the existence of a successful entrepreneur from that community has the wider (unpriced) benefit of acting as a positive role model to others in the community.

  - *Knowledge externalities.* Intangible benefits accrue from businesses working together formally or informally. Examples of this include the Emilia Romagna region of Italy (Piore and Sabel 1984) and the knowledge externalities so crucial to small business innovation and links with universities (Chapter 5).

  - *Network externalities.* Saxenian (1994) argues that long-run economic growth in Silicon Valley was dependent upon embedded social networks based upon 'strong' ties of collaboration, informal communication and learning between businesses (Chapter 8).

However, within the market failure framework, it is not sufficient *just* to demonstrate that, for example, there are spillovers or information imperfections or a lack of competition. These constitute a necessary, but not a sufficient, case for intervention. What is required is to demonstrate that society as a whole will be better off following the intervention. In making this assessment the benefits to society have to outweigh not only the social costs of the market failure, but also the costs of actually intervening (compliance costs). If the total costs of intervening are greater than the benefits, intervention would be undesirable even where there is a clear evidence of market failure. In short, is the country better off after the policy is implemented than beforehand?

To illustrate that there can be high intervention costs we take a US and a UK example. Blanchflower and Wainwright (2005) showed that one consequence of affirmative action programmes in the US was that some wives were used as 'fronts' for their husband's business because they could benefit from positive gender discrimination. This programme clearly had desirable aims, but its impact was less, and its costs more, than was intended.

The UK's Enterprise Allowance Scheme, below, is another example of where the 'costs' of enterprise support were high and these are set out in the Illustration below.

The Enterprise Allowance Scheme (EAS)

The EAS was introduced in 1982 by the UK. It provided the unemployed with a payment of £40 a week for a year, provided that EAS participants:

● had access to £1,000 capital;
● worked full-time on the business;
● were between 18–59; and
● had a business that was 'suitable for public support' (the last requirement was introduced after a massage parlour was funded in southern Wales).

At the end of the year, the EAS-supported business was meant to be self-sustaining. Greene (2002) identifies that the advantages of EAS were:

● It brought previously informal activity into the formal sector (discouraged 'moonlighting').
● It cost little or no more than unemployment benefit.
● There was a possibility that the business may take off and create further employment.
● Once on EAS, individuals no longer counted towards the unemployment total.

As Figure 19.4, shows, there was a dramatic growth in the EAS, from 3,000 participants in 1982/3 to a peak of nearly 200,000 in 1987/8. In total, nearly a million people participated in the EAS.

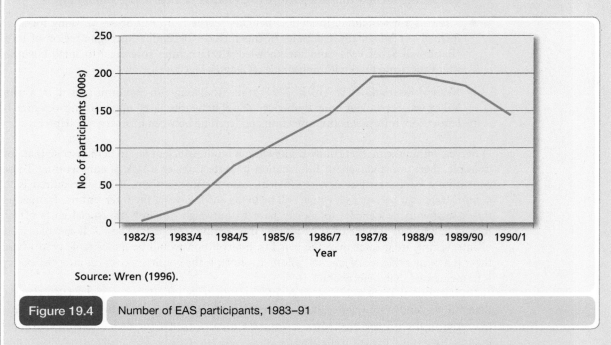

Source: Wren (1996).

Figure 19.4   Number of EAS participants, 1983–91

However, set against these advantages, Storey (1994) identified a number of issues with the EAS:

● The survival rates of EAS-supported businesses were only slightly lower than those of non-EAS businesses during the year in which they received the subsidy. However, once the year was over, and the subsidy was no longer available, closure rates rose very sharply. In short, employment was created for a year only to be followed by a high proportion of people returning to unemployment.
● Offering government support led to other 'unintended consequences'. One of these is called **deadweight**. This refers to businesses that would have set up regardless of the presence of public funding. Hence, public funds were wasted by being given to such businesses.

- Businesses were heavily concentrated in sectors that were easy to enter, but where growth opportunities were modest – such as hairdressers, vehicle repairers and window cleaners. The effect of the new entrants was to temporarily displace the existing providers – as a result of having the benefit of the public subsidy – and to be displaced themselves when the subsidy expired by new subsidised entrants. This effect is called **displacement**. In effect, taxpayers' money was used to help businesses start, but without any obvious net economic impact.

- Evidence pointed to the difficulty of increasing the number of new businesses in areas of high unemployment. This is because individuals in these areas either lack the skills to successfully run a business and/or because the local markets into which they sell their product/service lack buoyancy because of high unemployment. In other words, very many of the new businesses set up, particularly in areas of high unemployment, were likely to be of 'poor' quality. MacDonald and Coffield (1991) and MacDonald (1994, 1996), using case studies of young people who were unemployed, showed that many of them were enticed into enterprise by the prospects of £40 per week, but had no skills with which to run their business. The consequences for many of them were extremely serious since they incurred significant debt in operating the business, and their attempts to repay this debt continued to blight their life even after the business had closed.

- Evidence also pointed to the bulk of the job creation – in the medium term – occurring amongst a relatively small number of businesses that experienced rapid growth.

The fourth assumption underpinning the result that goods and services are allocated optimally through the price or market mechanism is that of 'willingness to pay reflecting demand'. This we will discuss in more depth in Section 19.6.

19.5 The political economy approach

Johnson (2005) argues that, in practice, the market failure framework pays too much attention to the first three assumptions of competition in the goods market, fully informed customers and suppliers, and an absence of externalities. By implication, insufficient attention is given to issues of equity and distribution. For example, there are wide differences in how wealth is distributed between groups in society or between different regions of an economy. This issue of equity is one of the main reasons why in most economies there are 'transfer' payments from richer to poorer people and regions. Johnson argues that the issue of equity is also related to spillover effects (externalities). He suggests that if someone is long-term unemployed, then they might be more likely to perpetrate anti-social or criminal behaviour. This has 'spillover' effects on the rest of society, so justifying policies that provide employment for that individual.

A second approach suggested by Johnson is within a public choice framework. Here the argument is that politicians are primarily interested in their own welfare, defined as enhancing their chances of being re-elected. This leads them to seek ways to ensure that they are seen as 'popular'. Classic examples of this are 'giveaway' budgets, designed to 'sweeten' the electorate prior to an election.

Applied to enterprise policy, these interventions may still produce increases in economic welfare. However, Johnson argues that such benefits are likely to be limited by two factors. First, politicians typically follow a short election cycle so they are more likely to favour short-term benefits. Second, politicians will be tempted to favour interventions that they judge will benefit particular electorally influential groups in society, rather than interventions that maximise overall economic welfare.

Johnson also identifies a third approach to understanding policy interventions. This is called the economic theory of bureaucracy. Instead of focusing on politicians, this approach suggests that government officials (civil/public servants) also have vested interests. Whilst not subject to reelection, the welfare of government officials is linked to better pay, higher status or greater power for themselves. Johnson argues that government officials are likely to favour interventions that maximise these objectives. Whilst these interventions may again coincide with increases in economic welfare, Johnson suggests that bureaucrats may maximise their own 'benefits' by favouring:

> . . . the establishment of larger and more resource-intensive programmes than might strictly be necessary; over-bureaucratic management and control structures; [show a] reluctance to undertake robust evaluations and [a] reluctance to curtail ineffective programmes for fear of loss of power or status for the policy makers and possibly loss of jobs or income for people who depend upon the continuation of state funding.
>
> *(p. 11)*

The final approach identified by Johnson examines the role of power relations, pressure groups and ideology. This approach largely uses a Marxist (class-based) framework to argue that any interventions pursued by the state are likely to benefit the ruling capitalist class in society rather than the ordinary worker. Hence, governments are likely to pursue an 'enterprise' agenda because they believe that it supports and enhances the ruling capitalist ideology of 'free enterprise' and the value of the market for allocating income and wealth. The suggestion is that interventions are more likely to favour larger, rather than smaller, businesses.

Coen and Dannreuther (2002) suggest a number of reasons for this:

● Governments can easily report that they have consulted the affected parties if they have had discussions with a small number of large businesses – who probably contribute a high proportion of employment and output in the particular sector.

● Responses are likely to be more homogeneous amongst large businesses, so the number of businesses that need to be consulted is fewer.

● Small businesses, because of their diversity, make the consultation process more complex and lengthy. This may be made easier if trade associations or small business lobby groups are involved, although these groups are often 'unrepresentative' of the population of small businesses.

● Large businesses are likely to have an individual, known to the relevant civil servant, who specialises in liaising with government. This is very unlikely to be the case for small businesses and so it means that, as legislation unfolds, it is the large, rather than the small, business that has the opportunity to influence enterprise policy.

The value of these political economy approaches is that they throw light on the wider reasons why policy makers intervene. They also illustrate some of the differences between the interests of small businesses and policy makers. Table 19.1 synthesises these key differences. It suggests that key features of small businesses are their independence, their ability to react quickly to opportunities and threats, and their clarity of vision about being customer and profit driven. Their priorities are also likely to be in terms of 'less is better' (regulation) and a desire to ensure that they keep more of their effort (profits) and give rather less away in taxes.

The contrast with the aims and objectives of public policy makers in Table 19.1 could not be starker. Policy makers are likely to seek interventions that show that they are 'doing something' which, in turn, will enhance their chances of getting re-elected. To achieve this, policy makers are likely to develop policies that satisfy large numbers of voters, of whom business

Table 19.1	Differences between small businesses and policy makers	
Dimension	**Small businesses**	**Policy makers**
Decision making	● Fast, since opportunities may be lost	● Inclusive so that all relevant parties are consulted
Priorities	● Profits	● Competitiveness
	● Low taxes	● Job creation
	● Low regulation	● Enterprise culture
		● Disadvantaged groups
Desirable characteristics	● Aware of opportunities	● Accountable
	● Prepared to take 'calculated' risks	● 'Evidence'-based
		● Reliable
Performance measures	● Profits	● Seen to be 'doing something'
	● Independence	● Being re-elected

owners are only one. This means policies have to be carefully – and slowly – assessed in terms of their impact upon different clusters of voters. Ideally, this requires consultation and the development of an 'evidence base' to support the intervention. Finally, because of the need for accountability for public money, the procedures that the small business has to undergo to obtain support are often, from their point of view, frustratingly bureaucratic and lengthy. In essence, therefore, small businesses and public policy makers have very different objectives, styles and timescales, and so bringing the two together is inevitably problematic.

Nevertheless, the crucial role that small businesses play in the economic and social life of a country means policy makers have increasingly to engage with small businesses. An example of how this dialogue can be facilitated is in New Zealand. Here the Labour government created a 'Small Business Advisory Group' made up of small business owners whose task is 'to give SMEs a greater voice in policy development and advise Ministers of issues facing SMEs'.

Overall, this section has reviewed the rationale for government support for small business – referred to as 'intervention' – according to two approaches that we call market failure and political economy.

The market failure approach views there to be a case for intervention if there is evidence of a lack of competition in the goods market, imperfectly informed customers and suppliers, or the presence of externalities. However, even if there is clear evidence of market failure, intervention is justified only if, following the intervention, there is expected to be a net addition to society's welfare.

The political economy approach emphasises that there are other reasons why policy makers intervene (e.g. public choice, bureaucracy, power relations, equity and distribution issues). What both approaches have in common is a recognition of the differences in the 'agendas' of small businesses and of policy makers. In the next section, we examine, at a general level, how enterprise policy may be characterised in different international economies. To illustrate this, we compare the development of two countries: the US and the UK.

19.6 Policy 'regimes': the US and the UK

The OECD framework discussed in Section 19.2 emphasised that policy makers have a wide range of policies available to them that may enhance entrepreneurs and SMEs. This section shows that the choices made by politicians vary markedly between countries. It uses the simple

Table 19.2	A typology of public policy towards small business	
Low direct assistance	Limiting (e.g. developing countries)	Competing (e.g. US)
High direct assistance	Compensating (e.g. EU countries)	Nurturing (e.g. US minority, Canada or New Zealand)
	High impediments	Low impediments

Source: Dennis (2004).

framework outlined by Dennis (2004) in Table 19.2 as a useful starting point for understanding how different economies have developed their policies. This shows a 2 × 2 matrix, the axes of which distinguish between countries that focus their policies more heavily upon the provision of assistance and countries that focus upon what Dennis calls the lowering of impediments. An example of an assistance policy – as was identified by the OECD (2008a) in Figure 19.2 – might be entrepreneurial capabilities (e.g. entrepreneurship education) whilst an example of an impediment might be administrative burdens for entry (see Figure 19.2 for more examples).

Dennis groups countries or sets of countries according to whether they are high or low on each measure. This generates four approaches to policy that are called: compensating, competing, limiting and nurturing.

Dennis suggests that most EU countries have a 'compensating' policy regime. This is because they tend to spend considerable amounts of taxpayers' money – high direct assistance – in providing 'hard' and 'soft' support to new and small businesses. 'Hard' support includes grants and loans – 'soft' support comprises advice and training. However, the EU also has 'high' impediments because they have high levels of regulation justified on the grounds that these protect consumers.

A very different approach is adopted in the US. Here direct assistance is low, but so too are the barriers to starting a business. Instead, competition is seen as the focus of policy and so the top right-hand box is labelled as 'competing'.

The US, however, does have some very major exceptions to this 'hands-off' approach – most notably its programmes to promote the interests of technology-based businesses and the promotion of minorities. Again, the barriers to starting businesses are low but a high level of direct assistance is provided to such enterprises. This is labelled as 'nurturing' in Table 19.2. Examples of other 'nurturing' economies are Canada and New Zealand. Both have quick, simple and cheap procedures for business start ups, coupled with greater publicly funded support to new SMEs.

Finally, there are many countries where the barriers to starting a business are high, but where public assistance is low. This cell is labelled as 'limiting' and tends to be the policy regime followed in many African, South American and eastern European countries.

The value of Table 19.2 is that it illustrates that policy makers have a wide choice on how, if at all, they wish to promote new and smaller businesses. It also illustrates that this leads to very different combinations of policies being delivered for small businesses.

The approach is, however, merely a way of categorising current choices. It does not seek to explain how or why those choices were made. It also ignores the wider impacts of policy making (e.g. taxation, immigration) on enterprise policy. We explore these more fully in Chapter 20.

Perhaps most importantly, because Table 19.2 is a 'snapshot', it also ignores the evolution of enterprise policy over time. To illustrate how current choices have evolved, we now consider two economies: the US which Dennis largely sees as 'competing', and the UK which Dennis sees as 'compensating'. We begin by examining the UK.

UK enterprise policies

Beesley and Wilson (1981) argued that, although there was some interest shown by the UK government in small business – most notably commissioning the Bolton Committee report in

1971 and the appointment of the first ever minister for small businesses in 1977 – it was not until the beginning of the 1980s that small enterprise policy became established.

The 1980s

Greene *et al.* (2008) argued that the election of Margaret Thatcher as UK prime minister in 1979 signalled a sea-change in attitudes towards small businesses and entrepreneurship for two reasons. First, the Thatcher government was ideologically committed to moving people away from a dependency (reliance on the state) to an enterprise (self-reliant) culture. This was part of a wish to reduce the size of government, to open markets, to limit union power, and to increase the choices available to people. A second motivation was the chronic unemployment of the 1980s in the UK.

Birch's (1979) results about the positive contribution that new and existing SMEs made to employment led UK policy makers to seek out means by which SMEs could 'soak up' the unemployed. In essence, if each small business took on one extra worker, the simple logic was that unemployment would be largely eliminated. Amongst the many problems with this calculation was that – as we saw in Chapter 3 – increasing employment is a very unlikely objective for a small business.

So, if a focus on existing small businesses was not possible, policy makers then switched their thoughts to supporting the creation of *new* businesses as a means of reducing unemployment. Greene *et al.* (2008) argue that this was the central enterprise policy thrust of the 1980s in the UK but, by the early 1990s, this policy was in disarray for three reasons (reflecting the experience of the Enterprise Allowance Scheme (EAS) discussed earlier):

- Even if new businesses (employment) could be created, it was also likely that there would be high business closure rates so that the impact on unemployment was modest.

- Encouraging the creation of new businesses had the 'unintended consequences' of high deadweight and displacement effects. In other words, there was little evident *net* benefit to the UK economy.

- The evidence showed that very many new businesses set up, particularly in areas of high unemployment, were likely to be of 'poor' quality.

The 1990s

For these reasons, in the 1990s, the general thrust of UK enterprise policy shifted away from a focus on the creation of new businesses and towards supporting *existing* SMEs. This was because:

- A policy focused on converting the unemployed into self-employed had the disadvantages noted above.

- Unemployment fell dramatically and there was a change of prime minister, from Margaret Thatcher to the less obviously ideological John Major.

- The number of UK businesses had increased by 50 per cent from 2.4 million in 1980 to 3.6 million in 1989. In other words, this was 'evidence' that the UK had shifted from a 'dependency' to an 'enterprise' culture.

- New evidence had emerged of the importance of fast-growth businesses in new sectors (see Chapter 15) such as computing (Jovanovic, 2001).

In the 1990s not only did the policy focus change, but so too did the way the policy was delivered. The first major change was that the UK sought to shift public policy provision away from being centrally provided, with decisions on enterprise priorities being made in London, to more local organisations called Business Links. These provided a 'one-stop shop' for assisting small businesses (Bennett 1995; Bennett and Robson 2003). The creation of Business Links represented:

> . . . a shift in emphasis from start-ups and micro-businesses towards established businesses with the potential to grow.
>
> *House of Commons Trade and Industry Select Committee (1996: xi)*

The second major change associated with the above focus on 'established businesses with the potential to grow' was the introduction of 'personal business advisors' (PBAs). As the name implies, the task of PBAs was to '. . . work proactively to develop long-term relationships with a portfolio of local businesses, focused particularly on small companies with growth potential' (DTI 1994: 9). The novelty of PBAs was that they used individuals with business experience, whose task was to provide tailored consultancy advice to small business clients – in this sense they provided 'personal' advice that was tailored to the specific circumstances of the business (Mole 2002). The logic underpinning the need for tailored advice was that the situations faced by small growing businesses were so different from other small businesses that advice had to be delivered by an expert who fully understood the precise circumstances of that particular business.

However, this strong focus on growth businesses constituted a major challenge for the public sector since it was presumed that public policy *can* devise and deliver appropriate support to such businesses. It required Business Links to be able to identify businesses with growth potential and then to provide them with tailored advice that enabled them to fulfil that potential. This was a challenging agenda for several reasons:

- Many small businesses with growth potential may choose *not* to seek advice from Business Links.

- The definition of a 'business with growth potential' was left vague but it was clear that it excluded the vast bulk of small businesses. Hence, the target population of businesses for each Business Link was small.

- The quality of PBAs was viewed by small business owners as patchy. Whilst some were well qualified in terms of experience, others were contemptuously dismissed as retired bankers/ civil servants supplementing their pension.

- The bringing together of a business with growth potential and a suitable PBA required considerable care. The personal chemistry, so crucial to a successful outcome, was very difficult to predict in advance.

The 2000s

In the 2000s, UK public policy towards entrepreneurs and SMEs continued to evolve. The Business Link/PBA policy focusing on growth businesses was regarded as a modest success but seemed to ignore other potential benefits (e.g. sustainability). Following an extensive review of the 'evidence base', a wider policy agenda was announced in 2004. Seven policy areas or 'pillars' were identified as the new focus of policy. These were:

- building an enterprise culture;

- encouraging a more dynamic start-up market;

- building the capability for small business growth;

- improving access to finance for small businesses;

- encouraging more enterprise in disadvantaged communities and under-represented groups;

- improving small businesses' experience of government services;

- developing better regulation and policy (SBS 2004).

Hence, in addition to recognising the value of entrepreneurs and small businesses in potentially reducing unemployment and improving economic growth (productivity), the UK government recognised that enterprise policy could allow for the development of 'enterprise for all'.

Arguably, these seven 'pillars' are only a re-formulation of the 1980s and 1990s policies. For example, the emphasis on 'enterprise for all' echoes the 1980s call for a shift from a 'dependency' to an 'enterprise' culture, whilst the second and third 'pillars' (dynamic start-up market and small business growth) simply reiterate the previous emphasis of the 1990s on improving productivity. But UK enterprise policy did 'mature' in two main ways during the 2000s.

First, what was particularly novel about the seven pillars was that they were derived from an 'evidence base' and that each pillar had a 'target' against which performance could be judged. (See Appendix 19.1.)

Second, the UK became the first country in the world to quantify the cost of its entrepreneurship and SME policies. These costs are reported in Table 19.3. It shows that in 2003/4 there were four main areas of expenditure: government departments; regional agencies;

Table 19.3	Support for smaller enterprises in 2003/4
Central government programme budgets	**Cost (£ million)**
Arbitration and Conciliation Advisory Service	46
Department of Environment, Food and Rural Affairs (excluding Common Agricultural Policy)	297
Department for Culture, Media and Sport	336
Department for Education and Skills	126
Department of Trade and Industry	425
Department of Work and Pensions/Job Centre Plus	331
Home Office	6
Learning and Skills Council (National)	1,672
Office of Science and Technology	49
Office of the Deputy Prime Minister	10
Small Business Service	271
UK Trade International	81
European Commission (Structural Funds)	276
TOTAL	3,926
Regional development agencies and local authorities	360
Tax incentives	
Corporation tax (20 per cent rate)	2,300
Corporation tax (zero rate)	350
SME R&D tax credit	260
Enterprise Investment Scheme	180
Venture capital trusts	15
EMI	60
VAT small traders	450
TOTAL EXPENDITURE ON TAX INCENTIVES	3,615
Common Agricultural Policy production subsidies	2,398
GRAND TOTAL	10,299

Source: PACEC (2005).

tax incentives; and agricultural subsidies. In terms of government departments, the 'host' department for enterprise policy at that time was the Department of Trade and Industry (DTI) and the dedicated agency responsible for policy was the (now defunct) Small Business Service (SBS).

Several points emerge clearly from Table 19.3:

- First, UK expenditure on enterprise support is considerable. The total figure is £10.3 billion, which is about £170 for every man, woman and child in the UK. In terms of small businesses, this equates to about £5,000 per small business.

- A second comparison is that UK taxpayers provide more funding for SMEs and entrepreneurs than for the police service or universities.

- However, in one respect, the enterprise support budget differs starkly from that of the police or universities. It is that the police or universities are the prime responsibility of a single government department. One department is the dominant budget holder and the same department has responsibility for overall policy formulation. This is not the case for SME and entrepreneurship policy.

- The department with overall responsibility for enterprise – the DTI – spent £696 million of which the agency with specific responsibility for small business (the SBS) spent £271 million. This meant the DTI was responsible for spending only 17.7 per cent of direct enterprise spending.

- The DTI expenditure was dwarfed by the £1.7 billion spent by the Learning and Skills Council in training for small business employees.

- Other major spenders are the Department of the Environment, Food and Rural Affairs (£297 million), the Department for Culture, Media and Sport (£336 million) and the Department of Work and Pensions/Job Centre Plus (£331 million).

- Finally, but very importantly, the table quantifies the massive scale of taxes and subsidies provided to small businesses. The tax assistance is £3.6 billion and the agricultural subsidies are £2.4 billion.

Ultimately, Table 19.3 makes two points: the first is the scale of taxpayer support for small business; and, second, that the main department with responsibility for delivering enterprise in Britain has only very modest control and influence over expenditure and, hence, over policy outcomes.

Does this matter? The answer is clearly yes, since shortly after these documents became public, the Chief Executive of the SBS, Martin Wyn Griffith, was called before the Public Accounts Committee of the House of Commons. A robust exchange of views took place between the Committee and Mr Wyn Griffith.

A Committee member, Richard Bacon, summarised matters thus:

> It sounds to me Mr Wyn Griffith, and I am sure you are doing your best, as though you are sitting there in this federal fiefdom system in Whitehall and you do not have any influence. You basically have responsibility without power, do you not? It boils down to well-meaning guff.

House of Commons (2007: p. 11)

By the time the Committee Report had been published, the Committee noted that:

> The Small Business Service was to be reformed (abolished) as a smaller policy unit within DTI . . . the old SBS failed to convince us that it was contributing cost effectively to the achievement of government objectives for small business, so we endorse its downsizing.

House of Commons (2007: 5)

However, within 15 months, the DTI had also been abolished, with many of its functions incorporated in the newly created BERR (Department of Business Enterprise and Regulatory Reform) (which, in turn, in 2009, became the Department for Business, Innovation and Skills) and the UK government had produced *Enterprise: Unlocking the UK's Talent* (HM Treasury, 2008). The seven pillars of 2004 had been converted into five 'enablers' intended to make the UK the most enterprising economy in the world:

● culture

● knowledge and skills

● access to finance

● regulatory framework

● business innovation.

So, at the end of close on 30 years of (small) enterprise policy in the UK, one thing is clear. It is that UK governments, both Labour and Conservative, have seen the small business sector as critical to achieving their long-term social and economic objectives. If anything, that commitment has increased over time. What has changed massively is the elements within that policy, how it is delivered and how it is assessed.

US enterprise policies

The US, like the UK, has an enterprise policy – even if it does not use this term. Indeed, if anything, the US has had formal enterprise policies for far longer than any other developed country. The origins of such support can be traced back to the setting up of the Reconstruction Finance Corporation in 1932 which gave out loans to small businesses as part of President Roosevelt's 'New Deal'. Enterprise policies, however, really began with the creation of the Small Business Administration (SBA) in 1953. As the lead agency responsible for small businesses, the SBA's aim is to '. . . aid, counsel, assist and protect, insofar as is possible, the interests of small business concerns' (SBA 2009). Subsequently, since the 1950s, the SBA has had responsibility for a range of small-business programmes. For example, it has responsibilities for the following key US programmes:

● The Small Business Investment Company (SBIC) Program (1958) which provides long-term debt and equity investments to high-risk small businesses.

● The creation of the Small Business Innovation Research (SBIR) Program to support high-tech innovation companies.

● Loan-guarantee programmes such as the 7(a) Loan Program.

● Counselling, training and the education of small business owners and entrepreneurs through programmes such as the Small Business Development Centers.

As in the UK, the SBA (2007) has a core range of strategic enterprise goals. These are:

● To expand America's ownership society, particularly in under-served markets.

● To improve the economic environment for small business.

● To ensure management and organisational excellence to increase responsiveness to customers, streamline processes, and improve compliance and controls.

Appendix 19.2 also identifies that it has a range of objectives to support these goals. These are linked to particular performance measures (SBA 2007).

Probably reflecting its lengthy history of policy in this area, the US appears to have far fewer, but much longer running, programmes, at least at the federal level, than the UK. US enterprise support also appears to be orientated more towards 'hard' rather than 'soft' support. Figure 19.5 shows two 'proxies' of such support: the SBIC Program (equity and debt investments) and its loan-guarantee programmes (e.g. 7(a) program). It shows clearly that these two programmes have increased markedly since the 1970s. Indeed, Craig *et al.* (2007) suggest that the US government, rather than the private banks, is the largest single creditor to small businesses.

But, if enterprise policy has a longer history in the US, the scale of such support is less clear. Unlike the UK, the US has never provided data on the general costs of its enterprise policies. Indeed, it is difficult to estimate the actual costs of enterprise support on a basis that is comparable with the UK. One clue to the cost of tax incentives is provided by Guenther (2005) who suggested that in 2005, these cost $7.96 billion. The OECD (2008*b*) also estimates that US agricultural subsidies were $41 billion (based on producer support measures in 2005). Gu *et al.* (2008) also estimated that the administrative cost of non-SBIR programmes was around $506 million whilst the SBIR programme cost $2 billion. This indicates, if we use these figures, that US enterprise support equates to around $174 per capita (US population of 296 million in 2005). This figure, however, does not include the expenditure of other US state departments nor, as Gu *et al.* (2008) point out, the various state enterprise policies.

Gu *et al.* (2008) also note that the publicly available evaluations of the various US schemes remain under-developed. They can only find one study (Benus, 1994) that 'appropriately' evaluates a particular enterprise programme. In contrast, there have been a variety of evaluations that have been conducted on UK programmes to evaluate the net benefits of particular enterprise support schemes (e.g. Wren and Storey, 2002, Meager *et al.*, 2003, Mole *et al.*, 2007).

Overall, our view is that the position of the US on the Dennis (2004) typology is not as clear as Dennis implies. This section has shown that, compared with the UK, the US seems to spend less per capita on enterprise support. This might suggest it should be classified as a 'competing'

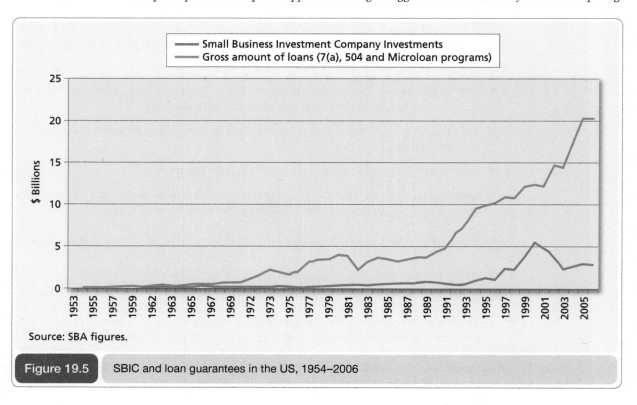

Source: SBA figures.

Figure 19.5   SBIC and loan guarantees in the US, 1954–2006

economy. However, this is not wholly clear for three reasons. First, US enterprise support seems to be more targeted towards the provision of hard (finance) support. This may seem at odds with Dennis' view that the US is an example of a 'competing' country. Second, it is difficult to judge the nature of US enterprise support without clear information on the costs of provision. Finally, there are very few appropriate evaluations of US programmes. Hence, programmes may say that they are 'competing' when, in fact, their net effect may be to either 'compensate' or 'nurture' businesses.

19.7 Segmenting enterprise policy: entrepreneurship and SME policies

So far, we have assumed that enterprise policy relates easily to SMEs and entrepreneurs. However, as we identified in Chapters 2 and 3, SMEs are very diverse – Coleman (1973) laconically suggested that '. . . the joys of defining "entrepreneurial" could fill a whole volume' (pp. 111–12).

Defining enterprise policy in terms of entrepreneurs and small businesses is likely to mirror these definitional difficulties. To address this, Lundstrom and Stevenson (2007) provide a useful distinction designed to segment entrepreneurship from SMEs. This is shown in Figure 19.6. First, there are a set of policies focused principally on the pre start-up and early stages of a business. Lundstrom and Stevenson (2007: 105) defined these as 'entrepreneurship policies' because they are:

> . . . aimed at the pre-start, the start-up and early post-start-up phases of the entrepreneurial process, designed and delivered to address the areas of motivation, opportunity and skills, with the primary objective of encouraging more people in the population to consider entrepreneurship as an option, move into the nascent stage of taking actions to start a business and proceed into the entry and early stages of the business.

(p. 105)

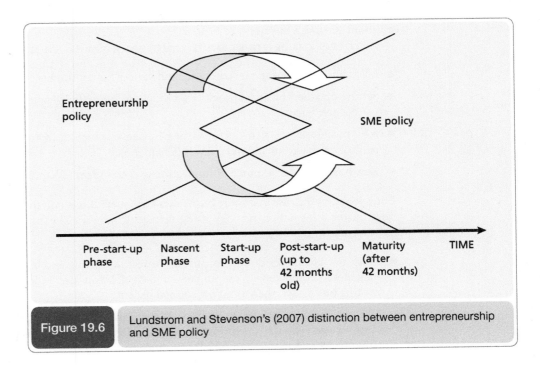

| Figure 19.6 | Lundstrom and Stevenson's (2007) distinction between entrepreneurship and SME policy |

Entrepreneurship policies have a role in primary, secondary and tertiary education; the promotion of entrepreneurship in the media and in society; the reduction of administrative, legislative and regulatory barriers; and support for people seeking to set up in business. It is also likely that the main type of support used to deliver these policies is 'soft' support (e.g. advice, awareness raising, signposting and training), as opposed to 'hard' policies such as the direct provision of financial assistance (e.g. loans and guarantee programmes).

Figure 19.6 shows that, in contrast, SME policies are focused around the post start-up phase of the *existing* business and its survival/growth. Lundstrom and Stevenson (2007) say:

> The primary aim of small business policy is to level the playing field for small firms through measures to overcome their disadvantages in the marketplace resulting from their 'smallness' and 'resource poverty', and to improve their competitiveness.
>
> *(p. 105)*

The implication is that SME policy has two main aims. The first is to reflect that these businesses are not disadvantaged by the (anti)competitive behaviour of (large) businesses. The second aim is to provide support that will allow SMEs to maximise their potential. It is likely, therefore, that an SME policy will focus on the business rather than the individual and that the provision will be on hard support (e.g. grants, loans).

As Figure 19.6 suggests, there are obvious linkages between SME and entrepreneurship policies since entrepreneurial activity (fast growth) may persist amongst some businesses as they develop, implying that entrepreneurship policies can extend into the SME policy 'arena'. Whilst Lundstrom and Stevenson's (2007) distinction is unlikely to fully capture the diversity of entrepreneurship and SME activities or policies, it does allow us to examine the arguments for and against supporting each policy. It is to this that we now turn.

Entrepreneurship policies

The case for entrepreneurship policy is based upon the argument that, without such policies, there would be either insufficient numbers, or the 'wrong types', of businesses started. In terms of market failure, entrepreneurship policies are justified on the grounds of imperfect information on the part of the person considering starting a business – basically they may not have even thought of the entrepreneurial option; or they may have very few ideas of how to go about starting a business.

In terms of making it easier for *everyone* to start a business, the arguments are:

- More businesses mean greater choice and variety for consumers.

- Setting up a new business provides a productive outlet for people enabling them to make use of their talents.

- New businesses are a threat to existing businesses, forcing them to become more competitive or risk going out of business (Chapter 6).

- New businesses are a source of innovation and new ideas (Chapter 5).

But is it always the case that more businesses are better? If it is not, then should policy seek to raise business formation rates by using taxpayers' money? The arguments against general entrepreneurship policies are:

- Most new businesses do not constitute a threat to existing and larger businesses. Instead, they merely compete with existing new and small businesses. Indeed, if they only displace existing businesses, there is no net societal benefit.

- The vast majority of new businesses are not innovative. Instead, they offer broadly the same service/products as existing businesses which perhaps explains their high closure rate (Chapters 9 and 10).

- In practice, it is extremely difficult to raise new business start-up rates, particularly in geographical areas where start up rates have been low. The clearest example of this was the attempt by Scottish Enterprise (Scotland's enterprise agency) to raise new business start-up rates to those of the average for Great Britain. Despite spending £140 million, there was no evidence that start-up rates in Scotland improved relative to the UK (Fraser of Allander 2001).

- If Baumol (1990) is correct (Chapter 2), then entrepreneurship is likely to be appealing only to a fixed proportion of the population. All that entrepreneurship policies can do is change the distribution between productive, unproductive and destructive entrepreneurship rather than create more entrepreneurship.

- Carree *et al.* (2002) suggest that countries can have too many, as well as too few businesses, to aid economic development. Hence, it is not always the case that 'more is better'.

An alternative argument is that whilst there may be no overall deficiency in the number of businesses created in an economy, there may be the wrong *types* of business, or there may be too few businesses established by certain groups in society. The following arguments are used to justify policies seeking to make it easier for *some people* to start a business:

- It is a desirable social objective for business ownership to broadly reflect the overall composition of society.

- Some ethnic groups are subject to discrimination, particularly in terms of finance (Chapter 17). Eliminating discrimination would lead to greater social diversity of business ownership.

- Women and young people are less likely to be business owners (see Chapter 8).

In response to these arguments, the following issues are relevant:

- Whilst it may be a desirable social objective to seek to equalise business ownership rates across groups, the ability to succeed in business may not be evenly distributed across all groups. On these grounds, encouraging individuals without the necessary skills to start a business may be counter-productive both for them and for society as a whole.

- It is not the case that all ethnic groups are 'under-represented' amongst the self-employed, although the evidence from Chapter 8 suggests some groups are likely to be.

- Business ownership rates amongst women have, in recent years, risen faster than men. Interventions, using taxpayer funds, may be unnecessary since male and female start-up rates may converge.

- Young people lack the necessary 'human capital' to run a business. It is counter-productive to 'fast track' them into business ownership prior to them developing the necessary skills and abilities to successfully run a business.

Overall, the arguments in favour of entrepreneurship policy require careful assessment. Even if there is agreement about a need to create more businesses, it remains open to question whether using taxpayer funds to raise awareness and provide information is effective. The Baumol option of changing the 'rules of the game' (Chapter 2) could be more cost-effective.

SME policies

A similar set of arguments for and against SME policy may be made. In terms of supporting *all* SMEs, the positive arguments are:

- SMEs are likely to have lower levels of productivity. It is, therefore, in the national interest to raise their productivity.

- Existing SMEs are major contributors to wealth and job creation, so enhancing their performance makes a major contribution to the economy.

The arguments against are:

- Whilst SMEs may contribute to job and wealth creation, this contribution is disproportionately concentrated amongst a tiny minority of businesses. The reality is that most SME owners do not wish to grow their business much above its current size so, if there is to be a SME policy it should focus on growing businesses rather than on SMEs in general.

- However, as we showed in Chapters 11–15, growth is poorly understood. It is unlikely, therefore, that one policy will fit all SMEs and as we saw in our review of UK policy, the public sector has, at the very least, too many differentiated/complex programmes.

As we also showed in our review of UK policy there is some experience of focusing policy upon those SMEs that seek to grow. The problems that emerged were:

- SMEs which are growing rapidly do not need assistance, because in part they are performing well, and in part because they are unlikely to use the assistance.

- Such businesses are difficult to find.

- Governments have traditionally found it difficult to develop policies that 'pick winners' because they do not share risks (e.g. take an equity stake) in the business.

- This approach is also politically sensitive because some SMEs will receive assistance and others will not. The reasons for making a decision to support one SME but reject another are likely to be highly subjective. Public servants are notoriously uncomfortable with making such decisions, which can be difficult to justify if challenged. Furthermore, when some of these decisions turn out to be incorrect – as inevitably they will – this may be difficult to reconcile with the need for risk avoidance in dealing with taxpayers' funds.

Overall, a focus on SME policies emphasises one of two approaches: the first is to 'level the playing field' to ensure all SMEs benefit. The second is to focus assistance on the small number of SMEs with the ability and motivation to grow. Both approaches have their advantages and disadvantages.

19.8 Policy choices

Up until now, we have broadly assessed the arguments for and against intervention. In this final section, we shall make the assumption – rightly or wrongly – that government has decided to intervene. Our final task is to outline the range of intervention choices available to policy makers.

A good way of structuring these intervention choices is to use Mole and Bramley's (2006) model. This suggests that policy makers have five main choices in designing and implementing enterprise policies. These five choices are in the form of five questions:

1 Who delivers . . . public, private or quasi (e.g. not-for-profit)?

2 What 'type' . . . generic, standard, tailored, regulated, face-to-face, e-based?

3 How is it rationed . . . time, sector, price, market segmentation?

4 How is it integrated . . . into other economic and social programmes?

5 How is it funded . . . by charges, by donations, directly from public funds?

To illustrate the Mole and Bramley framework we shall assume that the chosen policy is to supply publicly funded advice to SMEs.

Who delivers . . . public, private or quasi (e.g. not-for-profit)?

Business advice can be delivered in many ways. The advantage of using the public sector to provide support is, arguably, that it is *our* money and civil servants are best placed to ensure that it is spent well. This is the model favoured in Sweden and France.

The case for using the private sector (e.g. accountants, solicitors) is that their services have to be appropriate or they will face going out of business. This is different from civil servants who are less 'exposed' to the risks of providing advice since they are unlikely to lose their jobs if the programme fails. The private sector is also more likely to be seen as 'credible' by businesses. Finally, if there is too much support by the public sector, it may 'crowd out' private sector providers which may mean that businesses do not get the support they actually want. The use of the private sector is the model favoured in countries such as the US (e.g. Small Business Development Centers).

However, because of the tension between public accountability and the appropriateness of support, other countries such as the UK favour a mix of public/private support. Although this seems a good mix, the main problem with this choice is that the contract drawn up between the public funder and the private provider has to ensure both accountability for the public funder and profitability for the private provider. This is not straightforward. For example, lists of 'approved' suppliers have to be developed requiring the private provider to demonstrate their suitability. They are also likely to be required to keep details of their clients and report back on their performance. In essence, a mix of public/private support may just be as bureaucratic as direct public provision.

What 'type' . . . generic, standard, tailored, regulated, face-to-face, e-based?

Although business advice may best be offered on a face-to-face basis, the ability to do this varies according to geography: face-to-face business advice, for example, is considerably easier to deliver to 1,000 clients in Copenhagen than in the Northern Territory of Australia. Between these two extremes, however, matters are less clear. A second dimension of this policy choice is the form of that advice. In some cases, businesses may only want 'signposting' to an expert who can solve a specific problem. In other cases, the business owner may think they require an overall review of their business leading them to more accurately identify problem areas. A third case may be where the business owner identifies a specific problem – but only by talking the matter over with an 'expert' does it become clear that the fundamental problem lies elsewhere. The policy choice is, therefore, one of deciding on the proportion of the total advice budget that needs to be devoted to each of these very different forms of support.

How is it rationed . . . time, sector, price, market segmentation?

This is a crucial question. Since it is likely that – if the advice is thought to be useful – it will be over-subscribed, then rationing in some form will be needed.

Various rationing mechanisms can be used, although it is far from clear whether there is a 'best' method. One option is to restrict use of the advice only to those businesses or their owners that satisfy agreed conditions. For example, advice might be restricted to businesses in certain sectors – such as high technology businesses – on the grounds that they are most likely to experience or generate 'spillover' benefits. Alternatively, advice may be restricted to business owners with certain characteristics – young people, women, ethnic minorities, the unemployed or those without educational qualifications – on the grounds that such individuals are likely to lack business experience and so will benefit most from the advice. A third rationing approach is to focus only on new, rather than established, businesses since existing businesses are likely to be better informed. A fourth approach is to restrict access to those businesses in particular localities – such as those in areas of high unemployment.

Rationing, however, need not be determined just by the characteristics of the business or its owner. Instead, it could also be determined by time, with all businesses able to access a fixed number of hours or days of advice. A second time-related rationing could be that businesses are only able to access advice once – and so are not allowed to return for any follow up.

Public advice could also be – at least in part – rationed by price. Here businesses are only able to access the advice if they pay a proportion of the cost of providing that advice. The key argument in favour of rationing by price is that it provides a strong incentive to the customer to use the advice effectively. The argument against is that the purpose of the subsidy is to encourage greater use to be made of advice amongst those who are unaware of the benefits it may provide to their business. But, by the same token, by imposing a charge, this means that some, or perhaps most, of the 'target market' will be unwilling to seek the advice.

Rationing, however, may be used in different combinations. For example, the UK Marketing Initiative (1988–93) rationed its advice in the following way: by size (1–500 employees), by sector (manufacturing and business services), by ownership (British owned and independently owned), by time (a maximum of 15 days' advice and no 'repeats'), by price (50 per cent subsidy for 10 of the 15 days), and by location (urban locations) (Wren and Storey 2002).

Nonetheless, the central policy question is: 'What is the rationale for the rationing method(s) chosen?' The reality is that, whilst these issues may be examined by policy makers, we are not aware of any policy documents that describe how such policy decisions are actually made in practice.

How is it integrated . . . into other economic and social programmes?

The provision of publicly funded business advice is not an end in itself, only a means to having more/better small businesses. A simple example illustrates the point: if business owners are advised that it is in the best interests of their business to seek external equity finance, such advice is of little value if suppliers of equity finance are unavailable. Another example might be that entrepreneurship education programmes will only lead to frustration amongst students unless there are facilities made available to enable those students that wish to commercialise their ideas to do so.

Business advice, therefore, has to be part of an overall advisory package and not considered in isolation from other elements such as access to finance or the provision of premises.

How is it funded . . . by charges, by donations, directly from public funds?

There are several ways in which it is possible to fund the provision of business advice – from the private sector, from charitable donations, public funding, or by charging clients. Again, these funding choices may impact on the nature of the support. For example, whilst charging business clients may incentivise them, some groups or individuals may not be able to afford the charges.

In the UK, funding for business advice is provided from all the above sources. McLarty (2005), in his study of entrepreneurial graduates, found individuals had received business advice from a charity (The Princes Trust), a public organisation (Business Link) and a quasi-public organisation (Enterprise Agencies). In addition, at that time, he might have noted that large companies – most notably Shell – also devoted considerable resources to funding small business experience programmes such as Shell LiveWire (Greene and Storey 2004).

The source of funding is likely to influence both the take-up of the advice and perhaps the perceived value of the advice. As noted above, some businesses or potential business owners may avoid business advice for which they have to pay. Others may only use business advice for which they pay – on the grounds that 'free' advice may be worthless. The evidence on the perceived value of business advice is that publicly provided business advice is viewed as having less 'value' than that provided by the private sector (Greene *et al.* 2008) or that provided by charities (McLarty 2005).

Overall, this section has emphasised the many key policy choices that have to be made in designing and implementing a particular form of business support. Sometimes these choices are made explicitly, but our view is that far more frequently they are made implicitly – with politicians and their advisors often not being aware that there is a choice to be made.

Although we have only examined the issue of business advice, the Mole and Bramley framework can be used to examine key choices to be made in the delivery of other forms of enterprise support. The advantage of the framework is that it exposes the difficult choices policy makers have to make. It, therefore, indicates that one key to 'successful' policy formulation is to be clear about the objectives of the programme (its intervention 'logic') and the mechanisms for achieving these objectives.

Summary

This chapter identified four reasons given for using public funds to support entrepreneurs and SMEs: their job generation abilities; contribution to economic development; their sustainability benefits; and, finally, that SMEs and entrepreneurs represent a core political constituency. The chapter then went on to argue that this, by itself, was not a sufficient reason for intervention. What was needed was evidence of 'market failure'.

The chapter subsequently suggested that there were also other 'political economy' justifications for intervention. These were: issues of equity and the role of politicians, civil servants, and lobby groups who all have 'vested' interests in the small business agenda. What these alternative justifications showed was that there are profound and deep differences between how small businesses and policy makers 'look' at the world.

We then highlighted, using Dennis's typology, the different general policy choices available to different economies. Although a useful starting point, the chapter showed – using the examples of the UK and US – that policy 'regimes' in the UK in particular have changed over time. So, to fully understand the type of policy regime adopted by a particular economy, information was needed on the types of support and the costs of support available to businesses. We showed the UK has travelled further down this route than the US.

In the penultimate section, we detailed Lundstrom and Stevenson's (2007) distinction between entrepreneurship and SME policies. We showed that there are arguments both for and against for supporting the development of such policies. In the final section, we showed – using the Mole and Bramley (2006) framework – that policy makers have difficult choices to make in designing and implementing particular support policies.

Overall, what emerges from this review is that the sums of public money spent on this area are considerable, but that a valuable distinction can be drawn between public policies that have SMEs and entrepreneurs as their target, and more general public policies that impact – often powerfully – upon SMEs and entrepreneurs. The former we will call *micro* policies and responsibility for these policies normally rests primarily with the main small business ministry in government. These we will discuss in Chapter 21. Before that, in Chapter 20, we will turn our attention to more *macro* policies – defined as general government policies but which have an impact upon SMEs and entrepreneurs.

Questions for Discussion

1 Explain Dennis' (2004) typology for public policy towards small businesses. How useful is it in explaining international differences in small business policies?

2 What is 'market failure'? Does it adequately explain why SME and entrepreneurship policies/programmes are introduced?

3 Explain the distinction between entrepreneurship and SME policies. Evaluate who should be the recipients of public support.

4 Make a reasoned case for how 'free' business advice to SMEs should be rationed.

References

Audretsch, D.B. (2002) *Entrepreneurship: A Survey of the Literature*. Brussels: European Commission.

Audretsch, D.B. and Beckman, I.A.M. (2007) 'From Small Business to Entrepreneurship Policy', in Audretsch, D.B., Grilio, I. and Thurik, A.R. (eds) *Handbook of Research on Entrepreneurship Policy*. Cheltenham: Edward Elgar, 36–53.

Audretsch, D.B. and Thurik, A.R. (2004) 'A Model of the Entrepreneurial Economy', *Discussion Papers on Entrepreneurship, Growth and Public Policy*. Jena: Max Planck Institute, 1204.

Autio, E., Wallenius, H. and Arenius, P. (1999) 'Finnish Gazelles: Origins and Impacts'. Paper presented at the ICSB Conference, Naples, 20–23 June.

Baumol, W.J. (1990) 'Entrepreneurship: Productive, Unproductive and Destructive', *Journal of Political Economy*, 98, 893–921.

Beesley, M. and Wilson P.E.B. (1981) 'Government Aid to Small Firms in Britain', in Gorb, P., Dowell, P. and Wilson, P.E.B. (eds) (1981) *Small Business Perspectives*. London: Armstrong Publishing, 254–70.

Bennett, R. (1995) 'The Re-focusing of Small Business Services in Enterprise Agencies: The Influence of TECs and LECs', *International Small Business Journal*, 13(4), 35–55.

Bennett, R. and Robson, P. (2003) 'Changing Use of External Business Advice and Government Supports by SMEs in the 1990s', *Regional Studies*, 37(8), 795–811.

Benus, J.M. (1994) 'Self-employment Programmes: A New Re-employment Tool', *Entrepreneurship: Theory and Practice*, 19(2), 73–86.

Birch, D. (1979) *The Job Generation Process*. Cambridge, MA: MIT Program on Neighborhood and Regional Change.

Blanchflower, D.B. and Wainwright, J. (2005) *An Analysis of the Impact of Affirmative Action Programs on Self-employment in the Construction Industry*. NBER Working Papers 11793. London: National Bureau of Economic Research.

Boswell, J. (1973) *The Rise and Decline of Small Firms*. London: George Allen and Unwin.

Brock, W.A. and Evans, D.S. (1989) 'Small Business Economics', *Small Business Economics*, 1, 7–20.

Carree, M.A., Van Stel, A.J., Thurik, A.R. and Wennekers, A.R.M. (2002) 'Economic Development and Business Ownership: An Analysis Using Data of 23 OECD Countries in the Period 1976–1996', *Small Business Economics*, 19(3), 271–90.

Coen, D. and Dannreuther, C. (2002) 'When Size Matters: Europeanisation of Large and SME Business Government Relations', *Politique Européenne*, 7, 116–37.

Craig, B.R., Jackson, W.E. and Thomson, J.B. (2007) 'Small Firm Finance, Credit Rationing, and the Impact of SBA-Guaranteed Lending on Local Economic Growth', *Journal of Small Business Management*, 45(1), 116–32.

Dennis, W.J. (2004) 'Creating and Sustaining a Viable Small Business Sector'. Paper presented at the School of Continuing Education, University of Oklahoma, 27 October.

Disney, R., Haskel, J. and Heden, Y. (2003) 'Restructuring and Productivity Growth in UK Manufacturing', *Economic Journal*, 113, 666–94.

DTI (1994) *Policy Guidelines for Recruitment, Training and Development of Personal Business Advisers*. London: DTI.

Edgerton, D. (1996) 'The White Heat Revisited: The British Government and Technology in the 1960s', *Twentieth-century British History*, 7(1), 53–82.

Forum of Private Business (1996) 'Memorandum by the Forum of Private Business', in *Business Links*, House of Commons Trade and Industry Select Committee, Fifth Report, HC302-II. London: HMSO.

Fraser of Allander Institute (2001) *Promoting Business Start-ups: A New Strategic Formula; Stage 1: Progress Review; Final Report*. Glasgow: Fraser of Allander Institute for Research on the Scottish Economy, University of Strathclyde.

Galbraith, J.K. (1957) *American Capitalism: The Concept of Countervailing Power*. London: H. Hamilton.

Greene, F.J. (2002) 'An Investigation into Enterprise Support for Younger People, 1975–2000', *International Small Business Journal*, 20(3), 315–36.

Greene, F.J. and Storey, D.J. (2004) 'An Assessment of a Venture Creation Programme', *Entrepreneurship and Regional Development*, 16(2), 145–59.

Greene, F.J., Mole, K.F. and Storey, D.J. (2008) *Three Decades of Enterprise Culture: Entrepreneurship, Economic Regeneration and Public Policy*. London: Palgrave.

Gu, Q., Karoly, L.A. and Zissimopoulos, J. (2008) *Small Business Assistance Programs in the US: An Analysis of What They Are, How Well They Perform, and How We Can Learn More about Them*. WR-603-EMKF. Santa Monica: Kauffman-RAND Institute for Entrepreneurship Public Policy.

Guenther, G. (2005) *Small Business Tax Benefits: Overview and Economic Rationales, CRS Report for Congress*. Washington, DC: Congressional Research Service.

Harrison, B. (1994) *Lean and Mean*. New York: Basic Books.

HM Treasury (2008) *Enterprise: Unlocking the UK's Talent*. London: HM Treasury and BERR.

House of Commons, Public Accounts Committee (2007) *Supporting Small Businesses*, 11th Report of Session 2006–7. London: HMSO.

Johnson, S. (2005) 'SME Support Policy: Efficiency, Equity, Ideology or Vote-Seeking?'. ISBE 28th National Small Firms Policy and Research Conference, University of Lancaster, Blackpool, November 2005.

Jovanovic, B. (2001) 'New Technology and the Small Firm', *Small Business Economics*, 16(1), 53–5.

Lundstrom, A. and Stevenson, L.A. (2007) 'Dressing the Emperor: The Fabric of Entrepreneurship Policy', in Audretsch, D.B., Grilio, I. and Thurik, A.R. (eds) *Handbook of Research on Entrepreneurship Policy*. Cheltenham: Edward Elgar, 94–129.

MacDonald, R. (1994) 'Fiddly Jobs, Undeclared Working and the Something for Nothing Society', *Work, Employment and Society*, 11(4), 615–38.

MacDonald, R. (1996) 'Welfare Dependency, the Enterprise Culture and Self-employed Survival', *Work, Employment and Society*, 10(3), 431–47.

MacDonald, R. and Coffield, F. (1991) *Risky Business?: Riders, Fallers and Plodders*. London: Falmer Press.

McLarty, R. (2005) 'Entrepreneurship among Graduates: Towards a Measured Response', *Journal of Management Development*, 24(3), 223–39.

Meager, N., Bates, P. and Cowling, M. (2003) 'An Evaluation of Business Start-up Support for Young People', *National Institute Economic Review*, 186, 70–83.

Mole, K. (2002) 'Business Advisors' Impact on SMEs: An Agency Theory Approach', *International Small Business Journal*, 20, May, 139–62.

Mole, K.F. and Bramley, G. (2006) 'Making Policy Choices in Non-financial Business Support: An International Comparison', *Environment and Planning C: Government and Policy*, 24(6), 885–908.

Mole, K.F., Hart, M., Roper S. and Saal, D. (2007) *An Economic Evaluation of Business Link*. London: SBS.

OECD (2007) *Self-employment Rates: Total*. http://fiordiliji.sourceoecd.org/pdf//fact2007pdf//06-01-04.pdf (accessed 18 March 2008).

OECD (2008*a*) *Measuring Entrepreneurship*. Paris: Statistics Directorate.

OECD (2008*b*) *Producer and Consumer Support Estimates, OECD Database 1986–2007*. http://www.oecd.org/document/59/0,3343,en_2649_33727_39551355_1_1_1_1,00.html (accessed 3 September 2008).

PACEC (2005) *Small Business Service Mapping of Government Services for Small Business Final Report*. Cambridge: PACEC.

Piore, M. and Sabel, C. (1984) *The Second Industrial Divide*. New York: Basic Books.

Romer, P. (1986) 'Increasing Returns and Long-run Growth', *Journal of Political Economy*, 94(5), 1002–37.

Romer, P. (1990) 'Endogenous Technological Change', *Journal of Political Economy*, 98, 71–102.

Saxenian, A. (1994) *Regional Advantage: Culture and Competition in Silicon Valley and Route 128*. Cambridge, MA: Harvard University Press.

SBA (2007) *US Small Business Administration: Strategic Plan FY 2008–2013*. Washington, DC: SBA.

SBA (2009) *Overview and History*. http://www.sba.gov/aboutsba/history/index.html

Shutt, J. and Whittington, R. (1987) 'Fragmentation Strategies and the Rise of Small Units: Cases from the North West', *Regional Studies*, 21, 13–23.

Small Business Service (SBS) (2004) *A Government Action Plan for Small Business*. London: DTI.

Stanworth, M.J.K. and Curran, J. (1976) 'Growth and the Small Firm: An Alternative View', *Journal of Management Studies*, 13(2), 95–110.

Storey, D.J. (1982) *Entrepreneurship and the New Firm*. London: Croom Helm.

Storey, D.J. (1994) *Understanding the Small Business Sector*. London: Routledge.

Tracey, P. and Jarvis, O. (2007) 'Toward a Theory of Social Venture Franchising', *Entrepreneurship: Theory and Practice*, 31(5), 667–85.

Wren, C. (1996) 'Grant Equivalent Expenditure on Industrial Subsidies in the Post-war United Kingdom', *Oxford Bulletin of Economics and Statistics*, 58(2), 317–53.

Wren, C. and Storey, D.J. (2002) 'Evaluating the Effect of Soft Business Support upon Small Firm Performance', *Oxford Economic Papers: New Series*, 54(2), 334–65.

Appendix 19.1	Objectives and measures of success in UK enterprise policy

Objectives	Measures of success
1 Building an enterprise culture	● The number of young people involved in enterprise awareness activities. ● The proportion of young people aged 16–24 and the proportion of people aged over 25 considering going into business. ● The proportion of people who feel they have sufficient knowledge and understanding when considering business ventures.
2 Encouraging a dynamic start-up market	● Increases in the productivity of new businesses. ● Increases in the proportion of small businesses seeking external business advice during start up. ● Reductions in the barriers to start up.
3 Building the capability for small business growth	● The proportion of businesses reporting that they want to grow and are able to do so. ● The number of small businesses actively involved in product and process innovation. ● The take-up of external business advice by small businesses.
4 Improving access to finance	● A reduction in the number of small businesses reporting difficulties in obtaining finance for start up and growth. ● An increase in the number of equity investments in start-up and early-stage businesses. ● An increase in capital investment by small businesses.
5 Encouraging more enterprise in disadvantaged communities and in under-represented groups	● The gap between the number of people in the most and least deprived areas starting up in business. ● The gap between the self-employment rates of Black [and mixed race] groups and all groups. ● The gap between male and female self-employment rates.
6 Improving small businesses' experience of government services	● Increases in the number of small businesses saying they are satisfied with government services. ● Further improvements in Business Link market penetration and customer satisfaction. ● Improvements in small business perceptions that their concerns are being taken into account by government.
7 Developing better policy and regulation	● A reduction in the proportion of small businesses citing regulation as an obstacle to growth. ● To maintain or improve the UK's relative position in international comparisons of regulatory burdens. ● To increase awareness by small businesses of sources of advice and support on compliance issues and satisfaction with them. ● A reduction in the levels of crime affecting small businesses. ● More small businesses competing effectively for public sector contracts.

Source: SBS (2004).

| Appendix 19.2 | Strategic goals and objectives in US enterprise policy |

Expand America's ownership society, particularly in under-served markets	1 Improve access to SBA programmes and services by small businesses to drive business formation, job growth, and economic activity. 2 Support entrepreneurship in markets with higher poverty and unemployment, and in our military community. 3 Ensure stewardship and accountability over taxpayer dollars through prudent financial portfolio management and oversight.
Improve the economic environment for small business	1 Protect, strengthen and effectively represent the Nation's small businesses to minimise the regulatory burden. 2 Foster a more small business-friendly environment.
Ensure management and organisational excellence to increase responsiveness to customers, streamline processes, and improve compliance and controls	1 Deploy a skilled workforce capable of executing high-quality programmes. 2 Provide a safe and secure information system environment to support business decisions and agency operations. 3 Provide financial and performance management services to support efficient and effective programme delivery.

Source: SBA (2007).
Note: The SBA also has a strategic goal and set of objectives around disaster relief (e.g. Hurricane Katrina).

20 Macro policies towards small businesses and entrepreneurs

Key learning objectives

By the end of this chapter you should:

- Understand the constraints on the policy choices available to any small business ministry

- Be able to identify the types of macro-economic factors that influence SMEs and entrepreneurs

- Understand the rationale for the favourable tax treatment of SMEs and entrepreneurs and arguments against such policies

- Be able to critically evaluate the arguments for and against regulation

- Understand the influence of immigration policy

- Identify the reasons for competition and procurement policies.

20.1 Introduction

This chapter identifies those government policies that have a major impact upon SMEs and entrepreneurs in an economy. The unifying characteristic of these policies is that they do *not* have SMEs or entrepreneurs as their primary focus. Indeed, those responsible for some of these policies would be very unlikely to even consider the impact these may have upon either SMEs or entrepreneurs. However, what the chapter will show is the impact of such policies upon SMEs and entrepreneurs can be considerable. We refer to these as *macro* policies. Whilst they include traditional macro-economic policies, such as the management of aggregate demand through fiscal and monetary policy, they also include other highly influential public policies such as regulation, immigration and competition.

The crucial distinction between macro and micro policies is that the latter focus specifically upon SMEs and entrepreneurs. A second distinction is that micro policies are likely to be the responsibility of a government department – or sub-department – of small business or enterprise. In contrast, macro policies are the responsibility of another government department – frequently, but not always, the finance ministry.

20.2 Macro-economic factors

There can be little doubt about the general influence that macro-economic factors (such as interest rates) can have on entrepreneurship and small business policies. Shane (1996) showed that, in the US over the period 1899–1988, start-up rates were lower during times when interest rates were high. He attributes this to small business owners having to incur higher borrowing costs at times of high interest rates. Parker (1996) also found that self-employment is inhibited by higher real (excluding inflation) interest rates.

High interest rates are not the only macro-economic factor that is likely to influence entrepreneurial behaviour. Figure 20.1 shows the start-up and closure rates for Japanese businesses over the period 1975 to 2001. Until the period 1981–5, start-up rates were higher than closure rates. Arguably, this reflects the competitiveness of the Japanese economy which had managed to transform itself from a 'developing' economy in the early 1950s to the world's second largest economy (after the US) by the 1980s. However, Figure 20.1 shows that after 1986 start-up rates were *always* lower than closure rates.

JSBRI (2006) point to a range of factors that influence these changes. For example, there was the Plaza Accord (in 1985) which saw the yen appreciate against the US dollar. This made Japanese exports more expensive and reduced economic growth from more than 6 per cent in 1985 to just over 4 per cent in 1987 (Figure 20.2). To compensate for falling demand, the Japanese economy cut its base lending rate (the rate at which the central bank lends money). Figure 20.2 shows that this fell from 5 to 2.5 per cent between 1985 and 1987. This easing of monetary policy meant it became cheaper to borrow money. Figure 20.2 shows that GDP went up and unemployment went down. However, what is not shown is that property became much more expensive and the Nikkei (Japanese stock market) became overvalued. When the Japanese government increased its base lending rate to 6 per cent in 1990, this led to a massive downturn in the economy: Figure 20.2 shows that unemployment more than doubled, economic growth (GDP) fell and instead of increasing prices (inflation), prices fell (deflation). These macro-economic changes are clearly linked to the start-up and closure rates shown in Figure 20.1.

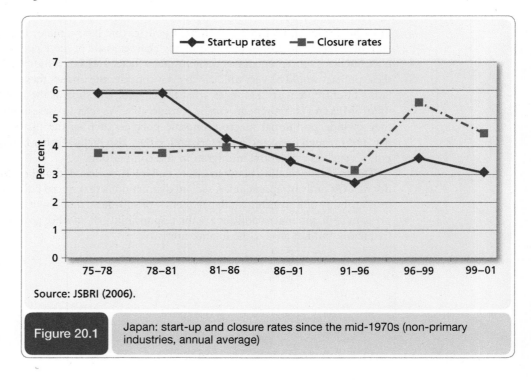

Source: JSBRI (2006).

Figure 20.1   Japan: start-up and closure rates since the mid-1970s (non-primary industries, annual average)

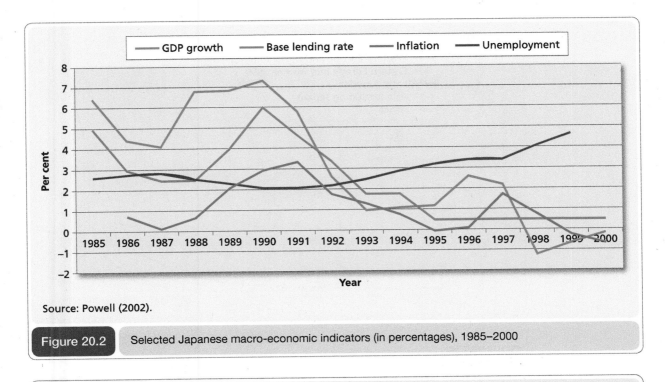

Source: Powell (2002).

| Figure 20.2 | Selected Japanese macro-economic indicators (in percentages), 1985–2000 |

Question

In 2007, the sub-prime crisis began in the US when it became clear that some property prices were overvalued. The sub-prime crisis became the 'credit crunch' as the full extent of the banks' over-exposure to 'toxic' assets became clearer. As with Japanese banks, this led to banks making it much harder for consumers and businesses to obtain credit. In response, governments across the world cut their base lending rate and tried to inject money into their financial systems. GDP and inflation fell but unemployment increased. What do you think is the likely impact of this on start-up and closure rates?

A second factor influencing small business activity is the *stability* of the macro-economy. Parker (1996) found that the self-employed were deterred by risks in the UK economy. Stiglitz (2000) also argues that macro-economic stability is fundamental to SME and entrepreneurship activity. One indicator of this is the level of income in a country. Figure 20.3 shows the GDP (national income) of the main economic 'blocs' from 1600 to 2001. Until the 1820s, there was little difference in incomes between these blocs but after 1913, incomes in western Europe and North America grew at a much faster rate. Income per person (also known as GDP per capita) in the 'West' was around US$28,000 by 2003. In Africa, in 2003, GDP per capita was around US$1,500 (Maddison 2003).

Levels of income obviously impact on the total demand for products and services and, thereby, shape the nature of entrepreneurial opportunities in an economy. Political instability is another factor influencing entrepreneurship. Klapper *et al.* (2007) show that the rate of business entry in Peru was directly associated with the incidence of political upheaval. They show that the Peruvian political crisis of 1999 led to a fall in business start ups of more than 5 per cent. When Peru moved to a transitional government in 2000 and then on to a new government in 2001, the impact was that the start-up rate increased in both 2000 and 2001 by more than 10 per cent per annum. Chemin (2009) showed that judicial frameworks can also have a pronounced impact on start-up rates. He evaluated the impact of judicial reforms designed to speed up the efficiency of the Pakistani judicial system and attributed judicial improvements to increases in the start-up rate in Pakistan.

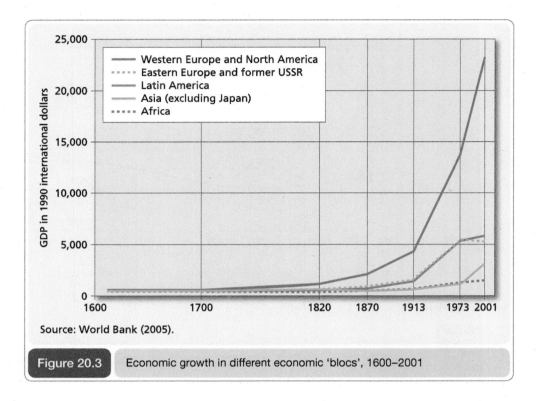

Source: World Bank (2005).

| Figure 20.3 | Economic growth in different economic 'blocs', 1600–2001 |

The World Bank (2005) also examined a range of factors that impact on the investment climate for businesses. Figure 20.4 shows the results of their survey of 26,000 businesses in 53 countries throughout the world. It shows that policy uncertainty and macro instability are the two most common constraints faced by businesses. Approximately 80 per cent of businesses report that this is some form of obstacle to their business. Noticeable also is the importance of constraints such as tax and corruption (see Section 20.3, below), regulations (see Section 20.4, below) and crime and infrastructure problems (e.g. poor telecommunications, poor roads/railways).

To illustrate the importance of crime and infrastructure, Figure 20.5 shows the percentage of businesses that pay for security to protect their business and the percentage identifying crime and disorder as major business constraints (World Bank, 2009). Figure 20.5 clearly shows that, outside of OECD countries ('developed' countries), crime and the threat of crime are major business constraints: more than 30 per cent of Middle Eastern/North African businesses pay for security whilst in South Asia it is more than 70 per cent. Similarly, concerns about crime and disorder range from about 7 per cent of OECD businesses to more than one third of businesses in Latin America.

Figure 20.6 also shows the importance of infrastructure to businesses. There are three measures. One is the number of power outages (failures) in a typical month. The second is the average number of water problems in a typical month and the third is the length of delay (in days) in obtaining a telephone connection. Figure 20.6 shows that in the OECD, the main constraint is obtaining a telephone connection. This takes – on average – 9 days across the OECD whilst in South Asia it takes more than 50 days. South Asia is also more likely to see disruptions to the electricity and water supply.

Overall, this section has shown that macro-economic factors (e.g. interest rates, aggregate demand) strongly influence entrepreneurial activity. This is unsurprising given that – as we argued in Chapter 1 – small businesses are more prone to external environmental uncertainties. What is also clear is the importance of the stability of the external environment (macro-economy). Very many businesses, particularly in developing economies, face real uncertainties about the quality of their country's infrastructure and its ability to provide support against

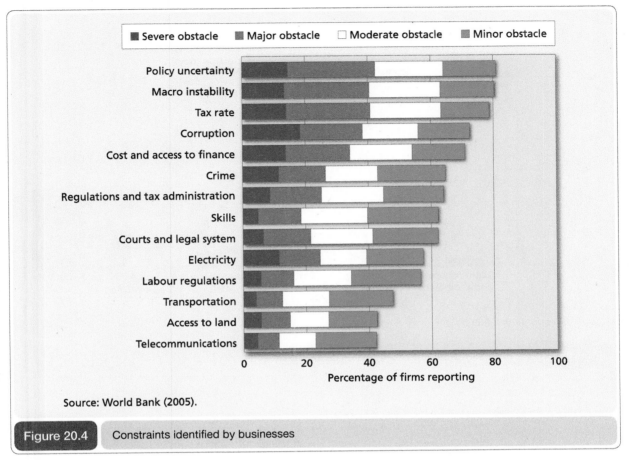

Source: World Bank (2005).

Figure 20.4   Constraints identified by businesses

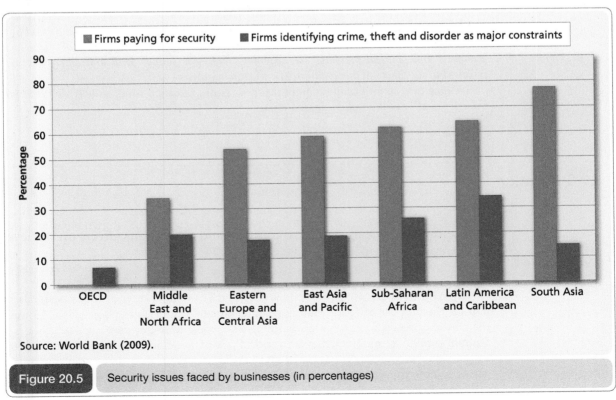

Source: World Bank (2009).

Figure 20.5   Security issues faced by businesses (in percentages)

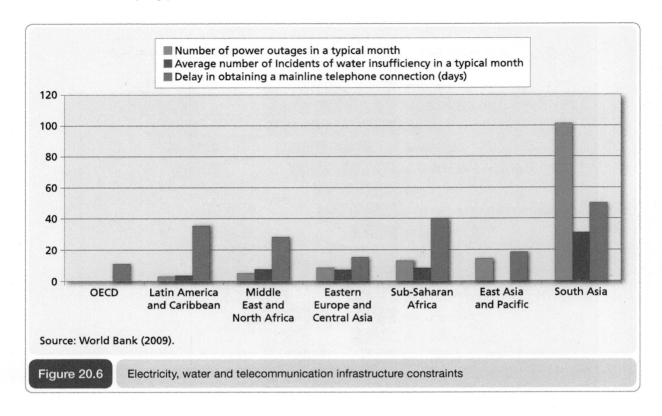

Source: World Bank (2009).

Figure 20.6 ┃ Electricity, water and telecommunication infrastructure constraints

criminal activity. It is also evident that the quality, continuance and direction of a country's political regime often govern the investment climate for very many businesses.

Faced with these difficulties, it is difficult to see how a dedicated small business ministry – on their own – can have a marked impact on outcomes for SMEs and entrepreneurs. Macro-economic factors (e.g. interest rates) are often set by the ministry of finance and entrepreneurs and SMEs are only one constituency. Equally, macro-economic stability is also a product of wider social, economic and political pressures. An economy may have 'sound' SME and entrepreneurship policies but see these fail due to failures in other policy areas.

We now turn to an examination of taxation. Again, taxation is not usually decided by the ministry dealing with small business affairs.

20.3 Taxation

> A country's tax system can have complex and ambiguous effects on the level of entrepreneurship.
>
> *Schuetze and Bruce (2004: 4)*

Governments raise taxes to pay for public goods such as security services, roads, hospitals, but also for the purpose of redistributing income, broadly from rich to poor people. However, the nature of a taxation system also incentivises people to follow particular behaviours. In Baumol's (1990) terminology, they are a critical 'rule of the game' since they influence whether an individual becomes or continues as a business owner, becomes or stays as an employee, or enters or exits from the labour market.

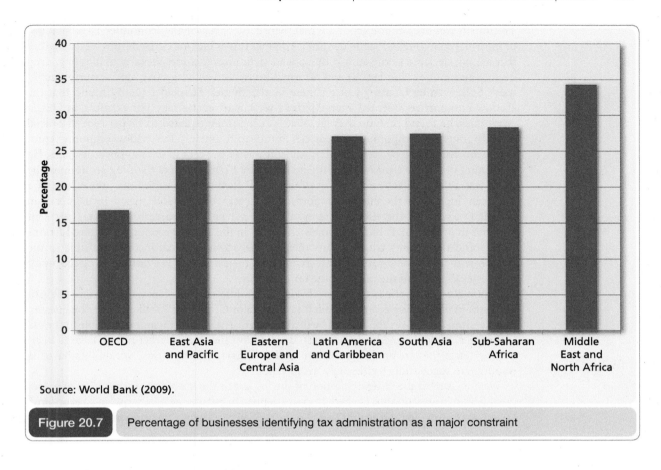

Source: World Bank (2009).

| Figure 20.7 | Percentage of businesses identifying tax administration as a major constraint |

The above quotation from Schuetze and Bruce, however, emphasises that these influences are not straightforward. Indeed, there are strongly conflicting views about the impact of the tax regime on the scale of business ownership/self-employment in a country.

Before turning to this debate, we begin with four important areas of 'common ground'. The first is that taxation compliance costs are regressive by business size, so that compliance costs are a much higher proportion of tax paid for small than for large businesses.

Both Crawford and Freedman (2008) and Chittenden *et al.* (2005) showed that the smaller the size of the business, the greater the cost per employee of tax compliance. Pope (2009) also showed that VAT compliance costs for SMEs in the EU were 2.6 per cent of total turnover whilst they represented 0.02 per cent of total turnover for larger businesses.

A second area of 'common ground' is that the owners of small businesses view tax administration as a major constraint on the growth of their business. Figure 20.7 shows that around 15 per cent of OECD businesses, and nearly 35 per cent of Middle Eastern and North African businesses, held this view.

A third area of common ground is that differences in how income tax rates are administered influence the self-employment/paid employment choice in three ways:

● Employees are taxed 'at source' whilst the self-employed declare their income to the tax authorities.

● Employees tend to have tax removed by their employers at weekly or monthly intervals, so the 'tax' money never comes to them. In contrast, the self-employed receive their income, and then have to pay the tax authorities in instalments and in arrears.

● The self-employed are able to claim expenses incurred to undertake their work (e.g. use of a work vehicle) that are not normally available to the employee.

The fourth area of common ground is that there exist, in very many economies, large 'shadow' or informal components. Schneider (2005) defines this as income derived from legal activities that are not declared to the authorities. Such a definition excludes illegal activities (e.g. drug dealing and money laundering) and informal household activities (e.g. do-it-yourself activities). Still, even by focusing just on these legal activities, Schneider (2005) found that the shadow economy represented a large part of very many economies. For example, in OECD economies, he found that, on average, shadow economies equated to 17 per cent of official GDP. In transition economies (e.g. eastern European countries), the shadow economy represented, on average, 38 per cent of GDP, whilst it was 41 per cent in developing economies. He also found that if the shadow economy increased by 1 per cent in developing economies, the effect was a 0.6 per cent reduction in official GDP. In transition economies, the effects of a 1 per cent increase in the shadow economy were larger – official GDP shrank by 0.8 per cent. In OECD countries, the effects were even larger: a 1 per cent increase led to a 1 per cent decrease in official GDP. In other words, increases in the shadow economy led to reductions in the official economy which means there is likely to be less tax income available to the economy. If this lowers government tax income, then a higher tax burden is placed upon businesses that are 'on the radar' of the tax authorities.

Figure 20.8 shows the net effect of this is that middle-sized businesses were more likely to pay taxes in developing economies such as Uganda or Cameroon. Unlike smaller businesses, middle-sized businesses are likely to be incorporated. This makes them more visible to the tax authorities. Middle-sized businesses also do not have the same market power as large businesses. Hence, they are unlikely to receive legal or illegal tax 'exemptions'. Nor do they have the resources to successfully legitimately 'avoid' taxes.

We now turn to the central question of the impact of the tax regime on the level of entrepreneurship in an economy. Do high tax rates depress or encourage 'enterprise' in an economy? We set out the case for and against (see also the specialist case study on taxation (Case study 8)).

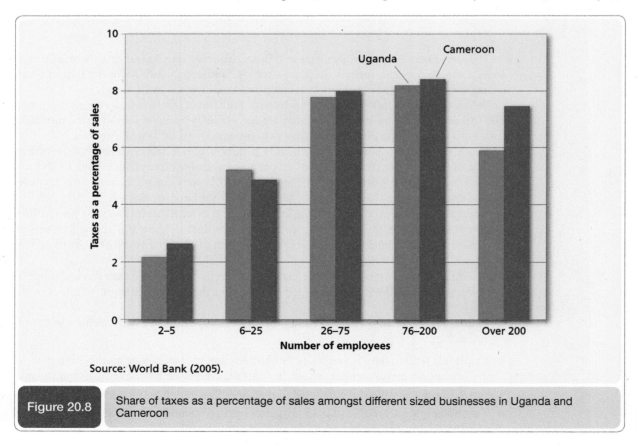

Source: World Bank (2005).

Figure 20.8   Share of taxes as a percentage of sales amongst different sized businesses in Uganda and Cameroon

Low tax rates encourage business ownership

The case that low tax rates encourage enterprise is based partly upon the views of business owners. Almost nobody enjoys paying taxes but, as we saw in Figure 20.1, a substantial proportion of business owners report that the collection and payment of taxes acts as a powerful disincentive to them to expand their business. On these grounds, it is also likely to discourage others from becoming a business owner.

In contrast, lower taxes mean that business owners will keep more of their rewards for their 'efforts'. In simple terms, why should the taxi driver work the extra hour if a substantial proportion of the earnings for this hour are 'given' to the government? Instead, if the taxi driver is able to keep more of their earnings then this would be more likely to encourage the extra hour to be worked.

In addition to the views of business owners, there is also macro-economic evidence that high tax rates can discourage self-employment effort. Folster (2002) showed, for Sweden, that reducing the tax burden by 10 per cent would increase the numbers of self-employed in employment by about 3 per cent. Similarly, Davis and Henrekson (1999) argue that Sweden's high business-tax regime explained the poor performance of the Swedish economy over several decades. They argued that the combination of high corporate tax rates combined with generous provisions for accelerated depreciation (allowing businesses to quickly depreciate the value of their capital) meant that the key beneficiaries were large businesses which were more likely to take advantage of depreciation provisions because they were more likely to spend on capital assets. By implication, these 'tax breaks' penalised SMEs because they are more likely to have modest capital assets.

Finally, there is clear evidence provided by Michaelas *et al.* (1999) that taxes which were levied on small company profits led to lower growth rates since retained profits were the prime source of funding for small business investments.

High tax rates encourage entrepreneurship

Schuetze and Bruce (2004) argue that a central reason why higher tax rates encourage self-employment is that it allows greater opportunity for both tax evasion and tax avoidance. It is important to distinguish between evasion and avoidance. Tax evasion is illegal since taxes which the law makes it clear should be paid, are not. Tax avoidance is legal – but of questionable morality. It involves taking actions which are strictly within the letter, but not the spirit, of the law so as minimise total tax paid.

As we noted earlier, the employee has their tax removed at source whereas the self-employed report their own tax liabilities, and do so in arrears. Clearly in a high-tax environment, these 'benefits' become particularly valuable since one avoidance strategy is to seek to delay payment for as long as possible – an option not open to the employee. A second avoidance strategy is to take professional advice on 'tax planning' which may involve adjusting reported income to ensure it takes advantage of the full range of allowances and exemptions.

Schuetze and Bruce (2004) argued that the self-employed are also likely to under-report their 'true' earnings – tax evasion. This is widely confirmed in several studies. Pope (2009) cited Slemrod (2004) who suggested that, in the US, 95.5 per cent of salary and wage workers are tax compliant compared with fewer than 50 per cent of small businesses. UK data also suggest that the smaller the business, the greater the likelihood of tax non-compliance: for example, 51 per cent of non-compliers were the self-employed/partnerships which underpaid their tax by £3.8 billion (HMRC, 2005). Pope (2009) also cited Swedish data which suggests that micro businesses were responsible for 39 per cent of the tax 'gap'. More recently Engström and Holmlund (2009) report that the self-employed under-report their income by 30 per cent.

In essence, therefore, the evidence indicates that tax avoidance and/or evasion are strong motivations for individuals to become self-employed. Schuetze (2000) found, for example, that as average income tax rates increased, there was a greater likelihood of more people becoming self-employed in Canada. Evidence from OECD countries also found that higher average rates of income tax lead to higher levels of self-employment (Parker and Robson 2004).

Adding complexity

Although there is good evidence that as the size of the tax burden increases so, too, does the rate of self-employment (Schuetze and Bruce 2004), the picture is clouded by several factors.

The first of these is the employee/self-employment decision is not only influenced by the tax rates, but also by the presence of other financial incentives that favour the business owner. The first of these are 'offset losses'. For example, if an individual is declared bankrupt, they may be able to 'exempt' or 'offset' their assets (e.g. their house and their pension arrangements) from any 'losses' they incur whilst running their business. So, higher offset losses will, all else being equal, make an individual more willing to undertake risky endeavours such as self-employment because effectively their downside losses are capped. This reduces the 'riskiness' of self-employment and makes it more attractive.

As Gropp *et al.* (1997) show, the presence of offsets has moral hazard consequences (see Chapter 17). Financial institutions will be more reluctant to make loans to businesses if they think that – because the bankrupt business owner keeps more in the event of failure – they will be less likely to be repaid. So, if the lender is less likely to be repaid, less money will be provided. This serves to lower the scale of enterprise in the economy.

A second complicating factor is that small businesses/self-employed individuals may be viewed as worthy of encouragement. This could be in the form of lower tax rates, exemptions from particular forms of taxation, relief from requirements to file 'full' accounts and additional burdens such as how loans are treated for tax purposes. As we saw in Chapter 19, the sums involved in such special treatment can be large, with this in the UK amounting to £4 billion in 2004, $8 billion in the US and, as Pope (2009) suggested, A$1 billion in Australia. The effect of these exemptions would be expected to increase the scale of enterprise in an economy.

Third, Parker and Robson (2004) showed that entry into self-employment was influenced by the rate of unemployment benefit offered by the state. They argued that if the unemployment benefit rate was high, there was little incentive for unemployed individuals to enter self-employment.

Rees and Shah (1994) also showed that what was often important to the self-employed was achieving a 'target' income. Hence, they observed that when the UK government cut income tax in the early 1980s, the effect was that the self-employed worked fewer hours because it was easier for them to achieve their 'target' income. The motivations of potential business owners, therefore, influence taxation-related incentives.

Fifth, Robson and Wren (1999) and Bruce (2000) also argued that it is not just average tax rates (calculated as the ratio of taxes paid to taxable income) but also marginal tax rates (calculated as the ratio of tax paid as income changes) that influence the self-employment decision. Both these studies suggested that lower marginal tax rates increased self-employment rates. However, they also found that increases in average tax rates increased self-employment rates because it offered opportunities – often denied to employees – for tax evasion and avoidance.

Gurley-Calvez and Bruce (2008) argued that marginal tax rates also influence how long the self-employed stay in business. They found that if marginal tax rates were cut for the self-employed, they stayed in self-employment longer. However, if marginal tax rates were reduced for employees, the self-employed stayed for a shorter time in self-employment as they saw more advantages in being employed.

Georgellis and Wall (2006), in their study of US states, found a 'U'-shaped relationship between marginal tax rates and self-employment. At low rates of tax, an increase in the marginal rates reduced the numbers of self-employed whilst at high rates of tax, an increase in marginal taxation increased the number of self-employed. They also examined the influence of offset losses (bankruptcy exemptions) on self-employment. They broadly confirmed the Gropp *et al.* (1997) findings that if these exemptions were low or very high, the impact was to reduce self-employment. However, if exemptions were between these two levels, the effect was to increase self-employment.

Sixth, the discussion so far has focused primarily on income tax. However, Henrekson and Stenkula (2010) point out that entrepreneurial income can be taxed in many different forms, including labour income, business income, current capital income (dividends and interest), or capital gains. All these influence the decision to start, remain in, or grow, a business.

A final ambiguity is whether taxation influences the scale of enterprise in an economy or whether it merely influences its distribution between 'forms'. For example, Chittenden and Sloan (2007) showed that by simply altering the tax treatment of incorporation, the UK was able to create large numbers of new limited companies. This was because there were distinctive tax advantages in becoming incorporated. What is much less clear, however, is whether these new companies were businesses that were wholly new, or whether they were businesses which otherwise would have existed but in some other legal form. The suspicion is that they were primarily the latter.

Overall, the evidence is that taxation policy can and does influence the risks and rewards of small business activity. Much of the evidence is focused on the self-employment entry decision and suggests that one of the primary motivations for becoming self-employed is that it is, relative to the employee, easier to avoid paying taxes, legally through avoidance or illegally through evasion. We concur with Schuetze and Bruce's (2004) review that:

> *The fact that self-employment seems to increase with income tax rates calls into question the common view that higher taxes hamper self-employment.*

(pp. 28–29)

Beyond this, the evidence indicates that the influence of taxation policies is ambiguous. After examining a broad range of business taxes (e.g. income tax, capital gains and estate taxes), Bruce and Moshin (2006) found:

> *. . . that tax policies can affect self-employment rates, [but] magnitudes are typically quite small and suggest that it would take a prohibitively large tax rate change to generate a noticeable change in self-employment activity.*

(p. 421)

The implication of this is that 'special' tax treatments (e.g. exemptions, lower taxes) for small businesses lead to piecemeal taxation policies:

> *. . . special tax treatment for small business generally relies on a complex raft of measures and qualifying rules, no doubt reflecting political lobbying, 'flavours' or whims of the time, and ensuing government reviews. Rationalisation in this area is long overdue.*

Pope (2009: 33)

Questions

1 There are a number of justifications for the favourable tax treatment of small businesses (e.g. encourages entrepreneurship, limits compliance costs). Do you see an argument for keeping such systems in place?

2 Alternatively, do you think that taxation policies should be as neutral as possible and just focus on minimising tax complexities and lowering taxes for all businesses?

3 Whose interest (prospective or actual business owner, the taxpayer) is best served if you were to continue with the status quo (favourable tax treatment) or, alternatively, seek to simplify the tax system?

4 If you were to simplify the tax system, what would be the impact on prospective and actual business activity?

20.4 Regulation

In this section, we examine the impact of regulation on small business activities. We consider arguments for and against regulation. Kitching defines regulation as:

> . . . the legal and administrative rules created, applied, and enforced by state institutions – at local, national, and supranational levels – that both mandate and prohibit actions by individuals and organisations, with infringements subject to criminal, civil, and administrative penalties.
>
> *Kitching (2006: 801)*

The Hampton Report (2005) argued that there are two main types of regulatory costs:

1 *Policy costs.* These are the costs of complying with a new piece of law which requires businesses to make changes in the way they conduct their business. For example, introduce a new 'greener' energy system to reduce its carbon footprint. Failure to comply may incur a fine.

2 *Administrative costs.* These are the regulator's costs in gathering information on the business and the business' costs in filling in forms or showing an inspector around the business.

The 'costs' to businesses of regulation are reportedly huge. Crain (2005) estimated that federal regulations cost businesses in the US $1.1 trillion. Open Europe (2009) estimated that the cumulative cost of regulation introduced to the 27 member countries of the EU between 1998–2008 was €1.4 trillion. The CBI (2009) also estimates that for individual member states such as the UK, the cost of regulation over 1998–2008 was £77 billion. The complaint about regulation is that it 'burdens' small-business activity with 'red tape' which retards people's efforts to set up and grow their business.

Djankov *et al.* (2002) used public choice theory to explain why regulation may not produce beneficial outcomes for the economy as a whole. It comes in two versions. The first suggests that regulation is inefficient. Instead of operating on behalf of the public good (the taxpayer), regulations serve the interests of existing businesses who use regulations to meet their own needs. For example, in Chapter 3 we showed that in France the Royer Law acted to protect existing retailers from the entry of larger (and potentially more efficient) retailers (Bertrand and Kramarz 2002). This version of public choice theory is called '*regulatory capture*'.

A second version is the '*tollbooth*' view. This suggests that the purpose of regulation is to serve not the interests of businesses (regulatory capture) – but the interests of politicians and bureaucrats. For example, politicians may seek – as we saw in Chapter 19 – to introduce new 'initiatives' (regulations) because it makes them more likely to be re-elected. Equally, regulations may benefit bureaucrats (e.g. career advancement). Regulations may, therefore, create opportunities for corrupt politicians and bureaucrats to 'tax' individuals and businesses. The net result is a reduction in the welfare of society because of such regulation.

The alternative theoretical case for regulation is derived from 'public interest' theory. This argues that regulation is necessary because of the presence of 'market failure'. For example, in Chapter 4, we showed that workers are much more likely to die if they work in a small business. Stringent employment regulations may be necessary to protect workers in such businesses. Equally, negative externalities are produced by polluters. Without environmental regulations, these businesses may not act responsibly to protect the environment.

We now review the arguments and evidence relating to the impact of government regulation on smaller businesses. Our focus is again to assess whether regulation, which is another of Baumol's 'rules of the game', influences the scale or the nature of entrepreneurship in an economy.

Arguments against regulation

Djankov *et al.* (2002) specifically tested whether public interest (pro-regulation) or public choice (anti-regulation) was a better explanation of the role of regulation in business entry. Using World Bank data, they examined the time and cost of business entry in 85 countries. Their conclusions were stark:

> we do not find that stricter regulation of entry is associated with higher quality products, better pollution records or health outcomes, or keener competition. But stricter regulation of entry *is* associated with sharply higher levels of corruption, and a greater relative size of the unofficial economy.
>
> *(p. 4, emphasis in original)*

The implication of this is clear: the 'tollbooth' version of public choice was a more appropriate view of why regulation was undertaken, particularly in poorer countries. Also, if countries wished to promote entrepreneurship, their aim should be to reduce the time and costs of business entry. Doing so would lead to societal benefits.

Newton *et al.* (2009) highlighted the positive impact of making business entry easier in the developing economy of El Salvador. Prior to 2006, business entry took, on average, 115 days and cost US$2,700 in fees plus the US$2,850 needed as minimum capital. The net result – in an economy where the average income per capita was US$2,145 – was that 38 per cent of businesses were started informally and, therefore, did not pay taxes. Newton *et al.* say:

> This meant less revenue for the government, less protection for consumers, and no social security benefits for employees. It also meant that companies usually stayed small. Investing in new machinery or a bigger office building was difficult without access to bank loans. And then there was the constant worry of being discovered by the authorities.
>
> *(p. 9)*

The European Commission (2008) also acknowledged that the perception of administrative barriers potentially deterred individuals from setting up a business. It found that, on average, 6.8 per cent of EU citizens believed that administrative barriers made it difficult to set up a business. This varied markedly from country to country: in Iceland only 0.8 per cent of individuals believed that administrative barriers made business entry difficult. In contrast, 17.7 per cent of Slovakians believed that administrative barriers impeded business entry.

Klapper *et al.* (2006) found, using data on European companies, that costly regulation inhibits business entry. Furthermore, Barseghyan (2008) examined entry costs in 97 countries. He found that if entry costs were reduced by 80 per cent, productivity increased by 22 per cent.

The World Bank (2009) has produced a 'league table' that ranks 181 countries in terms of the ease of starting a business. As Table 20.1 shows, the easiest countries in the world to set up a business (in terms of time, cost and minimum paid in capital required) tended to be from the developed English-speaking countries, and the hardest places tended to be former French African colonies.

The World Bank (2009) highlighted three benefits of reducing regulation to ease business entry. First, by reducing entry costs, businesses are more likely to enter the formal sector. Other things being equal, they are more likely to pay taxes and provide rights for workers. Second, fewer barriers to entry mean there is less opportunity for corruption by politicians and bureaucrats. Third, lower costs mean that more businesses are likely to enter. As we saw in Chapter 3, one potential consequence of increased entry is greater competition which, in turn, is likely to lead to stronger economic growth. An example from one country is shown in the box overleaf.

| Illustration | Barriers to business start up in Serbia |

For decades, starting a business in Serbia was time consuming and burdened with unnecessary bureaucratic hurdles – the rules inherited from the communist past were not business-friendly. Some of the biggest problems: the $5,000 minimum capital requirement for starting a limited liability company, the necessary inspections before a company could start operating, and the commercial courts checking every document. Sixteen commercial courts were in charge of registering enterprises, and 131 municipalities dealt with registering entrepreneurs. The practice was so inconsistent that even judges in the same court required different documents. As one lawyer says, 'I had to file the same form to the same court in 15 different ways depending on what judge handled my registration.' There were even cases when the courts refused to accept forms filled out electronically and instead insisted on handwritten materials (Jersild and Skopljak 2009: 15).

Table 20.1	Ease of starting a business: top and bottom ten 'league table' positions		
Easiest		**Hardest**	
New Zealand	1	Cameroon	171
Canada	2	Djibouti	173
Australia	3	Equatorial Guinea	174
Georgia	4	Iraq	175
Ireland	5	Haiti	176
US	6	Guinea	177
Mauritius	7	Eritrea	178
United Kingdom	8	Togo	179
Puerto Rico	9	Chad	180
Singapore	10	Guinea-Bissau	181

Source: World Bank (2009).

Business regulations impact on *existing* as well as new SMEs and, like tax, their impact is argued to be regressive. Table 20.2 shows the costs of regulation faced by US businesses. It shows this is greater for smaller businesses (fewer than 20 employees) than for large across all types of federal regulation. The only exception is that larger businesses (500+ employees) are more likely to face higher economic regulation costs (e.g. laws that place quotas on exporting/importing) whilst 'mid-sized' businesses (20–499 employees) face higher costs in terms of workplace regulations.

Table 20.2 is confirmed by other evidence. The OECD (2003) estimated, for example, that businesses with fewer than 20 staff have a regulatory burden that is five times greater than businesses with more than 50 staff. Small businesses also perceive that the weight of regulations they face is excessive. For example, the SBS (2006) found that 22 per cent of existing businesses said that 'regulations' were a barrier to business success.

The World Bank (2009) also showed regulations were a barrier to business development. They examined ten different types of regulations (starting a business, dealing with construction permits, employing workers, getting credit, protecting investors, paying taxes, trading across borders, enforcing contracts and closing a business) and ranked countries according to an index of the 'ease of doing business'. Table 20.3 shows the ten countries which were easiest, and the ten countries that were the hardest places, in the world to 'do' business.

Table 20.2	Costs of federal regulations to US businesses			
		Cost per employee for businesses with:		
Type of regulation	**All businesses**	**<20 employees**	**20–499 employees**	**500+ employees**
All federal regulations	$5,633	$7,647	$5,411	$5,282
Economic	$2,567	$2,127	$2,372	$2,952
Workplace	$922	$920	$1,051	$841
Environmental	$1,249	$3,296	$1,040	$710
Tax compliance	$894	$1,304	$948	$780

Source: Crain (2005).

Table 20.3	Ease of doing business: top and bottom ten 'league table' positions		
Easiest		**Hardest**	
Singapore	1	Niger	172
New Zealand	2	Eritrea	173
US	3	Venezuela	174
Hong Kong, China	4	Chad	175
Denmark	5	São Tomé and Principe	176
United Kingdom	6	Burundi	177
Ireland	7	Congo, Republic	178
Canada	8	Guinea-Bissau	179
Australia	9	Central African Republic	180
Norway	10	Congo, Democratic Republic	181

Source: World Bank (2009).

Djankov *et al.* (2006) used an earlier version of this World Bank data to investigate the relationship between business regulations and economic growth (GDP). They found that moving up the 'ease of doing business' league had profound benefits for an economy. For example, if a country moves from the bottom quarter of the 'doing' business league to the top quarter, annual GDP growth was enhanced by 2.3 per cent.

A number of other analyses have been conducted linking regulation with economic performance. Nicoletti and Scarpetta (2003) showed that more heavily regulated European countries were less productive than European economies that were less heavily regulated. Similarly, Bartelsman *et al.* (2005) compared productivity differences between the US and European countries. They found that the start-up and closure rates of businesses in both the US and the EU were broadly similar. Where they differed was that US businesses began smaller but, if they survived, grew much faster than EU businesses. They found that, on average, surviving US businesses had employment growth that was around 60 per cent whilst in the EU employment growth amongst survivors was around 3–35 per cent. They attributed this difference to the presence of greater regulation in the EU.

The critics of business regulation present what seems a compelling case. Increased regulation of business entry seems to only benefit politicians and bureaucrats whilst the taxpayer experiences a net reduction in economic growth (Schneider 2005). New entrepreneurs are also seemingly penalised by paying high costs which potentially forces them into the informal sector. Existing businesses also seem to suffer because regulations tend to be regressive. These costs also seem to inhibit growth.

The suggestion, therefore, is that there is a case for 'smaller' government. We saw earlier in Tables 20.2 and 20.3 that the World Bank (2009) identified that English-speaking countries were more likely to be the easiest places to start up and do business. Tables 20.2 and 20.3 also identified that the countries where starting and doing business were hardest tended to be former French African colonies. La Porta *et al.* (2008) argued that such differences are rooted in different legal systems. They found that countries whose legal system is based on French 'law' were much more likely to prohibit entry than countries whose laws were based on English 'common' law.

The implication of this view is that economies whose public policy is orientated towards a 'competing' SMEs and entrepreneurs policy framework (Dennis 2004 – see Chapter 19) are more likely to produce stronger entrepreneurial outcomes. This is a viewpoint shared by Nystrom (2008) who finds that self-employment rates are more likely to increase when governments are smaller, the rule of law is defended and where there was less regulation of credit, labour and businesses. Torrini (2005) also examined a range of OECD countries. He finds that self-employment was more likely in countries where employment in the public sector and unemployment benefits were both lower. The logic behind this is that:

> In a market with high levels of economic freedom, entrepreneurs have incentives to pursue economic profit by meeting consumer preferences. However, when economic freedom is diminished, rent-seeking may yield higher returns than productive activity.
>
> Gohmann et al. *(2008: 858)*

Arguments 'for' regulation

The argument for regulation is that it is necessary: without 'rules' there is no 'game'. For example, one of the basic regulatory needs of a business is to ensure that it has 'property rights' over its assets. The World Bank (2005) suggested that giving farmers 'title' over their land had a marked impact on farm productivity in developing economies. Regulation is also pivotal to innovation. Without adequate assurance of intellectual property rights (see Chapter 5), it is difficult to see how innovators can be incentivised to produce innovations. In the nineteenth century, one of the main complaints against the US was that it did not recognise the copyright of European authors. This meant that US publishers were able to reproduce books without having to pay royalties to European authors. Today, one of the main problems faced by music and software businesses is the illegal copying of their work. The OECD (2007) estimated that this cost around US$200 billion in 2005.

A second argument in support of regulation is that it protects the consumer. Anyone who has ever taken a taxi in London will be aware that the driver of the Hackney Cab knows where they are going. This is in stark contrast to other capital cities, such as Washington or Paris, or large cities such as Sydney, where the taxi service has 'light touch regulation'. Here a trip in a taxi can be a bit of a 'magical mystery' tour for the unfortunate passenger. But this 'consumer protection' provided in London does not happen by chance.

The concern for the consumer that London requires of its taxi drivers is unusual, but is in practice no different from many other occupations. In every country, it is accepted that doctors are required to undergo rigorous scrutiny and a long period of training before they can practise. Since many doctors ultimately become small businesses, their regulation is accepted almost without question.

Illustration	Putting London's cabbies to the test

Taxi drivers in London must pass a variety of tests before being legally allowed to operate.

Driving a black cab in London is not just a matter of picking up your keys and jumping in your cab, there are a few things you need to do before you can get your licence to drive.

- Firstly you have to be police checked to make sure you have a clean driving licence and no criminal record.

- You must also undertake a medical examination to ensure you're a fit and healthy person to drive a taxi.

- You have to pass the world's most intensive taxi training course known as the 'Knowledge'. The test itself dates back to 1865 and has changed little since. It requires a driver to have a detailed knowledge of central London within a radius of six miles of Charing Cross Station. There are some 25,000 roads and streets, 320 runs or routes across town, as well as places of interest, tourist attractions and important landmarks to learn – a goal that takes on average 40 months to achieve.

Source: London Taxi blog, 29 October 2008.

Make the case for and against the following business activities being regulated. Here regulation is defined to be:

1 a police check to eliminate those with a criminal record;
2 a lengthy apprenticeship period;
3 a licence which is periodically reviewed;
4 a test of competence associated with the issue of the licence;
5 regular audited accounts to confirm financial probity;
6 a transparent customer complaints procedure which can lead to licence revocation.

So, what businesses should be regulated in this way?

- Solicitors?
- Plumbers?
- Builders?
- Electricians?
- Taxi drivers?
- Child minders?
- Hairdressers?
- Convenience stores?

A second justification for regulation is to protect consumers from fraud. Ensuring that rogues are identified and prohibited from trading is clearly in the public interest, but implementing that protection may require, as a minimum condition for protecting the consumer, that businesses are registered. Yet, as we saw in the section above, business registration is seen as a 'regulatory burden'.

Illustration | **There's no business like showbusiness in Cardiff**

Hero of the week is Neil McEvoy, the Plaid Cymru deputy leader of Cardiff council. He's convinced the local hoteliers association to ban wannabe talent outfits. We've [*Mirror* newspaper] repeatedly exposed these shysters, who hold recruitment sessions in hotels where they fleece showbiz hopefuls. Most never find any work and, worse, are often passed on to other rip-off outfits. Neil took up the fight after one agency, Models Direct, told him he had a great future as a model, if he paid £128. 'Bear in mind I'm 39, and five foot six', he said.

Source: 'Here's One Place Where Rip-Off Showbiz Agencies are Banned, Thanks to Plaid Cymru', *Mirror*, 23 April 2009.

Question:

Is Neil McEvoy a hero of the week or is he an interfering regulatory bureaucrat?

Kitching (2006) argues, therefore, that 'arguments against' regulations are based upon a narrow view of the impact of regulation. He suggests, instead, that regulation was necessary for all economies and can actually do as much good as harm. For instance, he suggested that giving workers minimum wages in the UK caused little disruption to small businesses because they were largely able to pass these costs on to consumers. BERR (2008) also suggested that environmental regulations can open up markets and create societal benefits. An example of this is widespread government support and incentives to create new energy markets in renewable energy sectors (e.g. solar, wind and sea power).

There are also methodological issues in understanding the role of regulation. Kitching (2006) argued that studies which concentrated on small business owner perceptions of regulation tended to be flawed. For example, some owners may perceive regulation as negative but, in practice, actually use regulations to support or develop their business. Equally, much of the data used to measure regulation is imperfect (Crafts 2006). One example of this is that the 'arguments against' regulation tend to rely upon World Bank (2009) 'ease of doing business' data. The problem with this source is that it relies on the following definition of a 'typical' business:

- operates in the 'formal' economy;

- is a limited liability company;

- is 100% domestically owned and has five owners, none of whom is a legal entity;

- has start-up capital of ten times income per capita at the end of 2007, paid in cash (World Bank 2009).

There are three problems with this definition:

1 As Schneider (2005) showed, very many businesses in the world operate in the informal economy.

2 The 'typical' business looks nothing like the World Bank definition. A more typical small business might be one that is a sole proprietorship/partnership, has fewer than five employees (including owners) and starts up with very modest levels of finance.

3 Instead, the World Bank definition looks more like a definition of 'corporate entrepreneurship' (Acs *et al.* 2008). As such, the more typical business under its definition would be a medium-sized business. We have already seen that these types of business are more likely to pay more taxes as a percentage of their sales in developing economies.

Other evidence suggests that, in developed economies, the main impact of 'burdensome' regulation is primarily to change the nature, rather than the quantity, of entrepreneurship. Capelleras *et al.* (2008) showed there are marked differences between 'heavily' regulated Spain and 'lightly' regulated England when only registered businesses were examined. They showed that the Spanish businesses started larger and grew more slowly than the English businesses – confirming the result of Bartelsman *et al.* (2005). However, when all businesses were included (registered and unregistered), these differences in size and growth patterns disappeared. Capelleras *et al.* explain this by suggesting that regulation places a 'fixed' cost on a new business. So, it is rational only for the larger business to register if enforcement is imperfect. It means that government statistics that record the number of new businesses are strongly influenced by the regulatory regime and that the prime impact of licensing regulations is to influence the distribution of enterprises between the formal and the informal sectors, rather than influencing the total number of enterprises. van Stel *et al.* (2007) found similar results in their study of 39 countries.

Gohmann *et al.* (2008) and McMullen *et al.* (2008) also specifically examined the relationship between 'economic freedom' (an index of the level of deregulation in an economy) and entrepreneurial outcomes. Gohmann *et al.* (2008) found that the impact of economic freedom varied by sector whilst McMullen *et al.* (2008) found that the impact depended on the type of business set up.

Loayza *et al.* (2004) and Gørgens *et al.* (2003) also identify that most of the benefits of deregulation are found for developing economies with weak systems of government and heavy regulation rather than developing economies with mature regulatory frameworks.

Overall, Crafts' (2006) review suggested that:

> . . . in heavily regulated third-world countries recent deregulation has been good for growth, but that among the relatively lightly regulated OECD countries it has not made any difference.

(p. 197)

Overall, therefore, regulation does have benefits. This may be because consumers (taxpayers) see advantages in limiting and restraining the activities of some businesses or because 'active' regulation can enhance societal outcomes. Furthermore, the case for small business deregulating may be overstated either because of methodological weaknesses in the studies that have examined this topic or because, particularly in developed economies, the benefits are modest.

The regulatory policy challenge

Regulation is not binary: governments do not either regulate or not regulate. Instead, they have to make decisions on the balance of regulation. More regulation risks killing off or pushing underground enterprising individuals whose activities benefit the rest of society. It can also encourage rent-seeking schemes (e.g. corruption, bribery) on the part of bureaucrats. On the other hand, less regulation may lead to unsuitable individuals running businesses that might swindle customers, exploit their workers, and pollute the atmosphere.

Governments throughout the world have to face this delicate balance. Some will continue to see advantage in further deregulation. The World Bank (2009) argues that there are tangible benefits in following the lead of New Zealand which has a single unified online procedure for starting a business, no capital requirements and no judges involved in setting up a business.

However, what is more likely to happen is a greater emphasis on 'smart regulation' – defined as achieving the same regulatory goals, or perhaps even tighter ones – but in a much more cost-effective way. Hampton (2005), for example, argues that existing administrative costs can be reduced by co-ordinating amongst government departments the need for 'form filling' by using smart IT-based forms. Enforcement of regulations could also follow a 'lighter' touch so that businesses are given greater guidance rather than immediate fines when they contravene regulations. Another 'smart' initiative is the introduction of 'common commencement days' for regulation. The thinking behind such an initiative is that it saves business owners from having to constantly be aware of when separate regulations come into force. With one common commencement date, the business owner only has to scan for relevant regulations once or twice a year.

A second, but related, trend is the more extensive use of assessments to test the impact of new regulations on small businesses. Typically, these seek to consult a range of parties on the proposed regulation, investigate its likely costs and benefits, and how the regulation is likely to be monitored and evaluated after it has been introduced. The potential advantage of 'thinking small first' is that it is intended to reduce the regressive nature of regulatory costs on small businesses.

However, despite these good intentions, even for a lightly regulated economy such as the UK, regulation is pervasive. Hampton (2005) identified that there were 63 national regulators and 468 local authorities involved in regulation whilst, as we showed at the start of this section, the CBI (2009) identified that 'regulation' cost UK businesses £77 billion between 1998 and 2008. Of this, 70 per cent is attributable to EU regulations over which the UK has only a modest influence.

Overall, regulation is always likely to be a thorny issue of contention between government and the small business community. Despite promises of various political parties of a 'bonfire of regulations', the reality has consistently disappointed small businesses.

20.5 Immigration policies

In Chapters 8 and 14, we showed that immigration was an important explanation for why people set up and grow a business. We argued that immigrants could be seen as a self-selecting sample of individuals because they were likely to be more entrepreneurial than those who remained behind in their country. Public policy, therefore, may wish to attract such individuals so as to enhance the entrepreneurial skills and abilities of the host nation. Hence, an entrepreneurship policy may be to encourage higher education students to come to study in a country, in the expectation that they will remain in the host country and go on to develop their business there. Saxenian (2000), for example, found that many new Silicon Valley businesses were set up by immigrants from China and India who had come to the US to study.

Entrepreneurship and small business policy towards immigrants, however, may be much more *selective* than this. First, policy can encourage individual workers and businesses to re-locate from one area of a country to another. The expectation, again, is that this will help drive up productivity in the host country. Policy makers may also be active in selecting particular types of workers to come and work in (and hopefully run) successful small businesses. We showed in Chapter 14 that one early example of this was the active targeting of German Jews by the UK government. Loebl (1978) related that German Jews were more likely to successfully flee persecution from Nazi Germany if they had a business background and were willing to set up a business in an 'unfavoured' area of the UK.

Levie (2007) provides one of the few studies that investigate the relationship between in-migration, immigration and its links to the wider study of 'ethnicity'. His conclusions were that in-migrants (movers from one region to another) and immigrants were more likely to set up a business than 'life-long' residents. He suggested that this was due to the in-migrants and immigrants being better educated and more positive about entrepreneurial opportunities. However, he also found that ethnic minorities were *less* likely to set up a business. He suggested that the explanation for this was due to the individuals in his sample being younger. As we saw in Chapter 8, younger people are less likely to move into self-employment/business ownership.

Another implication of immigration is that it has potential benefits to the donor countries. Ghencea and Gudumac (2004) examined the role of remittances (money sent back) in supporting Moldovian businesses. They found that, whilst the number of business activities practised by the migrant families had not increased, the businesses were larger and more profitable than before the migration took place. McCormick and Wahba (2001) also showed that amongst literate Egyptians, business ownership upon return is more likely amongst those with savings accumulated overseas and amongst those who had spent a longer period abroad. They argued that any losses to the donor countries of enterprising individuals who migrated to work in more prosperous economies were only temporary. Indeed, it was the overseas work experience which provided them with a range of skills that they would never have accumulated by staying in their home country. Black and Castaldo (2009) provide similar results for returnees to Ghana and Côte D'Ivoire.

These findings help explain the active campaigns run by governments seeking to persuade those who have emigrated to return home, often with the intention of starting a business. High-profile campaigns have, for example, been run in Scotland and New Zealand. What is less clear is how well the businesses started by returnees subsequently performs (Black and Castaldo 2009).

It is clear that the migration of individuals across national borders is a source of entrepreneurship for host countries. However, the issue for policy makers is that a set of entrepreneurship and SME policies that encourage immigration may run counter to other policy objectives. The OECD (2008) estimated that, for example, 2.5 million temporary workers arrived in OECD countries in 2005. It also found the number of foreign students increased by 50 per cent over the period 2000–5.

Overall, the crucial issue is that decisions about these flows into countries, despite having potentially huge significance for entrepreneurship, are very unlikely to be made by the ministry responsible for small business. A much louder voice in government is likely to be the ministry responsible for security whose focus will be directed towards more selective and probably small-scale immigration. So, whilst government departments may agree that there is a positive relationship between immigration and entrepreneurship, the 'real politic' is that governments in the developed world are increasingly concerned about letting people into their country.

20.6 Competition policies and government procurement

In this final section, we examine competition policies and government procurement. In terms of competition policies, governments throughout the world have policies in place which are designed to allow 'free and fair' competition in the marketplace. They seek to ensure that the abuse of market power is prevented. Such abuses are where businesses operate a cartel whose members either formally or informally agree to not compete with each other on price, in particular areas or for particular customers.

Illustration	The airlines' cartel

A cartel was found to be operating in the airline industry: airlines such as Air France, KLM, Cathay Pacific, Martinair Holland and SAS Cargo were found to have fixed the price of international cargo rates. These companies were fined a total of US$504 million by regulators. Fines were also levied on other airline companies (e.g. Quantas, Korean Airlines, British Airways) for similar anti-competitive behaviour.

It may be thought that competition policies are likely to benefit small businesses because, other things being equal, they are more likely to be the abused than the abuser. In practice, however, many small business owners are unlikely to be easily persuaded that competition policy is in their best interests for the following reasons:

● The ultimate beneficiary of competition policies is the consumer. Increased competition should lead to lower prices and better quality offers to consumers. Many small business owners may recognise that enhancing competition could undermine the viability of their business.

● Many owners are fundamentally suspicious of all aspects of government, and view policy changes as yet another 'burden'.

● Many small business owners, even if affected by unfair competition, will be unaware of their rights of appeal.

● Many small business owners will not be able to distinguish between competition which is fair, but damaging to them, and that which is unfair (see Case study 1).

Storey (2005) showed that although one third of small businesses were aware of anti-competitive practices, and one quarter had experienced such practices, their most frequent reaction to anti-competitive behaviour was to ignore it. However, he also argued that responses varied. He found that educated, well-informed owners who were running growing businesses were more likely to take action against unfair competition, whilst those without these characteristics were more likely to ignore such practices and accept them as part of the 'cut and thrust' of business life.

Arguably, competition frameworks are well developed, at least in advanced economies. For instance, in the EU, businesses found guilty of anti-competitive behaviour can be fined as much as 10 per cent of their worldwide turnover and individuals involved can be imprisoned and disqualified from being a director. However, proving anti-competitive behaviour is difficult and, again, is a policy that is set for all businesses rather than for SMEs.

Where SMEs can benefit disproportionately from competition policy is in the area of finance. As we noted in Chapter 17, competition in the debt finance market is critical to ensuring SMEs have appropriate access to finance and are charged an interest rate that reflects the risk of the loan. The following Illustration reflects the efforts of the UK government to ensure this marketplace is competitive.

Illustration	The UK Competition Commission

In 2002, the UK Competition Commission published a review of the supply of banking services to SMEs. Its prime conclusion was that this marketplace could be characterised as a 'complex monopoly'. The Competition Commission held that there was insufficient effective competition amongst suppliers in this marketplace. The Commission's view was based upon the following six elements:

1 There is a significant market concentration with perhaps 90 per cent of liquidity (cash) management services being provided by four banks. This means that the providers of these services have considerable market power to raise their prices and obtain higher profits than would be the case if the marketplace were more competitive.

2 This market concentration has remained broadly unchanged for up to 20 years. Whilst there have been some mergers and takeovers, it is broadly the same four banks that have dominated the marketplace over this period of time.

3 Although the Commission was unable to provide clear evidence of this, its view was that the four banks colluded together since initiatives taken by one bank were usually followed very swiftly by the other banks following suit.

4 The profitability to the banks of lending to small businesses was high. At that time, the Commission estimated that profits to the banks on services to SMEs exceeded £2 billion per year. It also estimated that the average return on equity between 1998 and 2000 was 36 per cent, compared with an estimated cost of equity of about 15 per cent.

5 The Commission observed that relatively few businesses switched banks. It interpreted this as reflecting the difficulties that banks imposed on their customers wishing to switch, and the view of the customers that the four banks provided almost identical packages which would make switching of little value.

6 Whilst some building societies (mutuals) had converted into banks, there were almost no new entrants into the marketplace for providing finance to SMEs. Given that this marketplace was clearly highly profitable, the Commission inferred that the incumbent banks were able to deter new entrants.

Overall, therefore, the Commission concluded that this was a highly ossified marketplace in which banks were able to exploit a lack of choice on the part of SMEs. They were also able to deter entry of new competitors and the four banks, acting together, were able to exercise monopoly powers. The view of the Commission was that the marketplace could be made more competitive if more SMEs were able to switch.

However, this happened rarely. The Commission investigated this and came to the conclusion that this reluctance was for six reasons:

1 It was complex to switch and there were few finance benefits in the form of lower bank charges, access to finance or interest rate charged.

2 The perception on the part of the SME that the ability to access finance, particularly when the business was in difficulties, was heavily dependent upon maintaining good personal relationships with bank managers or with a particular bank branch.

3 The Commission reported, however, that in a number of cases the threat of the SME to switch banks did result in lower charges or improved service but curiously this threat seemed to be employed by few SME owners.

4 The Commission noted that many SMEs in the UK preferred to purchase all their financial services from a single supplier. This contrasted with somewhere such as Italy, where multiple banking was the norm for SMEs.

5 The Commission found that SMEs viewed the price thay paid for services and for loans was of secondary importance compared with what the SME perceived as the quality of the service. Hence, switching seemed to be primarily a response to bad service, rather than a response to high charges.

6 The Commission viewed the marketplace as a whole as characterised by a lack of transparency both in the determination of availability and the price of overdrafts and loans. In other words, it found that SMEs were not fully aware of the prices that they were paying or the price at which they could obtain such services

▶

from a competitor bank. In part, the Commission viewed this as a deliberate ploy on the part of the banks to be opaque.

The banks' response to the Commission's report was the following:

● They challenged the Commission's profitability figures which it will be recalled were averaged over the period between 1998 and 2000. The banks pointed out that this was a period of exceptional macro-economic prosperity during which time it was reasonable for the banks to make relatively high profits. They contrasted this with the recession in 1991 when banks were reportedly losing £2 million per day in bad debts in the SME sector. The banks emphasised that, if the government wished banks to perform a crucial economic function over a long period of time, then it was appropriate to examine profitability over the full duration of the economic cycle, rather than during a short period of prosperity.

● The banks provided a very different justification for the high levels of concentration. They argued that the reason why four banks dominated the marketplace was because they were able to obtain the benefits and economies of scale and not because of the raising of any artificial barriers. The banks pointed out that, although the number of financial institutions was stable over time, it reflected the unwillingness of organisations to enter this marketplace because it was too risky and fiercely competitive. This was because the existing banks had all accumulated considerable expertise in assessing propositions from SMEs. They had sophisticated credit scoring systems, developed in-house by each bank, which enabled them to accurately judge risky propositions. New entrants, understandably, lacked that expertise and the ability to make profitable lending and it was for this reason that entry rates were low. It was not because of artificial barriers being raised by the incumbent banks.

● The banks also responded to the comments by the Commission on switching. They argued that low switching rates were not, as the commission implied, because of restrictions imposed by the banks. Instead, the reason why comparatively little switching took place was because customers were happy with the services that they received. The banks pointed out that even the Commission had agreed that satisfaction levels were high, that the vast majority – perhaps 90 per cent – of SMEs seeking funding from banks were accepted, and for that reason customer satisfaction was high.

The government's response was broadly to favour the Competition Commission's interpretation over the banks. The government emphasised that its objective was to stimulate competition amongst providers of finance to the SME sector. It, therefore, made the following three key recommendations:

● Banks would have to provide interest to SMEs on monies deposited in current accounts. This presumably was intended to lower the profitability of the banks.

● To respond to the concern of the Competition Commission by making it easier for SMEs to switch, requiring banks to transfer information on credit history speedily to alternative banks.

● Finally, to enhance the quality of information, the government required banks to reduce the 'bundling' of services so as to make it more transparent to the SME what they are paying for, and to make it clear that they do not necessarily have to buy the whole of the bundle.

Questions

Matters have changed importantly since 2002. First, access to credit has become more difficult worldwide. Second, in several countries some banks have considerably greater public ownership than in the past.
Given those changes:

1 *What policies would you recommend to a government which has part ownership of a bank, if your purpose is to increase the scale of lending to small businessess?*

2 *What policies would you recommend to a government seeking to increase lending to small businessess when the bank is not in public ownership?*

3 *What difference does it make if some, but not all, banks are owned by the government?*

Governments are also major consumers of goods and services. Clark and Moutray (2004) estimated that the US federal government purchased $307.5 billion of goods and services in 2003. The Glover Report (2008) estimated that government procurement in the UK was £175 billion per annum or about 13 per cent of UK GDP. Morand (2003), however, shows that, whilst small businesses provide about 65 per cent of private sector sales in the EU, their share of public contracts won directly (excluding sub-contracting) was less than 25 per cent. Clark and Moutray (2004) also found that small businesses gained a similar share of US federal government procurement contracts.

It may be argued that this 'imbalance' is a natural outcome of the marketplace. There are several reasons for this:

1 Government contracts are often sizeable and it may be that small businesses do not have the resources to successfully deliver such projects.

2 Small businesses are risky. They have higher failure rates than larger businesses, making them less attractive to risk-averse politicians and civil servants.

3 Small businesses often lack a 'brand'. In practice, they are less likely than larger businesses to be 'known' to politicians and civil servants.

4 Tendering costs and procedures place high entry barriers on businesses. Because public money is at stake, politicians and civil servants often introduce procedures to vet businesses in the tendering process.

5 Government may also seek safeguards or guarantees once any tender has been offered. This is likely to involve significant administrative costs to the business. These costs are likely to be regressive: large businesses may be able to 'spread' these costs across a number of projects whilst a small business, going for only one project at a time, has less opportunity to spread costs.

To increase the 'share' of public procurement projects won by small businesses, several countries have changed their practices:

● Moving to e-procurement which offers the potential of reducing the administrative burdens faced by small businesses.

● Legislating to 'reserve' or 'set aside' a set number or percentage of government contracts specifically for small businesses.

● Standardising tendering documents and monitoring information to reduce the administrative costs of applying for, and managing, a government contract.

Although these may seem mundane reforms they can make a real difference to the ability of small businesses to submit informed tenders for government work. For example, a survey of Swedish small businesses showed that 85 per cent of them had successfully won government procurement contracts. The suggested reason for this high success rate was the visibility and accessibility of such programmes (cited in the Glover Report 2008).

Nonetheless, yet again, there are real issues in balancing the interests of the taxpayer with those of the small businesses. In the US, for example, government departments are mandated to set aside a proportion of their contracts for small businesses. This approach was considered in the UK, but the Glover Report (2008) rejected it, largely because it could lead to wider distortions in competition policies.

Overall, SMEs value a competitive market for finance and being given access to government contracts on the basis of a 'level playing field'. Delivering these requirements has, however, proved difficult for many governments.

Summary

The aim of this chapter has been to examine public policy in terms of macro-economic factors, taxation, regulation, immigration and competition policies. We showed that these are powerful influences on small business activity, particularly because SMEs and entrepreneurs are so exposed to uncertainties in the external environment. The impact of public policies – which seek to balance the interests of the taxpayer and businesses – are likely to be highly regressive, with the costs of complying with taxation and other forms of regulation falling disproportionately on SMEs and entrepreneurs.

There may be a case for giving small businesses special 'treatment' or for deregulation. This seems particularly beneficial for developing economies where there are undue restrictions on the entry and growth of small businesses in particular markets. There also seems particular value in addressing how government procurement contracts are administered and ensuring the market for SME finance is competitive. However, there is less of a consensus about the role that regulation and taxation play in developed economies. There are powerful arguments to suggest that instead of giving special tax treatment to small businesses the 'playing field' should be levelled to restrict opportunities for tax evasion and other distorting effects. Equally, there is also a balance to be struck in developed economies between the interests of taxpayers and businesses to ensure both efficiency and equity.

Public policy makers, therefore, face complex choices. What is very clear from this chapter is that although a small business ministry is often given ownership of 'small business' policies, very many of the decisions that directly affect small businesses are made by other government departments. For example, immigration policies are often decided by interior ministries whilst environmental and labour-market regulations are often administered and delivered by a multitude of different agencies, and taxation policies are always the province of the finance department.

Placing small businesses at the heart of government remains problematic for several reasons. First, entrepreneurs and SMEs are only two constituencies: a government may consider that what is more important is the interests of the general taxpayer or, in less just societies, politicians and civil servants may corruptly seek their own returns. Moreover, even if small businesses are placed at the centre of economic policy, there remains the problem that small businesses are heterogeneous and, subsequently, have different interests. This makes it more difficult for any small business ministry to effectively co-ordinate policy.

Our modest suggestion is that, as a minimum, each country should have a forum where small business issues and perspectives can be discussed at a strategic level within government. This perhaps would allow for more integrated policy choices to be made.

Questions for discussion

1 Should taxes be lower for smaller businesses?
2 Discuss the arguments for and against business regulation.
3 Does regulation impact on the scale or just the distribution of entrepreneurship between productive, unproductive and destructive entrepreneurship?
4 Review the evidence of whether governments can enhance the competitiveness of the market for SME finance.

References

Acs, Z.J., Desai, S. and Klapper, L.F. (2008) 'What Does "Entrepreneurship" Data Really Show?', *Small Business Economics*, 31(3), 265–81.

Barseghyan, L. (2008) 'Entry Costs and Cross-country Differences in Productivity and Output', *Journal of Economic Growth*, 13(2), 145–67.

Bartelsman, E., Scarpetta, S. and Schivardi, F. (2005) 'Comparative Analysis of Firm Demographics and Survival: Evidence from Micro-level Sources in OECD Countries', *Industrial and Corporate Change*, 14(3), 365–91.

Baumol, W.J. (1990) 'Entrepreneurship: Productive, Unproductive and Destructive', *Journal of Political Economy*, 98, 893–921.

BERR (2008) *Impact of Regulation on Productivity*. BERR Occasional Paper, 3. London: BERR.

Bertrand, M. and Kramarz, F. (2002) 'Does Entry Regulation Hinder Job Creation?: Evidence from the French Retail Industry', *Quarterly Journal of Economics*, 117(4), 1369–413.

Black, R. and Castaldo, A. (2009) 'Return Migration and Entrepreneurship in Ghana and Côte d'Ivoire: The Role of Capital Transfers', *Tijdschrift voor Economische en Sociale Geografie*, 100(1), 44–58.

Bruce, D. (2000) 'Effects of the US Tax System on Transitions into Self-employment', *Labour Economics* 7(5), 545–74.

Bruce, D. and Mohsin, M. (2006) 'Tax Policy and Entrepreneurship: New Time Series Evidence', *Small Business Economics*, 26(5), 409–25.

Capelleras, J.L., Mole, K.F., Greene, F.J. and Storey, D.J. (2008) 'Do More Heavily Regulated Economies Have Poorer Performing New Ventures?: Evidence from Britain and Spain', *Journal of International Business Studies*, 39(4), 688–704.

Carroll, R., Holtz-Eakin, D., Rider, M. and Rosen, H.S. (2001) 'Personal Income Taxes and the Growth of Small Firms', in Poterba, J. (ed.), *Tax Policy and the Economy*, Volume 15. Cambridge, MA: MIT Press, 121–48.

Chemin, M. (2009) 'The Impact of the Judiciary on Entrepreneurship: Evaluation of Pakistan's "Access to Justice Programme"', *Journal of Public Economics*, 93(1–2), 114–25.

Chittenden, F. and Sloan, B. (2007) 'Quantifying Inequity in the Taxation of Individuals and Small Firms', *British Tax Review*, 1, 58–72.

Chittenden, F., Kauser, S. and Poutziouris, P. (2005) 'PAYE-NIC Compliance Costs: Empirical Evidence from the UK SME Economy', *International Small Business Journal*, 23(6), 635–56.

Clark, M. and Moutray, C. (2004) *The Future of Small Businesses in the US Federal Government Marketplace*. Washington, DC: SBA.

Confederation of British Industry (2009) *Burdens Barometer 2009*. London: CBI.

Crafts, N. (2006) 'Regulation and Productivity Performance', *Oxford Review of Economic Policy*, 22(2), 186–202.

Crain, M.W. (2005) *The Impact of Regulatory Costs on Small Firms*. Washington, DC: SBA.

Crawford, C. and Freedman, J. (2008) *Small Business Taxation*. London: Institute for Fiscal Studies.

Davis, S.J. and Henrekson, M. (1999) 'Explaining National Differences in the Size and Industry Distribution of Employment', *Small Business Economics*, 12(1), 59–83.

Dennis, W.J. (2004) 'Creating and Sustaining a Viable Small Business Sector'. Paper presented at the School of Continuing Education, University of Oklahoma, 27 Oct.

Djankov, S., La Porta, R., Lopez-de-Silanes, F. and Schleifer, A. (2002) 'The Regulation of Entry', *Quarterly Journal of Economics*, CXVII(1), 1–37.

Djankov, S., McLiesh, C. and Ramalho, R.M. (2006) 'Regulation and Growth', *Economic Letters*, 92(3), 395–401.

Engström, P. and Holmlund, B. (2009) 'Tax Evasion and Self-employment in a High-tax Country: Evidence from Sweden', *Applied Economics* (forthcoming).

European Commission (2008) *Entrepreneurship Survey of the EU (25 Member States), US, Iceland and Norway*, Flash EB Series No. 192. Brussels: European Commission.

Folster, S. (2002) 'Do Lower Taxes Stimulate Self-employment?', *Small Business Economics*, 19(2), 135–45.

Georgellis, Y. and Wall, H.J. (2006) 'Entrepreneurship and the Policy Environment', *Federal Reserve Bank of St Louis Review*, 88(2), 95–111.

Ghencea, B. and Gudumac, I. (2004) *Labour Migration and Remittances in the Republic of Moldova*. Moldova: Soros Institute.

Glover Report (2008) *Accelerating the SME Economic Engine: Through Transparent, Simple and Strategic Procurement*. London: HM Treasury.

Gohmann, S.F., Hobbs, B.K. and McCrickard, M. (2008) 'Economic Freedom and Service Industry Growth in the US', *Entrepreneurship: Theory and Practice*, 32(5), 855–74.

Gørgens, T., Paldam, M. and Würtz, A. (2003) *How Does Public Regulation Affect Growth?* Working Paper 2003-14. Aarhus: University of Aarhus.

Gropp, R., Scholz, J.-K. and White, M.J. (1997) 'Personal Bankruptcy and Credit Supply and Demand', *Quarterly Journal of Economics*, 112(1), 217–51.

Gurley-Calvez, T. and Bruce, D. (2008) 'Do Tax Cuts Promote Entrepreneurial Longevity?', *National Tax Journal*, 61(2), 225–50.

Hampton Report (2005) *Reducing Administrative Burdens: Effective Inspection and Enforcement*. London: HM Treasury.

HM Treasury/BERR (2008) *Enterprise: Unlocking the UK's Talent*. HM Treasury/BERR: London.

Her Majesty's Revenue and Customs (HMRC) (2005) *Estimation of Tax Gap for Direct Taxes*. London: HMRC.

Japan Small Business Research Institute (JSBRI) (2006) *White Paper on Small and Medium Enterprises in Japan 2006: Small and Medium Enterprises at a Turning Point – Strengthening Ties with Overseas Economies and Population Decline in Japan*. Tokyo: JSBRI.

Jersild, T. and Skopljak, Z. (2009) 'How to Double Business Entry in Two Years', in *Celebrating Reform*. Washington, DC: World Bank, 15–19.

Kitching, J. (2006) 'A Burden on Business?: Reviewing the Evidence Base on Regulation and Small-Business Performance', *Environment and Planning C: Government and Policy*, 24, 799–814.

Klapper, L., Amit, R., Guillén, M.R. and Quesada, J.M. (2007) *Entrepreneurship and Firm Formation Across Countries*. Policy Research Working Paper 4313. Washington, DC: World Bank.

Klapper, L., Laeven, L. and Rajan, R. (2006) 'Entry Regulation as a Barrier to Entrepreneurship', *Journal of Financial Economics*, 82, 591–629.

La Porta, R., Lopez-De-Silanes, F. and Shleifer, A. (2008) 'The Economic Consequences of Legal Origins', *Journal of Economic Literature*, 46(2), 285–332.

Levie, J. (2007) 'Immigration, In-migration, Ethnicity and Entrepreneurship in the United Kingdom', *Small Business Economics*, 28(2–3), 143–69.

Loayza, N., Oviedo, A.M. and Serven, L. (2004) *Regulation and Macroeconomic Performance*. Policy Research Working Paper 3469. Washington, DC: World Bank.

Loebl, H. (1978) Government Financed Factories and the Establishment of Industries by Refugees in the Special Areas of the North of England 1937–1961. M. Phil. thesis, Durham University.

Maddison, A. (2003) *Historical Statistics for the World Economy: 1–2003 AD*. www.ggdc.net/maddison/Historical_Statistics/horizontal-file_03-2007.xls (accessed 7 May 2009).

McCormick, B. and Wahba, J. (2001) 'Overseas Work Experience, Savings and Entrepreneurship amongst Return Migrants to LDCs', *Scottish Journal of Political Economy*, 48(2), 164–78.

McMullen, J.S., Bagby, D.R. and Palich, L.E. (2008) 'Economic Freedom and the Motivation to Engage in Entrepreneurial Action', *Entrepreneurship: Theory and Practice*, 32(5), 875–95.

Michaelas, N., Chittenden, F. and Poutziouris, P. (1999) 'Financial Policy and Capital Structure Choice in UK SMEs: Empirical Evidence from Company Panel Data', *Small Business Economics*, 12(2), 113–30.

Morand, P.-H. (2003) 'SMEs and Public Procurement Policy', *Review of Economic Design*, 8(3), 301–18.

National Audit Office (NAO) (2006) *Supporting Small Businesses*. Report by the Comptroller and Auditor General, HC 972, Session 2005–6, 24 May. London: HMSO.

Newton, J., Solf, S. and Vicentini, A. (2009) 'Starting a Business (Quickly) in El Salvador', in *Celebrating Reform*. Washington, DC: World Bank, 9–14.

Nicoletti, G. and Scarpetta, S. (2003) *Regulation, Productivity and Growth: OECD Evidence*. New York: World Bank.

Nystrom, K. (2008) 'The Institutions of Economic Freedom and Entrepreneurship: Evidence from Panel Data', *Public Choice*, 136(3–4), 269–82.

OECD (2003) *From Red Tape to Smart Tape*. Paris: OECD.

OECD (2007) *The Economic Impact of Counterfeiting and Piracy*. Paris: OECD.

OECD (2008) *International Migration Outlook*. Paris: OECD.

Open Europe (2009) *Out of Control?: Measuring a Decade of EU Regulation*. London: Open Europe.

Parker, S.C. (1996) 'A Time Series Model of Self-employment under Uncertainty', *Economica*, 63, 459–75.

Parker, S.C. and Robson, M.T. (2004) 'Explaining International Variations in Self-employment: Evidence from a Panel of OECD Countries', *Southern Economic Journal*, 71(2), 287–301.

Pope, J. (2009) 'Favourable Small Business Taxation: To What Extent Is It Justified from a Tax Policy Perspective?', *Journal of Applied Law and Policy*, 21–34.

Powell, B. (2002) 'Explaining Japan's Recession', *The Quarterly Journal of Austrian Economics*, 5(2), 35–50.

Purohit, M. (2007) 'Corruption in Tax Administration', in Shah, A. (ed.), *Performance Accountability and Combating Corruption*. Washington, DC: World Bank, 285–301.

Rees, H. and Shah, A. (1994) 'The Characteristics of the Self-employed: The Supply of Labour', in Atkinson, J. and Storey, D.J. (eds), *Employment, the Small Firm and the Labour Market*. London: Routledge.

Robson, M. and Wren, C.M. (1999) 'Marginal and Average Tax Rates and the Incentive for Self-employment', *Southern Economic Journal*, 65(4), 757–73.

Saxenian, A. (2000) *Silicon Valley's New Immigrant Entrepreneurs*. Working Paper 15. San Diego, CA: Center for Comparative Immigration Studies University of California.

SBS (2006) *Annual Small Business Survey 2005*. London: SBS.

SBS (2006) *Annual Survey of Small Businesses*. URN 06/389a. London: SBS.

Schneider, F. (2005) 'Shadow Economies around the World: What Do We Really Know?', *European Journal of Political Economy*, 21, 598–642.

Schuetze, H.J. (2000) 'Taxes, Economic Conditions and Recent Trends in Male Self-employment: A Canada–US Comparison', *Labour Economics*, 7(5), 507–44.

Schuetze, H.J. and Bruce, D. (2004) *Tax Policy and Entrepreneurship*. Paper presented at Conference on Self-employment, 22 March, Stockholm: Economic Council for Sweden.

Shane, S. (1996) 'Explaining Variation in Rates of Entrepreneurship in the US: 1899–1988', *Journal of Management*, 22(5), 747–81.

Slemrod, J. (2004) 'Small Business and the Tax System' in Aaron, H.J. and Slemrod, J. (eds), *The Crisis in Tax Administration*. Washington, DC: Brookings Institution Press, 69–101.

Small Business Service (SBS) (2004) *A Government Action Plan for Small Business*. London: DTI.

Stiglitz, J. (2000) 'Unraveling the Washington Consensus: An Interview with Joseph Stiglitz', *Multinational Monitor*. http://multinationalmonitor.org/mm2000/00april/interview.html (accessed 7 May 2009).

Storey, D.J. (2005) 'The Competitive Experience of UK SMEs: Fair and Unfair'. Report to the Competition Commission. London: unpublished.

Torrini, R. (2005) 'Cross-Country Differences in Self-employment Rates: The Role of Institutions', *Labour Economics*, 12(5), 661–83.

van Stel, A.J., Storey, D.J. and Thurik, A.R. (2007) 'The Effect of Business Regulations on Nascent and Young Business Entrepreneurship', *Small Business Economics*, 28(2–3), 171–86.

World Bank (2004) *Costs of Corruption*. Washington, DC: World Bank.

World Bank (2005) *World Development Report 2005: A Better Investment Climate for Everyone*. Washington, DC: World Bank.

World Bank (2009) *Doing Business 2009*. Washington, DC: World Bank.

21 Policy in practice

Mini contents list

Key learning objectives

By the end of this chapter you should:

● Understand the justifications for SME and entrepreneurship policy interventions

● Be able to provide arguments for and against policy support for SMEs and entrepreneurs

● Be able to evaluate the success of SME and entrepreneurship policy support.

21.1 Introduction

In Chapter 19, we showed that governments in developed countries have a range of policies seeking to enhance the economic and social contribution of small businesses and to promote enterprise creation. A broad distinction was drawn between those policies that were explicitly focused on SMEs and entrepreneurs – which we call *micro policies* – and more general policies – which we call *macro policies*. An important distinction between the two is that the ministry responsible for small businesses has much greater influence over the micro than over the macro policies.

In Chapter 20, we reviewed the macro policies and showed that, although they rarely had SMEs or entrepreneurs as their prime target, their impact on them was often considerable.

In this chapter, we examine those policies that are specifically targeted at SMEs and entrepreneurs. We call these 'micro policies'. Typically, such policies are justified on the grounds of identifiable market failures (see Chapter 19). We examine five key types of intervention practised by governments throughout the world. These broadly correspond to the micro policy elements of the OECD (2008) framework, shown earlier as Figure 19.2:

● developing an 'enterprise culture';

● correcting 'market failure' in the access to, and provision of, finance;

● advice and assistance;

● supporting technology and innovation;

● supporting the entrepreneurial development of particular groups (e.g. women, ethnic minorities).

For each policy area, we begin by describing the rationale underlying the policy. We then provide examples of the policy in practice drawn from a variety of different countries. Finally, we review evidence – where this is available – of the impact of these policies. The role of gathering evidence – what is called monitoring and evaluation – and the reliability of that evidence are discussed in more detail in the fourth part of the public policy case study.

Key terms in this chapter are **additionality**, **deadweight** and **displacement**. Ideally, policy makers have policies that make something happen that would otherwise have not happened (or would not have happened as quickly). Such policies are said to have high additionality. They also seek policies where, for example, the increased sales of a business assisted by policy do not come about purely by the loss of sales from another business – without any benefit to the customer (displacement). Policies are said to have high displacement when any gain to one business is a pure transfer from another. This is viewed as providing little value to the taxpayer. Also, some policies may be prone to deadweight. For example, business support may be offered to young people in order to help them start up their business. However, some, or perhaps most, of these young people may have started their business regardless of the existence of such support.

21.2 Developing an 'enterprise culture'

The rationale for developing an 'enterprise culture' is that if individuals in society develop a more entrepreneurial 'mindset' (European Commission 2003) then there is a greater likelihood of them considering the entrepreneurial option for themselves (see Case study 7 on public policy). If policies can make business entry more attractive, individuals are, other things being equal, more likely to start up a business. These new businesses, in turn, may subsequently grow and deliver economic benefits to the rest of society, such as providing employment or taxes (Chapter 6). Equally, an 'enterprise culture' has important wider spillover benefits in that it reinforces positive cultural attitudes towards entrepreneurship (both in terms of setting up a business for one's self or acting in an intrapreneurial way inside a larger organisation).

Some public policy makers may also perceive that an additional rationale for public policy in this area is that there is an enterprise culture 'gap' between their country and 'competitor' countries. This is a particular concern of European countries (European Commission 2003) because, compared with the US, Europeans appear more cautious about entrepreneurial opportunities. For example, the European Commission (2008a) surveyed around 21,000 people in the EU, US, Iceland and Norway about their attitudes towards entrepreneurship. It found that:

- Around 60 per cent of US citizens preferred to be self-employed, whereas in the EU it was 40 per cent.

- Europeans were more likely to have negative beliefs about entrepreneurs (e.g. entrepreneurs exploit workers; entrepreneurs were only interested in their own 'wallets').

- US citizens saw self-employment as more desirable and feasible than EU citizens.

- 47 per cent of Europeans had never considered setting up a business compared with 27 per cent of Americans.

These differences are present despite the efforts of many EU countries to address this enterprise culture 'gap'. These policies have been primarily targeted at young people and cover changes to the education system, graduate self-employment and work placements in small businesses.

Changing the education system

Arguably, the easiest mechanism for developing an entrepreneurial 'mindset' is through the education system. This is thought necessary for three main reasons. First, youth unemployment (16–24-year-olds) generally is higher than amongst prime age workers (25–55-year-olds). Second, there is also no longer an expectation of a 'job for life' (OECD 2001) and young people's transitions into work have become longer and more difficult. Third, in very many societies – as we have seen in Chapter 8 – significant numbers of the working population are self-employed or have experience of self-employment. The rationale, therefore, for intervening in the education system is that young people need to develop more entrepreneurial skills and abilities, and the education system has a duty to 'prepare' them for the 'world of work'.

Different countries have, therefore, developed a range of policies to promote entrepreneurship at different stages of the education process:

1 *Primary education.* Programmes such as Primary 1 to plc (Scotland), Västerbotten project 'PRIO 1' (Sweden), Mini Society (US), 'entrepreneurial city' (the Netherlands). (Source: European Commission 2004*a*).

2 *Secondary education.* The Davies (2002) report in the UK argued that there was a need for secondary-level students to spend five days studying entrepreneurship. There are also a huge number of other schemes funded either by the public sector or by other means: e.g. Young Enterprise (UK), Junior Achievement (worldwide), Youth Enterprise Society (South Africa), CAEJE (Spain), YESS! (Youth Empowerment and Self-Sufficiency) (US), Young Achievement Australia, Young Enterprise (New Zealand).

3 *Tertiary education.* The key factor here has been the explosion of entrepreneurship courses. Kuratko (2005) identifies that in the US alone there were 2,200 entrepreneurship and small-business courses. This growth, he argued, has occurred since the 1980s. Wilson (2008) argued that similar developments have occurred in Europe since the 1980s.

Besides these initiatives, there have been numerous other 'extra-curricular' initiatives introduced since the 1980s. Some have sought to raise awareness of the entrepreneurial option amongst young people either through providing information and awareness support (e.g. Shell Livewire, 'Enterprise' Weeks) or by using the media.

Pittaway and Cope (2007) have argued that the net effect of these developments has been to increase entrepreneurial intentionality and propensity amongst UK higher education students. Greene and Saridakis (2008) also examined factors that influenced the take-up of self-employment immediately after finishing university. They found that managerial and leadership skills developed at university, and support provided by academics, were important factors for why some graduates entered self-employment. Athayde (2009) and Peterman and Kennedy (2003) found that participation on enterprise programmes led students to see self-employment as both desirable and feasible. More broadly, the European Commission (2008*a*) survey showed that entrepreneurial intentions are higher amongst EU young people than older people.

However, seven criticisms have been levelled against these interventions:

1 Entrepreneurship is a 'talent' which cannot be taught.

2 If it is to be taught, perhaps the only effective mechanism for entrepreneurial learning is through actually setting up a business. Delivery through 'simulated' businesses or through class-based learning is ineffective.

3 Setting up and running a business is an idiosyncratic experience so, even if students set up a 'real' business in school or university, this experience is unlikely to help them significantly in running a business 'in the real world'.

4 Young people are much more likely to see their business fail than older people (see Chapters 9 and 10). Promoting entrepreneurship encourages vulnerable young people to start and then fail, which can have a damaging long-term impact on their future work outcomes.

Promoting new businesses in the media

Television programmes like 'Dragon's Den' and 'The Apprentice' – and their spin-off merchandise – are just one way the media portrays new businesses and entrepreneurs.

Very many countries (e.g. the UK, Afghanistan, Canada, Finland, Nigeria, New Zealand) have broadcast TV programmes that allow new businesses to showcase their products to potential investors. These 'dragon den' reality TV formats are supplemented by other TV programmes that showcase the entrepreneurial skills and abilities of individuals (e.g. 'The Apprentice'). There are also numerous competitions around the world (e.g. Shell Livewire, Nescafé's Big Break, The Global Enterprise Challenge) that, again, attempt to provide role models of successful entrepreneurs.

5   In tertiary education, the favoured method for teaching entrepreneurship involves developing a business plan for a real or a simulated business. From Section 14.2 it will be recalled that Honig (2004) argues that there has been very little evaluation of whether the teaching of business planning actually leads to individuals going on to set up or grow a business. Bygrave *et al.* (2007) go further, arguing that:

> ... unless a would-be entrepreneur needs to raise substantial start-up capital from institutional investors or business angels, there is no compelling reason to write a detailed business plan before opening a new business.

(p. 1)

6   There is little policy coherence in the delivery of enterprise education. This is evident from the myriad of programmes that are available worldwide. For example, Hytti and O'Gorman (2004) identified 50 different programmes in Austria, Finland, Ireland and the UK alone.

Sometimes these programmes may even 'compete' with each other. It is also not clear what the objectives of many programmes are. Some programmes suggest that they are designed to support entrepreneurship outcomes (increased awareness amongst students of how to set up and run a business). However, other programmes seek to provide students with employability skills (e.g. initiative, self-confidence, ability to deal with financial information) that they may use as an employee. Finally, what are the outcomes of such a programme? Does dissuading an individual from setting up and running a business constitute a success?

7 Finally, it is incredibly difficult – if not impossible – to effectively evaluate the impact of enterprise education programmes for two reasons. The first is that they appear to have 'no lose' outcomes. If the person starts a business that is clearly a success, but if the person does not start, that, too, is a success because the course helped them make this decision. Second, if most people set up their business between the ages of 30 and 50, how easy is it to determine the influence of attitudes formed very many years previously? Although Greene and Saridakis (2008) showed that leadership and managerial skills formed at university and academics were influential factors when graduates set up a business immediately after graduation, they also found that these influences 'decayed' to being unimportant if graduates entered self-employment four years later.

Overall, policy makers have become interested in using the education system to promote entrepreneurial 'mindsets'. The rationale behind it is that education is a necessary part of a 'pipeline' leading people to go on to set up and grow their own business. A huge number of programmes around the world provide such education experiences. However, their value is unclear given the lack of policy coherence and the absence of an effective mechanism for evaluating outcomes.

Questions

1 Respond to each of the seven criticisms of enterprise education.

2 Do you think that the only students who need to know about small businesses – and how they differ from large businesses – are those who will start their own businesses?

3 Do you believe that an understanding of small businesses is required by those students who expect to work in large businesses?

4 What types of large private enterprises are most likely to require graduates with a key understanding of small businesses?

5 Is there a case for public sector employees learning about small businesses?

Graduate self-employment

In Chapter 14, we showed that a fairly consistent finding was the association between educational qualifications of the founder and the growth of their business. Broadly, businesses founded by graduates were more likely to grow than those established by non-graduates. It is, therefore, perhaps unsurprising that public policy makers are interested in supporting graduate entrepreneurship. The rationale for such policies is often framed not just in terms of the growth potential of graduate businesses but also in terms of the problems experienced by graduate entrepreneurs or potential entrepreneurs, most notably their relative lack of financial, social or human capital (e.g. level of indebtedness, lack of business contacts and lack of relevant experience).

| Illustration | Encouraging graduate entrepreneurship |

A number of programmes have been implemented since the early 1980s to encourage graduates to become self-employed. One of the earliest was England's Graduate Enterprise Programme which began in 1984. This was a formal course where aspiring entrepreneurs were provided with dedicated training and support over a number of weeks (Brown 1990). Since then, there have been many other schemes as well as increased teaching of entrepreneurship in higher education. Many of these schemes are run by universities themselves (e.g. summer schools, business plan competitions, advice and guidance by academics) as well as by organisations such as the National Council of Graduate Entrepreneurship (UK) or the Kauffman Foundation (US).

The question is: what is the impact of such support on graduate entrepreneurship? One measure might be changes in graduate self-employment rates. Brown (1990), for example, identified that the rate of self-employment amongst graduates six months after graduation was 0.3 per cent in 1983. A follow up study by Graduate Prospects (2005) found that the rate in 2003 was 2.3 per cent. This represents an increase of 767 per cent over the 20-year period.

Rosa (2003), though, investigated the outcomes of students who participated in a Graduate Enterprise Programme in the 1980s. He found that graduates tended '. . . to develop small and unimaginative businesses' (p. 435). Similarly, Greene and Saridakis (2008), after holding a range of other factors constant, found that graduate entrepreneurs earned less than their employed counterparts. They also suggested that, once out of self-employment, former graduate entrepreneurs did not return to self-employment within a four-year period. They argued that self-employment did not represent the realisation of a 'dream' but simply a transitory employment choice until better employment opportunities came along. Castagnetti and Rosti (2009) examined the employment destinations of Italian graduates. They found that higher 'quality' graduates went into waged employment whilst lower 'quality' individuals were effectively 'pushed' into self-employment, even if they wanted to go into waged employment.

In short, whilst it is the case that graduates, if they enter self-employment, have businesses that perform better than those started by non-graduates, this does not justify graduate enterprise programmes. This is because graduates will also earn more than non-graduates as employees. So, even if they can be encouraged to enter self-employment, it is unclear whether this is in the best interests of the graduates or of the country more widely.

Provide work experience for young people in small businesses

One of the objectives of modern education policies has been to ease the transition between the worlds of education and work. Reflecting this was the belief that too many students were leaving school and university without the requisite skills and abilities needed by employers (Weiner 1981). Hence, in secondary education, students have been encouraged to spend time working in a business to gain experience of the 'world of work'.

Higher education students have also been given the opportunity to gain work experience in a small business. Perhaps one of the best known examples is the Shell Technology Enterprise Programme (STEP). This provides undergraduates, in the summer vacation of their second year, with managed work experience in a small business. Their tasks might include writing software programmes, developing of a marketing strategy or scheduling production.

The evaluations of STEP produced two outcomes, one of which was expected, but the other was not. First, Fraser *et al.* (2006) showed, as expected, that STEP students are likely to enter work more quickly upon graduation than otherwise comparable students. However, they found that STEP students were *less* likely to work in a small business immediately after graduation. Fraser *et al.* attribute this to the STEP students being able to demonstrate, in an interview situation, that they had valuable practical experience of having solved challenging business problems, making them more attractive to potential employers of all sizes. Since it is large businesses that pay higher wages, it is with them that new graduates got their first job (see Chapter 4). Of course, it may be that such individuals will be more likely to work for smaller businesses, or start their own business, later in their career but this was not the case shortly after graduation. Again, such results raise questions about the value of policy making in this area. Whilst programmes such as STEP do improve the skills and abilities of under-graduates, the benefits accrue to the student in the form of higher earnings, rather than as a shift in behaviour towards entrepreneurship – at least in the short term.

In general, support for young people in the education system may serve as a useful trans-mission mechanism for developing an enterprise culture and there is evidence that there has been some attitudinal shift towards entrepreneurship, particularly in Europe. Nonetheless, despite the myriad of programmes, there is little compelling evidence pointing to the effectiveness of public policy interventions in these areas.

21.3 Access and provision of finance

We noted in Chapters 16–18 that small businesses are more likely to be subject to financial constraints than larger businesses. Governments have, therefore, chosen to use public funds to enable small businesses to overcome these constraints. This section reviews three micro approaches to overcoming the finance 'gap', in terms of either loans or equity (see also Chapter 20 for macro-economic factors such as governments attempts to enforce competition in finance markets). Again, we begin by describing the policy rationale and giving examples. We then make evidence-based observations about the impact of such policies.

Loan-guarantee schemes

As we argued in Chapter 17, the basic problem in small-business finance is 'informational opacity'. Debt-finance providers (e.g. banks) find it difficult to distinguish between 'good' and 'bad' borrowers and so collect information on the 'track record' of individuals. Since informa-tion collection is costly, the bank may decide that a better mechanism for distinguishing between a good and a bad borrower is to require collateral which compensates them in the event of a default. However, some good business propositions may not have access to collateral – not because the business owner lacks faith in the proposal, but because the business owner is poor and so does not have the required resources.

The basic rationale for a loan-guarantee scheme is that some small businesses may be denied debt finance *only* because they lack collateral. In other words, it is a business proposal that the bank would fund if collateral were available. The role of the public guarantee is then to provide assurance to the profit-seeking bank by underwriting a proportion of the loan in the event of a default by the borrower. Hence, although the borrower typically pays a premium – either in fees or in higher interest rates or both – for their loan, they are not denied debt finance. This resolves the credit constraint faced by smaller businesses which lack collateral.

Publicly funded loan-guarantee schemes (LGS) exist in many countries such as the US, Canada, the UK, Belgium, France and Germany. Their scale varies greatly: for instance, the size of the US's LGS makes it the biggest provider of debt finance to small businesses in the US (Craig *et al.* 2007). In contrast, the Graham (2004) report showed that the UK LGS was very modest in its scope and scale: in 2004, LGS-backed loans represented under 3 per cent of all bank lending to UK small businesses. This, however, changed radically in 2009 when £1 billion was set aside for a small-business guarantee programme.

Table 21.1 shows that the terms and conditions of Loan Guarantee Schemes vary from one country to another, but they normally contain two elements. The first is that not all the loan is underwritten by the government. Instead, typically between 50 per cent and 80 per cent is

| Table 21.1 | International comparisons of loan-guarantee schemes |

Country	US	Netherlands	Denmark	Belgium	France	Germany
Delivery agent	SBA Express	BBMKB	Vaekstkaution	SOWALFIN	SOFARIS	Burschafts-banken
Guarantee	Up to 50%.	Up to 50% for all businesses except for start ups and innovative companies where limit is 75%.	66.67% for loans of up to 350,000 euros. 50% for loans from 350,000 to 700,000 euros.	Up to 75%.	Varies – generally around 50% (average of 45% for 2001). Up to 70% for start ups.	Up to 80% (average between 50% and 80%).
Maximum size of loan	US$250,000.	1 million euros.	700,000 euros but minimum size 10,000 euros.	2.5 million euros.	No limit on loan size but SOFARIS' risk is limited to 750,000 euros.	1 million euros.
Cost of loan	Premium of 1% on loans of US$150,000, 2.5% on loans of US$150–700,000 and 3.5% for loans over US$700,000. An annual fee of 0.25% of the balance of the guaranteed sum is also charged.	One-off commission of 2% to 3.6%.	3% per annum in first two years, 1.5% thereafter.	1% per annum on guaranteed exposure (paid as a one-off and up front fee).	Annual fee of 0.45%–0.60% on the outstanding amount.	0.75% commission on amount guaranteed. Premium of 1% per annum (can be 1.2% for first operation, then 0.8%).
Interest rate	Fixed by lender but between 2.25% and 4.7% above base.	Fixed by government (usually equal to a low risk rate, but the commission is passed on by lenders to borrowers).	Fixed by lender.	Fixed by lender.	Fixed by lender (subject to restrictions ensuring it is a market rate).	Fixed by lender.
Length of loan	Maximum seven years.	Maximum six years (but 12 years for property lending).	3–10 years.	Maximum 10 years but lenders can request longer.	Length of loan guarantee matches length of underlying loan.	Up to 15 years but average of 10 years.
Target firms	Vast majority of SMEs.	Firms up to 100 employees. Special conditions for start ups and innovative companies.	SMEs in six focused areas.	All SMEs.	All SMEs in all phases of their existence. There are 10 different guarantee funds managed by SOFARIS.	All with a focus on start ups.

Source: Graham (2004).

covered – although in the Netherlands and US coverage is below 50 per cent. Second, the business is charged an interest rate premium, and possibly a fee, over and above the interest rate charged by the banks. This can be considered to be a 'risk premium', and is generally in the region of 1 per cent to 3 per cent.

Despite the prevalence of LGS, there have been very few publicly available evaluations of the impact of the schemes. The Graham (2004) report indicated that, because of high default rates of around 30 per cent, the actual cost of the UK LGS to the taxpayer was £60 million. Nonetheless, KPMG's (1999) review of the UK LGS indicated that LGS funding was 'additional' in the sense that without the LGS the loan would not have been provided. However, the wider economic benefits were less clear since there was thought to be high 'displacement' effects (the expansion of one business leads to contraction/loss of another with no clear benefit to the consumer).

More positive findings emerge from the review of the Canadian guarantee system by Riding and Haines (2001). They say that the loans guaranteed under the Small Business Loans Act (SBLA) provide an extremely efficient method of job creation with very low estimated costs per job. Riding *et al.* later (2007) confirm that this funding would not have been available without the SBLA and so the jobs created were genuinely 'additional'.

Grants to small businesses

The rationale for providing grants to small businesses is twofold. First, there are equity considerations: businesses in areas of relative regional deprivation provide jobs and so providing grants gives them an effective cost subsidy which, other things being equal, makes them more competitive. Second, if careful targeting of 'growth' businesses can be achieved, grants may enable businesses to invest more in equipment or training and consultancy support for their managers and employees. Potentially, this investment will enhance their competitiveness.

Roper and Hewitt-Dundas (2001) reviewed the impact of grants provided to small businesses in Northern Ireland and the Republic of Ireland. The provision of grants was substantial, with about half of businesses receiving grants in Northern Ireland and about one third in the Republic. Grants were used to subsidise capital equipment in Northern Ireland, and for training and consultancy in both countries. Their conclusion was that, whilst grants had no effect on profitability or turnover amongst businesses in either country, they did enhance job creation.

The problem with grants is that they may be both distortive and destabilising. The distortive aspect is that a grant may divert investment away from activities which would have been chosen in the absence of the grant: an illustration is where investment is made in plant and machinery in response to the availability of a subsidy, rather than in some other form of investment which would have yielded higher returns. In that case, the subsidy creates an undesirable market distortion. The destabilising effect of grants can also be that, in the long term, they induce a culture of 'grant-hunters' who devote more attention to obtaining subsidies than to running their business in an efficient manner. Lenihan and Hart (2006) in their study of grants provided to businesses in the Shannon region of Ireland find there is also high deadweight and displacement.

Equity finance provision by business angels

One of the typical aims of public policy is to improve the opportunities for business growth. One reason why this may be constrained is because of an inadequate supply of equity finance. As we saw in Chapter 18, equity finance might be more appropriate to the small fast-growth businesses than debt finance because, for example, a high technology business has fewer assets to offer as security for any loan. However, venture capital may not be forthcoming because of the high transaction costs that providers face in assessing a new start-up business. This means that informal equity investments by business angels may be the most appropriate form of support. However, such support may not be supplied for two main reasons:

1 Business angels may be reluctant to identify themselves. Therefore, a role for public policy may be to act as a market 'broker' identifying suitable business angels and businesses and then attempting to bring the two parties together. Publicly funded angel networks are found in, for example, Denmark and Canada. In Denmark, the government has funded the creation of a national business angel network: the Danish Business Angel Network. It matches business angels with entrepreneurs through regional angel networks and through an internet-based matching service. Canada has also adopted a regional approach through their Canadian Community Investment Plan. Mason and Harrison (1997) have argued that public sector 'market' broker services are important because such not-for-profit programmes tend to focus on smaller and newer businesses, whilst most for-profit networks tended to focus on larger 'deals' and bigger and older businesses.

2 There are not enough financial incentives in place to support the risky endeavour of investing in small businesses. This may constrain business growth and the development of an equity finance marketplace. Hence, there may be a justification for programmes to provide tax relief to wealthy individuals prepared to act as business angels. Such programmes have a long history in the UK. For example, the Business Expansion Scheme (BES) was set up in 1983 to provide tax incentives to encourage individuals to become a 'business angel'. Unfortunately, this did not prove a good use of public money: BES investments went into fine wines, racehorses and property. The BES was subsequently replaced by the Enterprise Investment Scheme (EIS) in 1993. This, again, was designed to provide tax relief to investors purchasing equity directly in smaller businesses. Venture capital trusts (VCT) were introduced in 1995, and were designed to allow individuals to invest more easily in venture capital trusts. Both VCT and EIS appear to have been more successful than the BES. Boyns *et al.* (2003) estimated that – although almost half of investors would have made the investment without the tax relief – for every £1 million in tax forgone, the EIS investee businesses increased their sales by £3.3 million and by 65 employees. Mason and Harrison (2003) argued, however, that VCT schemes missed the funding 'gap' by offering too small an amount of funding.

Overall, since 'information opacity' characterises small business finance, there is always evidence of market failure, implying a case for government intervention. It is for these reasons that programmes to address access to both loan and equity have been long established in many countries. Whilst such programmes have generally been able to show they did serve a valuable function, their role needs to be kept under constant review.

21.4 Free or subsidised advice

We now take two examples of public policies that provide information and advice to new and small businesses. As before, we begin by identifying the rationale for such policies, provide examples of such policies and then examine evidence of their impact.

Free or subsidised advice to individuals prior to starting, or currently operating, a new or existing small business

This type of support is justified on two grounds. First, many individuals who are considering starting a business have imperfect information about their own suitability for this task and the factors likely to influence the success of their business. Massey (2006), for example, shows that the New Zealand government provides 'signposting' services to private sector advice (e.g. accountants), general business advice and help with formulating a business plan.

Second, there is a 'spillover' benefit from providing advice and assistance. If assistance is given, the argument is that it will enable the business to grow, creating further employment and tax income for the government. Lambrecht and Pirnay (2005) show, for instance, that in the Walloon area of Belgium external consultancy support is provided to small businesses so that the businesses will go on to grow and develop.

These two rationales are similar to those discussed in relationship to training in the small business (Chapter 20). But, like them, the public provision of business advice can be critiqued on four grounds:

1 It is not immediately obvious why small business owners should persistently under-purchase advice and assistance if it is of value to them. If they are rational purchasers of other inputs (e.g. supplies), why are they not 'rational' purchasers of advice?

2 Mole and Bramley (2006) (see Chapter 19) showed that there is a huge diversity in the ways that advice can be provided. This means that different countries make different decisions on who provides the advice/assistance (e.g. public, private sectors), what type is it (e.g. tailored, e-based), how is it rationed (e.g. time, sector), how is it integrated into other programmes and how is it funded (e.g. charges, donations). What is not clear is which policy choice is 'best'.

3 The impact of a public subsidy for advice and assistance is to lower its price. Bennett (2006) shows that this is potentially problematic because potential and existing business owners place greater value on the advice they receive from private sector providers (e.g. banks, accountants) than they do on the advice from publicly funded organisations. The effect, therefore, may be for the public sector to effectively 'crowd out' valuable private sector advice because it is cheaper, but not necessarily better.

4 Although the situation is now changing to an extent (e.g. MED 2009; Mole *et al.* 2008), the prime evidence base for assessing the impact of business advice has been 'self-report' data from clients. One problem with this approach is that it may present an overly favourable picture of the impact of programmes, whereas studies that use business outcomes as the impact measure – such as survival and sales/employment growth – are much less positive. Probably the most positive findings emerging from a careful study using output-based measures comes from MED (2009). They report, as an upper bound, an impact of 4 per cent on sales and 6 per cent of business advice on productivity. A less positive finding emerges from Greene *et al.* (2008). They examined advice and assistance provided to new businesses in Teesside (an area of northern England) over the 1970s, 1980s and 1990s. They show that new small businesses' satisfaction with such support increased over the three decades. However, they also showed that the performance of new businesses in Teesside did not markedly improve over the three decades. A third evaluation of the impact of business advice was of the UK Marketing Initiative. Wren and Storey (2002) found that this programme had no overall effect, when all businesses were analysed. However, there was a positive impact upon businesses with between 10 and 80 employees.

The overall impact of public advice and assistance is difficult to measure, in part because it is delivered in a variety of different ways. The emergence of better forms of evaluation have led to a more informed debate on what constitutes best practice in this area but, at our current state of knowledge, it is fair to conclude that the impact that publicly funded advice has on the performance of small businesses is modest at best.

Subsidised visits to overseas trade fairs

Small businesses normally make the vast majority of their sales in local or regional, or to some extent, national marketplaces. However, businesses which grow rapidly are significantly more likely to sell overseas where markets are potentially much bigger. Governments in many countries, therefore, seek to widen the horizons of small businesses by providing subsidies to attend trade fairs and other marketing opportunities overseas. The justification for this is that the small business, without the subsidy, would not have sufficient resources to attend the trade fair but, if they do so, they may win orders which significantly enhance the growth of the business. From the government's perspective, these new orders then lead to additional employment and competitiveness, thereby justifying the use of taxpayers' funds.

Illustration	Improving access to export markets

The OECD (2008) showed that improving the access to international markets was integral to all developed and developing economies. Examples of such programmes include:

● *Turkey*: financial support for visits to international trade fairs.

● *The Netherlands*: the 'Programme for starters abroad' designed to help new exporters with their export plans.

● *Mexico*: the Exportable Supply Impellers Promotion Program (export support for SMEs).

● *Ireland*: 'Enterprise Ireland' (programmes to support market entry, trade fairs and market development).

● *Hong Kong*: an export marketing fund to support exporters.

Assessing the impact of such programmes is difficult because again each country makes different policy 'choices' as to how it operates such assistance. The OECD (2008) shows that the typical 'choice' is to focus on new or existing exporters and to seek to reduce barriers to international trade (e.g. support for attending trade fairs). However, other programmes provide financial assistance whilst others develop the skills and capabilities of the businesses themselves.

These programmes are delivered in a variety of ways. The OECD (2008) reports that Canada has 19 and France has 11 separate access to international markets programmes, making it difficult to identify the overall impact of such support. Furthermore, some small businesses would have sought, and succeeded, in overseas markets in the absence of public support. Finally, the 'take up' of such support is limited: the OECD (2008) found that only a third of export-orientated businesses used the support provided by their government.

The evidence is that the businesses that participate in these programmes generally report themselves satisfied or very satisfied with the experience but, again, relying exclusively upon the reported views of the businesses themselves is open to question on reliability grounds. This is because measuring satisfaction is not the same as measuring the economic impact of a programme (see part 4 of the public policy case study).

This section has taken two examples of advice and assistance for prospective and existing businesses. We have shown that such support is widely available in different countries. However, our view of the evidence is that it is difficult to make a persuasive case that this is a fruitful area for the use of public subsidies. In part, this is because of the diverse ways in which this policy is delivered. This makes it difficult to identify whether there are spillover benefits from such assistance, and it makes it difficult to develop 'best practice'.

A second problem is that justifying the subsidising of business advice assumes the business owner has imperfect knowledge of the advice available and of the benefits that it provides. However – as we also showed in terms of training (Chapter 4) – why business owners should be 'irrational' about acquiring advice and assistance is not made clear.

Third, as Bennett (2006) emphasises, most small business owners do make use of external information and advice. If they do, they favour obtaining it from the private sector which risks being 'crowded out' by the presence of public subsidies.

21.5 Technology and innovation

We showed in Chapter 5 that small businesses were often linked with innovation. Public policy makers see advantages in supporting the innovatory abilities of prospective and existing small businesses because they believe that such businesses will increase economic growth in their country. Such interventions are usually justified on the grounds of imperfect information or spillover 'market failures'.

In terms of imperfect information, there are two grounds for intervention:

1 Individuals who have the technical skills to commercialise their ideas but are either unaware of how to set up and run a business, or find there are barriers placed in their way. In many instances, these individuals have the highest possible academic qualifications and are often employed by, or closely associated with, a university.

2 The commercial worth of new technologies is often difficult to assess. Developing the business is also likely to require significant amounts of finance at different stages of the business (see Chapter 18). This raises the possibility of good business propositions being under-funded.

Acs and Audretsch (2003) argue that policy interventions in this area are also potentially necessary because of the advantages of spillovers. They suggest that this is important because small businesses diffuse their own business ideas or the ideas of other businesses to consumers. For example, they may be able to pick up on ideas developed in a university and seek ways to commercialise them. Hence, the argument is that public policy has a role in facilitating the development of such spillovers.

In this section, we examine two examples of policy interventions. As usual, we begin with the rationale for such policy and then proceed to provide examples and examine the evidence.

Business incubators

Business incubator is a term used to describe services, facilities or conditions which help businesses to develop. Tamasy (2007) has argued that since the early 1980s, the supply of incubator services for prospective and existing businesses has grown markedly. She suggests that the number of incubator units in the US grew from 12 (1980) to more than 1,000 (2006). She also suggests that similar growth is evident in the UK, Germany and South East Asia.

Bergek and Norrman (2008) argue that there are four particular features of incubator support:

1 Shared office accommodation. Typically, this is provided at a subsidised rate. The advantage of this is that it helps the new technology business to retain its working capital. This is very helpful for such businesses because it is likely to be spending heavily on R&D at this time and have minimal revenue flow.

2 Shared support services. Again, this provides a cost saving to the new business by reducing its overheads (e.g. running costs).

3 Professional business support and advice. The value of this support is that technology-orientated business founders are expected to bring with them 'technical' knowledge but may have little or no business knowledge. Providing expert advice and assistance is, therefore, designed to overcome this 'imperfect knowledge'.

4   Network provision. Another advantage for businesses in incubator units is that they can use the 'brand' of the unit to enhance the 'reputation' and legitimacy of their business. So, if the incubator unit is on a 'science park' or a university research facility, the new business becomes more credible to its customers and suppliers. Businesses can also develop linkages and networks with other businesses in the incubator.

Given these potential advantages, access to such incubator sites is often restricted to younger businesses (e.g. less than five years old) and/or high technology (e.g. nanotechnology, computer software) businesses. Government support for incubator units may also be closely associated with the economic role that universities are expected to play in knowledge transfer (Lambert 2003).

However, there are very real methodological problems in linking the provision of incubator support to subsequent economic outcomes. This is partly because incubator support '... can encompass almost anything from distinct organisations to amorphous regions' (Phan et al. 2005: 168). It is also because there are problems in assessing which particular part of the support mix (e.g. office accommodation, business advice or networking support) impacts on the economic outcomes experienced by the incubator businesses. Third, there is uncertainty over which economic outcomes should be examined: should it be the growth of incubator businesses or the success of the incubator site (Phan et al. 2005)? If it is the individual business, should success be measured only when the business is on the science park, or should it include those that have left? Equally, how successful is the site in promoting patent, licensing or spin-off activity from the incubator site?

Again the evidence that incubator units – particularly those on science parks – enhance the economic outcomes experienced by incubator businesses is mixed. Amongst those unconvinced are Colombo and Delmastro (2002) for Italy and Ferguson and Olofsson (2004) for Sweden. More positive findings on patenting come from Squicciarini (2008) for Finland and on network linkages from Fukugawa (2006) for Japan.

Despite the number of studies comparing on and off science park businesses, initiated by Monck et al. (1988), both Phan et al. (2005) and Tamasy (2007) argue that the area lacks reliable and robust data. Our view is that there is evidence that well-managed science parks provide a prestige location and often promote links between businesses and with the local university but that there are still doubts about the extent to which science parks enhance the survival and growth of new-technology-based businesses.

R&D funding

Financial support for new-technology-based businesses is justified by the spillovers from such businesses. As an illustration, the UK government offers four types of grant for R&D projects:

- *Micro projects* (duration of up to 12 months, maximum award of £20,000; business must have fewer than 10 employees).

- *Research projects* (to investigate the technical and commercial feasibility of innovative technology; lasts 6–18 months, awards of up to £100,000, fewer than 50 employees).

- *Development projects* (to develop a pre-production prototype of a new product or process that involves a significant technological advance, 6–36 months, up to £250,000, fewer than 250 employees).

- *Exceptional development projects* (these constitute significant technological advances that are strategically important for a particular technology or industrial sector, 6–36 months, grant up to £500,000, no size limit).

Illustration	The Small Business Innovation Research (SBIR) programme

The best known, and certainly the largest programme of this type in the world, is the US's Small Business Innovation Research (SBIR) programme. The SBIR is extremely large because participating departments (e.g. department of defence, education, energy) have to 'set aside' 2.5 per cent of their R&D expenditure for small businesses. In 2004, this meant that the SBIR budget was approximately $2 billion. The programme has two phases: Phase I awards (judged according to the technical merit or feasibility of an idea or technology, for a duration of up to six months, to a value of up to $100,000) and Phase II awards (for R&D work, lasting up to two years, and of a value of up to $750,000).

Both Lerner (1999) and Audretsch *et al.* (2002) provide broadly positive support for SBIR. They find that the businesses that obtained the assistance perform better than they would have performed without the assistance, although the evaluation approach is by no means the most sophisticated available (see Part 4 of the public policy case study). Aerts and Schmidt (2008) (Flanders and Germany), Gonzalez and Pazo (2008) (Spain) and Koga (2005) (Japan) all found that the provision of public R&D funding complements private sector R&D funding.

However, Link and Scott (2009) found that the commercialisation rate of SBIR supported projects was less than 50 per cent and that private sector funders were potentially better placed to make judgements about the use of such funds. Wallsten (2000) also showed that SBIR funding led to private R&D being 'crowded out'.

Overall, a persuasive market failure case can be made for public funding for new-technology-based businesses on the grounds of their potential positive spillover effects, the uncertainties over their access to funding and the potentially important role of networks in enhancing their performance. The evidence on the effectiveness of policies seeking to address these problems is not wholly consistent but, on balance, this looks to be a more cost-effective use of funds than many other areas of micro policy.

21.6 'Particular' groups

Finally, we examine a range of policies that have been directed towards particular groups in society – women, ethnic minorities, the unemployed and young people – so as to enable them to be more 'enterprising'. Although these programmes are expected to have economic outcomes, they are justified primarily on equity or distributional grounds (see Chapter 19). Enterprise support is intended to enable individuals to 'break free' from discrimination and disadvantage, obtain a better standard of life and, in doing so, provide role models for others to follow.

Women

As we saw in Chapters 8 and 14, women are less likely to go into business and less likely to own either large or fast-growth businesses. Public policy has been concerned about these issues. Prowess (2009) suggests, for example, that if the entrepreneurial 'deficit' by women could be made up in the UK there would be another 150,000 start ups per annum; that majority-owned women businesses contribute £130 billion to the UK economy; and that women are more likely to come from a background of unemployment than men.

Despite these suggested advantages in supporting female-owned businesses, the central policy question is whether outcomes reflect different endowments of talent, different choices made by women, or, instead, whether they reflect a market failure such as imperfect information or discrimination. If there is discrimination, then there is a clear economic, as well as social, case for intervention by government. If it is imperfect information, then the intervention has to be on 'social' grounds, perhaps implying some form of economic penalty in terms of output forgone, which is paid for by the rest of society.

The discrimination case, as we saw in Chapter 17, is often discussed in terms of access to finance. Our review of the evidence was that, whilst there were studies which implied that women had more difficulty accessing finance and obtaining similar terms and conditions to men, these differences frequently disappeared when a range of other factors were taken into account such as the sector and location of the business and the human capital of the owner. Nevertheless, Muravyev *et al.* (2009) has opened up the debate again by pointing to evidence of females being charged higher rates for loans, albeit most clearly in the less economically developed countries.

The European Commission (2004*b*) identified that there were 132 different programmes supporting female entrepreneurship in the EU. Programmes included the Women's Enterprise Agency (Finland) (designed to mentor and support new and existing female entrepreneurs), the Guarantee Fund for Women (France) (financial support for business development), Women in Business (WiB) Skills Training (Ireland), 'Mentoring Makes Success' (Luxembourg) and 'Women Into the Network' (UK). Other countries have similar services (e.g. 'Women's Business Centers (US)). In fact, Lundstrom and Stevenson (2005) reported that almost every developed country has publicly funded programmes to assist women entrepreneurs.

Regardless of how common such programmes are, it has proved difficult to establish if market failure occurs with regard to female entrepreneurship. This reflects the variety of explanations for the entry and performance of female-owned businesses (Chapters 8 and 14).

The value of 'female-only' business advice and support has also been questioned. Robson *et al.* (2008) argue in their study of Scottish service-sector businesses that what explained the use of business support was not gender but rather the characteristics of the business. Wilson *et al.* (2004) also argue that '. . . programming and policymaking based on the identification of gender deviation on a single variable ignores the richness of life and the often complex and conflicting priorities that people juggle' (p. 810). They also suggest that the case for public policy support for female entrepreneurship remains unproven given the lack of reliable information on its impact and the diversity of schemes that have been adopted. This is an obvious area for future research.

Ethnic minorities

Chapter 8 identified that self-employment rates amongst ethnic minorities varied considerably. Chapter 14 showed no clear evidence that the ethnicity of the founder influenced business growth rates. Nonetheless, ethnic minority businesses are a powerful political and economic grouping. Ram and Jones (2008) estimated, for example, that ethnic minority businesses contributed £15 billion to the UK economy. However, as with women, the central policy question is whether outcomes experienced by ethnic minorities reflect differences in individual talent, the choices made by individuals or some form of discrimination.

The evidence here is somewhat clearer than with women. Chapter 17 showed that there was robust evidence of discrimination against Blacks seeking finance in the US (Blanchflower *et al.* 2003). If this is the case, it presents a clear market failure and a strong justification for publicly funded programmes to overcome such discrimination.

The US has specific programmes to support ethnic minority businesses. One example of such support is the 8a business development programme, which offers marketing, managerial, technical, financial and procurement assistance. Other countries such as Canada, Australia and New Zealand also offer dedicated programmes of support for their indigenous communities.

The European Commission (2008*b*) identified 146 ethnicity-based policy measures and support programmes across 37 European countries. Levels of support for ethnic minority businesses varied considerably. The countries with the largest number of ethnic minority support schemes were northern European: the UK (32 schemes), Germany (22), the Netherlands (16) and Belgium (11). Support for ethnic minority businesses amongst southern and eastern European countries tended to be much lower. Similarly the funders, delivery agents, targets of support and types of policy all varied. The European Commission (2008*b*) showed, for example, that support was funded by a range of supranational (the EU), national, regional

Table 21.2	Policy types and delivery mechanisms to support minority enterprise		
	Types of policy (%)		**Types of delivery mechanism (%)**
Information	83	Individual	75
Advice	83	Workshop	69
Training	73	Publications	50
Networking	66	Regular	48
Mentoring	58	Electronic	38
(Access to) finance	54	Other	1
Other	1		

Source: EU (2008b).
Note: Table does not sum to 100 because more than one service is offered by support organisations.

and local providers and delivered by a range of public, private, non-governmental agencies and a mix of these approaches. In total, it identified 103 professional organisations supporting ethnic minority businesses, with 43 per cent of support being for native and immigrant businesses, 52 per cent only for immigrants and 5 per cent for the Roma.

The types of policy also varied in the kind of support that was offered. Table 21.2 shows the most common type of support offered was information and advice as well as networking and mentoring to minority businesses. The support was delivered in different ways (e.g. individual, workshops, electronically).

These programmes target ethnic groups who make less use of 'mainstream' business support because of language and cultural barriers. There is an argument, therefore, that support for ethnic minorities should be run *for* and *by* minorities. This is similar to the case for enterprise support by and for women.

However, given the myriad of policy choices, assorted delivery mechanisms and different groups (e.g. ethnic minorities and immigrants) supported, there are profound challenges to policy in this area. Deakins *et al.* (2003), for example, suggested that, in the UK, support was confused and was caught between trying to promote the economic advantages of business ownership amongst minority groups and wider concerns about the greater social inclusion of such groups. Ram and Jones (2008) also argued that there are dangers in focusing on 'ethnicity'. First, the reason why minority businesses may not use public support is that they, like 'mainstream' business owners, may not value public sector support. Second, as we showed in Chapters 8 and 13, 'ethnicity' may be a highly imperfect way of grouping business owners. For example, there are wide differences in start-up rates amongst different ethnic groups, differences between migrants and ethnic groups and differences in how individuals labelled as belonging to a 'minority' respond to public policies. The danger, therefore, is that policy may reduce individuals to ethnic stereotypes. Ram and Jones (2008) also argue that 'ethnic matching services' (support run by and for particular groups) have not been any better at meeting the needs of 'ethnic' businesses than other, more 'mainstream', services. More generally, there is an absence of evaluation studies which would enable a judgement to be reached on the effectiveness of interventions to support ethnic or minority businesses.

The unemployed

As we saw in Chapter 19, policies to support the conversion of the unemployed into business ownership have a clear attraction for policy makers. First, in all developed economies the state provides unemployment benefit which, for economic reasons alone, it would like to minimise. Second, unemployed people, particularly if they are long term unemployed, are also potentially more likely to experience other forms of social disadvantage (e.g. poor health). These outcomes may lead to negative 'spillovers' (e.g. the unemployed have less income which reduces overall demand). Third, there is geographical clustering of the unemployed and in such areas there is likely to be higher levels of deprivation and crime.

There are other justifications for supporting the unemployed to start a business. Unemployed people, all else being equal, may find that their routes into employment are blocked. They may also be more likely to suffer from a lack of confidence, be less aware of the self-employment option and have difficulties in accessing finance. All these reasons justify 'micro' support for some to make the transition into self-employment.

This was the context for the UK in the 1980s when unemployment was particularly high and the Enterprise Allowance Scheme was introduced (see Section 19.4 for further details) but such programmes did not disappear even in more prosperous times. For example, the 'new' EAS in the UK was the 'New Deal'. This provided an initial awareness session of self-employment, business planning support and a period of test-trading where participants can still – for up to six months – claim their unemployment benefit in full. Where the 'New Deal' differs, however, from EAS is that only around 4,500 people participated in 2005/06, compared with nearly 200,000 who were on EAS in 1987.

Similar programmes exist elsewhere the world (e.g. Canada where it operates in all the provinces and the US where it operates in some of the states). Perhaps one of the largest is provided by the German government. The government began by introducing a 'Bridging Allowance' (*Überbrückungsgeld*) in 1986 which paid unemployment benefit to the newly self-employed for up to six months. This was followed by another business 'Start-up Subsidy' programme (*Ich-AG*), introduced in 2003, that also subsidised self-employment activity but over a three-year period. In the first year, participants were given a monthly allowance of €600, €360 in the second year and €240 in the third year (Caliendo and Kritikos 2007).

Figure 21.1 shows the numbers participating in these two programmes. For the Bridging Allowance (BA) programme, around 100,000 individuals each year from East and West Germany participated during the period 1994–2001. After 2001, participation in BA increased steadily so that between 2003 and 2006 it reached a peak of around 150,000. For the Ich AG scheme (SUS in Figure 21.1), approximately 100,000 participated in 2003, around 175,000 in 2004 and around 100,000 in 2005. In total, there were approximately 850,000 participants on both programmes during 2003–5.

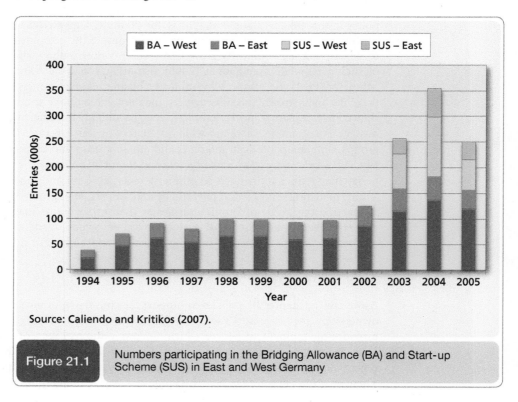

Source: Caliendo and Kritikos (2007).

Figure 21.1   Numbers participating in the Bridging Allowance (BA) and Start-up Scheme (SUS) in East and West Germany

In 2006, the programmes were combined into a single scheme called the 'start-up premium' (*Gründungszuschuss*) which gave new self-employed individuals unemployment benefits for up to 9 months.

Caliendo and Kritikos (2007) argued that these programmes were positive interventions by the German government because they found that the survival rates of participants were around 70 per cent and because the income levels of participants were higher (relative to previous period of employment) after two and a half years. Although, therefore, this looks like a 'successful' programme, one issue with this assessment is that they only measure individuals who participated in the programme. One difficulty with this is that the study does not provide a 'control' group that can be compared with those *not* on the programme. The primer on monitoring and evaluation (see part 4 of Case study 7) also highlights why this is important in evaluating the results of programmes.

In general, as Kellard *et al.* (2002) argue, programmes that seek to 'convert' the unemployed into self-employed have a poor track record. Pfeiffer and Reize (2000) also looked earlier at the German Bridging Allowance (BA) programme and found the allowances had no positive impact on job creation amongst supported businesses.

The problem faced by such programmes is that the individual who is unemployed often also lacks the human capital necessary to own and manage a successful business. Public programmes seeking to encourage the transition to self-employment are expected to focus disproportionately upon those individuals lacking the motivation to make such a move without the public funds. The problem is that if the business fails, the debts accumulated by that individual can mean they are in a considerably worse financial position than before they started the business.

Young people

There are three main justifications for support schemes directed at young people. First, young people have imperfect information about entrepreneurial opportunities and/or they lack information on how to start or grow a business compared with older people. Programmes address this by providing information, signposting, training and mentoring.

A second justification is that young people have restricted access to finance. Unlike older people who have had the opportunity to acquire resources throughout their lifetime, this is not the case for young people. Again, this potentially justifies micro-loan programmes targeted at young people.

Third, if support is provided then it will be 'rewarded' because young people have creative and novel ideas and the energy and enthusiasm to carry them through. Even if they fail, it is argued, they have plenty of time to learn from their experience and start again. In short, the returns to society for supporting enterprise amongst the young are considerably greater than assisting middle-aged or older individuals. Also, if they are successful, it has spillover benefits to other young people because they act as positive role models. Engaging young people in self-employment may also have other benefits because it may prevent negative spillover effects (e.g. unemployment, criminality).

Virtually every country in the developed world has programmes to support youth self-employment. Greene (2005) estimated there were 75 youth enterprise programmes in the EU alone. Lundstrom and Stevenson (2007) and Lewis and Massey (2003) also document youth entrepreneurship programmes in developed countries.

One notable example in the UK of a youth enterprise programme is the Prince's Trust, set up by Prince Charles in 1976. This programme targets young disadvantaged people (e.g. unemployed, ex-offenders, the disabled) aged between 18 and 30 years of age. It provides those contemplating starting a business with a range of grants, 'soft' loans, business planning and mentoring services. Another UK programme – which has been 'exported' internationally – is the Shell Livewire scheme. This provides two main types of support. First, it runs a signposting and information service. Second, it runs competitions each year which award cash prizes to competition winners. Italy has also enshrined youth enterprise into law: the De Vito Law (Law 44) was introduced in 1986 with the explicit aim of helping young Italians in the south of the country through the provision of financial subsidies for equipment, 'soft' loans and training and support.

Despite the ubiquity of youth enterprise programmes, assessments based on evidence, other than that of participants' opinions, are rare. Furthermore, assessments are normally confined to single programmes such as the Prince's Trust (Shutt and Sutherland 2003; Meager *et al*. 2003) or Shell Livewire (Greene and Storey 2004).

Shutt and Sutherland's (2003) study of the Prince's Trust suggests that such support enhances survival, although they found no impact of advice and mentoring services. Meager *et al*. (2003) found that the owners of Prince's Trust supported businesses were no more likely to earn more, have better survival rates or be more likely to be in employment subsequent to running their own business, than otherwise comparable individuals.

Greene and Storey's (2004) review of Shell Livewire found that only one in five that used the information and signposting services ever entered self-employment. Even amongst those that did, the perception was that Livewire information was not a key influence.

On balance, our view is that there is little compelling evidence pointing to the success of youth enterprise programmes. In part, our view is based on the small number of careful studies that have assessed these programmes – which generally point to minimal impact. Second, although the UK has had youth self-employment policies since the early 1980s, the self-employment rate amongst young people was *less* in 2003 than in 1983 (Chapter 3).

Overall, this section has examined enterprise support for women, ethnic minorities, the unemployed and young people. Support can also be justified in similar ways for other groups (e.g. the disabled, older people and ex-offenders). We showed that there is a huge range of support available in many countries to promote enterprise or entrepreneurship. Whilst the evidence base for judging policy impact is not extensive, or wholly reliable, policy can be criticised on three main grounds. The first is a lack of clarity on objectives – are these social or economic programmes? Second, even when objectives are clear, the bewildering range of available support begs the question of how coherent individual programmes actually are. This is important because, as Rouse and Kitching (2006) suggest, individuals do not exist purely as 'women', 'ethnic minorities', the 'unemployed' or 'young people'. Finally, the lack of clarity on expected outcomes from programmes in this area mean that assessing whether or not the taxpayer gets value for money for the funding is almost impossible.

Summary

This chapter has examined five key areas of what we call micro enterprise policy: developing an 'enterprise culture', access to, and provision of, finance, advice and assistance, technology and innovation and support for particular groups (e.g. women and minorities).

For each of these five areas, we provided examples of publicly funded enterprise policies seeking to address economic and/or social problems. In conducting this review, we were amazed at the diversity of programmes which we came across in a range of different countries. Our amazement at the diversity and ingenuity of the programmes is in stark contrast with our disappointment at the paucity of careful assessments of the impact of these programmes. In the vast majority of cases we are unable to find evaluations that go beyond reporting the views of recipients. However, even where there is some reasonably reliable evidence, this is often contradictory. At best it points to a modest impact, although this does vary somewhat between the five policy areas.

We are broadly persuaded that there is an economic case for public support for technology businesses in terms of R&D support. We also see the case that publicly funded loan-guarantee schemes are required.

The economic case for the use of public funds for other purposes is much less clear. There is some evidence that business support can enhance business performance but it does risk crowding out private sector advisory services. Where we feel the case is weakest of all is in attempts to create an 'enterprise culture'. This is partly on the grounds that this is unnecessary since, as Baumol (1990) demonstrates, 'the entrepreneur is always with us' and partly on the grounds that the evidence of policy effectiveness is so weak.

However, the chapter has emphasised that enterprise policy has a major social, as well as an economic, dimension. If there are strong social reasons for using taxpayer funds to advance social goals through grants to businesses, then the objectives of policy should be clear and an agreed system of appraisal be in place to determine whether these objectives are achieved. Sadly, this is not currently the case, given the lack of policy coherence.

In conclusion, whilst in the past researchers were prepared to give micro policy the benefit of the doubt over its impact, it appears that recently the sceptics have become more assertive. For example, Bridge *et al.* (2009: 481), following their comprehensive review, say:

> There appears to be no strong body of evidence to say that intervention has worked and a number of studies which suggest that so far intervention has failed. It seems reasonable to conclude that, overall, the evidence is that the methods so far applied have not worked in that they have not had the effect intended on improving rates of entrepreneurship or levels of business performance. Despite the similarities of policies and interventions across the world, there are few proven examples of successful 'best practice'. The adoption of interventionist policies appears to be due more to a 'me too' approach than any rigorous examination of their impact.

Davidsson (2008) concurs with such sentiments whilst Bill *et al.* (2009) also say: 'Numerous research studies have failed to find any positive correlation between support measures and development programmes on the one hand and firm growth and development on the other' (p. 1136).

There is, therefore, a clear contrast between the evidence of impact of micro policies in this chapter and the macro factors of taxation, regulation, immigration and competition policies (Chapter 20). We showed that macro factors were powerful influences on small business activity. However, based upon the evidence assembled here, governments could justify very few elements of micro policy.

Questions for discussion

1 Assess the case for, and against, all undergraduates being required to take an enterprise course whilst at university.

2 Using market failure based arguments, make the case for providing free advice to all young people considering starting a business.

3 What market failure do loan guarantee schemes address? What options are available to policy makers in delivering a loan guarantee scheme?

4 Are policy makers wise to support science parks?

5 Make the case for and against support for female entrepreneurship.

6 Should ethnic minorities have business advice programmes delivered solely by members of ethnic minorities? Make the case for and against.

References

Acs, Z.J. and Audretsch, D.B. (2003) 'Innovation and Technical change' in Acs, Z.J. and Audretsch, D.B. (eds), *Handbook of Entrepreneurial Research*. Dordrecht: Kluwer, 55–79.

Aerts, K. and Schmidt, T. (2008) 'Two for the Price of One? Additionality Effects of R&D Subsidies: A Comparison between Flanders and Germany', *Research Policy*, 37(5), 806–22.

Athayde, R. (2009) 'Measuring Enterprise Potential in Young People', *Entrepreneurship: Theory and Practice*, 33(2), 481–500.

Audretsch, D.B. and Lehmann, E.E. (2005) 'Do University Policies Make a Difference?', *Research Policy*, 34(3), 343–47.

Audretsch, D.B., Link, A.N. and Scott, J. (2002) 'Public/Private Technology Partnerships: Evaluating SBIR-Supported Research', *Research Policy*, 32(4), 145–58.

Baumol, W.J. (1990) 'Entrepreneurship: Productive, Unproductive and Destructive', *Journal of Political Economy*, 98, 893–921.

Bennett, R.J. (2009) 'Government SME Policy Since the 1990s: What Have We Learnt?' *Environment and Planning C*, 26(2), 375–97.

Bergek, A. and Norrman, C. (2008) 'Incubator Best Practice: A Framework', *Technovation*, 28(1–2), 20–8.

Bill, F., Johannisson, B. and Olaison, L. (2009) 'The Incubus Paradox: Attempts at Foundational Rethinking of the "SME Support Genre"', *European Planning Studies*, 17(8), 1135–52.

Blanchflower, D.G., Levine, P.B. and Zimmerman, D.J. (2003) 'Discrimination in the Small Business Credit Market', *Review of Economics and Statistics*, 85(4), 930–43.

Boyns, N., Cox, M., Spires, R. and Hughes, A. (2003) *Research into the Enterprise Investment Scheme and Venture Capital Trusts: A Report Prepared for Inland Revenue*. Cambridge: PACEC.

Bridge, S., O'Neill, K. and Martin, F. (2009) *Understanding Enterprise, Entrepreneurship and Small Business*. Basingstoke: Palgrave/Macmillan.

Brown, R. (1990) 'Encouraging Entrepreneurship: Britain's New Enterprise Program', *Journal of Small Business Management*, 28(4), 71–7.

Bygrave, W.D., Lange, J.E., Mollov, A., Pearlmutter, M. and Singh, S. (2007) 'Pre-Start-up Formal Business Plans and Post-Start-up Performance: A Study of 116 New Ventures', *Venture Capital*, 9(4), 1–20.

Caliendo, M. and Kritikos, S. (2007) *Start-ups by the Unemployed: Characteristics, Survival and Direct Employment Effects*. IZA DP 3220. IZA: Bonn.

Castagnetti, C. and Rosti, L. (2009) *Who Skims the Cream of the Italian Graduate Crop?: Wage Employment versus Self-employment*. MPRA Paper No. 13504. Munich: Munich Personal RePEc Archive.

Colombo, M.G. and Delmastro, M. (2002) 'How Effective Are Technology Incubators?', *Research Policy* 31(7), 1103–22.

Craig, B.R., Jackson, W.E. and Thomson, J.B. (2007) 'Small Firm Finance, Credit Rationing and the Impact of SBA-Guaranteed Lending on Local Economic Growth', *Journal of Small Business Management*, 45(1), 116–32.

Davidsson, P. (2008) 'Some Conclusions about Entrepreneurship and Its Support'. Paper presented to the World Entrepreneurship Forum, 13–15 November, Evian, France.

Davies, H. (2002) *Enterprise Britain: A Modern Approach to Meeting the Enterprise Challenge*. London: HM Treasury.

Deakins, D., Ram, M. and Smallbone, D. (2003) 'Addressing the Business Support Needs of Ethnic-minority Firms in the United Kingdom', *Environment and Planning C: Government and Policy*, 21, 843–59.

European Commission (2003) *Entrepreneurship in Europe: Green Paper*. Brussels: Enterprise Publications.

European Commission (2004*a*) *Helping to Create an Entrepreneurial Culture: A Guide on Good Practices in Promoting Entrepreneurial Attitudes and Skills through Education.* Brussels: European Commission.

European Commission (2004*b*) *Promoting Entrepreneurship amongst Women.* Brussels: European Commission.

European Commission (2008*a*) *Entrepreneurship Survey of the EU (25 Member States), US, Iceland and Norway.* Flash EB Series No. 192. Brussels: European Commission.

European Commission (2008*b*) *Entrepreneurial Diversity in a Unified Europe*, adapted from Tables 5 and 6. Brussels: European Commission. http://ec.europa.eu/enterprise/policies/sme/files/support_measures/migrant/eme_study_en.pdf, p. 26.

Ferguson, R. and Olofsson, C. (2004) 'Science Parks and the Development of NTBFs: Location, Survival and Growth', *Journal of Technology Transfer*, 29(1), 5–17.

FORA (2008) *Entrepreneurship Index 2007.* Copenhagen: Ministry of Economic and Business Affairs.

Fraser, S., Storey, D.J. and Westhead, P. (2006) 'Student Work Placements in Small Firms: Do They Pay Off or Shift Tastes?', *Small Business Economics*, 26(2), 125–44.

Fukugawa, N. (2006) 'Science Parks in Japan and their Value-added Contributions to New Technology-based Firms', *International Journal of Industrial Organisation*, 24(2), 381–400.

Gonzalez, X. and Pazo, C. (2008) 'Do Public Subsidies Stimulate Private R&D Spending?', *Research Policy*, 37(3), 371–89.

Graduate Prospects (2005) *Graduates in Self-employment.* Birmingham: National Council for Graduate Entrepreneurship.

Graham, T. (2004) *Review of the Small Firms Loan Guarantee.* London: HM Treasury.

Greene, F.J. (2005) *Youth Entrepreneurship: Latent Entrepreneurship, Market Failure and Enterprise Support.* CSME Working Papers, No. 87. Coventry: University of Warwick.

Greene F.J. and Saridakis, G. (2008) 'The Role of Higher Education Skills and Support in Graduate Self-employment', *Studies in Higher Education*, 33(6), 653–72.

Greene, F.J. and Storey, D.J. (2004) 'An Assessment of a Venture Creation Programme: The Case of Shell Livewire', *Entrepreneurship and Regional Development*, 16(2), 145–59.

Greene, F.J., Mole, K.F. and Storey, D.J. (2008) *Three Decades of Enterprise Culture: Entrepreneurship, Economic Regeneration and Public Policy.* London: Palgrave.

Hoffmann, A. (2007) 'A Rough Guide to Entrepreneurship Policy', in Audretsch, D.B., Grilio, I. and Thurik, A.R. (eds), *Handbook of Research on Entrepreneurship Policy.* Cheltenham: Edward Elgar, 140–71.

Honig, B. (2004) 'Entrepreneurship Education: Toward a Model of Contingency-based Business Planning', *Academy of Management Learning and Education*, 3(3), 258–73.

Hytti, U. and O'Gorman, C. (2004) 'What is "Enterprise Education"?: An Analysis of the Objectives and Methods of Enterprise Education Programmes in Four European Countries', *Education + Training*, 46(1), 11–23.

Kellard, K., Legge, K. and Ashworth, K. (2002) *Self-employment as a Route off Benefits. Department for Work and Pensions Research Report 177.* London: Department for Work and Pensions.

Koga, T. (2005) 'R&D Subsidy and Self-financed R&D: The Case of Japanese High-technology Start-ups', *Small Business Economics*, 24(1), 53–62.

KPMG (1999) *An Evaluation of the Loan Guarantee Scheme.* London: Department of Trade and Industry.

Kuratko, D.F. (2005) 'The Emergence of Entrepreneurship Education: Development, Trends, and Challenges', *Entrepreneurship: Theory and Practice*, 29(5), 577–97.

Lambert, R. (2003) *Review of Business–University Collaboration.* London: HM Treasury.

Lambrecht, J. and Pirnay, F. (2005) 'An Evaluation of Public Support Measures for Private External Consultancies to SMEs in the Walloon Region of Belgium', *Entrepreneurship and Regional Development*, 17(2), 89–108.

Lenihan, H. and Hart, M. (2004) 'The Use of Counterfactual Scenarios as a Means to Assess Policy Deadweight: An Irish Case Study', *Environment and Planning C-Government and Policy*, 22(6), 817–39.

Lenihan, H. and Hart, M. (2006) 'Evaluating the Additionality of Public Sector Assistance to Irish Firms', *Policy Studies*, 27(2), 115–33.

Lerner, J. (1999) 'The Government as Venture Capitalist: The Long-run Impact of the SBIR Program', *Journal of Business*, 72(3), 285–318.

Lewis, K. and Massey, C. (2003) *Youth Entrepreneurship and Government Policy*. Wellington: New Zealand Centre for SME Research, Massey University.

Link, A.N. and Scott, J.T. (2009) 'Private Investor Participation and Commercialization Rates for Government-sponsored Research and Development: Would a Prediction Market Improve the Performance of the SBIR Programme?', *Economica*, 76(302), 264–81.

Lundstrom, A. and Stevenson, L.A. (2005) 'Entrepreneurship Policy: Theory and Practice', in *ISEN International Studies in Entrepreneurship*. New York: Springer.

Lundstrom, A. and Stevenson, L.A., (2007) 'Dressing the Emperor: The Fabric of Entrepreneurship Policy', in Audretsch, D.B., Grilio, I. and Thurik, A.R. (eds), *Handbook of Research on Entrepreneurship Policy*. Cheltenham: Edward Elgar, 94–129.

Mason, C.M. and Harrison, R.T. (1997) 'Business Angel Networks and the Development of the Informal Venture Capital Market in the UK: Is There Still a Role for the Public Sector?' *Small Business Economics*, 9(2), 111–23.

Mason, C. and Harrison, R. (2003) 'Closing the Regional Equity Gap?: A Critique of the Department of Trade and Industry's Regional Venture Capital Funds Initiative', *Regional Studies*, 37(8), 855–68.

Massey, C. (2006) 'A New Conceptualisation of Business Development for SMEs: A Focus on Development Potential', *Environment and Planning C-Government and Policy*, 24(1), 37–49.

McAdam, M. and Marlow, S. (2007) 'Building Futures or Stealing Secrets? Entrepreneurial Cooperation and Conflict within Business Incubators', *International Small Business Journal*, 25(4), 361–82.

Meager, N., Bates, P. and Cowling, M. (2003) 'An Evaluation of Business Start-up Support for Young People', *National Institute Economic Review*, 186, 70–83.

Ministry of Economic Development (2009) *Evaluation of the Growth Services Range*. Wellington: Ministry of Economic Development.

Mole, K.F. and Bramley, G. (2006) 'Making Policy Choices in Non-financial Business Support: An International Comparison', *Environment and Planning C: Government and Policy*, 24(6), 885–908.

Mole, K., Hart, M., Roper, S. and Saal, D. (2008) *Assessing the Effectiveness of Business Support Services in England: Evidence from a Theory-based Evaluation*. CSME Working Paper No. 93. Coventry: University of Warwick.

Monck, C.S.P., Porter, R., Quintas, P., Storey, D.J. and Wynarczyk, P. (1988) *Science Parks and the Growth of High Technology Firms*. London: Croom Helm.

Muravyev, A., Talavera, O. and Schäfer, D. (2009) 'Entrepreneurs' Gender and Financial Constraints: Evidence from International Data', *Journal of Comparative Economics*, 37(2), 270–86.

OECD (2001) *Putting the Young in Business: Policy Challenges for Youth Entrepreneurship*. Paris: OECD.

OECD (2008) *Removing Barriers to SME Access to International Markets*. Paris: OECD.

Peterman, N.E. and Kennedy, J. (2003) 'Enterprise Education: Influencing Students' Perceptions of Entrepreneurship', *Entrepreneurship: Theory and Practice*, 28(2), 129–44.

Pfeiffer, F. and Reize, F. (2000) 'Business Start-ups by the Unemployed: An Econometric Analysis Based on Firm Data', *Labour Economics*, 7(5), 629–63.

Pittaway, L. and Cope, J. (2007) 'Entrepreneurship Education: A Systematic Review of the Evidence', *International Small Business Journal*, 25(5), 479–510.

Phan, P.H., Siegel, D.S. and Wright, M. (2005) 'Science Parks and Incubators: Observations, Synthesis and Future Research', *Journal of Business Venturing*, 20(2), 165–82.

Prowess (2009) *Prowess Facts and Figures*. http://www.prowess.org.uk/facts.htm (accessed 10 May 2009).

Ram, M. and Jones, T. (2008) 'Ethnic-minority Businesses in the UK: A Review of Research and Policy Developments', *Environment and Planning C-Government and Policy*, 26(2), 352–74.

Riding, A.L. and Haines, G. (2001) 'Loan Guarantees: Costs of Default and Benefits to Small Firms', *Journal of Business Venturing*, 16(6), 595–612.

Riding, A., Madill, J. and Haines, G. (2007) 'Incrementality of SME Guarantees', *Small Business Economics*, 29(1–2), 47–61.

Robson, P.J.A., Jack, S.L. and Freel, M.S. (2008) 'Gender and the Use of Business Advice: Evidence from Firms in the Scottish Service Sector', *Environment and Planning C-Government and Policy*, 26(2), 292–314.

Roper, S. and Hewitt-Dundas, N. (2001) 'Grant Assistance and Small Firm Development in Northern Ireland and the Republic of Ireland', *Scottish Journal of Political Economy*, 48(1), 99–117.

Rosa, P. (2003) ' "Hardly Likely to Make the Japanese Tremble": The Businesses of Recently Graduated University and College "Entrepreneurs" ', *International Small Business Journal*, 21(4), 435–59.

Rouse, J. and Kitching, J. (2006) 'Do Enterprise Support Programmes Leave Women Holding the Baby?', *Environment and Planning C-Government and Policy*, 24(1), 5–19.

Shutt, J. and Sutherland, J. (2003) 'Encouraging the Transition into Self-employment', *Regional Studies*, 37(1), 97–103.

Squicciarini, M. (2008) 'Science Parks' Tenants versus Out-of-Park Firms: Who Innovates More? A Duration Model', *Journal of Technology Transfer*, 33(1), 45–71.

Tamasy, C. (2007) 'Rethinking Technology-Oriented Business Incubators: Developing a Robust Policy Instrument for Entrepreneurship, Innovation, and Regional Development?', *Growth and Change*, 38(3), 460–73.

Wallsten, S.J. (2000) 'The Effects of Government–Industry R&D Programs on Private R&D: The Case of the Small Business Innovation Program', *RAND Journal of Economics*, 31(1), 82–100.

Weiner, M.J. (1981) *English Culture and the Decline of the Industrial Spirit, 1850–1980*. New York: Cambridge University Press.

Wilson, K. (2008) 'Entrepreneurship Education in Europe', in Potter J. (ed.), *Entrepreneurship and Higher Education*. Paris: OECD, 119–38.

Wilson, L., Whittam, G. and Deakins, D. (2004) 'Women's Enterprise: A Critical Examination of National Policies', *Environment and Planning C-Government and Policy*, 22(6), 799–815.

Wren, C. and Storey, D.J. (2002) 'Evaluating the Effect of Soft Business Support upon Small Firm Performance', *Oxford Economic Papers: New Series*, 54(2), 334–65.

Part 7

Case studies

This section of the book comprises in-depth case studies which take you to the heart of real businesses, and show you how the topics covered in this book interact with each other in practice.

This case study examines competition in the supply of funeral services by two small, family-run, funeral directors. The case charts the nature of this competition between the two businesses and asks you – as the competition watchdog – to adjudicate between their competing claims. The learning objectives of the case are that you should:

- become better aware of the hazards of making generalisations about competition between small businesses;
- be able to make judgements on the issue of market power and how it relates to smaller businesses.

The case begins with a brief overview of the legal background and then charts the nature of competition between the two funeral directors.

The legal background

Section 18 of the Competition Act 1998 addresses anti-competitive conduct. It states:

... any conduct on the part of one or more undertakings which amounts to the abuse of a dominant position in a market is prohibited if it may affect trade within the United Kingdom.

In terms of the Act, abuse includes:

... directly or indirectly imposing unfair purchase or selling prices or other unfair trading conditions.

Examples of this include: limiting markets or technical development to the prejudice of consumers; and applying dissimilar conditions to equivalent transactions with other parties, thereby placing them at a competitive disadvantage.

Competition or unfair practices?

The case involves two small funeral directors, Burgess and Austin. Both were family businesses: J.J. Burgess and Sons was run by Justin Burgess and his mother Margaret; whilst Austin's was chaired by John Austin and managed by his daughter Claire and her husband Peter Hope. Both also had long traditions of dealing with funeral arrangements. Burgess and Sons had been conducting funerals since 1839 whilst Austin's had been first a building business before in 1978 making the switch to funeral directing.

Both businesses were located in the same county of Hertfordshire, England. Burgess had branches in Codicote, Hatfield, Knebworth, St Albans and Welwyn Garden City. Austin's had branches in Stevenage and Hitchin (see

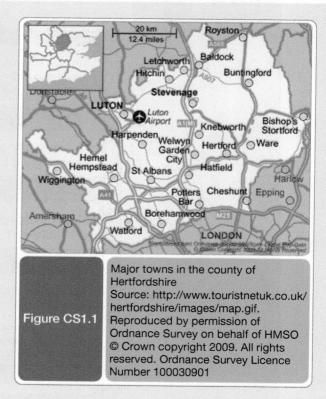

Figure CS1.1

Major towns in the county of Hertfordshire
Source: http://www.touristnetuk.co.uk/hertfordshire/images/map.gif.
Reproduced by permission of Ordnance Survey on behalf of HMSO © Crown copyright 2009. All rights reserved. Ordnance Survey Licence Number 100030901

Figure CS1.1). They had designed and built Harwood Park Crematorium in Stevenage in February 1997. This had allowed them to vertically integrate their business (i.e. provide both funeral directing services and crematorium services as a package). However, Austin's had been allowed to develop Harwood Park only on the basis that they would allow other funeral directors free access to their crematorium.

In 1998, Burgess and Sons had opened a branch of their business a mile (1.6 km) from Austin's crematorium. They had been steadily growing their share of the local market. They were able to do this because of the 'repeat' nature of funeral services. For example, suppose a family, unfortunately, saw a relative pass away. They then selected a funeral director to arrange the funeral and the cremation of the relative. When the family later on experienced another relative passing away, the usual way they dealt with the funeral arrangements was to return to the original funeral director (presuming the service was appropriate first time round) and seek to repeat the same funeral service. Alternatively, if someone attended a funeral and judged that the service from the funeral director had been appropriate, they might think of using that funeral service if there was, unfortunately, a need for such services within their own family.

Burgess and Sons began to find, however, that it was increasingly difficult to win this 'repeat' business when families chose to use the Harwood Park crematorium. Austin's, they felt, were putting active barriers in place to prevent Burgess and Sons from using the crematorium. This led to the breakdown of their working relationship in 2001. January 2001 saw Claire Austin – who was now the managing director of Austin's (having taken over from her father) – write to Justin Burgess to inform him that he was refused access to the crematorium.

Justin Burgess believed that he needed to make use of the crematorium because some of his customers, particularly those who had used pre-payment plans to pay for their funeral, had expressed a desire to be cremated at the Harwood Park crematorium. There were other customers who wished to see a 'repeat' of an earlier funeral service for a relative. Potential customers were willing to do this despite the prices at Harwood Park crematorium rising: indeed, over the period 1998–2003 they rose by more than 55 per cent which was by far and away the highest rises in the area. Nonetheless, Harwood Park continued to be used extensively.

Burgess and Sons, therefore, paid another local funeral director, Chas. A. Nethercott & Son, to conduct cremations at Harwood Park. In effect, this meant that Burgess and Sons were acting as a booking agent for Chas. A. Nethercott & Son. This allowed Burgess and Sons to continue to trade from the branch nearest to the crematorium. It also allowed Burgess and Sons to use Harwood Park for all its Hertfordshire customers – however far they were from Harwood Park. Nonetheless, Burgess and Sons' business suffered. Growth was stunted and the fact that they could not use Harwood Park meant that there people 'gossiped' about why it was that Burgess and Sons could no longer use Harwood Park. Burgess and Sons believed that this reduced the scope of their business.

Burgess and Sons' relationship with Chas. A. Nethercott & Son broke down when Austin's indicated to Nethercott's that the informal relationship they had with Burgess and Sons to use Harwood Park could no longer continue.

This put Justin Burgess and his mother under terrible strain. Burgess suggested that 'It's aged mum. The strain over three years has been incredible'. Burgess himself did not feel like going to work and, instead, wanted to 'pull the duvet over my head' and forget his business. He was also worried because this situation had arisen on his 'watch': he felt that he had responsibilities towards the generations of his family that had gone before him and the generations that would succeed him.

What was he to do? The obvious route was to take Austin's to the UK's competition watchdog – the Office of Fair Trade (OFT). Was this worth doing? It is likely that the OFT might take months or years to adjudicate on his case. By that time, would Burgess still have a business? What were his options? If he decided to take Austin's to the OFT, the basis of his claim would be that:

- Burgess and Sons were experiencing indirect price discrimination from having to pay Chas. A. Nethercott & Son to book cremations at Harwood Park.

- Customers were experiencing restraint on their choice of crematorium because they were effectively denied access to Harwood Park if they used Burgess and Sons.

- The activities of Austin's were having a negative impact on their business. They had to pay Chas. A. Nethercott & Son to book cremations which reduced their profitability.

- There was no other suitable crematorium in the vicinity that they could use.

Burgess knew, though, that Austin's would be likely to present powerful arguments in response. These were likely to be:

- Competition law should be there to support competition not competitors. Austin's had the right to trade with whoever they so wished. Austin's business model of a vertically integrated service had proved popular to the extent that it was able to open further branches in Welwyn Garden City and Knebworth. The claims of Burgess and Sons were just 'sour grapes' because they were not as competitive as Austin's. Burgess and Sons, like Austin's, were a family business. Just because they had been there a long time gave them no right or any guarantee to keep running the business. At the end of the day, Burgess and Sons had failed to understand and keep up to date with the modern practice of funeral services and provide a vertically integrated service.

- Burgess and Sons were the only funeral service to complain about being treated 'unfairly'. Other funeral services had not complained so any complaint had more to do with Burgess and Sons' businesses practices than anything to do with Austin's.

- Crucially, the Harwood Park crematorium is not the only crematorium in the vicinity. There are other crematoriums within a thirty-kilometre radius that could be used by Burgess and Sons.

- Hence, even if Austin's were 'dominant', there existed viable alternatives and, if this pushed Burgess and Sons out of the marketplace, that was a positive signal of the strength of competition in the supply of funeral services.

Questions   Your task is to consider the following questions:

1 What should be the judgement of the competition watchdog? Sift through the competing arguments and arrive at a reasoned judgement.

2 What do we learn about the nature of competition amongst small business from this case?

The aim of this case is to explore some of the difficulties surrounding the 'entrepreneurial status' of an individual. In very many countries, including the UK, it is often difficult to work out the employment or self-employment status of an individual. This matters because it shapes how we 'count' the number of self-employed in the economy. As Chapter 3 showed, for statistical purposes the self-employed are seen as 'entrepreneurs'. The 'entrepreneurial status' of an individual is also important because it has profound tax implications (see Chapter 20).

As Chapter 3 showed, there are four tests of self-employment status in the UK:

1 *Control*. Does the individual have to obey orders, and do they have discretion on hours of work?

2 *Integration*. Are they part of disciplinary/grievance procedures? Are they included in occupational benefit schemes?

3 *Economic reality*. How do they get paid? Are they free to hire others? Do they provide their own equipment? How do they pay tax? Who covers sick/holiday pay?

4 *Mutuality of obligation*. How long does the contract last? How regular is the work? Does the individual have the right to refuse work?

This case examines the decision by the UK tax authorities (Her Majesty's Revenue and Customs [HMRC]) that Mr Jon Bessell – the sole director of Dragonfly Consultancy Ltd – should pay a tax bill of £99,000 because HMRC judged he was an employee rather than a self-employed worker. Mr Bessell denied that he was liable for this tax bill because he was, in fact, self-employed rather than an employee. Mr Bessell took his case to a Special Commissioner (an individual in charge of appeals against tax decisions by HMRC). The case summarises the evidence heard by the Special Commissioner and gives his judgment. Your task is to examine the evidence and give your views. The learning outcomes of the case are that you should:

● increase your understanding of the ambiguity surrounding the status of the self-employed;

● increase your awareness of the difficulties presented in counting the number of self-employed in an economy.

We begin by introducing the background to the case, and then present the arguments given by both Dragonfly and HMRC. The case concludes with the summary given by the Special Commissioner.

Background to IR35

In 1999, the UK government became concerned that individuals were setting up their own 'service companies' to reduce their tax burden. The belief was that someone could resign from their job on a Friday, only to return on Monday to do the same job at the same company. However, by virtue of changing their job title to 'consultant', and through being employed by their own service company, their tax liabilities were reduced. The UK government enacted legislation in 2000 to limit this practice, introducing a new law – IR35 (so called after the press release that announced its arrival) – to clarify the tax situation of the self-employed. The aim of IR35 was:

> . . . to ensure that individuals who ought to pay tax and NIC as employees cannot, by the assumption of a corporate structure, reduce and defer the liabilities imposed on employees by the United Kingdom's system of personal taxation.
>
> *Source: Robert Walker in R (Professional Contractors Group)*
> *v IRC [2001] EWCA Civ 1945, (2002) STC 165, para. 51.*

Dragonfly vs HMRC

In December 2007, a Special Commissioner with powers to adjudicate on the rights and wrongs of this legislation had to decide on the following case:

> The sole director and 50 per cent shareholder of Dragonfly Consultancy Ltd is Mr Jon Bessell. Mr Bessell is an experienced IT systems tester. He had been hired by an agency, DPP International Limited, to provide IT services to the Automobile Association (AA) group. DPP was not connected to Dragonfly in any way. Mr Bessell worked on three separate projects for the AA between 2000 and 2003. On his tax return, he claimed his rightful allowances as a self-employed individual. HMRC did not agree that Mr Bessell was, in fact, self-employed. They demanded that Mr Bessell pay £99,000 in tax, because they claimed that he was an employee rather than self-employed.

The key facts found by the Special Commissioner were that some features of the work appeared to classify Mr Bessell as a self-employed contractor, while other features indicated that he was an employee. Some of the 'self-employed' features were that:

● Mr Bessell had a pass into the work site with a 'C' on it, to differentiate between him, as a contractor, from employees.

- Mr Bessell provided his own special chair to assist him with a back problem. This was at his own company's expense, and was used on the contractor's premises.

- Owing to his back problem, Mr Bessell was unable to work for a time, and received no payment during this period.

- Mr Bessell had a designated office at home, with two laptops, a fax machine, a scanner and office furniture.

- During the term of the contract Mr Bessell's company, Dragonfly, paid £400 for a training course for Mr Bessell, to benefit his work. The contractor did not reimburse him for this.

- Mr Bessell did not take holidays at times that were significantly inconvenient for the projects; but neither did he bill for time during which he was on holiday, nor did he receive any payment.

- Mr Bessell did undertake another contract during the period, but this formed a small part of his overall income.

The 'employee' characteristics were that:

- Mr Bessell was able to use the onsite canteen and was invited to attend staff social functions.

- Although Mr Bessell paid for it himself, his home computer was directly linked to the AA offices.

- Nobody told Mr Bessell how to do his work, but he was expected to complete tasks allocated to him by agreement with the team leader, and the standard of his work was monitored informally.

- Mr Bessell attended weekly team meetings and took part in ad hoc discussions.

The verdict

The Special Commissioner stated:

Overall I find nothing which points strongly to the conclusion that Mr Bessell would have been in business on his own account; by contrast, when I stand back and look at the overall picture I see someone who worked fairly regular hours during each engagement, who worked on parts of a project which were allocated to him as part of the [contractor]'s teams, who was integrated into the [contractor]'s business, and who had a role similar to that of a professional employee. Mr Bessell did not get paid for, or go to work to provide, a specific product; instead he provided his services to the [contractor] to be used by them in testing the parts of a project which from time to time were allocated to him. He was engaged in relation to the work to be done on a specific project but not to deliver anything other than his services in providing testing in relation to that project. In my opinion he would have been an employee had he been directly engaged by the [contractor].

Questions	
	1 Do you agree with the conclusion of the special commissioner?
	2 Using the four tests of self-employment, justify Mr Bessell's claim that he was self-employed.
	3 Justify HMRC's view that Mr Bessell was an employee.
	4 What does this case suggest about how we 'count' an 'enterprise' population?

Part 1 Runner & Sprue's business plan

The first part of this case study asks you to read the actual business plan written by two ex-students of Coventry University, Sam Tate and Nick Rutter. Sam Tate had graduated as an automotive design engineer but, following university, had moved into sales and marketing at a Coventry nightclub. Nick Rutter was a technology-design student at the university who had gone to Hong Kong to work as a freelance designer, working for, amongst others, the Dutch company, Phillips. He had seen how entrepreneurial people were in Hong Kong and how they could turn designs into products that sold.

Sam and Nick had come up with their idea for a smoke alarm in the spring of 1998 when they went round a house looking for domestic products that were poorly branded commodities in need of a new innovative spin. Nick Rutter explains:

> We were both at a time in our lives when we were looking to start something, accelerate our careers, make some money and we discussed the possibilities of starting a business. From that we started to build up a business model based on our experiences in business to date, and we stumbled across smoke alarms and thought, 'Here's a product which has seen no innovation since day one'. The products in the market, we felt, were very poor, so there was great opportunity for innovation. We invented the product over one evening with a few bottles of red wine, a sheet of paper and a biro. It wasn't like we needed millions of pounds of equipment at that stage.

Both Sam Tate and Nick Rutter subsequently enrolled on the twelve-week Graduates into Business course run by Coventry University, which aimed to take former students and guide them through the process of setting up a business. The course sought to develop their presentation skills, their understanding of legal and tax issues, and ultimately produce a business plan.

In this case, you are asked to read and evaluate their resulting business plan. The funding they are seeking is a £55,000 European grant administered by Coventry University. You are asked three questions:

1 On the basis of Table 1 (Personal details of founders) of the business plan, would you say that Sam Tate and Nick Rutter fit into your idea of what an 'entrepreneur' constitutes?

2 Would you give Sam Tate and Nick Rutter the grant? What is the basis for your decision?

3 If you were Coventry University, what stake, if any, would you ask for in Runner & Sprue?

Runner & Sprue Ltd.
The TechnoCentre
Puma Way
Coventry
CV1 2TT
Tel: (44) 1203 236 600
Fax: (44) 1203 236 024
1st November 1998

Graduate into Business Programme
Coventry University Enterprises Ltd.
The TechnoCentre
Puma Way
Coventry
CV1 2TT

Dear Panel Members

ERDF Funding from the GIB Panel

We welcome the opportunity to make a short presentation to the Graduate into Business (GIB) Panel on the 25th November 1998.

Please find attached a copy of Runner & Sprue's Business Plan. It goes into more detail about the proposed venture and demonstrates its viability.

We are asking for the maximum funding of £55,000 from the European Regional Development Fund (ERDF). The funding is to be used primarily to fund our working capital needs whilst we develop the Easyfit™ smoke detection system.

The £55,000 of funding we require has already been matched (in-kind) by a commercial organisation. We are also confident that the patent that we have filed for our innovative smoke detection system will, with the help of Coventry University, be granted.

We envisage that the ERDF funding will mean that we do not have to sign over a large percentage stake in Runner & Sprue in the future.

We look forward to seeing you on the 25th.

Yours sincerely,

Sam Tate and Nick Rutter
Runner & Sprue
PRODUCT DEVELOPMENT

Business Plan
Prepared for the GIB Funding Panel

November 1998

Executive Summary

- Runner & Sprue's smoke detection system – Easyfit™ – is a revolutionary new concept in the domestic smoke alarm market.

- It overcomes the three main problems with conventional smoke alarms: they take time to fit, batteries have to be maintained and they often go off at inconvenient times.

- Easyfit™ offers the consumer a system that fits in seconds, is maintenance free and is simple to reset.

- Globally, there are only two light fittings and two power ratings.

- Runner & Sprue is jointly owned by Nick Rutter and Sam Tate. Nick Rutter comes with a strong background and flair for product design whilst Sam Tate has robust sales and marketing experience.

- With the help of Coventry University, Runner & Sprue have filed for a patent for their innovative smoke detection system.

- We are looking for funding of £55,000 from the ERDF to turn the concept into a working product.

Runner & Sprue's milestones are:

1999	Launch the world's first consumer fit, mains powered, maintenance free smoke alarm
2000	Introduce two models to our range
2001	Break into the US market
2002	Forecasted turnover of £12 m with a gross profit of £4.5 m
2003	After the second generation of alarms is launched we sell the entire operation

Background

Runner & Sprue have come along way in the last year. The company began when we recognised that there was an opportunity in the consumer product market. As a generalisation, this market can be split into two different groups:

1 'Big Brands' – these are companies that supply a high quality product to well established highly stable markets. Dominated by global companies, they take their products from conception to the retailer. On the downside, they often have incredibly long lead times, are bureaucratic and need mature markets. This means that they need to sell high volumes to cope with low profit margins.

2 'B Brand Manufacturers' – are companies that seek to minimise all costs (fixed and variable) and to sell products as commodities. Such businesses have little or no market research, design or development functions. Their products often have little or no added value and are typically sold through discount houses (K-Mart, Target, etc.). What advantage they do have is that they are able to push a product very quickly – on an incredibly tight development budget – into emerging markets and fulfil the needs of lower volume specialist markets.

We have set out to compete against 'B Brand Manufacturers' by preying on weak market sectors which supply a mediocre product that has little or no design ethic and provide questionable consumer benefit. In particular, our aim is to attack mature markets where pricing issues dominate by offering a clear user benefit to the consumer.

We have spent a year developing the idea for a second generation smoke alarm. We have just completed a Graduate into Business programme run by Coventry University. Runner & Sprue is now a limited company registered in England and Wales. The share distribution of the company (A class shares) is 50% Sam Tate and 50% Nick Rutter. The owners of the company are currently in negotiation with Coventry University over the equity return to the University for financing the filing of the patent.

The Product

The familiar battery-powered domestic smoke alarm was launched in the 1960s and then heavily marketed and promoted throughout the 1970s. By the early 1980s, these units were selling in excess of 25 million units a year in the US alone.

There are only three different types of sensors in smoke alarms:

- Ionisation sensors detect an imbalance in current flow between two minute plates coated in a radioactive foil.

- Optical detectors compare light beams inside and outside of a sealed glass tube to detect smoke. They are highly effective but expensive.

- Rate of rise detectors monitor the ambient temperature and trigger the alarm when the temperature rises very quickly. They are suitable for detecting flash fires (e.g. kitchen, garages) but are costly.

Over 95% of domestic smoke alarms use the ionisation smoke detector. Central to these alarms is the use of a very small amount of radioactive Amercium 241. This is manufactured only by two companies worldwide: Amersham International in Buckinghamshire, UK and NRD in New York, US. Manufacture of finished ionisation alarms is almost exclusively undertaken in Mexico for the North American markets whilst the EI Company supplies such units for the European market.

Existing domestic smoke alarms typically require a nine volt battery: consumers need DIY skills to install them.

Also, although UK building regulations now make the fitting of mains-powered smoke alarms compulsory, the vast majority of consumers have failed to do so because wiring houses to the high voltage ring main is not something they can do easily. That has meant that mains powered consumer units are almost exclusively sold through the building trade.

EasyFit system™ the maintenance free smoke alarm

Our innovative smoke alarm system overcomes the problems of first-generation smoke alarms. Installation is simple: the system plugs into an existing light fitting and the light bulb fits in underneath.

A real problem with conventional smoke alarms is their reliance on batteries. Consumers fit the wrong battery, forget to replace the battery or actively disarm the battery. No wonder, then, that 39% of smoke alarms were found to have battery problems (Figure 1).

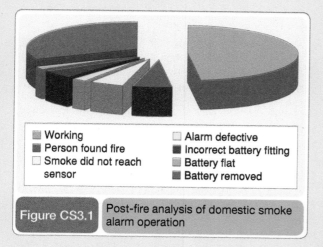

- Working
- Person found fire
- Smoke did not reach sensor
- Alarm defective
- Incorrect battery fitting
- Battery flat
- Battery removed

Figure CS3.1 Post-fire analysis of domestic smoke alarm operation

In the US, although household ownership of smoke alarms runs at 90%, there are real issues with the utility of conventional smoke alarms: 'We put 50 million smoke detectors in buildings in America in a two-year period, and our fire loss and death rate goes up' (Gordon Vickery, former head of US Fire Administration, Source: *Fire Engineering*); and 'John C. Gerard, Fire Chief of the Los Angeles Fire Department cited national statistics showing battery-powered devices have a 50–80 per cent failure rate' (Source: *Fire Control Digest*, 6, 10)

The Easyfit™ system solves this problem because it is maintenance free. The rechargeable Lithium batteries will last for six months without the light switch ever being used. The system has an additional benefit to the consumer in that active disarming is prevented because all consumers have to do to reset the alarm is to flick the light switch three times. This will also cut down on the number of nuisance alarms.

Unlike conventional smoke alarms which typically retail at around £5, the Easyfit™ system provides an opportunity for charging premium prices.

The Market

Currently, the consumer market for smoke alarms is saturated. Worldwide sales have slumped from over 30 million units p.a. in the mid-1980s to around 15 million.

The standard smoke alarm is a commodity. Retailers across the board stock one type of unit: the battery operated ceiling mounted unit for around £4. The only other models which are similar to the ceiling mounted unit are a unit with an escape light or a unit with a ten-year battery supply. The ten-year alarm has not proved popular because of the bulkiness of the batteries.

Manufacture of the conventional smoke alarms is dominated by large companies in the UK such as BRK, Dicon and EI Company. BRK has 32%, Dicon has 18% and EI has 15% of the UK's £92 million market for smoke alarms (Source: *Mintel, Personal and Home Security Report*, 1997). BRK and Dicon are North American owned, whilst EI was bought out in an MBO from General Electric. It is estimated that if 60% of households in the UK, Germany, France, Italy and the US have a smoke alarm; the potential market size is 123 million households.

Reaching the Market

Because of the innovative nature of the Easyfit™ system, we anticipate that the product will give us a gross profit margin of 42%.

Manufacturers of traditional smoke alarms spend very little on marketing. What matters, instead, is the price of the good. Also significant is the fact that such manufacturers tend to rely on free exposure from governments and fire brigades to promote their product.

Our radical system has clear benefits to the consumer. This alone will help sell it. Governments and fire brigades are also looking for a distinctive solution to the problems of active disarming and nuisance alarms. We intend to work closely with fire brigades in the first instance to remind them of the problems with conventional alarms and then how the Easyfit™ system overcomes these problems. Such free promotion will help convince the consumer of the value of the product.

Another route being considered is to approach insurance companies, offering them a discount scheme, similar to the car/burglar alarm policies.

The benefits of manufacturing exclusives are important. The major DIY retailers (whose own branded products currently account for 16% of the market) will be targeted so that a joint promotional campaign, perhaps through television advertising, can be launched.

Finally, the packaging of the product is also key. Consumers will not be familiar with the product so the product should be packaged in an eye-catching manner.

Production and Operations

Having already specified the initial production model, the next stage is the production of manufacturing ready circuitry. Once the exact circuitry dimensions are done, prototyping of the mouldings can be achieved. There is then a subsequent need to ensure that the product complies with all of the approval bodies (e.g. BS, CE, Kite marking, TUV and UL).

As we have never sought to manufacture, the intention is to use an ionisation chamber which can be bought as a complete unit. These are guaranteed for ten years and so a full ten-year warranty will be provided on the products.

As the Easyfit™ system has a high volume potential (only two fittings and two power ratings worldwide) and is relatively straightforward to manufacture, South East Asia has always been the preferred site of manufacture. Nick Rutter has both experience and contacts in Hong Kong and Shenzhen. Manufacturing in such areas is also cheaper even if the economic situation in South East Asia is of concern at the moment: the high mark up of the Easyfit™ system allows Runner & Sprue to cope with a certain amount of fluctuation.

There are many third-party manufacturers in southern China which specialise in turnkey packages (price for the finished goods on a boat) for plastic-based electronics goods.

To ensure quality, companies such as Inchcape (owned by Seagrams) whose core business is quality control for overseas clients could be used. Such a company may prove expensive but would ensure that production quality does not become eroded. Nick would also use his experience here to good advantage.

Tooling costs are difficult to estimate without more information on moulding. Tool burn out, though, is likely to be a big issue but it is anticipated that tool life is likely to be around 500–750,000 units. If so, a second set of tools will be required after sales begin to pick up.

Our filed patent also has the benefit that it is for any combination of light fitting and smoke alarm whether integral or not. This gives us the opportunity to produce not only several variants for the consumer market but also smoke alarms in ceiling roses, track lights and florescent strip lights for the construction industry. Hence, besides the entry level model (Easyfit™) the product has other applications: Easyfit™ with an escape light; an energy saver model and, for the deaf, a model with a strobe instead of a piezo electric buzzer.

Because the entry level system and variants share identical tooling and circuit boards, costs will be minimised. Adopting a modular tooling system means that the main unit for each product will be moulded in cheap but highly resistant plastic (e.g. Polybutylene Terephthalate (PBT)). Alternatively, there is the option of compression moulding in a thermoset such as Phenolic. Materials and tooling for this would be cheaper but Phenolic does tend to be very brittle.

The variants (Easyfit™ with an escape light, energy saver and a strobe) all will require different materials (e.g. clear plastic for escape light unit) and perhaps alternative tooling but any increase in cost can be more than compensated by the higher unit price charged.

Any manufacturer used would be responsible for packing and containerisation of the product (approx. 6,300 units). We will not have to deal with production in a physical sense.

Management

The owners – Sam Tate and Nick Rutter – have known each other for five years and have a strong friendship and a similar sense of humour. Both have a very Northern, down to earth outlook on life, which includes a hard-work ethic, a natural tenacity and a total inability to suffer fools gladly. We have given up well-paid jobs and are 100% dedicated to the project.

Nick Rutter comes with a strong background and flair for product design, particularly in Hong Kong. Sam Tate has excellent sales and marketing experience gained through the automotive and entertainment industries (see Table 1 for further information).

Finance

Runner & Sprue's main problem is cashflow (see Three-Year Profit and Loss and Cashflow in Tables 2a–c and 3a–c). Working capital is required to finance the business to a stage in the development whereby all the necessary approvals have been given and an order book can be opened. We have, so far, received £55,000 of in-kind support from Coventry University. This has no impact on the equity structure of the business.

We are seeking £55,000 of ERDF funding from GIB to allow for the development of the Easyfit™ system. This will be used to pay the owners a subsistence salary, provide an administrative assistant and, most importantly, fund the product development phase.

It is estimated that a further £400,000 will be needed to get the product into the market. Having the ERDF funding will mean that signing over a large percentage stake in Runner & Sprue and its potentially very lucrative intellectual property will be avoided.

Working with a strategic partner could unlock the required funding. These could be:

1 A manufacturer of a complementary product (e.g. fire extinguishers) who has a strong brand;

Table 1	Personal details of founders

Nick Rutter
Design and Development Director

Age	**26**

Experience	**Product Designer**
	Designed Portable Audio for Philips Corporate Design in Hong Kong. Worked as one of six product designers in a studio responsible for the design and development of Philips entire mainstream audio range (approximately 17 million units per annum). My main responsibility was to create and present new designs in line with the company's corporate design philosophy and then work closely with the manufacturer to ensure quality was upheld into production.
	Freelance Design Consultant
	Worked on a diverse range of projects for both Western and Chinese companies based in Hong Kong. During this time I was responsible for many areas of the design process including concept development, production of model drawings, commissioning and checking of models, inspection of copper tooling impressions, packaging concepts, design of brochures and instruction manuals and market mapping studies.
Qualifications	**Honours Degree in Transport Design**
	BTEC HND in Engineering
Key Skills	*Creative flair*
	Holistic approach to design
	Experience in Asia

Sam Tate
Business Development Director

Age	**29**

Experience	**Programme Manager**
	Responsible for developing the customer base and range of products on offer for the Planet Night Club in Coventry. Through effective marketing and promotion succeeded in increasing business by 26% per annum and turned an artist budget of £250,000 into direct revenue exceeding £620,000.
	Operations Manager
	Working for Coventry Students' Union and Planet Night Club as the Operations Manager I was responsible for all operational issues, including in excess of 250 part-time staff and a budget of £150,000.
	Dealership Service Manager
	At the age of 21, I was the Service Manager of a large Nissan dealership in the north of England. My main tasks included managing staff and dealing with (usually disgruntled) customers.
Qualifications	**Degree in Automotive Engineering Design**
	BTEC OND Vehicle Studies
	City and Guilds Technicians
Key Skills	*Negotiating*
	Logical thinking
	Turning investment into profit

2 A manufacturer or retailer with a strong world-wide distribution network who is able to accelerate market penetration; or

3 A supplier of components (e.g. ion chambers) who could further develop the business.

Exit Strategy

There are no sacred cows for Runner & Sprue. The owners aim to establish the true market potential of the Easyfit™ and then sell the company at its height to obtain the maximum possible revenue. This should take a maximum of five years from concept to sale:

1999 Launch the world's first consumer fit, mains powered, maintenance-free smoke alarm

2000 Introduce two models to our range

2001 Break into the US

2002 Forecasted turnover of £12 m with a gross profit of £4.5 m

2003 After the second generation of alarms is launched we sell the entire operation

Table 2a Profit and loss forecast for Runner & Sprue, YEAR 1

						Month							
	Nov	Dec	Jan	Feb	Mar	Apr	May	Jun	Jul	Aug	Sept	Oct	Total
	1	2	3	4	5	6	7	8	9	10	11	12	
Selling on price	£6.00	£6.00	£6.00	£6.00	£6.00	£6.00	£6.00	£6.00	£6.00	£6.00	£6.00	£6.00	
Sales per month	0	0	0	0	0	0	0	0	30,000	5,000	7,500	7,500	50,000
Sales/Revenue	0	0	0	0	0	0	0	0	180,000	30,000	45,000	45,000	300,000
Less cost of sales:													
Buying in price	3.40	3.40	3.40	3.40	3.40	3.40	3.40	3.40	3.40	3.40	3.40	3.40	
Purchases	0	0	0	0	0	0	0	0	105,000	17,500	26,250	26,250	175,000
Direct wages	0	0	0	0	0	0	0	0	0	0	0	0	0
Cost of goods sold (COGS)	0	0	0	0	0	0	0	0	105,000	17,500	26,250	26,250	175,000
Gross profit (GP)	0	0	0	0	0	0	0	0	75,000	12,500	18,750	18,750	125,000
Gross profit margin	0	0	0	0	0	0	0	0	41.67	41.67	41.67	41.67	41.67
OVERHEADS													
Salaries	5,000	5,000	5,000	5,000	5,000	5,000	5,000	5,000	5,000	5,000	5,000	5,000	60,000
Training	100	100	100	100	100	100	100	100	100	100	100	100	1,200
Rent and rates	300	300	300	300	300	300	300	300	300	300	300	300	3,600
Product development costs	1,250	1,250	1,250	1,250	1,250	1,250	1,250	1,250	1,250	1,250	1,250	1,250	15,000
Electricity	40	40	40	40	40	40	40	40	40	40	40	40	480
Postage/Stationery/Photocopying	83	83	84	83	83	84	83	83	84	83	83	84	1,000
Repairs and renewals	100	100	100	100	100	100	100	100	100	100	100	100	1,200
Travelling and motor expenses	1,100	1,100	1,100	1,100	1,100	1,100	1,100	1,100	1,100	1,100	1,100	1,100	13,200
Telephone	150	150	150	150	150	150	150	150	150	150	150	150	1,800
Professional fees (patent charges)	700	700	700	700	700	700	700	700	700	700	700	700	8,400
Marketing	583	583	584	583	583	584	583	583	584	583	583	584	7,000
Insurance	200	200	200	200	200	200	200	200	200	200	200	200	2,400
Bank charges	60	60	60	60	60	60	60	60	60	60	60	60	720
Depreciation	500	500	500	500	500	500	500	500	500	500	500	500	6,000
TOTAL OVERHEADS	10,166	10,166	10,168	10,166	10,166	10,168	10,166	10,166	10,168	10,166	10,166	10,168	122,000
Total profit (Loss) (GP – Overheads)	–10,166	–10,166	–10,168	–10,166	–10,166	–10,168	–10,166	–10,166	64,832	2,334	8,584	8,582	3,000

Table 2b   Profit and loss forecast for Runner & Sprue, YEAR 2

	Nov	Dec	Jan	Feb	Mar	Apr	May	Jun	Jul	Aug	Sept	Oct	Total
Month	1	2	3	4	5	6	7	8	9	10	11	12	
Selling on price	£6.00	£6.00	£6.00	£6.00	£6.00	£6.00	£6.00	£6.00	£6.00	£6.00	£6.00	£6.00	£6.00
Sales per month	10,000	10,000	7,500	7,500	15,000	20,000	25,000	30,000	35,000	45,000	55,000	65,000	325,000
Sales/Revenue	60,000	60,000	45,000	45,000	90,000	120,000	150,000	180,000	210,000	270,000	330,000	390,000	1,950,000
Less cost of sales:													
Buying in price	3.40	3.40	3.40	3.40	3.40	3.40	3.40	3.40	3.40	3.40	3.40	3.40	3.40
Purchases	34,000	34,000	25,500	25,500	51,000	68,000	85,000	102,000	119,000	153,000	187,000	221,000	1,105,000
Direct wages	0	0	0	0	0	0	0	0	0	0	0	0	0
Cost of goods sold (COGS)	34,000	34,000	25,500	25,500	51,000	68,000	85,000	102,000	119,000	153,000	187,000	221,000	1,105,000
Gross profit (GP)	26,000	26,000	19,500	19,500	39,000	52,000	65,000	78,000	91,000	117,000	143,000	169,000	845,000
Gross profit margin	43.33	43.33	43.33	43.33	43.33	43.33	43.33	43.33	43.33	43.33	43.33	43.33	43.33
OVERHEADS													
Salaries	12,460	12,460	12,461	12,460	12,460	12,461	12,460	12,460	12,461	12,460	12,460	12,461	149,524
Training	200	200	200	200	200	200	200	200	200	200	200	200	2,400
Rent and rates	600	600	600	600	600	600	600	600	600	600	600	600	7,200
Product development costs	1,250	1,250	1,250	1,250	1,250	1,250	1,250	1,250	1,250	1,250	1,250	1,250	15,000
Electricity	60	60	60	60	60	60	60	60	60	60	60	60	720
Postage/Stationery/Photocopying	192	192	191	192	192	191	192	192	191	192	192	191	2,300
Repairs and renewals	250	250	250	250	250	250	250	250	250	250	250	250	3,000
Travelling and motor expenses	1,500	1,500	1,500	1,500	1,500	1,500	1,500	1,500	1,500	1,500	1,500	1,500	18,000
Telephone	400	400	400	400	400	400	400	400	400	400	400	400	4,800
Professional fees (patent charges)	667	667	666	667	667	666	667	667	666	667	667	666	8,000
Marketing	1,000	1,000	1,000	1,000	1,000	1,000	1,000	1,000	1,000	1,000	1,000	1,000	12,000
Insurance	417	417	416	417	417	416	417	417	416	417	417	416	5,000
Bank charges	92	92	91	92	92	91	92	92	91	92	92	91	1,100
Depreciation	688	688	688	688	688	688	688	688	688	688	688	688	8,250
TOTAL OVERHEADS	19,776	19,776	19,773	19,776	19,776	19,773	19,776	19,776	19,773	19,776	19,776	19,773	237,294
Total profit (Loss)	6,225	6,225	−273	−276	19,225	32,228	45,225	58,225	71,228	97,225	123,225	149,228	607,706

Table 2c Profit and loss forecast for Runner & Sprue, YEAR 3

	Month												
	Nov	Dec	Jan	Feb	Mar	Apr	May	Jun	Jul	Aug	Sept	Oct	Total
	1	2	3	4	5	6	7	8	9	10	11	12	
Selling on price	£5.10	£5.10	£5.10	£5.10	£5.10	£5.10	£5.10	£5.10	£5.10	£5.10	£5.10	£5.10	£5.10
Sales per month	70,000	80,000	65,000	70,000	75,000	80,000	85,000	90,000	95,000	90,000	95,000	105,000	1,000,000
Sales/Revenue	357,000	408,000	331,500	357,000	382,500	408,000	433,500	459,000	484,500	459,000	484,500	535,500	5,100,000
Less cost of sales:													
Buying in price	£3.20	£3.20	£3.20	£3.20	£3.20	£3.20	£3.20	£3.20	£3.20	£3.20	£3.20	£3.20	3.40
Purchases	224,000	256,000	208,000	224,000	240,000	256,000	272,000	288,000	304,000	288,000	304,000	336,000	3,400,000
Direct wages	0	0	0	0	0	0	0	0	0	0	0	0	0
Cost of goods sold (COGS)	224,000	256,000	208,000	224,000	240,000	256,000	272,000	288,000	304,000	288,000	304,000	336,000	3,400,000
Gross profit (GP)	133,000	152,000	123,500	133,000	142,500	152,000	161,500	171,000	180,500	171,000	180,500	199,500	1,700,000
Gross profit margin	37.25	37.25	37.25	37.25	37.25	37.25	37.25	37.25	37.25	37.25	37.25	37.25	33.33
OVERHEADS													
Salaries	25,126	25,126	25,126	25,126	25,126	25,126	25,127	25,126	25,126	25,127	25,126	25,126	301,514
Training	533	533	534	533	533	534	533	533	534	533	533	534	6,400
Rent and rates	920	920	920	920	920	920	920	920	920	920	920	920	11,040
Product development costs	3,333	3,333	3,334	3,333	3,333	3,334	3,333	3,333	3,334	3,333	3,333	3,334	40,000
Electricity	73	73	74	73	73	74	73	73	74	73	73	74	880
Postage/Stationery/Photocopying	238	238	239	238	238	239	238	238	239	238	238	239	2,860
Repairs and renewals	500	500	500	500	500	500	500	500	500	500	500	500	6,000
Travelling and motor expenses	1,750	1,750	1,750	1,750	1,750	1,750	1,750	1,750	1,750	1,750	1,750	1,750	21,000
Telephone	600	600	600	600	600	600	600	600	600	600	600	600	7,200
Professional fees (patent charges)	1,500	1,500	1,500	1,500	1,500	1,500	1,500	1,500	1,500	1,500	1,500	1,500	18,000
Marketing	1,000	1,000	1,000	1,000	1,000	1,000	1,000	1,000	1,000	1,000	1,000	1,000	12,000
Insurance	1,000	1,000	1,000	1,000	1,000	1,000	1,000	1,000	1,000	1,000	1,000	1,000	12,000
Bank charges	100	100	100	100	100	100	100	100	100	100	100	100	1,200
Depreciation	875	875	875	875	875	875	875	875	875	875	875	875	10,500
TOTAL OVERHEADS	37,548	37,548	37,552	37,548	37,548	37,552	37,549	37,548	37,552	37,549	37,548	37,552	450,594
Total profit (Loss) (GP – Overheads)	95,452	114,452	85,948	95,452	104,952	114,448	123,951	133,452	142,948	133,451	142,952	161,948	1,249,406

Table 3a Cashflow forecast for Runner & Sprue, YEAR 1

		Nov	Dec	Jan	Feb	Mar	Apr	May	Jun	Jul	Aug	Sept	Oct	Total
Month		1	2	3	4	5	6	7	8	9	10	11	12	
INCOME														
Units sold		0	0	0	0	0	0	0	0	0	0	30,000	5,000	35,000
Selling on price		6	6	6	6	6	6	6	6	6	6	6	6	
Cash received		0	0	0	0	0	0	0	0	0	0	180,000	30,000	210,000
Capital and/or loans introduced		0	0	0	0	0	0	0	0	0	0	0	0	0
Other income		0	0	0	0	0	0	0	0	0	0	0	0	0
Total Cash IN		0	0	0	0	0	0	0	0	0	0	180,000	30,000	210,000
EXPENDITURE														
Purchases														
No. of units bought in		0	0	0	0	0	0	0	0	30,000	5,000	7,500	7,500	50,000
Manufacturing costs		3.5	3.5	3.5	3.5	3.5	3.5	3.5	3.5	3.5	3.5	3.5	3.5	3.5
Total		0	0	0	0	0	0	0	0	105,000	17,500	26,250	26,250	175,000
Wages														
No. of employees (1)		3	3	3	3	3	3	3	3	3	4	4	4	3.5
Total		4,043	4,043	4,043	4,043	4,043	4,043	4,043	4,043	4,043	7,871	7,871	7,871	60,000

Table 3a continued

OVERHEADS (indirect costs)	1	2	3	4	5	6	7	8	9	10	11	12	Total
Training	100	100	100	100	100	100	100	100	100	100	100	100	1,200
Rent and rates	300	300	300	300	300	300	300	300	300	300	300	300	3,600
Product development costs	3,000	4,000	3,000	5,000	0	0	0	0	0	0	0	0	15,000
Electricity	0	0	120	0	0	120	0	0	120	0	0	120	480
Postage/Stationery/Photocopying	150	150	150	150	50	50	50	50	50	50	50	50	1,000
Repairs and renewals	0	0	0	0	200	200	200	200	200	200	0	0	1,200
Travelling and motor expenses	1,100	1,100	1,100	1,100	1,100	1,100	1,100	1,100	1,100	1,100	1,100	1,100	13,200
Telephone	450	0	0	450	0	0	450	0	0	450	0	0	1,800
Professional fees (patent charges)	700	0	500	0	1,000	500	0	0	0	0	5,700	0	8,400
Marketing	0	1,000	1,000	2,000	0	3,000	0	0	0	0	0	0	7,000
Insurance	600	0	0	600	0	0	600	0	0	600	0	0	2,400
Bank charges	100	60	60	60	60	60	60	0	60	60	60	0	720
Total	5,450	5,650	6,380	7,650	3,550	6,280	2,750	1,750	3,170	2,750	8,870	1,750	56,000
Capital equipment													
Tooling	0	0	0	0	0	9,000	0	9,000	0	12,000	0	0	30,000
Office equipment (2)	10,000	0	0	0	0	0	0	0	0	0	0	0	10,000
Total	10,000	0	0	0	0	9,000	0	9,000	0	12,000	0	0	40,000
Total Cash OUT	−19,493	−9,693	−10,423	−11,693	−7,593	−10,323	−6,793	−14,793	−121,213	−40,121	−35,871	−42,991	−331,000
Net cashflow	−19,493	−9,693	−10,423	−11,693	−7,593	−10,323	−6,793	−14,793	−121,213	−40,121	144,129	−12,991	−121,000
Balance brought forward	0	−19,493	−29,186	−39,609	−51,302	−58,895	−69,218	−76,011	−90,804	−212,017	−252,138	−108,009	
Balance carried forward	−19,493	−29,186	−39,609	−51,302	−58,895	−69,218	−76,011	−90,804	−212,017	−252,138	−108,009	−121,000	−121,000

Notes: (1) 1 office assistant @ £275 av. per week (£14,300); 2nd office worker @ £2,331 per month (months 10–12) (£13,986); two directors @ £1,472 each (months 1–9) (£26,496) and @ £2,331 each (months 10–12) (£5,993). (2) Laser printer £300; scanner £300; inkjet printer £280; CD burner £300; zip drive £150; 2 laptops £3,000; desktop PC £900; monitor £700; network set up £200; office furniture £2,000.

Table 3b	Cashflow forecast for Runner & Sprue, YEAR 2

Month

	Nov	Dec	Jan	Feb	Mar	Apr	May	Jun	Jul	Aug	Sept	Oct	Total
INCOME													
CASH/CHEQUES RECEIVED													
Units sold	7,500	7,500	10,000	10,000	7,500	7,500	15,000	20,000	25,000	30,000	35,000	45,000	205,000
Selling on price	6	6	6	6	6	6	6	6	6	6	6	6	
Sales/Revenue	45,000	45,000	60,000	60,000	45,000	45,000	90,000	120,000	150,000	180,000	210,000	270,000	1,320,000
Capital and/or loans introduced	0	0	0	0	0	0	0	0	0	0	0	0	0
Other income	0	0	0	0	0	0	0	0	0	0	0	0	0
Cash inflows	45,000	45,000	60,000	60,000	45,000	45,000	90,000	120,000	150,000	180,000	210,000	270,000	1,320,000
EXPENDITURE													
Direct costs													
Number of units bought in	10,000	10,000	7,500	7,500	15,000	20,000	25,000	30,000	35,000	45,000	55,000	65,000	205,000
Manufacturing costs	3.4	3.4	3.4	3.4	3.4	3.4	3.4	3.4	3.4	3.4	3.4	3.4	
Total	34,000	34,000	25,500	25,500	51,000	68,000	85,000	102,000	119,000	153,000	187,000	221,000	1,105,000
Wages													
No. of employees (1)	4	4	4	5	5	5	5	5	5	5	5	5	
Total	8,092	8,092	8,367	13,459	13,459	14,064	13,459	13,459	14,064	15,486	13,459	14,064	149,524

Table 3b continued

													Total
OVERHEADS													
Training	200	200	200	200	200	200	200	200	200	200	200	200	2,400
Rent and rates	600	600	600	600	600	600	600	600	600	600	600	600	7,200
Product development costs	2,000	3,000	5,000	5,000	0	0	0	0	0	0	0	0	15,000
Electricity	0	0	180	0	0	180	0	180	0	0	0	180	720
Postage/Stationery/Photocopying	375	175	175	175	175	175	175	175	175	175	175	175	2,300
Repairs and renewals	250	250	250	250	250	250	250	250	250	250	250	250	3,000
Travelling and motor expenses	1,500	1,500	1,500	1,500	1,500	1,500	1,500	1,500	1,500	1,500	1,500	1,500	18,000
Telephone	0	0	1,200	0	0	1,200	0	1,200	0	0	0	1,200	4,800
Professional fees (patent charges)	0	0	1,000	0	0	1,000	0	2,000	0	0	0	4,000	8,000
Marketing	0	0	0	2,000	5,000	5,000	0	0	0	0	0	0	12,000
Insurance	1,000	0	1,000	0	0	1,000	0	1,000	0	0	0	1,000	5,000
Bank charges	0	0	250	0	0	250	0	300	0	0	0	300	1,100
Total	5,925	5,725	11,355	9,725	7,725	11,355	2,725	7,405	2,725	2,725	2,725	9,405	79,520
Capital equipment													
Tooling	0	0	0	0	0	0	0	0	0	0	0	50,000	50,000
Office equipment	5,000	0	0	0	0	0	0	0	0	0	0	0	5,000
Total	5,000	0	0	0	0	0	0	0	0	0	0	50,000	55,000
Total Cash OUT	−53,017	−47,817	−45,222	−48,684	−72,184	−93,419	−101,184	−118,184	−140,469	−171,211	−203,184	−294,469	−1,389,044
Net cashflow	−8,017	−2,817	14,778	11,316	−27,184	−48,419	−11,184	1,816	9,531	8,789	6,816	−24,469	−69,044
Balance brought forward	−121,000	−129,017	−131,834	−117,056	−105,740	−132,924	−181,343	−192,527	−190,711	−181,180	−172,391	−165,575	−165,575
Balance carried forward	−129,017	−131,834	−117,056	−105,740	−132,924	−181,343	−192,527	−190,711	−181,180	−172,391	−165,575	−190,044	−190,044

Notes: (1) 1 office assistant @ £275 av. per week (months 1–3), £303 per week (months 4–12) (£15,392); 2nd office worker @ £2,331 per month (£27,972); two directors @ £2,331 each (months 1–3) and @ c. £3,333 (months 4–12) per month (£73,980).

Table 3c Cashflow forecast for Runner & Sprue, YEAR 3

								Month					
	Nov	Dec	Jan	Feb	Mar	Apr	May	Jun	Jul	Aug	Sept	Oct	Total
INCOME													
CASH/CHEQUES RECEIVED													
Units sold	55,000	65,000	55,000	65,000	70,000	80,000	65,000	70,000	75,000	80,000	85,000	90,000	735,000
Selling on price	6	6	5.1	5.1	5.1	5.1	5.1	5.1	5.1	5.1	5.1	5.1	
Sales/Revenue	330,000	390,000	280,500	331,500	357,000	408,000	331,500	357,000	382,500	408,000	433,500	459,000	4,468,500
Capital and/or loans introduced	0	0	0	0	0	0	0	0	0	0	0	0	0
Other income	0	0	0	0	0	0	0	0	0	0	0	0	0
Cash inflows	330,000	390,000	280,500	331,500	357,000	408,000	331,500	357,000	382,500	408,000	433,500	459,000	4,468,500
EXPENDITURE													
Direct costs													
Number of units bought in	70,000	80,000	65,000	70,000	75,000	80,000	85,000	90,000	95,000	90,000	95,000	105,000	850,000
Manufacturing costs	3.2	3.2	3.2	3.2	3.2	3.2	3.2	3.2	3.2	3.2	3.2	3.2	
Total	224,000	256,000	208,000	224,000	240,000	256,000	272,000	288,000	304,000	288,000	304,000	336,000	3,200,000
Wages													
No. of employees (1)	5	5	5	8	8	8	8	8	8	8	8	8	
Total	13,459	13,459	14,068	28,618	28,618	29,608	28,618	28,618	29,608	28,618	28,618	29,604	301,514

Table 3c continued

OVERHEADS (indirect costs)

	1	2	3	4	5	6	7	8	9	10	11	12	Total
Training	400	400	400	400	600	600	600	600	600	600	600	600	6,400
Rent and rates	920	920	920	920	920	920	920	920	920	920	920	920	11,040
Product development costs	5,000	5,000	5,000	5,000	5,000	5,000	10,000	0	0	0	0	0	40,000
Electricity	0	0	220	0	0	220	0	0	220	0	0	220	880
Postage/Stationery/ Photocopying	440	220	220	220	220	220	220	220	220	220	220	220	2,860
Repairs and renewals	500	500	500	500	500	500	500	500	500	500	500	500	6,000
Travelling and motor expenses	1,750	1,750	1,750	1,750	1,750	1,750	1,750	1,750	1,750	1,750	1,750	1,750	21,000
Telephone	0	0	1,800	0	0	1,800	0	0	1,800	0	0	1,800	7,200
Professional fees (patent charges)	0	0	4,000	0	0	4,000	0	0	5,000	0	0	5,000	18,000
Marketing	0	0	0	0	2,000	5,000	5,000	0	0	0	0	0	12,000
Insurance	0	0	3,000	0	0	3,000	0	0	3,000	0	0	3,000	12,000
Bank charges	0	0	300	0	0	300	0	0	300	0	0	300	1,200
Total	9,010	8,790	18,110	8,790	10,990	23,310	18,990	3,990	14,310	3,990	3,990	14,310	138,580
Capital Equipment													
Tooling	0	0	0	0	0	50,000	0	0	0	0	0	0	50,000
Office equipment	20,000	0	0	0	0	0	0	0	0	0	0	0	20,000
Total	20,000	0	0	0	0	50,000	0	0	0	0	0	0	70,000
Total Cash OUT	−266,469	−278,249	−240,178	−261,408	−279,608	−308,918	−369,608	−320,608	−347,918	−320,608	−336,608	−379,914	−3,710,094
Net cashflow	63,531	111,751	40,322	70,092	77,392	99,082	−38,108	36,392	34,582	87,392	96,892	79,086	758,406
Balance brought forward	−190,044	−126,513	−14,762	25,560	95,652	173,044	272,126	234,018	270,410	304,992	392,384	489,276	489,276
Balance carried forward	−126,513	−14,762	25,560	95,652	173,044	272,126	234,018	270,410	304,992	392,384	489,276	568,362	568,362

Notes: (1) 1 office assistant @ £275 av. per week (months 1–3), £303 per week (months 4–12) (£15,392); 2nd office worker @ £2,331 per month (£27,972); two directors @ £2,331 each (months 1–3) and @ c. £3,333 (months 4–12) per month (£73,980).

After five years, if a suitable deal cannot be negotiated, the intention is to start up dedicated companies to handle the manufacture, sale and supply with new directors buying into the companies. If so, the owners will keep a majority shareholding but will not get involved in the day-to-day running of the business.

Part 2 Developing and commercialising Runner & Sprue

In April 2000, Runner & Sprue's founders, Nick Rutter and Sam Tate, faced a difficult decision. They needed money to continue to finance the business, but it might mean that they had to give up control of their business which they had invested the last two years of their lives developing.

New investments also had implications for Coventry University, which had provided key support for Runner & Sprue. Indeed, Runner & Sprue was a university spin-out, and it is unlikely that it would have ever got off the ground without the help of the University.

Finally, any new investors would also have their own concerns. Although Runner & Sprue were an exciting new innovation-led company, the business had still made little headway in terms of sales and there were doubts about how much funding it would need in the future.

This second part of the case study of Runner & Sprue begins by examining the progress that the business had made since approaching the Graduate Enterprise Programme for a £55,000 grant in November 1998. It then describes the situation in April 2000 and the nature of the funding opportunity available to Runner & Sprue. It asks you to consider the interests of three parties:

1   The founders of Runner & Sprue

2   Coventry University

3   The 'business angels' proposing to invest in Runner & Sprue.

Developing the FireAngel

By the start of 1999, Nick Rutter and Sam Tate had received the £55,000 grant award that they had applied for in November 1998 (see Part 1 of this case study). This grant represented an opportunity to develop the business. However, both founders were realistic about what the grant meant. Nick says: 'We got that money, and don't get me wrong, £55,000 in personal terms is a hell of a lot of money, but in business terms it puts you in a position to write a business plan and put your case.'

In essence, the founders had a choice to make.

- Option 1: Were they to spend the grant to develop the product?

- Option 2: To use the money to leverage further funding?

- Option 3: Or to get a deal in place whereby they could license their product to a smoke-alarm manufacturer or a business looking to move into the smoke-alarm industry?

These are perennial choices faced by many new-technology-led businesses. In terms of using the money to leverage further funding, the grant gave them credibility and legitimacy because it showed that they had successfully won funding to support their business. They could use this money to go to other investors, an important choice because both founders recognised that they would need much more than £55,000 to develop and commercialise their smoke alarm.

The second option was to use the money to develop and patent the product. The advantage of using the money in this way would be that they could have a tangible product at the end of the process. They also had support from Coventry University, which had facilities to produce prototypes of the product, and access to facilities at Warwick University which, like Coventry University, had strong engineering departments. Both Sam and Nick were also trained engineers, having taken the design degree courses at Coventry University. Hence, although they had been successfully building their careers after their degree, engineering was 'what they knew'.

The third choice was to develop and then license the smoke alarm. By licensing the smoke alarm there was the opportunity to receive royalty payments. However, since the product was still uncertain commercially, there was a real chance that any licence deal would mean that their royalty 'cheques' would be extremely modest. Second, after having worked in Hong Kong for two years and seen how successfully products could be produced, Nick Rutter was convinced he had the contacts and know-how to successfully see their product manufactured in China.

The founders discussed the options with their adviser at Coventry University, Bill Peapal, prior to receiving the award. They decided that they would use the £55,000 to develop the product and the patent (Option 2). Rutter explains their rationale for product development and patent activity: 'Without patents, no one would invest – end of story.'

They believed that without a working prototype of the smoke alarm, it might be difficult to get funding. 1999 was the start of the internet boom, and investors were principally interested in internet-based business opportunities rather than products. Another, more important, reason for developing the prototype was that it potentially placed them in a stronger position with any outside investor. Also, they firmly believed that they could beat competition from other smoke alarm manufacturers. Nick Rutter said: 'Our rivals seemed so poor.'

By this time, Sam Tate and Nick Rutter each owned 40 per cent of Runner & Sprue, with the other 20 per cent being owned by Coventry University which had supported them through the Graduates into Business course, given them an office in its incubator space (Coventry Technocentre) and helped them with filing their initial patent of the smoke alarm in October 1998. The role of the University was pivotal, as Tate acknowledged: '. . . it would be impossible to put a price on the work that they [Coventry University] have carried out on our behalf'.

Coventry University had also supported the early proto-typing of the smoke alarm product. Indeed, Coventry's Rapid Prototyping Unit had already in July 1998 investigated whether solar energy could be used to power the smoke alarm. This use of solar energy, however, was found to be unfeasible. Nonetheless, in September 1998, the Rapid Prototyping Unit continued to work with Runner & Sprue and helped them produce the initial bayonet light fitting design (see Part 1 of this case study) and a casing for the first alarm design that was used in their pitch for the £55,000.

Sam Tate and Nick Rutter decided, however, that even if they were to concentrate on developing the product, they still needed to develop their finance, sales and marketing channels. They decided to split their roles. Nick was to be principally responsible for developing the product, whilst Sam was to be in charge of the commercial side of the business. Nick, then, continued to work with Coventry University but also with Warwick University, to develop the product. By the end of 1998, a second bayonet light fitting smoke alarm had been developed, and further prototypes were produced using computer-aided design.

Further work continued in 1999 to develop the product. This was in two areas. First, there was the design of the packaging. Both Sam and Nick knew that this was important if they were to be able to approach potential clients with the product. The second area involved the very real issues of the actual technical specification of the smoke alarm. For example, there were issues to be dealt with around the dynamics of smoke flow, the production of silicon moulds for vacuum casings, and generally resolving the electronics of the smoke alarm. Nick Rutter knew from his previous experience of working in Hong Kong as a designer for Phillips that these issues were often difficult and time consuming to resolve, no matter how much assistance was provided by Coventry and Warwick Universities. The actual cost of resolving these product development issues was rapidly eating away at their grant funding.

Nick and Sam's smoke alarm boasted three crucial benefits: it was easy to fit, mains-powered, and easy to reset via the light switch. Realising these key benefits of the product, however, was difficult, since each aspect needed to be technically built into the features of the product. This was not the only chal-lenge. Just as big a job – if not bigger – was commercialising the product. Both founders recognised that a vital barrier to the competition from existing smoke alarm manufacturers and those with more financial 'muscle' was to defend their intellectual property. As their smoke alarm was a product, there was a need to ensure that they followed through on their initial patent applications. The problem with patents is that they take time, energy and money to turn from patent filings into actual patents granted. The founders also decided that they needed to defend their product by using trademark protection. Their initial idea (see Part 1) was to use the brand name 'Easyfit'. One problem with trying to trademark the name Easyfit was that it could be deemed too generic and, if so, was unlikely to be granted by the patent office (the body which grants trademarks). The founders, therefore, sought to develop a 'better', more unique identity for their smoke alarm.

Subsequently, they developed the brand of 'FireAngel' which they submitted as a potential trademark in April 1999. Sam Tate was also extremely busy trying to develop the sales channels for their new 'FireAngel' brand. Initially, they had thought of three main channels: the public sector (fire brigades), insurance companies and major DIY chains (see Part 1 of this case for their background market research on these three channels). What became increasingly clear in 1999 was that the public sector, in particular, was wary of their smoke alarm. Whilst they could see the benefits it proposed, the product was still being developed and, more importantly, did not meet safety standards such as being 'kitemarked'. Again, getting a product – particularly a new innovative product – approved is resource-intensive in terms of both time and money. Without safety certification, though, it was unlikely that fire brigades or insurance companies would be comfortable endorsing their FireAngel.

Potentially, an 'easier' sell might be to approach buyers from the DIY chains. Sam found, however, that no matter how persistent he was or how hard he worked developing contacts amongst buyers, it remained an extremely 'hard' sell. One reason for this was that he had no background experience in DIY retailing. It took time and effort to understand the industry. Sam says: 'It's really important to be able to get your message across in 30 seconds flat. If you get the chance to speak to a buyer, you need to be able to sock it to them – they're extremely busy people. It's definitely down to trial and error so I would recommend rehearsing your sales pitch in front of anyone who will listen, and not delivering it for the first time to the top buyer at a potentially major client.'

Another problem was that the smoke alarm industry was mature (see Part 1 of this case), indicating that there was an inbuilt conservatism amongst very busy buyers as to the value of the product. Third, Runner & Sprue were proposing to sell their product at around £20. Whilst the great advantage to the retailer is that margins would be healthier, there was the chance that consumers would be unwilling to pay this amount for a smoke alarm when they were more used to paying around £5–£10 for a traditional smoke alarm. Finally, Runner & Sprue were an unknown entity, with an unproven and untested product. It is hard to build credibility and legitimacy amongst buyers when the business is new. Commercialising the product, therefore, proved to be very difficult throughout 1999.

The core problem faced by Nick Rutter and Sam Tate throughout 1999 was money – or rather the lack of it. The £55,000 award was being quickly spent: there were rapid prototyping costs, design and packaging costs, costs involved in marketing, the costs of developing sales channels, costs to rent and run their tiny space in Coventry University's Technocentre. There were also their costs of living. Both founders quickly realised that they needed to 'sweat' the £55,000 if they were every to see the dreams of building a successful business realised.

From September 1999, though, they began to experience very real financial difficulties. There was very little money left from their grant, and they were behind in paying their bills to Coventry University. Tate says: 'We were hours away from bankruptcy at the end of November 1999, and you think: how can we keep this thing going?' Talking to public sector funders, they managed to win another £10,000 grant – again brokered by Coventry University – to tide them over. This allowed them to limp through Christmas 1999 and into 2000.

Their accounts for the year ending January 2000 showed how parlous their position was. These are shown in Tables CS3.1, CS3.2 and CS3.3 (below). Over the course of the financial year, Table CS3.1 (profit and loss account) shows that their only turnover was £2,000 they had managed to gain from doing work external to the business. Their administrative expenses of nearly £66,000 – largely product development and commercialisation activities – outstripped their other operating income (grant income), leading to a loss of around £18,000. Table CS3.2 (balance sheet) shows that by the end of January 2000 they had only £242 in the bank, but creditors

of £25,000. Table CS3.3 (cashflow statement) shows that their net funds at the end of the year were around −£9,000.

The new year of 2000 brought good days and bad days. On the good days, there was the promise of some extra funding or some good news on the development of the product. Bad days witnessed Sam and Nick actively considering giving up their dream of running a successful business. To tide them over, they managed to scrape together a personal loan of £10,000. But by April 2000, all their money was gone. No matter how good their product was, there just wasn't enough money to commercialise it.

Sam and Nick had been trying very hard through 1999 and early 2000 to gain extra funding. Despite winning two awards in 1999 – the 'Graduate Company with the Most Export Potential' Award, and Coventry and Warwickshire's Shell 'LiveWIRE' Business Start-Up Award – their options were limited. Since they had no money to put into the business themselves, no house which they could mortgage, no business assets – other than their intangible assets of patents pending on their smoke alarm – and no sales to speak of, the bank would not touch them for a term loan or any other type of funding. Grant funding brokered by Coventry University had also reached the end of the line. The awards they had won – like their grants – had increased their visibility, but done nothing to increase the success in winning funding. For example, they had tried venture capitalists but there was little appetite for a 'traditional' manufacturing business during the dot.com

Table CS3.1	Profit and loss account for Runner & Sprue
	Period ended 31 January 2000 £
Turnover	2,000
Cost of sales	–
Gross loss	(9,702)
Administrative expenses	(65,763)
Other operating income	57,200
Operating loss	(18,265)
Interest receivable and similar income	252
Interest payable and similar charges	(17)
Loss on ordinary activities before taxation	(18,030)
Taxation	–
Loss for the period	(18,030)

Table CS3.2	Balance sheet for Runner & Sprue
	Period ended 31 January 2000 £
Fixed assets	
Tangible assets	3,636
Current assets	
Debtors	3,657
Cash at bank and in hand	242
	3,899
Creditors: amounts falling due within one year	(25,465)
Net current liabilities	(21,566)
	(17,930)
Capital and reserves	–
Called up share capital	100
Share premium account	–
Profit and loss account	(18,030)
Total equity shareholders' funds	(17,930)

Table CS3.3	Cashflow statement for Runner & Sprue

	Period ended 31 January 2000 £
Reconciliation of operating loss to cash flow from operating activities	
Operating loss	(18,265)
Grant income	(57,200)
Depreciation	1,998
(Increase)/decrease in debtors	(3,637)
Increase in creditors	16,079
Net cash flow from operating activities	(61,025)
Return on investment and servicing of finance	
Interest received	252
Interest paid	(17)
	235
Capital expenditure and financial investment financing	
Payments to acquire tangible fixed assets	(5,634)
Net cash flow before financing	(66,424)
Issue of shares	80
Movement on directors' loans	9,371
Grant income received	57,200
	66,651
Increase in cash in period	227
Reconciliation of net cash flow to movement in net (debt)/fund	
Increase in cash in period (above)	227
Cash flow from movement in debt financing	(9,371)
Movement in net debt	(9,144)
Net debt at start of period	–
Net (debt)/funds at end of period	(9,144)

boom, and once the dot.com bust had started, such investors tended to be very nervous about any types of investments in high technology businesses.

One advantage of operating out of a tiny space in an incubator unit such as Coventry's Technocentre was that it meant that both Sam and Nick came into contact with other people who rented a unit, and who were also either interested in innovations or were business angels seeking to finance new innovations. Sam and Nick's experience of business angels had not been terribly positive. One angel offered to support the business but was unwilling to actually put his own money into the business. Another told Nick to sell his car – his only real asset – to fund the business.

Sam and Nick, therefore, were nervous about business angels, and were also nervous about talking about their business, fearing that someone else might develop their intellectual property. They did, however, build a rapport with Graham Whitworth.

Whitworth was a serial entrepreneur. His background was that he was born into a third-generation family business. Instead of working in his family's engineering construction company, he had branched out on his own, working in machine tooling and developing experience in countries such as France and Australia. In 1982, he had begun working for Computervision (a computer software company) as a salesman. Over the next 14 years, his responsibilities grew so that he ended up managing director and executive vice-president of European, Middle Eastern and African operations. His next move was away from 'corporateville' to setting up his own business: Datavine. This business, which focused on transferring and viewing engineering data over the internet, proved an enormous success. He was able to sell the business to a large US corporate.

This left him with time on his hands, so he decided to see what opportunities there were available for developing other business projects from his space in the Technocentre. He was intrigued by the founders of Runner & Sprue. They were determined, ambitious and hard working. Whitworth commented that: 'Seeing these guys' raw enthusiasm with this [their product] was outstanding'. Their product – which he had learnt about after signing a non-disclosure agreement – offered enormous potential, and fitted in with the sort of opportunities he was used to dealing with. However, Sam Tate and Nick Rutter had no money, were, arguably, 'just' former students or recent graduates, and had little experience of the 'realities' of setting up and running other businesses. Was it worth working with them, or had they taken it as far as it could go?

Finally, having looked at their finances, Whitworth's experience told him that Runner & Sprue needed significant investment of at least £200,000. This was more than he as a single business angel was prepared to pay. He needed to see if any of his contacts were interested in looking at the Runner & Sprue opportunity. By April 2000, he had made up his mind: he and four other business angels were interested in putting £200,000 into Runner & Sprue.

Questions

- Suppose you were Graham Whitworth and you were charged by the other business angels to arrange a deal. What percentage equity would you want for the money and what terms, if any, would you place on the deal? How would you arrive at this decision?

- Suppose you were the founders of Runner & Sprue: what deal would you be prepared to negotiate? How would you negotiate the deal? What terms and conditions might you like to see placed on any deal with the business angels? Have Sam Tate and Nick Rutter really explored all of the options for financing the business?

- Suppose you are from the technology transfer office of Coventry University. Runner & Sprue represents a very strong example of your university 'spin out' policy. If the founders were to go ahead with negotiating with the business angels, what would you be looking for in terms of any deal? How would you like to structure this deal?

Part 3 The IPO

Graham Whitworth and his fellow business angels invested £200,000 in Runner & Sprue in April 2000. This signalled a change for the business. The third part of this case study charts Runner & Sprue's metamorphosis into Sprue Aegis plc. It begins by charting the production, sales and marketing and finance developments that took place between May 2000 and April 2001. It then provides an overview of Sprue Aegis plc's decision to embark on an initial public offer (IPO). This saw Sprue Aegis float 16 per cent of the company on the Ofex stock exchange at 34p a share. The aim was to raise £1.2 million.

This part of the case study asks you to consider:

1 Would you invest in the IPO?

2 Why would you invest – what do you think of the market entry strategy of Sprue Aegis plc?

3 Is an Ofex listing the best finance option for Sprue Aegis and potential shareholders?

Table CS3.4	Profit and loss account for Runner & Sprue

	Year ended January 2001 £
Turnover	–
Cost of sales	–
Gross loss	–
Administrative expenses	(358,552)
Other operating income	8,359
Operating loss	(350,193)
Interest receivable and similar income	1
Interest payable and similar charges	(692)
Loss on ordinary activities before taxation	(350,884)
Taxation	–
Loss for the period	(350,884)

May 2000 to April 2001 (IPO offer)

There were a number of organisational changes following on from the deal struck between Graham Whitworth and his fellow business angels, Nick Rutter and Sam Tate, and Coventry University. Essentially, Runner & Sprue became a wholly owned subsidiary of a new company – Sprue Aegis Ltd (later to become Sprue Aegis plc in March 2001). Graham Whitworth became the new chief executive of the business, whilst Nick Rutter became director of technology and Sam Tate became director of sales and marketing.

Runner & Sprue's accounts for the year ending January 2001 show that it was a company in some financial difficulties. Table CS3.4 shows that it had made no sales, but had made a loss of £350,884 mainly due to administrative expenses – again,

largely due to product development and commercialisation activities. Its balance sheet (Table CS3.5) for the same period showed that its net current liabilities were –£358,814 whilst its cashflow statement (Table CS3.6) reflects the losses it had made. The balance sheet (Table CS3.7) for the parent company – Sprue Aegis plc – reflects some of these difficulties but its cash position – a key measure of business survival in any small business – is much stronger. Nonetheless, Sprue Aegis plc had still made no sales and was very weak financially.

Product development

Part of the reason for the financial difficulties faced by the new Sprue Aegis was that it needed to continue work to develop and certify the product. Between April and September 2000,

Table CS3.5	Balance sheet for Runner & Sprue

	Year ended January 2001 £
Fixed assets	
Tangible assets	2,542
Current assets	
Debtors	3,451
Cash at bank and in hand	4,439
	7,890
Creditors: amounts falling due within one year	(369,246)
Net current liabilities	(361,356)
	(358,814)
Capital and reserves	–
Called up share capital	110
Share premium account	9,990
Profit and loss account	(368,914)
Total equity shareholders' funds	(358,814)

Table CS3.6	Cashflow statement for Runner & Sprue

	Year ended January 2001 £
Reconciliation of operating loss to cash flow from operating activities	
Operating loss	(350,193)
Grant income	(8,359)
Depreciation	1,094
(Increase)/decrease in debtors	1,459
Increase in creditors	353,167
Net cash flow from operating activities	(2,832)
Return on investment and servicing of finance	
Interest received	1
Interest paid	(692)
	(691)
Capital expenditure and financial investment financing	
Payments to acquire tangible fixed assets	–
Net cash flow before financing	(3,523)
Issue of shares	10,000
Movement on directors' loans	(10,624)
Grant income received	8,359
	7,735
Increase in cash in period	4,212
Reconciliation of net cash flow to movement in net (debt)/fund	
Increase in cash in period (above)	4,212
Cash flow from movement in debt financing	10,624
Movement in net debt	14,836
Net debt at start of period	(9,144)
Net (debt)/funds at end of period	5,692

Sprue Aegis continued to use Coventry University's facilities to develop prototypes that would narrow the distance between a prototype and a final product. There was also the issue of certification of the smoke alarm. Between September 2000 and March 2001, Nick Rutter worked hard with his colleagues to test their product so that by March 2001 it had received CE mark approval for its smoke alarm (BS5446 – 2000), lamp holders (BS EN 61184) and electrical safety (BS EN 60065). All of this, however, took time and resources, particularly since the innovative nature of the smoke alarm – trademarked as the FireAngel PS101 – was something not previously seen by the certification authorities.

Getting the product ready for production – a process that had been ongoing for $2\frac{1}{2}$ years (September 1998 to March 2001) – was only one strand of the production process. The next question was: who was going to manufacture it, and where? Nick Rutter had always believed that the most appropriate place to produce their smoke alarm was China. He knew Chinese producers after his two years in Hong Kong, and knew how they operated. Graham Whitworth, with his wide international experience, also knew that a main issue was ensuring the security of their intellectual property. Their patent on the smoke alarm and the new fire extinguisher foam was still 'patent pending' (and so did not yet have legal IPR protection in the UK or abroad). Even if they were granted these patents in the UK – which was a very costly process – could they still guarantee the integrity of their products? China had a poor reputation for supporting intellectual property rights, but was

manufacturing in the UK likely to be any better? It certainly would be more expensive, even after shipping from China was factored into the costs. The real danger was that one of the existing smoke alarm manufacturers would get hold of the Sprue Aegis product and 'reverse engineer' it. Although Sprue could seek damages and losses for infringement of its patent, any legal action would be costly and might take years to resolve. By the time that had been resolved, the financially weak Sprue Aegis might have missed its opportunity.

Table CS3.7	Balance sheet for Sprue Aegis plc

	Year ended January 2001 £
Fixed assets	
Investments	148,594
Current assets	
Debtors	300,342
Cash at bank and in hand	66,602
	366,944
Creditors: amounts falling due within one year	(150,036)
Net current assets	216,908
	365,502
Capital and reserves	
Called up share capital	358,055
Share premium account	7,447
Total equity shareholders' funds	365,502

In November 2000, Sprue Aegis decided to enter into a strategic manufacturing contract with AEA Technology plc to build and package the FireAngel PS101. This contract agreed that AEA would produce the FireAngel PS101 at its CICAM factory situated in Shenzhen, China, and would receive 3 per cent of the equity of Sprue Aegis. Production was due to commence in April 2001, with shipping of the FireAngel PS101 and another new product – the FireAngel foam fire extinguisher – to the UK in May 2001, and sales commencing in June 2001.

Sales and marketing

In the period leading up to the proposed flotation on Ofex, Sam Tate and Graham Whitworth had been working hard on increasing the visibility of the FireAngel PS101 smoke alarm. In November 2000 they exhibited their smoke alarm at a trade show – Fire 2000 – where it aroused considerable interest, increasing the awareness and visibility of the product. Their sales and marketing strategy is outlined in greater detail in the later section which specifically examines the IPO offer.

Finance

Given that the Sprue Aegis plc was a still a company with no sales and likely to incur significant development costs, there was a pressing need to raise further finance. Graham Whitworth reviewed his options. First, by using his investment as collateral, he could potentially seek bank finance by leveraging the amount already invested in the business. Although theoretically possible, this was not a real option: bank finance would

need to be serviced (interest charged), and there would still be a loan to pay off. It was also unlikely, as Sprue Aegis had no assets – although he (unlike Nick Rutter and Sam Tate) could have used his house as security. However, the loan needed to be very large, making it unlikely that a bank would see value in lending to the business. Another option was to go back to venture capitalists (see Part 2 of this case study). With the benefit of Whitworth's experience, this was now a more realistic option. There were, however, issues. Whitworth explains: 'Venture capital is highly dilutive and with two student founders it can be difficult for private equity sources to take us seriously.' Nonetheless, they approached a range of venture capitalists: the consensus was that they were likely to ask for between 45 to 60 per cent of Sprue Aegis. Whitworth rejected this, because it would too severely dilute the equity of the shareholders in the business.

The last option seriously considered was flotation on a stock exchange. Indeed, this is the main reason why Sprue Aegis had been changed from a limited liability company to a public limited company. Flotation on the London main stock exchange (the LSE) was not an option because of their size. However, there were two other options: flotation on the AIM or the Ofex stock exchanges. The advantage of the AIM stock exchange was that it was the more 'senior' of the two 'junior' stock exchanges available to new companies like Sprue Aegis. This meant that it had greater credibility and legitimacy in the marketplace for shareholders. The market for AIM shares was also more liquid, in that there were more buyers and sellers. This meant that shares were more likely to be easily traded. The disadvantages of AIM, however, were that disclosure and oversight of the company were greater – pushing up compliance costs. Another main disadvantage was that the costs of listing the company were significantly higher. This was principally because the advisers to an IPO offer – rather than the directors of the company – were responsible for ensuring the accuracy of any projected flotation. This pushed up the 'due diligence' costs of the projected flotation. With Ofex, although credibility and legitimacy was relatively lower and the market less liquid, the advantages for Sprue Aegis were that there were fewer compliance costs, and listing costs were lower because the directors were responsible for ensuring the accuracy of the information contained in the IPO. Sprue Aegis decided to go for an IPO on Ofex.

The Ofex IPO (April 2001)

The subscription list for Sprue Aegis opened in April 2001. 3,329,412 ordinary shares (16 per cent of the issued share capital) were offered at 34p per share. This gave a market capitalisation of £7.5 million. The aim of the offer was to raise £1.2 million gross, which would – after expenses and other payments – leave Sprue Aegis with £900,000 of working capital.

The offer identified the main benefits of the FireAngel PS101 (Figure CS3.1):

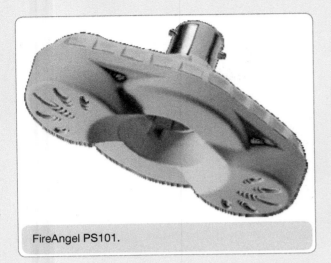

FireAngel PS101.

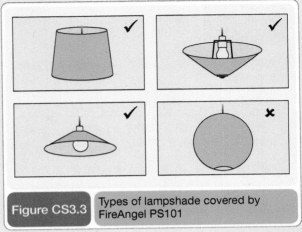

Figure CS3.3   Types of lampshade covered by FireAngel PS101

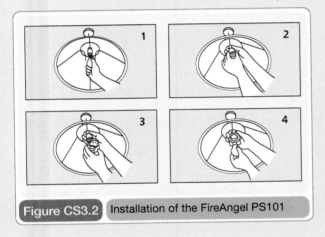

Figure CS3.2   Installation of the FireAngel PS101

- It was mains-powered consumer fit – Figure CS3.2 shows that it could be easily installed.
- There was no need for battery replacement (would last for 60 days even without mains power to recharge the battery).
- It could be easily reset and tested using the light switch.
- It could be used with most lightshade designs (Figure CS3.3).

Sprue Aegis also suggested in their offer that the FireAngel foam fire extinguisher was the first in a range of other fire safety products. The aim was to shift Sprue Aegis from a single-product, smoke-alarm business to a fire-security business, with a range of products supporting the prevention and treatment of domestic fires. This represented a radical departure from the initial plan of Runner & Sprue (see Part 1 of this case). Sprue Aegis saw the value in developing the following range:

- enhancements of the FireAngel PS101;
- lock-in smoke alarms that could be hard wired into new houses, student and sheltered accommodation;

- optical sensors for more efficiently sensing slow smouldering fires;
- plug-in carbon monoxide alarms.

The ambition also was to move very quickly – after the introduction of the initial product in the UK (see sales and marketing strategy below) – to sell the product in Europe and the US. The plan was to start selling the FireAngel PS101 through European distributors in October 2001 and in the US – again through distributors – in April 2002. These markets were huge. For example, Sprue Aegis estimated – based upon research from the US consumer products safety commission – that 16 million 'traditional' smoke alarms were not working. The main reasons for this were that people often took the battery out (because of frustration due to 'false' alarms), poorly positioned smoke alarms, failure of smoke alarm to detect fires or because of faulty batteries.

The UK market, although smaller, also presented strong opportunities. Sprue Aegis estimated, based upon Home Office data (see Part 1 of this case), that 6.4 million traditional smoke alarms did not work. Sprue Aegis believed that the marketing and sales strategy for the UK, therefore, should be focused on the following channels:

1 DIY superstores
2 supermarkets
3 mail order catalogues
4 trade distributors
5 fire services
6 retail distributors
7 general wholesalers
8 direct sales via the internet.

The existing management team – Graham Whitworth (CEO), Nick Rutter (Technology), and Sam Tate (Sales and Marketing) – was to be complemented by the introduction of a sales

Table CS3.8	Illustrative financial projections for IPO made by directors		
Based on the minimum subscription of £900,000	**Full year**	**Full year**	**Full year**
	2001	2002	2003
	£	£	£
Revenue	1,400,000	8,281,000	18,690,000
Gross margin	454,000	3,421,000	7,630,000
Operating margin	(318,000)	2,323,000	6,110,000
Taxation	–	501,000	1,833,000
Post-tax profit	(318,000)	1,822,000	4,277,000

consultant – initially on a part-time basis – to support the sales and marketing activities of Sprue Aegis. The company had already had favourable discussions with large-scale DIY retailers such as B & Q and Homebase, as well as other retailers such as Sainsbury's (a supermarket chain with non-food lines) and Mothercare (a large specialist retail chain of products for expectant and new parents). The plan was to sell the product at a premium price of £20: well above the price offered by other smoke alarm manufacturers (typically £5 to £10).

Sprue Aegis identified the following illustrative financial projections (Table CS3.8). This identified a loss of around £320,000 for 2001. For 2002, Sprue Aegis' directors projected a move into profit of around £1.8 million and, in 2003, £4.3 million. This was based upon projected sales of 8 million in 2002 and 18 million in 2003. If Sprue Aegis were to achieve this, they would have to move very quickly from no sales to becoming the dominant smoke detector business in the UK between 2001–3.

Questions

The IPO of Sprue Aegis raises a number of points both about the company and the appropriateness of listing on the Ofex stock exchange.

- In terms of the listing, have Sprue Aegis fully considered all of the finance options for the business?

- Are potential shareholders' interests best served by a junior stock market such as Ofex?

- In terms of Sprue Aegis, would you invest? What would motivate your decision?

- Is Sprue Aegis right to seek to manufacture in China?

- How would you evaluate the sales and marketing channels proposed by the company?

- Does Sprue Aegis need to be aggressive in the marketplace or should its strategy be more conservative?

- Does it need to move quickly to a full portfolio of fire security products to diversify its risks and solidify its position in the marketplace against other more mature (and larger) smoke alarm and fire security companies?

- Finally, investing in a new start-up company such as Sprue Aegis plc would likely see you benefit from a UK government-run scheme to support such businesses. This scheme – called the Enterprise Investment Scheme – allowed individuals tax relief at 20 per cent on investments of up to £150,000. Hence, potentially, an investment of £150,000 would cost only £120,000. Also, if the investment was sold after three years, there would be no capital gains tax to be paid (so, for example, if the £150,000 investment had grown to £200,000 in value after three years, the £50,000 capital gain was not liable for tax). Does the presence of these tax advantages have any influence on your decision to invest in Sprue Aegis?

Part 4 Reaching for the 'Stars and Stripes'

Sprue Aegis' IPO on the Ofex stock market was a success. In fact, the share offer had been over-subscribed. In this fourth part of the case, our aim is to chart Sprue Aegis' movement into the US market. For the sake of clarity, this part of the case artificially separates Sprue Aegis' US activities from the activities of its UK parent. In reality, of course, these are inter-related. The company's UK activities are dealt with in the fifth and final part of the case (Part 5 of this case study).

The aim of Sprue Aegis' US subsidiary – FireAngel Inc. – was to break into the large and potentially hugely lucrative US market. This was estimated to be around 16 million units (see Part 3 of this case). Sprue Aegis, therefore, actively pursued the development of its subsidiary.

This part of the case charts this activity. However, just as the company was about to ship 500,000 units of FireAngel PS101 to its US subsidiary, Sprue Aegis was asked to enter into a strategic licensing agreement with DuPont, one of the largest companies in the world.

In this case, the principal question is: should Sprue Aegis enter the US market on their own or with DuPont?

The North American activities of Sprue Aegis

One of the choices that any business seeking to enter an inter-national market faces is how it chooses to be perceived in a foreign marketplace. At one extreme, a new entrant can choose to follow the example of Ikea, which unashamedly brands itself as a Swedish store. Despite the original Ikea stores being red and white in Sweden, Ikea chose to brand its international stores in Sweden's national colours, blue and yellow. The names of their products – drawn from Scandinavian words – also do not offer any concessions to other languages. At the other extreme, a new entrant may elect to hide its 'origins'. For example, although Burger King and McDonald's restaurants share a similar corporate 'identity', they are in fact mostly franchises run locally by outside businesses. Similarly, the optician chain Specsavers is, in fact, a series of franchises under a corporate umbrella.

The choice facing Sprue Aegis was the format of its entry into the North American market. One option was to set them-selves up as an unashamedly UK operation. The second option was to set up a North American operation but 'pretend' to be an American company by setting up North American subsidi-aries. The final option was to seek to license their technology to an existing North American company.

There are advantages and disadvantages with each of these three options. If Sprue Aegis set up an independent company – either as a UK or North American brand – the main advant-age would be that future profits from the large and potentially lucrative North American market would wholly belong to Sprue Aegis. The advantage of branding FireAngel as a UK brand is that it may add credibility and legitimacy to the over-all efforts of Sprue Aegis to become a market leader in fire security. Brand recognition would allow for the opportunity for continued premium pricing in an industry where the norm was for manufacturers to have no 'brand'. The disadvantage of this approach is that Sprue Aegis would have two major 'hard' sells: to convince American consumers of the value of their technology, and to overcome any potential bias that American consumers have against foreign companies. Whichever route – UK or US branded goods – still presented Sprue Aegis with the challenges of gaining a US patent, going through the American safety certification process and selling, marketing and distributing their products.

There were also advantages and disadvantages in licensing their products to a North American-based company. One advantage was that – despite Graham Whitworth's North American experience – there was little 'know-how' in Sprue Aegis about how the North American fire security market operated. A third party, therefore, could provide this 'know-how'. A second advantage of licensing was that, given the vast size of the American marketplace, it was easier to license their products to US distributors and gain subsequent royalty payments. Under this arrangement, although Sprue Aegis would continue to be responsible for the manufacturing and shipping of its products, the actual sales, distribution and marketing of their technology would be done by a third party. The main disadvantage of this 'royalty' route was that it would mean lower profits from the North American operation, since each distributor would require a 'cut'. Also, Sprue Aegis was an independent business with a track record of setting up and running its own business. Its 'culture', therefore, was more attuned to acting independently. Besides losing control, there was also always the chance that the licensee would not be so committed or passionate about fire security products as Sprue Aegis.

Sprue Aegis plc decided to set up two North American subsidiaries: in May 2002, FireAngel Inc. was set up in the US, and in July 2002, the AngelEye Corporation was set up in Canada. Sprue Aegis plc was the sole shareholder in both these companies. In other words, Sprue Aegis – like Runner & Sprue (see Parts 1 and 2 of this case study) – made a strategic decision to forgo licensing their technology and sought, via their North American subsidiaries, to act 'as if' they were American companies.

Following the establishment of these two subsidiaries, Sprue Aegis formally appointed John Walsh as President of its North American operations in July 2002. Walsh had significant experience of the US market, having been formerly a president of Dicon Holdings – one of the largest manufacturers and sell-ers of smoke alarms in the world. Walsh's task was to take the FireAngel PS101 smoke alarm and sell it to fire and safety authorities and DIY chains such as Home Depot. The oppor-tunity was vast, because around 50 per cent of all the world's sales of smoke alarms are made in North America.

Besides the challenge of successfully selling and marketing the FireAngel, there was also the need for the US patent authorities to grant a patent on the technology. This proved both time consuming and costly. It was also onerous to achieve safety certification in North America. Although technically the main difference between the UK and US market is the light fitting (bayonet fitting in the UK; screw (Edison) fitting in North America), Sprue Aegis also faced the challenges of convincing sceptical US safety authorities. As with the UK safety certifiers, the US certifiers had not seen a product such as the FireAngel PS101 before. It was not until October 2003 that final approval for the product was granted by the US safety authorities. The costs of these investments in product development and certification were £127,683 (2002) and £182,277 (2003).

By 2004, Sprue Aegis and its two North American subsidiaries were ready. Distribution partners were in place and strong encouragement had been received from retailers. A significant media campaign involving TV adverts was planned using a US marketing agency to develop their 'Go to Market' strategy. 2004 also saw Sprue Aegis manufacture and ship $500,000 worth of stock, ready for an autumn 2004 launch.

DuPont

In July 2004, DuPont (full name EI DuPont de Nemours) began formal negotiations with Sprue Aegis about their FireAngel PS101 smoke alarm. DuPont is one of the oldest and most innovative of US companies. It was set up in 1802 by Éleuthère Irénée du Pont de Nemours, a French immigrant to the US. From its beginnings as a gunpowder manufacturer, DuPont became a major chemical producer in the twentieth century by developing polymers that led to successful materials such as Vespel, Neoprene, Nylon, Teflon, Kevlar and Lycra. DuPont had also successfully expanded into the refrigeration industry through its Freon (CFCs) series and later by developing more environmentally friendly refrigerants. In the paint and pigment industry, it also created synthetic pigments and paints. By 2004, it had five major divisions: Coatings and Color Technologies, Performance Materials, Safety and Protection, Agriculture and Nutrition and, finally, Electronic and Communication Technologies. Overall, turnover over these five 'platforms' was $26 billion. Unsurprisingly, each of the platforms was a substantial business in its own right: for example, Safety and Protection had a turnover of $4.7 billion in 2004.

DuPont proposed that the FireAngel PS101 should form part of its portfolio of Safety and Protection products. Well-known brands in this platform included Kevlar, Tyvek, and Nomex. The platform also ranged across a wide range of customers from construction, transportation, communications, to industrial chemicals, oil, gas, manufacturing, defence and safety consulting.

Du Pont proposed a licence agreement with Sprue Aegis covering the US, Canada and Mexico. This licensing agreement would be for a minimum period of five years, and would see Sprue Aegis receive an advance royalty payment of $1.4 million. The deal also suggested that there were options to extend the deal beyond this five-year period and, potentially, into new territories. Sprue Aegis would continue to be acknowledged as the owner of the technology.

Although the DuPont licensing deal was attractive, was it the right deal for Sprue Aegis? There were advantages to having such a deal. First, there was the immediate up-front royalty payment of $1.4 million. This would be important for recovering some of the costs of the North American investments and would help offset the costs of sending the $500,000 worth of stock back to China to be rebranded and then reshipped to North America. DuPont is a well-known and highly regarded business. This, if nothing else, would help legitimise the brand to retailers and consumers. After all, DuPont's strapline was 'The Miracles of Science', pointing to its comfort with taking on innovative products and developing them into commercial successes. It also had substantial economies of scale, huge resources for marketing and selling, and it was easy to see how the FireAngel smoke alarm could easily complement their existing range of safety and protection products.

There were, however, disadvantages. First, a licence deal – although giving an advance royalty immediately – should eventually prove to be a less profitable course of action for Sprue Aegis in the longer term. Second, Sprue Aegis had spent considerable energy and resources getting ready for market entry into North America. Arguably, small innovative and aggressive companies are better placed through clever marketing and sales strategies to exploit new and innovative products. There were also doubts about the ability of DuPont to deliver. The FireAngel PS101 would be only one of very many safety and protection products distributed and sold under the DuPont brand. Would DuPont really understand the product? Would they be committed to the product? The FireAngel might end up only being sold by a small number of consultants. In this case, there would be little that Sprue Aegis could do to prevent a limp introduction into the US consumer market for its product.

> ● What would your advice to the Sprue Aegis board be? Grasp the opportunity presented by DuPont or, instead, follow the 'culture' of Sprue Aegis and seek to introduce the FireAngel through its North American subsidiary?

Part 5 Growing pains?

In Part 3 (the IPO flotation stage) of this case, Sprue Aegis outlined an aggressive multi-channel strategy for exploiting its products. Sprue Aegis called this its 'Reach and Range' strategy. The 'Reach' element was covered in Part 4 of this case study, which explored the activities of Sprue Aegis in North America. This final part of the case examines the 'Range' strategy in the UK. It charts the movement of Sprue Aegis from a single-product business (FireAngel PS101) to it becoming a fully fledged fire-security business.

The case asks you to evaluate the strategic development and performance of the business post IPO, to December 2006. It then asks you to consider what future strategic directions the business needs to take.

June 2001 – December 2002

In their IPO offer, Sprue Aegis' directors projected – on an illustrative basis – that the company would make a loss of around £318,000 for the full year 2001. Up until June 2001, as

the profit and loss account for that period (see profit and loss accounts – Table CS3.9) shows, the business made a loss of £545,050. By June 2001 – as projected (see Part 3 of this case) – no sales had been made, but there was the promise of sales in excess of £500,000 through DIY chains (e.g. B & Q), supermarkets (e.g. John Lewis, Tesco, Waitrose) and other retailers (e.g. Comet), as well as through Fire brigades in Avon, Kent, Merseyside and the West Midlands. Sprue Aegis also won two awards in 2001 for its smoke alarm – the 'Real Business/CBI Growing Business Award for New Product of the Year' and the 'Good Housekeeping Institute and Innovations of the Year Award'. Such accolades were important, representing free publicity and raising the brand value and awareness of Sprue Aegis.

Table CS3.9	Profit and loss accounts of Sprue Aegis plc, 2001–6					
	31/12/2006 12 Months GBP Cons. UK GAAP	31/12/2005 12 Months GBP Cons. UK GAAP	31/12/2004 12 Months GBP Cons. UK GAAP	31/12/2003 12 Months GBP Cons. UK GAAP	31/12/2002 18 Months GBP Cons. UK GAAP	30/6/2001 14 Months GBP Cons. UK GAAP
Turnover	3,383,968	2,208,992	1,457,166	2,424,104	3,031,986	
UK turnover	3,383,968					
Overseas turnover						
Cost of sales	−2,041,430	−1,137,339	−917,148	−1,470,588	−2,061,177	−97,319
Exceptional items pre GP						
Other income pre GP						
Gross profit	1,342,538	1,071,653	540,018	953,516	970,809	−97,319
Administration expenses	−1,583,789	−1,277,165	−1,507,691	−1,393,637	−1,784,623	−446,923
Other operating income pre OP	10,225					
Exceptional items pre OP						
Operating profit	−231,026	−205,512	−967,673	−440,121	−813,814	−544,242
Other income		22,964	124,288	11,730	30,798	2,845
Total other income and int. received	12,390	22,964	124,288	11,730	30,798	
Exceptional items						
Profit (Loss) on sale of operations						
Costs of reorganisation						
Profit (Loss) on disposal						
Other exceptional items						
Profit (Loss) before interest	−218,636	−182,548	−843,385	−428,391	−783,016	−541,397
Interest received	12,390					
Interest paid	−120,411	−52,736	−52,469	−50,258	−4,875	−3,653
Paid to bank	−119,056					
Paid on hire purchase						
Paid on leasing						

Table CS3.9 continued

	31/12/2006 12 Months GBP Cons. UK GAAP	31/12/2005 12 Months GBP Cons. UK GAAP	31/12/2004 12 Months GBP Cons. UK GAAP	31/12/2003 12 Months GBP Cons. UK GAAP	31/12/2002 18 Months GBP Cons. UK GAAP	30/6/2001 14 Months GBP Cons. UK GAAP
Other interest paid	−1,355					
Net interest	−108,021	−52,736	−52,469	−50,258	−4,875	
Profit (Loss) before tax	−339,047	−235,284	−895,854	−478,649	−787,891	−545,050
Taxation	90,631	43,223	61,221	62,594	68,318	
Profit (Loss) after tax	−248,416	−192,061	−834,633	−416,055	−719,573	−545,050
Extraordinary items						
Minority interests						
Profit (Loss) for period	−248,416	−192,061	−834,633	−416,055	−719,573	−545,050
Dividends						
Retained profit (Loss)	−248,416	−192,061	−834,633	−416,055	−719,573	−545,050
Depreciation	6,487	7,463	5,195	6,945	15,273	994
Depreciation owned assets	6,487					
Depreciation other assets						
Audit fee	19,650	13,490	19,019	10,012	12,500	10,000
Non-audit fee						
Tax advice						
Non-tax advisory services						
Other auditors services						
Total amortisation and impairment	17,292	17,292	17,292	17,292	25,939	18,382
Amortisation	17,292					
Impairment						
Total operating lease rentals	32,122					
Hire of plant and machinery						
Land and building or property rents and other	32,122					
Research and development						
Foreign exchange gains/ losses	20,922					
Remuneration	634,192	580,313	596,676	594,926	615,871	166,786
Wages and salaries	566,450	528,602	542,734	543,321	559,368	
Social security costs	64,941	51,711	53,942	51,605	56,503	
Pension costs						
Other staff costs	2,801					
Directors' remuneration	311,308	222,635	220,157	219,273	279,741	159,399
Directors' fees	311,308	222,635	220,157	219,273	279,741	
Pension contribution						
Other emoluments						
Highest paid director	83,615	66,015	67,572	65,108	81,134	48,224
Number of employees	14	15	15	17	12	6

Table CS3.10	Balance sheet of Sprue Aegis plc, 2001–6

	31/12/2006 12 Months GBP Cons. UK GAAP	31/12/2005 12 Months GBP Cons. UK GAAP	31/12/2004 12 Months GBP Cons. UK GAAP	31/12/2003 12 Months GBP Cons. UK GAAP	31/12/2002 18 Months GBP Cons. UK GAAP	30/6/2001 14 Months GBP Cons. UK GAAP
Fixed assets						
Tangible assets	17,328	18,773	11,176	15,431	16,491	5,353
Land and buildings	0	0	0	0	0	0
Freehold land						
Leasehold land						
Fixtures and fittings	7,295	18,773	11,176	15,431	16,491	5,353
Plant and vehicles	0	0	0	0	0	0
Plant						
Vehicles						
Other fixed assets	10,033	0	0	0	0	0
Intangible assets	59,433	76,725	94,017	111,309	128,601	154,540
Investments						
Fixed assets	76,761	95,498	105,193	126,740	145,092	159,893
Current assets						
Stock and WIP	505,129	406,109	689,318	216,195	62,428	62,153
Stock		406,109	689,318	216,195	62,428	62,153
WIP		0	0	0	0	0
Finished goods	505,129					
Trade debtors	1,198,603	396,683	341,954	527,638	724,554	
Bank and deposits	645,257	460,232	195,675	383,162	266,002	885,545
Other current assets	336,364	197,191	106,208	205,435	112,359	48,694
Group loans (asset)	0	0	0	0	0	0
Directors loans (asset)	0	0	0	0	0	0
Other debtors	107,901	197,191	106,208	205,435	112,359	48,694
Prepayments	70,855					
Deferred taxation	157,608					
Investments						
Current assets	2,685,353	1,460,215	1,333,155	1,332,430	1,165,343	996,392
Current liabilities						
Trade creditors	−472,335	−217,500	−339,355	−479,178	−323,198	−83,329
Short-term loans and overdrafts				−6,791	−12,195	
Bank overdrafts				−2,059	0	
Group loans (short term)				0	0	
Director loans (short term)				0	0	
Hire purch. and leas. (short term)				−4,732	−12,195	
Hire purchase (short term)						
Leasing (short term)				−4,732	−12,195	
Other short-term loans				0	0	
Total other current liabilities	−481,081	−335,247	−328,966	−379,678	−465,464	−184,568

Table CS3.10 continued

	31/12/2006 12 Months GBP Cons. UK GAAP	31/12/2005 12 Months GBP Cons. UK GAAP	31/12/2004 12 Months GBP Cons. UK GAAP	31/12/2003 12 Months GBP Cons. UK GAAP	31/12/2002 18 Months GBP Cons. UK GAAP	30/6/2001 14 Months GBP Cons. UK GAAP
Corporation tax	0	0	0	0	0	0
Dividends	0	0	0	0	0	0
Accruals and def. inc. (short term)	−210,643	−126,666	−104,766	−77,505	−129,276	−49,585
Social securities and VAT	−59,507	−111,184	−116,700	−127,694	−131,284	−56,698
Other current liabilities	−210,931	−97,397	−107,500	−174,479	−204,904	−78,285
Current liabilities	−953,416	−552,747	−668,321	−865,647	−800,857	−267,897
Net current assets (liabilities)	1,731,937	907,468	664,834	466,783	364,486	728,495
Net tangible assets (liabilities)	1,749,265	926,241	676,010	482,214	380,977	733,848
Working capital	1,231,397	585,292	691,917	264,655	463,784	−21,176
Total assets	2,762,114	1,555,713	1,438,348	1,459,170	1,310,435	1,156,285
Total assets less current liabilities	1,808,698	1,002,966	770,027	593,523	509,578	888,388
Long-term liabilities						
Long-term debt	−1,912,447	−925,000	−500,000	−500,000		
Group loans (long term)	0	0	0	0		
Director loans (long term)	0	0	0	0		
Hire purch. & leas. (long term)	0	0	0	0		
Hire purchase (long term)						
Leasing (long term)						
Other long-term Loans	−1,912,447	−925,000	−500,000	−500,000		
Total other long-term liab.						
Accruals and def. inc. (long term)						
Other long-term liabilities						
Provisions for other liabilities						
Deferred tax						
Other provisions						
Pension liabilities						
Balance sheet minorities						
Long-term liabilities	−1,912,447	−925,000	−500,000	−500,000		
Total assets less liabilities	−103,749	77,966	270,027	93,523	509,578	888,388
Shareholders funds						
Issued capital	565,841	557,175	557,175	474,912	474,912	441,914
Ordinary shares	565,841					
Preference shares						
Other shares						
Total reserves	−669,590	−479,209	−287,148	−381,389	34,666	446,474
Share premium account	2,283,397	2,228,163	2,228,163	1,299,289	1,299,289	991,524
Revaluation reserves	0	0	0	0	0	0
Profit (Loss) account	−2,952,987	−2,707,372	−2,515,311	−1,680,678	−1,264,623	−545,050
Other reserves	0	0	0	0	0	0
Shareholders funds	−103,749	77,966	270,027	93,523	509,578	888,388

| Table CS3.11 | Cashflow of Sprue Aegis plc, 2001–6 |

	31/12/2006 12 Months GBP Cons. UK GAAP	31/12/2005 12 Months GBP Cons. UK GAAP	31/12/2004 12 Months GBP Cons. UK GAAP	31/12/2003 12 Months GBP Cons. UK GAAP	31/12/2002 18 Months GBP Cons. UK GAAP	30/6/2001 14 Months GBP Cons. UK GAAP
Net cash in(out)flow operating activity	−845,812	−97,344	−1,278,169	−330,964	−975,496	−401,677
Net cash in(out)flow return on investment	−108,021	−48,039	−38,452	−38,528	10,004	−808
Taxation	25,000		123,669		19,710	
Net cash out(in)flow investing activity						
Capital expenditure and financial investment	−5,042	−15,060	−940	−5,885	−5,496	−1,602
Acquisition and disposal					−1,036	−3,790
Equity dividends paid						
Management of liquid resources	300,195	−300,195	123,014	−22,715	700,301	−800,600
Net cash out(in)flow from financing	1,118,900	425,000	1,006,405	492,537	332,771	1,293,422
Increase (Decrease) cash and equivalent	485,220	−35,638	−64,473	94,445	80,758	84,945

| Table CS3.12 | Financial ratios for Sprue Aegis plc, 2001–6 |

	31/12/2006	31/12/2005	31/12/2004	31/12/2003	31/12/2002	30/6/2001
Current ratio	2.82	2.64	1.99	1.54	1.46	3.72
Liquidity ratio	2.29	1.91	0.96	1.29	1.38	3.49
Shareholders liquidity ratio	−0.05	0.08	0.54	0.19		
Solvency ratio (%)	−3.76	5.01	18.77	6.41	38.89	76.83
Asset cover	1.44	1.68	2.88	2.92		
Gearing (%)				541.89		
Shareholders funds per employee (unit)	n.s.	5,198	18,002	5,501	42,465	148,065
Working capital per employee (unit)	87,957	39,019	46,128	15,568	38,649	−3,529
Total assets per employee (unit)	197,294	103,714	95,890	85,834	109,203	192,714

Integral to the sales strategy of Sprue Aegis in 2001 was the UK's Home Office initiative to promote fire prevention, beginning in September 2001. However, September 2001 saw the Twin Towers of the World Trade Center destroyed in New York in the 9/11 attack. This external event led to the postponement of the Home Office's initiative until early 2002, and meant that Sprue Aegis's sales of its FireAngel – at a retail price of £19.99 – were retarded.

In 2002, there were some significant highlights for the company. It won further awards, including:

- Best Security Product category in the DIY and Housewares Industry.
- Best New Business category in the Sage 2002 Business Awards.
- An award for Innovation from the Shell LiveWIRE.

Table CS3.13	Profitability ratios for Sprue Aegis plc, 2001–6					
	31/12/2006	**31/12/2005**	**31/12/2004**	**31/12/2003**	**31/12/2002**	**30/6/2001**
Profit margin (%)	−10.02	−10.65	−61.48	−19.75	−25.99	
Return on shareholders funds (%)	n.s.	−301.78	−331.76	−511.80	−103.08	−52.59
Return on capital employed (%)	−18.75	−23.46	−116.34	−80.65	−103.08	−52.59
Return on total assets (%)	−12.27	−15.12	−62.28	−32.80	−40.08	−40.40
Interest cover	−1.82	−3.46	−16.07	−8.52	n.s.	n.s.
Stock turnover	6.70	5.44	2.11	11.21	32.38	
Debtors turnover	2.82	5.57	4.26	4.59	2.79	
Debtor collection (days)	129.28	65.55	85.65	79.45	130.84	
Creditors payment (days)	50.95	35.94	85.00	72.15	58.36	
Net assets turnover	1.87	2.20	1.89	4.08	3.97	
Fixed assets turnover	44.08	23.13	13.85	19.13	13.93	
Salaries/Turnover (%)	18.74	26.27	40.95	24.54	20.31	
Gross margin (%)	39.67	48.51	37.06	39.33	32.02	
Berry ratio	0.85	0.84	0.36	0.68	0.54	−0.22
EBIT margin (%)	−6.46	−8.26	−57.88	−17.67	−25.83	
EBITDA margin (%)	−5.76	−7.14	−56.34	−16.67	−24.47	
Turnover per employee (unit)	241,712	147,266	97,144	142,594	168,444	
Average remuneration per employee (unit)	45,299	38,688	39,778	34,996	34,215	23,827
Profit per employee (unit)	−24,218	−15,686	−59,724	−28,156	−43,772	−77,864

Sprue Aegis also sought to extend its three sales channels:

- *Retailers.* By the end of the year, it had contracts in place and was selling its FireAngel PS101 in more than 3,500 outlets (e.g. B & Q, Dixons, Homebase, Sainsbury's, Waitrose and Woolworths).

- *Public and not-for-profit agencies.* Working with 14 of the 62 UK fire brigades as well as Help the Aged.

- *Distributors.* It had deals in place with direct order magazines (e.g. expertverdict, innovations and findmeagift. com), as well as deals with an Irish distributor.

The business also launched its FireAngel FE-909 SuperFoam Fire Extinguisher at the DIY and Home Improvement Show in 2002. Yet, by the end of 2002, despite these developments, Sprue Aegis posted another loss. Although turnover had grown to more than £3 million for the 18-month period (June 2001–December 2002, profit and loss accounts – Table CS3.9), its losses were £787,891. Also, its share price, which had traded at 63p soon after the IPO was finished, had slipped to 45p per share. Nonetheless, in terms of market share, Sprue Aegis had around 8 per cent by volume and 15 per cent by value of the UK smoke detector industry.

Fire security market 2003–6

The market for fire security products remained extremely buoyant during 2003–6. UK Government statistics (*Fire Statistics, United Kingdom, 2005*, Department for Communities and Local Government: London) showed that the number of smoke alarms in domestic homes had increased from 8 per cent of accommodation in 1988 to around 70 per cent in 1994 but that, although this had subsequently grown to 78 per cent in 2003, there was still considerable room for replacement and new smoke alarms to be fitted into people's homes.

Also, recognising that smoke alarms were absent in 47 per cent of home fires, the government judged that smoke alarms were an important element in reducing the 'discovery' time between a fire being ignited and it causing death.

A major cause of the failure of smoke alarms that were present in households was that the batteries were removed. In other words, Sprue Aegis' core proposition remained sound.

There were also economic pressures on the need to reduce the number and extent of fires. The UK government estimated that fires cost the UK economy £7 billion in 2004. The government's strategy for dealing with this was to, first, increase fire brigade funding in real terms by over 25 per cent over the period 1998–2008 (*Rising to the Challenge* (2008) Audit Commission, London). This meant that by 2008, funding would be £2.1 billion. Second, the government shifted the emphasis towards community fire safety; in other words, the emphasis was on prevention and detection strategies. As a consequence, the fire service – through the 46 fire brigades – was given a target to install 2.4 million smoke alarms between 2004 and 2008.

The government also promoted fire prevention in the social housing sector through its Home Fire Risk Check scheme. This provided capital grants to local councils to purchase and install smoke alarms. Funding available for this scheme would amount to £25 million for the period 2004–9.

In essence, Keynote's (2006) *Fire Protection Equipment* report suggested that the overall market for active (e.g. smoke alarms) and passive (e.g. fire extinguishers, fire doors) prevention was £1.12 billion in 2005 and that the market would grow by more than 3 per cent by annum. One reason for this was the level of new build construction of private and social housing. Also important was that new legislation was introduced that placed an emphasis on commercial as well as domestic properties to take fire prevention seriously. AMA Research's (2007) report, *Active and Passive Fire Protection Market UK 2007*, also indicated that the total fire protection market was worth £1.25 billion, split between the active fire protection market (£400 million in 2006) and £850 million in the passive market.

Financial performance 2003–6

Throughout the three-year period of 2003–2006, Sprue Aegis continued with its 'Reach and Range' strategy. It sought to produce four types of fire safety product, and to extend its range of products. Extending its range meant moving from its single patented product into other types of smoke alarms, carbon monoxide alarms, wi-safe fire products (for launch in 2007) and other products (i.e. fire blanket and foam extinguisher). This product-led development was designed to continue the process of moving the company from a single product business to a fully fledged fire security business. Besides the FireAngel PS101, Sprue Aegis sought to develop a ten-year, battery-operated smoke alarm, a 'toast'-proof alarm, and a digital-display, carbon monoxide alarm. The types of customers served by these fire safety products were also extended to include heavy sleepers, the visually and hearing impaired, and those with mobility problems.

After reaching £2,424,104 at the end of financial year 2003, turnover fell by 40 per cent at the end of financial year 2004 (£1,457,166), reflecting the hot summer in the UK and the prolonged time it took to set up contracts with local councils and social housing associations. By 2005, turnover increased to near 2003 levels. Only in 2006 did turnover increase beyond the 2003 level, to £3,383,968, a 40 per cent increase on 2003 (see profit and loss Account – Table CS3.9). Throughout this

period, Sprue Aegis sought to extend its reach amongst existing stockists of its products. It continued to work with DIY retailers and supermarket chains to generate further new and repeat sales. One notable success was securing the supply to Tesco of its entire fire safety range: a whole product range over Tesco's 732 stores.

Sprue Aegis also won new contracts in 2006 to supply Mothercare and Focus DIY. Its expanded range of products was also beginning to break through, and B & Q was expected to be the 'launch' customer for its new range in 2007.

Sprue Aegis' improving relationship with the Fire Brigades – aided by becoming an approved supplier of domestic smoke alarms – was also supported by a move into social housing. Hence, it won contracts with social housing providers in the UK and local councils.

Figure CS3.4 reflects this 'U'-shaped turnover pattern. So, too, as can be expected, do costs of sales, as these are variable costs. Indeed, gross profit margin (turnover minus costs of sales) (see profitability ratios in Table CS3.12) remained around 40 per cent. However, as Figure CS3.4 shows, administration expenses were broadly flat: indeed, in 2004 these expenses were more than £1.5 million. Subsequently, the loss in 2004 was around £835,000.

Figure CS3.5 further reflects the performance of the business. It shows for each of the years (2003–6) three key illustrative ratios: profit margin, return on assets and return on capital employed. Each of these three ratios is negative.

Given this financial performance, Sprue Aegis needed significant working capital to fund its operations. In early 2003, Sprue Aegis secured a commercial loan for £500,000. This was charged at 9 per cent per annum, and could be repaid

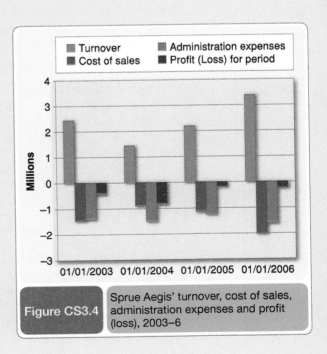

| Figure CS3.4 | Sprue Aegis' turnover, cost of sales, administration expenses and profit (loss), 2003–6 |

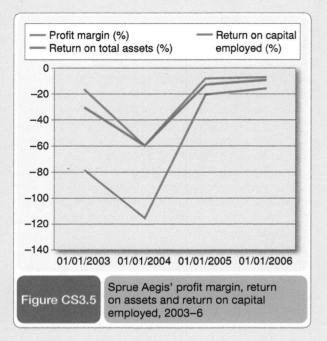

Figure CS3.5	Sprue Aegis' profit margin, return on assets and return on capital employed, 2003–6

at any time without penalty. At the start of 2004, a further £223,980 (net of expenses) was raised by Sprue Aegis by placing 895,918 ordinary shares at 25 pence per share. Further private placings took place in March 2004: the gross proceeds from this were £775,750. This money was, again, to fund working capital needs.

It was also not the end of attempts to raise additional working capital. For example, Sprue Aegis received another £425,000 of secured loan funding in 2005. In 2006, 433,333 ordinary shares were placed to raise £65,000. In September 2006, it issued another £1 million of convertible loan stock. In essence, over the period 2003–6, Sprue Aegis raised around £3 million of funding, and the number of shares in the company had grown from around 22 million to 28 million.

There were also boardroom changes at Sprue Aegis. Whilst Graham Whitworth remained CEO and Nick Rutter head of technology, one of the original founders, Sam Tate, moved to become a non-executive director of the company.

Questions

● By September 2005, Sprue Aegis' share price was around 13p per share. It was at this same price at the start of 2006. This meant that the share price now had fallen more than 60 per cent from its IPO price of 34p per share. In other words, the market capitalisation of the business had fallen from £7.5 million at the IPO offer (April 2001) to £3.82 million (September 2005). At the beginning of 2006, would you sell your shares in Sprue Aegis? Do you think that you could find a buyer?

● Suppose you had been invited in to examine the business. You are asked to consider four options set out below. Which one would you recommend?

1 *The selling of Sprue Aegis to a competitor (trade sale) or a private equity (e.g. venture capitalist) buyer.* Who would you recommend?

2 *Replacing the board of Sprue Aegis.* The share price has collapsed and, after examining their business and their financial accounts, you see little prospect of the current management team delivering on the promise of Sprue Aegis. They have had enough time. What sort of team do you think should replace the existing management team?

3 *Re-focusing the business's 'reach and range' strategy.* The market for fire security products has been buoyant and will continue to be buoyant. Sprue Aegis needs a new strategy. The current board has been wedded to a strategy that is ill-suited for the fire security market. The question is, what would you recommend in terms of changing the strategic direction of the business?

4 *Recommend no substantive changes to the strategy or management team of the business.* Sprue Aegis has an experienced serial entrepreneur running the business who has a track record in raising finance for the business. The 'rounds' of finance that Sprue Aegis has gone through since its inception are part and parcel of the development of a new innovative business. Such businesses have high cash 'burn' rates. It is also important that Sprue Aegis continue with their 'reach and range' strategy because the only way to become dominant in the market is to complete the shift from a smoke alarm producer to a fire security business. The business also needs to continue to evolve and develop new products. Replacing the team now would be extremely disruptive, just when the business is finally about to turn the corner.

Stuart Roberts' retail chain of 13 Two Seasons stores had proved remarkably successful. Selling ski, snowboard, surfing and skating equipment, footwear and clothing, he had managed to build Two Seasons up from one store in 1983 by following a simple formula. Focused in urban locations in the Midlands of the UK, he had pitched his sports equipment retail offer between volume stores such as Sportsworld.com and outright specialist retailers like snow+rock. His stores appealed to those seeking sports equipment but also those wanting urban brands.

But having successfully grown the business by internal growth, Stuart Roberts now faces a tricky decision on the future direction of the business. He and his management team have to re-evaluate the business proposition offer of Two Seasons. Should he go for more aggressive growth? How is he to fund it – borrowing from the bank? Getting formal (venture capital) or informal (business angel) finance? Should he, instead, focus on a trade sale? Alternatively, should Roberts continue with the status quo?

The start up of Two Seasons

Stuart Roberts has always been interested in extreme sports. As a teenager, he liked nothing better than spending time going skiing in the winter and surfing in the summer. Two Seasons grew out of this passion. He explains: 'Basically, it was a lifestyle choice for me setting up the business in 1983. I set up the business when I was 19 and all I wanted to do was to have enough money to pay the rent, buy a beer at the weekend and have enough to fund my skiing and surfing trips.'

Stuart Roberts got a lot of support from his parents. In the early 1980s, his father had run an import business and the original concept behind Two Seasons was to sell samples of skiwear and skis that his father had imported. His mum also agreed to do his accounts so that he could keep a rein on his cashflow. In 1984, though, his father's import business went into administration. This meant very real challenges for Stuart. The first was that there was no financial help available from his parents so there was very little capital available. Second, the advantage of selling his father's samples was that he was getting skiwear and skis cheaper than if he went elsewhere. Without these samples, Stuart Roberts had to negotiate with existing suppliers. This was tough because the economic conditions in the early 1980s were difficult. The UK at that time was coming out of a very deep recession.

Nonetheless, Stuart Roberts put the success of his first store down to a number of factors. He says: 'I realised fairly quickly

that trade was initially going to be on a fairly hand-to-mouth basis. I had very limited funds so the first thing I sought to do was limit my overheads in my first store in Northampton. There was initially only me and one other employee who worked in the store. I also had no borrowings. Costs, therefore, were as low as I could get them. Equally important was for me to negotiate with suppliers for credit. Getting a discount was a must. To get this, I had to turn stock around fast which meant that I had to have the right sales techniques. I was on the shop floor all of the time and people could see that I was putting lots of effort into the store. In fact, after a while I became "Mr Two Seasons" to the local community.'

Developing the Two Seasons concept

Stuart Roberts' business model is based on learning as much from your mistakes as from your successes. He explains: 'What I realised fairly early on was that cashflow is the key indicator of success and is the oxygen for any small business. Another key lesson I learnt was to take a team approach to building the business. From day one it was important to bring in the person with the right technical knowledge so even in a team of two there needed to be complementary skills.'

This key focus on building the team was integral to the development of the business. At one level, Two Seasons looks like any other family business. Stuart Roberts' father joined the business in the mid 1980s until he retired in 2000. His mother continued to do his accounts. His sister also joined Two Seasons, after a season in the Alps, to manage her own store. Subsequently, his brother joined the business in 2000.

Stuart Roberts explains the value of having family members on the management team: 'Besides being able to draw on their own business abilities and knowledge, having the family as both shareholders in the business and actually working in the business means that we have a tight control on finances and a strong work ethic.'

Stuart Roberts, however, believes that any team needs to be properly balanced. As the business developed, he sought to bring in non-family members to complement the existing strengths of the family. Motivating and retaining key managers is a challenge in any retail business but Stuart – with his family's support – decided to give away 10 per cent of the equity of the business to non-family members. He says: 'Key to our expansion has been people like our commercial director Adrian Flowers. Adrian now has an equity stake in the business and has managerial control over our buying. My sister, for example, although she is a shareholder, understands that it is Adrian rather than her that makes buying decisions for Two Seasons. Saying that, my sister – like all our other store managers – is encouraged to take on additional responsibilities and to make decisions on store performance and training.'

Stuart Roberts, however, believes that whilst you can go a long way with the right team and the right incentives, the retail offer also had to be focused on what the customer wants. The Two Seasons' concept is based upon its core demographic groups which are students and young professionals (18–28 years old). However, what is unique about the positioning of the Two Seasons product mix is that it appeals to all age groups who are interested in the extreme sports of surfing and snow sports.

Competitive environment

Competition in Two Seasons' marketplace is severe. Although the sports goods retail market was worth £5.6 billion in 2007 and had grown by 19 per cent over the period 2002–7 (source: Mintel 2008 *Sports Goods Retailing, June 2008*), there was a wide range of retail provision:

- The largest volume producer of sports goods (clothing and equipment) in 2008 was Sports Direct International (trading under the name of Sportsdirect.com or Sports World). In 2008, it had turnover of £1.26 billion and operated 375 stores as well as under the fascias of businesses it had acquired (e.g. Lillywhites, Gilesports, Hargreaves and Streetwise). It had also acquired brands such as Dunlop, Karrimor, Lonsdale and Kangol. Like other volume retailers (e.g. JJB Sports, JD Sports) Sports Direct International grew in the 2000s in three ways: acquiring other store groups, developing sites out of town rather than in town locations and, perhaps most importantly, by selling own brand goods such as Kangol.

- Besides these volume sports retailers, there exist a range of department stores (e.g. M & S, Next, BHS) retailing sports goods as well as more specialist equipment stores such as snow+rock or Blacks. Snow+rock was also – like Two Seasons – founded in the early 1980s but had been sold in 2004 when the founder decided to retire. Since 2004 it has increased its trading floor space by around 65 per cent. Blacks, however, was struggling by 2008 and had instituted a major turnaround strategy to combat its loss-making stores.

- There were also 'lifestyle' urban fashion stores such as Fat Face and White Stuff. Fat Face, for example, in 2008, had 154 stores and had entered into a partnership with John Lewis (department stores) and had opened stores in Abu Dhabi and Bahrain.

The key concept underlying Two Seasons is to focus on two key niches. First, it wants its clothing, equipment, footwear and accessories to meet the needs of those interested in keeping up to date with mainstream fashions. Hence, it focuses on brands such as Quiksilver, Animal, Element, Billabong, Nixon, O'Neill, Fox, Roxy and Oakley. Second, it wants to meet the needs of those interested in using sports equipment such as surfboards, skiing, snowboarding and skating equipment.

However, where Two Seasons has sought to differentiate itself from the competitors is by focusing on the 80–20 rule. Stuart Roberts says: 'There are basically two types of retailers out there that we are competing against. One group you could call the "fashion guys" and the other the "technical guys". With Two Seasons what I have been trying to do is compete to some extent by providing fashionable lines balanced with technical equipment and relevant hardware giving us authenticity with our customers. I reckon that is about 80 per cent of the market in our area. The other 20 per cent is customers who are following very specific fashion trends or who have very specialised technical requirements of their equipment. That 20 per cent is not our market. In other words, what we do – unlike any other major retailer in our space – is to blend street fashion with boardsports and the relevant hardware.'

Two Seasons' turnover had grown markedly over the period 2003–7. The year on year increases are shown in Figure CS4.1. For example, in 2004 turnover was up 14.9 per cent on 2003 whilst turnover in 2007 was up 30.4 per cent on 2006 (see financial accounts in Tables CS4.1a and CS4.1b for further information). Indeed, compared with 2003, turnover in 2007 was 73.8 per cent up. Part of the reason for this was that store numbers had increased from one back in 1983 to 13 in 2007. Yet, like others in the marketplace, Two Seasons' profit margins continued to be thin. Figure CS4.2 shows that for the years 2003–7, profit margins had never exceeded 5 per cent of total turnover. Also, costs remained remained difficult as wages, rents and rates were, as may be expected from a retail business, high.

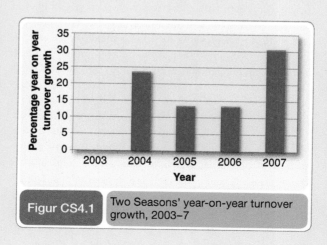

| Figur CS4.1 | Two Seasons' year-on-year turnover growth, 2003–7 |

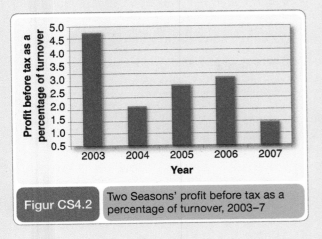

Figur CS4.2	Two Seasons' profit before tax as a percentage of turnover, 2003–7

2 Go to the bank for a loan to fund further business opportunities?

3 Go to formal or informal private equity investors to fund further business opportunities?

4 Seek a trade sale?

Stuart Roberts sat down with his management team and his family and reviewed these four options. There were advantages and disadvantages with each of these options.

In terms of Option 1 – the status quo – the main advantage was that he and his team had successfully built up the Two Seasons concept over the last 25 years. The question was 'if it is not broke, why fix it?'. Future organic growth continued to be a possibility by continuing to develop successful brands and moving into online retailing. Stuart Roberts and his team were also emotionally attached to the business. He explains: 'We had been through very tough times and – at times – struggled to keep the business afloat. This meant the management team was very tight and as we grew the business it became an extension of our personal successes.'

The rain and generally poor weather of the previous summer of 2007 had, though, been terrible for retailing in the UK. Against this background, the main danger for Two Seasons of pursuing Option 1 is that it could leave it exposed to further competition. Despite having 13 stores, Two Seasons

The four options facing Two Seasons

Subsequent to the production of the video (www.pearsoned.co.uk/storeygreene), Stuart Roberts increasingly realised that the business had reached a crossroads. As far as he could see, there were four options available to the business:

1 Remain with the status quo of 13 stores and continue to fund further growth from retained profits?

Table CS4.1a	Profit and Loss Accounts for Two Seasons, 2003–7				
	31/7/2003 **£**	**31/7/2004** **£**	**31/7/2005** **£**	**31/7/2006** **£**	**31/7/2007** **£**
TURNOVER	3,466,202	3,983,974	4,516,885	4,618,690	6,023,461
Costs of sales	2,059,853	2,296,623	2,627,220	2,659,841	3,430,777
GROSS PROFIT	1,406,439	1,687,351	1,889,665	1,958,849	2,592,684
Administrative expenses	1,252,273	1,605,343	1,773,006	1,876,017	2,523,916
	154,076	82,008	116,659	82,832	68,768
Other operating income	12,000	15,000	4,888	60,237	20,130
OPERATING PROFIT	166,076	97,008	121,547	143,069	88,898
Exceptional item	–	29,292	125,355	143,069	
Interest receivable and similar income	3,346	1,108	953	1,937	957
	169,422	68,824	124,404	145,006	89,855
Interest payable	4,828	4,160	9,985	13,824	32,002
PROFIT BEFORE TAX	164,594	64,664	114,419	131,182	57,853
Tax	32,838	35,739	34,008	34,196	29,826
PROFIT AFTER TAX	131,756	28,925	80,411	96,986	28,027
Dividends	51,069	39,780	44,250	58,250	
(DEFICIT) RETAINED PROFIT	80,687	–10,855	36,161	38,736	

Table CS4.1b	Balance Sheets for Two Seasons, 2003–7

	31/7/2003 £	31/7/2004 £	31/7/2005 £	31/7/2006 £	31/7/2007 £
FIXED ASSETS					
Intangible assets	23,552	13,168	3,601		6,103
Tangible assets	566,437	584,464	590,785	643,481	1,022,903
Investments	1	1	1		
TOTAL	589,990	597,633	594,387	643,481	1,029,006
CURRENT ASSETS					
Stocks	581,506	714,195	820,083	807,450	1,141,263
Debtors	25,603	25,158	14,783	10,352	4
Prepayments and accrued income	25,567	28,259	39,179	47,517	95,080
Cash at bank and in hand	9,753	3,129	3,318	4,448	18,010
TOTAL	642,429	770,741	877,363	869,767	1,254,357
CREDITORS					
Amounts falling due within one year	535,472	697,744	730,474	712,545	1,352,354
NET CURRENT ASSETS	106,957	72,997	146,889	157,222	−97,997
TOTAL ASSETS LESS CURRENT LIABILITIES	697,047	670,630	741,276	800,703	931,009
CREDITORS					
Amounts falling after more than one year	−165,797	−127,969	−151,714	−169,919	−305,471
PROVISION FOR LIABILITIES AND CHARGES	–	−22,266	−33,006	−35,492	−48,379
NET ASSETS	531,250	520,395	556,556	595,292	577,159
CAPITAL AND RESERVES					
Called up share capital	10,000	10,000	10,000	10,000	10,000
Revaluation reserve					50,841
Profit and loss account	521,250	510,395	546,556	585,292	516,318
SHAREHOLDER FUNDS	531,250	520,395	556,556	595,292	577,159

was still a small-scale retailer. This meant that it had fewer economies of scale. And, with profit margins being so tight, there was a possibility that the status quo would have poor outcomes for the business. Stuart Roberts explains the problem: 'We were using the same systems that we had when we had three stores and our warehousing and finance was all being pushed to breaking point. We simply needed to have major investment to continue the growth path. We were also excited by the opportunity of independent competitors exiting the market but how could we take advantage of this with limited resourses?'

Option 2 – debt finance – was attractive. Two Seasons had built up a strong rapport with its bank. The bank was very positive about lending to Two Seasons and had always done so in the past. Having bank finance also meant that the Roberts family and the management team would not see their shareholding diluted. Stuart Roberts explains why this is often important for entrepreneurs: 'Having control over

your own destiny and ownership kept the team very focused and fosters an independent attitude that takes responsibility for its actions'. Extra bank funding also could fund future development of the business either through organic growth (opening new stores) or by acquiring other businesses. This meant that growth could be managed from internal resources and planned. This would mean that the business would remain focused as it was their debt: not someone else's. This discipline had stood Two Seasons in good stead over its development as Stuart Roberts explains: 'When you have your own money – in my case my own home – on the line it concentrates the effort and really focuses your cost commitments. We had seen other companies expand recklessly through misreading the market. This had led to their demise so we were nervous of outside intervention.'

The costs of the bank finance option for Two Seasons, however, were both financial and emotional. Debt finance has to be serviced – principally from cashflow – and given that

Two Seasons is inevitably a seasonal business, there were wide fluctuations in its cashflow over the year. Stuart Roberts was also aware of how critically the bank looked at the gearing of the business. He knew that banks do not like providing term loans which were greater than or approaching the size of their existing asset base. Stuart Roberts takes up the story: 'Just before we were thinking through the four options, there arose an opportunity to acquire a competitor. It had two stores. One of these was haemorrhaging money but the other one was very profitable. I knew it was the right opportunity. I went to the bank and they were keen to lend to me but they wanted my house as security. Earlier on in developing the business, my parents had kindly offered to put their house up as security for the business. They were now retired: if anything I didn't want their house as security. Still, I knew it was the right opportunity. I talked to my wife. I explained that it could be a step too far but she saw the logic of the opportunity. My family were also supportive but, in the end, it was my house on the line. I wasn't 19 anymore with no worries other than where the next ski trip was to. The bank were also asking more questions about the asset value of the security [house] as it did not cover the full extent of the loans/overdraft.'

Private equity provided by either formal (venture capital) or informal (business angels) investors was a third option. The main advantage of venture capital finance is that it could raise serious amounts of funding to develop the business. It was a model that had been successfully applied to the Two Seasons marketplace. For example, the urban lifestyle retailer, Fat Face, had been able to grow their business through successful rounds of venture capital finance. This had made the original founders rich: an obvious benefit for any entrepreneur who had spent most of his working life developing his business. Venture capital finance also meant that the business could grow very quickly either organically or through acquisitions. This would give it greater economies of scale thereby reducing its cost base because the more volume it developed, the cheaper the price of suppliers. Venture capital also presented the potential that Two Seasons could develop its own brand. This was advantageous because it meant that it effectively cut out the 'middleman' – thus improving profit margins. This had already been successfully done by JD Sports which had developed its own brand 'Mackenzie'. Also, if they could develop a brand, this would make the business more appealing to investors in any further finance rounds.

Business angels also presented real advantages. Stuart Roberts knew a number of such private investors who were interested in the success of Two Seasons. Besides bringing finance, Stuart Roberts recognised that potentially business angels could bring with them invaluable business expertise and contacts for the business. This – like venture capital – could really drive the growth of the business. Developing his team was important to Stuart Roberts: 'I have always believed that our staff – from those who work in the store through to

buyers and support staff and senior management team – need to see a future for themselves. Developing the people side is often key in developing a business.'

The potential problem with business angels is that Stuart Roberts felt that you might run the risk of the relationship breaking down. He explains: 'The issue with business angels is that it is all on the individual. They could be fantastic or they could turn out to be like a football chairman who decides that he is not happy with the team's performance and decides to take his ball home.' This could cause very real problems in the business. So, too, could involving venture capitalists. Because they tended to be more 'professional' managers, there was a risk over the short to medium term that if they experienced a downturn in profits, the management team could find themselves replaced. This would be hard to take, explains Stuart Roberts: 'Finding the right match of someone who could understand the business and give us the freedom to continue to drive our own vision was a real concern.'

There was also no guarantee that the equity finance would work. They may find themselves growing the business too quickly. There was also no guarantee that if they embarked on trying to develop their own brand it would be successful. Stuart Roberts explains: 'There are plenty of businesses out there who have tried to develop their own brand and failed. We would have to invest a lot and our core expertise was in retailing. Sure, we could develop this expertise but it was time consuming, expensive and uncertain.' Another problem was the amount of finance that Two Seasons was looking to potentially raise: £1 million. It was unlikely that any single business angel would be prepared to invest this amount without taking over the business. To keep equity in the business would need a syndicate of business angels. Whilst this might work – and there were people interested – it might create management tensions between the existing team and the business angels. There were also problems with approaching venture capitalists for £1 million: 'If we were asking for £5 million it was there on the table. However, because we were asking for £1 million that was at the lower end of what they could do. Their problem [venture capitalists] is that they have diligence costs and we might be too small for them to consider.'

Finally, Option 4 was a trade sale of the business. This had advantages. One was that if they could get the right business to sell to, Two Seasons could move forward rapidly. For example, if a supplier bought the business, there would be no 'middleman' involved which would be positive for profit margins. This had been (in reverse) the model adopted by Sports Direct International. The right partner could also bring along with it business expertise in logistics, potentially, a brand or suite of brands and extra finance. Stuart Roberts explains the advantage of this option: 'With profit margins under pressure and cost of high street retailing growing, we desperately needed our own brand to deliver the extra margin. One way of resolving this at a stroke would be a trade purchase. The main problem was the lack of options and the main suppliers were already building their own network of stores. Also we had no dominant brand, so no obvious suitor.'

Another advantage would be that they could 'harvest' the business for all shareholders. This would give a return to the shareholders. Also, if the right partner could be found, they might recognise that one of the key strengths of the business was not just its retail offer but its management team and staff. For example, one option was to go with the UK based surf brand Animal or someone bigger like Billabong or Oakley. Stuart explains: 'Animal had recently purchased a distressed retailer and experimented with a multi brand store concept. This experiment had not proved successful so they converted the stores to stores selling just Animal merchandise. However, we knew that they were aggressive, wanted more stores and greater retail presence so were potentially worth meeting.'

The key disadvantage of a trade sale was that it might signal, either now or in the future, the end of Stuart Roberts' involvement with Two Seasons. Even if he stayed on after any sale, there may still be tensions with any new buyer and the way he had run the business. Another danger of a trade sale is that the business might find itself saddled with a supplier of brands that were beginning to lose their lustre. This had occurred with the Kangol and Karrimor brands which had become devalued subsequent to their purchase by Sports Direct International.

Stuart Roberts and his management team evaluated the four options. They have to make a decision. Option 1 was definitely viable. Option 2 was equally viable and he had already approached the bank to sound them out. They were very supportive of providing extra finance. Stuart Roberts also held positive meetings with a number of venture capital businesses that were keen on his business. He had also been approached by business angels. A range of suppliers also showed real interest in buying the business. This left him with the following questions:

1 Had he considered all of the finance options for Two Seasons?

2 If he carried on with Option 1, how could he sustain the business?

3 Bank finance was attractive but was it too much of an emotional rollercoaster?

4 Equity finance looked very possible but if he was to go with this option who should he go with (venture capitalist or business angel) and what sort of deal should he be looking for?

5 Finally, if Option 4 was possible, what sort of supplier should he be looking for and, again, what sort of deal would he looking to reach?

6 Which of the four options should he take?

We know from Chapters 9 and 10 that small businesses are more likely to close than large businesses. We also know that most close without incurring any debts because the business owner either retires or becomes an employee.

There are, however, some spectacular exceptions to this and the case below is one of these. Please read the case and then address the questions posed at the end.

Tahir Mohsan: running out of time?

In June this year, the Asian Business Federation held its annual dinner at King George's Hall in Blackburn in Lancashire. The ABF founder and chairman, Tahir Mohsan, a local entrepreneur in his early 30s and still with a boyish plumpness to his cheeks and brightness to his gaze, gave his customary uplifting speech. This year his theme was the need for multi-racial business initiatives to help dissolve prejudice. 'Money', he concluded, 'is colour-blind.'

Mohsan seemed well qualified to make such generalisations. Since the late 1980s, despite the fact that Blackburn and nearby Burnley had become two of the most racially polarised places in the country, he had built up a racially integrated business empire in the area that was large enough to attract the attention of national newspapers and politicians. His busily proliferating companies were involved in, among other enterprises, property, retail, making plasma screens for televisions, internet service provision and manufacturing the two remaining big-selling brands of British personal computers, Time and Tiny computers, which together once accounted for a third of British PC sales. Mohsan was a regular inclusion in lists of the most successful British Asian businessmen, of the country's most promising digital entrepreneurs, of the richest young Britons.

In 1997, Paddy Ashdown, then the leader of the Liberal Democrats, had attended the tenth anniversary celebrations of Mohsan's businesses. 'Time Computers produces quality goods by quality workers', Ashdown said. 'Special tribute must be paid to Tahir.' In 1999, Ashdown became a non-executive director of Time Computers, and remained one for three years. In 2001 and 2004, Jack Straw, the MP for Blackburn, former home secretary and now foreign secretary, spoke at ABF events and praised its work.

Yet, in July this year, Mohsan's status as an uncomplicated role model abruptly came to an end. With almost no warning, seven of his companies went into administration with debts of £70 m. Granville Technology Group Ltd, VMT Ltd and the other five enterprises formed the core of his personal computer and plasma screen business. Between 1,000 and

1,500 people – accounts differ – lost their jobs immediately. Thousands of customers who had paid in advance for goods and warranties (much of Mohsan's business was mail order) faced battles for refunds or, in the case of debit card and cash payers, the likelihood of losing their money altogether.

Company collapses are rarely neat or happy events. And the rise and apparent fall of Mohsan contains broader, more melancholy lessons: about the recent history and future prospects of British manufacturing, and the British computer industry in particular.

But the demise of his companies also contains several mysteries. Granville Technology Group, the most important of the seven, went into administration having failed to file audited accounts covering any period after June 2003. In a letter to creditors this September, the company's administrators, Grant Thornton, also noted that 'stock records are incomplete', that 'there is significant concern as to missing quantities of stock', and that 'under 50% of the stock listed [at the company's chain of Computer Shop stores] has been recovered'. Other puzzles Grant Thornton has struggled with include the precise ownership structure of the companies; the resignation of several directors shortly before the companies went into administration; the establishment of foreign subsidiaries with apparently questionable prospects; and a general lack of records. 'I wouldn't use the word fishy', says Martin Ellis, one of the administrators, 'but it is unexplained.'

Other people have been less restrained in their language. Since July, parts of the internet have throbbed with allegations against Mohsan (some, possibly, motivated by former employees' desire for revenge) of dubious commercial practices: excessive secrecy, knowingly selling shoddy goods, and switching assets between companies to avoid creditors. Ever-lengthening chains of 'evidence' have been assembled and presented, part anecdote, part rumour, part fact. Anti-Mohsan websites have been established. In the next few weeks, as required by law, Grant Thornton will send a report on the Granville implosion to the Department of Trade and Industry. Nigel Evans and Kitty Ussher, the MPs whose constituencies include the main company premises and much of its former workforce, have both called for the DTI to investigate whether Granville has been managed, in Ussher's words, 'within the law'.

In Burnley, the local branch of the Computer Shop is on the main shopping street between an amusement arcade and a children's shop that sells multi-packs of socks for £1. In October, there were still two pieces of A4 paper sellotaped to the Computer Shop's windows, unceremoniously printed and slightly askew, that read, 'We apologise for any inconvenience caused but this store will be closed today for a year-end stock take'. The notices had been up since July.

Old promotional posters were also still in the windows. They combined hard sell with a hint of desperation: 'Selected cameras half-price'. Through the shutters, the interior of the shop was just visible: empty boxes scattered about, empty shelves, extension cables with empty sockets left lying on the floor.

The Granville headquarters were a few miles out of town, beyond Burnley's derelict and patched-up Victorian mills, in a wide, pretty valley like an advertisement for a more modern kind of industrial location, below the wealthy village of Simonstone. Inside a long fence there were two large, low buildings. Unexpectedly, their lights were still on. At the front of the compound several dozen cars were parked, a striking proportion of them expensive ones. Even before July, there was a degree of speculation about Mohsan. He almost never gave interviews – only two in national newspapers in an eighteen-year business career – and he was almost never photographed. In 2003, he moved to Dubai to set up a new company, Time Group (Middle East). In 2004, he ceased to be a director of Granville, but continued to own 60 per cent of the company and maintain an undefined degree of influence.

This summer and autumn, in the wake of Granville's collapse, Mohsan gave no interviews. At the ABF, where he remains chairman, they were keen to emphasise Mohsan's distance from July's disasters. They agreed to pass on some questions but did not sound optimistic. A week later there was a quick, flat Lancashire voice on my phone. Before I could ask anything, Mohsan began denying one of the allegations: '. . . The stock that was missing . . . The implication is I took it. I couldn't take the stock from 80 shops. And I was not involved with the business then . . .' He trailed off. Then he said he was coming to Lancashire in November. He would see me then.

Last week, there were a few more cars and a few more lights on in the Simonstone compound. But inside the main building, at two on a Tuesday afternoon, reception was almost deserted. After a few minutes, a tall, faintly nervous man who said he worked for one of Mohsan's surviving companies appeared and led the way down a freezing, dim corridor. He opened a door and we were in a panelled boardroom. The heating was on but had not been for long. The man made conversation. 'I was made redundant from Granville for three weeks', he mentioned, 'until I was asked to come back.' Then the door opened and in walked Mohsan. He was wearing a pinstripe suit with a wide gold tie. His round, smooth face showed no signs of anxiety. He walked briskly to the table and sat down, then leaned back in his chair. The first of his many smiles revealed pointed white teeth.

We started with his activities in Dubai. 'We are building the largest consumer electronics factory in the Middle East', he said. 'Basically, to target the Indian market. We are going to be making flat-screen TVs, PCs, notebook computers.' Without hesitating, he drew an obvious, but possibly unwise comparison: 'it is going to be similar, in terms of the value proposition, the brand proposition, to what Granville was doing in the latter stages'. Mohsan stopped. A note of caution,

that he would deploy only intermittently during the afternoon, entered his voice. With a smile, he suggested we move on to another, less problematic part of his history: Granville's early years.

The details of this period acquired a romantic, slightly blurred quality when Mohsan became a public role model, but a reasonably solid outline can be constructed. He founded the company with his older brother, Tariq, in 1987. Tahir was 16, and was living with his parents and siblings above a corner shop on Granville Road, a modest, mainly Asian street near the centre of Blackburn. He had just left school. 'I was planning to go to college. I wanted to be a lawyer.' But before that he intended to have a year off, and was not sure what to do. Tariq, who was a decade older and working as a pediatrician, was interested in computers and had written software programs establishing feeding routines for vulnerable babies. Tahir was 'into computers' too, and had been since 'the age of 11'. The brothers decided to collaborate, selling Tariq's software to hospitals. To raise some capital, Tariq persuaded Tahir to put his Amstrad computer up for sale in the local paper.

In 1987, the early boom in British computer manufacturing initiated by Clive Sinclair, Alan Sugar and other less-remembered geeks and entrepreneurs was already deflating. Competition from America, unworldly business thinking and over-optimistic sales forecasts had already done for many British computer start ups, which were typically run – with Sugar the exception that proved the rule – by white, middle-class postgraduates. But the public appetite for owning a PC was still growing rapidly – faster than computer manufacturers and retailers could satisfy it. 'There was a waiting list for Amstrads at Dixons', said Mohsan, 'and the prices were high.' He sold his through the paper within a week. Having improved the computer's specifications himself and raised its price accordingly, he made a profit of £300.

Tahir and Tariq quickly dropped their idea of supplying software to hospitals, and began buying Amstrads wholesale, upgrading them, and selling them locally through newspaper advertisements. 'One sale a week became two a week, then four, then eight', said Tahir. Word spread that two 'very nice kids', as a former neighbour puts it, were performing miracles with computers. Tahir and Tariq's father had himself followed an entrepreneur's trajectory of sorts, from working in a mill as a Pakistani immigrant in the 1960s to running a corner shop to buying property, but his sons' upward path was more modern and much faster. Within a year, the narrow family flat was too full of circuit boards and boxes, and the business moved out, its annual turnover already £0.5 m. By 1990, Granville Technology was too big to occupy a shop and moved into an old Blackburn textile mill. In 1993, with a turnover of £100 m, the company moved to Simonstone.

Tariq continued practising as a pediatrician, but Tahir worked for the business obsessively. 'I lost my friends very, very quickly. The business takes all your time.' As their enterprise grew, so Tahir and 'Dr Tariq', who owned 60 per cent and

40 per cent respectively, recruited two other Mohsans, their younger brothers Zia and Zubhair, to help out, and subdivided the business into separate companies, sometimes with related names (Time Computers, Time Computer Systems), sometimes not (MJN Technology, the Internexus Group). Some of these companies frequently changed their names as well. 'Manufacturing and retailing and property don't mix', explained Mohsan. 'So you have them in separate companies.' But he conceded that the complexity of it all has aroused suspicions: 'It's very difficult for people to understand corporate structures.'

During the 1990s, however, the Mohsan strategy seemed to be working very well, and was rarely challenged. The brothers moved on from upgrading and selling other manufacturers' computers mail order to assembling their own from bought-in components. With schools and homes and hospitals acquiring their first PCs, and the price of upmarket brands staying high, the opportunities for anyone who could make and sell cheaper machines were enormous. The American computer company Dell had been doing this since 1984. Mohsan acknowledges its example as an influence, but in such a favourable market, being completely original was not a precondition for being successful.

'We used to make incredible amounts of money', said Mohsan. 'The profit margins in the late 90s were about 45 per cent.' As the British market for PCs widened, so the Mohsans started to also sell through shops, which they believed working-class computer buyers preferred to mail order. They began by selling through concessions in other people's stores, then through supermarkets, then by opening their own retail premises. 'We used to open a shop on a Friday', said Mohsan. 'By Monday afternoon, it had paid its overheads for the whole year.'

Up at Simonstone, with its Pennine mists and good motorway connections, the Mohsans' private industrial estate was given the name the Time Technology Park. Well-kept lawns and flowerbeds surrounded the buildings. Male staff wore shirts and ties, even on the production line. And some of Burnley and Blackburn's tensions were left at the factory gates. 'The great thing about Time was that it was very multicultural', says someone who worked there who is no ally of the Mohsans. 'I had lots of Asian friends. It was quite an island of calm.'

In recent years, unemployment in Burnley and Blackburn has not been as high as their more desolate areas sometimes suggest – neither place was in the worst 10 per cent for joblessness in England and Wales at the last census. But during the 1990s, the local papers carried news of vacancies at Simonstone as eagerly as they carried advertisements for the Mohsans' products. In July 1999, the Lancashire *Evening Telegraph* reported that more than 1,500 people queued up outside the factory for several hours to attend a recruitment fair where 500 vacancies at Simonstone were on offer. However, the opportunities inside the gates did not always live up to expectations. 'It's pretty old-fashioned for new media', says someone who works at Supanet, the brothers' still-functioning internet service provider. 'It's very much ruled from above.

We call it Victorian.' Graham Coxon, Lancashire organiser of the GMB union, which has had members at Simonstone since the 1990s, is more specific: 'Granville treated the workforce, I thought, disgracefully. There was a fear factor in the place. People were dismissed if they didn't fall into line.'

Not all past and present employees see it in these terms. 'Tahir used to bob in quite a lot. He was a really nice chap', says someone who worked in customer warranties in 2000. 'He'd say "Hi" to staff, "You all right?"' But like all the other employees I spoke to, none of whom had stayed at Simonstone for more than two years, she conceded that staff turnover was very high. 'The canteen was full of people talking about how they hated the management, hated the company.' The most frequently voiced grievance concerned relations with customers. As enterprises based on competitive prices, the Mohsans' companies have always emphasised low-cost production. 'In meetings', says the person who works at Supanet, 'it's always, "I want it cheaper, faster".' Someone who worked for the Mohsans' computer businesses between 1999 and 2001 says, 'If we found a problem with a newly issued model of PC, production continued and PCs were still shipped. It would then be down to technical support to gather the returns, and then pass the faulty PCs to evaluations for them to be examined. Only then would the model [be] put on hold.'

During the 1990s, Time Computers began to attract attention in the press for its faults as well as its enticing prices. Judging the representativeness of individual complaints from customers can be difficult, and the Simonstone management was quick to suggest that the problems were being exaggerated: 'Our stance has always been that one customer with a genuine grievance is one too many', wrote Time's then national sales manager, Colin Silcock, to *The Independent* in 1995. But the complaints continued. In 2003, the consumer magazine *Which?* asked several thousand computer users whether they would recommend the brand they owned to a friend. Only 14 per cent of Time owners said yes and 8 per cent of Tiny owners – making them the least popular of the brands surveyed by a large distance. In 2005, *Which?* included a question about reliability in a similar survey: Tiny scored respectably, but Time came bottom. In Lancashire and on the internet, a substantial spin-off industry grew up around fixing Mohsan hardware. 'I smile at all the faulty Time PCs brought in here', says the owner of a Burnley computer-servicing shop, a line of Simonstone computers in various stages of repair still standing in front of his cash register. 'They were basically using customers to test their stuff.'

With characteristic confidence – some would say chutzpah – Tahir Mohsan blames the complexity of the machines and the limited technical knowledge of most buyers. 'The industry sells a product to customers that is difficult. We sold PCs to people who didn't know what to do with them', he told me. He put the poor ratings of his machines compared with other makes down to his products' sheer ubiquity: 'The quality was the same [as other brands].'

Yet, whatever the reason, the customer service departments at Simonstone, with their low ceilings and tight clusters of desks, were busy and not very happy places. One of the ways the companies made money was by selling warranties and paid access to telephone helplines; when products went wrong, or were felt to have gone wrong, customer negotiations with Simonstone followed; in these transactions, too, Time and Tiny acquired poor reputations. In the 2003 *Which?* survey, Time's helpline performed even worse than its computers.

'People would be in the phone queue for an hour and a half', says someone who answered customer calls for six months during 2005. 'You were discouraged from telling them that they were paying when they were on hold.' On other occasions, he continues, 'You would be passing people on to departments where you knew the staff weren't there.' The woman who worked in warranties in 2000 describes her department's philosophy more bluntly: 'Put them off, put them off, until the machine goes out of warranty.'

On this subject, Mohsan lost his usual expansiveness. 'Customer service', he said, 'was not good enough in the 90s.'

Yet, the business seemed to expand regardless of its flaws. 'Because the market for PCs was growing so fast', says Michael Dean of the National Computing Centre, the Mohsans' success did not necessarily rely on 'the same people buying another Time computer'. In 1999, Tahir reportedly turned down an offer from Freeserve to buy his business for £300 m. In 2000, Time Computers won an out-of-court settlement from IBM of a very large unconfirmed sum after IBM had allegedly supplied Time with faulty components. Reporting the story, the online computer-industry journal, *The Register*, presented the companies, without any irony, as peers, referring to 'the two PC heavyweights'.

But then the climate for computer makers, benign for so long, began to change. From 2000, the upward graph of PC sales started to dip: a lot of people had a computer now. At the same time, sudden shortages affected the supply of essential components such as memory cards, and their cost shot up accordingly. Finally, as selling PCs became more difficult, every manufacturer reduced its prices. The Mohsans' big advantage was gone.

'We did not see the price deflation coming', said Mohsan. 'A PC fell from £1,500 in 2000 to £300 in 2005. And our margin went down from 45 per cent to 20 per cent. In other words, from £600 to £60 per computer.' Suddenly, the large chain of high-street shops the Mohsans had built up, with all their associated costs, became a liability. 'Granville was a very bad retailer', said Mohsan. 'We were not professional retailers. We didn't do it properly, sell ink and paper as well, all the accessories. We did not realise that supermarkets would hurt the high street.'

In 2000, the business nearly went into administration. Only a loan from HSBC prevented a collapse, but, publicly, the situation was played down. 'This is a temporary rather than a terminal issue', one of the Mohsans' executives told *The Evening Telegraph*. But shop closures and redundancies at Simonstone followed; these were noted in the Lancashire papers and the computer press. Yet, in the national media, such problems, like the problems with Granville's computers and customer service, continued to receive less attention than Tahir's youth and wealth and achievements.

'I didn't pretend to be a role model', he says now. His reluctance to give interviews seems to support this. But perhaps something of the media's persistent faith in him rubbed off. From 2000 to 2004, he responded to his companies' new vulnerability by being more ambitious, not less.

In 2002, the Mohsans bought Tiny Computers, then the biggest British PC maker. The fact that Tiny was in administration, having been undone by the same combination of over-expansion and worsening market conditions as the Mohsans two years earlier, did not seem to put Tahir and his brothers off. They also began acquiring foreign subsidiaries: a company to sell their computers in France, Time Group (Middle East) to make them in Dubai. In 2004, the Mohsans diversified into making plasma screens, which, unlike PCs, could still be sold with high profit margins. The launch of the new product line last September was, Tahir said, 'exceptionally successful'.

Ten months later, the administrators were called into Simonstone. The precise sequence of events in those months, like the precise structure of the Mohsan companies, remains a matter of debate – that may only be resolved when the administrators send their report to the DTI, and perhaps not even then. But it most likely included the following: the proposed sale of Granville to a management team appointed by the Mohsans; resistance to this idea from HSBC, mindful of the company's debts and uncertain prospects; a period of stalemate and drift; the injection of £2 m into Granville by the Mohsans in June; the resignation of the management team in early July; and abortive last-minute talks at Simonstone between Tahir and HSBC. And there is one important detail on which all parties are agreed: the employees were told absolutely nothing.

For several months before July, shopfloor rumours had circulated at Simonstone that Granville was in trouble. In June, staff were paid late. Over the summer, sections of the Mohsan compound were closed off and rented to outside businesses. People also noted that senior managers were not making their usual rounds.

But most employees did not pay much attention. They were used to uncertainty: about exactly which Mohsan company they worked for; about their job prospects even in normal times, as the Simonstone workforce constantly expanded and contracted; and about the long-term future of the companies after the near-collapse of 2000. It was not until mid-July, when some assembly staff were instructed to take a week off, unpaid, that rumours of a new crisis became widespread. The following Monday, July 25, the Mohsans' shops closed for their unscheduled 'stock take'. At Simonstone, some sales staff, realising that the end was imminent, began suggesting to customers who rang to order goods that they pay by credit card only, the one sure way of getting a refund.

On the morning of 27 July, at about 10 a.m., a junior employee tried to leave the main Granville building to fetch something from his car. He was told by a security guard, one of the usual Simonstone contingent, that anyone who stepped outside would be sacked. Soon afterwards, at the local GMB office, Coxon says, 'I got a phone call saying, "We've been locked in." I told them to call the police.' By the time he got to Simonstone, the yard was full of furious staff with police vans and television cameras in attendance. Granville was in administration; most of the staff had read the news on the internet. A reader comment in one of the online computer industry journals expressed a fairly common sentiment: 'Good ridance [sic] to crap PC maker.'

Does Mohsan regret how things ended? He picked up one of the Granville placemats from the boardroom table and fiddled with it with his fingers. He made one of his disarming admissions: 'The employees were appallingly handled.' Then he switched into one of his equally characteristic evasions: '. . . But by whom? Legally, I was handcuffed.' His answer became a broad expression of regret about how banks and administrators had to behave in Britain when companies fail.

His responses to the other allegations against him also moved quickly and nimbly away from the specific to the general. Of the lack of records at the failed companies, he said: 'Every board meeting I went to, there was a board minute . . . [But] I can't comment on actual records. I wasn't around.' Of the notion that he and his brothers transferred assets from Granville to other companies shortly before it went into administration, he said that his critics had got things precisely the wrong way round: 'Every single company we have has bad debt from Granville. We are owed in excess of £30 m.' But Ellis says Mohsan's use of the word 'debt' here is too vague to have much meaning.

On Granville Road in Blackburn, the events at Simonstone are discussed in more concrete terms. At the barber opposite the Mohsans' old flat, a middle-aged Asian man who used to know the family says quietly, with small nods of disapproval: 'Quite a few worked for Time from around this area. Six or seven of my relatives did. They've got to pay the mortgage. What do they do now?'

Half a mile away, where the treeless terraced streets give way to detached villas and views of distant hills, some of the Mohsan brothers still live in a gabled Victorian house the size of a hotel. The electric gates are guarded by a CCTV camera and the nameplate of a private security firm. Since July, many of the former Simonstone staff have, in fact, found new jobs, but a sense of bitterness has lingered, sometimes with a vicious edge. At tinycon.com, an outspoken website for ex-employees that was shut down by lawyers in August, 'One out of every 20 posts would be racist', says Matt Ashworth, the site's founder. 'We had to delete the posts and ban the users.'

Tahir said he was not aware of any racial backlash. Then again, he continued, 'I was the figurehead. People need someone to blame.' And he was ready, he said, to accept 30 per cent of the responsibility for the Granville meltdown. 'I hired the management team.'

But then his tone shifted. 'If you look at some of the great people in the world', he said, 'they rise and fall.' He paused and looked restlessly round the boardroom. 'You can sit here. You can have regrets. But we are going to continue in the UK. We are going to launch a PC company again. We intend to be in business for many, many years to come. Yes, I regard Granville as a disappointing part of my business life. I've learned a lot of lessons. I'll make sure it doesn't happen again. But listen . . .', he said the words more slowly than usual: 'We are in the business of taking risks.'

At the end of the interview, I asked if I could look round the premises. The man who met me in reception guided me into a maze. There were endless office partitions and empty hallways, corners full of upended furniture and piles of computer monitors. There were darkened open-plan areas with infinities of empty desks. And there were sudden areas of light and warmth where young people in neat clothes were still sitting at desks answering telephones. As we passed, one of them was saying to a customer, slightly impatiently, 'You have to request it, right?'

We ended the tour on a balcony looking down on the old Granville assembly line. It was almost deserted. But one whole section, perhaps the size of a tennis court, was piled with large brown boxes. Stickers said they had plasma screens in them. 'That wasn't here yesterday', said the man from reception, matter-of-factly. 'There must be some plan for them.'

Source: *The Guardian*, 2 December 2005

Questions for discussion

1 Assume Tahir is now seeking funding for a new venture. What case would he make to justify funding on the basis of his record in business?

2 Would you fund Tahir in another business venture? Give reasons for your answer.

3 Do you think Tahir made a positive contribution to the economy of Burnley? Justify your answer.

4 How much of the demise of Tiny Computers was bad luck and how much was poor management?

5 Could Tahir have done more to avoid the collapse of Tiny Computers? If so, what?

The case below examines small business closure. It is in two parts:

- The first is the reported view of the business owner.
- The second part consists of two perspectives upon the closure, which we refer to as the cynic and the optimist.

Having read both the case and the two perspectives, you will be asked to make a reasoned case from the evidence available from the case and your knowledge of small business closure about whether you side with the cynic or the optimist.

The business owner

Three years ago Peter Durose made the life-changing decision to quit his £250,000-a-year job running the fresh produce section at Tesco. Weary of starting each day with a 6.45 a.m. car journey to the supermarket's headquarters in Cheshunt, Hertfordshire, he abandoned the prospect of a seat on the board, and the £1.5 m pay package that came with it, to open a gourmet corner shop in the nearby village of Buntingford.

The tiny new venture promised Durose the chance to spend more time with his wife, Marion, and their young daughters, Grace and Lauren. It was a far cry from his days at Tesco in charge of £2 billion of sales and 160 people, but the family had almost paid off their mortgage and could afford to take the financial gamble. They sank £100,000 of their savings into the venture and in March 2007, after months of painstaking planning, The English Grocer opened its doors.

It stocked the good-quality fare that middle-class food lovers rave about – beautiful breads, cheeses from Neal's Yard dairy, hams and pickles, as well as cream teas, scones and coffees – all the ingredients for a perfect picnic basket. Sales grew steadily and by the first Christmas the family were taking orders for £100 luxury hampers. The following year trade was steady.

After only two years, though, the dream has died. The English Grocer shut last month and Durose is back working round the clock for a fraction of what he earned during his highflying days at Tesco. He could be forgiven for being bitter at the business's demise but in an interview with *The Sunday Times* this weekend the Duroses were sanguine about its failure.

Sitting at the kitchen table in their 200-year-old converted barn, he said: 'We had a lot of fun setting up the shop. I learnt more in the past three years than in the previous ten. There is something all-encompassing about starting a business.' However, starting their own business was not easy.

When Durose resigned from Tesco he was forced to spend 13 weeks serving his notice – instead of preparing his new venture. Once he left Tesco, and with The English Grocer still in its planning stages, he teamed up with a friend to set up a small consultancy business advising growers on how to find the best market for their products. Once the shop opened, Durose was spending a lot of time on his consultancy work while his wife spent most of her time at the store.

He said: 'I found it difficult to organise my time. I quickly found I was doing seven days a week again. It's easy to lose that balance and you have to stop and think – remember what we are doing here.' His wife said: 'We both did a lot of work in the evening. We would put the kids to bed and then at 8 p.m. we would both be sat there with our laptops.' She threw her energies into the store, but it was proving a hard grind, made worse after she became pregnant with their third child. 'I would go to all the food shows and there would be 900 people selling new jams. After a while I thought: the jam we've got is really good and it tastes nice – do we need to look at any more?'

Once the recession hit, trade remained steady. 'I kept saying I can't believe we seem to be bucking the trend', she said. But last November, just as she gave birth to her son, sales slumped. It couldn't have come at a worse time. Endless advertising leaflets in the run-up to Christmas yielded little response. When customers did spend money they were ordering £30 hampers in place of the £100 hampers a year earlier.

In January the couple were forced to inject more cash to keep the business afloat. Desperate measures were required and they called their landlord to ask for a 25 per cent cut in their rent – but even that was not enough to save them. 'I kept thinking that maybe trade would pick up when the weather got better. But it didn't get better – it snowed in March', said Marion. The final blow came when the local council abolished free car parking in the village and erected bollards to restrict cars. 'The works meant the high street was shut for three weeks and after they finished the browsers never came back.'

The Duroses decided to pull the plug. They reassigned the lease to a new coffee shop within three weeks and sold off their stock. 'The hardest part, I guess, was that we could have carried on', said Durose. 'It wasn't just a commercial decision – it was an emotional decision. Alistair Darling may think there are green shoots out there, but I am not sure anyone agrees with him. We found we were consistently talking about the year after next year – and for a small business that is a heck of a gamble.'

'It looks like there could be 18 months before there are any real green shoots', he said. His wife added: 'We would look like fools if we sank all our money into it and then next year we were flat stony-broke. The saddest thing from a personal level is that a food movement that was just getting going about good-quality, home-cooked, locally sourced food has been lost because people say they want cheap food and they will buy whatever is being sold at Tesco for two-for-one or half-price.'

So, would Durose ever go back to working for a big company like Tesco? 'I would never say never', he said hesitantly, ignoring his wife's glowers. 'Recruitment companies still call me – in fact one called me this morning. I heard about a job at Coles in Melbourne and we both thought oooh . . .' 'But then we decided let's not even discuss it', said his wife, 'because we will suddenly find we're there'. Durose said: 'I do miss having a team and working with a team. Before this, the smallest business I had worked for was Boots the Chemist. But in our hearts I don't think The English Grocer is over for ever. Maybe another time . . . another place. There is definitely a place for it.'

These days he may be working round the clock again doing consultancy work, but he can do it in the rather more relaxed surroundings of his home. Dressed casually in white and blue checked shirt, with no tie, he is grappling with his five-month-old son in the kitchen during our conversation. Outside in the huge sunlit garden the couple's two golden brown mini-dachshunds, Jasper and Jason, are tumbling playfully on the grass. 'I don't regret any of it, not at all', said Durose. And does he ever see the Tesco executives racing to work at 6.45 a.m.? 'No. I'm in bed asleep at that time', he laughed.

Source: *The Sunday Times*, 26 April 2009.

The cynic's perspective

Doesn't this case perfectly illustrate everything in the chapter about small businesses that close? First – the fault never lies with the owner. Instead, blame lies squarely with a factor or set of factors outside the control of the individual: in this case, we have almost all the 'usual suspects': we have the recession, of course, and the government (Chancellor Alastair Darling). But we also have the blame distributed amongst a wide range of parties: Tesco for making him work his notice, his wife for becoming pregnant with their third child, the weather – after all it snowed in March! And, of course, the Council finished it off by abolishing free parking in the village.

In contrast, there is almost no apparent awareness that this was the type of business that could only survive at the top of a historically unprecedented credit boom when people had money to spare. There is no recognition that perhaps they over-extended themselves; maybe the premises were too expensive; maybe their internal controls were not strong enough. The really sad thing about this case is that they still believe the business model is sound . . . they believe there is a place for it. Perhaps the only redeeming feature is that at least they got out before losing all their own funds.

The entrepreneurial perspective

Well done to the Duroses! You came up with a great idea and you implemented it. It was a venture that brought the two of you together and enabled Peter to get off the appalling treadmill of working unsocial hours for a large multinational and never seeing his children.

You were just unlucky. Hardly anyone in the world saw the recession of 2008–9 coming and your idea of providing high-quality food was very sound – especially since you were able to bring to the business your expertise in this area that you accumulated in your years with Tesco.

To your eternal credit, you quit whilst you were ahead and are still able to generate an income from your consultancy activities. As you say, 'We had a lot of fun setting up the shop. I learnt more in the past three years than in the previous ten. There is something all-encompassing about starting a business.'

Are you with the cynic or the entrepreneur? Justify your answer.

The four case studies below are designed to help you consider some of the challenges faced in the provision of public support to entrepreneurs and small businesses. The first case begins by asking you to come up with a working definition of entrepreneurship.

The second case asks you to reach a judgement about the level of entrepreneurship in your country. It offers a range of entrepreneurial 'measures' that can be used to assess the development of enterprise in your country.

The third case takes the six 'determinants of entrepreneurship' identified by the OECD (2008) (see Chapter 19). It asks you to pick one of these six determinants and make a reasoned case for a policy intervention in one of these areas. It subsequently asks you to work through the choices involved in designing and implementing your policy choice.

The final case asks: How would you know that the policy choice you made in the third part will work? To support you, we provide a short primer that introduces some of the main issues involved in assessing entrepreneurship and small business policies/programmes.

Part 1 Defining 'entrepreneurship'

This case study assumes that you have just started work in a dedicated small business ministry in your country. Your new minister has asked you to 'go back to first principles' to develop your country's entrepreneurship policy. Your initial research has found that there is no simple definition of entrepreneurs, entrepreneurship or small businesses. The best definition that you have found from fellow policy makers is the one from the EU. It states: 'Entrepreneurship is the mindset and process to create and develop economic activity by building risk-taking creativity and/or innovation with sound management, within a new or existing organisation'.

You realise that this definition looks appealing because it seems to combine familiar concepts. For example, it emphasises 'mindset'. This suggests entrepreneurs have a way of looking at opportunities quite separate from others in the population. 'Process', meanwhile, points to the fact that entrepreneurship is not a one-off event. People take time to develop their business. Equally, once established, business owners continually have to adjust to changing circumstances. The EU definition also mentions 'risk taking'. It also suggests that it involves a 'new or existing organisation'.

However, there may be problems with this definition. First, 'mindset' or 'risk taking' seems to imply that policy makers believe that entrepreneurs are special people. Second, it implicitly assumes that entrepreneurship policy is about changing people's attitudes to entrepreneurship. You know from reading Baumol (1990) that this may not be the case.

You are also aware that the EU definition mixes up its unit of analysis. The first part talks as if it has to do with the entrepreneurial personality; the second talks of 'process'; and the third looks at the new or existing business.

> Based upon your reading and what you know, what would your definition of entrepreneurship be? More importantly, your minister wants to know why you have chosen this definition.

Part 2 Measuring 'entrepreneurship'

Your minister is now worried. The main opposition party assert that your country is under-performing. The minister, as a result, has had some unfavourable press reports that question if, indeed, your country is 'entrepreneurial'. Your minister has called upon your expertise in small business and entrepreneurship policy to develop some key 'messages' to show that your country is, in fact, highly 'entrepreneurial'.

The problem you face is that you know – even if the minister doesn't – that there are a number of measures of what it means to have an 'entrepreneurial' society.

These are:

- high rates of new business formation;

- a high rate of business closure or maybe a low rate of business closure;

- a high proportion of people who had considered, or who are considering, starting a business of their own;

- a low proportion of people motivated to start their own business because of a fear of, or actual, unemployment;

- a high proportion of new businesses in 'growth' as opposed to 'traditional' sectors;

- a high proportion of rapidly growing small businesses.

Your initial research has led to the development of Table CS 7.1. This identifies the advantages and disadvantages of each approach.

Table CS 7.1	Measures of entrepreneurship		
Indicator	**Background**	**Advantages**	**Disadvantages**
High rates of new business formation	Sharma and Chrisman (1999: 18) define entrepreneurship as ' . . . the process whereby an individual or group of individuals, acting independently of any association with an existing organization, create a new organization'	Reflects the novelty and risk of entrepreneurship. Data are available on new businesses in many countries, often over a long time span.	Under-estimates the aggregate level of enterprise in an economy: what about the 'quality' (e.g. innovativeness) of an economy? Different definitions used in differing countries make comparisons very difficult. It is particularly difficult when official statistics under-estimate the scale of the informal economy. What is the appropriate measure: the stock or population based measure?
A high rate of business closure	Schumpeter's (1950) 'gale of creative destruction' is only partly about creating something new. There is also a need to destroy the old because resources need to be released and then re-allocated from their old inefficient uses to their more efficient uses.	Encapsulates the concept of destruction which is a necessary pre-condition for entrepreneurship.	Taking business closures alone provides an imperfect measure since it could reflect a collapsing economy if there is no evidence of new activity replacing the old. People close businesses for a variety of reasons (e.g. ill-health, retirement). They may also be acquired or sold. Business 'deaths' may be greatly exaggerated in official statistics.
A high proportion of people who had considered, or who are considering, starting a business of their own	People in a country with an entrepreneurial 'mindset' are a pre-condition for enterprise.	Useful for an economy that wishes to have people who can identify entrepreneurial opportunities when they come along. Can be measured using Global Entrepreneurship Monitor (GEM) data. This identifies those that are 'nascents' (in the process of setting up their own business) and young businesses. Also GEM's coverage includes businesses below/outside official data because they look at very small businesses, very new businesses and, potentially, those that operate in the informal economy.	Only measures intentions not actions. It is known that not everyone who thinks about starting a business actually does. It is also known that many who start a business spend almost no time thinking about it.

Table CS7.1 continued

Indicator	Background	Advantages	Disadvantages
A low proportion of people motivated to start their own business because of a fear of, or actual, unemployment or under-employment	So far, we have assumed that 'more is better'. However, we have not looked at the 'quality' of entrepreneurship. It could be that there are the 'wrong' types of entrepreneur. For example, take two countries, A and B. Country A has low unemployment and so very few new businesses begin as a direct result of unemployment or the threat of unemployment facing the founder. By contrast, Country B has higher rates of new business formation, but these are mainly started by people experiencing or threatened by unemployment. Does this mean that Country B is more entrepreneurial than Country A?	Entrepreneurship might seem to be about choice but very many people in the world have little choice but to follow a self-employment route. These are 'necessity' entrepreneurs. Measuring these proportions using data like GEM might indicate how few/many people are necessity entrepreneurs. This is beneficial because necessity entrepreneurship may be associated with businesses that do not generate a great deal of wealth.	Evidence on necessity entrepreneurship leading to poorer-performing businesses is mixed at best. The role of entry is to exercise a credible threat to those in business, disciplining them to perform efficiently. That threat is most effective when there are clearly many potential businesses eager to take their marketplace. It matters little why those people wish to start a business, only that they constitute a credible threat.
A high proportion of new businesses in 'growth', as opposed to 'traditional' sectors	It is better to have businesses in higher 'quality' sectors because they lead more clearly to economic development.	Technology based business appear to be a major driver of social and economic change. The US appears to be 'entrepreneurial' because of its ability to develop leading technology companies (e.g. Microsoft, Google or Dell).	Not all technology businesses display fast growth. It is also the case that the vast majority of rapidly growing businesses are not in technology sectors. How do you measure growth (e.g. employment, sales, assets)? Is the government the best agent for picking relevant sectors?
A high proportion of rapidly growing small businesses	Independent of sector, some businesses grow rapidly.	Without growing businesses, it is hard to see how an economy can generate further wealth.	How do you measure growth (e.g. employment, sales, assets)? Is the government the best agent for picking relevant growth businesses?

- One task now is to decide which one, or combination, of measures is the most appropriate for measuring how entrepreneurial your society is.

- Your minister has also asked you to identify evidence that will support the claim that your country is more entrepreneurial now than it was 20 years ago.

- You recognise that if you say that all six measures are important, then the entrepreneurial 'message' may become lost in the detail. You know that the minister wants you to pick on just one measure: it provides a clear focus.

- Alternatively, do you go to the minister and say that all of the measures are of equal importance?

Part 3 Policy choices

The last minister lasted three months in the job and you now have a new minister. Her first task was to go to Paris to an OECD meeting with other small business ministers. There she was told that Denmark was the 'world leader' in framing entrepreneurship policy and has asked you to look at their policy regime.

Now that she has returned she has asked you to identify which of the six 'determinants of entrepreneurship' (OECD 2008) should be the focus of future policy developments (see Figure CS 7.1). Having identified a determinant, your task is to choose one of the policy sub-categories within this determinant that you think needs most development.

She has also brought back her notes on the Danish policy regime (Table CS 7.2) so you presume she will ask you about how your proposals compare with those of the Danes. You, therefore, need to get a better understanding of the Danish framework than is provided by her notes.

Determinants					
Regulatory framework	R & D and technology	Entrepreneurial capabilities	Culture	Access to finance	Market conditions
Administrative burdens for entry	R & D investment	Training and experience of entrepreneurs	Risk attitude in society	Access to debt financing	Anti-trust laws
Administrative burdens for growth	University/Industry interface	Business and entrepreneurship education (skills)	Attitudes towards entrepreneurs	Business angels	Competition
Bankruptcy regulations	Technological co-operation between firms	Entrepreneurship infrastructure	Desire for business ownership	Access to VC	Access to the domestic market
Safety, health and environmental regulations	Technology diffusion	Immigration	Entrepreneurship education (mindset)	Access to other types of equity	Access to foreign markets
Product and labour-market regulation	Broadband access			Stock markets	Degree of public involvement
Court and legal framework	Patent system; standards				Public procurement
Social and health security					
Income, wealth, business and capital taxes					

Source: OECD (2008).

Figure CS7.1   Entrepreneurship determinants: policy areas

Table CS 7.2	Entrepreneurship benchmarking: the Danish approach

The new Danish government in 2001 set out the ambitious goal that, by 2015, Denmark should have the world's highest share of growth entrepreneurs. It specified two growth indicators:

1 The share of new enterprises with more than 15 employees with sales growth of more than 60 per cent between 2003 and 2005 and annual sales growth in each year of at least 20 per cent.

2 The share of new firms with more than 15 employees that had employment growth of more than 60 per cent between 2002 and 2004 and at least 20 per cent each year.

The OECD countries that perform best on these measures are the US, Korea, Ireland and Canada.
    Denmark 'benchmarks' its policy regime against these countries since it has been shown that there is a strong correlation between Framework conditions and entrepreneurship activity (Hoffman 2007).
    In total 24 policy elements are identified of which 18 are quantified and constitute the Framework Conditions. These are:

- Tech transfer/regulation
- Entry barriers
- Access to foreign markets
- Loans
- Venture capital
- Exit
- Wealth and bequest tax
- Capital taxes
- Restart possibilities
- Entrepreneurship education
- Traditional business education
- Entrepreneurship infrastructure
- Personal income tax
- Business tax and fiscal incentives
- Bankruptcy legislation
- Administrative burdens
- Labour-market regulation
- Entrepreneurial motivation

The Danish government then reviews its progress periodically both on the policy regime and on its performance in progressing towards its 2015 target (FORA 2008).

This minister – unlike the last one – also understands that there are two basic rationales for public intervention to support small businesses and entrepreneurs: market failure and political economy. How do you convince the minister of your likely chosen policy? What is your intervention logic? What are the likely economic and social impacts of your policy choice?

Table CS 7.3	Mole and Bramley's policy choice framework

Q1	Who delivers . . .	public, private or quasi?
Q2	What 'type' . . .	generic, standards, tailored, regulated, face-to-face, e-based?
Q3	How is it rationed . . .	time, sector, price, market segmentation?
Q4	How is it integrated . . .	into other economic and social programmes?
Q5	How is it funded . . .	by charges, by donations, directly from public funds?

Any policy that you seek to develop involves important choices. Your minister has asked you to work through the Mole and Bramley (2006) framework to arrive at the best way of designing and implementing your chosen policy (see Table CS 7.3). On what basis can you justify how you have chosen to design and implement your policy choice?

Part 4 Assessing the policy choice

The minister is now very enthusiastic about the policy proposal you have developed. There is a good chance that it will be adopted and become part of a new package of support for small businesses and entrepreneurs. A senior colleague, however, has had a quiet word with you. Their advice is that, if the policy is taken further, your name – and hence your reputation – will become associated with the policy choice and that this will have long-term impacts on your career. The biggest danger is – after the current minister has left the small business ministry or even after the current government has been replaced – that the policy choice will be scrutinised to see if it has worked.

What types of evidence should you collect to demonstrate if the policy proposal works? You talk to the policy evaluation team in your ministry. They have provided you with the attached primer on monitoring and evaluating policy programmes (see Appendix following). Again, you are faced with choices:

1 If you choose to 'monitor' the programme, it is likely that your policy choice will be seen to be effective. It may also lead to improvements in how the programme is run. However, there is a risk that it will be reviewed by 'experts'

and there is a strong chance that they may be sceptical about the impact of the programme and your attempts to put in place a satisfactory mechanism for judging its effectiveness. Such scepticism may be widely reported in the media.

2 However, if you choose to 'evaluate' the programme, there is an opportunity to properly appraise the effectiveness and efficiency of the programme. It, too, may lead to managerial improvements but there is a chance that it will be misunderstood by colleagues and, relative to a monitoring approach, show that the programme is not a success.

Your task is to read the supporting information in the Appendix and make a reasoned recommendation of whether the programme should be monitored or evaluated.

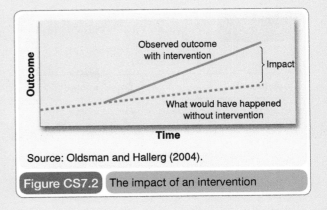

Source: Oldsman and Hallerg (2004).

Figure CS7.2   The impact of an intervention

Appendix A monitoring and evaluation primer

This primer begins by identifying the four reasons why assessments of policy choices are necessary. It then defines what is meant by monitoring and evaluation and then examines their advantages and disadvantages. Finally, it presents a typology for comparing monitoring and evaluation techniques.

Four reasons for assessing a policy

OECD (2008) gives four prime reasons for assessing the impact of entrepreneurship and small business policies:

- Substantial sums of taxpayers' money are used for administering and delivering small business and entrepreneurship policies.
- A responsibility to the taxpayer – it is public money and there is a need to ensure that it is spent effectively.
- Political imperative – in democratic societies there is a need to ensure accountability.
- Efficient policy delivery – public money should be spent wisely.

Defining monitoring and evaluation

Assessments of the impact of a particular policy/programme impact are undertaken through monitoring and evaluation. Monitoring approaches rely primarily upon the views of managers, stakeholders and participants on the efficiency and effectiveness of the programme. These views are usually derived from surveys (e.g. surveys of the perceptions of participants),

case studies (e.g. identification of 'best' practice) or peer reviews (e.g. surveys of 'experts'). The typical aim of monitoring is to describe the inputs of a programme (e.g. levels and types of activities undertaken by the programme) and using self-report data to estimate outputs (e.g. number of jobs created).

Evaluation seeks to assess the *net* effect of a policy – the effect observed compared with doing nothing (the counterfactual). Evaluation takes place only when there is an explicit counter-factual. For example, suppose a small business was receiving publicly funded business advice so as to boost the sales of the business. Prior to receiving the business advice, we observe sales (the dotted line in Figure CS 7.2). However, once the advice is received, or acted upon, we only observe the continuous line. It is tempting to believe that the impact of the business advice is the area under the continuous line. However, this ignores the fact that sales were both positive and rising prior to receiving the advice. Instead, what is necessary is to work out what would have happened to sales if the business did not receive the business advice. This is the counter-factual (the dotted line). The problem is that the counter-factual cannot be easily measured since the only observable 'state' is that the business received the advice. In practice, entrepreneurship and small business policy evaluations have compared businesses in receipt of policy – often called the 'treatment' group – with otherwise similar businesses that did not benefit from the policy – called the 'control' or 'non-treatment' group.

The aim of an evaluation, therefore, is to formally assess the impact of a policy/programme by making some assessment of its net impact on participants. Often, a second aim is to provide recommendations on how a particular programme can be improved, or to highlight the 'lessons' from the programme. Typically, evaluations tend to make use of large-scale surveys and employ statistical techniques, because such studies often seek to be 'representative' of participants in a particular programme, and compare participants with some form of 'control' group.

Advantages and disadvantages of monitoring and evaluation

Table CS 7.4 identifies the advantages and disadvantages of the two approaches. The main advantage of monitoring is

Table CS 7.4	Advantages and disadvantages of monitoring and evaluation

Monitoring		Evaluation	
Advantages	**Disadvantages**	**Advantages**	**Disadvantages**
Engages participants in policy learning	Respondents and interviewers may be biased or poorly informed	Clear answers on impact	Cost of data collection and technical demands
Can vary the scale and hence cost	Rarely provides a clear answer	If well done will get close to true impact	Lacks information on context and mechanisms behind policy impacts
Deeper understanding of processes leading to impacts	Tend to 'describe' rather than 'evaluate'	Can be independently verified	Absence of pure control groups
Should be easy to interpret	Risks including 'un-representative' groups		Possible false impression of precision
Can assess against a wide range of evaluation criteria	No opportunity for independent verification		Narrow focus on effectiveness and efficiency
Picks up unintended consequences	Hard to judge efficiency and effectiveness		Difficult to use on indirect interventions that seek to influence the business environment
Better understanding of policy options and alternatives	Hard to establish cause and effect		

that it can provide valuable qualitative information from participants, programme managers and 'experts' on a programme. From this information a deeper understanding of the programme's processes may potentially be gained. This may generate a fuller appreciation of any 'unintended' consequences of a programme (outcomes that occur, but which were unexpected). Finally, the use of qualitative material means that the benefits of the programme are likely to be more easily understood than by presenting 'dry' statistics.

However, monitoring has disadvantages. Essentially, the problem is that monitoring tends to 'describe' rather than evaluate the positive or negative impact of a policy/programme. One symptom of this is that qualitative data collection often trades in-depth 'insights' into processes for a loss of representativeness and generalisability. Hence, those who take part in a monitoring study may be unrepresentative of the wider population. This means an absence of independent verification, making it hard to judge the overall value or impact of the programme.

With evaluation studies it is much easier to establish cause and effect. Indeed, evaluation studies can provide much clearer, independently verifiable, assessments of the impact of a particular programme. In other words, they are much more likely to meet the OECD (2008) criteria of providing accountable information on the cost, efficiency and effectiveness of a particular policy/programme.

Evaluation studies, however, do have disadvantages. They are costly, often need evaluators with sophisticated and specialist statistical skills, and may be difficult to comprehend. Also they tend to rely on a comparison between programme participants and a 'control' group. Establishing these control groups can often be difficult and may – even with the best

of intentions – result in 'impure' control groups since they do not exactly match programme participants. Hence, evaluations may give a false impression of precision, and the results may over- or under-estimate the actual impact of a programme. This is even more likely given that programmes usually do not have one single, clear objective, and there are a variety of performance measures against which the programme may be measured. Again, this makes comprehension of the evaluation difficult. Curran (2000) argues that evaluations may miss the heterogeneity of small businesses and fail, practically, to identify – because of the focus on effectiveness and efficiency – what the key benefits are of a particular programme for small businesses and entrepreneurs.

Comparing monitoring and evaluation methodologies

The OECD (2008) provides a typology for comparing monitoring with evaluation. This is the 'six steps' approach. Table CS 7.5 identifies each of the 'six steps', what questions each of the 'steps' answers and the difficulties each step faces. Fundamental to the six steps approach is the distinction between monitoring (steps 1–3) and evaluation (steps 4–6).

A Step 1 approach identifies programme take-up but gives no indication of how this satisfies programme objectives or if the programme is effective. So, it provides information on the number, and perhaps the characteristics, of the businesses that apply and benefit. It may also provide an important audit function ensuring that public money is spent legally, but it provides no assessment of whether the programme had an impact.

Table CS 7.5	The 'six steps' approach

	Questions addressed	Problems with the approach
Step 1 Take-up of programme	● How many businesses participated? ● What sectors were they in? ● What locations were they in? ● How big were these businesses? ● How much money was spent?	● Tells you almost nothing about policy effectiveness. ● Tells you almost nothing about satisfying objectives.
Step 2 Recipients' opinions	● Did recipients value the service? ● Were there problems in accessing the service?	● Even if recipients say they like it, it may not influence performance or behaviour. ● Only offers insights into policy delivery not into whether the service adds value.
Step 3 Recipients' views of the difference made by the assistance	● Did businesses think it provided 'additionality'? ● Would businesses have done it anyway? (deadweight) ● Does it cause displacement?	● No way of checking the answers. ● Suspect some may over-estimate and some may under-estimate impact. ● Can only examine responses of surviving businesses, which could be an important bias.
Step 4 Comparison of the performance of 'assisted' with 'typical' businesses	● How does employment and sales growth in treated businesses compare with 'typical' businesses? ● How does the survival of assisted businesses compare with typical businesses?	● Assisted businesses are not necessarily typical.
Step 5 Comparison with 'match' businesses	● How does employment and sales growth in treated businesses compare with match businesses, i.e. taking account of age, sector, ownership and geography? ● How does the survival of treated businesses compare with that of match businesses?	● More 'motivated' businesses may apply, so the 'match' businesses are not an ideal control group. ● Attribute differential performance to scheme and not to motivation.
Step 6 Taking account of selection bias	● How can account be taken of self- and committee-selection bias in assessing the impact of assistance on the survival and growth of businesses?	● Although statistical methods have been used to address selection bias, policy makers (and some academics) feel uneasy about statistical 'adjustment'. ● The second approach – randomised trials. Use of randomised trials could mean public money is given to businesses/ people who it is known in advance will not benefit, and money, therefore, is not given to businesses that will benefit.

Asking recipients for their views – Step 2 – is an approach to assessing the impact of the programme. It is particularly helpful in providing policy makers with insights into aspects of programme delivery or 'process' but any estimates of impact are likely to be unreliable. This is primarily because there is no way of accurately assessing the reliability of 'self-report' data.

Step 3 does seek to address this by implicitly posing a counter-factual. It asks respondents to estimate what the impact on their business would have been if they had not benefited from this policy. The problem with this approach is that it is liable to interview and cognitive biases. There are, therefore, major problems with reliability over self-report information – especially where there is no explicit control group.

Steps 4–6 constitute evaluation because they make a comparison between the recipients of policy – the treatment group – and the control group. A second characteristic of these steps is that they rely primarily on 'outcome' measures of policy impact – such as sales, employment or survival in the assisted businesses. Step 4 takes the control group as the 'average' or 'typical' unassisted businesses, and so compares their performance with that of the treated businesses. However, the latter may, or may not, be a 'typical' business. For example, they might be in only certain sectors or geographical areas. It, therefore, cannot be assumed that if the treated businesses perform better (or worse) than the control group, this is because of the policy: it might merely reflect sectoral or geographical differences. An example of a Step 4 evaluation is detailed in the Illustration below.

Context

Small Business Development Centers provide a full programme of support from running a business start up through to technology support for existing businesses. They have been operational since 1977 and operate across the US. The centres are funded by the US federal government through population-based grants with the expectation that this is matched by other sources at the local or state level. Support is generally free. Administration of the programme is conducted by the Small Business Administration (SBA) but individual centres are given a degree of latitude to tailor their programmes to local and state needs.

The evaluations

SBDCs have been the subject of a number of evaluations over the period 1985–2005 (Chrisman 2005, 1999, 1989; Chrisman *et al.* 2005; Chrisman and McMullan 2004, 2002, 2000, 1996; Chrisman *et al.* 2002; Chrisman and Katrishen 1994; Chrisman and Leslie 1989; Chrisman *et al.* 1987; and Chrisman *et al.* 1985). These evaluations all showed consistent and positive performance by SBDCs. For example, Chrisman *et al.* (1985) showed that those SBDC clients that received in-depth counselling were '. . . more likely to survive, prosper and grow' (p. 10) and suggested that the overall benefits, relative to costs, supported the programme. Twenty years later Chrisman and McMullen (2004) found that SDBC clients were more likely to survive whilst Chrisman *et al.* (2005) found that they were more likely to grow in terms of both sales and employment.

A critique of these evaluations

This Step 4 approach has the following limitations:

- Many of the samples used involved very low numbers. For example, in the 1985 study (Chrisman *et al.* 1985), there were just 19 usable responses for South Carolina, limiting the use of statistical testing.
- The control group is 'typical' businesses. This means that any differences in performance may be because SBDC clients differed in terms of sector, size or age, or a myriad of other observable features.
- But, even if they had controlled for 'observables', it might be that SBDC clients were more likely to wish to grow. The case is that they are more motivated, because otherwise they would not have applied for SBDC assistance. Hence, they also differ in terms of 'unobservables'. This is important because it implies that, even if there had been no SBDC advice, these businesses would have grown faster. This, in turn, means the evaluators are attributing the growth amongst clients to SBDC services, when it would have happened without the services. This is one dimension of 'selection bias'.
- Finally, much of the evaluation focuses upon the responses of the businesses. The subjective responses of business owners who choose to visit advice centres may be generally positive since to report otherwise would imply they made a mistake in their decision to seek the advice.

A Step 5 approach seeks a better match between the two groups. It ensures that there are no differences in terms of age, size and location of the two groups of business. This means that any differences in performance are not attributable to these factors and more likely to reflect the real impact of the policy. Whilst the Step 5 approach ensures that observable differences such as sector and geography are taken into account there may also be unobservable factors that are different between the treatment and the control groups. If there are, then the assumption that the two groups are identical – other than that the treatment group benefits from the policy – is invalid. The main unobservable factor is selection.

Step 6 approaches seek to take account of two forms of selection – self-selection and committee selection. Self-selection is important if participant businesses/individuals are more motivated to grow than other businesses – even when account is taken of factors such as sector and geography. The reason this is important is that such businesses would have performed better than 'average' even without the programme, so account has to be taken of this. A second potential selection problem could be that not all eligible applicants are allowed to participate. Instead their suitability is assessed and the 'unsuitable' ones are rejected – perhaps by a committee. If the selectors are good at their job this means programme participants are better than a random draw of applicants – and account has to be taken of this.

Two approaches to addressing the problems posed in Step 6 have been adopted. The first is statistical and derives from the work of Heckman (1979) and seeks to control for sample selection bias. In simple terms, if the aim is to observe the impact of advice on business sales but it is known that the take-up of advice is influenced by other factors unrelated to the sales of the business, then the Heckman two-step approach is used first to explain the take-up of advice and then use that in the equation that explains performance. In practice, this presents difficulties in finding a variable that influences advice without influencing performance. An example of a Step 6 approach is detailed in the Illustration below.

Illustration

The impact of soft business support on small business performance: the UK Marketing Initiative

Context

The advice assessed here was subsidised marketing-consultancy advice provided to small businesses in the manufacturing and allied sectors (Wren and Storey 2002). All businesses received one free consultancy day. They could then purchase either five or 15 days' subsidised consultancy. For most businesses the subsidy was 50 per cent. The programme operated between 1988 and 1994.

The evaluation

All businesses that participated between 1988 and 1994 were tracked in 1996. This was a Step 6 study because the control group was the performance of businesses that purchased less than the full 15 days' advice. Their performance was then compared with the businesses that purchased the full 15 days. The evaluation showed that, overall, those business purchasing 15 days' advice performed no better than the control group. However, the key target businesses – those with between 10 and 80 employees – did perform significantly better than the control group, implying the programme provided additionality for them.

Critiquing the evaluation

This is a Step 6 evaluation since it has an explicit control group and addresses the issue of selection bias. However, even this is not ideal since it uses those applicants that did not purchase the full 15 days as the control. Whilst this has the major advantage of being a group of businesses that had some aspirations for growth – since they applied for the programme – their choice can be criticised on the grounds that if they were identical to the participants then they would have proceeded with the programme. In short, it may be that they were also less motivated, and it is this that makes them drop out of the programme.

Of course, lack of motivation is likely to be only one of many reasons why businesses dropped out of the programme, but it does illustrate the difficulty of identifying the perfect control group, without using randomised trials.

A technically better approach to overcoming selection bias is the use of randomised trials. If, for example, an evaluation of financial assistance/business advice to small businesses were required then a randomised trials experiment could take place. Here all applicants' eligibility would be assessed and a final list drawn up. Then, all businesses would be placed in a lottery, with the winners getting the finance/advice. Subsequently the winners and losers would be tracked over time and any difference in the performance of the two groups would accurately measure the impact of the finance/advice. One of the few examples of a randomised trial in this area is detailed in the Illustration below.

Illustration   Randomised trials

Benus (1994) conducted a randomised trial on two self-employment assistance programmes in Washington and Massachusetts, US. To achieve this, unemployed individuals interested in becoming self-employed were randomly assigned to a treatment group (that received programme services) or a control group (who only received unemployment benefit). The conclusion based on this was that '. . . self-employment assistance programs [in the US] are viable policy tools to promote the rapid re-employment of unemployed workers' (Benus 1994: 73). The problem with the use of randomised trials is that they are expensive, complex and involve the denial of support to individuals who may need such support.

The use of different evaluation methodologies appears to impact on evaluation results. Greene (2009) compares four evaluations that have been conducted of the UK's Prince's Trust. One was a Step 1 approach, two were Step 4 approaches and the fourth was a Step 6 approach. He suggested that simpler forms of monitoring and evaluation tend to lead to more favourable outcomes for the Prince's Trust. Hence, using the Step 1 and Step 4 approaches provided the Prince's Trust with 'favourable' assessments of its impact. However, the Step 6 evaluation (Meager *et al.* 2003) identifies less favourable outcomes.

These differences were because the stronger evaluation methodologies were more able to robustly estimate the outputs and outcomes of a programme. In other words, the weaker methodologies tended to inflate the impact of the programme by including factors that were not explicitly attributable to programme impact. So, in the case of the Prince's Trust, Meager *et al.* are able to isolate more precisely the impact of the programme because they can hold constant a range of human capital factors such as education and age of participants.

Conclusions

This short primer has identified that there are real issues and choices involved in assessing small business and entrepreneurship policies/programmes. Chiefly, these consist of the choice of monitoring or evaluation and what particular evaluation methodology is to be used.

References

Baumol, W.J. (1990) 'Entrepreneurship: Productive, Unproductive and Destructive', *Journal of Political Economy*, 98, 893–921.

Benus, J.M. (1994) 'Self-employment Programmes: A New Reemployment Tool', *Entrepreneurship: Theory and Practice*, 19(2), 73–86.

Chrisman, J.J. (1989) 'Strategic, Administrative and Operating Assistance: The Value of Outside Consulting to Pre-Venture Entrepreneurs', *Journal of Business Venturing*, 4, 401–18.

Chrisman, J.J. (1999) 'The Influence of Outsider-generated Knowledge Resources on Venture Creation', *Journal of Small Business Management*, 37(4), 42–58.

Chrisman, J.J. (2005) 'The Performance of the SBDC Program in the US', in *Small Business Development Centers: New offerings for a new economy*. Committee on Small Business, House of Representatives, 109th Congress, First Session, Serial No. 109-X. Washington, DC: US Government Printing Office.

Chrisman, J.J. and Katrishen, F. (1994) 'The Economic Impact of Small Business Development Center Counseling Activities in the US: 1990–1991', *Journal of Business Venturing*, 9(4), 271–80.

Chrisman, J.J. and Leslie, J.D. (1989) 'Strategic, Administrative and Operating Problems: The Impact of Outsiders on Small Firm Performance', *Entrepreneurship: Theory and Practice*, 13(3), 37–51.

Chrisman, J.J. and McMullan, W.E. (2000) 'A Preliminary Assessment of Outsider Assistance as a Knowledge Resource: The Longer Term Impact of New Venture Counseling', *Entrepreneurship: Theory and Practice*, 24(3), 37–53.

Chrisman, J.J. and McMullan, W.E. (2004) 'Outsider Assistance as a Knowledge Resource for New Venture survival', *Journal of Small Business Management*, 42(3), 229–44.

Chrisman, J.J., Hoy, F., Robinson, R.B., Jr. and Nelson, R.R. (1987) 'Evaluating the Impact of SBDC Consulting: A Reply to Elstrott', *Journal of Small Business Management*, 25(1), 72–5.

Chrisman, J.J., McMullan, W.E. and Hall, J. (2005) 'The Influence of Guided Preparation on the Long-term Performance of New Ventures', *Journal of Business Venturing*, 20(6), 769–91.

Chrisman, J.J., Nelson, R.R., Hoy, F. and Robinson, R.B., Jr (1985) 'The Impact of SBDC Consulting Activities', *Journal of Small Business Management*, 23(3), 1–11.

Curran, J. (2000) 'What is Small Business Policy in the UK for? Evaluation and Assessing Small Business Policies', *International Small Business Journal*, 18(3), 36–50.

FORA (2008) *Entrepreneurship Index 2007*. Copenhagen: Ministry of Economic and Business Affairs.

Greene, F.J. (2009) 'Evaluating Youth Entrepreneurship: the Case of the Prince's Trust', *Environment & Planning C: Government & Policy*, 27(2), 216–29.

Greene, F.J. and Storey, D.J. (2007) 'Issues in Evaluation: The Case of Shell Livewire', in Audretsch, D.B. and Thurik, A.R. (eds), *The Handbook of Entrepreneurship Policy*. Alphen aan den Rijn: Kluwer, 213–33.

Heckman, J. (1979) 'Sample Selection Bias as a Specification Error', *Econometrica*, 47, 153–61.

Hoffmann, A. (2007) 'A Rough Guide to Entrepreneurship Policy', in Audretsch, D.B., Grilio, I. and Thurik, A.R. (eds), *Handbook of Research on Entrepreneurship Policy*. Cheltenham: Edward Elgar.

Johnson, S. (2005) 'SME Support Policy: Efficiency, Equity, Ideology or Vote-Seeking?'. Paper presented at the ISBE 28th National Small Firms Policy and Research Conference, University of Lancaster, Blackpool, November, 2005.

Meager, N., Bates, P. and Cowling, M. (2003) 'An Evaluation of Business Start-up Support for Young People', *National Institute Economic Review*, 186, 70–83.

Mole, K.F. and Bramley, G. (2006) 'Making Policy Choices in Non-financial Business Support: An International Comparison', *Environment and Planning C: Government and Policy*, 24(6), 885–908.

OECD (2007) *OECD Framework for the Evaluation of SME and Entrepreneurship Policies and Programmes*. Paris: OECD.

OECD (2008) *Measuring Entrepreneurship: A Digest of Indic-ators*. Paris: OECD.

Oldsman, E. and Hallerg, K. (2004) 'Evaluating Business Assistance Programs', in *Evaluating Local Economic and Employment Development: How to Assess What Works among Programmes and Policies*. Paris: OECD, 229–50.

Schumpeter, J.A. (1950) *Capitalism Socialism and Democracy*. New York: Harper and Row.

Sharma, P. and Chrisman, J.J. (1999) 'Toward a Reconcilia-tion of the Definitional Issues in the Field of Corporate Entrepreneurship', *Entrepreneurship: Theory and Practice*, 23(3), 11–28.

Wren, C. and Storey, D.J. (2002) 'Evaluating the Effect of Soft Business Support upon Small Firm Performance', *Oxford Economic Papers*, 54, 334–65.

You are chair of the fictitious Small Business Advisory Group set up by the government to review tax differences between unincorporated businesses (sole traders and partnerships) and incorporated businesses (limited companies).

The government has long believed that one of the best ways to incentivise entrepreneurial activity is through the tax system. Evidence (see Section 14.3) has suggested that high-growth businesses tend to be incorporated. On this basis, the government has introduced policies that provide tax incentives to small, incorporated businesses, in the hope that this will stimulate entrepreneurial activity.

However, recent international evidence has called into question the value of such incentives. The government has now established a review of whether its tax policies are cost-effective in promoting entrepreneurship.

You have been asked to advise the government on the best way forward, and have developed three policy options:

1 **Radical reform**: this would eliminate the tax incentive to incorporate;

2 **Incremental reform**: this would reduce but not eliminate the incentive to incorporate; and

3 **No change**: the status quo would be maintained.

You have drafted a short consultation note (see below) which details differences in the taxes paid by unincorporated and incorporated businesses, and outlines your three policy options. You have received two responses to your consultation: one from a lobby group ('FairTaxes') in favour of the radical option of abolishing the incentive to incorporate, and another from a small business lobby group ('SmallBiz') which strongly favours the status quo. These responses can also be found below.

> It is your task to recommend to the government which of these approaches they should take. Examine the consultation note and read the responses received from FairTaxes and SmallBiz. Provide an argument to defend which of the three policy proposals you propose.

Consultation note – Small Business Advisory Group seeks views on its review of the small business tax system

The Small Business Advisory Group has been reviewing the taxes paid by the owners of UK small businesses. What has emerged is that the amount of tax paid differs significantly depending on the legal form of the business. This stems from differences in the ways in which unincorporated and incorporated businesses are taxed.

Unincorporated business owners pay income tax and social security (National Insurance) contributions on the entire profits of their business under the standard income tax system. Incorporated business owners, on the other hand, face two levels of taxation: 1) the company pays corporation tax on its profits (after taking into account wage costs); 2) the company owner is taxed on any income she takes out of the company.

There are two ways in which the incorporated business owner can take money out of the company: a) as a wage; b) as a dividend (which is the return to holding shares in the company). If the money is taken as a wage, then it is taxed under the standard income tax system, in the same way as unincorporated business owners. If instead the money is taken as a dividend, then dividend tax is paid. Because the dividend tax rate is lower than the combined income and social security tax rate, it is more tax efficient for the incorporated business owner to take their money out of the company in the form of a dividend.

Moreover, because the combined dividend and corporation tax rate (which the incorporated business owner pays on her income) is lower than the combined income tax and social security tax rate (which the unincorporated owner pays on her income), there is a tax incentive to be incorporated rather than unincorporated.

For example, at the time of our review, the owner of an unincorporated business making £25,000 per year would face a total tax bill of £5,372.60 (21.5 per cent of £25,000). If we assume that the owner of an incorporated business (also making £25,000 per year) takes their income in the most tax efficient way, then this owner would face a total tax bill of £3,970.27 (15.9 per cent of £25,000). The incorporated business owner would pay £1,402.33 (5.6 percentage points) less in tax than the unincorporated business owner.

The government's aim in introducing and maintaining such an incentive stems from its belief that incorporated businesses are more likely to grow and stimulate entrepreneurial activity than unincorporated businesses, and that this should be encouraged through the tax system. However, recent international evidence (including Schuetze and Bruce 2004; Chittenden and Sloan 2007; Crawford and Freedman 2008; and Pope 2009 (see Chapter 20.3)) has called into question the value of such incentives.

On the basis of this evidence, we have developed three policy options. We invite interested parties to comment on these three policy options before we make recommendations to the government. The policy options are as follows:

1 **Radical reform.** This would involve increasing the small companies' corporation tax rate to 28 per cent (from 21 per cent). Such an increase would bring the combined dividend and corporation tax rate (paid by incorporated business owners) into line with the combined income tax and social security contributions rate (paid by unincorporated business owners), thus eliminating the tax incentive to incorporate.

2 **Incremental reform.** This would involve a small increase in the small companies' corporation tax rate which would reduce (but not eliminate) the tax incentive to incorporate.

3 **No change.** The status quo would be maintained.

Response 1 – response from 'FairTaxes'

Chairman
Small Business Advisory Group

Dear Madam

Re: consultation on small business taxation

We are writing in response to your recent consultation on small business taxation. We would like to express, in the strongest possible terms, our recommendation that you should adopt the radical reform set out in your consultation note, that is, to increase the small companies' corporation tax rate to 28 per cent.

We are strongly of the opinion that a reduced corporation tax rate is NOT the correct way in which to support small businesses. Our evidence to support this is the following:

- As we have seen in the UK in recent years, there has been a substantial increase in the number of companies being set up, following reductions in the small companies' rate of corporation tax. However, the majority of these new companies came from the ranks of already-established unincorporated businesses rather than being entirely new businesses. (For example, the graph below, Figure CS8.1, shows a decrease in the number of unincorporated businesses – and a significant increase in the number of companies – over the period (2002–2005) when a 0 per cent corporation tax rate was in place for very small companies.) Such a rearrangement of activity surely cannot be viewed as increasing entrepreneurship. Indeed, your government has already recognised that substantially reducing the corporation tax rate for small companies was an ill-judged policy, and we would encourage you to view the current situation in a similar light.

- The current blanket tax incentives for small companies assume that ALL small companies are entrepreneurial. In reality, however, very many of the new businesses set up and currently in existence are never likely to generate substantial future employment and economic prosperity; they are merely businesses that provide employment to one or, at most two, people and should be seen as an alternative form of employment. Very many of them can also hardly be described as innovative. Moreover, even if such businesses do grow, there is plenty of evidence to suggest that employment in small businesses provides workers with fewer benefits than those provided by larger businesses.

- The tax system is NOT the correct place for small businesses to be 'rewarded' for the additional 'risks' it is

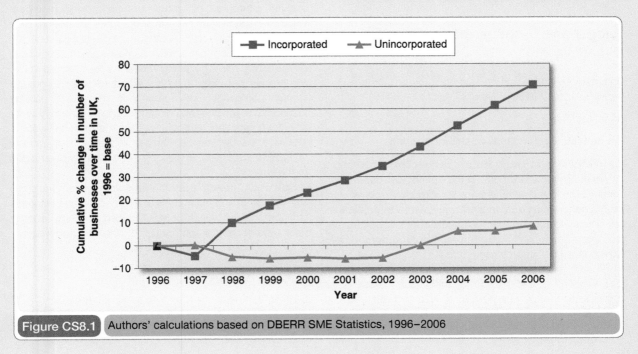

Figure CS8.1 | Authors' calculations based on DBERR SME Statistics, 1996–2006

often argued that they bear. A better mechanism would be to rely upon the market, with the 'risks' of running a small business reflected in the form of higher prices charged to consumers. This is exactly what happened with the introduction of the UK minimum wage: while it was argued that the legislation would have a disastrous effect on the ability of small businesses to hire workers and so on, small businesses instead simply passed these higher wage costs on to consumers in the form of higher prices.

- The current tax system encourages tax avoidance. As representatives of a very large number of taxpayers, we are disappointed that the government would provide a legal shelter for certain types of businesses to avoid tax. The net effect of this tax avoidance is a serious loss to the taxpayer of tax revenues, with no discernable economic benefit in return.

We would, on the basis of this evidence, strongly recommend that the small companies' rate is increased to 28 per cent, as outlined in your proposal.

If, however, your government did want to offer more support to small businesses – regardless of legal form – it could take further steps to address some of the market failures that they face. For example, small businesses may find it difficult to access the start-up capital that they need. While we are aware that much is already being done to help such businesses, we believe that it is these types of schemes – rather than blanket tax incentives available to anyone who starts up a company – that are more likely to encourage entrepreneurship in the long run.

Yours faithfully,
Chairman of FairTax

Response 2 – the response from 'SmallBiz'

Chairman
Small Business Advisory Group

Dear Madam

Re: consultation on small business taxation

We are writing in response to your recent consultation on small business taxation. Of the options set out in your consultation document, we would strongly urge you to maintain the status quo. Indeed, we would like to take this opportunity to suggest that you should in fact *reduce* (rather than increase) the small companies' rate of corporation tax to help small businesses even further.

Small businesses are the engine of growth. They create jobs and wealth, and provide the innovation necessary to keep our economy growing. We believe that reduced tax rates are the perfect way to reward *all* small companies for the risks they take and the benefits they offer for us all. Your government has also recognised the advantages that such a strategy has to offer. May I remind you of what the UK Paymaster General said:

> businesses growing beyond a certain size will often be companies. We believe that cutting corporation tax is an effective way of targeting support at small and growing businesses . . . We want to create growth and economic activity, and to sustain entrepreneurial activity.
>
> *(House of Commons Standing Committee F16, May 2002, cols. 114–115).*

Some people argue that the risks taken by small businesses are adequately accounted for by market prices, and that no further incentive is necessary. But those individuals forget that small businesses are price takers – not price makers – and cannot possibly charge a higher price for their product when they are trying to compete with already-established businesses. The tax system, therefore, is the best mechanism for ensuring the appropriate balance between risk and reward.

Moreover, we would argue that substantially increasing the small companies' rate is more likely to *reduce* government revenues from corporation tax than it is to increase them. A higher tax rate may lead some entrepreneurs to choose not to start up their businesses and others to move abroad to start up their businesses. This would not only diminish corporation tax revenues, but would also reduce the degree of competition in the economy (with potentially detrimental effects on productivity growth), and reduce the amount of innovation in the economy. More worryingly, however, there may also be a marked increase in tax evasion. Of course, I'm certain that none of our members would engage in such practices, but there are bound to be unscrupulous individuals out there who would do so.

It is our opinion that small businesses are the backbone of the economy. The entrepreneurs who start up these businesses deserve to be rewarded for their efforts to stimulate innovation, drive economic growth and provide jobs for so many people. We consider it political suicide for any government to radically reform the existing system. The net impact will be a sizeable reduction in the number of entrepreneurs, which, in the long run, will be very damaging to the economy.

We would, therefore, strongly recommend that the small companies' rate is maintained at 21 per cent (as outlined in your proposal) or, even better, reduced to 15 per cent to reflect the economic contribution of small businesses.

Yours faithfully,
Chairman of SmallBiz

Case written by Claire Crawford and Francis Greene

absorptive capacity how well a business is able to learn in order to manage current circumstances and predict future developments.

additionality refers to the sum of direct and indirect impacts directly due to a government intervention.

adverse selection reflects an information asymmetry in which the one party – typically the Principal (see agency theory) – struggles to distinguish between 'good' and 'bad' agents. This makes the selection of good from bad applicants difficult.

agency theory an economic theory describing a relationship between two parties – the Principal and the Agent – wherein the Principal takes some action which benefits the Agent, but from which the Principal expects a payback. Central to the theory is the ability of the Principal to control or influence the Agent, normally through an agreed contract.

anchoring and adjustment heuristic a 'rule of thumb' by which a person makes a decision based on known information about other people in similar circumstances.

arbitrage (aka pure arbitrage) the process of exploiting the difference between two prices in order to make a profit (see temporal and spatial arbitrage).

asset-based finance a term which covers three basic types of financing: factoring, invoice discounting and stock finance.

asset finance a process whereby a business can hire or lease an asset – such as equipment or machinery – by making regular payments to the owner of that asset.

availability heuristic a 'rule of thumb' which lets a person compare their situation to whatever comparable information is easily available, retrieved or recalled.

bankruptcy a formal legal procedure for people (in the UK) and people and businesses (most other countries) that can no longer pay their creditors.

base year when tracking the performance or growth of a business, this is the first year for which data is collected – although it is not necessarily the business's first year of trading.

'born globals' start-up businesses which, from inception, make observable and significant commitments of resources (e.g., material, people, financing, time) in more than one nation.

business angels wealthy *individuals* (as opposed to businesses) who provide equity capital for new businesses.

business closure occurs when a transacting entity stops its activities and does not transfer its ownership to another business and is independent of an existing business.

business incubators accommodation – often provided on science parks – which typically offer new and/or technology-orientated businesses a package of services (e.g. access to shared office costs).

corporate ventures new businesses or business activities initiated by an existing, generally large, business.

deadweight refers to the level of activity that would have occurred without government intervention.

debt finance finance, often provided in the forms of loans, made available to a business, most commonly by a bank or other external organisation, based on the promise of timely repayment by the business, together with interest payments.

deregistration the process whereby a business ends its inclusion in a register, such as sales tax or a trade directory. It is often used as a measure of business closure.

desire for autonomy an individual who places value on freedom and independence.

displacement the impact of a government intervention on businesses that have been affected, normally adversely, by a government intervention designed to support other businesses.

disruptive innovation (aka radical innovation) the introduction of something new and different (e.g. a method of production, a market, supplier, organisation or good) to an established industry or sector.

dynamic capabilities the ability of a business to learn and to change in response to events.

'elephants' large businesses that employ lots of people but do not generate many new jobs.

endogenous literally, originates from 'within' – in an economic context, used to describe trends, effects and changes in a system which are the result of internal forces.

enterprise an entity engaged in economic activity, otherwise known as a business.

entrepreneurial orientation (E-O) a business's strategic entrepreneurial outlook, judged by its innovativeness, proactiveness, and risk taking.

entry barriers the obstacles a business may encounter when trying to enter a new sector or market.

equity finance the process of selling part ownership of a business (often in the form of shares) to an outside person or organisation often in return for a cash sum.

establishment a place where economic activity takes place, such as a factory or an office.

exit the movement of a person or business out of one market state and into another.

exogenous literally, originates from 'outside' – in an economic context, used to describe trends, effects and changes in a system which are the result of external forces.

factoring a form of asset-based finance which involves a business *selling* its invoices (its sales not yet paid) to a third party (a 'factor') in return for a proportion of the yet unpaid invoices.

formality the presence of written procedures, rules and policies to design, measure and regulate business processes.

franchise a contractual relationship between a franchisor (owner of a brand, product, service) and a franchisee in which the franchisee uses the services of the franchisor in return for payment.

'gazelles' fast-growth businesses which meet certain criteria in terms of their growth in sales, growth in employee numbers, and age.

Global Entrepreneurship Monitor (GEM) an annual international survey which examines the rate of people in the process of setting up a business (nascent entrepreneurs) and actual new business owners in an economy.

grant a non-repayable payment that is usually provided by a public organisation.

Gross Domestic Product (GDP) is the total value of goods and services of a country.

human capital attributes factors such as the education and background experiences of the individual.

illusion of control the tendency to over-estimate the extent of personal control over outcomes.

incremental innovation the introduction of something new to extend the value of an existing innovation by building on existing know-how.

informality a reliance on upon custom and practice and an absence of written procedures within a business.

information asymmetries the phenomenon of information (for example, about a business or market) being unequally shared amongst the concerned parties.

invoice discounting a form of asset-based finance which involves the business *borrowing* against its unpaid invoices, for a fixed proportion of the value of the invoices.

impression management like politicians who 'spin' events, the entrepreneur may try to place the blame for poor performance on other factors, or take credit for good performance.

insolvency a status applied to limited companies which are no longer able to pay their debts in full.

intentionality the concept that those seeking to set up a new business have to form some intentions towards explicitly setting up their business.

intrapreneurship the ability or tendency of employees in a large organisation to act 'entrepreneurially'.

intrinsic motivation the concept that individuals who perform tasks for their own sake are likely to be better motivated than individuals who are motivated by some external feature.

liquidation occurs when the assets of the business are distributed amongst the creditors of the business.

locus of control an entrepreneurial trait or characteristic that places the responsibility for achievement either within (internal locus of control) or outside (external locus of control) the person.

macro-economic policies government policies which do *not* have SMEs or entrepreneurs as their primary focus, but which may affect them anyway as part of the wider economy.

management buy out a business that is formed through being bought out by the existing managers.

market failure occurs when the Agent is encouraged to favour a more risky outcome by not having to incur full 'downside losses'.

'mice' small businesses that start out small and only contribute marginally to employment growth.

micro-economic policies government policies which focus specifically upon SMEs and entrepreneurs.

moral hazard a type of information asymmetry in which there is a risk that one or both parties will act differently to that set down in their contract.

nascent entrepreneurs people who are in the process of setting up a business.

need for achievement (NAch) an entrepreneurial trait or characteristic that means a person is achievement motivated, undertakes tasks of moderate difficulty, actively seeks out taking responsibility and welcomes feedback on their actions.

network closure approach a theory which emphasises the importance of stability and strength of network ties as the most important aspects or characteristics of a network.

network content how entrepreneurs access resources – this may be in terms of financial or physical resources, but more typically it is intangible resources such as advice, information or emotional support.

network governance how networks are governed. Often the emphasis is on 'trust' as the 'glue' linking people together.

network magnitude approach a theory which emphasises size as the most important aspect or characteristic of a network.

network position approach a theory which emphasises the importance of the entrepreneur correctly establishing their appropriate 'place' between existing networks as the most important aspect or characteristic of a network.

network structure the size of the network, its density (the number of connections in relation to its potential number of connections), its diversity (mix of strong and weak ties) and where the individual sits in a network (centrality).

niche a small restricted marketplace, in which higher than average profits can be made by offering some form of specialist service or product.

overdraft a facility or option to borrow, provided by a bank, which is flexible in the sense of being able to borrow up to an agreed limit whenever required.

over-optimism the tendency for entrepreneurs to be more confident about their chances of success than their circumstances actually warrant.

overtrading the state where a company has more business than it can adequately fund.

planning fallacy the belief that a plan can be put in place quicker than is actually possible.

population ecology a theoretical model which uses a biological metaphor (of birth, growth, maturity, and eventual death) to explain business dynamics.

portfolio entrepreneurship owning more than one business at the same time.

preferred creditors people to whom a business owes money, and who are repaid either in full, or who take priority over other creditors, if the business fails.

price maker a business that is able to influence prices in a market by withholding supplies.

price taker a business that has to accept that the price received for their product/service is beyond their control.

private equity equity provided to more established businesses involved in, for example, management buy outs and 'turnarounds'.

process innovation the introduction of new ways of working or methods of production that result in a more efficient, cheaper operation.

product innovation the introduction of new ideas or processes that result in a new product.

productivity a measure of the efficiency by which inputs such as capital equipment or labour are used to produce outputs (goods or services).

radical innovation (aka disruptive innovation) the introduction of something new and different (e.g. a method of production, a market, supplier, organisation or good) to an established industry or sector or even the creation of a wholly new industry or sector.

representative heuristic a 'rule of thumb' which assumes that an action or event can be categorised and understood based on similarities with other situations.

Resource Based View (RBV) a view of a business which focuses on the internal resources of the business – rather than the external environment – as an explanation for business performance.

risk taking propensity the likelihood that an individual will undertake a risky act.

'rules of the game' the legal and financial structures within which businesses have to operate.

scale economies the reduction in unit costs that comes with increased size.

Schumpeter Mark I a theory which argues that the entrepreneur is central to innovation and economic development, because of their ability to radically and disruptively transform, undo and remake routines.

Schumpeter Mark II a theory which argues that large businesses play a more important role in innovation and economic development than independent businesses or lone entrepreneurs because only large businesses can finance the undertaking of large-scale research and development.

science parks physical clusters of high-technology, R&D-led businesses often adjacent to universities.

self-efficacy the belief that a person can control their own destiny in a particular area or aspect of their life.

serial entrepreneurship having owned more than a single business, but never more than one at the same time.

Small and Medium-sized Enterprises (SMEs) a term used to define small and medium-sized businesses based on number of employees, turnover or balance sheet total.

social capital the sum of the actual and potential resources embedded within, available through, and derived from the individual's social network.

social enterprises businesses run for social purposes and often without a profit motive or where the profit motive is secondary to social outcomes.

social network the network of social relationships possessed by an individual or social unit.

spatial arbitrage buying a good or service in one particular place, then selling it on at a profit in another place.

spillovers the benefits obtained by businesses, usually in terms of knowledge or cost savings, through their interaction with, or proximity to, other businesses.

stage models theoretical models which characterise business growth as happening in clearly defined stages.

stock finance a form of asset-based finance which raises finance *against* the stock a business holds.

subsidised loans loans which are repayable, but at an interest rate which is often below commercial rates.

substantive capabilities the ability of a business to transform its assets (e.g. people, management structures and routines) to solve problems.

temporal arbitrage buying a good or service at one particular time, in the expectation of selling it on at a profit at a later time.

term loans loans made by banks or other financial institutions for a fixed period of time, normally not exceeding three years.

tolerance for ambiguity the ability to cope with situations where information is limited and events uncertain.

Total Entrepreneurship Activity (TEA) the combined measure of the rate of people in the process of setting up a business (nascent entrepreneurs) and actual new business owners in an economy.

trade credit a source of finance by which the business owner acquires the use of an asset – such as a machine – without having to pay for it until some point in the future.

unsecured creditors people to whom a business owes money, but who, in the event of the business failing, are not repaid until after the preferred creditors have been repaid.

utility the benefits (such as income and lifestyle) that an individual stands to gain from any given form of employment.

venture capitalist (VC) a group or individual who provides funds in return for *part* ownership of a business, with a view to facilitating the long-term growth of such a business. The VC expects to sell this ownership at some point in the future when, because of its growth, the valuation of the business will be considerably higher than when the shares were purchased.

Index